W9-CWS-009

Dependency Syntax

SUNY Series in Linguistics
Mark Aronoff, Editor

DEPENDENCY SYNTAX: THEORY AND PRACTICE

Igor A. Mel'čuk

State University of New York Press

Published by
State University of New York Press, Albany

© 1988   State University of New York

For information, address State University of New York Press,
State University Plaza, Albany, N.Y., 12246

Library of Congress Cataloging-in-Publication Data

Mel'čuk, I. A. (Igor' Aleksandrovič), 1932–
   Dependency syntax.

   (SUNY Series in Linguistics)
   Bibliography: p. 400
   Includes indexes.
   1. Dependency grammar. 2. Grammar, Comparative and
general—Syntax. 3. Typology (Linguistics) 4. Grammar,
Comparative and general—Ergative constructions.
5. Linguistic models. 6. Russian language—Syntax.
I. Title. II. Series.
P162.M45   1987   415   86-14542
ISBN 0-88706-450-7
ISBN 0-88706-451-5 (pbk.)

10 9 8 7 6 5 4 3 2 1

To friendship and affection,
those necessary ingredients of any serious scientific activity;
To all who share these feelings with me—from Montreal with love.

CONTENTS

FOREWORD

Webster's III makes a nice distinction between a foreword and a preface. While a preface is "the author's introduction to a book explaining the object and scope of what follows," a foreword is "front matter likely to be of interest but not necessarily essential for the understanding of the text of a book and commonly written by someone other than the author of the text."

Only after discovering this distinction did I consent to provide a foreword to Igor Mel'čuk's book, for although I do hope that my remarks will be of some interest, I cannot pretend to add anything essential to the understanding of the work. Having thus been absolved by Merriam-Webster of all responsibility toward either the reader or the author, and having conversely freed these, I am now at liberty to go forward. But in what direction and to what purpose? Since I have defined away all responsibility my status is no longer clear. What should I say about this book that the author couldn't or wouldn't and how can I help the reader without usurping the author's role? What follows is a partial response to these questions.

First and most essentially, this is the work of a great outsider, with all the virtues that such a position entails. For almost twenty years, Mel'čuk was the Soviet linguist best known outside the Soviet Union. At the same time, in part because of his Western connections, his work was considered inappropriate in correct academic circles inside the Soviet Union, with all of the sanction, official and unofficial, that follows when one is put beyond the pale. As one person who studied in Moscow in the 1960s told me, "Mel'čuk's ideas were well known, but they could not be used." In 1977 Mel'čuk, having been forced to leave the Soviet Union, came to North America where he took up a position at the Université de Montréal. He has joined the editorial boards of journals, and has published widely, both books and articles, but to most North Americans he is a Soviet linguist, an outsider still.

This might be considered accidental, or the common fate of an exile, but in Mel'čuk's case there are other reasons. Being outside has allowed him to preserve his independence. Thus, for many years, he carried on an active correspondence with Roman Jakobson, and Jakobson has clearly had a major influence on his work, yet he never became a Jakobsonian.

To the reader, what is most interesting about all this is the way it comes out in the work. Most strikingly, this book is remarkably free of the kind of theory-comparison that is so common today. There are no attacks on other peoples' views, no demonstrations of the superiority of the author's. Linguistics, for Mel'čuk, is above politics. He seeks neither to convert nor to offend. Instead, he has provided an entire framework laid bare for the reader's dispassionate perusal. As an outsider, he will not presuppose familiarity, and so almost nothing is left out. The analyses are all laid out with extreme care and he has tried to be as comprehensive as possible in coverage, down to the smallest details of lexical semantics. There is much more explicit presentation of methodology than we are used to and there are many definitions, all arriving out of a desire to be as explicit and as open as possible.

One other characteristic pervades the work—love of language. There is a sense of awe in the book, a joyful marvel at the systematicity of language, coupled with a humble respect for its mysterious complexity. There is also fine wit and a great deal of play. For Mel'čuk, as for Sapir, language is not something to be conquered, but something to wonder at and rejoice in.

The result is a remarkable work, a triumph of modern linguistic method that spans all social, factional and national boundaries. Those who can read it carefully and thoughtfully, with as much passionate openness as it was written with, will be rewarded amply on many levels of human experience.

MARK ARONOFF
Stony Brook, New York

ACKNOWLEDGEMENTS

This book would never have seen the light of day, at least not in its present form, if it weren't for a number of people who offered me their unqualified support. Now that I have put the final stop at the end of the manuscript, I have the pleasant obligation of returning to the beginning and thanking them. The people who helped me were many, and many were the ways in which they were helpful. Therefore, I will divide the names into groups and take up each group in turn.

First, the following bodies and organizations have granted me their kind permission to reprint or otherwise use material that was previously published under their auspices. I am happy to acknowledge here the friendly cooperation of the following:

Annual Review of Anthropology for Mel'čuk 1981a
Berkeley Linguistics Society (M. Macaulay) for Mel'čuk 1979b
Forum Linguisticum (A. Makkai) for Mel'čuk 1981c
KAROMA Publishers (Th. L. Markey) for Mel'čuk 1979a
Linguistic Research Inc. (A. Vanek and B. Comrie) for Mel'čuk 1981b
Linguistic Society of America for Mel'čuk 1980b
Linguistics (W. Klein) for Mel'čuk and Savvina 1978
Sørensen Festschrift Committee (H. Crag) for Iordanskaja and Mel'čuk 1981.

Second, many of my American friends and colleagues have been instrumental in translating, editing or correcting my texts so that my message could get through to my American audience in spite of all the problems and obstacles one has to face when writing in a foreign tongue. These people are (in alphabetical order): J. Augerot, J. Barnstead, L. Bazer, S. Carrol, B. Comrie, S. Franks, M. Green, R. Kittredge, I. Mackenzie, E. Macklovitch, P. McMullan, J. Nichols, and P. Roberge. Last but not least, I would mention Margalit Fox, who copyedited my manuscript for the State University of New York Press, hunting down and exterminating even the smallest bugs that remained.

Third, still more friends and colleagues, both back in Moscow and in North America, took the trouble to read parts of the present book, sometimes in many consequent versions. They are too numerous to be listed here, but most important criticisms, remarks and suggestions have been received from the following people:

Chapter 1:   T. D. Korelskaja and R. Kittredge.
Chapter 2:   L. L. Elnitsky, R. Kittredge and J. Nichols.
Chapter 3:   Ju. D. Apresjan, I. M. Boguslavskij, Y.-Ch. Morin, N. V. Pertsov and E. V. Savvina.
Chapter 4:   Ju.D. Apresjan, I. M. Boguslavskij, B. Comrie, R. M. W. Dixon, L. L. Iomdin, N. V. Pertsov, A. Wierzbicka, A. A. Zaliznjak and A. K. Zholkovsky.
Chapter 5:   R. Hetzron, N. V. Pertsov and E. N. Savvina.
Chapter 7:   L. L. Iomdin, A. E. Kibrik, I. A. Murav'ëva and N. V. Pertsov.
Chapter 8:   Ju. D. Apresjan, L. L. Iomdin, the late A. A. Xolodovič, and A. K. Zholkovsky.
Chapter 9:   L. L. Elnitsky.
Chapter 10:   Ju. D. Apresjan, J. Nichols, E. V. Paducěva, N. V. Pertsov and A. A. Zaliznjak.
Chapter 11:   Ju. D. Apresjan, L. L. Iomdin, N. V. Pertsov and Ju. A. Šixanovič.

Moreover, Ju. D. Apresjan and N. V. Pertsov read the whole manuscript; I did my best to take into consideration their numerous fundamental comments. Several incongruities and omissions were spotted by James McCawley, who served as a reader for the State University of New York Press.

Fourth, Mark Aronoff invited me to publish this book in a series he had launched with the State University of New York Press.

Fifth, four people ensured a quick and efficient preparation of the book for the printer: Johanne Mercille, who typed the whole manuscript; Line Arès, who made the numerous corrections; Lucie Cusson, who compiled the indexes and the bibliography and drew the diagrams; and Lidija Iordanskaja, who shared with me the tedious job of proofreading. Special thanks are due to the Faculty of Arts and Sciences of the University of Montreal (Mr. B. Landriault, assistant to the Dean), for help in typing my complex manuscript.

Sixth, Lidija Iordanskaja, more than anybody else, has contributed to the book intellectually, during the difficult period of its slow gestation. My first, n-th and last reader, she read every word of the text many times. All key problems were discussed repeatedly with her; in many places she kept me from saying things that I did not mean, and in as many places she helped me to say things that I did mean. As the result, the book embodies much of her effort, which I value more highly than I can express in words.

To these people—to all of them and to each of them—goes my most heartfelt gratitude.

IGOR A. MEL'ČUK
University of Montreal

LIST OF COMMONLY USED ABBREVIATIONS AND SYMBOLS

Anaph~	anaphoric (as in *AnaphS* 'anaphoric structure')
c	grammatical case
C	conditions (in a rule)
CO$^{(agent)}$	(agentive) complement [a typical agentive complement is the *by*-phrase with English passives]
D~	deep (as in *DSyntS* 'deep-syntactic structure')
D-	dependency (as in *D-syntax*)
DS~	deep-syntactic
"DS"	direct speech
Δ	a standard syntactic subtree [e.g., Δ NP = 'noun phrase standard subtree', etc.]
EC	ergative construction
ECD	explanatory combinatorial dictionary
GO$^{(dir/indir/obl)}$	grammatical object (direct/indirect/oblique)
GP	government pattern
GS	grammatical subject
L	lexeme
$\mathcal{L}$	a given language
LF	lexical function
Morph~	morphological (as in *MorphR* 'morphological representation')
MTM	Meaning-Text model

MTT	Meaning-Text theory
MV	main verb
n	grammatical number
N	noun
NAP	neutral assertive prosody
NE	numerical expression
NP	noun phrase
Num	numeral
N(V)	noun being an actant of the verb V
OC	object clause
p	grammatical person
Phon~	phonetic
PP	prepositional phrase
Pros~	prosodic (as in *ProsS* 'prosodic structure')
PS	phrase structure
r_i	surface-syntactic relation i
~R	representation
Я	rheme (= comment)
~Rel	relation
S~	surface (as in *SSyntS* 'surface-syntactic structure')
~S	structure
Sem~	semantic (as in *SemR* 'semantic representation')
SemObj	"semantic object"
SemSubj	"semantic subject"
SS~	surface-syntactic
Synt~	syntactic (as in *SyntS* 'syntactic structure')
Ⱦ	theme (= topic)
$V_{(tr/itr)}$	(transitive/intransitive) verb
$VAL_{pass/act}$	passive/active valency
VP	verb phrase
w	wordform
χ	a whole morphological characteristic (of a wordform; as in $L_χ$ 'a lexeme with a morphological characteristic χ')
$χ_i$	a specific morphological variable (= part of a χ)
X→Y	Y depends on X
Y◄--►X	X and Y are co-referential
X⇔Y	X corresponds to Y, and vice versa
Y | X	X is a set of conditions bearing on Y
$\{X_i\}$	set of elements X_i
X(V)	a sentence element syntactically depending on the verb V
Ø	linguistic₁ zero element (see Introduction, note 5)
Λ	the empty string or the empty set
'X'	the meaning of X
X	linguistic₁ sign **X** (see Introduction, note 5)

Part **I**

DEPENDENCY SYNTAX: AN OVERVIEW

INTRODUCTION

I. THE CASE "DEPENDENCY VS. PHRASE STRUCTURE"

This book has been written in order to plead the case for DEPENDENCY SYNTAX in modern linguistics. Dependencies as a formal means of representing the syntactic structure of sentences have been the staple diet of traditional syntacticians for centuries, especially in Europe and particularly in Classical and Slavic domains. Their popularity culminated in the brilliant work of Lucien Tesnière (Tesnière 1959), which laid the groundwork for all subsequent explorations in the area—but which, most unfortunately, is all but ignored by the mainstream of today's syntactic research. (For more titles on dependency syntax see the end of Chapter 1, p. 39.)

However, in North America in the early 1930s, dependency syntax was eclipsed by what then was called "immediate constituency" (or IC-analysis) and later became known as "phrase structure" (or PS-analysis). Neatly formulated by Leonard Bloomfield (Bloomfield 1933: 161 ff.; cf. also Wells 1947 and Percival 1976), phrase-structure representation in syntax was strongly promoted by the Structuralist school during the thirties, forties and fifties (cf., for instance, Hockett 1958: 147–156). It became the only syntactic representation ever seriously discussed in the work of Noam Chomsky and the Transformational-Generative School he founded in the late fifties. As a result of the triumphal offensive of the transformational-generative approach throughout the world, phrase-structure syntax forced dependency syntax into relative obscurity. Dependency syntax came to be virtually unknown to vast populations of linguists; it is not taught in linguistic courses at major universities, never considered in major theoretical discussions and not used in major syntactic descriptions. Dependency syntax is now treated like a quasi-extinguished exotic language in which a few old people still prattle but which—unlike Dyirbal (see Chapter 4, the last paragraph of Section I, p. 154)—fails to attract the attention of field workers and analysts.

True, there were some attempts to defend the positions of dependency syntax. Let me mention first the pioneering work by two Americans, Hays 1960, 1961, 1964b and Robinson 1970a, b; several Russians (including the present writer), Czechs, Germans, Britons, etc. (see Chapter 1, p. 39) have also contributed to the cause of dependency syntax. But all these attempts were to no avail: pockets of dependency resistance were easily overrun by advancing transformational armor, so that phrase-structure syntax very quickly established itself as the unopposed authority.

How can this easy victory be explained? PS-syntax's main working principle is CONSTITUENCY and CONSTITUENT CATEGORIES, which tends to insist on taxonomy, i.e. classification and distribution. Dependency (= D-) syntax is based on RELATIONS between ultimate syntactic units, and it therefore tends to be concerned with meaningful links, i.e. semantics. (A brief systematic comparison of both approaches is offered in Chapter 1, p. 13–17.) Given this, I think there are (at least) four reasons for the present dominance of PS-syntax in general linguistics.

1. English as Mother Tongue of the Founding Fathers of Modern Syntax

Even though this sounds a bit too Whorfian, I am fairly sure that PS-syntax could not have been invented and developed by a native speaker of Latin or Russian. Such languages feature an incredibly flexible (but far from arbitrary) word order and very rich systems of morphological markings; word arrangements and inflectional affixes are obviously contingent here upon relations between word-forms rather than upon constituency. To promote PS-representation in syntax, one has to be under the overall influence of English, with its rigid word order and almost total lack of syntactically driven morphology.[1]

However, English is very exotic in that it uses constituency almost as its only expressive device in syntax, i.e., as the only device for encoding syntactic structure in actual sentences. In other words, constituency (marked by word order + prosody) is in English the principal observable phenomenon used to indicate on the surface, albeit indirectly, the underlying syntactic relations. Let me emphasize: constituency is a MANIFESTATION of syntactic structure, not syntactic structure itself. But thinking in or even simply working mostly with English lures the researcher into mistaking this idiosyncratic surface trait of a particular language (i.e., relying mostly on word order and prosody to mark syntactic relations) for a universal mechanism of syntactic representation. It is, then, to be expected that in languages that do not use constituency as the main surface expressive device, the constituency, or phrase-structure, formalism will perform poorly as a means to represent syntactic structure.[2]

Notice that dependencies, on the contrary, are not a surface-observable phenomenon at all and therefore they are not language-specific. Being abstract relations, they possess enough generality to accomodate any type of syntactic organization. (This becomes clearer after the more detailed discussion of D-syntax which is offered in Chapter 1.)

2. Exaggerated Formalistic Drive

The *Sturm und Drang* years of modern syntax began with a crusade against "mentalism"; for more than two decades, only surface, directly observable data were admitted as legitimate. The Chomskyan revolution, with its emphasis on deep structures and underlying representations, changed the course of events, but to my taste, not radically enough. The "objective" approach, which rejects introspection as the main linguistic tool and values above all the formality and rigor of descriptions, still dominates the scene. This atmosphere is not favorable for syntactic dependencies: they are much less directly observable than constituency and therefore require more intuition-based steps to relate them to immediately tangible surface forms. In other words, it is more difficult to develop discovery procedures for syntactic dependencies than for constituency; and although, from the dominant point of view of modern linguistics, discovery procedures do not enjoy the kind of prestige they used to have before Chomsky, this fact is still perceived as a flaw.

3. Available Mathematical Apparatus

Modern linguistics, and especially syntax, is, in conformity with general tendencies of contemporary science, strongly biased toward mathematization. Linguists have made it a point of honor to borrow from mathematics as much as possible. The trend is clearly visible from Bloomfield (his "Set of Postulates for the Science of Language," 1926) to Harris to Chomsky and his followers. I find this phenomenon highly productive for linguistics; but the mathematical zeal of early prophets turned out to be harmful to dependencies. The fact is that until now, for describing the syntax of mathematical languages, mathematics has been using the PS-formalism almost exclusively. Especially in mathematical logic and programming languages the best known descriptive devices (= formal grammars) are consistently geared to PS-syntax: cf. Post production rules or Backus-Naur normal form (or, more generally, semi-Thue rewriting systems). All this was easily borrowed and adapted to the needs of PS-syntax. There was nothing comparable in mathematics that one could use ready-made for D-syntax.

4. Isolationist Attitude Toward Semantics

Even today, the basic working hypothesis in modern syntax is that of the centrality of syntax: syntactic structures are thought of as generated out of nowhere and only later on "interpreted" by semantic rules, i.e., converted into a semantic representation. Such an asemantic generation of syntactic structures lends itself better to PS-description. Had linguistics taken a different course, i.e. producing syntactic structures from underlying semantic representations, the situation would be much more favorable for dependencies. For semantics, relations viz. dependencies between semantic units are of the utmost value. Therefore, the fact that modern linguistic theories fail to put enough emphasis on dependencies seems to follow from the autonomist treatment of syntax ("generate structures first, and ask questions about meaning later").

There might be other reasons as well that explain the actual preponderance of PS-syntax in modern linguistics; however, for our purposes here it suffices to mention just these four:

1. English as the mother tongue of researchers and the main source of data
2. formalistic drive
3. available mathematical apparatus
4. lack of interest in semantics

The factors mentioned are not as valid today as they were fifteen or twenty years ago.

1'. As of mid-seventies, linguistics has been dealing with a greater variety of languages than ever before. The diversity and richness of factual data currently available in syntax are simply unprecedented, and English has obviously ceased to be the primary model for syntactic description. The need for a D-representation is thus emerging from the study of a large number of languages. (For instance, the proponents of Relational Grammar—cf. Perlmutter 1983—draw on their research of a few dozen languages, from Cebuano to Kinyarwanda, from Seri to Spanish, etc.)

2'. Linguistics' appetite for formalization has been largely satisfied. It has created its own formalisms (due mostly to the Chomskyan school) and no longer suffers from an inferiority complex with respect to mathematics; it can easily afford the risks of working with less formalized representations and techniques with a view towards formalizing them.

3'. In connection with 2', linguistics is not as dependent on mathematics as was the case some years ago. Linguists are less hesitant nowadays to develop formalisms of their own and let mathematicians worry about how to accommodate them. At the same time, within mathematics more interest is felt toward new, more sophisticated formalisms, biased toward dependencies. (I mean, in the first place, so-called "specification languages," being developed in computer science for the description of the state of affairs to which a particular algorithm must apply. These languages are based on predicate calculus and show much relational structure.)

4'. Semantics has become much more important than it was in the 60s and is continuously tightening its grip on linguistics, which entails new interest in relations, viz. in dependencies of all kinds.

These developments must be responsible, at least in part, for the trend clearly seen in present-day theoretical syntax: that towards a departure from the strict principles of PS-representation for syntactic structures. I would like to mention four most visible manifestations of this trend.

Bresnan's **lexical-functional grammar** (Bresnan 1982b) retains the PS-tree for representing the surface-syntactic structure of a sentence but introduces additional machinery to explicitly express grammatical relations: the so-called "functional structure," which is essentially a specification of dependency relations over the set of lexemes of the sentence under description.

Fillmore's **case grammar**, launched in the late sixties (Fillmore 1968), also starts from PS-trees but proposes semantically labeled dependencies, called "deep cases," between elements of the sentence.

Perlmutter's **relational grammar** (Perlmutter 1983, Perlmutter and Postal 1983) constitutes a decisive shift from PS- to D-representation in syntax: "grammatical relations must be considered to be primitive notions [of linguistic theory—I.M.] and must figure in syntactic representations" (Perlmutter 1983: xi), a grammatical relation (such as 'be the subject of' or 'be the direct object of') being nothing more than a syntactic dependency.[3]

And, finally, Hudson's **word grammar** (Hudson 1984) is already explicitly and consistently based on syntactic dependencies. In his book, Hudson discusses such problems as dependency direction, multiple and mutual dependencies, different dependency relations, similarities and differences between D- and PS-syntax, and so forth.

This is not the place to characterize these or similar approaches in detail. Suffice it to say that the recent trend in theoretical work shows that the time is ripe to speak about dependencies more broadly and more assertively. I have been working actively with dependencies and promoting them as a basic tool for syntactic representation for the last twenty-five years (Mel'čuk 1962, 1963, 1964a, etc. up to Mel'čuk 1979a; cf. also Mel'čuk and Pertsov 1987). Therefore, I feel I should share my experience in the domain with other linguists, which is my purpose in this book.

II. ORGANIZATION OF THE PRESENTATION

Dependency Syntax: Theory and Practice is by no means a thorough and systematic compendium on syntactic dependencies (for a real *Handbuch* on the matter see Kunze 1975). It is instead a collection of (relatively) self-contained studies covering a number of syntactic problems and trying to solve them within the framework of D-syntax. I do not develop a consistent and exhaustive theory of syntactic dependencies (although I do offer a brief outline of a D-formalism in Chapter 1 and an in-depth analysis of the notion of dependency in Chapter 3); rather, I propose to show how one can use dependencies to deal successfully with several notorious theoretical topics of syntax.

However, for my exposition to be convincing (and even sufficiently understandable), the book must show a certain unity. Therefore, its organization acquires quite a special importance; to facilitate the reader's access to the book's contents, I must dwell on these matters and justify the choices I have made. More specifically, two points call for discussion: (1) composition of the book (what is included in it), and (2) sequence of the parts (in what order they are included).

1. Composition of the Book

First, besides the introductory part, *Dependency Syntax* contains two gravitational centers: one group of studies dealing with the ergative construction and syntactic typology, and another group of studies concerning several very specific problems of Russian syntax. These two groups may seem, at first glance, to have little to do with each other, almost as if they were two different books under the same cover. But such an impression is wrong. These two topics, however distant and unrelated they might appear, have been chosen on purpose in order to illustrate the efficiency of dependency formalism in different domains. The greater the intellectual distance between two subject areas picked up to test a syntactic formalism, the better they fulfill their role (just like bearing supports in engineering: the wider the distance between their bottom ends, the more stable the whole structure). Let us be reminded that in physics, for instance, the most general theories are tested in different domains that are extremely remote from each other. Thus, the relativity theory was shown to hold both in astrophysics and nuclear physics; that is, from the depths of the universe to the depths of the atom. This by no means detracts from the unity of the theory, but on the contrary, enhances it. Similarly, introducing the dependency formalism in syntax necessitates the demonstration of its successful applicability in at least two quite different domains.[4]

Second, to evaluate the appropriateness and advantages of the dependency formalism, the latter has to be considered within a particular linguistic$_2$ framework.[5] In our case, this is the Meaning-Text approach, which puts forward the Meaning-Text Model (= MTM) of natural language. This approach has to be introduced, albeit briefly, to serve as a theoretical basis for further deliberations. The MTM lays a heavy emphasis on semantics and, more specifically, on the lexicon; syntax is viewed as determined and controlled both by the semantic representation and dictionary entries. Therefore, *Dependency Syntax* must include a large chapter on the MTM and on the very special dictionary that it presupposes: the Explanatory Combinatorial Dictionary. This chapter may seem like a foreign body within the book, but it is absolutely necessary. Many crucial notions, such as the deep syntax vs. surface syntax distinction, linguistic$_1$ representations of various levels, lexical functions and a host of other concepts, cannot be properly introduced except in such a chapter. I take very seriously de Saussure's famous saying that language is a system where everything is interrelated ("un système où tout se tient"); and because of this, I am in no position to talk about a syntactic formalism without a serious discussion of my general approach.

Third, *Dependency Syntax,* besides presenting the D-formalism and introducing a number of fundamental dependency concepts, has to cover at least the following three aspects: syntactic theory, syntactic description, and syntactic methodology (= principles of syntactic research); otherwise, the advantages of D-syntax are difficult to demonstrate. This, however, forces me to admit several rather heterogeneous studies into the book.

As a result, it is impossible to avoid the impression that *Dependency Syntax* is organized in a peculiar way; but such an organization is inevitable and, given the circumstances, fully justified.

2. Sequence of the Chapters

Since the present book is, as indicated above, not a systematic treatise, its chapters cannot be easily arranged in a linear sequence. Logical relations between chapters are basically multidimensional; in many cases any order is arbitrary and violates some logical requirements, so that pragmatic compromises have to be found.

Generally speaking, the parts into which *Dependency Syntax* is divided appear in the order of decreasing generality, so that the broadest and very general problems considered at the beginning of the book, and the narrowest and very specific ones are considered at the end. (Notice, however, that the theoretical value of a very specific problem may be very high.) In this connection, two clarifications are in order.

First, the chapter on the Meaning-Text model should, from a purely logical viewpoint, precede anything else. But this would be too hard on the reader; it seems advisable to let him warm up with less formal characteristics of D-syntax in general, which is, in addition, much more directly related to the book's main subject. Accordingly, the description of the MTM follows the introductory description of the D-formalism.

Second, the chapter on syntactic zeroes is rather theory-oriented, and for this reason it should go into the part dealing with syntactic theory, nearer to the beginning of the book. However, it constitutes an excellent logical bridge between all the ergative chapters and the Russian syntax chapters. Taking this into consideration, I preferred to put it at the end of the syntactic description part.

As a result, this book's content is organized as follows:

Part I, "Dependency Syntax: an Overview," contains two chapters in addition to the present Introduction. Chapter 1 sketches the notion of syntactic dependency, indicating its main properties and comparing it to phrase structure. Chapter 2 presents a general outline of the Meaning-Text Model, so that references can be made to different levels of linguistic$_1$ representation or to different components of natural language as appearing in this model.

Part II, "An Important Concept of Dependency Syntax: Surface-Syntactic Relations," includes only one chapter (Chapter 3), which deals with different major classes of dependencies, distinguishes syntactic dependencies (as opposed to semantic and morphological ones) and states several criteria for the presence, direction and type of a syntactic dependency.

Part III, "Syntactic Theory: The Ergative Construction," is dedicated to a syntactic phenomenon that is extremely popular nowadays, namely, ergativity. Intimately linked to the problem of voice, the problem of ergativity has prompted revision of PS-representation. In fact, lexical-functional grammar and relational grammar both started from the discussion of passives and related topics. Part III has three chapters. Chapters 4 and 5 analyze what is thought to be an ergartive construction in two specific languages, Dyirbal and Lezgian, while Chapter 6 offers a tentative definition of the concept itself.

Part IV, "Syntactic Description: Surface-Syntactic Models and Notions," concentrates, in two chapters, on descriptive aspects of syntax. Chapter 7 contains a formal syntactic description (in terms of dependencies) of a fragment of an exotic language, Alutor. Chapter 8 discusses zero lexemes—elements of a language's lexicon that play an important role in its syntactic structures, especially in connection with grammatical voices and voice-like phenomena.

Finally, Part V, "Syntactic Methodology: Some Thorny Questions of Russian Syntax," demonstrates, in its three chapters, the techniques of syntactic argumentation in a dependency framework. Chapter 9 describes a peculiar Russian construction: non-speech verbs introducing direct speech (such as *Počemu ty ne prišël? - rasserdilsja Džon,* lit. '"Why didn't you come?", became-angry John' [i.e., 'asked John angrily']. Chapter 10 analyzes an interesting case of adjectival agreement in animacy and the category of animacy in Russian. And Chapter 11 examines "difficult" constructions exhibiting peculiar case government of numeral phrases by quantitative prepositions. Four methodological principles, to be used in syntactic argumentation, are stated at the end of Part V.

From this survey, one sees immediately that my source data stem exclusively from languages other than English. I can give two reasons for this. As already indicated above, English is pedagogically far from ideal to illustrate the advantages of syntactic dependency; languages of quite a different type are needed to fully demonstrate the strong points of the dependency representation. Furthermore, a description of English surface syntax in terms of dependencies is now available: Mel'čuk and Pertsov (1987), so that anyone eager to see how dependencies apply to English can refer to that title.

In conclusion, let me make two points. First, in a book such as this, it is really impossible to supply full bibliography. Given the astronomical number of publications in the relevant domains, I am in no position to guarantee a balanced representation of references, even for specialized subjects. Second, I would greatly appreciate any remarks, suggestions, criticisms, counterexamples, etc., concerning not only the bibliography but the essence and form of this book.

NOTES

1. (Page 4.) The only traces of morphological agreement or government in English are: the verbal suffix *-s* in 3sg of the present indicative, different number-person forms of BE, singular — plural opposition *this* vs. *these* and *that* vs. *those,* as well as the oblique-case forms of personal pronouns *me, us, him, her, them* and of the interrogative pronoun *whom*; the status of the nominal possessive form in -'s is dubious (see Mel'čuk 1986: 48-52).

2. (Page 5.) Following the same line of reasoning, one could point out that the transformational bias of modern syntax stems as well from the specific nature of English. Compared with Russian, for instance, English features a plethora of syntactic processes for which nothing similar exists in Russian: *Tough*-Movement, *There*-Insertion, *Do*-Insertion, Clefting, Tag Question, Extraposition, Dative Movement; different Raisings, although they are marginally present in Russian, are by no means as common there as their English counterparts. (The lack of syntactic processes in Russian is explained by much freer word order in this language.) "A large number of meaning-invariant syntactic processes in English provided rich material for a theory of grammatical transformations . . . [and] suggested the idea that a theory of syntactic processes can also serve as a theory of paraphrase" (Nakhimovsky 1983: 120). Such Anglo-centricity is found even in some of the most recent American syntactic theories. As Nichols (1986:115) points out, "Chomsky's analysis of case and government (Chomsky 1982: 48ff.) can be read as making the following implicit assumption(s): . . . Every dependent must bear the marker of its syntactic relation. ... The effect [of this] is to build into the fundamentals of core grammar the dependent-marking nature of English (and generally Indo-European) morphosyntax."

3. (Page 7.) Note that even within the PS-approach itself the need for distinguishing between head (= governor) and modifier (= satellite, dependent) was strongly felt from the very beginning: cf. Pittman (1948); then X-bar theory (Chomsky 1970) etc. to Hawkins (1984). But systematically and explicitly distinguishing governors and dependents in a sentence means switching to D-syntax. This is very clearly stated by Hudson (1984: 94), who says the following: indicating the modifier-to-head relation or linking an NP that is a sister of a particular verb to this verb by an index etc., "would presumably be exactly equivalent to a dependency arrow. Once this device, and all its attendant machinery, is introduced into a phrase-structure grammar, it would be very close in power to a dependency grammar; . . . However, the question which would then arise would be whether all the bits of phrase-structure theory which distinguished it from dependency theory (notably, higher nodes) were really necessary; and if the answer was no, then the resulting change would in effect mean that phrase-structure grammar had become dependency theory."

4. (Page 8.) Note that besides this general consideration, there are specific and substantive links between the ergative construction and the problems of Russian syntax dealt with in this book. In particular, discussing the ergative construction inevitably entails the problem of voice; discussing voice brings one to the problem of syntactic zero subjects; syntactic zero subjects are very typical of Russian and have to be analyzed within the appropriate context. So that our two topics are, after all, not as distant as one might think.

5. (Page 8.) The English adjective *linguistic* is ambiguous between 'pertaining to language(s)' (= German *sprachlich*) and 'pertaining to linguistics' (= German *sprachwissenschaftlich*). Since in many contexts this distinction is crucial, but by no means obvious, I will use subscripts: *linguistic$_1$* denotes the first sense, and *linguistic$_2$* the second. (However, where this ambiguity does not seem harmful, I will write simply *linguistic*.)

Chapter *1*

BASIC ELEMENTS OF DEPENDENCY REPRESENTATION IN SYNTAX

I. INTRODUCTORY REMARKS

The term **dependency theory** (as opposed to **phrase-structure theory**) is found quite frequently in the literature; it seems to have originated with Hays (1960, 1964b). The term **dependency grammar** is also in current use, e.g., Robinson (1970a). However, in this chapter I do not by any means propose a THEORY of syntax. To do so, I would have to state certain postulates and then try to deduce from these a system of valid statements concerning the syntax of natural languages; however, I will not do anything of the kind. Nor will a formal grammar or grammars be discussed, with the concomitant questions of generative capacity, decidability problems, etc. Therefore, the reader will find neither of the terms *dependency theory* or *dependency grammar* in my presentation.

All I intend to do is to suggest an artificial FORMAL LANGUAGE, or a formalism, for describing natural sentences at the syntactic level. (Cf. my general preoccupation with linguistic$_2$ metalanguage, Chapter 4, I, p. 154.)

By its logical nature, dependency formalism cannot be "proved" or "falsified." Leaving aside simple errors and inconsistencies, it can be evaluated solely in terms of expediency or naturalness, not in terms of truth or falsity. Dependency formalism is a tool proposed for representing linguistic$_1$ reality, and, like any tool, it may or may not prove sufficiently useful, flexible or appropriate for the task for which it has been devised; but it cannot be true or false.

To be sure, I am making a certain claim about the dependency formalism:

||Namely, I claim that dependencies are much better suited to the description
||of syntactic structure (of whatever nature) than constituency is.

One can argue for or against this claim. But in the present chapter I will simply explain what the dependency formalism means and what the reasons are for its introduction. The remainder of the book demonstrates various facets of its application and in this indirect way substantiates it. But there will be no systematic discussion of its advantages or disadvantages.

Thus, Chapter 1 is devoted to the specification of a particular formal language, in this case dependency, or D-, language.

II. DEPENDENCY LANGUAGE VS.
PHRASE-STRUCTURE LANGUAGE

As is well known, there are two diametrically opposed methods of describing the syntactic structure of natural sentences: **dependency (D-) trees** and **phrase-structure (PS-) trees**. Obviously, combinations of the two methods are possible, with lines of compromise being drawn at different points; but there is no essentially distinct third possibility. Since the reader may be more familiar with PS-language, I will offer a first, impressionistic characterization of D-language in terms of the former.

There are five major respects in which D-language is different from PS-language:

1. Constituency vs. Relations
A PS-tree of a natural-language expression shows which items of the latter —wordforms or phrases—"go together" (i.e., combine) with which other items to form tight units of a higher order. A PS-tree reveals the structure of an expression in terms of groupings of its actual elements: maximal blocks, which consist of smaller blocks, which consist of still smaller blocks, etc.:

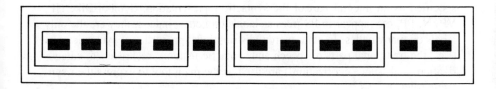

The PS-approach concentrates on CONSTITUENCY and is, therefore, rightly called the "(immediate) constituent method/system." The main logical operation in this approach is set inclusion (to "belong to a phrase" or "belong to a category"). Under the PS-approach, an actual sentence is, so to speak, cut into (generally two) major constituents, each of which is subsequently cut in its turn, etc. This approach thus favors the analytical viewpoint.

A D-tree, on the other hand, shows which items are related to which other items and in what way. A D-tree reveals the structure of an expression in terms of hierarchical links between its actual elements:

The D-approach concentrates on the RELATIONSHIPS between ultimate syntactic units, i.e., wordforms. The main logical operation here is the establishing of binary relations. Under the D-approach, an actual sentence is, so to speak, built out of words, linked by dependencies. This approach thus favors the synthetic viewpoint.

Note that a D-tree allows for a natural representation of groupings as well: a grouping, i.e., a word and its phrase (e.g., *the* **tidbit** *most important from a practical point of view*), appears in D-language as a node with the corresponding complete subtree hanging from it. For instance, all of the important properties of constituents listed in Zwicky (1978) can be as easily (in some cases, I would say even more easily) expressed in terms of dependencies.

At the same time, a "pure" PS-tree does not allow for a natural representation of relations between wordforms. A distinction as important as that between a syntactic head and its satellite, or modifier, recognized since the very beginning of the PS-era, cannot be stated at all within a strict PS framework. (We can of course add head-vs.-satellite marking to a PS-tree, but that would mean having recourse to D-formalism; cf. Note 3 in the Introduction.) The so-called configurational expression of some relation (such as 'to be the subject of' or 'to be the object of') does not in fact indicate a D-relation between wordforms. Rather, it signals the role played by a grouping within a larger grouping: once again, this is a distributional, and not a relational, characteristic.

2. Categorization and Its Function

In a PS-tree, the syntactic class membership (i.e., categorization) of an item is specified as an integral part of the syntactic representation. Symbols like NP, VP, N, PP, etc. appear in PS-trees as labels on nodes; indeed, they are the only labels on many nodes. In other words, distributional properties of syntactic units (i.e., the traditional parts of speech and syntactic features, rechristened 'categorization' and 'subcategorization') are used as the main tool to express their syntactic roles.

In a D-tree, on the other hand, the symbols representing the syntactic class membership and other syntactic properties of an item are not admitted as immediate elements of syntactic structure. All such information is relegated to the dictionary entry of the item (i.e., **lexeme**, see page 54) in question, more specifically to its syntactics;[1] this information is utilized when a Synt(actic) S(tructure) is constructed, but within the latter it remains behind the scenes. I believe that data on distributional (i.e., combinatorial) properties of an item cannot properly represent its actual syntactic role in a text. (In a D-tree, syntactic roles are indicated explicitly, by special labels; see below, p. 16.)

3. Terminals and Non-terminals

In a PS-tree, most nodes are non-terminal: they represent syntactic groupings or phrases and do not correspond to the actual wordforms of the sentence under analysis. Under certain transformations of PS-trees, many parasitic non-terminals are created, so that a special technique of "pruning" PS-trees had to be devised.

A D-tree, on the contrary, contains terminal nodes only; no abstract representation of groupings is needed. This statement should not be construed as implying that all the nodes in a D-tree stand in one-to-one relation to the wordforms of the sentence in question. On the one hand, a surface D-tree might have nodes corresponding to zero wordforms (see Chapter 8), such as the Russian zero copula in the present tense:

Russian *Ivan učënyj*, lit. 'Ivan scientist' $\Longleftarrow$

$$BYT'_{ind, pres} \text{ 'be'}$$

where BYT' $_{ind, pres}$ is manifested in the sentence as a zero word form.

On the other hand, an amalgamated wordform can be represented by two nodes in the D-tree:

French *au* /o/ 'to the' $\Longleftrightarrow$ À LE

and so forth.

In a deep D-tree, structural words are not represented at all, and certain fictitious lexemes, lexical functions, idiom symbols, etc. may appear, although all these do not necessarily have a direct equivalent in the sentence (Chapter 2, pp. 60ff.) However, except for a number of systematic discrepancies stated explicitly for each language, a node in a D-tree represents a wordform, never a phrase. (As indicated above, any phrase can be easily specified in a D-tree, if need be, by indicating its head and the complete subtree hanging from it.)

4. Linear Order of Nodes

In a PS-tree, nodes must be ordered linearly. The order is not necessarily that of the actual wordforms of the sentence, but some linear order is unavoidable. Therefore, any word-order rule has to be formulated as a reshuffling of the initial wordform string (all the while keeping track of the changes, since the initial word order might be meaningful). The PS-language is essentially linear.

In a D-tree, on the other hand, the nodes are in no linear order at all. The linear order of wordforms in the sentence is an expressive means used by actual languages to encode something different from this order itself, namely syntactic relations, and therefore, linear order should not be present in syntactic structures. The D-language is essentially two-dimensional.

Let it be reminded that in the Meaning-Text framework, linear order of symbols is never allowed to carry information in semantic and syntactic representations; whatever has to be stated should be expressed exclusively by means of explicit symbols.[2] (Cf. the remarks in Chapter 2, pp. 53 and 60.) Thus, the absence of linear order in our D-trees is a corollary of this general principle.

5. Labeling Syntactic Roles

A PS-tree does not specify the type of syntactic link existing between two items (and cannot do so, at least not in a natural and explicit way).

A D-tree, on the other hand, puts particular emphasis on specifying in detail the type of any syntactic relation obtaining between two related items. The meaningful labeling of all branches in a D-tree constitutes an important feature of the Meaning-Text approach. It raises an interesting question about the inventories of universal deep-syntactic relations and language-specific surface-syntactic relations—a question that cannot even be asked within the PS-framework. (Failing to compile a list of syntactic relations is very much like failing to compile a list of phonemes or of grammatical categories of a language.)

Chapter 3 below discusses at length several criteria proposed for establishing inventories of surface-syntactic relations; tentative inventories have been suggested for several languages:

English	Mel'čuk and Percov (= Pertsov) (1973b, 1987)
French	Kulagina (1970: 40–44), Percov and Polovko (1979: 8–13), Apresjan et al. (1984: 45–54)
Russian	Mel'čuk (1963: 490–493), Hays (1964a), Klimonov et al. (1969: 71–77), Mel'čuk (1974a: 221–234), Apresjan et al. (1978: 265–269)
Somali	Žolkovskij (1971: 12–13)

I cannot undertake here a detailed comparison of PS-trees and D-trees, nor elaborate on their (non-)equivalence and respective merits and disadvantages; nor will I discuss attempts to devise a combined method of syntactic representation that embodies the best aspects of both formalisms while trying to circumvent their drawbacks. Instead, I refer the reader to (in particular) Padučeva (1964), Gaifman (1965), Gladkij (1966: 8–29; 1968, 1971, 1981), Beleckij (1967), Fitialov (1968), Robinson (1970a, b) and Hudson (1976, 1980a, b, 1984: 92–98), and limit myself to a comparison of PS-and D-formalisms on the basis of an example.

Let us take an English sentence, e.g., (1) and then draw its PS-structure (1′) and its D-structure (1″).

(1) *She lov'd me for the dangers I had pass'd, And I lov'd her that she did pity them* (Shakespeare).

See Figs. 1-1 and 1-2 on pages 18 and 19, respectively.

The PS-structure needs sixty-one nodes to represent a sentence of 18 word-forms; the D-structure uses exactly eighteen nodes. In the PS-structure, the linear order of nodes is relevant: for instance, if we destroy it, there is no way of distinguishing between *She loved me . . . and I loved her . . .* and *I loved her . . . and she loved me.* In the D-structure, the linear order of nodes is absolutely irrelevant: all the information is preserved through labeled dependencies. (To emphasize this, I use a quite arbitrary order of nodes in the graphic layout of the D-structure.) It is also obvious that, while the PS-structure is filled mostly with non-terminal categorization symbols, there are no such symbols in the D-structure.

III. THE RATIONALE BEHIND SYNTACTIC DEPENDENCIES

In order to shed additional light on the dependency approach in syntax, we need to discuss the following two points: (1) the nature of syntactic relations and (2) the nature of syntactic structure.

1. The Nature of Syntactic Relations

As is well known, natural language has only two major types of expressive means—lexical and non-lexical—to encode the information a sentence carries.

Lexical means are simply words. The set of lexical means used in a sentence is the list of all wordforms, or lexeme occurrences, that constitute it.

Non-lexical means are of three varieties:
- linear order of wordforms
- prosody (intonation contours, pauses, phrase and sentence stresses)
- inflections (i.e., morphological categories)

Of these three varieties, word order is the most important and the most universal, being necessarily present in every language and in every sentence. It is imposed by the physiologically conditioned linearity of human speech. Inflections, on the other hand, are the least important (from the syntactic point of view), because they are the least universal linguistic$_1$ means: some languages lack them entirely; in all languages there are uninflected words, which, however, are syntactically linked to other words in a sentence. Prosody occupies an intermediate position.

There are no other types of linguistic$_1$ expressive means.

(1')

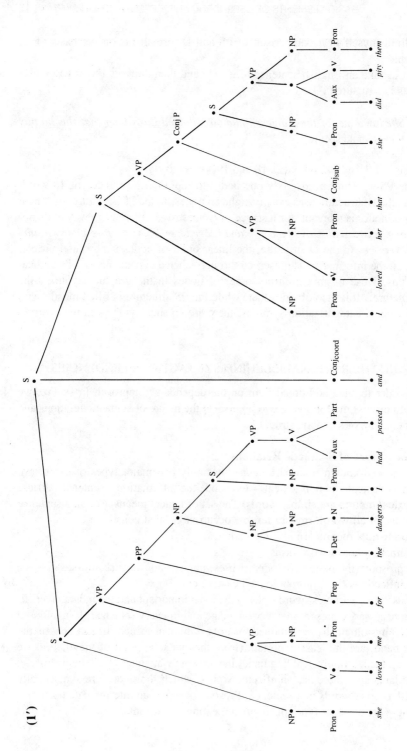

Figure 1-1
The PS-structure of Sentence (1)

18

(1″)

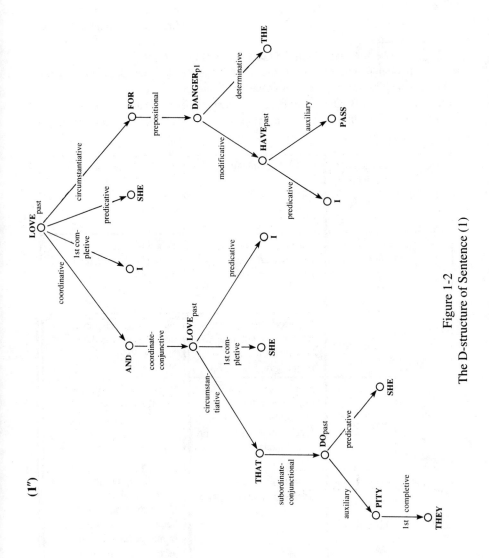

Figure 1-2
The D-structure of Sentence (1)

19

Both lexical and non-lexical expressive means of a language can be used in one of the following two ways:

- Either in a SEMANTIC capacity, i.e., to convey meaning immediately, being directly connected to a portion of the Sem(antic) R(epresentation) of the sentence.
- Or in a SYNTACTIC capacity, i.e., to mark relations between linguistic₁ entities, while being connected to the SemR only indirectly, through the syntactic structure.

This may be summarized in the table below (Fig. 1-3).

Non-lexical means in a syntactic capacity are called **syntactic means** for short; syntactic means are enclosed within the box in the bottom right corner of the table in Fig. 1-3. Our list of syntactic means types is exhaustive: all links between wordforms in a sentence, which as a whole might be called **syntactic in-**

Type of linguistic₁ means \ Capacity in which it is used		Semantic	Syntactic
Lexical means		Full words; *decision, way, intend, because (of), usually, window, kiss*, . . .	Function words: (strongly) governed prepositions and conjunctions, auxiliary verbs, . . .
Non-lexical means	Word order	Wordform arrangements marking communicative structure: theme *vs.* rheme, given *vs.* new, . . .	Wordform arrangements marking constructions: N + N, Prep + N, Adj + N, Adv + Adj, . . .
	Prosody	Prosodies marking assertions, questions, exclamations, . . . , or focus, emphasis, . . . , or irony, menace, anxiety, . . .	Prosodies marking constructions, borders of constituents, . . .
	Inflections	Inflections marking number in nouns, or tense and aspect in verbs, . . .	Inflections marking grammatical case in nouns, or gender, number and case in adjectives, or number and person in verbs, . . . (agreement and government categories)

Figure 1-3
Linguistic₁ Means and their Possible Usages

formation, are expressed either by word order, or by prosody, or by inflections or by a combination of these. Once again, word order is the most important and universal of syntactic means: it is actively exploited by all languages, while inflections in a syntactic capacity are by no means characteristic of all languages; prosody is used by all, but its role can vary greatly from language to language.

It seems fairly obvious that syntactic means, i.e., devices used by natural languages to encode syntactic structure in actual sentences, cannot be part of the structure itself: otherwise, we have a flagrant *contradictio in terminis*. Therefore, syntactic word order, prosody and inflections should be banned from the representation of syntactic structure. All the more so insofar as the three syntactic means are highly ambiguous, interdependent and inexplicit; they convey syntactic information in a very complicated and cumbersome way. Thus, the same word order can signal different constructions, while one construction can manifest itself in different word orders, and so forth. But ambiguity and inexplicitness should not be permitted in the representation of syntactic structure. This is one more reason to exclude order, prosody and inflections in their syntactic capacity from the SSynt-representation.[3]

However, syntactic means do convey information; we cannot simply omit them. They have to be replaced by a formal device, which will fulfill their function while being free of their major drawbacks, i.e., ambiguity and inexplicitness. This device must indicate the INTERACTIONS, or relations, among wordforms, since wordforms of a sentence are ordered, intonated and inflected one in relation to another (for example, "X stands to the right/left of Y"; "X has a higher/lower contour than Y"; "X has the same gender and number as Y"; etc.). This leads us to a conception of the syntactic structure of a sentence as a pair consisting of two sets:

— the set of all the wordforms appearing in the sentence, or more precisely, of all the reduced **D(eep-)Morph(ological) R(epresentations)**, or DMorphRs, of the wordforms (a DMorphR is a lexeme occurrence subscripted for all meaning-bearing grammemes, see below, p. 61);

— a set of *n*-ary relations defined over the first set (i.e., a set of syntactic relations).

The requirement of maximal simplicity and uniformity entails positing a set of **binary** relations. On the one hand, the reduction of *n*-ary relations (with arbitrary *n*) to a system of binary relations is formally always possible. On the other hand, all facts of natural language known to me show that natural syntax lends itself readily to description in terms of binary relations. Therefore, I propose the use of binary syntactic relations between wordforms as the sole means for representing the syntactic structures of natural sentences. The question immediately arises as to what kind of relations these should be.

First, a syntactic relation must be **antisymmetric**:

if X→Y, then ⌐ (X←Y).

This follows from the existence of such pairs as *value restriction* vs. *restriction value* or *symbol sequence* vs. *sequence symbol* etc., since VALUE ←RESTRICTION (= *value restriction*) and VALUE→RESTRICTION (= *restriction value*) clearly contrast semantically.

Second, a syntactic relation must be **antireflexive**:

⌐X⟲.

This follows from the fact that no wordform can be linearly ordered or inflected with respect to itself. (Moreover, the antireflexivity of a binary relation follows from its antisymmetry.)

Third, a syntactic relation must be **antitransitive**:

if X→Y and Y→Z, then ⌐(X→Z).

This means, in other words, the observance of the following principle: "The direct dependent of my direct dependent is never my own direct dependent." This follows from the existence of such expressions as [*a*] *usually reliable source,* where *usually* is by no means directly related to *source* (cf. [*a*] *source usually reliable* [*in that* . . .]), or *locate the sunken submarine,* with no direct relationship between *locate* and *the* or between *locate* and *sunken*. (Note that both the antisymmetry and antireflexivity of a syntactic relation follow from its complete antitransitivity; that is, if for any n, from X→Y$_1$, Y$_1$→Y$_2$, . . . , Y$_{n-1}$→Y$_n$ it follows that ⌐(X→Y$_n$), then the relation → is antisymmetric and antireflexive.)

Fourth, a syntactic relation must be **labeled**, i.e., distinguishable: in language $\mathcal{L}$, there must be several pairs of syntactic relations, of the type $\overset{r_1}{\rightarrow}$ and $\overset{r_2}{\rightarrow}$, where $r_1 \neq r_2$. This follows from the existence of such pairs as, for instance, Russian *žena-vrač*, lit. 'doctor-wife = the wife who is a doctor' vs. *žena vrača* 'doctor's wife'. In a dependency syntactic structure (SyntS) without labeled dependencies, both expressions would become identical:

ŽENA$_{sg}$→VRAČ$_{sg}$

To distinguish these two phrases in a dependency SyntS, we need different types of syntactic relations, so that ŽENA$_{sg}\overset{r_1}{\rightarrow}$VRAČ$_{sg}$ represents *žena-vrač* and ŽENA$_{sg}\overset{r_2}{\rightarrow}$VRAČ$_{sg}$, represents *žena vrača*. A corresponding English example is [*He will*] *do* [*it*] *naturally* vs. [*He will*] *do* [*it*], *naturally*. The labels on syntactic relations must then be indicative of the syntactic constructions they represent.

To sum up: If the syntactic means of natural languages (i.e., word order, prosody, inflection) are banned from the representation of syntactic structure, then the latter has to use binary relations between wordforms, these relations being antisymmetric, antireflexive and antitransitive; moreover, they are sorted, i.e., labeled with the names of the particular constructions they stand for. (I will not go into more detail here, since all of Chapter 3 is dedicated to this question.)

The relations I am talking about are called **syntactic dependencies** and are represented by arcs with arrows: X→Y. We will say that Y **depends** on X or, conversely, that X **governs** Y; X is called the (syntactic) **governor** of Y, and Y is called a (syntactic) **dependent** of X. (I will avoid the more current terms **head** vs. **modifier** for the following reasons. First, Y is by no means always a modifier of X: Y can be an object or the subject of X, its complement or attribute, its conjunct, etc.; I feel it is embarrassing to call, e.g., an object a modifier. Second, the term **head** is better used in the sense of 'top node', see immediately below. Consider, for instance, the expression *for all my important guests*; I would like to say that *for* is the governor of the phrase *all my important guests* (but not its head), while *guests* is the head of this phrase (but not its governor). In fact, the **head** of P is then a component of P which is the governor of all other components of P.)

2. The Nature of Syntactic Structure

The above observations give rise to the following preliminary notion of syntactic structure: namely, a set of wordforms linked by syntactic relations, the latter as specified in the preceding subsection. Such a structure is best represented by a **connected directed labeled graph**; its **vertices**, or **nodes**, are labeled with reduced DMorphRs of wordforms, and its **arcs**, or **branches**, are labeled with the names of syntactic relations. (This graph must be CONNECTED, since no component of a sentence can be fully detached from it without destroying its integrity. The graph must also be DIRECTED since its arcs depict antisymmetric relations.) This preliminary notion needs to be refined in light of certain linguistic₁ facts.

First, a syntactic structure must contain exactly one node that does not depend on another node; this unique non-governed node is called the **top node**, or **root**. Let X, Y, Z be nodes of a syntactic structure; then:

$$\text{in a SyntS, } (\exists X), (\forall Y) \urcorner (X \leftarrow Y) \text{ and } (\not\exists Z \mid Z \neq X), (\forall Y) \urcorner (Z \leftarrow Y).$$

This condition follows from the fact that, in principle, a natural sentence can be reduced to just one word (this is not true of any sentence in any language). In English this is only possible with imperatives (*Go!*), but in many languages (Russian, Spanish, Japanese, to name a few) a one-word complete sentence is a regular phenomenon.

Second, in a syntactic structure, no node may simultaneously depend on two or more other nodes:

$$\text{in a SyntS, } (\forall X, Y, Z) \urcorner (Y \rightarrow X \leftarrow Z)$$

This is the principle of the uniqueness of the syntactic governor: every node, except the top node, must have just one governor. This condition follows from the fact that in most typical cases, if the positioning of a word in a sentence is a function of other words, it depends on just one other word; the same is roughly true of prosody and inflection. (For some exceptions in case of inflection, see the next section.)

These two conditions, namely the obligatory presence of one absolute syntactic governor in a sentence and the uniqueness of the syntactic governor for every syntactic unit, fully determine the form of syntactic structure as we understand it. This structure proves to be a **rooted tree** (in the mathematical sense), specifically a D-tree.[4]

That is how we arrive at the concept of dependency tree as a formal means for representing the syntactic structure of a sentence. Two final observations are not out of place here, as they provide further justification of our choice.

First, dependency trees have been independently accepted in many grammatical traditions, beginning from Antiquity. In particular, so-called "traditional parsing," widespread at the pedagogical level throughout the nineteenth and twentieth centuries, is nothing more than dependency language, albeit non-formalized (cf., in this connection, McCawley 1973). Constituent trees, on the contrary, were devised (according to Percival 1976) only at the beginning of the twentieth century by the German psychologist Wilhelm Wundt, from whom they were borrowed and introduced into linguistics by Bloomfield in the early thirties. To be sure, this is not a sound scientific argument; but the overwhelming allegiance of grammarians and language teachers to syntactic dependency constitutes, at least to my mind, an important indication of its validity.

Second, in the theoretical framework we adopt here, the syntactic dependency tree constitutes (as we will see in Chapter 2, Fig. 2-1) an ideal bridge between the semantic network and the morphological/phonological chain.

IV. CURRENT FALLACIES CONCERNING SYNTACTIC DEPENDENCIES

In the literature one finds a number of unjustified criticisms leveled at dependency formalism that claim its insufficiency or inadequacy. These can be divided into three major groups: (1) "Double Dependency," (2) "Mutual Dependency" and (3) "No Dependency." As far as I can judge, all of these are due to logical confusions — mostly to the failure to distinguish purely syntactic dependencies from other types of relations, in particular semantic and morphological dependencies (see Chapter 3). It should be helpful to discuss briefly a few sample cases.

1. "Double Dependency"

Some say that in a natural sentence a wordform can simultaneously depend on two different wordforms, its "clause mates"; therefore, the principle of uniqueness of the syntactic governor is unacceptable and a syntactic structure cannot, generally speaking, be a rooted tree. Typical examples include constructions of the following type:

(2) a. *Wash the dish* **clean.**
   He pounded the box **flat.**
   He sanded the stick **smooth.**
   b. *We found John* **working.**
   We heard Mary **singing.**
   The watchdog smelled us **coming.**

The boldface adjective (or present participle) is said to be simultaneously dependent on the verb and on the preceding noun (which is the direct object of the verb).

   The same construction in a language such as Russian is even more revealing, since here the adjective in a similar role takes its grammatical case (the instrumental) from the verb, while receiving its gender and number from the direct object of the verb:

(3) Russian *My našli*
      we found

$$\left\{ \begin{array}{lll} zal & pust + \mathbf{ym} \\ \text{hall[masc]} & \text{empty} & \text{MASC.SG.INST} \\ komnatu & pust + \mathbf{oj} \\ \text{room[fem]} & \text{empty} & \text{FEM.SG.INST} \\ zaly \;/\; komnaty & pust + \mathbf{ymi} \\ \text{halls} \quad \text{rooms} & \text{empty} & \text{PL.INST} \end{array} \right\}$$

But there is no double SYNTACTIC dependency in (2) and (3). What really happens here is that the adjective in question, which is syntactically dependent on the verb only, is semantically related to (i.e., predicated of) the direct-object noun, and in Russian it is, in addition, morphologically controlled by this noun. With proper distinction of different major types of dependencies no problem arises. (See Nichols 1978 for a careful analysis of such syntactic constructions; cf. also Nichols 1981.)

   A further example is the case of relative clauses with the relative pronoun; the pronoun is said to depend both on the verb of the relative clause and on its antecedent, as in (4a):

(4) a. Russian

$$\left\{ \begin{array}{lll} \textit{žurnal,} & kotor + \mathbf{yj} \\ \text{magazine[masc]} & \text{which} & \text{MASG.SG.ACC} \\ \textit{kniga,} & kotor + \mathbf{uju} \\ \text{book[fem]} & \text{which} & \text{FEM.SG.ACC} \\ \textit{pis'mo,} & kotor + \mathbf{oe} \\ \text{letter[neut]} & \text{which} & \text{NEUT.SG.ACC} \\ \textit{žurnaly} \;/\; knigi \;/\; pis'ma, & kotor + \mathbf{ye} \\ \text{magazines} \quad \text{books} \quad \text{letters} & \text{which} & \text{PL. ACC} \end{array} \right\} \begin{array}{l} \textit{my čitaem} \\ \text{we read} \end{array}$$

Here, the gender and the number of the relative pronoun come from its antecedent, while its case comes from the verb.

However, once again, the relative pronoun depends syntactically only on the main verb of the relative clause. True, it depends on its own antecedent as well, but solely morphologically; moreover, there is also an anaphoric link between *kotoryj* 'which' and its antecedent. But all this is irrelevant from the viewpoint of syntactic dependency. (Syntactically speaking, the relative clause depends — via its top node, the main verb — on the noun modified, i.e., on its antecedent:

b.

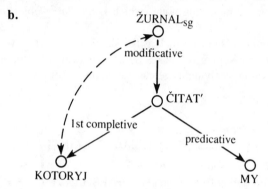

The broken line shows the coreference between *žurnal* and *kotoryj*.)[5]

2. "Mutual Dependency"

Fairly often, grammarians insist on mutual dependency between the main verb of a sentence and its grammatical subject: the verb, so to speak, represents the whole sentence, but the grammatical subject (GS) controls its form, as in *The child **is** playing* vs. *The children **are** playing* etc. However, it must be clear now that this is one more case of confusion between the syntactic dependency of the GS on the main verb and the morphological dependency of the verb on the GS. (For more details see Chapter 3, p. 108.) Let me remark here that in many languages a transitive verb agrees not only with its GS, but also with its direct object (for instance, in Alutor: Chapter 7); however, this fact does not belie the universality of the dependent status of direct objects.[6]

3. "No Dependency"

It is commonly believed that in coordinated phrases no syntactic head can be found, i.e., there is no dependency between conjoined items. The reason is the presumed symmetry of coordination: *John and Mary* is basically identical to *Mary and John*. However, this symmetry obtains only at the semantic level and only for purely logical uses of conjunctions such as 'and' or 'or'. In the majority of cases there is no reversibility in coordinated structures:

(5) **a.** *He stood up and gave me the letter* ≠ *He gave me the letter and stood up.*

b. *Go to bed, or I'll spank you!* ≠ **I'll spank you, or go to bed!*
c. *not only a good worker but also a nice man* ≠ *not only a nice man but also a good worker*

Malkiel (1959) and Cooper and Ross (1975) cite several dozen types of conjoined phrases that are not reversible. Moreover, the right-hand component of a conjoined construction, that is, the conjunction plus the conjunct it introduces (i.e., the conjunction phrase), is always omissible, while the left-hand component (i.e., left conjunct) is not:

(6) a. *John, but not Mary, came ⇒ John came*
⇏ **But not Mary came*
b. *several interesting and beautiful magazines*
⇒ *several interesting magazines*
⇏ **several and beautiful magazines*

To me, this clearly indicates that from the strictly syntactic viewpoint, the left conjunct and the conjunction phrase are not equal: there is a dependency relation between them. Since the passive syntactic valency of a conjoined construction is that of its left conjunct, and by no means that of the conjunction phrase, we must conclude that the conjunction phrase depends syntactically on the left conjunct. Within the conjunction phrase itself, the conjunct introduced by the conjunction depends on it (since it is the conjunction that determines the passive syntactic valency, or distribution, of the conjunction phrase):[7]

c. *John → and → Mary*
John → but not ⟵Mary
interesting → and → beautiful
stood → up and → gave

Confusing genuine syntactic dependencies with morphological and semantic ones is the most important but by no means the only source of the unwarranted reproaches directed against dependency trees. There are at least two others: the unwillingness to distinguish, on the one hand, deep vs. surface syntactic structures and, on the other hand, syntactic vs. communicative structures. (For more details concerning both distinctions see Chapter 2.) Let me illustrate this with two examples.

First, it is said that within a dependency tree one cannot naturally express the essentially lexical character of numerous word-like phrases: analytical forms (such as *have done, will stick, was struck, more beautiful, the most beautiful*), compound prepositions (*with respect to, in connection with*), phrasal verbs (*give up, turn over, set aside, stake out*), genuine idioms (*hit the hay* 'go to bed,' [*be left*] *holding the bag* '[be left] with the responsibility or blame for failure'), compound proper names (*Mount Everest, St. Lawrence River, Nova Scotia*), and the like. All such expressions behave and "feel" like single words, but in a dependency tree they must be represented in exactly the same way as regular phrases (i.e., syntactically free combinations of words), which—in the opinion of dependency tree opponents—distorts their nature. To that it could be answered that on the surface-syntactic level the expressions in question ARE phrases, not words. But on the deep-syntactic level, such an expression is represented by a single node and thus its lexical character is fully expressed. The paradoxical status of an analytical form or a phrasal verb etc. is exactly its being a "word" in the DSyntS and a phrase in the SSyntS. In this way, granted the deep vs. surface distinction, the dependency tree captures quite well the specificity of wordlike phrases.

Second, it is claimed that in a dependency tree it is impossible to indicate the semantic difference between the following two readings of sentence (7):

(7)   *He gave three talks on human rights in Chicago in 1982*

means either

(7′)   'He gave three talks on human rights, and it happened in Chicago in 1982' [there were no other talks on human rights by him] or

(7″)   'He gave three talks on human rights in Chicago, and it happened in 1982' [his talks on human rights in other places may have occurred at different dates]

The problem is to indicate whether the time adverbial *in 1982* modifies the verb *gave,* along with the place adverbial *in Chicago,* or whether it modifies the whole constituent *He gave . . . in Chicago.* To that it could be answered that in the syntactic structure as such this distinction should not be expressed at all: it is absolutely irrelevant from the syntactic point of view. To be sure, it is essential for the proper understanding of sentence (7) but it belongs to the communicative structure, rather than to syntax. The distinction in question is reducible to the topic vs. comment division (theme vs. rheme, in our terms: page 58 ff.). Namely, for the (7′) reading, the theme **Ⱡ** is 'He gave . . . rights', and 'in Chicago in 1982' is the rheme **Я**; for the (7″) reading, the **Ⱡ** is 'He gave . . . in Chicago', the **Я** being 'in 1982'. Therefore, I think that the incapacity of a dependency tree to express this distinction (in sharp contrast to a phrase-structure tree, which cannot avoid expressing it) is one of its advantages over PS-trees.[8]

V. SOME INSUFFICIENCIES OF SYNTACTIC DEPENDENCY

Despite the foregoing evidence, there do exist some constructions which do not lend themselves to a satisfactory description in terms of D-language alone. These are, for instance, modification structures in which an element (*X*) modifying the head of a phrase can contrast semantically with the same element modifying the whole phrase:

(8)

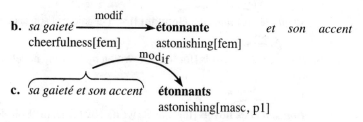

Let us take an example.

(9) French **a.** *sa gaieté*   *et*   *son*   *accent* —modif→ **étonnant**
                his cheerfulness   and   his   accent[masc]   astonishing [masc]

        b. *sa gaieté* —modif→ **étonnante**   *et   son   accent*
                cheerfulness[fem]   astonishing[fem]

        c. *sa gaieté et son accent*   **étonnants**
                                            astonishing[masc, pl]

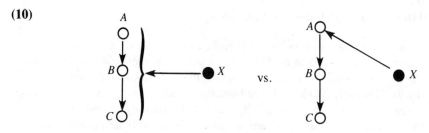

Using only dependency, one cannot supply, in a natural way, two different structural descriptions for (9b) vs. (9c): in both cases, *étonnant* must be described as dependent on *gaieté*, and relevant information is lost ((9b) means that only his cheerfulness is astonishing, (9c) means that both his cheerfulness and his accent are astonishing).

An opposite situation obtains when modification of an element (*X*) by a phrase as a whole contrasts with the modification of *X* by separate elements of the same phrase:

(10)

Here is an English example of this phenomenon:

(11) **a.** *Bob* → *and* → *Dick's* **novels** 'novels written by the team "Bob + Dick"'
        vs.
        b. *Bob's* → *and* → *Dick's* **novels** 'novels written by Bob and novels written by Dick'.

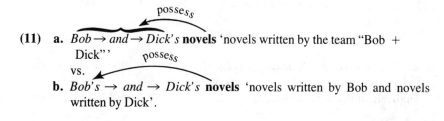

There is no way of naturally representing the observed difference by means of D-language.

To be sure, we could use one of the following three devices in order to safeguard the status of syntactic dependencies.

First, there is the logical possibility of attaching a special label to a dependency in order to indicate that it connects an element with a whole phrase rather than with its head only:

(12) **a.** *sa gaieté et son accent* **étonnant** [for 'sa gaieté étonnante et son accent']
    vs.
    sa gaieté et son accent **étonnant** [for '(sa gaieté et son accent) étonnants'];

    b. *Bob and Dick* **novels** [for 'novels written by Bob and novels written by Dick']
    vs.
    Bob and Dick **novels** [for 'novels written by the team "Bob + Dick"'].

While technically irreproachable, this method seems highly unnatural and is therefore rejected.

Second, we could consider constructions of the type illustrated in (9c) and (11b) as being elliptical and assume that the full forms of these latter are, respectively,

(9c′)   *sa gaieté étonnante et son accent étonnant*
and
(11b′)   *Bob's novels and Dick's novels,*

which do not pose any problem for D-representation. There do indeed exist elliptical utterances for which the D-tree in its pure form cannot be used; but then a PS-tree is not good for them, either (something like *Dick kissed Susan, and Joe, Mary*). However, (9c) and (11b) obviously do not fall into this category: these sentences are not perceived as elliptical (on the contrary, their "full" variants (9c′) and (11b′) are strongly marked and somewhat artificial); moreover, a PS-tree would easily capture the semantic distinction between (9a) and (9c):

(13)   *sa gaieté et (son accent* **étonnant**)
    vs.
    (sa gaieté et son accent) **étonnant**

(For (11a) vs. (11b) the PS-language is equally helpless.) Consequently, we cannot accept the "ellipsis" solution, either.

Third, the inflections showing the contrast we are interested in could be considered meaning-bearing (cf. page 61) and retained in the syntactic structure. For (9c), we should then preserve the plural marker on *étonnant* (and thus indicate the relation of this adjective to the whole conjoined string; for (11b), the repeated possessive marker should be retained (so that it indicates the "disjunctive" meaning of the phrase).

This is a really attractive possibility, since natural languages feature numerous constructions where morphological categories ordinarily taken to be syntactically induced acquire a full-fledged semantic status. Take, for instance, the following Russian phrases:

(14) Russian

a. *n´jujorksk* + ***ij***   *i*   *čikagsk* + ***ij***
New York   MASC.SG.NOM   and   Chicago   MASC.SG.NOM
universitet +   *y*
university[masc]PL.NOM
vs.
n´jujorksk + ***ie***   *i*   *čikagsk* + ***ie***   *universitet* + *y*
                   PL.NOM   and   PL.NOM

The first phrase refers to two universities: one in New York and one in Chicago; the second, to several universities in New York and several in Chicago.

b. *Daj*   *mne*   *čaj* + *∅*   'Give me tea' [and not coffee, wine, etc, . . .]
give   me   tea   ACC
vs.
Daj   *mne*   *čaj* + *u*   'Give me some tea.'
                   tea   PART(itive)

In Russian, grammatical number in adjectives and grammatical case in nouns are syntactically induced (by agreement and government, respectively); yet in (14) they are meaning-bearing and have to be retained in the syntactic structure in order to avoid loss of information.

Note that in this connection, PS-language does not fare any better than D-language—both are insufficient for expressing the desired distinction— unless some additional machinery is introduced. (This solution to the problem of constructions of the type exemplified in (14), i.e., admitting syntactically-conditioned grammemes into the syntactic structure when they become meaning-bearing, is convincingly argued for in Iomdin 1979.)

The use of "semanticized" grammemes in the syntactic structure is a powerful device sufficient to close all the gaps in D-formalism. Since semanticized grammemes must be admitted anyway, we could have recourse to them wherever needed and thus eliminate the problem of D-language's insufficiency. But I wish to avoid an unwarranted exploitation of semanticized grammemes; that is, I choose to use these only where there is no other recourse (such is the case in (14) but not in (9) or (11)). In other words, I prefer a more natural description: if the problem for D-formalism is created by a contrast between dependency of or on the whole phrase and dependency of or on the head of this phrase, this contrast should be expressed as such, explicitly and systematically. Therefore, I introduce **groupings** into D-formalism. A grouping is a complete subtree taken as a whole; groupings must be indicated in D-trees wherever this is relevant. To return to examples (9) and (11), the contrasts we are concerned with must be expressed as follows (the horizontal bracket indicates a grouping):

(15)   a.   *gaieté → et → accent   étonnant* [= (9a), i.e., only the cheerfulness is astonishing]

vs.

gaieté → et → accent   étonnant [= (9c), i.e, both the cheerfulness and the accent are astonishing]

(15)   b.   *novels → Bob → and → Dick* [= (11b), i.e., novels written by Bob plus those written by Dick]

vs.

novels → Bob → and → Dick [= (11a), i.e., novels written by Bob and Dick together]

D-language is thus supplemented by a device resembling PS-language (since groupings are logically equivalent to phrases). Let it be emphasized, however, that a grouping is not a constituent, because unlike a constituent, (1) its elements are not linearly ordered, (2) dependency relations among them are explicitly shown and (3) there is no higher node to represent the grouping as a whole.

Moreover, I allow the grouping device only in strictly controlled contexts: for instance, in conjoined structures of the types illustrated and in a few other structures in which the syntactic scope of "operator" words (such as negation or *only*) may play a role. For the time being, I do not know whether groupings are generally confined to coordination and "operator"-word constructions or whether there are other SSynt-constructions where groupings may prove necessary. (It is interesting to see that such a staunch partisan of dependencies as Hudson also found it unavoidable to use constituency in order to describe coordinate constructions: Hudson 1984: 211 ff.) In any event, contrary to the viewpoint of the proponents of combined syntactic representations, where groupings are used extensively along with dependencies (cf., e.g., syntactic groups of Gladkij: 1968, 1971, 1981), I admit only an occasional use of groupings, and do so if and only if the D-language proves insufficient. My principal aim is to exploit the possibilities of dependency representation to the fullest extent.

The above exposition has, I believe, shown that D-language is sufficient for the representation of the syntactic structure of natural sentences, with the following two provisos:

1. Three important distinctions must be strictly observed: namely, the distinction between syntactic and semantic/morphological dependencies; that between surface and deep syntactic structures; and that between syntactic and communicative structures.
2. Grouping is invoked only in a number of strictly circumscribed cases.

To be more convincing, I have tried to show that known objections to D-trees as the basic means of syntactic representation miss the point. The discovery of new, valid ones would be an interesting challenge.

VI. SOME ADVANTAGES OF SYNTACTIC DEPENDENCIES

Syntactic dependencies have proved useful in many respects but I am in no position to discuss this topic here in depth. Yet I would like to point out four areas of general syntax where serious progress has been achieved due mostly to the consistent use of D-formalism.

1. Syntactic Typology of Languages

It was shown many years ago (Mel'čuk 1964b) that the directions of the syntactic and the morphological dependencies linking two given wordforms of a sentence can be opposite:

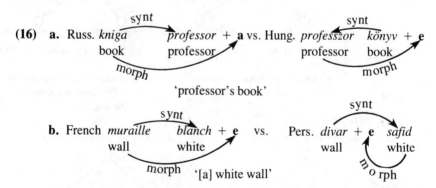

(For more examples and a systematic analysis see Chapter 3, Section II.) This means that in some constructions of some languages the syntactic governor is morphologically marked under the influence of the dependent (cf. the Hungarian and Persian phrases in (16)), while other languages choose to morphologically mark the dependent under the influence of the governor (Russian and French in (16)). That is, some languages opt for governor-marking, and some for dependent-marking. Nichols (1986) thoroughly investigates these two patterns and demonstrates that they have significant implications for linguistic typology as well as for historical linguistics. Languages use one or the other marking pattern very consistently throughout their grammar, and the choice of the pattern explains certain word-order and related phenomena. "One reason for the neglect [of the difference between morphological governor-marking and dependent-marking—I. M.] may lie in the fact that it is easily observed and described in dependency grammar, but is less obvious to constituency grammar" (Nichols 1986: 56).

2. Voice and Voice-like Categories

The voice in general (or passivization in particular) involves changing the syntactic relations between the deep-syntactic and the semantic actants (roughly, arguments) of a verb; it is a kind of conversion (in the logical sense: $R(a, b) = R^{-1}(b, a)$). Compare:

(17) a. English

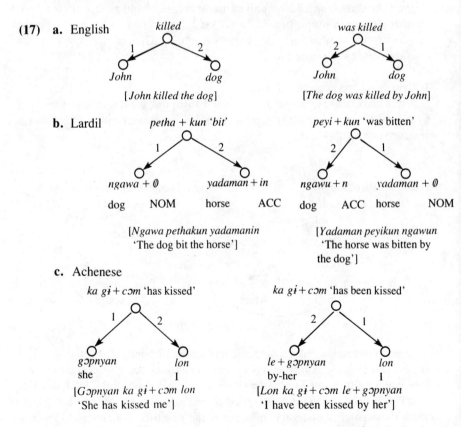

[*John killed the dog*]

[*The dog was killed by John*]

b. Lardil

[*Ngawa pethakun yadamanin* 'The dog bit the horse']

[*Yadaman peyikun ngawun* 'The horse was bitten by the dog']

c. Achenese

[*Gɔpnyan ka gi+cɔm lon* 'She has kissed me']

[*Lon ka gi+cɔm le+gɔpnyan* 'I have been kissed by her']

[In the Achenese example, *ka* marks the perfect, and the prefix *gi* marks lsg.]

Let me make it quite clear that the deep-syntactic actant labels "1" and "2", appearing in (17), are by no means to be confused with syntactic labels "1", "2", etc. of Relational Grammar. An actant DSyntRel *i* of the Meaning-Text theory, say

$$X \xrightarrow{\ i\ } Y,$$

covers all syntactic elements *Y* depending on *X* that can express, at the DSynt-level, a given semantic argument of 'X'. Our "1" marks the DSynt-actant that corresponds (on the surface) to the grammatical subject. Our "2" marks the DSynt-actant that corresponds to the "closest" or "strongest" surface comple-ment present: therefore, this "2" can refer to a direct or indirect object or even to a "chômeur" (in Relational Grammar terminology): these further distinctions are made at the SSynt-level, while at the DSynt-level they are ignored. Our "3" marks the DSynt-actant that corresponds to the second "closest" surface comple-ment, and so forth. In *The dog was killed by John*, the phrase *by John* is the "closest" surface complement, and it is taken to be the DSynt-actant 2 of the pas-sive verb. (With a transitive verb, the DSynt-actant 2 is the direct object.) For more about actants and actant DSyntRels see Chapter 2, II, **2**, pp. 63ff.

It is clear that voice transformations cannot be properly characterized using only word classes, word order, grammatical case or verbal morphology. (For co-gent arguments, see Perlmutter and Postal 1983.) We need syntactic relations ex-plicitly shown and labeled, in order to ensure useful generalizations and an ade-quate cross-linguistic account of what happens when a sentence is passivized. It is no accident that a calculus of possible voices and a unified description of voice-like categories for a large variety of languages were first proposed within the D-framework (Mel'čuk and Xolodovič 1970, Xolodovič 1974, Xrakovskij 1978, 1981). Nor is it an accident that a systematic inquiry into the diversified problems of voice triggered the elaboration of Relational Grammar (Perlmutter 1983), which is essentially based on labeled dependencies. And it is no accident that a careful description of the syntax of Polynesian languages, where voice dis-tinction play such an important role (Chung 1978), is carried out in terms of grammatical relations, i.e., dependencies, rather than constituency.

3. Word Order

Using dependencies in the highly formalized framework of automatic text pro-cessing quickly led (around 1960) to the discovery, by Hays and Lecerf, of an extremely important property of word order: so-called **projectivity**.

A sentence is called **projective** if and only if among the arcs of dependency linking its wordforms:

(*i*) no arc crosses another arc [* ]

(*ii*) no arc covers the top node [* 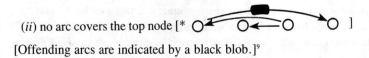]

[Offending arcs are indicated by a black blob.][9]

It turns out that most sentences of a language are projective. For instance, the English sentence (18) is projective:

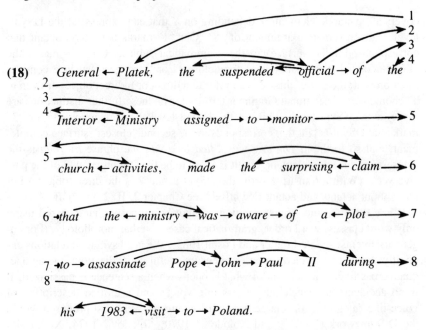

(18)

There exist, to be sure, several types of non-projective sentences but all of them are somehow marked: emphatically, stylistically, communicatively (emphatic topicalization tends to cause numerous violations of projectivity, especially in colloquial speech), or else they contain special syntactic elements, such as clitics. Here is a small selection of non-projective sentences from different languages (the offending arcs are marked as above):

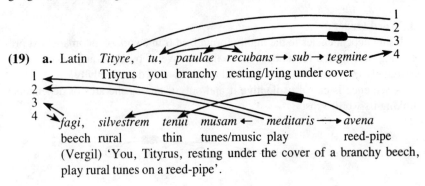

(19) a. Latin *Tityre, tu, patulae recubans* → *sub* → *tegmine*
           Tityrus you branchy resting/lying under cover

fagi, silvestrem tenui musam ← *meditaris* → *avena*
beech rural   thin tunes/music play   reed-pipe

(Vergil) 'You, Tityrus, resting under the cover of a branchy beech, play rural tunes on a reed-pipe'.

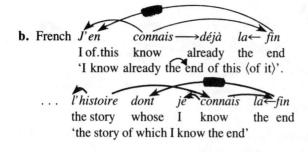

b. French J'en   connais ⟶ déjà   la ← fin
I of.this know   already the end
'I know already the end of this ⟨of it⟩'.

... l'histoire dont   je   connais la ← fin
the story whose I   know   the end
'the story of which I know the end'

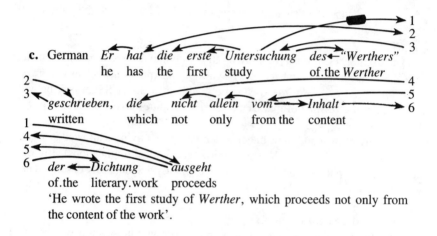

c. German Er   hat die   erste   Untersuchung des ← "Werthers"
he   has the first   study   of.the Werther

geschrieben, die   nicht allein vom ⟶ Inhalt
written   which not   only   from the content

der ← Dichtung   ausgeht
of.the literary.work proceeds
'He wrote the first study of *Werther*, which proceeds not only from the content of the work'.

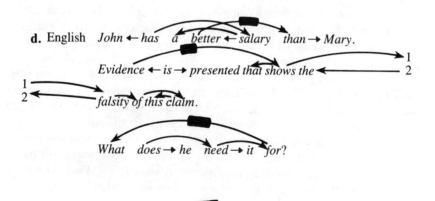

d. English John ← has   a   better ← salary   than ⟶ Mary.

Evidence ← is ⟶ presented that shows the ←—————— 2

falsity of this claim.

What does ⟶ he   need ⟶ it for?

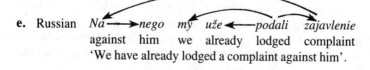

e. Russian Na ⟶ nego   my uže ← podali zajavlenie
against him we already lodged complaint
'We have already lodged a complaint against him'.

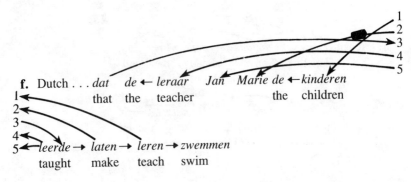

f. Dutch . . . *dat   de ← leraar   Jan Marie de ← kinderen*
that   the   teacher   the   children

leerde → laten → leren → zwemmen
taught   make   teach   swim

. . . 'that the teacher taught Jan to make Marie teach the children to swim'.

Dutch sentences of this type were brought to linguists' attention by Bresnan et al. (1982). Note that I represent the SSyntS of an expression such as *teach John to swim* as *teach→John to→swim*, i.e., without a direct SSynt-link between *John* and *swim*. In spite of that, sentence (19f) features unavoidable non-projectivity.

The study of the conditions under which non-projectivity is allowed is a fascinating task (which has, by the way, serious typological implications). But once again, here is a phenomenon which can be explicitly and naturally described only within the framework of D-formalism.

4. Restricted Lexical Co-occurrence

Syntactic dependencies supplied the framework within which it was possible to develop a powerful formal device for the description of restricted lexical co-occurrence: **lexical functions** (Žolkovskij and Mel'čuk 1967, Mel'čuk 1982). Lexical functions will be briefly characterized in Chapter 2. pp. 61 ff. Suffice it to say here that it would be next to impossible to establish anything of a similar nature within PS-formalism.

Three other domains where one easily sees the advantages of D-syntax are discussed in Hudson (1984: 120ff). These are (1) active valency of lexemes (semantic and syntactic)—what requires what as its dependent etc. (cf. van Megen 1985), (2) co-occurrence restrictions imposed either by the governor on its dependent or vice versa and concerning morphological form or word order (e.g., *enough* follows its governor: *good enough* vs. **enough good*) and (3) displacement of a sentence element along the dependency chain (e.g., **What** *did you say he said*?, from the underlying *You←did→say he←said→***what**?).

This concludes my brief introduction to syntactic dependency. But before we proceed to the real business, to the substantive syntactic problems tackled in Parts II through V, I would like to offer to an interested reader a fairly representative bibliography of theoretical works on syntactic dependency. It is organized essentially in chronological order:

Tesnière (1959)
Hays (1960, 1961, 1964a, b)
Lecerf (1960)
Hirschberg (1961)
Lynch (1961)
Fitialov (1962, 1968)
Mel'čuk (1962, 1963, 1964a
  [especially 17–27], 1970,
  1973c, 1974a [especially
  208–235], 1979a)
Mel'čuk and Percov (= Pertsov)
  1973a, b, 1975, 1987)
Iordanskaja (1963, 1964, 1967)
Beleckij, Grigorjan and
  Zaslavskij (1963)
Beleckij (1967)
Padučeva (1964)
Marcus (1965a, b)
Gaifman (1965)
Baumgartner (1965)

Gladkij (1966: 8–29, 1968, 1973;
  228–310, 1981)
Galdkij and Mel'čuk (1983: 151–187)
Kunze and Priess (1967–1971)
Kunze (1975)
Dolinina (1969)
Robinson (1970a, b)
Heringer (1970)
Goralčiková (1973)
Jelitte (1973)
Vater (1975)
Machová (1975)
Happ (1976, 1977, 1978)
Dönnges and Happ (1977)
Hudson (1976, 1980a, b, 1984)
Korhonen (1977)
Garde (1977)
Apresjan et al. (1978)
Dahl (1980)
Matthews (1981: 71–95)

To this I would like to add a few titles that do not use or discuss D-language in its pure form but that are obviously concerned with problems crucial from the dependency viewpoint (such as the head vs. modifier distinction or syntactic roles). I will cite these in chronological order as well: Starosta (1975, 1981), Van Valin and Foley (1980), Gazdar and Pullum (1981), Hawkins (1984).[10]

NOTES

1. (II, **2**, p. 15.) **Syntactics** is the third component of a linguistic₁ sign, which is an ordered triplet

⟨'signatum'; /signans/; (syntactics)⟩.

The syntactics of a sign is, roughly, a set of specifications concerning all possible combinations of this sign with other signs, these specifications being such that they cannot be deduced either from its signatum or its signans. The most typical components of syntactics include, among others:

a. Part of speech
b. Syntactic features
c. Grammatical gender of nouns
d. Government pattern
e. Declension or conjugation type
f. Lexical functions

For more on syntactics see Mel'čuk (1982: 26ff).

2. (II, **4**, p. 16.) This principle runs counter to the viewpoint adopted in most modern linguistic approaches. One of the rare exceptions is Sanders (1972: 95) where it is required that "all terminal semantic representations be free of ordering relations" and that "there be no reordering" in a grammar. A comprehensive discussion of the problem is found in Meisel and Pam (1979).

3. (III, **1**, p. 21.) Word order, prosody and inflections that appear in their semantic capacity, i.e., that convey meaning directly, are reflected in the syntactic representation, but not as constituent elements of the syntactic structure. Meaning-bearing word order is depicted by the syntactic-communicative structure; meaning-bearing prosody by the syntactic-prosodic structure (see Chapter 2, p. 66), and meaning-bearing grammemes appear as subscripts to lexical nodes.

4. (III, **2**, p. 24.) One often finds in the literature a further condition imposed on D-trees; e.g.:

> "if *A* depends directly on *B* and some element *C* intervenes between them (in linear order of string), then *C* depends directly on *A* or on *B* or on some other intervening element" (Robinson 1970: 260).

This condition, however, defines a special subclass of D-trees, so-called **projective trees**, and concerns not so much the D-trees proper as word order in natural languages. I will discuss the property of projectivity later in this chapter (VI, p. 35)

5. (IV, **1**, p. 26.) There are more complicated cases of "double dependency" challenging the adequacy of D-trees. For instance, in his careful and thorough study (1979–1980), Sannikov introduces the following series of examples ("lexico-semantic coordination," as he calls the phenomenon):

(i) Russian *Nikto   i   nikomu   ne   pomogaet.*
nobody   and   to-nobody   not   helps
lit. 'Nobody and to nobody helps' = 'Nobody helps nobody'.

(ii) Russian *Kto   i   komu   pomog?*
who   and   to-whom   helped
lit. 'Who and whom helped?' = 'Who helpled whom?'

(iii) Russian *Ja   govorju   s   poètom   i   o   poète.*
I   talk   with   poet   and   about   poet
lit. 'I talk with a poet (and) about a poet'.

In all such constructions, different elements of the sentence (the grammatical subject and an indirect object in (i) and (ii), two different prepositional objects in (iii)) are conjoined, to produce highly idiomatic Russian expressions, possible only in restricted contexts (the conjunction must be *i* 'and'; the conjoined elements must be negative or indefinite pronouns or the occurrences of the same lexeme). Sannikov argues for double syntactic dependency of the right-hand members in such conjoined strings: on the left-hand member (hence coordination) and on the governing verb (hence subordination); according to him, the dependency structure of (i) is as follows:

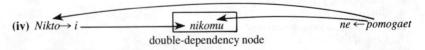
(iv) *Nikto→ i ————————▶ nikomu ————————ne ◀─pomogaet*
double-dependency node

But I think that in (iv) we observe, once again, a confusion between syntactic and semantic/morphological dependencies: *nikomu* does not depend on *pomogaet* syntactically; *nikomu* does depend on *pomogaet* both semantically and morphologically. To see that this is so, we need only try putting *i nikomu* in the normal linear position assigned to objects:

(v) *Nikto ne pomogaet nikomu,*
 but not
 *Nikto ne pomogaet i nikomu.

As far as word order and syntactic prosody are concerned, *nikomu* depends exclusively on *i* and, via *i*, on *nikto*. For purely syntactic dependency all other considerations are irrelevant.

6. (IV, **2**, p. 26.) A curious case of what is erroneously considered to represent double dependency is analyzed at length in Mel'čuk (1985: 59–81). This is the case of Russian phrases "Numeral + Noun": *dva stol+a* 'two tables', *pjat´ stol+ov* 'five tables' etc., where the numeral controls the genitive of the noun. It is shown that syntactically the numeral always depends on the noun; morphologically, however, the opposite direction of dependency is possible in specific contexts.

7. (IV, **3**, p. 27.) Coordination, which has always been a stumbling block for many linguistic theories, possesses a rich literature, of which I will indicate here Dougherty (1970–71), Hudson (1984: 211–240) and Gazdar et al. (1985: 169–181). However, most published discussions are dedicated to the semantic properties of coordinate structures, to logical constraints on coordination, etc., more or less shunning its strictly syntactic aspects. Since our dependency description of coordination could be regarded by some as counterintuitive, a serious justification of it is in order, but I cannot offer it here, as it would constitute an additional chapter. Instead, I will hint at main logical factors on which the proposed treatment is based:

1) In a phrase of the form *X and Y,* no element can remain "independent," i.e., unrelated to any other element. (This follows from obligatory connectedness of a SyntS, see page 23.)
2) In the phrase *X and Y,* the conjunction cannot be the head, since the distribution of the phrase is determined by its conjuncts and by no means by the conjunction. (This follows from Criterion B.I. for the direction of a Synt-dependency, see Chapter 3, page 132.)
3) *X* is the head of the phrase, since the distribution of *X and Y* is that of *X,* and by no means that of *and Y.*
4) In the chunk *and Y,* the conjunction is the head: it determines the distribution of the expression to a greater degree than *Y.* (Once again, this follows from the aforementioned Criterion B.I.)

As a result, we have:

$$X \xrightarrow{\text{coordinative}} and \xrightarrow{\text{coord-conjunctive}} Y.$$

8. (IV, **3**, p. 28.) Take the case of linear ordering of modifying adjectives:

(i) *I would like to see a few* $\left\{ \begin{array}{c} \textit{interesting Chinese} \\ \\ \textit{Chinese interesting} \end{array} \right\}$ *novels.*

The meaning is different in each variant: either those of all Chinese novels that are interesting, or those of all interesting novels that are Chinese. Should we say that in the first variant, the adjective *interesting* modifies the phrase *Chinese novels,* while in the second one, *Chinese* modifies the phrase *interesting novels*? I do not think so: the observed difference lies, as I believe, in the communicative organization, rather than in syntactic structure.

9. (VI, **3**, p. 36.) The term **projectivity** stems from a different formulation of the concept:

> Let there be a dependency-tree diagram drawn over an actual sentence so that each node is linked to the corresponding word of the sentence by a vertical line. Then the PROJECTION of the domain of each node (i.e., the complete subtree that hangs down from this node, including the node itself) is a continuous line segment, corresponding to a continuous piece of linear text.

Another term sometimes used for the same concept is **adjacency** (Hudson 1984: 98ff.).

10. (At the very end of the chapter, p. 39.) A good review of the present state of art concerning the PS approach and a rich bibliography can be found in Gazdar et al. 1985.

Chapter 2

THE MEANING-TEXT LINGUISTIC MODEL AS THE FRAMEWORK FOR DEPENDENCY SYNTAX

I. BASIC POSTULATES AND MAIN PROPERTIES
OF A MEANING-TEXT MODEL

The Meaning-Text approach to language was put forward in Moscow more than twenty years ago by Alexander K. Zholkovsky and the present writer (Žolkovskij and Mel'čuk 1965).[1] Conceived as a general framework for the study and description of natural languages, this approach is based on the following three postulates.

Postulate 1

A speech event, which is considered as given, involves, in addition to the speaker, the addressee and the physical channel linking them, another three essential components:[2]

a. A certain CONTENT, or hierarchically organized pieces of information to be communicated (by the speaker), which we will call **meaning(s)**. Meanings are taken to be distinguishable entities forming a denumerable (i.e., infinite) set.

b. Certain (linguistic$_1$) FORMS, or hierarchically organized physical phenomena to be perceived (by the addressee), which we will call **text(s)**. Similarly, texts are distinguishable entities and also form a denumerable set.

c. A many-to-many CORRESPONDENCE, or mapping, between the set of meanings and the set of texts. This correspondence constitutes **language proper** (or "language in the narrow sense of the term").

Our view of natural language can then be diagrammed as follows:

(1) $\{\text{MEANING}_i\}$ $\underset{\text{LANGUAGE}}{\overset{\text{language proper}}{\Longleftrightarrow}}$ $\{\text{TEXT}_j\} \mid 0 < i, j \leq \infty$

In other words, (1) means that a natural language is viewed as a logical device that establishes the correspondence between the infinite set of all possible meanings and the infinite set of all possible texts and vice versa. For a given meaning, this device must ideally produce all the texts that, in the judgement of native speakers, correctly express this meaning, thus simulating SPEAKING; from a given text, the device must extract all the meanings that, according to native speakers, can be correctly expressed by the text, thus simulating SPEECH UNDERSTANDING.

The following three remarks are in order:

1. The words *meaning* and *text* are used here as purely technical terms whose content must be specified by convention. 'Meaning' stands for 'invariant of synonymic transformations' and refers only to information conveyed by language; in other words, it is whatever can be extracted from or put into an utterance solely on the basis of linguistic₁ skills, without any recourse to encyclopedic knowledge, logic, pragmatics or other extralinguistic abilities. 'Text' stands for 'the physical form of any utterance' and refers to all linguistic₁ signals (words, phrases, sentences, etc.,); it has nothing to do with *text* in the sense of so-called "text grammar". i.e., with discourse.

2. Rather than dealing with meanings and texts as such, we deal with their symbolic representations: Sem(antic) R(epresentation)s for meaning, and Phon(etic) R(epresentation)s for text. SemRs and PhonRs are formal entities— expressions in artificial languages, or "transcriptions", that must be devised for this purpose. Consequently, we can rewrite (1) in a more precise form (2):

(2) $\{\text{SemR}_i\}$ $\overset{\text{language proper}}{\Longleftrightarrow}$ $\{\text{PhonR}_j\} \mid 0 < i,j \leq \infty$

The nature of SemR and PhonR will be discussed below.

3. The correspondence between the set of SemRs and the set of PhonRs in a language is many-to-many. All natural languages are ridden with SYNONYMY (a SemR corresponds to many different PhonRs) and HOMONYMY/POLYSEMY (a PhonR corresponds to many different SemRs). This fact, especially the existence of widespread synonymy, is crucial to the Meaning-Text approach (cf. Postulate 3 below).

Postulate 2

Devices of the type presupposed by our view of natural language (cf. (1) and (2) above) can be described by so-called **cybernetic models**, with the actual language considered as a kind of "black box" where only the input and output can be observed, but the internal structure cannot.

A **cybernetic model of X** is (roughly) a system of rules approximating the observed behavior of X. In our case, X is a language, and its observed behavior is the Meaning-Text correspondence; therefore, our linguistic$_1$ model is called a **Meaning-Text Model** (MTM).

In more rigorous terms, then, an MTM of language $\mathcal{L}$ is a finite set of rules specifying the many-to-many correspondence between the denumerable (i.e., infinite) set {SemR$_i$} of semantic representations of $\mathcal{L}$ and the denumerable set {PhonR$_j$} of its phonetic representations.

This statement requires four important qualifications:

1. The MTM is by no means a generative or, for that matter, transformational system: it is a purely EQUATIVE (or translative) device. The rules of the MTM do not generate (i.e., enumerate, specify) the set of all and only grammatically correct or meaningful texts. They simply match any given SemR with all PhonRs which, in accordance with native speakers' linguistic$_1$ intuition, can convey the corresponding meaning; inversely, they match any given PhonR with all SemRs that can be expressed by the corresponding text.

   Therefore, a SemR is not transformed into a PhonR. A parallel can be drawn with a cake recipe that controls the making of a cake: in no way is the recipe as such converted into the cake, although all its prescriptions are faithfully reflected in the cake. Similarly, a given SemR is but a set of descriptive statements according to which a relevant text is to be produced. But this set itself is not affected by the process of text production—the initial SemR does not change at all. (As a result, the MTM does not need any complex machinery to keep track of the rules applied to an initial representation, of its modifications, of the order of operations, and the like.)

2. The rules of the MTM represent the mapping {SemR$_i$} $\Leftrightarrow$ {PhonR$_j$} quite STATICALLY, i.e., as correspondences between elementary fragments of SemRs and elementary fragments of PhonRs. The transition mechanism, i.e., the dynamic device, or procedure, for moving from actual complex SemRs to actual complex PhonRs and vice versa is not considered. I believe that such a dynamic device, while necessary to put the above static mapping to work, lies outside the field of linguistics, at least as yet. The MTM can be compared to a bilingual dictionary, which presupposes, but does not include, rules for looking up the words it contains; then the dynamic device driving the MTM corresponds to the psychological ability of a human to use these rules in order to actually look up any given word. It stands to reason that such an ability is not part of the dictionary and should not concern the lexicographer too much. (As a result, the MTM does not need its rules to be ordered: all linguistically$_1$ relevant information has to be encoded explicitly in the rules themselves; all the other ordering factors belong to the dynamic device, therefore being of no interest to us. Cf. note 12, p. 90.)

3. In the MTM, the mapping $\{SemR_i\} \Leftrightarrow \{PhonR_j\}$ is bidirectional: it represents the production of speech (from meanings to texts) as well as the understanding of speech (from texts to meanings). Logically, both directions are, of course, equivalent. But linguistically₁ they are not: language gives a more prominent place to the speaker than to the addressee. A speaker is possible even in the absence of an addressee (one can speak to oneself, to God, . . . to the posterity, etc.), while an addressee is inconceivable without a speaker. In all languages we say *Do you speak . . . ?*, and this is a typical cliché; in all languages there is a special verb to refer to the production of speech— *speak* —but there seems to be none that refers exclusively to the understanding of speech (you can *understand* anything, not just speech). In an idealized situation of linguistic₁ communication, the speaker knows what he is going to say: he proceeds from complete information, and his only task is to use his linguistic₁ skills properly; whereas the addressee does not know anything beforehand, and has to decipher the utterance, actively using his logic, his extralinguistic knowledge, etc.

Therefore, first, purely linguistic₁ skills are not as important to the addressee as to the speaker, and second, the addressee never uses them alone, in pure form. For this reason the viewpoint of the speaker is more advantageous for linguistics: it allows one to avoid confusion with non-linguistic₁ data and ensures a correct perspective. Notice, for example, that the English expression *to make a mistake* presents no problem from the analytic (i.e., the addressee's) viewpoint, but shows an interesting problem as soon as the researcher looks at it from the synthetic (i.e., the speaker's) viewpoint: we say *to make ⟨*do⟩ a mistake ⟨a decision⟩* but *to do ⟨*make⟩ a favor ⟨one's job⟩* etc. The MTM is developed and presented strictly in the SYNTHESIS DIRECTION: from meanings to texts.[3] (As a result, the MTM does not have to cope with the messy problem of disambiguation that plagues so many linguistic₂ works.)

4. The MTM is no more than one component of a global model of human linguistic behavior:

(3)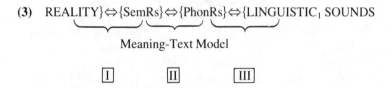

REALITY} ⇔ {SemRs} ⇔ {PhonRs} ⇔ {LINGUISTIC₁ SOUNDS

Meaning-Text Model

Ⅰ   Ⅱ   Ⅲ

As we see, in the chain of actual linguistic₁ production, the MTM is joined to two other models.

Model Ⅰ, or the Reality-Meaning Model, is the subject of a science that does not yet exist as a unified discipline. Presently, its domain is unevenly distributed among philosophy, psychology, cognitive science, logic, documentation, artificial intelligence, etc. The Reality-Meaning model presumably has a very complex structure, of which, at the present state of our knowledge, one can only advance hypotheses. It is clear, however, that this model must include a component that produces a discrete cognitive representation of observed continuous reality. There must also be another component that ensures the interaction between the cognitive representation, the internal thesaurus of the speaker, the pragmatics of a given speech situation and the like, in order to produce the SemR of a future utterance.

Model ⟦III⟧, or the Text-Sound Model, is the subject of acoustics and articulatory phonetics. A text-reading computer program, such as, for example, "Smooth Talker" for the Apple Macintosh computer, is an excellent illustration of what a model of this type should be like.

Model ⟦II⟧, or the Meaning-Text Model, is the genuine subject of linguistics. However, not even fragment ⟦II⟧ is represented quite fully in our MTM. In order to simplify our task of constructing the latter, we disgregard a number of relevant aspects and properties of natural language. (But we hope that all these can be taken into consideration as soon as an MTM, of at least passable quality, is available for the language under consideration.)

In its present form, the MTM has the following six limitations:

1) The temporal dimension is excluded from discussion: the extremely important problem of language acquisition and that of linguistic change are deliberately ignored.

2) The social dimension is excluded: the question of how a language functions in a linguistic community is deliberately ignored.

3) The psychological-neurological dimension is excluded as well: no attempts have been made so far to relate the MTM experimentally with psychological or neurological reality (aphasiology, psychology of speech production/perception, etc.)

4) Only the communicative function of natural language is dealt with seriously, to the exclusion of all other functions (poetic, phatic, emotive, metalinguistic, etc.)

5) As indicated above, only the static aspect of linguistic systems is reflected, to the exclusion of the dynamic aspect. In particular, the feedback between meanings and texts in the actual processes of speaking and understanding (possible changes in the original message determined by the text already synthesized and uttered) is deliberately ignored.

6) The analysis of meaning itself goes beyond the scope of an MTM: it does not distinguish "normal" meanings from absurdities, contradictions or trivialities. Discovering that something is stupid or absurd or detecting contradictions is by no means a linguistic$_2$ task.

It should be clear that these limitations are tactical, not inherent: we can eliminate them whenever we decide that the MTM in question is sufficiently developed.

An MTM represents, or simulates, a language; however, as stated above, it does not deal with actual linguistic$_1$ utterances but only with their representations. The concept of a linguistic₁ REPRESENTATION is thus central to the Meaning-Text approach.

I have already mentioned the two "end" representations: the SemR and the PhonR, as well as the fact that the correspondence linking them is many-to-many. It is especially rich and complex in the SYNTHESIS direction (synonymy): a fairly complex meaning can have, in a given language, hundreds of thousands of expressions.[4] One can even say that, a natural language is essentially a system designed to produce a great many synonymous texts for a given meaning. This makes it practically impossible to establish a direct match between a SemR and a PhonR, so the need for intermediate levels of representation arises. Introducing such levels is also prompted by language itself: it clearly features (at least) two different tiers of organization, the sentence and the wordform, each of which is governed by its own set of hierarchical regularities. Thus we obtain the Synt(actic) and the Morph(ological) R(epresentations).

Postulate 3

Utterances of natural language will be described by using, beside a SemR and a PhonR, two intermediate-level representations: a SyntR and a MorphR.

The general picture becomes then as follows:

(4)   {SemR}⇔{SyntR}⇔{MorphR}⇔{PhonR}

The intermediate representations are supported as well by formal considerations. A SemR, as we will see in the next section, is an (almost) arbitrary NETWORK, a graph with practically no formal restrictions imposed on it. On the contrary, a PhonR is obviously a string of phonetic symbols, i.e., a CHAIN, the simplest of all possible graphs, with the maximum of restrictions imposed on it. So, too, is a MorphR of a sentence: it is a strictly ordered string of wordforms. To establish a many-to-many mapping between arbitrary networks and chains, a convenient bridge is needed, that is, a graph formally situated halfway between arbitrary networks, on the one hand, and chains, on the other. This happens to be a TREE, a formal entity traditionally used to depict sentence structures and chosen as the main descriptive device in our approach as well (Chapter 1). See Fig. 2-1 on the next page.

On all the levels thus established, with the exception of the semantic one, two types of phenomena or properties are readily distinguished: those dependent on and oriented towards meaning and those dependent on and oriented towards sound. Based on corresponding considerations, we split each of the three upper levels into two sublevels: a **deep** one, geared to meaning (D~), and a **surface** one, geared to physical form (S~). This gives us a total of seven representation levels:

DEPTH

1. Semantic Representation (SemR), or the meaning

2. Deep-Syntactic Representation (DSyntR)

3. Surface-Syntactic Representation (SSyntR)

4. Deep-Morphological Representation (DMorphR)

5. Surface-Morphological Representation (SMorphR)

6. Deep-Phonetic Representation (DPhonR; commonly called "phonemic representation")

7. Surface-Phonetic Representation (SPhonR; commonly called simply "phonetic representation"), or the text

SURFACE

(5)

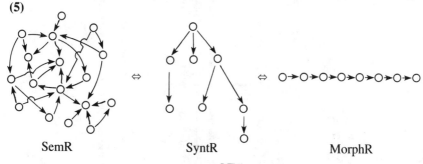

SemR   SyntR   MorphR

Figure 2-1

Typical Formalisms for Different Levels of Sentence Representation
[arbitrary networks for the SemR, trees for the SyntR, and chains for the MorphR
(and, obviously, the PhonR)]

In the Meaning-Text approach, then, an utterance is simultaneously characterized by seven different representations, each of these specifying the utterance in
the perspective of the corresponding level (cf. Mel'čuk 1972, 1973c and 1974a:
31ff.) Let it be emphasized that any representation carries ALL the information
contained in the utterance considered; all the seven MTM representations encode
the SAME informational content, but by means of different units and different sets
of relations. Any two MTM representations differ then only in that one presents
more explicitly and makes more available different properties of the utterance
than the other. (In the transformational-generative theory this is not the case:
here, the deep and surface syntactic structures encode different information using
essentially the same set of units and relations, cf. Nakhimovsky 1983: XIX–
XX.)

Notice, that, consequently, a representation of level n preserves all the linguis-
tic$_1$ information available at a more surface level $n + 1$; therefore, as we go
from level $n + 1$ to a deeper level n, linguistic$_1$ ambiguity may only decrease. In
other words, a MTM representation of level n is never more ambiguous than the
corresponding representation of level $n + 1$.

Each representation level is mapped onto the adjacent one by a separate component of the MTM, which thus has six major components, the latter corresponding to traditional linguistic disciplines. See Fig. 2-2:

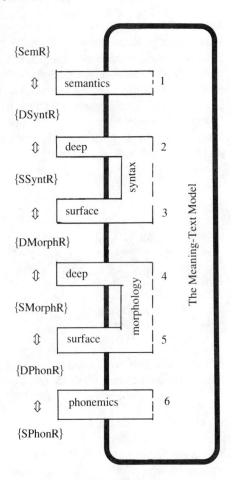

Figure 2-2
Levels of Utterance Representation and
Corresponding Components of the Meaning-Text Model

Thus the MTM is a stratificational system, very much in the spirit of Lamb's (1966) and Sgall's (1967) models.

A systematic survey of different level representations and the major components of the MTM is offered in Section II below. This survey cannot avoid being rather sketchy. I do not mention any alternative solutions or provide justifications; nor do I draw any parallels with other related linguistic$_2$ models. Likewise, I find it impossible to discuss here general scientific philosophy underlying our approach, although it is quite different from what is currently believed in mainstream modern linguistics, especially in North America. (An interested reader can consult Sussex 1974, Nichols 1979 and Nakhimovsky 1983: IX–XX.)

II. UTTERANCE REPRESENTATION AT DIFFERENT LEVELS

1. Organization of a Linguistic$_1$ Representation

In the MTM approach, a linguistic$_1$ representation is a set of formal entities called **structures**:

$$R = \{S_1, S_2, \ldots, S_n\}$$

The number of structures varies according to the level of representation. In any given representation, one structure is distinguished and called the **main** structure; all the others specify its additional characteristics. The main structure of a representation may stand alone (although it will not provide a complete characterization of the represented linguistic$_1$ unit), but the rest of the structures cannot appear without the main one.

Each structure is designed to depict a certain aspect of the unit considered at a given level. Instead of seeking a homogeneous representation of a given linguistic$_1$ unit as a whole, the MTM puts emphasis on formally distinguishing what is linguistically$_1$ distinct in nature. Therefore, for instance, the syntactic relations, anaphoric links and communicative organization of a sentence are expressed by means of three different structures, which belong to the SyntR of the sentence. A structure is, as it were, only *one* projection of the unit portrayed; taken together, the structures of a given level form the corresponding representation.

Utterance representations are written in artificial formal languages devised by the researcher, i.e., in special linguistic$_2$ metalanguages. The elaboration of such metalanguages is one of the prime tasks in the MTM framework.

2. Survey of MTM Linguistic$_1$ Representations

I will start with a SemR representing a family of synonymous Russian sentences, and then I will work up through the representations of all the levels. Here is a sample sentence corresponding to our initial SemR:

(**6**) Russian *Kak soobščaet amerikanskaja pečat', prezident polagaet, čto objazannost'ju naroda Soedinënnyx Štatov javljaetsja aktivnoe sodejstvie razvitiju èkonomiki afrikanskix stran,* lit. 'As the American press says, the President believes that a duty of the people of the United States is active aid to the development of the economy of African countries'.

The same meaning can be expressed by another sentence, which contains almost none of the lexemes of (6), except for such technical terms as 'development', 'economy' or 'country':

(**7**) Russian *Po soobščenijam pressy SŠA, Belyj Dom priderživaetsja togo mnenija, čto amerikanskij narod objazatel'no dolžen okazyvat' stranam Afriki samuju ènergičnuju pomošč' v dele razvitija ix èkonomiki,* lit. 'According to reports by the press of the USA, the White House has the opinion that the American people should obligatorily give to the countries of Africa its most energetic support concerning the development of their economy'.

The SemR of sentences (6) and (7) is fairly complicated and may stun a newcomer. The reader should have been trained first, by a selection of simpler examples, to identify the components of such representations. Since, however, for lack of space, such a pedagogically justifiable approach is out of the question here, I had the choice between using a toy SemR or exposing the reader to the astonishing complexity of the real thing. Not without hesitation, I opted for the second alternative.

Semantic Representation

In the MTM approach, a semantic representation specifies the meaning of a set of synonymous utterances, i.e., utterances having the same meaning. Meaning is taken to be an invariant of synonymic transformations between such utterances; the synonymy of utterances is considered as given in the linguistic$_1$ intuition of native speakers. In other words, a native speaker forms a set of utterances having the same meaning, identity of meaning being an elementary, unanalyzable notion; then what is common to all these utterances is considered to be their meaning and is expressed by means of a SemR. Thus, as we see, the concept "meaning" is based on the concept "same meaning".[5]

Our SemR is characterized by two important properties, which I state here informally.

First, a SemR represents the meaning of an utterance regardless of its linguistic$_1$ form. Thus, the actual distribution of the meaning among words, clauses or sentences is ignored in a SemR, as is its expression through different linguistic$_1$ devices: lexemes, grammatical categories, syntactic constructions or prosody. The SemR seeks to present any meaning homogeneously, using the same formal means for all types of meaning (see below), and in a manner that is as independent as possible of the way this meaning is presented in the given language.

Second, a SemR does not seek an "absolute" precision. Describing equisignificant utterances, the SemR captures relative, or approximate, synonymy, reflecting only those semantic contrasts that are indeed observed by the speaker in actual discourse; it may (and sometimes must) ignore potential semantic distinctions, irrelevant in a given context. Notice that a certain degree of approximation in the SemR is necessary, if we want to obtain linguistically$_2$ interesting results. (See Note 4, p. 86.)

A sample SemR, presenting the meaning of sentences (6) and (7) and of all other sentences synonymous with them (cf., e.g., (15)), is given on page 54 as (8) (= Fig. 2-3). It can be worded very roughly as follows (the capital letters with numbers in square brackets in (8') refer to the rows and columns of diagram (8)):

(**8'**) 'More than one [= plural; A1] periodical being a newspaper or a magazine [= 'press'; B2] of which the publication is located in the USA [= 'American'; A1]

communicates to the people who read them, the moment of the communication being identical to the moment of this speech act [= present tense; C1], that

the president of the USA believes [the present is rendered in the same way] that

the population of the USA has the duty to apply intensively their resources to the growth of African economy, having the goal of thereby facilitating [= 'to actively help'; B3]

the causation, by more than one nation located in Africa [= 'African countries'; C3], of the growth of their economy [= 'economic development'; C2]'.

Note that in order to avoid overburdening the diagram, I have omitted temporal specifications for the last "chunks" of meaning. Strictly speaking, it has to be indicated that 'having the duty', 'applying resources' etc. are also cotemporaneous with the moment of speech — in much the same way as before.

Formally speaking, the SemR of an utterance consists of three structures: (1) the Sem(antic) S(tructure), (2) the Sem(antic)-Comm(unicative) S(tructure) and (3) Rhet(orical) S(tructure), so that

SemR = {SemS, Sem-CommS, RhetS}

The **Sem(antic) S(tructure)** is the main structure of the SemR. It specifies what might be loosely called the "objective" meaning, i.e., the state of affairs that the speaker wishes to characterize. (Note that the state of affairs also includes internal states, attitudes or value judgments of the speaker himself.) The "subjective" part of the meaning, i.e., the organization of the message and its style (in a broad sense of the term), is reflected in two other structures of the SemR.

Formally, a SemS is a **network**: a simple connected directed graph without circuits; it is composed of **vertices** or **nodes**, linked by **arcs**.

Let it be emphasized that the nodes of a SemS are linearly UNORDERED: we do not permit order to carry information in our semantic representation. Anything meaningful must be expressed explicitly by a symbol. (Cf. Chapter 1, p. 16.)

The physical layout of nodes in our illustrative diagrams has, therefore, no scientific relevance; it is dictated by typographical or pedagogical considerations.

(8)

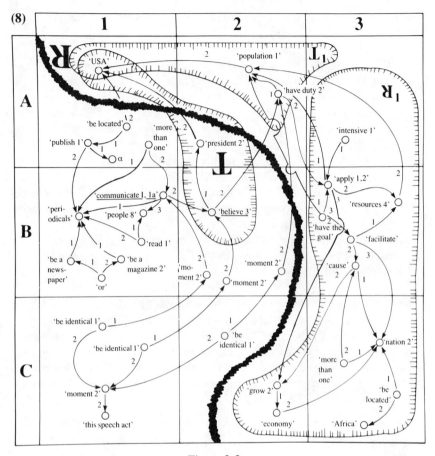

Figure 2-3
The SemR of Sentences (6) and (7)
and of all the Sentences Synonymous with Them

A **vertex**, or **node**, of a SemS is labeled with a semantic unit, or **semanteme**, of the language. A semanteme corresponds to a specific sense of a word; it is the signatum of a **lexeme** (a lexeme being a word taken in one well-defined sense). Such a sense is identified by a numerical index accompanying the word; in our illustrations, the indexes are taken from *The American Heritage Dictionary*. Thus *magazine 2* identifies 'a periodical in the form of a book with a paper cover . . .', as opposed to *magazine 1* 'warehouse . . .' and *magazine 3* 'a compartment of a firearm . . .'

[The letters **A–C** and the numbers **1–3** that appear at the left side and the top of the diagram are not part of the SemR: they are used for referring to locations in it. The shaggy lines mark the boundaries of theme and rheme, cf. below.]

Two major classes of semantemes are distinguished:

1. FUNCTORS, further subdivided into three unequal groups:
   A. predicates (relations, properties, actions, states, events, etc.), numbering hundreds of thousands
   B. quantifiers ('all', 'there exist', and all numbers)
   C. logical connectives ('and', 'or', 'if', 'not', . . .), just a few of them.
2. NAMES (OF CLASSES) OF OBJECTS, also very numerous. (This class also includes all proper names.)

As in logic, the current notation of predicate calculus is used. Thus, to represent *Mary discovered the loss of her flask*, the functors 'discover$_2$', 'disappear$_1$', 'belong to$_2$', 'be the moment of$_2$' and 'be before$_2$' are needed; the names are 'Mary' and 'flask' (all semantemes are put in single quotes). The functors are distinguished by the number of arguments they can take: this number is indicated as a subscript in our example. Another important element of the SemS is the notion of 'this speech act', which we use as a reference point. So, we can write:

'discover$_2$'('Mary'; 'disappear$_1$'('flask')); 'belong$_2$'('flask'; 'Mary');

'before$_2$'('discover$_2$' ($\bigcirc$); **t**); and 'be the moment of$_2$' (**t**; 'this speech act')

[$\bigcirc$ stands as an abbreviation for the contents of the parentheses after the preceding occurrence of 'discover'.]

However, to avoid the linearity of this notation and all the technical problems that flow from it we have recourse to a different graphical device: the relations between a functor **F** and its arguments **a**, **b**, **c**, . . . are indicated by numbered arcs with arrows pointing from **F** to its arguments, rather than by spatial position and linear ordering of the latter. Therefore:

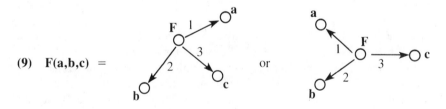

(9)   F(a,b,c) =   or

Thus, *John likes Mary* has the SemS (10):

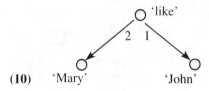

(10)   'Mary'   'John'

Both types of semantemes can receive arrows but only a functor can be the starting point of an arrow. If a node is labeled with a functor semanteme having *n* arguments, then exactly *n* arrows should start from it. A functor also imposes semantic restrictions on its arguments, but we will not discuss these here. Let it be noted that an object or a particular event is represented in the SemS by a single node such that all relevant functors "converge" on it. Therefore, there is no coreference in the SemS; an utterance such as *Mary says she will go* is represented (minus the tense) as:

(11)

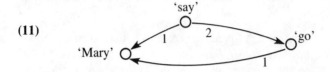

An argument of a functor is also called its **semantic actant**; cf. below, pp. 63 and 69, the notions of **deep syntactic** and **surface syntactic actant**.

A semanteme can be either elementary (i.e., a **seme**) or—in most cases—complex. A complex semanteme can be represented, in its turn, by a semantic network, which specifies its semantic decomposition. For instance, the semanteme 'facilitate', found in (8), (B3), can be decomposed as follows:

(12)

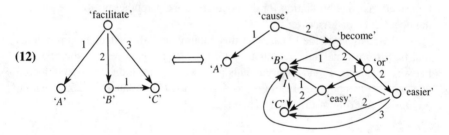

(12) can be read in the following way: '*A* facilitates *B* of *C* for *C*' means '*A* causes that *B* of *C* become easier [than *B* was before] or easy for *C*'.

In principle, semantic decomposition can be carried on until semes are reached. I will not discuss here the problem of semes, or semantic primitives, and that of semantic analysis in general, but I will rather limit myself to stating two hypotheses on which the MTM semantic approach rests.

First, we believe that there are semantic primitives in natural language and that they will be arrived at by consistent analysis of lexical items. A definitive list of semantic primitives is not yet available, but some likely candidates can be indicated: 'more than', 'this speech act', 'time', 'or', 'and'. (But cf. a much more definite view of semantic primitives: Wierzbicka 1972 and 1980a, where a set of thirteen semantic primitives is proposed and argued for. In several subsequent works, Wierzbicka effectively demonstrates how her primitives work in hundreds of elaborate and astoundingly astute semantic decompositions of English —and other—lexemes and grammemes: 1982, 1984a, b, 1985, [to appear].)

Second, in a SemS, one should not necessarily try to decompose all the semantemes into semes. Such a decomposition would make the semantic network unreadable and unmanageable. What is more, "a [complete — I.M.] decomposition [of a semanteme—I.M.] is a description of the language user's lexical competence; his performance on any particular occasion may not fully exploit that competence" (Miller and Johnson-Laird 1976: 326–327). In other words, in actual speech, speakers use as little decomposition as they can in a particular situation, although they are always able to push it deeper if they want to. Therefore, in the MTM the "canonical" SemS is required to be as shallow as possible, that is, as close to the actual utterance as it can be. However, the door is open to ever deeper and deeper decompositions, down to the level of semantic primitives.

An important corollary of this principle is that an utterance has a large number of (equivalent) SemSs, obtainable by expanding the semantemes (contained in a given SemS) into the corresponding semantic networks. Because of this, the SemS is not canonical in the following sense: two synonymous sentences of a language may have non-identical, although equivalent, SemSs. Notice that the "depth" of a particular SemR depends on the richness of the set of synonymous utterances whose meaning invariant this SemR is called upon to specify. The more synonymous utterances are to be represented, the more "decomposed" (i.e., the deeper) will be the resulting SemR.

An **arc**, or arrow, of a SemS is labeled with a symbol that has no meaning of its own but is needed to differentiate the various arguments of the same functor. Natural numbers are used for this purpose; thus in (12), numbers on the arcs stemming from 'facilitate' mark A, B and C as the 1st, the 2nd and the 3rd arguments of this functor, respectively: who/what [= A] facilitates what [= B] for whom [= C]. (Note that with 'facilitate', its 3rd argument, i.e., C, must necessarily be the 1st argument of its 2nd argument, i.e. of B, this B representing an activity of C, or a process that C undergoes, or the like.) In this way, arc labels are strictly distinctive and asemantic. The "semantic" role of an argument with respect to its functor is specified by the decomposition of the functor into simpler functors. So the decomposition of 'facilitate' in (12) shows clearly that A is the causer (= the 1st argument of 'cause'), B is what changes its state (= the 1st argument of 'become'), and C is simultaneously the agent of B and the beneficiary of A's activities (C = the 2nd argument of 'easier' and 'easy').

A more complex example is provided by the comparison of

English 'like' (A,B) =   'like' [2 → 'B', 1 → 'A']   and French 'plaire' (A,B) =   'plaire' [2 → 'B', 1 → 'A']

These functors are converse with respect to each other, so that 'Mary likes John' = 'John plaît à Mary' ('Mary plaît à John' means 'John likes Mary'). The "semantic" role of A in 'like' is identical with that of B in 'plaire' and vice versa. To see this, one has to decompose both functors:

(13)   **a.** 'like'(A, B) = 'A has an emotion E toward B'

      b. 'plaire'(A,B) = 'B has an emotion E toward A'

[the nature of the emotion E remains to be specified].

An argument of a functor is called its **semantic actant**; there will be more discussion of semantic actants in connection with the ergative construction in Part III.[6]

The **Sem(antic)-Comm(unicative) S(tructure)** specifies the manner in which the speaker wants his message to be organized: what should be presented first and what should be added later; what should be explicitly asserted and what can be only presupposed; what should be emphasized and what can be left in the background. All this constitutes an important part of the "subjective" meaning. One and the same "objective" meaning reflecting a given situation can be encoded in quite different messages according to what the speaker actually wants to say. To put it slightly differently, two distinct utterances can have the same SemSs but different Sem-CommSs:

(14)   **a.** *One day, Van Campen came into the room and found the empty bottles in the closet*

      vs.

  b. *One day, the empty bottles in the closet were found by Van Campen, who had come into the room.*

(To be sure, (14a) and (14b) receive the same SemS only if we agree to ignore such latent semantic differences as that between coordination and modification: *X came and found* vs. *X, who had come, found*, or, rather, if we relegate them to the Sem-CommS.)

The Sem-CommS shows the following five contrasts:

1. Theme (i.e., topic; notation: $\mathbf{L}$) vs. rheme (i.e., comment; notation: $\mathbf{Я}$). $\mathbf{L}$ is the starting point of the utterance, or that part of its meaning of what the message says something; $\mathbf{Я}$ is what is communicated about $\mathbf{L}$. Thus, $\mathbf{L}$ and $\mathbf{Я}$ specify the itinerary through the situation chosen by the speaker from among all the other possible itineraries.

2. The old (i.e., given) vs. the new. The "old" is known to both interlocutors, the "new" is what is communicated by the speaker for the first time.

3. Foregrounded information vs. backgrounded information. Foregrounded information is what is presented as main predications (i.e., full clauses), backgrounded information is relegated to attributes and morphological derivations.

4. The asserted vs. the presupposed.

5. The emphatically stressed vs. the neutral. Emphasis indicates a particular psychological or emotional attitude of the speaker.

In our illustrations, only the $\bot$ vs. $\bot$ contrast is shown. In (8), $\bot$ is 'the president of the US believes' and $\bot$ is 'the population of the US should intensively help the development of African countries' economy'. Note that there can be different layers of the theme-vs.-rheme division. For example, within $\bot$ in (8), a $\bot_1$ and $\bot_1$ of second order can be distinguished:

$\bot_1$ = 'the population of the US should'
$\bot_1$ = 'intensively help . . . economy'

Semantic-communicative information, expressed in the Sem-CommS, stands in approximately the same relationship to the semantic network (i.e., SemS) as do suprasegmental prosodic phenomena to the segmental phonemic string that makes up (the signans of) a sentence.

At this point, it seems convenient to quote a Russian sentence that has the same SemS as sentences (6) and (7), but a different Sem-CommS:

(15) *Po mneniju prezidenta SŠA, ukazyvaet amerikanskaja pressa, pomogat' samym aktivnym obrazom razvitiju èkonomiki v stranax Afriki est' važnaja objazannost' amerikanskogo naroda,*

lit. 'According to the opinion of the president of the US, the American press says, to help, in the most active way, the development of the economy in Africa's countries is an important duty of the American people'.

In (15), the theme is *pomogat' . . . v stranax Afriki*, and the rheme is *est' . . . naroda*.

Sentence (15) is an additional illustration of incredible synonymic flexibility of natural language.

The **Rhet(orical) S(tructure)** specifies the style and the rhetorical characteristics that the speaker wants to impart to the utterance: whether it should be highly technical or colloquial, smack of journalese or be poetic, be couched in slang or sound neutral or informal. The corresponding labels determine lexical choices and particular syntactic configurations. Rhetorical components of an utterance undoubtedly serve expressive purposes, that is, carry meaning of their own; this justifies the inclusion of the RhetS into the SemR. (True, the rhetorical meaning is part of "subjective" meaning, so that the RhetS is closer to the Sem-CommS than to the SemS; however, we cannot discuss this problem here.)

Deep-Syntactic Representation

A **deep-syntactic representation** specifies the organization of a particular sentence, considered from the viewpoint of its meaning. To illustrate this point, I give, in Figs. 2-4 (p. 67) and 2-5 (p. 68), the DSyntRs of sentences (6) and (7). Both of them have the same SemR (shown in (8), Fig. 2-3).

Formally speaking, the DSyntR of a sentence consists of four structures: (1) the D(eep-)Synt(actic) S(tructure), (2) the D(eep-)Synt(actic)-Comm(unicative) S(tructure), (3) the D(eep-)Synt(actic)-Anaph(oric) S(tructure) and (4) the D(eep-)Synt(actic)-Pros(odic) S(tructure). Thus we have:

DSyntR = {DSyntS, DSynt-CommS, DSynt-AnaphS, DSynt-ProsS}

The **D(eep-)Synt(actic) S(tructure)** is the main structure of the DSyntR. It specifies the syntactic organization of the sentence in terms of its words and relationships between them.

Formally, a DSyntS is a (dependency) **tree**: a network in which a node can receive only one (entering) arc and in which there is only one node that receives no arc at all. (For a discussion of dependency trees see Chapter 1.)

║ Very much like the SemS, the nodes of the DSyntS (and for that matter, of
║ the surface-syntactic structure as well) are linearly UNORDERED, and for the
║ same reasons (cf. p. 53).

Word order is considered a means for expressing—on the surface—syntactic relations between words; therefore it cannot be present in a syntactic structure.

A **node** of a DSyntS is labeled with a **generalized** (i.e., deep) **lexeme** of the language.

A generalized lexeme is one of the following four items:

1. A **full lexeme**. (Semantically empty lexemes, such as governed prepositions and conjunctions, as well as auxiliary verbs, are not represented in the DSyntS.)
2. A **fictitious lexeme**. Two types of fictitious lexemes are presently distinguished:
   a. A lexemic unit presupposed by the symmetry of the derivational system, yet non-existent (such as the verb **compromiser* in French, from *compromis* '[a] compromise'; cf. *accord* 'agreement' / *s'accorder* 'agree', *lutte* 'struggle' / *lutter* '[to] struggle' etc.).
   b. A lexeme postulated by the researcher to represent a meaning that is expressed in the given language by an idiosyncratic syntactic construction (such as preposing the noun to the modifying numeral in Russian, which means very roughly 'approximately': *sto metrov* '100 m' vs. *metrov sto* 'approximately 100 m'). Let it be emphasized that the meaning in question does not correspond to an actual lexeme of the language.[7]
3. A **multilexemic phraseological unit** which is semantically a whole, i.e., an idiom, such as the notorious *kick the bucket*. (An idiom is thus represented by a single node in the DSyntS. Some idioms—specifically, those that are sentence-like, i.e. that include a main verb and a grammatical subject, such as *The cat got one's tongue* etc.,—create problems for a single-node rep-

resentation in the DSyntS. This is, however, too special a question to be discussed here.) In (23) and (24), we find two examples of idioms: SOEDINËNNYE ŠTATY 'USA' and BELYJ DOM 'The White House'.

4. A **lexical function**: see below.

A generalized lexeme in a DSyntS is subscripted for all its **meaning-bearing morphological values**, such as number in nouns, or tense and aspect in verbs. Meaning-bearing morphological values are derived from the SemS; in other words, they are freely chosen by the speaker. (Syntactically conditioned morphological values are induced by syntactic rules, such as government and agreement. They are not represented in a SemS and they are not shown in a SyntR, particularly in a DSyntS. These latter values include: case in nouns; person and number in verbs; gender, number and case in adjectives. Cf. Fig. 1-3 in Chapter 1, p. 20.)

Two definitions seem to be useful at this point:

An individual morphological value is called a **grammeme**; for instance: 'nominative case'; 'plural'; '2nd person'.

A lexeme name subscripted for all and only meaning-bearing grammemes is called the **reduced** D(eep-)Morph(ological) R(epresentation) of the corresponding wordform. (The **complete** DMorphR of a wordform contains all the grammemes it expresses, including those that are syntactically induced.)

Now we can say that the nodes of a DSyntS are labeled with reduced DMorphRs of generalized lexemes.

The concept of lexical function is an important innovation of the MTM approach. A (**standard simple**) **lexical function** (LF) $\mathbf{f}$ is a semantico-syntactic relation that obtains between a lexical unit (i.e., a word or phrase) W (the **argument**, or **key word**, of $\mathbf{f}$) and a set $\mathbf{f}(W)$ of other lexical units (the **value** of $\mathbf{f}$) in such a way that the following four conditions are met:

(i)   For any W^1 and W^2, if $\mathbf{f}(W^1)$ and $\mathbf{f}(W^2)$ exist, then both $\mathbf{f}(W^1)$ and $\mathbf{f}(W^2)$ bear an identical relation (with respect to meaning and deep-syntactic roles) to W^1 and W^2, respectively; thus, we have
      '$\mathbf{f}(W^1)$': 'W^1' $=$ '$\mathbf{f}(W^2)$': 'W^2'.

(ii) In most cases, $\mathbf{f}(W^1) \neq \mathbf{f}(W^2)$; this means that $\mathbf{f}(W)$ is phraseologically bound by W.

(iii) There are many different Ws that can be arguments of $\mathbf{f}$. (That is, the meaning of $\mathbf{f}$ is general and abstract enough for $\mathbf{f}$ to co-occur with a great number of meanings.)

(iv) $\mathbf{f}$ has many linguistic[1] expressions as its possible values. (That is, the set of all $\mathbf{f}(W_i)$ is sufficiently rich.)

A lexical function is, as we see, a function in the mathematical sense; it is called "lexical" because its arguments and values are lexical units.[8]

In the MTM, about fifty standard simple LFs are used.[9] Here are some examples (only some of possible values are given).

Syn is a synonym; **Syn$_\supset$**, **Syn$_\subset$** and **Syn$_\cap$** designate, respectively, synonyms with broader, narrower and intersecting meanings.
Syn (*for instance*) = *for example, e.g.*
Syn$_\supset$ (*assist 1*) = *help*

S$_0$ is a substantival derivative, having the same meaning as the source lexeme (roughly, *nomen actionis/qualitatis*).
S$_0$ (*to move*) = *movement*
S$_0$ (*to refuse*) = *refusal*
S$_0$ (*to help*) = [*the*] *help*
S$_0$ (*to invite*) = *invitation*

Oper$_i$ stands for an empty verb[10] such that its 1st DSynt-actant is the *i*-th participant in the situation denoted by the key word *W* and its 2nd DSynt-actant is *W* itself.

Oper$_1$ (*visit*) = *pay*	**Oper$_2$** (*visit*) = *have*
Oper$_1$ (*doubt*) = *have*	**Oper$_2$** (*trial*) = *stand, undergo*
Oper$_1$ (*trip*) = *take*	**Oper$_2$** (*blow*) = *receive*

Func$_i$ stands for an empty verb such that its 1st DSynt-actant is the key word *W* and its 2nd DSynt-actant, the *i*-th participant in the situation 'W'.

Func$_1$(*responsibility*) = *rest with*	**Func$_2$** (*responsibility*) = *include*
Func$_1$ (*proposal*) = *come, stem from*	**Func$_2$** (*change*) = *affect*

The following three LFs represent the meanings of phasal verbs:

Incep 'begin'
Fin 'cease'
Cont 'continue'
    IncepOper$_1$ (*fire 9*) = *open*
    IncepOper$_2$ (*power 4*) = *fall under*
    FinOper$_1$ (*faith*) = *lose*
    ContOper$_1$ (*influence*) = *maintain*

(These are in fact **compound** LFs, see note 9, p. 89.)

Real$_i$ means 'fulfill a demand or requirement of *W* being its *i*-th participant'.

Real$_1$ (*mine 4b*) = *strike*	**Real$_2$** (*examination*) = *pass*
Real$_1$ (*policy*) = *follow*	**Real$_2$** (*test 1*) = *withstand*

Magn means 'very', 'to a high degree' [an intensifier].
Magn(*disgusted*) = *thoroughly*
Magn(*belief*) = *staunch*
Magn(*cold*) = *enough to freeze balls off a brass monkey*
Magn(*to blush*) = *deeply*
Magn(*to agree*) = *wholeheartedly*

I have to stop here; the interested reader may refer for more details to Mel'čuk 1982.

LFs play a crucial role [*play* = **Oper₁** (*role*), *crucial* = **Magn** (*role*)] in two respects. First and foremost, they are used to describe restricted lexical co-occurrence. All the LFs of a lexeme are stored in its lexical entry in a special dictionary that constitutes the pivot of the Semantic Component of our MTM: see below, in Section III, pp. 74 ff., and Appendix, pp. 92 ff. Second, LFs are central to the rules for synonymic paraphrase at the DSynt-level; I will return to this later, III, **2**, Sem-Component, 8, p. 77. In our examples (Figs. 2-4 and 2-5), the following LFs are shown: **S₀**, **Magn**, **Oper₁** and **Oper₂**; **Adv₂** appearing in (24) below stands for a derived adverb meaning something like 'undergoing W', so that **Adv₂** (*communicate*) = *as* [X *communicates*] (i.e., 'being the object of the communication').

An **arc**, or **branch**, of a DSyntS is labeled with a **D(eep-)Synat(actic) Rel(ation)** (DSyntRel). These relations are supposed to be language-independent, i.e., universal. Each DSyntRel stands for a family of specific syntactic constructions of particular languages, representing them in a generalized way.

A DSyntRel is one of the following nine binary relations (they are antireflexive, antisymmetrical and antitransitive, see above, pp. 22 ff.):

1.–6. Six **actant** relations, notated simply 1, 2, . . . ,6. An actant DSyntRel connects a semantically predicative lexeme, i.e., a lexeme whose meaning is a functor, with its 1st, 2nd, . . . ,6th arguments, respectively. Actant DSynt-relations represent "Verb-Subject", "Verb-Object" and "Verb-Complement" constructions of particular languages, as well as the transforms of such constructions. For instance:

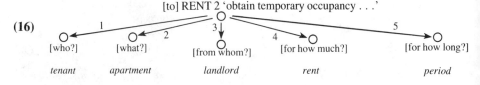

(16)

[to] RENT 2 'obtain temporary occupancy . . .'
[who?] [what?] [from whom?] [for how much?] [for how long?]
tenant *apartment* *landlord* *rent* *period*

In sharp contrast to the SemR, the numbers used as names of actant DSynt-relations are meaningful, not simply distinctive: each refers to a vast class of syntactic constructions serving the same semantic argument of a predicate. Thus "1" refers to grammatical subjects and their transforms expressing the first argument of a functor, and "2" through "6," to objects and complements of different types expressing the second, third, . . .,sixth argument (of a functor); cf. the comment in Chapter 1, after (17), p. 35.

7. The **attributive** relation, notated ATTR, which covers all kinds of modifiers, circumstantials and attributes (in the broadest sense of the term):

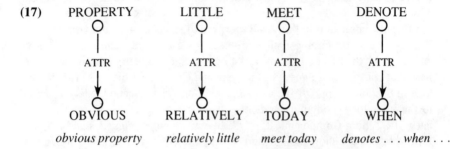

(17)

PROPERTY	LITTLE	MEET	DENOTE

obvious property   *relatively little*   *meet today*   *denotes . . . when . . .*

8. The **coordinative** relation, notated COORD; it accounts for all conjoined (= coordinate) constructions in which the right-hand conjunct is linked to the left-hand one, the latter being the syntactic governor:[11]

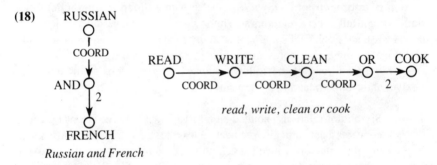

(18)

read, write, clean or cook

Russian and French

9. The "**appendancy**" relation, notated APPEND; it subsumes all parentheticals, interjections, direct addresses, and the like:

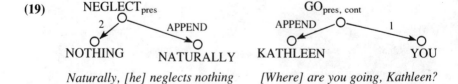

(19)

Naturally, [he] neglects nothing   *[Where] are you going, Kathleen?*

Space considerations prevent me from justifying or even explaining particular DSynt-representation I use in the examples; they should be accepted as simple illustrations.

Let it be emphasized that DSynt-relations, although they are meaningful, should by no means be construed as being semantic, i.e., corresponding each to a semantic invariant—they are not. A DSynt-Rel represents a FAMILY OF SYN-TACTIC CONSTRUCTIONS of the same structural type, regardless of their semantic content. Thus, DSyntRel "1" will be used indiscriminately to represent any grammatical subject, whatever its actual semantic function:

The soldier⟵¹kills the enemy, The enemy⟵¹is killed by the soldier, This restaurant⟵¹seats twenty, 1984⟵¹saw a surge of interest in . . . , etc. (For the important distinction between semantic and syntactic relations see Chapter 3.) If a meaning is expressed in the given language only syntactically, i.e., by a particular construction (without lexemic support), it must be rendered in the DSyntS by a fictitious lexeme (see above). For instance, the semantic distinction between two Russian phrases *ledokol-pobeditel'* 'victorious icebreaker' and *ledokol "Pobeditel'"* 'icebreaker *Victor*' is reflected, at the DSynt-level, by means of two fictitious lexemes (in double quotes):

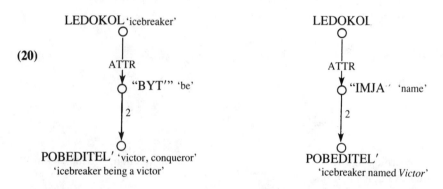

(20)

LEDOKOL 'icebreaker'

ATTR

"BYT'" 'be'

2

POBEDITEL' 'victor, conqueror'
'icebreaker being a victor'

LEDOKOL

ATTR

"IMJA" 'name'

2

POBEDITEL'
'icebreaker named *Victor*'

The main reason behind the introduction of DSynt-relations is to be able to describe syntactic phenomena in a GENERALIZED way, ignoring distinctions that are language-specific and idiosyncratic. For instance, the following English expressions having different surface-syntactic organization are represented, in terms of DSyntRels, in the same way, which reveals their actual syntactic relatedness:

(21)   **a.**   *a xerox* **of** *the article*
        a proposal **to** *cut taxes*
        an investigation **into** *the affair*
        the conclusion **that** *Bill is a fool*
     b.   *xerox*———²———▶*article*
        proposal——²—▶*cut* → *taxes*
        investigation—²▶*affair*

        conclusion   *Bill* ← *be* → *fool*
(Adapted from Nakhimovsky 1983: 24–25.)

Or compare two representations of a syntactic transformation (passivization) expressed in surface-syntactic and deep-syntactic formalisms, (22a) and (22b), respectively:

(22) a.

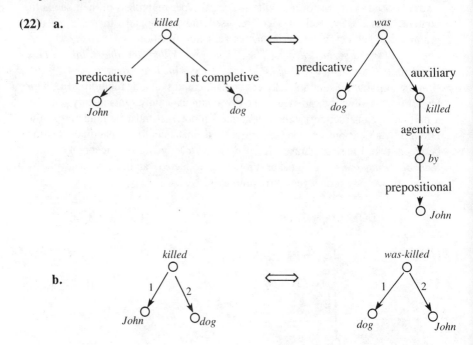

(Concerning the DSynt-representation of passive construction, see the comment after example (17), on page 35.)

The DSynt-relations provide for much more systematic and insightful representation. We will better see its advantages in Part III, when dealing with ergative construction and voice problems.

An element of the sentence depending on its DSynt-governor via one of the actant DSynt-relations is called a **deep-syntactic actant** of this governor.

The **D(eep-)Synt(actic)-Comm(unicative) S(tructure)** specifies the division of the sentence into theme and rheme, old and new, etc. Part of what constitutes the Sem-CommS is encoded, at this level, in the lexical choices made: for instance, adjectives and other types of modifiers vs. finite verbs, as well as the choice of corresponding articles etc. In other words, some data from the Sem-CommS go into the DSyntS. However, other important data concerning the communicative organization of the sentence are still preserved as components of the DSynt-CommS.

The **D(eep-)Synt(actic)-Anaph(oric) S(tructure)** specifies coreferentiality; we can see examples of it in (23)–(24), where a broken line connects the coreferential nodes STRANA 'country' and the coreferential nodes NAROD 'people'.

The **D(eep-)Synt(actic)-Pros(odic) S(tructure)** represents all meaning-bearing prosody: namely, prosody that is not syntactically conditioned but that derives directly from the SemS, such as question vs. affirmation, menace vs. indignation, irony, doubt, tenderness, secretiveness and the like. Prosody must be specified at this level as intonation contours, pauses, emphatic stresses, timbres. In (23) and (24), the DSynt-ProsS is indicated by the acronym NAP (Neutral Assertive Prosody).

(23)

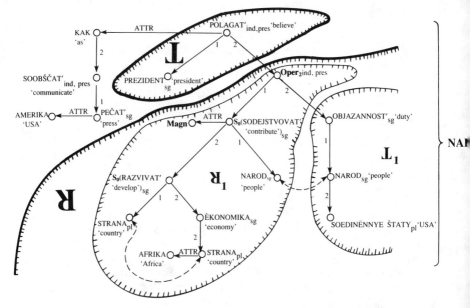

Figure 2-4
The DSyntR of Sentence(6)

Surface-Syntactic Representation

A **surface-syntactic representation** specifies the organization of a particular sentence, much as a DSyntR does; but unlike the latter, a SSyntR is geared to the surface form: to morphologization and linear ordering. In Fig. 2-6, (25), p. 70, the SSyntR of sentence (7) is shown; it corresponds to the DSyntR (24) of Fig. 2-5.

The SSyntR of a sentence consists of four structures corresponding to the four structures of the DSyntR (replacing D[eep-] by S[urface-]):

SSyntR = {SSyntS, SSynt-CommS, SSynt-AnaphS, SSynt-ProsS}.

(24)

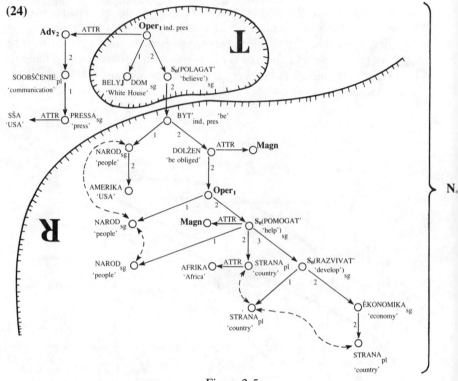

Figure 2-5
The DSyntR of Sentence (7)

The **S(urface-)Synt(actic) S(tructure)** is also the main structure of the
SSyntR. It is a dependency tree quite like the DSyntS, but its composition and labeling differ from those of the DSyntS.

A **node** of a SSyntS is labeled with an ACTUAL LEXEME of the language. Five
differences between the nodes of a SSyntS and those of a DSyntS should be indicated. First, in a SSyntS all the lexemes of the sentence are present, including
semantically empty (i.e., structural) words. Second, all the idioms are expanded
into actual surface-syntactic trees. Third, the values of all the lexical functions
are computed (using a special dictionary, see below) and spelled out as actual
lexemes, replacing the LF symbols. Fourth, all the fictitious lexemes of the
DSyntS are expressed in the SSyntS by the corresponding SSynt-relations and
thus disappear. And fifth, all the pronominalizations (under lexical and/or referential identity) are carried out, so that a SSyntS node can be a pronoun. However, generally speaking, there is no one-to-one mapping between the nodes of a
SSyntS and the actual wordforms of the sentence: as indicated in Chapter 1 (p.
15), either a SSynt-node may correspond to a zero wordform, or two SSynt-
nodes may correspond to one amalgamated wordform.

As is the case for DSyntS, a lexeme assigned to a SSynt-node is subscripted for all its meaning-bearing grammemes; in other words, a node of a SSyntS is the reduced DMorphR of the corresponding wordform. However, with two afore-mentioned exceptions, the wordforms represented in a SSyntS are all ánd only actual wordforms of the sentence, rather than wordforms of generalized lexemes, which appear in a DSyntS.

An **arc**, or **branch**, of a SSyntS, is labeled with a **S(urface-)Synt(actic) Rel(ation)** (SSyntRel). These relations are language-specific; they describe particular syntactic constructions of particular languages. The inventory of SSynt-relations for language $\mathcal{L}$ is established empirically, according to several criteria, discussed in Chapter 3, pp. 129 ff.; references to tentative lists of SSynt-relations for several languages are given in Chapter 1, p. 16.

Among the SSyntRels of $\mathcal{L}$ a few are distinguished, so that the corresponding dependent is called a **surface-syntactic actant**. SSynt-actants of a verb include its grammatical subject, its objects and its complements (if any). Actants are opposed to circumstantials; the line between the former and the latter is drawn according to a number of criteria that cannot be considered here. (The main criterion is that the actants are lexically specified by a given verb, while circum-stantials are freely added to any verb.)

The correspondence between semantic, deep-syntactic and surface-syntactic actants of a lexeme (i.e., its **diathesis**) is specified for this lexeme by what we call **government pattern** (GP): a matrix whose columns give the pairs "Sem-actant/DSynt-actant" and whose rows contain indications as to the SSynt-actants and their morphological realizations. See the examples of GPs in the Appendix, pp. 94 and 97.

Let it be recalled that, as is the case with the DSyntS, the nodes of the SSyntS are not ordered linearly. (Linear ordering of actual sentence elements is a means to mark the syntactic relations properly speaking; therefore, it should not appear in a SyntS, be it a deep or surface structure.)

The **SSynt-CommS**, the **SSynt-AnaphS** and the **SSynt-ProsS** are more or less analogous to their deep counterparts; I will not discuss the divergences here since they are marginal to our main topic.

Deep-Morphological Representation

A **deep-morphological representation** specifies the form of a particular sentence in terms of the wordforms and the phrases that constitute it and their linear order, without regard to the internal organization of the wordforms themselves.

Formally, the DMorphR of a sentence consists of two structures: the D(eep-)Morph(ological) S(tructure) and the D(eep-)Morph(ological)-Pros(odic) S(tructure), so that:

DMorphR = {DMorphS, DMorph-ProsS}

(25)

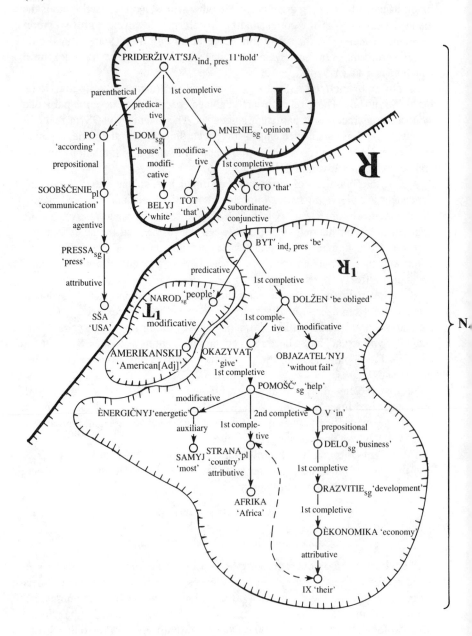

Figure 2-6
The SSyntR of Sentence (7)

The **D(eep-)Morph(ological) S(tructure)** of a sentence is the main structure in its DMorphR. It is an ordered string (i.e., a **chain**) of D(eep-)Morph(ological) R(epresentations) of all the wordforms that make up the sentence, given in the linear order they actually have in it.

The DMorphR of a wordform **w** is the name of the lexeme to which **w** belongs subscripted for all its grammemes. DMorphR(**w**) unambiguously specifies **w** (up to wordform homonymy), while the DMorphS of the sentence unambiguously specifies the word order in it.

The **D(eep-)Morph(ological)-Pros(odic) Structure** of a sentence indicates the pauses, intonation contours, and the like. It is on this level that the phrase structure of the sentence is specified: prosodically distinguished phrases are part of the DMorphR.

In Fig. 2-7 (= (26)) the DMorphR of a fragment of sentence (7) is shown.

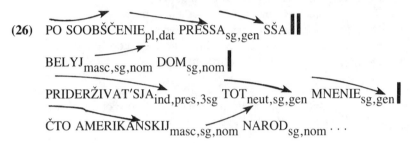

(26) PO SOOBŠČENIE$_{pl,dat}$ PRESSA$_{sg,gen}$ SŠA ‖

BELYJ$_{masc,sg,nom}$ DOM$_{sg,nom}$ |

PRIDERŽIVAT′SJA$_{ind,pres,3sg}$ TOT$_{neut,sg,gen}$ MNENIE$_{sg,gen}$ |

ČTO AMERIKANSKIJ$_{masc,sg,nom}$ NAROD$_{sg,nom}$ · · ·

['As reports the press of the USA, the White House has the opinion that American people . . .']

Figure 2-7
The DMorphR of a Fragment of Sentence (7)

Surface-Morphological Representation

A **surface-morphological representation** is similar to the DMorphR, but it stresses the internal morphemic organization of wordforms:

SMorphR = {SMorphS, SMorph-ProsS},

where the SMorphS consists of linearly ordered SMorphR of wordforms and the SMorph-ProsS plays the same role as the DMorph-ProsS. The SMorphR of wordform **w** is the set of morphemes making up the wordform. I will limit myself to three examples of SMorphRs of Russian wordforms:

(27) **a.** {SOOBŠČENIE} + {PL.DAT} = *soobščenijam*
  b. {BEL(YJ)} + {MASC.SG.NOM} = *belyj*
  c. {PRIDERŽIVA(-T′SJA)} + {IMPERF} + {IND.PRES} + {3SG}
    + {REFL} = *priderživaetsja*

There is no reason to consider here the two phonetic levels that are distinguished in the MTM. For the purposes of syntactic discussion, the D~ and SPhonRs can be safely replaced with conventional spelling.

III. MAJOR COMPONENTS OF A MEANING-TEXT MODEL

1. General remarks

As stated above, an MTM of a language maps the set of its SemRs onto the set of its SPhonRs and vice versa; this is done through the five intermediate levels listed in Section II, pp. 48–49. Accordingly, the MTM includes six major components:

1. The Semantic Component, or **semantics**, for short.
2. The Deep-Syntactic Component, or **deep syntax**.
3. The Surface-Syntactic Component, or **surface syntax**.
4. The Deep-Morphological Component, or **deep morphology**.
5. The Surface-Morphological Component, or **surface morphology**.
6. The Deep-Phonetic Component, or **phonemics**.

The Surface-Phonetic Component, which provides for the correspondence between the SPhonR and actual sound, falls outside the scope of the MTM.

Each component of the MTM is a set of rules having the trivial form:

$$X \Leftrightarrow Y \mid C$$

Here X stands for a fragment of utterance representation at level n (counting from the SemR), Y stands for a fragment of utterance representation at level $n + 1$, and C is the set of conditions under which the above correspondence holds; these conditions, expressed by Boolean formulas, bear on X, Y or the correspondences between the two. The two-headed double arrow means 'corresponds' (rather than 'is transformed into').

The MTM rules have two important properties. First, as I have already said, these rules are static, not dynamic. They simply state what corresponds to what, but they do not transform or generate anything. When, for instance, the transition from a given SemR 'X' to a corresponding DSyntR Y takes place, the rules of the semantic component do not change 'X' in the least. With 'X' used as a blueprint, these rules are applied to construct Y by a dynamic mechanism, which is not part of the MTM, because it is deemed not to be linguistic₁ in nature.

Second, the MTM rules are logically unordered. All relevant information about the language is expressed by symbols within the rules, but never by the order of the rules. Each rule is self-contained in the sense that it itself determines the proper moment and point of its application; this makes individual rules more complex than they could be otherwise, but greatly simplifies the rule system, which becomes modular and easily manageable. Once again, the mechanism that computes the appropriate (or best) order for rule application in a particular situation is not linguistic$_1$ in nature and should not detract linguists from their professional tasks.[12]

I will briefly characterize only the first three components of the MTM, leaving the others aside for the same reason that I did the three nearest-to-surface representations. (Concerning morphology within the MTM framework see, e.g., Mel'čuk 1973a, b, 1976 and 1982.)

2. Survey of the MTM components

Semantic Component

The Semantic Component of the MTM establishes the correspondence between the SemR of an utterance and all the synonymous sequences of DSyntRs of the sentences that make up the utterance. To do this, the Semantic Component must be able to perform eight main operations, which can be thought of as main divisions, or problem domains, of semantics.

1. **Sentencialization**. Proceeding from the original SemR 'X', "smaller" SemRs are constructed, such that their sum equals 'X' and each of them corresponds, in its semantic "size," to a sentence. Language-specific and style-sensitive rules are needed for the job, since different languages differ greatly in regard to the degree of physical length and semantic loading they tolerate in a sentence.

2. **Lexicalization**. Generalized lexemes (i.e., nodes of the DSyntS) are selected by means of semantic rules that put together bundles of semantic units appearing in the initial semantic network such that each such bundle is expressed by a lexemic unit of the language in question. Four types of semantic rules are needed to carry out the operation (corresponding to the four types of generalized lexemes); roughly speaking, they relate semantic subnetworks to deep-syntactic subtrees.

   a. A **lexico-semantic rule** maps a semantic subnetwork onto a lexeme (with its DSynt-actants); for instance:

(28) Russian

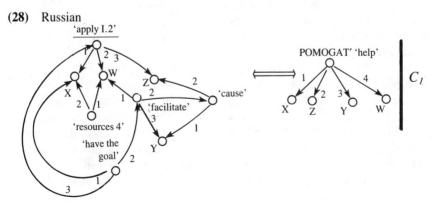

[The semanteme 'apply I.2' in the left-hand part of the rule is underlined to show its foregrounding with respect to all other semantemes: 'X applies W to Z with the goal . . . ,' rather than, e.g., 'X has the goal to apply W to Z . . . .']

C_1 is the set of conditions (or restrictions) on contextual uses of POMOGAT'. In fact, (28) is the dictionary entry for this Russian lexeme. In particular, the left-hand part of the rule is nothing but a lexicographic definition in a network form; we can present it in prose as follows: *X pomogaet Y-u v Z-e W-em* 'X helps Y in Z with W' = 'X applies his resources W to Z, which Y is causing, with the goal that it facilitates for Y the causation of Z'.

Lexico-semantic rules are fairly numerous: in any language, their number is of the order $10^5 \sim 10^6$ (about one million). This is not so surprising, since every particular word sense needs a separate rule of this kind.

b. A **phraseologico-semantic rule** is very much like a lexico-semantic rule, with the following difference: instead of a lexeme, it contains in the right-hand part a phraseme, i.e., a multilexemic idiomatic expression. For instance:

(29) Russian

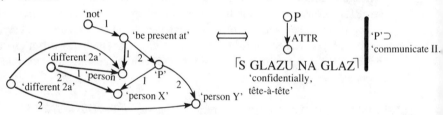

The Russian phraseological expression S GLAZU NA GLAZ, lit. 'from eye to eye', is an adverb meaning 'with no witnesses (present)'; it is used as a modifier of a verb whose meaning includes the idea of an 'exchange of ideas, communication' (*Oni pogovorili s glazu na glaz* 'They conversed with no witnesses present', but not **Oni podralis' s glazu na glaz* 'They fought with no witnesses present').

Lexico-semantic and phraseologico-semantic rules make up a dictionary of a new type: the Explanatory Combinatorial Dictionary (ECD), which constitutes an integral and very important component of any MTM. I cannot elaborate here on this crucial concept of the MTM approach (see Mel'čuk et al. 1984, Mel'čuk and Zholkovsky 1984, Mel'čuk et al. 1981, with all the relevant references). Let it be stated only that an entry of the ECD includes, in addition to a full SemR of the headword, a completely formalized and exhaustive description of its restricted co-occurrence, syntactic as well as lexical. The syntactic co-occurrence is represented by means of the **government pattern** (see above), which specifies, as indicated for every semantic actant of the headword, the corresponding deep-syntactic actant and possible surface realizations of the latter, including the compatibility of different realizations, etc. The lexical co-occurrence is described in terms of **lexical functions**, cf. above, p. 61. At the end of this chapter, a lexical entry from a Russian ECD and a lexical entry from a French ECD are offered as illustrations (see Appendix, p. 92ff.).

c. A **lexico-functional(LF)-semantic rule** specifies a sense of a lexical function:

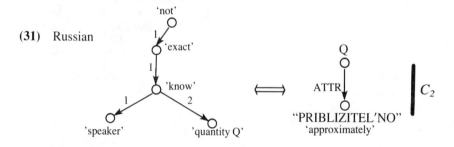

In other words, the LF **Magn**, being a modifier of a lexemic unit, predicates 'intensive' on its meaning.

d. A **syntactico-semantic rule** specifies a fictitious lexeme representing a meaning to be encoded by a syntactic construction:

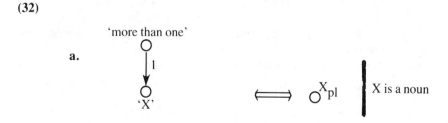

The fictitious (i.e., deep-syntactic) Russian lexeme "PRIBLIZITEL′NO" ('approximately', 'about') is manifested at the SSynt-level through an idiosyncratic approximate-quantitative SSyntRel. This is a construction that preposes the noun to the numeral; cf. *desjat′ tonn* '10 tons' vs. *tonn desjat′* 'about ten tons'.

3. Morphologization. Proceeding from the original SemR, **morphologico-semantic rules** establish meaning-bearing grammemes:

(32)

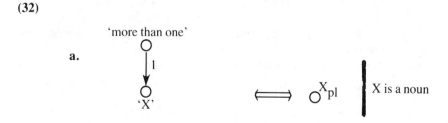

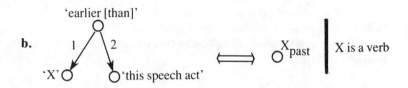

Here, the meanings of the plural in nouns and the past tense in verbs are represented.

4. **Syntaxization**. The DSyntS, i.e., a DSynt-tree, is constructed out of the available lexemes subscripted for meaning-bearing grammemes.

5. **Topicalization**. The DSynt-CommS is provided: the topic—comment, the given—new, the presupposed—asserted and similar divisions are established, using the data contained in the Sem-CommS.

6. **Anaphorization**. Coreference is established for the lexical nodes that have appeared as a result of the forcible duplication, in the DSyntS, of certain semantic nodes. (Because of the strictly linear nature of speech, the speaker is obliged to use several consecutive lexical units to refer back to the same object or event.)

7. **Prosodization**. The meaning-bearing prosody of the sentence-to-be is computed by **prosodico-semantic rules**. For example:

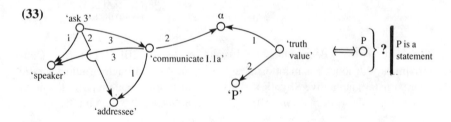

The meaning 'the speaker asks the addressee to communicate to him α, which is the truth value of the statement *P*' is rendered, at the DSynt-level, by the specific interrogative prosodics, represented in rule (33) by the symbol "**?**". (I cannot even touch here on the serious problem of representing, in the SemR, pragmatic aspects of meaning, such as the imperative, for example, which underlies questions: 'How old are you? = 'Tell me your age!') Note that other syntactic means—inversion or interrogative particles—can, of course, also be used at the same time to express questions; these must be accounted for by other types of rules.

All meaning-bearing prosodic phenomena are represented in the SemR in the same way as other meanings (lexical, morphological, or syntactic), but in the

DSyntR they are reflected differently, since suprasegmental means (i.e., prosody) differ so greatly from segmental means.

8. **Synonymic Paraphrasing.** For each $DSyntR_i$ produced, the semantic component constructs (ideally) all synonymous DSyntRs such that their synonymy with this $DSyntR_i$ can be exhaustively described in terms of lexical functions. In other words, the construction of the set of all synonymous DSyntRs for a given SemR may be viewed as being carried out in two stages:

(34)

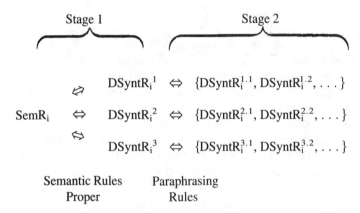

$$\text{SemR}_i \Leftrightarrow \begin{cases} \text{DSyntR}_i^1 \Leftrightarrow \{\text{DSyntR}_i^{1.1}, \text{DSyntR}_i^{1.2}, \dots\} \\ \text{DSyntR}_i^2 \Leftrightarrow \{\text{DSyntR}_i^{2.1}, \text{DSyntR}_i^{2.2}, \dots\} \\ \text{DSyntR}_i^3 \Leftrightarrow \{\text{DSyntR}_i^{3.1}, \text{DSyntR}_i^{3.2}, \dots\} \end{cases}$$

Semantic Rules   Paraphrasing
Proper   Rules

Remark. Other types of linguistic₁ synonymy are accounted for either by lexico-semantic rules that can group semantic units into semantemes corresponding to particular lexemes in different ways or by rules of surface syntax that carry out synonymic surface transformations, such as different types of nominalizations, etc.

The calculus of synonymous DSyntRs is ensured by means of a **paraphrasing system**, a subcomponent of the semantic component. The paraphrasing system defines an algebra of correspondences between those DSyntRs where the DSyntS contains LF symbols; this is achieved by means of the following two major classes of rules:

● **Lexical Paraphrasing Rules** represent either semantic equivalences or semantic implications, both expressed in terms of lexical functions. Because of this fact, their number is limited (about sixty) and they are universal, i.e., they are valid for any language. For example:

(35) **Equivalences**

a. *W* $\Leftrightarrow$ **Conv**$_{21}$ (*W*)   *This set contains [W] the point* **M** $\Leftrightarrow$ *The point* **M** *belongs [***Conv**$_{21}$ *(W)] to this set.*

b. W $\Leftrightarrow S_0(W) + Oper_1 (S_0 (W))$ *He warned* [W] *them* $\Leftrightarrow$ *He issued* [$Oper_1$] ($S_0(W)$)] *a warning* [S_0 (W)] *to them.*

c. Real$_2$ (W) $\Leftrightarrow$ **Ady$_{1B}$** (**Real$_2$** (W)   *He followed* [**Real$_2$** (W)] *her advice* [W] *to enroll* $\Leftrightarrow$ *He enrolled on* [**Adv$_{1B}$**(**Real$_2$**(W)] *her advice* [W].

(36) Implication
    PerfCaus (W) $\Rightarrow$ **PerfIncep** (W)   *He started* [**PerfCaus** (*run 11*)] *the motor* $\Rightarrow$ *The motor started* [**PerfIncep** (*run 11*)].

- **Syntactic Paraphrasing Rules** specify the necessary changes in the DSyntS that are entailed by the application of particular lexical paraphrasing rules. Only four basic syntactic operations exist for labeled dependency trees: (1) merger of two nodes (= contraction of a branch), (2) splitting of a node in two (= growing a new branch), (3) transfer of a node (together with its entering branch) to another governor and (4) renaming of a branch. Moreover, as stated above, only nine DSynt-relations are distinguished at the DSynt-level in the MTM. Therefore, the number of elementary deep-syntactic tree processing rules is not very large (below 100). Any particular syntactic rule describing a change in our DSyntS can be represented as a sequence of these elementary rules.

To operate the lexical paraphrasing rules in (35), the following syntactic rules are needed:

(37) a.

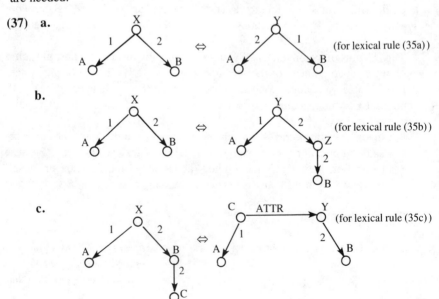

Generally speaking, a syntactic paraphrasing rule, because of its abstract character, may serve several different lexical paraphrasing rules. (For a formalism describing the processing of unordered dependency trees — so-called Δ-grammar — see Gladkij and Mel'čuk 1969, 1974, 1975, 1983: 151–187.)

The eight major operations of the semantic component have been listed in what may be called logical order—for the ease of reading. But this pedagogical ordering by no means reflects the chronological sequence of the above operations. There are, to be sure, intrinsic factors which require, for instance, that syntaxization be done after lexicalization: until lexemes are selected, they obviously cannot be arranged within the DSynt-tree. However, besides such factors, the general question of which operations precede and/or follow which other operations during the passage from a SemR to a corresponding DSyntR is not even asked within the present framework. It is quite probable that in actual speech production these operations are intermingled or carried out in parallel, but for present purposes we will not be concerned with this question: the mechanisms underlying or governing any such ordering are beyond linguistics as such, as was claimed above.

Deep-Syntactic Component

The Deep-Syntactic Component of the MTM establishes the correspondence between a DSyntR and all the SSyntRs of the various sentences that can implement it on the surface. To do this, the DSynt-component performs seven main operations corresponding to the main divisions, or problem domains, of deep syntax. (Note that, as before, the ordering of these operations is adopted for expository purposes only; nothing is presupposed as to their actual order.)

1. **Computation of the values of lexical functions**. Proceeding from the LF symbols in the DSyntS, the DSynt-component computes for them the corresponding values by means of rules such as (38):

(38)

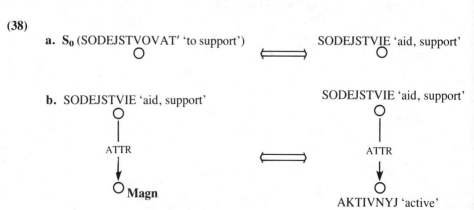

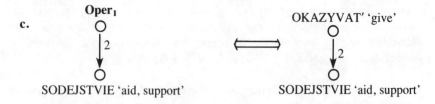

c.

2. **Phraseme expansion**. For every lexical node representing a phraseological unit, the DSynt-component constructs the actual surface tree.

Operations 1 and 2 are carried out according to the Explanatory Combinatorial Dictionary, where the values of LFs (for a given key word) and the SSyntSs of phrasemes are stored.

3. **EQUI-Deletion**. The DSynt-component finds and marks all lexical nodes that occur in anaphoric relations and should not appear in actual texts. This is done partly on the basis of dictionary information, and partly in conformity with general rules of syntax. Cf., for instance, sentence (39a) and its DSyntS (39b):

(39)   **a.** *Dick asked Susan to visit him.*

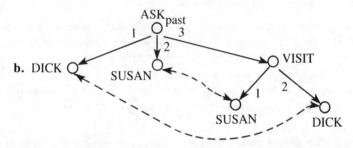

According to the information contained in the government pattern of ASK (in the dictionary), VISIT should be realized as an infinitive; according to a general rule of English syntax, the 1st DSynt-actant of any verb should not appear in the SSyntS, if this verb is to be represented as an active infinitive (not in a FOR-TO construction). Therefore, the branch $\xrightarrow{1}$ SUSAN, which hangs from VISIT, is eliminated:

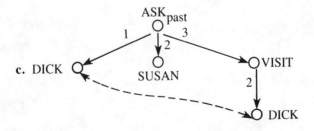

As we see, the two coreferential nodes labeled DICK remain, in order that the second one (= depending on VISIT) may be replaced by HE, see below.

4. Pronominalization. Under referential identity, appropriate nodes are replaced by pronouns; for instance, (39c) is pronominalized to become (39d):

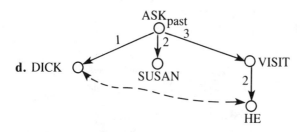

5. SSyntS construction. The DSynt-component constructs the SSyntS of the sentence-to-be by means of the following three types of DSynt-rules:

a) Rules of the type "a DSyntRel ⇔ a SSyntRel."
A deep-syntactic (i.e., universal) relation is expressed, in a particular context, by a surface-syntactic (i.e., language-specific) relation. For example:

(40) English

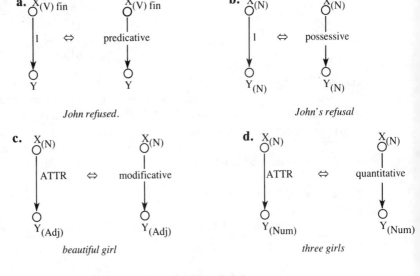

b) Rules of the type "a DSynt-node ⇔ a SSyntRel."
A fictitious deep lexeme is expressed by a surface-syntactic relation. For example:

(41) Russian

$$X(N) \xrightarrow{\text{ATTR}} Y(\text{Num}) \xrightarrow{\text{ATTR}} Z_{\text{"PRIBLIZITEL'NO"}} \quad \Leftrightarrow \quad \text{approximate-quantitative} \quad X(N) \rightarrow Y(\text{Num})$$

c) Rules of the type "a DSyntRel ⇔ a SSynt-node."
A DSynt-relation is expressed by a function word. For example:

(42) English

$$X_{(V, \, 2[ON])} \xrightarrow{2} Y \quad \Leftrightarrow \quad X_{(V, \, 2[ON])} \xrightarrow{\text{1st completive}} ON_{\text{prepositional}} \xrightarrow{} Y$$

The notation $X_{(V, \, 2[ON])}$ indicates a lexeme that is a verb and whose second DSynt-actant must be expressed in the SSyntS by a phrase introduced by the preposition ON, e.g., DEPEND or INSIST; this information is stored in the dictionary entries of the corresponding lexemes (i.e., in the government pattern).

6. SSynt-CommS construction.

7. SSynt-ProsS construction.

A small fragment of the DSynt-component for Russian is presented in Mel'čuk (1974a: 237–259).

Surface-Syntactic Component

The Surface-Syntactic Component of the MTM establishes the correspondence between the SSyntR of a sentence and all the alternative DMorphRs that are realizations of it. To do this, the SSynt-component performs four main operations. (All the remarks made above in connection with the DSynt-component apply here as well.)

1. **Morphologization**. All syntactically conditioned grammemes are determined. These include: grammatical case of nouns; gender, number and case of adjectives; person and number of finite verbs. In other words, agreement and government are implemented. After that, the nodes of the SSyntS have complete DMorphRs of wordforms associated with them.

2. **Linearization**. The actual word order of the sentence is determined.

3. **SSynt-ellipsis**. Various kinds of reductions and omissions, possible or obligatory in a given context, are carried out.

4. **Prosodization**. The correct prosody of the sentence is computed on the basis of the SSynt-ProsS (i.e., meaning-bearing prosody) and the SSyntS (i.e., syntactically induced prosody). It is here that the phrase structure of the sentence is fully determined. This includes: major pauses, intonation contours, and the like.

The SSynt-component uses five major types of rules:

—**Syntagms**, or **Surface-Syntax Rules**, which serve as the basic tool of morphologization and linearization of the SSyntS. A fairly complete list of English syntagms is found in Mel'čuk and Pertsov (1987); a representative sample of Alutor syntagms and a more detailed discussion of this type of SSynt-rules is offered below in Chapter 7. This allows me to limit myself to three English examples, without any general explanations:

(**43**)   English

$$
\begin{array}{c}
X_{(V)} \\
O \\
| \\
\text{predicative} \;\Leftrightarrow\; \\
\downarrow \\
O \\
Y_{\Delta NP}
\end{array}
\left\{
\begin{array}{l}
(1)\; Y_{\textbf{not}\; \text{obj}} + \ldots + X \\
\\
(2)\; X + \ldots + Y_{\textbf{not}\; \text{obj}}
\end{array}
\right|
AGREE_{V(N)}
\left|
\begin{array}{l}
\textbf{not} \\
INVERS_{\text{Subj-V}}^{\text{oblig}}\,(Y, X) \\
\\
INVERS_{\text{Subj-V}}\,(Y, X)
\end{array}
\right.
$$

This SSynt-rule (i.e., syntagm) says that a predicative construction having a **standard subtree** Δ NP[13] as the grammatical subject (GS) features the following properties:

• Morphologically, the GS must not be in the objective case (relevant only for personal pronouns: *me, us,* . . . and for the interrogative pronoun *whom*);

the verb must agree with the GS in accordance with the **standard func-tion**[14] AGREE$_{V(N)}$, i.e., "agreement of the verb with the GS."
- Linearly, the GS must precede the verb if yet another standard function, INVERS$_{Subj-V}^{oblig}$, i.e., "obligatory inversion of the GS with respect to the main verb," does not apply; it must follow the verb otherwise; and it may either precede or follow the verb if a similar function, "non-obligatory inversion," applies.

(44) English

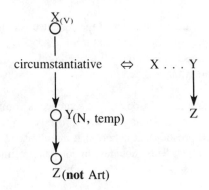

This SSynt-rule describes temporal adverbials of the type *last week, next year, the same day*. It says that a noun with the syntactic feature "temp(oral)" having a dependent other than an article expresses the circumstantiative dependency on a verb with no morphological changes required and can be placed before or after the verb: *Last week we traveled to Boston* or *We traveled to Boston last week*. (The actual position of a temporal circumstantiative NP is determined by word order rules of further types, see below.)

(45) English

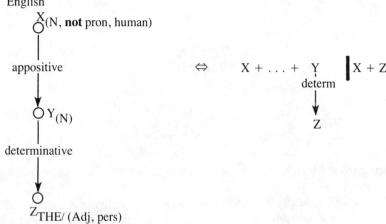

This SSynt-rule describes the appositive construction such as *my friend the director* or *Jack the Ripper*. In this construction, a noun governing the definite article or a possessive adjective (*my, your, . . .*) follows a human noun it modifies, so that its determiner follows the latter immediately.

—**Patterns for elementary phrases** (e.g., *these four interesting German books* vs. **German four these interesting books*).

—**Global word order rules**, which determine the best word order possible for the given SSyntS on the basis of various data:
- indications contained in syntagms
- topic—comment, given—new etc. divisions (including emphasis)
- specific properties of some lexemes marked in the dictionary (for instance, MEAN [something *by* something] shows a tendency towards preposing of the second actant: **By free trade** *we mean such an arrangement that . . .*)
- avoiding possible syntactic ambiguities produced by specific arrangements (There are perhaps some other data to be used for fully determining word order in an English sentence.)

These rules are aimed at minimizing the value of a utility function that represents the "penalty" assigned (by the linguist) to certain unfelicitous arrangements. This is done by reshuffling the constituent phrases within a prospective DMorphS of the sentence with an eye to the value of the utility function. (Global word order rules for Russian, a language famous for its involved word order, were published twice: Mel′čuk 1967 and 1974a: 268–300.)

—**Ellipsis rules**.

—**Prosodic rules**.

Let me add that the SSynt-component of an MTM for Russian is outlined in Apresjan et al. (1978), and the SSynt-component of an MTM for French is outlined in Apresjan et al. (1984).

NOTES

1. (I, the very beginning, p. 43.) Some of the central ideas of the Meaning-Text approach may be traced back to Žolkovskij et al. (1961) and Žolkovskij (1964). The first major presentation of the Meaning-Text theory appeared in Žolkovskij and Mel′čuk (1967); it was soon translated into English and then into French. Shortly afterwards, Jurij D. Apresjan, who was already well known for his work on lexical semantics, joined us; thus was formed the nucleus of our team. Over a ten-year period, some twenty linguists contributed to the work on a Meaning-Text Model of Russian. Basic general readings, in addition to the two titles just mentioned, include Mel′čuk (1970, 1973c) [see now in Gladkij and Mel′čuk 1983: 151–187], 1974a, 1981a), Mel′čuk and Žolkovskij (1970), Rozencvejg (1974); cf. also Nichols (1979) and Nakhimovsky (1983). A fairly complete bibliography of works realized in the Meaning-Text framework is found in Mel'čuk (1981a: 58–62) and in Hartenstein and Schmidt (1983).

2. (I, Postulate 1, p. 43.) The reader will easily recognize here the Jakobsonian six-element scheme of linguistic₁ communication: Jakobson (1960: 353–357).

3. (I, Postulate 2, Remark 3, p. 46.) In the meaning-sound union, both partners are equal, but the meaning, in Orwellian fashion, is more equal than the sound. Or, as Lewis Carroll's Duchess put it: "Take care of the sense, and the sounds will take care of themselves." In the MTM, we have been following this advice.

4. (II, between Postulate 2 and Postulate 3, p. 48.) To show how thousands of paraphrases for a given meaning can be produced, let me give an example.

Let there be sentence (i):

(i) *The Food and Drug Administration has seriously cautioned expectant mothers to avoid one of life's simple pleasures: a cup of coffee* (*Newsweek*, Sept. 15, 1980).

The meaning of (i) can be expressed by (ii), as well:

(ii) *Pregnant women have been earnestly warned by the FDA against drinking coffee, one of the small pleasures of life.*

Except for the function words (articles, auxiliaries) and such technical terms as *the FDA*, *coffee* and *pleasures of life*, all the other words in (i) have been changed, as has the syntactic structure. Yet the meaning has been preserved (more or less) intact. True, if we really want to, we can find semantic differences between (i) and (ii): thus the meaning of *seriously caution* is not, strictly speaking, quite identical with that of *earnestly warn*, etc. But the important fact is that, in normal situations, people never speak strictly: potential semantic contrasts are often ignored in actual contexts as irrelevant to the main point of the message. This ability of the speaker not to notice semantic nuances if he does not need them is, in my view, an important property of natural language that has to be accounted for. Therefore, here as elsewhere, when considering two sentences as (nearly) synonymous, I consciously disregard obvious semantic distinctions that I think are "neutralized" in the given context. Contextual neutralization of actual semantic distinctions is extremely important to any semantically-based theory of language and especially so to the MTM theory. Nevertheless, this phenomenon is not directly relevant to dependency syntax, and I cannot enter here into a serious discussion of it. Let me only mention that a profound analysis of semantic neutralization is offered in Apresjan 1974: 158–163, 239–242, 281–283.

From (i) and (ii), it can be seen that the underlying meaning consists of roughly eight fragments, or blocks, each of which will be represented by one column in Fig. 2-8 below, p. 87. Each column contains (nearly) synonymous expressions that convey the corresponding "piece" of meaning; the figure in boldface under a column indicates the number of expressions, or variants, in it. Any variant from one column combines with almost any variant from another column, for instance:

(iii) *The FDA has addressed a stern caution to ladies to the effect that while expecting a baby they should abstain from coffee, something that is one of life's small joys.*
(iv) *The FDA has made public a strong warning addressed to mothers-to-be: they should not indulge in consuming coffee, one of the simple pleasures of life.*

This allows us simply to multiply the number of variants in each column:

Top table

1	2	3	4	5
FDA	serious(ly) earnest(ly) stern(ly) strong(ly)	caution warn forewarn counsel put on guard address a caution issue a warning {a caution / a warning} make public	pregnant women expectant mothers mothers-to-be {during pregnancy / while expecting a baby} {women / ladies}	to avoid to abstain from should {avoid / abstain} should not not to
1	4	9	7	6

Bottom table

6	7	8
coffee {drink(ing) / consum(ing) / cup of coffee} coffee (indulge in)	one of something that {is one of / constitutes}	{small / simple} {pleasures / joys} {life's / of life}
6	3	8

Figure 2-8
Paraphrastic Variants for Sentences (i)–(iv) in Note 4

$1 \times 4 \times 9 \times 7 \times 6 \times 6 \times 3 \times 8 = 217{,}728$ paraphrases!

True, some of these paraphrases will be sifted out by selectional restrictions and other co-occurrence constraints; however, a native speaker can easily think of more variants, so that the order of magnitude for the number of (nearly synonymous) paraphrases of a given idea shown above must be correct. It is interesting to quote, in support of the last claim, the introductory article by Ohmann to *The American Heritage Dictionary* (1971: XXXI–XXXXII): "Put before 25 speakers a fairly simple drawing, ask them to describe in a sentence the situation it portrays, and they will easily come up with such examples as:

A bear is occupying a telephone booth, while a tourist impatiently waits in line.
A man who was driving along the road has stopped and is waiting impatiently for a grizzly bear to finish using the public phone.
A traveler waits impatiently as a bear chatters gaily in a highway phone booth.

Almost certainly, each of the 25 sentences will be different from all the others, yet each will adequately describe the drawing . . . An analysis by computer shows that the 25 sentences about the bear in the phone booth yield the materials for 9.8 billion sentences, all describing just one situation."

5. (II, **2**, SemR, the very beginning, p. 52.) Interestingly, the same is true of many physical notions. The notion of 'weight' is based on that of 'the same weight', the weight being the only property all the objects of the same weight have in common; similarly, the notion of 'length' is based on 'the same length'; etc. Identity/non-identity of two weights, lengths, speeds, etc. is more readily available to human perception (than the abstract notion of weight, length or speed), via comparisons made using some kind of instrument, including human "instruments" (arms or eyes). Note that the precision of such comparisons is always relative, contingent upon the task (weighing potatoes at a grocer's vs. weighing some chemicals for a medicine) and of course upon the measuring device. The same holds with regard to meaning: the precision with which we establish the equisignificance (i.e., synonymy) of two texts must be allowed to vary as a function of the nature of the task (a journalistic description vs. a legal formulation) as well as of the speaker involved, who represents the "measuring device." Cf. the remarks in Note 4.

6. (II, **2**, SemR, after (13), p. 58). As can be seen from the preceding exposition, in the MTM framework no explicit marks for semantic roles are allowed: we do not use meaningful relational labels on the arcs as presupposed, for instance, by Fillmore's "deep cases" or their latest development in transformational grammar, the so-called "Theta-roles" (short for 'thematic roles'). The reasons for our decision are of two sorts: formal and substantive.

Our main formal reason is as follows. Suppose we require that every relation between a functor **F** and its argument **a** be labeled by a MEANINGFUL name **n**:

$$\mathbf{F} \xrightarrow{\mathbf{n}} \mathbf{a};$$

but since this **n** is itself a functor (i.e., a binary relation, of the type 'be the causer of', 'be a perceiver of', 'be the source of', etc.), we should label the relations between **n** and its arguments, **F** and **a**, again with meaningful names **n′** and **n″**:

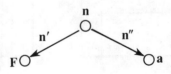

These **n'** and **n"** are also functors; we are obliged again to label the relations between them and their arguments, and so forth. This means that we fall into infinite regression. The only way to avoid this is to allow the relations between some chosen functors and their arguments to be unlabeled. However, this would constitute an arbitrary decision, aggravated by the fact that the same functors that label arcs may appear on nodes of the SemR: e.g., for sentences such as *John will be the* **beneficiary** *of my will* or *The* **source** *of my knowledge is The New York Times*. Should then the relations between 'beneficiary' (or 'source') and its arguments be semantically labeled—and if so, then how?

The main substantive reason is that all repertories of so-called "semantic roles" known to us are wanting. On the one hand, they contain some roles that are in fact not semantic, but rather syntactic: 'be the subject of', 'be the theme of', 'be the object/goal of'. On the other hand, they do not contain many other roles that should be distinguished— if the roles we are after are to be really semantic. Interestingly, Apresjan discovered twenty-five semantic roles (1974: 125–126), and still he believes that his "list is, most probably, incomplete."

I think that semantic relation labels are nothing more than holdovers of the syntactic era in linguistics and can be safely abandoned.

7. (II, **2**, DSyntR, Fictitious Lexeme, p. 60.) For instance, the meaning of the Russian approximate-quantitative construction is not identical with that of the lexeme PRIBLIZITEL'NO or PRIMERNO (both meaning 'approximately, about'). This construction expresses the subjective uncertainty of the speaker rather than an objective, albeit approximate, measure. Thus, someone asked about the coming birthday of a friend—'How old will Ann be on Tuesday?'—may answer in Russian:

(i) *Ne znaju točno, let dvadcat'*, lit. '[I] don't know exactly, maybe twenty'
while to say
(ii) *Ne znaju točno, *priblizitel'no ⟨*primerno⟩ dvadcat' let*, lit. '[I] don't know exactly, approximately twenty'

is impossible for obvious semantic reasons.

Moreover, this construction readily admits the combination with such lexemes as PRIBLIZITEL'NO 'approximately':

(iii) *Èto stoit problizitel'no dollarov dvesti*, lit. 'This costs approximately maybe $200'.

To distinguish fictitious lexemes from actual lexemes, we enclose the former in double quotes: thus PRIBLIZITEL'NO 'approximately' is a regular Russian lexeme, while "PRIBLIZITEL'NO" is a fictitious lexeme standing for the approximate-quantitative SSynt-construction.

8. (II, **2**, DSyntR, Lexical Functions, p. 61.) A most infelicitous ambiguity of the term **argument** must be noted here. The term is used in two clearly distinct senses: (1) to denote an argument of a functor, as in 'love(John, Mary)', where *John* and *Mary* are the arguments of the predicate *love*; (2) to denote the argument, or key word, of a lexical function, as in **Magn**(*supporter*) = *staunch*, where *supporter* is the argument of the LF **Magn**. I will do my best to avoid confusion.

9. (II, **2**, DSyntR, Lexical Functions, p. 62.) There are also non-simple and non-standard LFs, of which only a few words can be said here.

Non-simple LFs include **compound** LFs. A compound LF is a combination of syntactically related simple LFs that has a unique lexical expression (covering the meaning of the combination as a whole). For example:

AntiMagn(*applause*) = *thin* **AntiMagn**(*arguments*) = *weak*
IncepOper₁(*despair*) = *sink into* **IncepOper₁**(*treason*) = *take the path of*
AntiReal₂(*examination*) = *fail* **AntiReal₂**(*application*) = *turn down*

A **non-standard** LF is a meaning that is idiomatically expressed depending on the key word but has either a strongly limited semantic combinability, or a strongly limited range of expressions, or both. Non-standard LFs are written in standardized natural language.

10. (II, **2**, DSyntR, LFs, *Operᵢ*, p. 62.) To avoid misunderstanding, let me indicate that the term **empty**, as used here, should not be construed as 'absolutely deprived of meaning'. I call a linguistic₁ expression X empty in context A if X is implied by A (i.e., X is automatic) and the meaning of X repeats, or duplicates, a part of the meaning of A. Thus *pay* is empty in the context of *visit* or *attention* [*pay a visit/attention*] just as *on* is empty in the context of *depend* [*depend on*].

11. (II, **2**, DSyntR, DSyntRel, p. 64.) Our way of representing coordinate structures on the deep-syntactic level as follows:

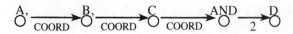

$$\underset{\text{COORD}}{\overset{A,}{\bigcirc}\longrightarrow} \underset{\text{COORD}}{\overset{B,}{\bigcirc}\longrightarrow} \underset{\text{COORD}}{\overset{C}{\bigcirc}\longrightarrow} \underset{2}{\overset{AND}{\bigcirc}\longrightarrow} \overset{D}{\bigcirc}$$

was argued for in Chapter 1, p. 41. Note that conjunctions, as well as prepositions have only DSyntRel 2, but not DSyntRel 1 issuing from them: a conjunction or a preposition necessarily has a complement but is unable to have a subject. (Semantically, a conjunction or a preposition is obviously a two-place predicate; but its 1st semantic argument is its syntactic governor, not its actant. Cf.:

(i) *beer in bottles*

(ii) SemS:

'in'

'beer' 1 2 'bottles'

(iii) DSyntS: BEER ——ATTR——→ IN ——2——→ BOTTLES

See Chapter 3 for a comparison of semantic and syntactic dependencies.)

12. (III, **1**, p. 73.) Rule ordering is such an important and complicated theoretical issue that I am not in a position to discuss it here. For a good exposition of the views of the opponents of extrinsic rule ordering and relevant references, see Koutsoudas (1978) and Koutsoudas and Sanders (1974). To date, the most thorough study of rule ordering is Pullum (1979), which also rejects extrinsic ordering.

Incidentally, I think that there exist no ways of LOGICALLY proving the indispensability of extrinsic rule ordering. Admitting more complex rules and/or a sufficiently sophisticated processor (more powerful than naive sequential devices presupposed by modern linguistic₂ theories) one can always get rid of ordered rules. The question is not whether we can do so, but whether we want to. My answer (within the MTM framework) is an unqualified yes. It is based on two very general principles:

(i) In a scientific description, nothing should be expressed implicitly, for instance, by means of order; all we have to state must be stated via explicit symbols (see pp. 53 and 60).

(ii) Linguistic₂ rules as such should express only linguistic₁ knowledge; information controlling the application of rules must be rigorously separated from them.

13. (III, **2**, SSynt-Component, **Syntagms**, p. 83.) A **standard (sub)tree** (Δ) is a means for a more economic representation of syntagms. It is an abbreviation: it stands for a class of syntactic constructions that behave as a unit and are roughly equivalent to a word class. Thus Δ NP is a family of dependency (sub)trees representing any noun phrase or any of its syntactic equivalents. Standard (sub)trees are specified separately from syntagms; a Δ is usually exploited by several syntagms.

14. (III, **2**, SSynt-Component, after (41), p. 84.) A **standard function** (in computer programming, called also a **standard subroutine**) is a closed set of rules designed to carry out a specific class of tasks. In a linguistic₂ model, standard functions (not to be confused with **lexical functions**) provide for different types of agreement, inversion, coordination, ellipsis, and the like. A standard function thus specifies a particular linguistic₁ phenomenon quite independently of more comprehensive rules and may be repeatedly used by different rules. In this way, recourse to standard functions enhances the generality and logical transparency of syntactic rules in particular. Thus, a standard function is, like a standard subtree, a means for a more economic representation of syntagms — more specifically of their conditions. It is an abbreviation standing for a complex condition that appears in several syntagms. As an example, see the standard function AGREE in SSynt-rules for Alutor, in Chapter 7, pp. 279 ff.

APPENDIX:
TWO SAMPLE ENTRIES
OF THE
EXPLANATORY
COMBINATORIAL
DICTIONARIES
OF FRENCH
AND RUSSIAN

The reader interested primarily in dependency syntax might not immediately see the point of including an appendix about the Explanatory Combinatorial Dictionary (ECD) in the book. But the fact is that a presentation of the ECD, at least a very sketchy one, is a must. The ECD constitutes the very foundation of the Meaning-Text theory, the framework within which the present D-formalism is argued for. Therefore, to be reasonably confident of the validity of D-syntax, the reader needs to see for himself what the ECD is about and how it works. This is all the more necessary in that there is no readily available detailed description of the ECD in English. Moreover, the following three notions crucial to syntactic argumentation have to be illustrated (and actually are) by ECD entries: deep-syntactic actant, government pattern (related to **diathesis** and **voice**, see Chapter 4) and lexical function. Also, as indicated in the Introduction, this Appendix helps the reader better grasp the semantic and lexicographic orientation of the whole approach espoused in this book.

In this Appendix, I chose as illustrations a French and a Russian lexemes that are equivalent under translation: French ADMIRATION = Russian VOSXIŠČENIE, both meaning roughly 'admiration'. The Appendix is divided into two sections: in Section I the two entries are given, in Section II several examples of translation between French and Russian by means of an ECD are analyzed.

I. SAMPLE ENTRIES

The sample entries are borrowed, respectively, from Mel'čuk et al. (1984: 54–56) and Mel'čuk and Zholkovsky (1984: 215–217). I have made several simplifications and modifications (e.g., I have replaced original definitions, formulated in French and Russian, by English glosses; I have omitted sense-distinguishing indices, which generally accompany polysemous words; etc.). Also, I do not provide additional explanations for the lexical functions not introduced before and for many other specific details, hoping that the linguistic[1] material itself is clear enough.

NOTATIONS AND SYMBOLS

~	head word
A	adjective
A_{poss}	possessive (pronominal) adjective
ART	⎧ with article
Ø/ART	the head word ⎨ without article, with the exception of cases
	is used ⎪ when it is modified by an adjective
~	⎩ without article
C_i	surface-syntactic actant (of the head word) corresponding to the i-th deep-syntactic actant
$C_{i.j}$	surface means j expressing the i-th surface-syntactic actant
G(X)	syntactic governor of X; if X is not explicitly indicated, G is the governor of the immediately preceding item
M_i	i-th deep-syntactic actant
N	noun
|X	X is a condition whose scope includes any expression to the left of vertical bar up to the first semicolon
Λ	empty set (e.g., $C_1 = \Lambda$ means that C_1 cannot be expressed at all)
//X	X is the "fused" value of the corresponding lexical function (i.e., an expression whose meaning covers the meaning of the function together with the meaning of its key word)
Wh	relative word (meaning 'where', 'when', . . .)

French ADMIRATION, noun, fem.

1. no plural. *Admiration de X devant Y pour son Z* = Emotional attitude of X, favorable with respect to Y, which is caused by the following fact: X believes that actions, state or properties Z of Y are completely extraordinary; this attitude is such that one normally has in such situations.

Government Pattern[1]

1 = X	2 = Y	3 = Z
1. *de* N 2. A_{poss} 3. A	1. *de* N 2. *pour* N 3. *devant* N 4. *envers* N	1. *pour* A_{poss} N

1) $C_{2.4}$: N denotes a person
2) C_3 without C_2 ⎤
3) $C_{1.1} + C_{2.1}$ ⎬   : impossible
4) $C_{2.2} + C_{3.1}$ ⎦

l'admiration du public, son admiration, l'admiration nationale; son admiration des ⟨pour/devant les⟩ tableaux anciens; l'admiration de Pierre devant ⟨envers⟩ Jacques pour son courage

Impossible: **l'admiration envers ces tableaux* (1) [= *l'admiration pour ces tableaux*];
            *l'admiration de Pierre pour le courage (2) [= *l'admiration de Pierre envers Jacques pour son courage*];
            *l'admiration de Pierre de son père (3) [= *l'admiration de Pierre pour son père*];
            *l'admiration pour son père pour son courage (4) [= *l'admiration envers son père pour son courage*]

Lexical Functions

$Syn_\subset$	: enthousiasme
$Syn_\cap$	: ravissement, émerveillement
Anti	: aversion
Gener	: sentiment [d'~] │ $C_1 = \Lambda$
V_0	: admirer
$S_{1\subset}$	: admirateur
S_2	source, objet [de ∅/ART~] // admiration 2 [*Il devint l'admiration de la superbe Ninive*]
A_1	: plein, rempli [de ∅/ART~], dans [ART~], en [~] // admiratif 1 [*Elle est admirative pour tout ce qu'il dit*]
$Able_1$	: sujet, enclin, porté [à ART~]
$Able_2$	: digne [de ∅/ART~] // admirable
Adv_1Able_2	: // admirablement [*Une rivière aux eaux admirablement claires*]

$PredAble_2$	: mériter [ART/de ART$\sim$]
Magn	: grande, vive, profonde $<$ immense $<$ sans bornes
PredMagn	: ne plus connaître de bornes
AntiVer + Magn	: excessive, démesurée, exagérée
$Magn_1^{quant}$	: commune $<$ générale, universelle
IncepPredPlus	: grandir, s'accroître, augmenter 1, se développer
CausPredPlus	: accroître, augmenter 2
IncepPredMinus	: diminuer 1, faiblir
CausPredMinus	: diminuer 2, affaiblir [ART$\sim$]
Ver_1	: justifiée, fondée
$AntiVer_1$	: injustifiée; de commande
AntiBon	: aveugle, irréfléchie, béate
Adv_1	: dans un moment [d'$\sim$]; avec [$\emptyset$/ART$\sim$] $\mid M_2\,(G) = Y$
Adv_2	: à [l'$\sim$] $\mid$ either $C_1 \neq \Lambda$ or $A \rightarrow Magn_1^{quant}$ [*Il remporta la victoire, à l'admiration de ses copains*]
Propt	: par [$\sim$] $\mid$ no modifier, except for *seul* and $C_{2.2}$ [*par seule admiration*]; sous l'effet [de ART$\sim$] $\mid C_i = \Lambda$
$Oper_1$	: éprouver, ressentir, avoir, nourrir [ART / de l'$\sim$], être [en$\sim$/ dans ART$\sim$] $\mid C_2 \neq$
Magn + $Oper_1$	: brûler [de $\emptyset$/ART$\sim$] $\mid C_2 \neq \Lambda$
$Oper_1$ + W$\xleftarrow{1}$A.$\xrightarrow{2}$Y	: partager [1'$\sim$de N = W] $\mid C_2 \neq \Lambda$
$IncepOper_1$	: tomber [en$\sim$] $\mid C_2 \neq \Lambda$
$ContOper_1$	: rester [en $\sim$ / dans ART$\sim$]; garder [ART$\sim$] $\mid C_2 \neq$
$FinOper_1$	: perdre [ART$\sim$] $\mid C_2 \neq \Lambda$
Magn + $Caus_{(2)}Oper_1$	: remplir [N de $\emptyset$/ART$\sim$]
$Oper_2$	: s'attirer, attirer [ART$\sim$] $\mid C_1 \neq \Lambda$; inspirer [ART/de l'$\sim$ chez N]
$ContFunc_0$	: durer
$FinFunc_0$	: s'éteindre, s'évanouir, s'épuiser, cesser, disparaître
$LiquFunc_0$	: mettre fin [à ART$\sim$], **coll** liquider [ART$\sim$]
$Perm_1Manif$ or $Perm_1Func_0$	: céder [à ART$\sim$]
$notPerm_1Manif$ or $notPerm_1Func_0$	: retenir, refréner, réprimer [ART$\sim$]
Magn + $Func_1$	: remplir, transporter [N]
$IncepFunc_1$	: saisir, gagner [N] $\mid$ preferably in the passive voice; s'emparer [de N], naître [en son âme $\langle$ coeur $\rangle$]
(W$\xleftarrow{1}$A.)$\xleftarrow{1}$$CausFunc_1$	: [N = W] communiquer [1'$\sim$ à N = X]
$Caus_{(2)}Func_1$	: causer, provoquer, allumer, susciter, éveiller, déclencher, exciter [ART/de l'$\sim$ chez N]

	[*Le père a causé une grande admiration chez les enfants pour cet artiste*]
$Caus_2Func_3$	: gagner, forcer [1'~ par N] $\mid C_1 \neq \Lambda$, Y
	<small>denotes a person</small>
$Magn + Labor_{21}$	: **lit** soulever, frapper [N de Ø/ART~]
facial expression ←² Manif	: se peindre ⟨ se refléter ⟩ sur le visage [de N = X]
$Conv_{21}Manif$	: [N] traduire [ART~], montrer, exprimer [ART/de l'~]
in spite of X, $Conv_{21}Manif$	:[N] trahir [ART~]
A_2Manif	: [N] plein, rempli, empreint [de Ø/ART~] // admiratif 2, admirateur 2 [*Il pose sur elle un regard admirateur*]
$MagnManif$	: éclater [Loc_{in} N] [*L'admiration éclatait dans chaque ligne de sa lettre*]
$Caus_1Manif$	: manifester, montrer [ART/de l'~], exprimer [ART~]
orally $Caus_1Manif$	: dire < crier [A_{poss}~]; **lit** professer [ART/de l'~ à l'égard de N]
by talking much about Y, $Caus_1Manif$	: // avoir la bouche pleine [de N = Y]
Adv_1Caus_1Manif	avec [Ø/ART~] // admirativement [*regarder quelqu'un admirativement*]
$notPerm_1Manif$	: cacher, dissimuler [ART~]
$A_2notPerm_1Manif$	: secrète
$Degrad^{motor}(body)$— $Sympt_{23}$	: se pâmer [d'~]
$Excess^{fulg}(eyes)$— $Sympt_{13}$	: ses yeux brillent, étincellent, brûlent [de Ø/ART~]
whistle—$Sympt_{23}$	: siffler [d'~]
S_0(whistle—$Sympt_{23}$)	: sifflement [d'~]
S_0(whisper—$Sympt_{23}$)	: murmure [d'~]

With the right-side brace annotation: N = *regard, voix, ton, parole, visage, geste, . . .*

Examples

En même temps, il ne pouvait se retenir d'éprouver une secrète admiration pour ce Biturige qui alliait la fierté et l'adresse [G. de Sède]. Il me parle avec admiration du docteur de Martel qui vient de sauver sa femme [A. Gide]. Je reste longtemps dans l'admiration de son tronc énorme et de sa ramification puissante [A. Gide]. Les Anglais en particulier ont une grande admiration pour son talent. Ce pauvre Sandy a gagné l'admiration des humains. Ce discours improvisé souleva d'admiration l'auditoire. En le voyant sauter l'obstacle, il poussa un long sifflement d'admiration. Elle professe à son égard une admiration qu'il ne mérite pas. Il force l'admiration par son courage. A ces mots, un murmure d'admiration s'éleva de la foule.

Russian VOSXIŠČENI|E 〈 VOSXIŠČEN′|E 〉, *ja*, noun, neuter, no plural.

Vosxiščenie X-a pered Y-om = Emotional attitude of X, favorable with respect to Y, which is caused by the following fact: X believes that actions, state or properties of Y are completely extraordinary; this attitude is such that one normally has in such situations.

Government Pattern

1 = X	2 = Y
1. N_{gen} 2. A_{poss}	1. N_{instr} 2. *pered* N_{instr} 3. *tem, čto / Wh* + CLAUSE

vosxiščenie publiki, moë 〈*Katino*〉 *vosxiščenie; ego vosxiščenie starymi kartinami; vosxiščenie publiki pered artistom; eë vosxiščenie tem, čto u nix tak mnogo knig* 〈*skol′ko u nix xorošix knig*〉

Lexical Functions

$Syn_{\subset}$	: èntuziazm
$Syn_{\cap}$	: vostorg
Anti	: otvraščenie
Gener	: čuvstvo [~ja]
V_0	: vosxiščat′sja
$S_{1\cap}$	: poklonnik
S_2	: ob″ekt, **lit** predmet [~ja]
A_1	: polnyj, ispolnennyj [~ja pered N_{instr}] // vosxiščënnyj 1
A_1 + Magn	: preispolnennyj [~ja/~em]
$Able_2$	: dostojnyj [~ja] // vosxititel′nyj
$PredAble_2$	: byt′ dostoin, zasluživat′ (vsjačeskogo) [~ja]
Magn	: glubokoe < bezmernoe, neopisuemoe; soveršennoe, polnoe │ G(V.) = (Incep)$Oper_1$ or $IncepLabor_{21}$
AntiVer + Magn	: preuveličennoe
$Magn_1^{quannt}$	: vseobščee
IncepPredPlus	: rasti

IncepPredMinus	: umen'šat'sja
CausPredMinus	: umen'šat' [~e]
Ver_1	: iskrennee, nepoddel'noe
AntiVer_1	: delannoe, pritvornoe
Adv_1	: v [~i] $\mid C_2 = V$; s [~em] $\mid G = Y$
Adv_2	: k [~ju] $\mid$ either $C_1 = \Lambda$ or V.$\rightarrow \text{Magn}_1^{\text{quant}}$
Oper_1	: ispytyvat' [~e pered N_{instr}], byt' polon [~ja pered N_{instr}]; byt' [v ~i (ot N_{gen})] $\mid$ V. has no dependent
$\text{Oper}_1 + \text{W} \xleftarrow{\perp} \text{V}.\xrightarrow{\;3\;} \text{Y}$	: razdeljat' [~e N_{gen} = W] ['have admiration for the same thing as W']
IncepOper_1	: prixodit' [v ~e (ot N_{gen})]
$(\text{W} \xleftarrow{\perp} \text{V}.) \xleftarrow{\perp} \text{CausOper}_1$	: [~e N_{gen} = W] peredaëtsja [N_{dat}]
IncepOper_2	: vyzyvat' [u N_{gen}/v N_{prep}~e], vnušat' [N_{dat}~e]
FinFunc_0	: proxodit'
$\text{Caus}_2\text{Func}_0$	: zavoëvyvat' [~e] $\mid$ either $C_1 \neq \Lambda$ or V. $\rightarrow \text{Magn}^{\text{quant}}$
Labor_{12}	: otnosit'sja [k N_{dat} s ~em]
IncepLabor_{21} or CausOper_1	: privodit' [N_{acc} v ~e N_{instr} = P(X)] [*On privël vsex v vosxiščenie svoej xrabrost'ju*]
facial expression $\xleftarrow{2}$ Manif	: vyražat'sja na lice [N_{gen} = X]
$\text{Conv}_{21}\text{MagnManif}$	: [N] dyšit [~em] $\mid C_2 = \Lambda$, N denotes a message of X [*Ego pis'mo dyšit vosxiščeniem*]
A_2Manif	: [N] polnyj, ispolnennyj [~ja] // vosxiščënnyj 2 $\mid C_2 = \Lambda$; N = *vzgljad, golos, ton, slova, žest, . . .*
such a sound of voice in which notMagnManif	: notka [~ja]
$\text{Caus}_1\text{Manif}$	: vyrazit' [(svoë) ~e]
in spite of X, $\text{Caus}_1\text{Manif}$	: ne moč' sderžat' [(svoego) ~ja]
$\text{Adv}_1\text{Caus}_1\text{Manif}$	: s [~em] $\mid C_2(\text{V.}) = \Lambda$ // vosxiščënno
$\text{Perm}_1\text{Manif}$	: ne skryvat' [(svoego) ~ja]
$\text{A}_2\text{Perm}_1\text{Manif}$	: neskryvaemoe
$\text{A}_2\text{notPerm}_1\text{Manif}$	: tajnoe
$\text{Degrad}^{\text{motor}}(body)$—$\text{Sympt}_{23}$	: zameret' [ot ~ja/v ~i]], zastyt', ostanovit'sja [v ~i] $\mid C_2 = \Lambda$
$\text{Excess}^{\text{fulg}}(eyes)$—$\text{Sympt}_{23}$	: [u N_{gen}] glaza svetjatsja, sijajut [ot ~ja/ ~em] $\mid M_1$ denotes a person, $C_2 = \Lambda$
Exclam—Sympt_{23}	: axnut' [(ot ~ja)]

Examples

Pis'mo ego dyšalo vosxiščeniem i ljubov'ju. On smotrel na učitelja s neskryvaemym vosxiščeniem. Krome ruž'ja, ja dal emu nož, ot kotorogo on prišël v polnoe vosxiščenie. "I ty skazal èto?"—v ego golose poslyšalas' notka vosxiščenija.

II. TRANSLATING BY MEANS OF AN ECD

Now I will show (using data from Jørdanskaja and Arbatchewsky-Jumarie 1982) how a French speaker who does not know Russian can translate a French sentence into Russian by means of an ECD. In doing this I will completely ignore grammatical problems and concentrate exclusively on lexical choices.

Let us take sentence (1):

(1) French *Les Anglais avaient une grande admiration pour son talent*
'The British had great admiration for his talent'.

The problem is that its literal translation (2):

(2) Russian **Angličane imeli bol'šoe vosxiščenie dlja ego talanta*

is completely ungrammatical. The best target equivalent should be (3):

(3) Russian *Angličane ispytyvali glubokoe vosxiščenie ⟨byli polny glubokogo vosxiščenija⟩ pered ego talantom,*
lit. '. . . experienced ⟨were full of⟩ profound admiration before his talent'.

Using an ECD, our French speaker is able to find the required equivalent (3); to do so, he needs to perform the following five operations:

1) Find (in a bilingual index) the Russian equivalent of ADMIRATION, namely VOSXIŠČENIE.

2) Understand that *grande* (with *admiration*) is a value of a particular LF, namely **Magn**(*admiration*), and *avoir* is a value of another particular LF: **Oper₁**(*admiration*).

3) Look up **Magn**(*vosxiščenie*) and **Oper₁**(*vosxiščenie*) in the Russian ECD and, since there are alternative variants, make his choice according to the conditions stated in the corresponding lexical entry. Thus, he will choose *glubokoe*, rather than *bezmernoe*, as a modifier of *vosxiščenie*, since in French *grande* is the lowest degree of **Magn**. He will not choose *byt'* (*v*) as the value of **Oper₁** because this **Oper₁** does not admit any modifier with *vosxiščenie*, while there is a modifier (i.e., *glubokoe*).

4) Understand that *pour* (with *admiration*) is a surface marker of the 2nd syntactic actant.

5) Look up the corresponding marker in the government pattern of the Russian **Oper$_1$**, in this case, of *ispytyvat'* or *byt' polon*; it is *pered . . . [talantom]*.

I invite the reader to carry out this modest exercise himself.

In many cases, however, a particular expression cannot be translated into another language this easily. For example, the LF **f** defined for X$_1$ in $\mathcal{L}_1$ may not be defined at all for X$_2$ in $\mathcal{L}_2$: $\mathcal{L}_2$ lacks a value of **f** for X$_2$. Thus, consider the French sentence (4):

(4)   French *Son admiration pour ce pays durait toujours*
'His admiration for this country lasted forever',

where *durer* 'last' is **ContFunc$_0$**(*admiration*). This sentence cannot be rendered in Russian in a structurally similar way: there is no value of **ContFunc$_0$** for Russian VOSXIŠČENIE. In this case, we invoke the paraphrase system mentioned above, Chapter 2, p. 77, specifically, the universal equivalence (5):

(5)   **ContFunc$_0$** $\Leftrightarrow$ **notFinFunc$_0$** (compare the equivalences in (35), pp. 77–78).

It happens that the LF **FinFunc$_0$** does have a value for VOSXIŠČENIE: *proxodit'*, lit. 'pass'. So the French sentence (4) featuring the LF **ContFunc$_0$** can be translated by Russian sentence (6) using LF **FinFunc$_0$** plus negation:

(6)   Russian *Ego vosxiščenie ètoj stranoj ne proxodilo*,
lit. 'His admiration for this country did not pass'.

A similar difficulty for a translator arises in the French sentence (7):

(7)   French *L'admiration éclatait dans chaque ligne de sa lettre*,
lit. 'Admiration was exploding in every line of his letter'.

Here, *éclater* is the value of LF **MagnManif** (**MagnManif** $\cong$ 'manifest itself in an intensive way'). But in Russian, this LF is not defined for VOSXIŠČENIE: we cannot say anything like (8):

(8)   Russian **Vosxiščenie vzryvalos' v každoj stroke ego pis'ma*
[Russian *vzryvat'sja* = French *éclater*].

However, we have for VOSXIŠČENIE the LF **Conv$_{21}$MagnManif**: *dyšat'* 'breathe'; this provides for a translation equivalent, following the equivalence (9):

(9)   head word $\xleftarrow{1}$ **Manif** $\xrightarrow{2}$ U $\Leftrightarrow$ U $\xleftarrow{1}$ **Conv$_{21}$Manif** $\xrightarrow{2}$ head word

The translation obtained is (10):

(10)   Russian *Každaja stroka ego pis'ma dyšala vosxiščeniem*,
         lit. 'Every line of his letter was breathing with admiration'.

We now take an example of translation in the opposite direction, from Russian into French. The equivalence (11):

(11)

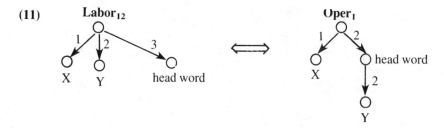

allows us to translate the Russian sentence (12), which contains the LF **Labor$_{12}$**, not defined for Fr. ADMIRATION, with the French sentence (13), using **Oper$_1$**:

(12)   Russian *Druz'ja otnosjatsja* [= **Labor$_{12}$**] *k Jure s vosxiščeniem*,
         lit. 'Friends treat Yura with admiration'.

(13)   French *Les amis éprouvent de l'admiration pour Jura*,
         lit. 'Friends experience admiration for Yura'.

NOTES

1. (I, ADMIRATION, p. 94.) Government Pattern (GP), used in the MTM approach since 1965, is an important formal device designed to relate the semantic and the syntactic actants of the same lexeme. This means that the GP of lexeme L specifies L's **diathesis** — a correspondence between L's semantic and syntactic actants. (Such pairings were called "lexical forms" in Bresnan 1980: 97.) The diathesis is discussed more in detail in Chapter 4, pp. 176 ff.

AN IMPORTANT CONCEPT OF DEPENDENCY SYNTAX: SURFACE-SYNTACTIC RELATIONS

Proceeding from the general framework put forth in Part I, the present part sets out to introduce and characterize a notion that is crucial to any surface-syntactic dependency formalism: SURFACE-SYNTACTIC RELATION. In this connection, Part II has to deal with a few related notions, especially with semantic and morphological dependencies. A review of these is necessary in order to better delineate our main target here, syntactic dependency proper.

Part II includes just one chapter, Chapter 3, which analyzes and compares semantic, syntactic and morphological dependencies and then describes the surface-syntactic relation by a number of criteria which determine the presence of such a relation between two given wordforms, its direction and its type.

Chapter 3

TYPES OF SYNTAGMATIC DEPENDENCIES BETWEEN WORDFORMS OF A SENTENCE AND SURFACE-SYNTACTIC RELATIONS

A short article published more than twenty years ago (Mel'čuk 1964b) introduced the distinction between three major types of syntagmatic dependencies that can link the wordforms of a sentence in any language, namely: (1) MORPHOLOGICAL dependency, (2) SYNTACTIC dependency and (3) SEMANTIC dependency. Main ideas from that article were later taken up and developed, in an interesting way, by Garde (1977). It now seems appropriate to return to this subject once again and to refine it further. This chapter will attempt to do so.

The chapter is divided into three sections:

I. Types of syntagmatic dependencies between wordforms of a sentence.

II. Possible combinations of types of syntagmatic dependencies between two arbitrary wordforms of a sentence.

III. Syntactic dependency: a logical analysis of an important concept.

I. POSSIBLE TYPES OF SYNTAGMATIC DEPENDENCIES
BETWEEN WORDFORMS OF A SENTENCE

In the following discussion, the ELEMENTARY (i.e., unanalyzable at this level) UNITS of the sentence are wordforms or, more specifically, the **deep-morphological representations** of wordforms (since the physical aspect of wordforms—their phonological structure, their prosody and so forth—is not relevant to this study).

The **Deep-Morphological Representation**, or DMorphR, was introduced in the preceding chapter (p. 71). The DMorphR of wordform **w** will be notated as

$$L\chi,$$

where L is the corresponding lexeme, i.e., the lexeme that includes **w** (i.e., the wordform in question); and χ is the morphological characteristic of **w**, that is, the string of values of all its morphological variables or grammemes. (The notions of "morphological variable" and "grammeme" are taken for granted in what follows.) For example:

(1) **a.** DMorphR(*canals*) = $CANAL_{pl}$
   b. DMorphR (*is*) = $BE_{indic, pres, 3sg}$
   c. French DMorphR (*fraîches*) = $FRAIS_{fem, pl}$ 'fresh'
   d. DMorphR(*walks*) = $\begin{cases} WALK\ 1_{pl}\ [noun] \\ WALK\ 2_{indic, pres, 3\ sg}\ [verb] \end{cases}$
   e. DMorphR(*building*) = $\begin{cases} BUILD_{pres, participle}\ [verb] \\ BUILDING\ 1_{sg}\ [noun] \\ BUILDING\ 2\ [adjective] \end{cases}$

The forms *walks* and *building* are morphologically ambiguous—with a double ambiguity in the first example and a triple one in the second.

At least three major types of SYNTAGMATIC DEPENDENCIES linking wordforms of a specific sentence can be differentiated:

1) morphological, or strictly formal, dependency
2) syntactic, or mixed, dependency—half formal, half conceptual
3) semantic, or strictly conceptual, dependency

These three dependency types do not describe all the syntagmatic links that exist between the wordforms of a sentence. For example, two more types can be noted:

—**Anaphoric links**. When two wordforms in an utterance, w_1 and w_2, denote the same real object or the same real phenomenon, there is an anaphoric link between w_1 and w_2 (marked in (2) below by bidirectional broken-line arrows):

(2) **a.** French *Il n'a jamais exprimé le désir de rester plus longtemps au pays* [w_1] *ou d'y* [w_2] *retourner* (A. Gide)
'He never expressed a desire to remain in the country longer or to return to it'.

b. French *C' était une fille* [w_1] *sage* / *A bouche que veux-tu, J'ai croqué dans son* [w_2] *corsage* / *Les fruits défendus* (G. Brassens)
'She was a good girl / With a greedy mouth, / I plucked from the bodice (of her robe) / The forbidden fruit'.

—**Communicative links**. These occur, for example, between two wordforms that simultaneously belong to the theme (i.e., topic, focus) or to the rheme (i.e., comment, nucleus) of the sentence. Cf. (3):

(3) French *Ce que j'ai promis de faire,* | *je le ferai* (G. Bernanos)
'What I promised to do, I will do',

where all wordforms before | belong to the topic, and those after | belong to the comment.

However, the anaphoric and communicative links are hardly examples of dependency (especially since they are symmetrical),[1] so they will not be discussed here. I will consider only the three dependency types mentioned above.

1. Morphological Dependencies

In a sentence, wordform w_1 directly depends morphologically on wordform w_2, if and only if the value of at least one morphological variable of w_1 is determined by w_2.

It does not matter whether this value is determined by (the value of) a morphological variable of w_2 or by (the value of) a feature of its syntactics (i.e., by its inherent, or lexical, properties).[2]
For example, in French sentence (4):

(4) French *C'est l'extase langoureuse,* / *C'est la fatigue amoureuse,* / *C'est tous les frissons des bois* . . . (P. Verlaine)
'It's the languorous ecstasy, / It's the amorous fatigue, / It's all the rustle of the forest'

the following morphological dependencies are observed:

— the adjectives *langoureuse* and *amoureuse* are morphologically dependent on the nouns *l'extase* and *la fatigue* (according to number and grammatical gender variables: thus, *langoureuse* is in the singular feminine, because *l'extase* is feminine and in the singular; the same is true of *amoureuse* and *la fatigue*).

— The articles *l'*, *la*, *les* and *des* are morphologically dependent on the nouns *extase*, *fatigue*, *frissons* and *bois*, respectively (also according to number and grammatical gender).

— The pronominal adjective *tous* is morphologically dependent on the noun *frissons* (once again according to number and grammatical gender: plural masculine).

— The verb *est* is morphologically dependent on the pronoun *ce* (according to the variables of person and number).

Other types of morphological dependency occur in Russian sentence (5):

(5) Russian *I na grudi ee bulyžnoj / Blestit rosa serebrjanym soscom* (V. Xleb-nikov)
'And on her stony breast, / [A] dew [drop] glistens like a silver teat'.

(This verse refers to one of the ancient female statues, crudely hewn in stone by nomad tribes, and found in the steppes of southern Russia.)

Setting aside the adjectival agreement of *bulyžnoj* 'stony' with *grudi* 'breast', and *serebrjanym* 'silver' with *soscom* 'teat' (according to the variables of number, gender and case), the noun *grudi* is morphologically dependent on the preposition *na* (for case, since another preposition could require a different case: *s grud'ju* 'with the breast', etc.), and the verb *blestit* 'glistens' is morphologically dependent on the grammatical subject, the noun *rosa* 'dew' (for number and person: compare *Blestit rosa* '(A drop of) dew glistens' to *Blestjat rosy* 'Dew drops glisten' or to *Ty blestiš'* 'Thou glistenest'). At the same time, the grammatical subject *rosa* is morphologically dependent on the main verb *blestit* according to the case variable (there are a few Russian verbs that require the genitive case of the subject, for example, *Rosý xvataet* 'There is enough dew', lit. 'Dew suffices'; other, more numerous verbs require their subject to be in the genitive if they are negated).

Morphological dependency has the following three important properties.

First, all languages have words that are morphologically invariable and that because of this invariability, are never morphologically dependent on another word. In English, these words are adverbs, prepositions, conjunctions, particles and interjections. There are also words that vary morphologically, but not because of other words: for instance, nouns in English or in French, where the choice of singular or plural is usually not based on another word but is made according to the meaning to be expressed (this variability is thus directly determined by semantics).

The presence of such words suggests that, within a sentence, morphological dependencies do not necessarily create a CONNECTED structure. Consider, for example, French sentence (2b′), where morphological dependencies are shown with arrows (pointing from the governor to the dependent):

(2b′)   *J'*$\xrightarrow{\text{morph}}$*ai* $\xrightarrow{\text{morph}}$*croqué dans son*$\xleftarrow{\text{morph}}$*corsage*
les$\xleftarrow{\text{morph}}$*fruits*$\xrightarrow{\text{morph}}$*défendus.*

Discontinuities in the chain of morphological dependencies are obvious.

Moreover, isolating languages (Chinese, Vietnamese, Khmer, Thai, a number of Tibeto-Burmese languages, Indonesian, etc., as well as a wide range of West African languages such as Yoruba) lack morphological dependencies completely. In these languages, the morphological form of a word never depends on any other word.

All this suggests that, in a sense, morphological dependency is a marginal type of syntagmatic dependency—since some languages do without it occasionally and others do not use it at all.

Second, a morphological dependency can be bilateral, that is, w_1 can depend morphologically on w_2 according to its variable $\chi_i(w_1)$, whereas w_2 depends morphologically on w_1 according to another variable $\chi_j(w_2)$; $i \neq j$. Consider, for example, the Russian expression *dve volny* 'two waves'. The numeral *dve* is morphologically dependent on the noun *volny* according to gender: *dv*+*e* receives the feminine ending because VOLNA 'wave' is feminine (cf. *dv*+*a* *vola* 'two steers', where VOL 'steer' is masculine). At the same time, *voln*+*ý* (singular genitive form) is dependent on *dve* according to number (cf. *pjat' voln* 'five waves', where *voln* is the plural genitive form) and case (cf. *dvadcat'odna voln*+*a* 'twenty-one waves', where *volna* is nominative singular, or *Volny nesutsja* 'The waves rush by' with *vóln*+*y* in nominative plural). Thus we have:

$$dve \overset{\text{morph}}{\underset{\text{morph}}{\rightleftarrows}} volny$$

This point will be discussed later, when we analyze syntactic dependency within the Russian numeral phrase [Num + N]; see pp. 125–126, (23).

A bilateral morphological dependency is very common in languages with the **ergative construction** (see Part III) such that the case of the grammatical subject is dependent on the tense and aspect of the main verb while the person and number of the main verb depend on the person and number of the subject. For example:

(6) Georgian

    a. *Is*   *amb + ob + s*   *rom . . .*
        he-SG.NOM   say   PRES 3SG   that
        'He says that . . .'
        vs.
        Man   *tkv + a*   *rom . . .*
        he-SG.ERG.   say   AOR.3SG   that
        'He said that . . .'
        [*amb-* and *tkv-* are suppletive roots of the same verb *tkma* 'to say']

        Mas   *u + tkv + am + s*   *rom . . .*
        he-SG.DAT   say   PERF 3SG   that
        'He has said that . . .'

        But cf.:

    b. *Isini*   *amb + ob + en*   *rom . . .*
        they -PL.NOM   say   PRES 3PL   that
        'They say that . . .'
        vs.
        Mat   *tkv + es*   *rom . . .*
        they-PL.ERG   say   AOR.3PL   that
        'They said that . . .'
        vs.
        Mat   *u + tkv + am + (s)t*   *rom . . .*
        they-PL.DAT   say   PERF 3PL   that
        'They have said that . . .'

As we see, the grammatical case of the Georgian subject is determined by the tense of the main verb (the nominative for the present, the ergative for the aorist, and the dative for the perfect); however, the form of the verb reflects the number of the subject: the singular in (6a) and the plural in (6b) (the form of the verb also reflects the subject's person, which is not shown in our example).

A similar situation was mentioned for Russian (in the analysis of (5) above), except that in Russian this bilateral morphological dependency between the main verb and the grammatical subject is a lot less developed, and as a result, less evident.

In languages with polypersonal verb conjugation and case declension in nouns, a bilateral morphological dependency links the transitive verb not only to its grammatical subject, but also to its direct object. This phenomenon is also found in languages of the Chukchee-Kamtchatka stock as well as in Georgian. The case of the object depends on the governing verb while the object person and number of the verb depend on the person and number of the governed object;[3] for more details, see Chapter 7 below.

Third, since a word can have several morphological variables, it can be morphologically dependent on several wordforms at once.

Example 1

(7)   Russian
    a. *Ona   kažetsja   sovsem   bol'n* + **oj**
        She   seems   completely   ill   FEM.SG.INSTR
    b. *On   kažetsja   sovsem   bol'n* + **ym**
        He   seems   completely   ill   MASC.SG.INSTR

The adjective BOL'NOJ 'ill' is dependent in gender and number on ONA 'she' in (7a), and on ON 'he' in (7b); but the same adjective is dependent in case on the verb KAZAT'SJA 'to seem'. Compare similar sentences with another verb:

(7′)   **a.** *Ona ležit sovsem bol'n* + **aja**   ⟨ **bol'noj* ⟩
                                FEM.SG.NOM
        lit. 'She is in bed completely ill'.
   b. *On ležit sovsem bol'n* + **oj**   ⟨ **bol'nym* ⟩
                               MASC.SG.NOM
        lit. 'He is in bed completely ill'.
This case was mentioned in Chapter 1, p. 25.

Example 2

A Georgian verb can depend morphologically on three different nouns at once: on the grammatical subject, the direct object and the indirect object.

Example 3

In Tabassaran (Soviet Daghestan), the finite verb can be morphologically dependent on the grammatical subject according to its nominal class, and at the same time, on the object, on the adverbial complement or even on a possessive attribute that modifies the subject (or the object, or the complement) according to person and number:

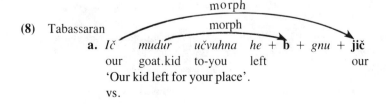

(8)   Tabassaran
    a. *Ič   mudúr   učvuhna   he* + **b** + *gnu* + **jič**
        our   goat.kid   to-you   left   our
        'Our kid left for your place'.
        vs.

morph   morph

b. *Ič*   *mudur*   *učvuhna*   *he* + **b** + *gnu* + **čvuhna**
   our   kid   to-you   left   to-you
'Our kid left for your place'.

(8a) and (8b) are optional variants that express the same meaning 'Our goat kid has left for your place'. The element *-b-* in the verbal wordform represents the nominal class of the grammatical subject (cf. *Murad he-***r***-gnu* 'Murad has-left', with the subject of another class, which calls for *-r-* instead of *-b-*) The different suffixes (*-jič* and *-čvuhna*) represent the person and number either of the attribute of the subject (*ič* 'our'), or those of the adverbial complement (*učvuhna* 'to you = for your place').

2. Syntactic Dependencies

A **syntactic unit** U of a language $\mathcal{L}$ is an occurrence of a lexeme (that is, a wordform), a phrase, a clause or a sentence. The list of constructions of $\mathcal{L}$, or more precisely, the list of the surface-syntactic roles in which U can appear either as a dependent (i.e., marginal, modifying) component or as an absolute head (i.e., an element that is dependent on nothing) will be called the **passive surface-syntactic valency** [passive SS-valency] of U. U's capacity not to depend on anything in the syntactic structure of a sentence is understood as a special instance of its capacity to depend on specific units U^1, U^2, etc. The passive SS-valency of U is notated as $VAL^{SS}_{pass}(U)$. Notice that passive SS-valency of U can be loosely called U's distribution.[4]

The passive SS-valency of a noun (and of a noun phrase) in English, for example, includes, among others, the following syntactic roles:

- **a.** grammatical subject
- **b.** object of a verb
- **c.** copulative verb complement
- **d.** preposition complement
- **e.** modifying [i.e., left] component of a nominal compound (**paper** *bag*, **op-position** *movement*)
- **f.** apposition
- **g.** adverbial complement of duration (*He spent one* **week** *there*)
- **h.** head of an absolute construction (*The* **war** *finished, my parents came to Paris*)
- **i.** head in titles, labels, exclamations, etc. ("*A* **language** *with a double causative construction*"; *What a beautiful* **day**!), etc.

Before proceeding to describe syntactic dependency, it is appropriate to state the following two important assumptions:

(I) Although I will speak of sentences, it is not the sentence as such that is considered in this syntactic dependency discussion, but rather the surface-syntactic representation of the sentence, of which the main part is the surface-syntactic structure, presented in the form of a dependency tree, as defined in Part I, Chapters 1 and 2. Therefore, the SS-valency of a syntactic unit is considered only WITHIN SURFACE-SYNTACTIC STRUCTURES, never in actual sentences.

(II) In a surface-syntactic structure (SSyntS), an actual wordform appears as its deep-morphological representation (see page 106) in REDUCED form, that is, as a DMorphR from which all morphological values indicating or induced by its syntactic role (i.e., agreement and government markers) are removed. Thus, the VAL_{pass}^{SS} of a wordform **w** must be interpreted as the VAL_{pass}^{SS} of the corresponding lexeme $L(\mathbf{w})$. In other words, the SS-valency, that is, the SS-potential, of a wordform is determined only by its INHERENT, LEXICAL PROPERTIES. The syntactically induced morphological values of a wordform are considered as saturation marks of the valency slots satisfied by this wordform. For example, the grammatical case of a Russian noun does not change its passive SS-valency, which is characteristic of its stem and of its stem only. The case, absent from SSyntS, shows up in the deep-morphological structure of the sentence to indicate that the corresponding noun actually fills a particular SS-role.

With these two assumptions in mind, we can proceed to the definition of surface-syntactic dependency. It must be defined by a complex SYSTEM OF CRITERIA (for which see Section III below, pp. 129 ff.). Here, however, a preliminary simplified outline seems in order. Therefore, only one—the most important—of the criteria to be described later will be mentioned.

In a sentence, wordform $\mathbf{w}_1$ directly depends syntactically on wordform $\mathbf{w}_2$ if the passive SS-valency of the phrase $\mathbf{w}_1 + \mathbf{w}_2$ is (at least largely) determined by the passive SS-valency of wordform $\mathbf{w}_2$.

Consequently, the passive SS-valency of the phrase $\mathbf{w}_1 + \mathbf{w}_2$ (where $\mathbf{w}_2$ is the SS-head) is only slightly dependent, if at all, on the passive SS-valency of wordform $\mathbf{w}_1$. (The reader should remember that passive valency is a list of syntactic roles, so that when I say "largely determines the valency", I mean 'determines the majority of elements on the list of syntactic roles'.)

A direct syntactic dependency of $\mathbf{w}_1$ on $\mathbf{w}_2$ is notated as $\mathbf{w}_1 \xleftarrow{\text{synt}} \mathbf{w}_2$

Symbolically, the criterion above can be expressed as (9):

(9)
$$\mathbf{w}_2 \xrightarrow{\text{synt}} \mathbf{w}_1 \underset{\text{DEF}}{\equiv} VAL_{pass}^{SS}(L(\mathbf{w}_1) + L(\mathbf{w}_2)) \cap VAL_{pass}^{SS}(L(\mathbf{w}_2)) >$$

$$VAL_{pass}^{SS}(L(\mathbf{w}_1) + L(\mathbf{w}_2)) \cap VAL_{pass}^{SS}(L(\mathbf{w}_1))$$

[with $>$ used to mean 'is bigger than', i.e., 'contains more elements than'].

Garde (1977) builds his definition of syntactic dependency along the same lines. The only apparent difference occurs in that Garde speaks of "information on syntactic relations between the phrase and what is outside it" (Garde 1977:8), whereas I prefer the concept of "passive SS-valency" of the phrase in question (and that of the morphological contact point, which will be discussed in Section III, page 135). Let me mention also the definition of Bazell: "One member of a syntagma is said to subordinate the other if the first is characterized by such features as are also characteristic of the whole syntagma" (1950:11). Here, it is only the vague concept of "feature" that can be criticized.

The system of SS-dependencies in a sentence can be illustrated as follows:

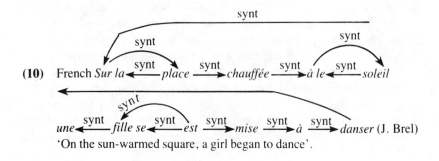

(10)   French *Sur la place chauffée à le soleil une fille se est mise à danser* (J. Brel)
'On the sun-warmed square, a girl began to dance'.

Some explanations are required:

—*la* is syntactically dependent on *place, le* on *soleil* and *une* on *fille*, since it is the noun that imposes its passive valency on the noun phrase NP (the same holds for the dependency between *place* and *chauffée*);

—*place* depends on *sur* and *soleil* on *à*, since the passive valency of the prepositional phrase PP, completely different from that of the embedded NP, comes from the preposition[5];

—*danser* depends on *à* for the same reason as above (VAL$_{pass}^{SS}$($à$—danser) is determined by the preposition rather than by the verb);

—*à* (*danser*) depends on *mise* since the whole phrase *mise à danser* is used like *mise* and not like *à* (*danser*);

—finally, *fille* depends on the verb form *est*, considered to be the absolute SS-head of the sentence, because the passive valency of a sentence (for example, its capacity to become a subordinate clause in a complex sentence) is based on the passive valency of the main verb. Thus, sentence (10) can be used as a subordinate clause in (10′):

(10′)   **On me dit que** *sur la place, chauffée au soleil, une fille s'est mise à danser* 'I hear that on the sun-warmed square, a girl began to dance' whereas the expression (11), without a finite verb as the head, does not allow such embedding:

(11) *une fille qui s'est mise à danser sur la place, chauffée au soleil* 'a girl who began to dance on the sun-warmed square'

(11′) *On me dit qu'une fille qui s'est mise à danser sur la place, chauffée au soleil* 'I hear that a girl who began to dance on the sun-warmed square'

These explanations are clearly far from sufficient, but it is impossible to examine here all the problems of a general syntactic theory or even all the principles that underly a specific syntactic description such as the one adopted here for (10). The reader will have to accept the analysis of (10) as a working hypothesis. In Section III, the notion of syntactic dependency and the criteria for such dependency will be discussed in greater detail. If, after reading Section III, the reader considers (10) again, our analysis will perhaps seem more natural and better justified.

Before proceeding farther, however, a very important point should be clarified. The reader may have the impression that the criterion for surface-syntactic dependency suggested on page 113, contains a vicious circle. Namely, surface-syntactic dependency is defined in terms of passive SS-valency, while passive SS-valency is defined in turn in terms of the capacity of a surface-syntactic unit to depend syntactically on certain types of lexemes. However, this circularity is eliminated because the concept of passive SS-valency includes capacity of the unit in question to be the absolute head of an utterance. This capacity is postulated in this book for the finite verb.

The dominant syntactic role of the finite (i.e., tensed) verb is intuitively evident. Taking it for granted, one proceeds by induction, the finite verb constituting the induction basis. The other cases of syntactic dependency are reduced, sometimes in several steps, to dependency on the finite verb, that is, on the grammatical predicate of the sentence.

This reasoning presupposes a recursive procedure. Syntactic roles and passive SS-valencies must be introduced by "layers" or "ranks." Initially, first-rank dependencies are considered: all units that are linked directly to the main verb depend on it; the first-rank SS-roles and the first components of the VAL_{pass}^{SS} are thus obtained. Then, the units linked to those units directly dependent on the main verb are considered; and so on. It is not necessary to expand here this procedure any farther; the sole purpose of my remark is to reassure the reader that it can be done.

In connection with the specific and privileged status of the finite verb, it can be said that as a word class, the verb is defined basically by its exclusive capacity to be the absolute SS-head of the sentence. As the brief remarks about the analysis of (10′)–(11′) try to demonstrate, this definition is not arbitrary; it is possible to prove, by linguistic[1] data, the absolute syntactic primacy of the finite verb at the clause or sentence level. But since it is a fiercely debated matter, which merits more meticulous study, we will accept the property mentioned as a postulate to head off objections and criticism that are not relevant to our purpose.

Syntactic dependency properties are clearly different from morphological dependency properties. **First**, contrary to morphological dependency, syntactic dependency is universal. There is no language that does not have syntactic dependencies and no language has words that—while in a sentence—can remain free from syntactic dependency. For all languages, in every non-elliptical sentence, syntactic dependencies link all wordforms, that is, they always form a CON-NECTED structure. A sentence cannot contain any wordform that is not syntactically joined to another wordform of the sentence. (Otherwise, the sentence would be incoherent.)

Second, syntactic dependency cannot be bilateral. If, in a sentence, the wordform w_1 depends syntactically on w_2, then in this sentence, w_2 can never be syntactically dependent on w_1:

On the one hand, this condition follows from our interpretation of syntactic dependency in terms of the imposition, by the syntactic governor, of its passive SS-valency on the whole "governor + dependent" phrase. On the other hand, such are the formal properties of the dependency tree as a mathematical object chosen for representing syntactic dependencies.

Third, in a sentence, any wordform can depend syntactically on only one other wordform; this is the uniqueness of the syntactic governor: $*w_2 \rightarrow w_1 \leftarrow w_3$ (cf. Chapter 1, p. 23). This condition follows from the same linguistic[1] and formal properties as those underlying the unilaterality condition.

3. Semantic Dependencies

Let 'X' stand for the meaning of unit X, and the symbol '$X_n(. . .)$' for a predicate X with n arguments (in semantic or logical sense of the term **predicate**).

> In a sentence, wordform w_1 directly depends semantically on wordform w_2 if and only if the meaning of lexeme $L(w_2)$ is described (in the language's dictionary) by a predicate '$L(w_2)_n(. . .)$' and in the sentence in question the meaning '$L(w_1)$' is an argument of this predicate:
> '$L(w_2)_n(. . ., L(w_1), . . .)$'.

For "w_1 is an immediate semantic dependent of w_2" we will write $w_1 \xrightarrow{\text{sem}} w_2$.

For example, in sentence (10), the wordform *place* 'square' depends semantically on *chauffée* 'warmed' since 'chauffé' is a two-place predicate: 'chauffé(X,

Y)' = 'X is warmed by Y'; and in (10), 'place' is an argument of 'chauffé': 'chauffé(place, soleil)'. In the same way, the preposition *sur*, as a two-place predicate, semantically subordinates *place* and *danser*: '[être-]sur(danser, place)' = '(her) dance is-located-on the square'. *Danser* is semantically dependent on *mise*, or rather on *s'est mise*, considered as a whole because *se mettre (à)* is (just as *chauffer* and *[être-]sur)* a two-place predicate: 'se mettre(fille, danser)'. An article (*le, la, les, un, une*) is a one-place predicate that attributes to its argument the semantic property of definiteness or indefiniteness: 'la(fille)', 'une(fille)'; thus, the noun depends semantically on the article that determines it. The noun *(une) fille* depends semantically on *se mettre*, but it also depends on *danser*: 'danser(fille)' and on *une*: 'une(fille)'. On the other hand, the two occurrences of the preposition *à* play no semantic role at all in sentence (10) and as a result, are not part of the sentence's semantic dependency system.

Let me briefly summarize semantic dependency properties. **First**, semantic dependency is universal (almost to the same degree as syntactic dependency). Semantic dependency occurs in all languages and applies to all words of a language—except the words which are semantically empty in a particular context (cf. Chapter 2, Note 10, p. 90). In every sentence, semantic dependencies form a connected structure, including all its semantically full words (i.e., words that must be represented at that level; the function words, which are the exception, do not even appear at the semantic level. Thus, in (10″) below, the two occurrences of the preposition *à* are only added to assist comprehension).

Second, again like syntactic dependency, semantic dependency is unilateral. Within the boundaries of one sentence, there cannot simultaneously be:

$$\text{`}L(w_1)_n(L(w_2))\text{'} \text{ and } \text{`}L(w_2)_n(L(w_1))\text{',}$$

$$\text{that is, } *w_1 \overset{\text{sem}}{\underset{\text{sem}}{\rightleftharpoons}} w_2$$

Third, contrary to syntactic dependency and just like morphological dependency, semantic dependency does not presuppose any uniqueness of the governor: in the same sentence, for the same argument, it is logically possible to affirm more than one predicate at once. Thus, in (10), *fille* simultaneously depends semantically on *une*, on *danser* and on *se mettre; place* on *la*, on *sur* and on *chauffée; danser* on *se mettre* and on *sur*, etc.

The system of semantic dependencies in sentence (10) is expressed as follows:

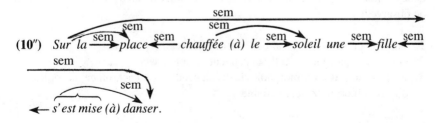

(10″) *Sur la* →place← *chauffée (à) le* →soleil une →fille←

— s'est mise (à) danser.

Different properties of morphological, syntactic and semantic dependencies linking wordforms in a sentence can be compared in the following chart:

Properties of dependency \ Dependency type	Morpho-logical	Syn-tactic	Se-mantic
1. Universality: is the type necessarily present in every language, in every sentence and for every wordform?	NO	YES	YES*
2. Connectedness: does this type affect all wordforms in a sentence?	NO	YES	YES*
3. Unilaterality: from $w_1 \rightarrow w_2$, does it necessarily follow that $w_1 \nleftarrow w_2$?	NO	YES	YES
4. Uniqueness of governor: from $w_1 \rightarrow w_2$, does it necessarily follow that $w_3 \nrightarrow w_2$ (if $w_3 \neq w_1$)?	NO	YES	NO

*With the exception of function words.

Figure 3-1
Properties of Dependency Types

As a general rule, morphological dependencies are used to indicate syntactic dependencies. Syntactic dependencies, in turn, generally indicate semantic dependencies. However, fairly often, this is not the case: $w_1 \xrightarrow{morph} w_2$ does not necessarily imply $w_1 \xrightarrow{synt} w_2$, and $w_1 \xrightarrow{sem} w_2$ does not imply $w_1 \xrightarrow{synt} w_2$. Moreover, a morphological dependency between two particular wordforms does not necessarily entail the presence of a direct syntactic dependency between them. The same is true of syntactic and semantic dependencies.[6]

II. POSSIBLE COMBINATIONS OF SYNTAGMATIC DEPENDENCY TYPES BETWEEN TWO WORDFORMS OF A SENTENCE

The three types of syntagmatic dependencies described above are logically independent. It can thus be expected that all possible combinations of them can be found in natural languages.

When the matter is examined from the viewpoint of morphological dependency, three different relations between wordforms w_1 and w_2 in a sentence can be observed:

1. There is no morphological dependency between w_1 and w_2.
2. Only w_1 is morphologically dependent on w_2 or vice versa.
3. Both w_1 and w_2 are morphologically dependent on each other (according to different morphological variables).

To these three situations, we should add the presence or absence of a direct syntactic dependency between $\mathbf{w}_1$ and $\mathbf{w}_2$. Taking into account coincidence and divergence of the direction of the two dependencies (such as in (b4) and (b5) below), there are seven possibilities:

		MORPH		SYNT	
(a)	1.	$\mathbf{w}_1$	$\mathbf{w}_2$	$\mathbf{w}_1$	$\mathbf{w}_2$
	2.	$\mathbf{w}_1$	$\mathbf{w}_2$	$\mathbf{w}_1 \longrightarrow \mathbf{w}_2$	
(b)	3.	$\mathbf{w}_1 \longrightarrow \mathbf{w}_2$		$\mathbf{w}_1$	$\mathbf{w}_2$
	4.	$\mathbf{w}_1 \longrightarrow \mathbf{w}_2$		$\mathbf{w}_1 \longrightarrow \mathbf{w}_2$	
	5.	$\mathbf{w}_1 \longrightarrow \mathbf{w}_2$		$\mathbf{w}_1 \longleftarrow \mathbf{w}_2$	
(c)	6.	$\mathbf{w}_1 \underset{\longleftarrow}{\overset{\longrightarrow}{}} \mathbf{w}_2$		$\mathbf{w}_1$	$\mathbf{w}_2$
	7.	$\mathbf{w}_1 \underset{\longleftarrow}{\overset{\longrightarrow}{}} \mathbf{w}_2$		$\mathbf{w}_1 \longrightarrow \mathbf{w}_2$	

Symmetrical cases need not be distinguished here; that is, in (a2), for example, $\mathbf{w}_1 \overset{\text{synt}}{\longleftarrow} \mathbf{w}_2$ is not considered, since it results in the same thing: the absence of a morphological dependency between two wordforms, one of which is syntactically dependent on the other. Similarly, in (b3), $\mathbf{w}_1 \overset{\text{morph}}{\longleftarrow} \mathbf{w}_2$ is not considered, and so forth.

As for correlations (c6) and (c7), they add nothing specific to the (b) situations; (c6) is equivalent to (b3), and (c7) can be identified with either (b4) or (b5). Consequently, (c) situations are not considered within the calculus of all possible combinations of dependency types that can link two wordforms. (Nevertheless, a few corresponding examples are presented in item 11 in the list below.)

Semantic dependencies can now be introduced:

			MORPH		SYNT		SEM	
(a)	1.	1.	$\mathbf{w}_1$	$\mathbf{w}_2$	$\mathbf{w}_1$'	$\mathbf{w}_2$	$\mathbf{w}_1$	$\mathbf{w}_2$
	1.	2.	$\mathbf{w}_1$	$\mathbf{w}_2$	$\mathbf{w}_1$	$\mathbf{w}_2$	$\mathbf{w}_1 \longrightarrow \mathbf{w}_2$	
	2.	3.	$\mathbf{w}_1$	$\mathbf{w}_2$	$\mathbf{w}_1 \longrightarrow \mathbf{w}_2$		$\mathbf{w}_1$	$\mathbf{w}_2$
	2.	4.	$\mathbf{w}_1$	$\mathbf{w}_2$	$\mathbf{w}_1 \longrightarrow \mathbf{w}_2$		$\mathbf{w}_1 \longrightarrow \mathbf{w}_2$	
	2.	5.	$\mathbf{w}_1$	$\mathbf{w}_2$	$\mathbf{w}_1 \longrightarrow \mathbf{w}_2$		$\mathbf{w}_1 \longleftarrow \mathbf{w}_2$	
(b)	3.	6.	$\mathbf{w}_1 \longrightarrow \mathbf{w}_2$		$\mathbf{w}_1$	$\mathbf{w}_2$	$\mathbf{w}_1$	$\mathbf{w}_2$
	3.	7.	$\mathbf{w}_1 \longrightarrow \mathbf{w}_2$		$\mathbf{w}_1$	$\mathbf{w}_2$	$\mathbf{w}_1 \longrightarrow \mathbf{w}_2$	
	3.	8.	$\mathbf{w}_1 \longrightarrow \mathbf{w}_2$		$\mathbf{w}_1$	$\mathbf{w}_2$	$\mathbf{w}_1 \longleftarrow \mathbf{w}_2$	
	4.	9.	$\mathbf{w}_1 \longrightarrow \mathbf{w}_2$		$\mathbf{w}_1 \longrightarrow \mathbf{w}_2$		$\mathbf{w}_1$	$\mathbf{w}_2$
	4.	10.	$\mathbf{w}_1 \longrightarrow \mathbf{w}_2$		$\mathbf{w}_1 \longrightarrow \mathbf{w}_2$		$\mathbf{w}_1 \longrightarrow \mathbf{w}_2$	
	4.	11.	$\mathbf{w}_1 \longrightarrow \mathbf{w}_2$		$\mathbf{w}_1 \longrightarrow \mathbf{w}_2$		$\mathbf{w}_1 \longleftarrow \mathbf{w}_2$	
	5.	12.	$\mathbf{w}_1 \longrightarrow \mathbf{w}_2$		$\mathbf{w}_1 \longleftarrow \mathbf{w}_2$		$\mathbf{w}_1$	$\mathbf{w}_2$
	5.	13.	$\mathbf{w}_1 \longrightarrow \mathbf{w}_2$		$\mathbf{w}_1 \longleftarrow \mathbf{w}_2$		$\mathbf{w}_1 \longrightarrow \mathbf{w}_2$	
	5.	14.	$\mathbf{w}_1 \longrightarrow \mathbf{w}_2$		$\mathbf{w}_1 \longleftarrow \mathbf{w}_2$		$\mathbf{w}_1 \longleftarrow \mathbf{w}_2$	

Therefore, in principle, fourteen correlations can be found between any two wordforms in a sentence according to direct morphological, syntactic and semantic dependencies between them. It will help to give linguistic examples for each of the fourteen correlations.

1. (= a1.1) Absence of any direct dependency between two wordforms. For example, the wordforms *fille* and *soleil* in (10), page 114, are not linked by any direct morphological, syntactic or semantic dependency.

2. (= a1.2) Two wordforms are linked only by a semantic dependency, which is not supported by any direct syntactic or morphological dependency. Thus the noun *fille* in (10) is semantically dependent on *danser*, even though there is no direct morphological or syntactic link between the two wordforms.

3. (= a2.3) Only a syntactic dependency is present that is not supported by any morphological or semantic dependency. This is typical of quantitative adverbs in Japanese; cf. (12):

(12) Japanese
  Huransugo + *no* *hon* + *o* *takusan* *yomimasita*
  French-language GEN book ACC many (has) read
  lit. 'He many-ly read French-language book' = 'He has read many French books'.

In (12), the morphologically invariable adverb *takusan* 'many' is syntactically dependent on the verb *yomimasita* '(has) read', whereas, from a semantic viewpoint, *takusan* is only linked with *hon* 'book', since sentence (12) speaks of 'many books'.

A more common example (in many European languages) is the so-called "displaced negation" (Boguslavskij 1978a, b, 1985: 40-53): a morphologically invariable negative particle depends syntactically on one word while semantically it bears on another; cf. (13):

(13) **a.** *All computers do not have three memory levels*
    [semantically, 'all' is negated, and not 'have'].
  b. *They did not die for the glory*
    [semantically, 'for the glory' is negated, and not 'die'].

The same situation is characteristic of other modal particles, such as *only*.

4. (= a2.4) Two wordforms are linked by a syntactic and a semantic dependencies whose directions are the same; no morphological dependency is present. For example, such is the "Verb + Object" construction in a language that lacks the grammatical case of the noun as well as the objective conjuga-

tion of the verb (Chinese, English, French: *to read (a) newspaper*, etc.). One can also classify here the expressions such as *his* $\xleftarrow{\text{synt}}$ *arrival* or *his* $\xleftarrow{\text{synt}}$ *jumps*, because semantically, they are 'arrive(he)' and 'jump(he)'.

5. (= a2.5) A semantic dependency and a syntactic dependency go in opposite directions with no direct morphological dependency between the two word-forms. For example, take the attributive adjective in a language where adjectives are invariable, such as in English. In *special effects, human life*, etc. we have Adj + N with no morphological link between Adj and N. Another example is the phrase V + Prep, or V + Adv in several languages:

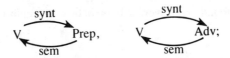

prepositions and adverbs do not vary morphologically.

6. (= b3.6) In Tabassaran, morphological dependency subordinates the main verb *hebgnu***jič** to a possessive attribute of its grammatical subject (i.e., to *ič* 'our': see (8) on page 111). However, there is no direct semantic of syntactic link between *hebgnujič* and *ič*.

The same dependency pattern appears in languages where a finite verb governing an infinitive can itself depend morphologically on an object of the infinitive. Thus, in Hungarian:

(14) Hungarian
    a. *Minden* + *t* $\xleftarrow{\text{synt}}$ *tud* + *ni* $\xleftarrow{\text{synt}}$ *akar* + *∅*
         everything   ACC   know INF   want   PRES.3SG
         'He wants to know everything'.

    b. *Az* + *t* $\xleftarrow{\text{synt}}$ *tud* + *ni* $\xleftarrow{\text{synt}}$ *akar* + *ja*
         that   ACC   know INF   want   PRES.OBJ.3SG
         'He wants to know that'.

The choice of the appropriate form of the verb *akar-* 'to want' (the non-objective form *akar* vs. the objective form *akar + ja*) is made as the function of the definiteness or indefiniteness of the direct object governed by *tud + ni* 'to know'. (*Minden* 'everything' is indefinite in Hungarian; *az* 'that' is definite.) Therefore, *akar* in (14a) and *akar + ja* in (14b) depend morphologically on *minden + t* and *az + t*, while there is no direct semantic or syntactic dependency between *akar-* and the object of *tud + ni*.

In West Flemish (Hudson 1984: 107), the subordinate conjunction 'that', which introduces a complementive clause C, morphologically depends on the grammatical subject of C: the conjunction appears as *da* or *dan*, according to whether the latter is singular or plural; but no direct semantic or syntactic link connects a subordinate conjunction (i.e., a complementizer) with the GS of the verb it introduces.

7. (= b3.7) A real example for this particular combination of dependencies:

could not be found. However, a hypothetical example can be constructed such as:

(15)   *My father + **ode** returned exhausted*

in which the form *father + ode* is morphologically dependent on the presence and the properties of the co-predicative (i.e., attributive) adjective *exhausted*, whereas *exhausted* is not dependent on the wordform *father* (the suffix *-ode* marks the presence of a qualitative co-predicative adjective). Consider the following artificial examples:

(16)   **a.** *My father + **ane** returned alone*
           (the co-predicative is not qualitative and therefore requires a different suffix on the grammatical subject)
       b. *My father returned*
       c. *My sister + **ode** returned exhausted*
           (the co-predicative does not change its form in relation to the subject's grammatical gender).

In (16), lexeme occurrences *father* and *exhausted* are not directly linked syntactically. Semantically, there is a dependency: 'exhausted (father)', that is, *exhausted* $\xrightarrow{\text{sem}}$ *father*.

8. (= b3.8) Morphological and semantic dependencies are opposed as to their direction in the absence of a direct syntactic dependency in common French constructions:

(17)   French **a.** *Le carré semblait blanc* 'The square seemed white'
                   and
           b. *La ligne semblait blanche* 'The line seemed white'

where the gender and number of *blanc* and *blanche*, respectively, are determined by those of the grammatical subject: *carré* $\xrightarrow{\text{morph}}$ *blanc* and *ligne* $\xrightarrow{\text{morph}}$ *blanche*. At the same time, there is *blanc* $\xrightarrow{\text{sem}}$ *carré* and *blanche* $\xrightarrow{\text{sem}}$ *ligne*, since 'blanc(carré)' and 'blanc(ligne)'.

Another example of the same type is the Japanese construction with numerals:

(18) Japanese

    a. *zibiki   + o   san + satu   kaimasita*
        dictionary ACC   three   BOOK.FORM bought
        '(He) bought three dictionaries'.

    b. *Empitu + o   san + bon   kaimasita*
        pencil   ACC   three   LONG   bought
        '(He) bought three pencils'.

    c. *Kuruma + o   san + dai   kaimasita*
        car   ACC   three   VEHICLE   bought
        '(He) bought three cars'.

In each of the three sentences in (18), the numeral depends syntactically on the verb, but it is morphologically dependent on the direct object, which determines its form, that is, *zibiki* 'dictionary' $\xrightarrow{\text{morph}}$ *san + satu, empitu* 'pencil' $\xrightarrow{\text{morph}}$ *san + bon, kuruma* 'car' $\xrightarrow{\text{morph}}$ *san + dai*. However, the object is semantically dependent on the numeral: 'three(dictionary)'. 'three(pencil)', 'three(car)'.

9. (= b4.9) A Japanese construction with nominalized sentences (described and analyzed in Xolodovič 1971: 121–131) can serve as an example for this dependency combination:

(19) Japanese

    a. *Kuruma + ga   kowareta   + no   + o   naosimasita*
        car   NOM   was-damaged the.fact.that ACC   repaired
        lit. '(He) repaired the fact that his car was damaged [= repaired the damagedness of his car]', that is, '(He) repaired his damaged car'.

    b. *Suruto Sugiko + ga   mon + kara deru + no   + ni*
        then   Sugiko   NOM   door   ABL go.out the.fact.that DAT
        atta
        met
        lit. '(He) then met with the fact that Sugiko was going out of the door' [= met with the going out of the door by Sugiko], that is, '(He) met Sugiko who was going out the door'.
        [The verb ARU 'meet' governs the dative.]

    c. *Tabemono + ga   tumetaku natta + no   + o*
        food   NOM coldly   became   the.fact.that ACC
        attameta
        heated
        lit. '(He) reheated the fact that the food became cold' [= reheated the becoming cold of the food], that is '(He) reheated the food that had become cold'.

In (19), a nominalized verb in *-no* is syntactically and morphologically dependent on the main verb, the latter governing the accusative in (19a) and (19c) and the dative in (19b), even though no semantic dependency exists between the two units: 'repair(car)' but not *'repair(damagedness)'; 'meet(Sugiko)' and not *'meet(going out)'; 'reheat(food)' and not *'reheat(having become cold)'.

Another revealing example of this type is given by Hale and Kitagawa (1976–77: 51):

d. *John + wa   Hanako + ga   heya + kara tobidasite kita*
John   as.for Hanako   NOM room   ABL running   came
tokoro + ni   dekuwasita
moment   DAT met
lit. 'John met the moment [the verb DEKUWARU 'meet', 'run into' governs the dative] when Hanako came running out of the room', that is, 'John met Hanako when [= at the moment] she was running out of the room'.

As can be seen, Japanese has a marked tendency toward the discrepancy between semantic and syntactic dependencies; this is a far less common phenomenon in Indo-European languages.

However, some examples of the combination X $\overset{\text{morph}}{\underset{\text{synt}}{\curvearrowright}}$ Y (with no semantic link between X and Y) are found even in languages such as French. Consider an adjective used as attributive of an action noun with which it agrees, while semantically this adjective modifies the semantic subject of the corresponding action:

(20) French **a.** *un silence* **confus** *de l'enfant* 'the child's confused silence'
and
b. *une plainte* **confuse** *de l'enfant* 'the child's confused whine'

where the adjective is morphologically and syntactically dependent on *silence* and *plainte*, while being linked semantically to *l'enfant*: 'confus(enfant)'.

10. (= b4.10) It is a widespread case. In particular, one can cite nominal objects and complements of verbs and of prepositions in languages with grammatical cases. For example, in Russian:

(21) Russian

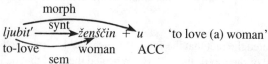

ljubit' $\xrightarrow{\text{synt}}$ *ženščin + u*   'to love (a) woman'
to-love   woman   ACC

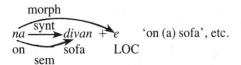

'on (a) sofa', etc.

In French, verbs governing an infinitive are a good example:

(22) French

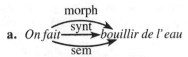

lit. '(They) make the water boil' = 'The water is being boiled'.

b. *Je le vois* *partir* 'I see him leave'.

11. (= b4.11) Morphological and syntactic dependencies both go in the same direction, but semantic dependency goes in the opposite direction. This is a very common situation, illustrated by the modifying adjective which must agree with the noun (e.g., in German, *ein schön* + **er** *Berg* 'a beautiful mountain', *eine schön* + **e** *Frau* 'a beautiful woman', *ein schön* + **es** *Kind* 'a pretty child', where we have the following configuration of dependencies:

The same phenomenon exists in Slavic, Romance, Semitic and languages from several other families.

The case of Russian numerals merits special mention since a few of them are characterized by bilateral morphological dependency. Cf. (23a) and (23b):

(23) Russian

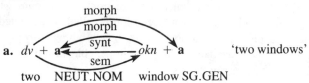

'two windows'

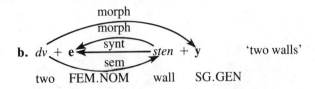

b. *dv* + e ⟵ *sten* + y   'two walls'

two   FEM.NOM   wall   SG.GEN

In (23), the numeral (Num) *dva/dve* is morphologically dependent on the N, which determines the gender of the Num, and at the same time, the N is morphologically dependent on the Num, which determines the noun's grammatical case and number (cf. *pjat' okon* 'five windows', with *okon* PL.GEN). Or consider:

(24)   *dvadcat' odn* + **o** *okno* 'twenty-one windows', but
        dvadcat' odn + **a** *stena* 'twenty-one walls'

where the case and gender of Num *odin* are dependent on N, whereas the number of N (singular) is dependent on *odin*. (For more details see Mel´čuk 1985: 326 ff.)

12. (= b5.12) A real example for this dependency combination could not be found, but it is easy to construct one, using example (20) transposed into a so-called "izafa language" of the Persian type (see directly below, item 13). The attributive adjective (in this case, *confus*) is morphologically invariable and the noun reacts to its presence by different suffixes (i.e., the noun is morphologically dependent on the adjective). Therefore, we have *un si-lence-**ode** confus de l'enfant* but *un silence de l'enfant*.

13. (= b5.13) Morphological and semantic dependencies go in the same direction, but syntactic dependency goes in the opposite direction. This happens in various syntactic constructions where the morphological marker of the syntactic dependency is attached to the governor rather than to the dependent (cf. Nichols 1986). The typical example is the so-called "izafa construction" of a Turkic-Persian type. Compare, for example, Tajik phrases *bino* + **i** *nav* '(a) new building' or *daftar* + **i** *man*, lit. 'workbook I', in which *bino* = 'building', *daftar* = 'workbook', *nav* = 'new', *man* = 'I', and **-i** is the izafa, that is, a noun suffix which signals the presence of a modifier depending syntactically on the noun to which this suffix belongs.

   Another example is the attributive construction of two nouns where the governing (i.e., head) noun has a special form (called "constructed state") that signals the presence of a nominal attribute: Hebrew *sifreị limúd*, lit. 'books-of study' = 'manuals', with *sifreị* in the constructed state opposed to the absolute state *sfarím* 'books', that is:

(25)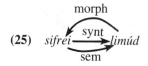

Contrary to the izafa of the Persian type, which is an autonomous segmental unit (a suffix) added to the governor, the constructed state of Hebrew nouns is manifested by a non-segmental unit, that is, by a meaningful alternation, or an apophony, within the governor.

The Russian numeral constructions of (23) and (24) could have been presented in item 13 as well, because of the bilateral nature of the morphological dependency in them.

14. (= b5.14) The same direction for syntactic and semantic dependencies and an opposite direction for the morphological dependency are observable in predicative and completive constructions of languages that have a polypersonal conjugation but that do not have noun cases. Thus, the Abkhaz we have:

(26) Abkhaz *Ḳwasta Nadš´a   i + l   + i + teiṭ   ašʷqʷə*
              Kwasta Nadsha it   to.her   he   gave book
              'Kwasta [masc] gave the book to Nadsha [fem].'

where the three nominal actants are invariable and where the form of the verb, that is, the presence of prefixes *i-* (inanimate direct object, 3 sg), *l-* (animate indirect object, feminine, 3 sg) and another *i-* (animate subject, masculine, 3 sg) depends on the actants. Compare, for example, (26'):

(26') Abkhaz
      a. *Sara Nadš´a   i + l   + əs + teiṭ   ašʷq̇ʷə*
            I   Nadsha it   to.her   I   gave book
            'I gave the book to Nadsha'.

where, instead of the second (subjectival) *i-* indicating 3 sg, subjectival *s-* (1 sg) is found (-ə- before *s-* is an automatic linking vowel):

      b. *Ḳwasta   sara   i + s + i + teiṭ   ašʷqʷə*
            Kwasta I   it   to.me he   gave   book
            'Kwasta gave me the book.'
      c. *Ḳwasta   Nadš´a   s + l   + i + teiṭ   sara*
            Kwasta Nadsha me   to.her   he   gave   I
            'Kwasta gave me to Nadsha'.

Among the most common examples of combination 14, I must cite the possessive construction of several Ural-Altaic languages, illustrated by the following examples from Hungarian:

(27) Hungarian
    a. *a   könyv   felépítés + e*
        the   book   structure   of
        'the structure of the book'
    b. *az   apá + m   haź + a*
        the   mother my   house   of
        'the house of my mother'

where *-e* and *-a* are phonologically conditioned variants of the possessive marker, which signals, in the governing noun, the presence of a nominal complement of this noun. Therefore, strictly speaking, *felépítése* means 'structure of . . .', and *háza* means 'house belonging to . . .' (cf. Mel'čuk 1973b).

As already stated, considering morphological dependencies of the bilateral kind would not create new types of combinations. Cases of bilateral dependency can be analyzed indiscriminately under two different items. Thus, in Hungarian, the predicate of a sentence represented by a transitive verb is morphologically dependent on its direct object (the type of verb conjugation—objective or objectless—is determined by the definite/indefinite character of the object). At the same time, this object is morphologically dependent on the verb that determines its case (i.e., the accusative). Compare (28a) to (28b):

(28) Hungarian
    a. *Ez + t   a   pohár + t   kér   + i*
        this   ACC   the   glass   ACC   request   PRES.OBJ.3SG
        '[He] requests this glass.'
    b. *A   törött pohár helyett   egy másik + at   kér   + ∅*
        the broken glass instead.of a   other   ACC request PRES.3SG
        '[He] requests another glass, instead of the broken one'.

Here, the accusative of wordforms *pohár + t* 'glass' in (28a) and *másik + at* 'other' in (28b) is imposed by the transitive verb *kér + ni* 'to request', whereas the different verb forms, *kéri* in (28a) and *kér* in (28b), are dependent on the direct object according to its definiteness/indefiniteness (*ezt a pohárt* is definite and *egy másikat*, indefinite in Hungarian). In this way, cases of type (28):

can be discussed as much here in item 14 as in item 10.

III. SYNTACTIC DEPENDENCY: A LOGICAL ANALYSIS
OF AN IMPORTANT CONCEPT

I am unable to propose a rigorous definition of syntactic dependency. However, since this notion is extremely important and, at the same time, not quite clear, some preliminary considerations seem to be in order. These considerations, although far from being fully formal, help to make the notion of syntactic dependency more explicit and precise.

First of all, it is necessary to state the following three relevant assumptions, adding them to the two adopted in Section I, p. 113.

(III) $\|$ All that is said below concerns only the SURFACE-SYNTACTIC LEVEL (SS-level) of the linguistic$_1$ representation. It is thus a matter only of pSS-connectedness, SS-dependency, and so forth.

(IV) $\|$ Only GRAMMATICALLY COMPLETE AND CORRECT SENTENCES (that is, their SSyntSs) will be considered, since elliptical or colloquial utterances could show peculiarities irrelevant for the present study.

(V) $\|$ All surface-syntactic dependencies between wordforms of a sentence are described only in terms of ANTISYMMETRIC, ANTIREFLEXIVE AND ANTITRANSITIVE BINARY RELATIONS, of which different types are distinguished (in the SSyntS, each relation must be labeled with its type).

(This assumption has already been introduced in Section I, p. 116, in a less precise form; in fact, it follows the line drawn in Chapter 1.)

A definition of SS-dependency presupposes three groups of criteria.

A. SS-CONNECTEDNESS criteria, that is, criteria establishing the presence of SS-dependency between wordforms w_1 and w_2 (in a sentence). In other words, $w_1 \text{———} w_2$ or $*w_1 \text{———} w_2$?

B. SS-DEPENDENCY DIRECTION criteria, that is, criteria deciding which of the two syntactically linked wordforms, w_1 and w_2, is the syntactic governor of the other. In other words, if $w_1 \text{———} w_2$, then $w_1 \rightarrow w_2$ or $w_1 \leftarrow w_2$?

C. SS-DEPENDENCY TYPE criteria, that is, criteria determining whether SS-dependency types, or suface-syntactic relations (SSRels), in two phrases $w_1 \rightarrow w_2$ and $w_3 \rightarrow w_4$ are identical or not. In other words, if $w_1 \overset{r_1}{\rightarrow} w_2$ and $w_3 \overset{r_2}{\rightarrow} w_4$, then $r_1 = r_2$ or $r_1 \neq r_2$?

Each group of these criteria will be discussed briefly.

A. Criteria for the presence of an SS-dependency

The criteria of type A must be formulated according to the following two properties:

- linear correlation of the wordforms linked by an SS-dependency

- prosodic correlation of the wordforms linked by an SS-dependency.

These two properties must be present simultaneously; this means that for two wordforms, w_1 and w_2, to be considered directly linked by a surface-syntactic dependency, it is necessary that w_1 and w_2 be simultaneously both in linear and prosodic correlation. (The meaning of these two expressions will become clearer later on.)

However, for the present, it is not known whether these properties are logically independent, that is, whether it is possible to find two wordforms which would be correlated linearly without also being prosodically correlated, or vice versa. It is also not known whether these two properties are sufficient (in the mathematical sense); perhaps there exist natural languages having syntactic constructions in which two wordforms are correlated linearly as well as prosodically but in which, despite this, the direct SS-dependency between the two wordforms would not exist.[7]

Criterion A.I (linear correlation of syntactically linked wordforms)

> In a sentence, wordforms w_1 and w_2 are directly linked by an SS-dependency, if the linear position of one of them cannot be determined without reference to the other.

This in no way means that, with two linearly correlated wordforms, one determines the position of the other in a unique manner. It is completely possible to have these two situations:

$$w_1 + \ldots + w_2 \quad \text{or} \quad w_2 + \ldots + w_1$$

(perhaps along with some specific conditions). The essential is that, in speaking of the position of wordform w_2, it is necessary to mention w_1. For example, "w_2 must be placed before w_1" ("before" = to the left of), "w_2 must be placed either before w_1, or after it (according to the factors to be made more precise)", etc.

In a sentence like (29):

(29) *La diane chantait dans les cours des casernes* (Baudelaire)
'The reveille sounded in barracks yards'

the position of the preposition *dans* 'in' cannot be specified without referring to *les cours* 'the yards' ("*dans* must of necessity precede *les cours*: **les cours . . . dans*") and to *chantait* 'sang' ("*dans* and its governed NP can follow or precede *chantait*, based on several factors"); the article *la* 'the' must be placed before *diane* 'reveille'; and so forth.

Criterion A.II (prosodic correlation of syntactically linked wordforms)

> In a sentence, wordforms w_1 and w_2 are directly linked by an SS-dependency if:
> (i) either w_1 and w_2 can form a prosodic unit in the language;
> (ii) or w_1 and w_2, taken as such, cannot form a prosodic unit, but one of them, for example w_1, can form a prosodic unit with an independent prosodic unit φ consisting of syntactically linked wordforms, such that in φ, wordform w_2 is the SS-head, or top node.

The formulation of Criterion A.II calls for the following three important comments:

1) The concept of "prosodic unit" will not be clarified here. Although it is used in a fairly vague way, it is hoped that an approximate understanding is enough to grasp the underlying idea of Criterion A.II. The foundations of a theory insisting on links between prosody and syntactic structure have been laid down in the promising work of Martin (1977, 1978), and it is along these lines that this concept is expected to be developed. For the moment, a prosodic unit is said to be specified by several factors, the most important of which are its ability to form an independent utterance (i.e., to appear between two full pauses), the presence of a single tonal contour, and a particular distribution of stress, external sandhis (such as French **liaisons**), and pauses. In other words, our prosodic unit is (roughly) what is currently called a **phrase** or **constituent**.

2) The second condition of Criterion A.II is needed because of the SS-dependency between a full word and a function word (a preposition, a conjunction, etc.) that introduces another full word. Thus in (29) above, the string *la diane chantait* represents a prosodic unit, while *chantait dans* does not. However, since *chantait dans les cours* et *dans les cours* are prosodic units and the surface-syntactic head of the prosodic unit (i.e., phrase) *dans les cours* [= φ] is the preposition *dans* [= w_2], the string *chantait dans* satisfies the second condition of Criterion A.II. As a result, it can be considered SS-connected, which boils down to saying that there is an SS-dependency between *chantait* and *dans* in sentence (29).

3) There is no circularity in the second condition of Criterion A.II: the SS-connectedness and the SS-head of the prosodic unit φ are established by means of all necessary criteria prior to the application of Criterion A.II to w_1 + φ. Let it be recalled that our approach to the concept of syntactic dependency is designed to use a recursive procedure for determining SS-dependencies between sentence elements (Section I, p. 115).

To establish surface-syntactic connectedness between the wordforms of a given sentence, it must be broken into independent fragments (each of which may constitute an utterance). In (29), for example, there are thirteen such independent fragments (actually, prosodic units):

1) *La diane chantait dans les cours* 'The reveille sounded in the yards'
2) *La diane chantait* 'The reveille sounded'
3) *la diane* 'the reveille'
4) *chantait dans les cours des casernes* 'sounded in the yards of the barracks'
5) *chantait dans les cours* 'sounded in the yards'
6) *chantait* 'sounded'
7) *dans les cours des casernes* 'in the yards of the barracks'
8) *dans les cours* 'in the yards'
9) *les cours* 'the yards'
10) *les cours des casernes* 'the yards of the barracks'
11) *des casernes* 'of the barracks'
12) *les casernes* 'the barracks',
as well as
13) the sentence in its entirety.

By examining these fragments in terms of Criteria A.I and A.II and by observing the three above assumptions, the following system of SS-links (for the moment, without direction) can be established in (29):

$$\text{(30)} \quad La \xrightarrow{\text{synt}} diane \xrightarrow{\text{synt}} chantait \xrightarrow{\text{synt}} dans\ les \xrightarrow{\text{synt}} cours \xrightarrow{\text{synt}}$$

$$\xrightarrow{\text{synt}} de\ les \xrightarrow{\text{synt}} casernes.^{8}$$

B. Criteria for the direction of an SS-dependency
Two criteria for the direction of an SS-dependency are known:

• imposition of passive SS-valencies (the criterion that has already been presented in Section I and which will be discussed here in greater detail)

• morphological contact point.

Criterion B.I (imposition of passive SS-valencies)
Let there be two wordforms directly linked at the SS-level: w_1——w_2.

‖ The SS-head of the phrase w_1——w_2 is the wordform that determines the
‖ passive SS-valency of the phrase to a greater degree than the other wordform.

To give this criterion a stricter form, let us use the symbolic notations, introduced above: L(w) stands for the lexeme to which wordform w belongs, and $\text{VAL}_{\text{pass}}^{\text{SS}}$(L), for the passive surface-syntactic valency of lexeme L in the language under consideration (pp. 112–113).

For a wordform pair $\mathbf{w_1}$——$\mathbf{w_2}$, linked by a direct SS-dependency, three different passive SS-valencies can be considered:

$$VAL_{pass}^{SS}(L(\mathbf{w_1}))$$

$$VAL_{pass}^{SS}(L(\mathbf{w_2}))$$

$$VAL_{pass}^{SS}(L(\mathbf{w_1})\text{——}L(\mathbf{w_2}))$$

The following principle should be emphasized because it is essential for the formulation of Criterion B.I:

(31) In several cases, one of two wordforms, for example $\mathbf{w_1}$, can never be used alone (that is, without $\mathbf{w_2}$) as a dependent element in syntactic roles where the whole phrase $\mathbf{w_1}$——$\mathbf{w_2}$ appears. In such a case, the passive SS-valency of $\mathbf{w_1}$ is that of the phrase $\mathbf{w_1}$——$\mathbf{w_2}$, on the condition, however, that the latter is different from $VAL_{pass}^{SS}(L(\mathbf{w_2}))$.

The clearest example is a prepositional phrase (PP) in many languages. Look at the PP *to Paris*; the $VAL_{pass}^{SS}(to\ Paris)$ is completely different from the $VAL_{pass}^{SS}(Paris)$. But *to* is not used alone (without a noun or an infinitive); therefore, the passive SS-valency of any PP of the *to Paris* type will be attributed to the preposition *to*.

It is important that $VAL_{pass}^{SS}(L(\mathbf{w_1})) \neq VAL_{pass}^{SS}(L(\mathbf{w_2}))$; otherwise Criterion B.I could not apply.

Thus, we have:

(9′) If and only if $VAL_{pass}^{SS}(L(\mathbf{w_1})\text{——}L(\mathbf{w_2})) = VAL_{pass}^{SS}(L(\mathbf{w_2}))$ or, at least, $VAL_{pass}^{SS}(L(\mathbf{w_1})\text{——}L(\mathbf{w_2})) \cap VAL_{pass}^{SS}(L(\mathbf{w_2})) > VAL_{pass}^{SS}(L(\mathbf{w_1})\text{——}L(\mathbf{w_2})) \cap VAL_{pass}^{SS}(L(\mathbf{w_1}))$, then woodform $\mathbf{w_2}$ is the SS-governor of $\mathbf{w_1}$, that is, $\mathbf{w_1} \overset{synt}{\longleftarrow} \mathbf{w_2}$.

(9′) is a simple reformulation of (9), cited on page 113. Here are three examples to illustrate the application of Criterion B.I:

Example 1

Let there be a prepositional phrase PP: **in** *(this) house,* **at** *(her) home,* **for** *John.* $VAL_{pass}^{SS}(Prep + N)$ differs considerably from $VAL_{pass}^{SS}(N)$; since the preposition is not used without a noun, according to principle (31), $VAL_{pass}^{SS}(Prep) = VAL_{pass}^{SS}(Prep + N)$. To apply (9′), Prep is $\mathbf{w_2}$ and N is $\mathbf{w_1}$; the preposition will result as the SS-head of the PP. Common sense gives us the same solution. The difference between the passive SS-valency of the PP and that of the noun could only be explained by the presence of the preposition, which by virtue of this, must be considered the SS-governor of the noun.

Example 2

The passive SS-valency of the Russian clause *Mal'čik kačalsja* 'The boy was swinging' is identical to that of the verb KAČAT'SJA 'to swing' but completely different from that of the noun MAL'ČIK 'boy'. In fact, along with *kogda mal'čik kačalsja* 'when the boy was swinging', there is *kogda kačalsja* 'when was swinging'—but **kogda mal'čik* 'when the boy' is not allowed in Russian as a connected phrase. The passive SS-valency of the clause *mal'čik kačalsja* is fully determined by the passive valency of its main verb; consequently, *kačalsja* is the surface-syntactic governor for *mal'čik* (which fact does in no way prevent, as emphasized before on page 108, *mal'čik* from governing the number and gender of *kačalsja*, that is, it does not prevent the subject noun from being the morphological governor of the finite verb).

Example 3

The passive SS-valency of the Russian phrase *okolo desjati kilometrov* 'about ten kilometers' is determined by the passive SS-valency of the approximation marker *okolo* 'about, some'. In fact, the phrase with *okolo* is only found in a syntactic position requiring the nominative or the accusative (but not after a preposition), whereas without *okolo*, the phrase *desjat' kilometrov* 'ten kilometers' is accepted in any SS-position that takes simple nouns or NPs. Consider the following:

(32) *Ostavalos'* ⟨*My prošli*⟩ *okolo desjati kilometrov* 'We had about ten kilometers left' ⟨'We covered about ten kilometers'⟩

although utterances of (33) type are excluded:

(33) **a.** **k okolo desjati kilometram* 'to about ten kilometers' [after a preposition]
   b. **On zainteresovalsja ètimi okolo desjat'ju kilometrami* 'He began to show interest in these ten-odd kilometers' [in a position requiring the instrumental].

Without *okolo*, expressions (33) are perfectly acceptable:

(33') **a.** *k desjati kilometram* 'to ten kilometers'
   b. *On zainteresovalsja ètimi desjat'ju kilometrami* 'He began to show interest in these ten kilometers'.

Since the approximation marker *okolo*[9] is not used without a NP, its VAL$_{pass}^{SS}$ is taken—according to principle (31)—to be that of the whole phrase *okolo* + NP. Thus, following (9'), *okolo* is the SS-head of the phrase in question, despite the fact that *okolo* can always be omitted in the sentence's SSynt-structure without ever affecting its grammaticality. (However, *desjat' kilometrov*, which is its dependent, cannot be omitted: for more details, see below, page 139.[10])

It is interesting to note that in the six cases analyzed by Garde (1977: 8–12), the results from applying Criterion B.I coincide with Garde's conclusions:

$$\text{Adj}\xleftarrow{\text{synt}}\text{N}, \quad \text{V}\xrightarrow{\text{synt}}\text{N}\ [= \text{object}], \quad \text{V}\xrightarrow{\text{synt}}\text{N/Adj}\ (= \text{attribute}),$$

$$\text{V}\xrightarrow[\text{(auxiliary)}]{\text{synt}}\text{V}_{\text{(full)}}, \quad \text{N}\ [= \text{gram.subject}]\xleftarrow{\text{synt}}\text{V}, \quad \text{Prep}\xrightarrow{\text{synt}}\text{N}.$$

Criterion B.II (morphological contact point)
Let there be two wordforms directly linked at the SS-level: $\mathbf{w}_1\text{———}\mathbf{w}_2$.

> The SS-head of the phrase $\mathbf{w}_1\text{———}\mathbf{w}_2$ is the wordform whose morphological links with the phrase's external context are more important than those of the other wordform (that is, the SS-head is the wordform that constitutes the morphological contact point of the phrase).

The relative importance of morphological links is established as follows: the morphological marker(s) of the passive SS-role of a phrase (i.e., of its syntactic role as a dependent element) is supposed to be more important than the marker(s) of its active SS-role (i.e., of its influence on its dependents).

A phrase's morphological contact point is thus its element that either is itself morphologically inflected under the control of the external governing context, or controls morphological inflections of some elements of the context. The other element of the phrase is not able to undergo or impose similar changes: it is morphologically passive in this respect.

Remark 1
Criterion B.II is likely to raise some doubts. After the insistence in Sections I and II on mutual logical autonomy of syntactic and morphological dependencies, morphological phenomena should not be easily accepted as indicators of direction for an SS-dependency. However, some small liberties are justified here: first, because Criterion B.II uses morphology on an abstract level (it is not a matter of a specific, concrete morphological dependency having a certain direction, and so forth; on the contrary, it is only a question of the presence of any morphological link); second, because some correlations exist, after all, between two dependency types. This can favor the use of morphological considerations in syntax, if only very judiciously.

Remark 2
The description of Criterion B.II is very sketchy. It does not clarify the concept of external context (of a phrase) and omits some relevant details.

Criterion B.II is indispensable for phrases composed of lexemes of the same syntactic class. In such a situation, the passive SS-valency of the phrase $\mathbf{w}_1\text{———}\mathbf{w}_2$ coincides, quite clearly, both with $\text{VAL}^{\text{SS}}_{\text{pass}}(\text{L}(\mathbf{w}_1))$ and with $\text{VAL}^{\text{SS}}_{\text{pass}}(\text{L}(\mathbf{w}_2))$, so that Criterion B.I becomes inapplicable. However, Criterion B.II itself is applicable only in languages having syntactic morphology and only for constructions in which the morphological links of one of the two elements of a phrase with an external context are more important than those of the other, at least for certain lexemes. Here are two examples.

Example 1

The Russian genitive construction is composed of two nouns, the second of which is in the genitive:

(34) *kniga studenta* 'the student's book', *list dereva* 'the tree's leaf', *mat'*
Ivana 'John's mother', etc.: $N^1 + N^2_{gen}$.

Since $VAL^{SS}_{pass}(N^1) = VAL^{SS}_{pass}(N^2) = VAL^{SS}_{pass}(N^1 + N^2)$. Criterion B.I does not apply here. However, N^1 is the morphological contact point; this noun is the only one to react to the requirements of the governing context, N^2 remaining invariable:

(34′) *dlja kni**g**i studenta* 'for the student's book'
*Vižu kni**g**u studenta* 'I see the student's book'
*s kni**g**oj studenta* 'with the student's book', etc.

Consequently, according to Criterion B.II, noun N^1 is the SS-head of the phrase $N^1 + N^2_{gen}$ and the SS-governor of N^2.

Example 2

Let us now consider the appositive construction of two Russian nouns of the following type:

(35) *druz'ja-tovarišči*, lit. 'companions-friends', *vek-volkodav,* lit. 'century-wolfhound' (O. Mandel'štam), *jubka-štany*, lit. 'skirt-pants', *aèrosani-glisser*, lit. 'hoversleigh-glider', etc.: $N^1_{case} + N^2_{case}$.

Criterion B.I obviously does not apply here (both elements belong to the same syntactic class); the government of the external context does not help us either because the two nouns of the appositive construction are always in the same case, that is, they react identically to the commands "from above." Nevertheless, they behave differently towards their syntactic inferiors: namely, the first element imposes agreement on the modifying adjective characterizing the whole phrase and on the finite verb (when the phrase is the grammatical subject).

(36) **a.** *jubka   -stany,   sšitaja   ⟨*sšitye⟩ . . .*
skirt-SG[fem] pants-PL   made-FEM.SG   made.PL
lit. 'skirt-pants made . . .'
The modifier *sšitaja* agrees with *jubka*, not *štany*.

b. *Aèrosani   -glisser   pojavilis'*
hoversleigh-PL glider-SG[masc]   have-appeared-PL
⟨*pojavilsja⟩ . . .
     has-appeared-MASC-SG
'The glider hovercraft has appeared . . .'
The verb *pojavilis'* is in the plural because of *aèrosani*, a *plurale tantum*.

The fact that all grammatical agreements outside the phrase in question are produced with the N^1 and not with N^2 gives N^1 the status of SS-head of the phrase. Therefore we have:

synt   synt
drúz´ja-tóvarišči, *jubka-štany*, etc.

Criterion B.II was proposed in Ward (1973: 4–6) and developed in Uryson (1982).[11]

Let us now discuss hierarchical relations between Criteria B.I and B.II and their logical status (necessity and sufficiency).

Criterion B.I is considered superior to B.II because it is more universal and more "syntactic." In contrast to B.II, Criterion B.I applies even in languages without syntactic morphology and in constructions composed of morphologically invariable elements. The superiority of Criterion B.I means that in applicable cases, that is, where $L(w_1)$ and $L(w_2)$ belong to different word classes, Criterion B.II's indications are simply not taken in consideration.

In light of available syntactic data, it seems that in most cases, Criteria B.I and B.II do not contradict each other. If both apply, then their indications coincide. Nevertheless, it is not a logical necessity, and there is at least one case of divergence between the two criteria: the Russian construction Num(eral) + N(oun) in a syntactic position that requires the nominative or the accusative. Consider (37):

(37)   **a.**   *V kupe naxidilos'* ⟨ *naxodilis'* ⟩ **tri passažira**
              'In the compartment, there were three travelers.'
       b.   *Ja uvidel* **pjat' mašin** 'I saw five cars.'

The quantitative phrase (in boldface) is in the nominative in (37a) and in the accusative in (37b). However, although, according to Criterion B.I, the noun is the SS-governor in this phrase (because the passive SS-valency of the quantitative phrase is that of the noun rather than that of the numeral), the dependent (= the numeral) rather than the governor is the morphological contact point taking the form of the grammatical case imposed by the external context on the phrase as a whole. The numeral is in the nominative in (37a) and in the accusative in (37b), but the noun is invariably in the genitive (singular in (37a) and plural in (37b)), which is not allowed by this context, if the numeral is omitted.

When speaking of the necessity/sufficiency of Criteria B.I and B.II, it is necessary to distinguish: (1) the logical-mathematical meaning and (2) the current meaning of these terms.

From the logical-mathematical perspective, the two criteria are sufficient. This means that if Criterion B.I applies, then the wordform that determines the passive SS-valency of the phrase is obligatorily considered as its SS-head; if, on the contrary, Criterion B.II applies (and Criterion B.I does not), the phrase's morphological contact point is considered its SS-head.

(However, I am not completely convinced that Criteria B.I and B.II never contradict the researcher's intuition regarding the direction of syntactic dependencies. There may be constructions whose SS-heads are obvious from the viewpoint of linguistic$_1$ intuition, but are not treated as such by these two criteria. In this sense, logical sufficiency of Criteria B.I and B.II is postulated but not guaranteed.)

Considering the current meaning of the word *sufficient*, Criteria B.I and B.II are clearly not sufficient. Situations where neither of the two criteria applies are easily found, such as a non-coordinated construction composed of lexemes of the same syntactic class in an isolating language (e.g., Vietnamese or Chinese). A general theory of surface syntax needs still more criteria for the direction of the SS-dependency. Here are two possible avenues for the development of such criteria.

a) Meaning considerations. In phrase w_1——w_2, take as the SS-dependent the element whose omission leads only to a REDUCTION in the meaning of the utterance that includes the phrase in question, but not to an essential RESTRUCTURING of meaning.

b) Form considerations. In the phrase w_1——w_2, take as the SS-dependent the element whose behavior in the text (regarding the linear position and prosody) is similar to that of other SS-dependents in a language.

The criteria of these two types must be placed farther down in the criteria hierarchy than Criteria B.I and B.II; that is, they will be used only in cases where these two do not apply.

As for necessity, in the logical-mathematical sense Criteria B.I and B.II must be considered necessary. This means that if B.I applies to the phrase w_1——w_2 and does not indicate that w_1 is the head of it, then w_1 cannot be considered as such. The same is true of B.II.

(However, similar to what was said above, it may be the case that these criteria contradict linguistic$_1$ intuition. I do not insist on their logical necessity, just as I have not insisted on their sufficiency.)

In conclusion, it would perhaps be useful to mention two other criteria currently used to determine the direction of SS-dependencies. These, although well known, are inadequate and must be rejected.

First, omissibility criterion: "In phrase w_1———w_2, the SS-dependent is omissible whereas the SS-governor is not." This criterion works well for most constructions; however, there are cases where it is applicable but produces unacceptable results. In other words, there exist constructions in which the SS-governor itself, but not the dependent, can be omitted. One such construction has already been mentioned: the Russian phrase with an approximation marker or with the preposition PO in the distributive sense;[12] cf. (38):

(38)   **a. okolo** *pjati tonn* 'about five tons'
       b. ne bolee *milliona dollarov* 'not more than one million dollars'
       c. svyše *pjatisot frankov* 'more than five hundred francs'
       d. po *zdorovomu ogurcu* 'a giant cucumber each'

In (38), the approximation marker and *po* (printed in boldface) are obviously syntactic governors, and yet they can always be omitted from the surface-syntactic structure (without affecting the grammaticaity of the corresponding sentences), while the rest of the phrase can in no way be omitted; see (39)–(40):

(39)   **a.** *Oni polučili* **okolo** *pjati tonn* 'They received about five tons'.
       b. *Oni polučili pjat' tonn* 'They received five tons'.
       c. **Oni polučili* **okolo** 'They received about'.
(40)   **a.** *Každoj dostalos'* **po** *zdorovomu ogurcu* 'They received a giant cucumber each'.
       b. *Každoj dostalsja zdorovyj ogurec* 'Each received a giant cucumber'.
       c. **Každoj dostalos'* **po** 'They received each'.

A similar phenomenon can be observed in French:

(41)   **a.** *J'ai acheté* **beaucoup** *de livres* 'I bought many books'.
       b. *J'ai acheté des livres* 'I bought books'.
       c. **J'ai acheté beaucoup* 'I bought many'.

In *beaucoup de livres* 'many books', the SS-governor is *beaucoup*, but in spite of this, *beaucoup* 'many' can be omitted without problems, but *livres* 'books' cannot.

N.B.: The reader should recall again (see Assumption (I), page 113) that omission of sentence elements is considered only WITHIN A SURFACE-SYNTACTIC STRUCTURE, that is, in a syntactic tree, and not within the actual sentence, with all the morphological markers and word order established.

The phrases of the type illustrated in (38)—(41) clearly show that there is no one-to-one correspondence between the property of "being ommissible" and the property of "being a syntactic dependent." Therefore, omissibility should not be considered as a criterion for the direction of an SS-dependency. This does not prohibit, however, using omissibility as a quite efficient heuristic means, since, in most cases, SS-dependents are omissible—whereas SS-governors are only rarely so.

Second, predictability criterion: "In phrase w_1——w_2, the SS-dependent is the element that (statistically) predicts the whole phrase." For example, if conditional probability of the phrase after w_1 is superior to that after w_2, the element w_1 is the dependent. This criterion is based on the hypothesis that any modifier (i.e., dependent) predicts its head (i.e., governor) and that this predictability goes only one way. This is true in some cases, e.g., for adjectives: an Adj predicts the phrase Adj + N (or N + Adj) far stronger than a N does. (In other words, in a text, the percentage of adjectives that are not modifiers of a noun is much lower than that of nouns that do not have an adjective modifier.)

Predictability is directly related to omissibility: Because of the mere fact that the omissible element appears less frequently, it predicts its environment more strongly than this environment would predict it. However, the two concepts are not equivalent. Predictability seems more practical to use since it is also applicable to constructions that do not allow the omission of any of their elements. Such is the case for the construction Prep(osition) + N, where neither Prep nor N is usually omissible (i.e., for an exocentric construction). But it is precisely in constructions of this type that the inadequacy of predictability as a criterion for the direction of SS-dependencies becomes obvious. A Prep predicts the prepositional phrase more strongly than a N, and a Conj(unction) predicts the construction Conj + V more strongly than a V. However, for several other reasons, it is evident that Prep and Conj are the governors and not the dependents in each of these constructions. (Applying Criterion B.I gives the same result.)

Thus it can be seen that, although the predictability of a phrase by one of its elements constitutes an important property of the phrase, this property has no necessary logical link with the direction of the SS-dependency within the phrase. This feature has already been discussed in the brief but interesting note Bazell (1950).

I hope to have thus shown that omissibility and predictability cannot be accepted as criteria for the direction of SS-dependencies. The representability criterion, mentioned in note 10 (page 146), does not have a well defined meaning, since its formulations are too vague. Consequently, having no other alternatives than Criteria B.I and B.II, these must be recognized as indispensable for a surface-syntactic theory.[13]

C. Criteria for the SS-dependency type

Let there be two phrases $w_1 \xrightarrow{r_1} w_2$ and $w_3 \xrightarrow{r_2} w_4$, where r_i is a surface-syntactic relation. How can we know whether r_1 and r_2 are two different (types of) surface-syntactic relations (SSRel), that is, whether $r_1 \neq r_2$—or rather it is necessary to recognize that $r_1 = r_2$, allowing in this way that w_2 be linked to w_1 by the same type of SSRel that w_4 is to w_3?

Mel'čuk (1979a: 91–150) discusses three criteria likely to help the researcher to answer such questions:

- semantic contrast in minimal pairs

- reciprocal substitutability of subtrees

- repeatability of a SSRel

Here succinct formulations and simplified examples of these criteria will be presented.

Criterion C.I (semantic contrast in minimal pairs of phrases)

Let there be, in language $\mathcal{L}$, two phrases G_1 and G_2 that satisfy the following four conditions:

1) G_1 and G_2 consist of the same lexemes X and Y, possessing the same meaning-bearing morphological characteristics, or grammemes.[14]

2) X and Y are linked in G_1 as well as in G_2 by a direct surface-syntactic dependency with identical orientation. In other words, either $G_1 = X{\rightarrow}Y$ and $G_2 = X{\rightarrow}Y$, or $G_1 = X{\leftarrow}Y$ and $G_2 = X{\leftarrow}Y$.

3) The signantia of G_1 and G_2 (i.e., their DMorphRs), are different.[15] (From conditions 1 and 2 above, it follows that the two signantia differ only by purely syntactic means, whose function is to mark the SS-dependency between X and Y.)

4) G_1 and G_2 can appear in the same syntactic role. Then $\mathcal{L}$ possesses pairs of utterances $\langle U_i^1, U_i^2 \rangle$ such that U_i^1 contains G_1, U_i^2 contains G_2 and besides that, there is no other difference between U_i^1 and U_i^2. The utterances of the pair $\langle U_i^1, U_i^2 \rangle$ are called **matrix utterances** for G_1 and G_2.

> Two different SS-relations r_1 and r_2 $(r_1 \neq r_2)$ are used for representing G_1 and G_2 in the surface-syntactic structures of $\mathcal{L}$ if and only if among all the utterance pairs $\langle U_i^1, U_i^2 \rangle$, U_i^1 and U_i^2 being matrix utterances for G_1 and G_2, there is at least one pair $\langle U^1, U^2 \rangle$ whose utterances are semantically distinct: 'U¹' $\neq$ 'U²'.

Example 1

Take Russian phrase *desjat' rublej* '10 rubles' and *rublej desjat'* 'about/ approximately 10 rubles'. The difference between their signantia is purely syntactic: namely, word order. A pair of non-synonymous matrix utterances for them could be (42):

(42)   *Ja polučil desjat' rublej* 'I received 10 rubles'.
      Ja polučil rublej desjat' 'I received about 10 rubles'.

In this case, there is *desjat'* $\xrightarrow{r_1}$ *rublej* and *rublej* $\xrightarrow{r_2}$ *desjat'*, where $r_1 \neq r_2$ (r_1 is the quantitative SSRel, r_2 is the approximate-quantitative SSRel).

Example 2

Russian *čem Lena* '(more) than Lena [nominative]' and *čem Lenu* '(more) than Lena [accusative]'. The difference between signantia is also purely syntactic: namely, two different cases (nominative vs. accusative). The pair of non-synonymous matrix utterances could be:

(43)   *Ja ljublju Mašu men'še, čem Lena* 'I like Masha less than Lena likes her'.
       Ja ljublju Mašu men'še, čem Lenu 'I like Masha less than I like Lena'.

In this case, there is *čem*$\xrightarrow{r_1}$*Lena* and *čem*$\xrightarrow{r_2}$*Lenu*, where $r_1 \neq r_2$ (r_1 is the predicative conjunctive SSRel, while r_2 is the completive conjunctive SSRel).

Criterion C.II (reciprocal substitutability of subtrees)

This criterion will be cited in a simplified form considering that its exact formulation is too complicated (cf. Mel'čuk 1979a: 115–118).

Let there be, in language $\mathcal{L}$, wordforms of the type X, Y, Z and W, complete terminal subtrees Z_Δ and W_Δ (i.e., subtrees having as their top nodes wordforms of the Z and W types), and an SSRel r.

We will say that r has **the Kunze property** if and only if, for any pair of correct SSyntSs of $\mathcal{L}$ that contain $X{\rightarrow}Z_\Delta$ and $Y{\rightarrow}W_\Delta$, respectively, replacing Z_Δ by W_Δ (or inversely) does not affect the correctness. (J. Kunze is a German researcher who seems to be the first to have analyzed the reciprocal substitutability of different dependent elements of an SSRel; see Kunze 1972.)

This means that all dependent elements of an SSRel r that has the Kunze property must be reciprocally substitutable in all correct SSyntSs of $\mathcal{L}$.

> Any SSRel used in the description of the SSyntSs of language $\mathcal{L}$ must possess the Kunze property. If, for an SSRel r, this is not the case, it must be split into two (or several) different SSRels.

Note that in the transferred subtrees Z_Δ and W_Δ, we allow purely syntactic transformations that enable the "adjustment" of Z_Δ or W_Δ to their new surface governor. In fact, it is allowed to delete, to introduce or to replace the function word constituting the SS-head of the transferred subtree (for example, a governed preposition) or else to transpose Z_Δ and W_Δ into other parts of speech while performing the remaining required adjustments (for example, the transferred subtree can be nominalized if the new context requires it).

Example 1

The SSRel r_1 and r_2 appearing in English phrases *the*←*rule* and *analytical* ←*method* must be different. The proof is as follows: Let there be *rule* = X, *method* = Y, *the* = Z, *analytical* = W. Suppose that the article and the adjective are dependent elements of the same SSRel that subordinates them to the noun. Then, if in the phrase *the analytical method* (which has, of course, a correct SSyntS) the adjective [W] is replaced by the article [Z] borrowed from another correct structure (= *the rule*), the resulting expression will have an incorrect SSyntS: *the the method*. In this way, Criterion C.II ensures that, in that case $r_1 \neq r_2$ (r_1 is the determinative SSRel, and r_2 the attributive SSRel).

Example 2

In Russian, there are SS-relations r_1, r_2 and r_3 which appear, for example, in phrases (44):

(44)   **a.** $iz \xrightarrow{\ r_1\ } štanin$ 'from pant legs'

      b. $čtoby \xrightarrow{\ r_2\ } dostal$ 'so that (he) take (something) out (of something)'

      c. $i \xrightarrow{\ r_3\ } štanina$ 'and the pant leg'

According to Criterion C.II, these three SS-relations must be different:

—SS-relations r_1 and r_2 cannot be identical since the SSyntS *čtoby→štanina 'so that the pant leg' (obtained by replacing *dostal* in (44b) by *štanina* of (44a) under the hypothesis of the identity of r_1 and r_2) is incorrect.

—SSRel r_1 and SSRel r_3 can also not be identical because there are two correct SSyntSs $i \xrightarrow{r_3} iz \xrightarrow{r_1} štanin$ 'and from pant legs' and $dlja \xrightarrow{r_1} štanin$ 'for pant legs'; if the subtree $iz \xrightarrow{r_1} štanin$ is transferred from the first phrase to the seond, being attached to SSRel r_1 which issues from *dlja* we get an incorrect SSyntS: $*dlja \xrightarrow{r_1} iz \xrightarrow{r_1} štanin$.

—SSRel r_2 and SSRel r_3 are also different, because the SSyntS *čtoby→ štanina is incorrect.

The above reasoning leads us to postulate that:

   r_1 is the prepositional SSRel

   r_2 is the subordinate-conjunctive SSRel

   r_3 is the coordinate-conjunctive SSRel

Criterion C.III (repeatability of an SSRel with the same node)

If, in language $\mathcal{L}$, a SSyntS of the form $Y \xleftarrow{\ r_i\ } X \xrightarrow{\ r_i\ } Z$ is correct, the SSRel r_i is called **repeatable**. In other words, if the SSRel r_i is repeatable, it is possible to have more than one branch labeled r_i issuing from the same node.

> Any SSRel used in the description of SSyntSs of language must be either non-repeatable, or repeatable with any dependent elements. If, for an SSRel r, this is not the case, r must be split in two (or several) different SS-relations.

Therefore, in language $\mathcal{L}$, for any units Y and Z, in SSyntS $Y \xleftarrow{\ r_i\ } X \xrightarrow{\ r_i\ } Z$ is always correct or always incorrect. However, if $Y \xleftarrow{\ r_i\ } X \xrightarrow{\ r_i\ } Z$ is correct for some Ys and Zs but incorrect for other Ys and Zs, Criterion C.III requires splitting the SSRel r into two different relations.

Example

In phrases (45):

(45)   [*They*] *returned rich men* and [*They*] *returned* $\xrightarrow{\ r_2\ }$ *all*,

with r_1 arcing over *returned rich men*.

the SSRel r_1 and the SSRel r_2 must be different. In fact, if it were only one SSRel $r(?)$, it would be repeatable with some Ys and Zs but non-repeatable with other Ys and Zs:

(46)   **a.** [*They*] *all* $\xleftarrow{\ r(?)\ }$ *returned rich men*

with $r(?)$ arcing over *returned rich men*.

   b. *[*They*] *returned* $\xrightarrow{\ r(?)\ }$ *heroes rich men*

with $r(?)$ arcing over *returned ... rich men*.

As can be seen from (46), the SSRel $r(?)$ would only be repeatable on the condition that at least one of its dependent elements be a pronominal adjective of a certain type; two nouns attached to the same governor by means of the two occurrences of the same SSRel $r(?)$ are inadmissible. In this way, Criterion C.III ensures that in these specific phrases $r_1 \neq r_2$ (r_1 is the subjective-copredicative SSRel; r_2 is the pronominal-copredicative SSRel).

It is necessary to emphasize that the last three criteria do not help to determine what type of SSRel must be used in what phrase. In other words, Criteria C.I–C.III do not help to make syntactic IDENTIFICATION of different phrases, they only help their differentiation. The identification of SS-relations is possible—as happens in all the domains of natural language—based only on considerations of similarity, although this approach still defies formalization (at least, in the present linguistic$_2$ framework). The situation is quite familiar in phonology. There exist fairly formal criteria for deciding if two sounds [f_1] and [f_2] can belong to the same phoneme /f/ or if they must be considered as belonging to two different phonemes. However, no formal criteria exist for deciding if two sounds must be included in the same phoneme. This last decision must be made based on non-formal reasoning (physical similarity of specific sounds, etc.).

Translated from French by Patricia McMullan, a Master's Translation student at the University of Montreal.

NOTES

1. (I, before 1, p. 107.) A direct dependency is, as defined in Chapter 1, an antireflexive, antisymmetrical and antitransitive binary relation, that is, an **order relation** (in the mathematical sense of the term). In this chapter, only direct dependencies are considered.

2. (I, 1, before (4), p. 107.) Syntactics is the third component of a linguistic sign, besides the signatum and the signans of de Saussure (i.e., **signifié** vs. **signifiant**); it includes all the information on the combinatorics, or the cooccurrence properties, of the sign that cannot be deduced from its meaning (i.e., from its signatum) or from its form (i.e., from its signans). See Chapter 1, Note 1, page 39.

3. (I, 1, after (6), p. 111.) An analogy could be drawn between this instance of a bilateral morphological dependency linking a transitive verb with its object and what is found in the French construction of the type *la lettre qu'il a écrite* 'the letter that he has written'. If *a écrite* is considered as a single verb form, we can say that it is morphologically dependent on *que* and, therefore, on its antecedent *lettre* (according to gender), while *que* — as opposed to *qui* — is morphologically dependent on the form *a écrite*, which, as a transitive verb, governs the object form of the relative pronoun, i.e., *que*.

4. (1, 2, p. 112.) The **active surface-syntactic valency** of a syntactic unit U is the list of the other units U'_i that can be subordinated to U. In English, for example, the active SS-valency of the verb BELONG or of the adjective EQUAL includes the preposition TO; $VAL^{SS}_{act}(see)$ includes the noun phrase NP, the infinitive, and the present participle (the two latter always appearing with an NP): *Mary sees him cut(ting) the grass*; the active SS-valency of a French preposition like SANS 'without' includes both the noun phrase and the infinitive (*sans moi* 'without me', *sans bouger* 'without moving'); and the VAL^{SS}_{act} of a noun (in most languages) includes, among other things, the adjective.

5. (I, 2, after (10), p. 114.) The VAL^{SS}_{pass} of a PP includes the capacity to be an adverbial complement, an object or a complement to a verb governing this particular preposition, etc. The problem of a preposition's valency will be taken up again later, p. 133.

6. (I, after (10″), p. 118.) The intermediate nature of syntactic dependency (situated between morphological and semantic dependency) was noted by Bazell (1950: 9): "By fundamental syntactic relations, we shall understand only such relations between terms in the chain of discourse as may be defined without reference either to meaning or to expression, but which, once defined, may be applied to both alike."

7. (III, A, p. 130.) In this connection, it is interesting to mention the problem raised by the syntactic description of French pronominal nonsubject clitics in Iordanskaja (1982).

If one assumes with Iordanskaja that in French a nonsubject pronominal clitic is syntactically dependent on the same wordform as its antecedent noun (i.e., the noun replaced by this clitic), the properties of prosodic and linear unity would not be sufficient for an SS-dependency. The reason is that under this assumption, a French pronominal clitic can form a prosodic and linear unit with a wordform other than the syntactic governor of the cliticized noun, namely, with its host word. Consider for example, sentences (i) and (ii), (ii) being the source of (i):

(i) French *J'en ai* [*ai* is the host word of *en*] *commencé le premier chapitre* 'I began the first chapter of it',

(ii) French *J'ai commencé le premier chapitre* $\xrightarrow{\text{synt}}$ *de ce traité* 'I began the first chapter of this treatise'.

In (i), where *en* replaces the prepositional phrase *de ce traité*, the clitic *en* is considered to be syntactically dependent on *chapitre*, whereas linearly and prosodically, this clitic forms a unit with *ai*.

This problem seems to admit of at least three solutions:

1) Iordanskaja's approach can be rejected, so that the pronominal clitic is not considered to be necessarily dependent on the same wordform that was the syntactic governor of

its source, i.e., of the cliticized noun. In this case, the surface-syntactic dependency structure of a sentence would change under cliticization.

2) We can add to the two properties introduced on p. 130 a condition that forbids their application to pronominal clitics. This boils down to recognizing the insufficiency of these properties.

3) Finally, the concept of prosodic and linear unity can be generalized in such a way as to cover the case of French nonsubject pronominal clitics. In principle, this is possible, because the host word of a clitic (i.e., the wordform to which the clitic is "affixed" linearly and prosodically), is itself defined in terms of the surface-syntactic governor of the clitic, which allows us to treat the linear and prosodic unity of the clitic and its host as the generalized unity of the clitic and its governor.

At present, I am unable to make a well-founded choice between these three solutions. Nevertheless, it seems that the least painful solution would be solution 3.

French is not exceptional with regard to clitics. In some common cases in English, such as:

   (iii) *How'm I doing?*
   (iv) *We'll consider it.*
   (v) *Your Daddy's coming.*

and many others, the syntactic head of the sentence, the finite verb, is converted into a clitic, which, linearly and prosodically, is subservient to the preceding word.

It is evident that clitics require special treatment—because of their intermediate status between that of an independent word and that of a word part.

8. (III, the very end of A, p. 132.) B.V. Suxotin (1973, 1976) put forward a very promising idea for formally determining the surface-syntactic connectedness of wordforms of any sentence. Let there be, in $\mathcal{L}$, two classes of wordforms, A and B. Probability $P_{A,B}$ of their cooccurrence in the same sentence in $\mathcal{L}$ is calculated, after which one can determine, in terms of $P_{A,B}$, reciprocal probabilistic predictability of classes A and B for language $\mathcal{L}$ in general. Then, for any sentence Φ of $\mathcal{L}$, the set **SSynt** of all its logically possible surface-syntactic structures is created: each wordform of Φ is taken in turn as the absolute head of a syntactic structure, and all the other wordforms are made to depend on it (not necessarily directly) in all possible ways. And finally, in **SSynt**, the structure that features a maximum sum of reciprocal predictabilities of all its syntactically directly linked wordforms is chosen as the correct SSynt-structure for Φ. Similarly, Suxotin defines *morph* as a phonemic string characterized by a maximum sum of reciprocal predictabilities of the adjacent phonemes that constitute it.

9. (III, B, after (33'), p. 134.) The approximation marker *okolo* is a homonym of the preposition (adverb) *okolo* 'near, around'; furthermore, the two homonyms require the genitive in the same way:

   (i) *okolo jaščikov* 'near the boxes', 'besides the boxes'
   (ii) *okolo dvadcati jaščikov* 'about [= some] twenty boxes', 'approximately twenty boxes'.

10. (III, B, after (33'), p. 134.) The criterion of imposing passive surface-syntactic valency can seem to be only a reformulation of the so-called "representability criterion" (Kuryłowicz 1960); cf. also Xolodovič 1970: 332: "The governing element (= the head) of a phrase is that which represents it in its external relations, that is, which supports all the phrase's external links."

But in such a form, the representability criterion does not have a precise meaning. To make it more specific, it is necessary to clarify the expressions *external relations* ⟨*links*⟩ (of a phrase), since these relations can be active or passive, and so forth, and *to represent a phrase externally* ⟨*to support the phrase's external links*⟩. It is very likely that by attempting to clarify these expressions, the criterion of imposing the passive SSynt-valency will of necessity be obtained. Also compare Criterion KI in Kunze and Ljudskanov (1975) (note 13, below, page 148).

11. (III, B, after (36), p. 137.) The situation for noun appositives in Russian is more complex than my illustrations suggest. Humesky (1964) quotes a few dozen noun phrases with noun apposition created by the great Russian poet V. Majakovskij. In these phrases, agreement sometimes marks as the SS-head the preceding noun and sometimes the following one (the morphological contact point and the ending that it requires are printed in boldface):

(i) *čtoby vzvi*l*sja* **flag**-*malina* 'May the raspberry flag unfurl'.
(ii) *Spada*jut **štany**-*garmoška* 'The accordion pants fall'.
(iii) *Korot*ka **smeta**-*plat′ice* 'The dress estimate is short'.

On the other hand, we have:

(iv) *Priboj-***revoljucija** *vbrosil*a *v Zimnij* . . . 'The backwash of the revolution' [lit. 'backwash revolution'] pushed into the Winter Palace . . .'
(v) **Vaša** *podrostok-***strana** 'Your young country' [lit. 'adolescent country'].

In the folkloric expression *put′-doroga* 'path road', the second element (feminine noun) serves as a morphological contact point:

(vi) *V put′-***dorogu** *dal′n*juju *ja tebja otpravlju* 'I will send you on a long road' [Soviet song].
(vii) *V golubye snega put′-***doroga** *legl*a 'A road is lost in the blue snow' [Soviet convict song].

It is easy to give more examples but it is not necessary. The law that governs this surface variation is almost obvious—the morphological contact point (i.e., the syntactic head of all these phrases, according to Criterion B.II) is always the semantically dominant noun. In this way, in (i), flags are talked about and therefore the noun *flag* 'flag' is the syntactic head, 'raspberry' (*malina*) being only a metaphoric attribute here. In (v), the topic of countries is discussed and *strana* 'country' determines all the external agreements with the whole phrase (while *podrostok* 'adolescent' appears also as a metaphoric qualification), and so forth.

There might be found apparent counterexamples, as in the following sentenꞒꞓ of M.A. Bulgakov:

(viii) *Čërnaja ptica-šofër na letu otvintil pravoe koleso* 'The blackbird driver, while airborn, loosened the right wheel'.

Here, *ptica* 'bird' [feminine] requires the feminine form of the adjective *čërnaja* 'black' whilst *šofër* 'driver' [masculine] determines the masculine gender of the verb *otvintil* 'loosened'. However, it is not a matter of two morphological contact points. Quite simply, the noun *šofër*, the SS-head of the phrase, is modified by the whole phrase *čërnaja ptica* 'black bird'. But the problem seems too technical and marginal to be analyzed here in more detail.

12. (III, preceding (38), p. 139.) The Russian preposition *po*, which is polysemous, allows, in one of its several meanings, a construction that is completely foreign to English syntax (and rather exceptional in Russian syntax). It is the so-called "distributive" sense:

(i) *V universitety goroda prišlo pis'mo* 'A letter was received by the city's universities' [the same letter]
vs.

(ii) *V universitety goroda prišlo* **po pis'mu** 'A letter was received by each of the city's universities' [it could be different letters].

(iii) *My s''eli bifšteks* 'We ate a steak' [everybody was eating the same steak]
vs.

(iv) *My s''eli* **po bifšteksu** 'We each ate a steak'.

The important thing is that the prepositional phrase introduced by distributive *po* can only be used in the syntactic position of grammatical subject or of direct object, i.e. in a position requiring the nominative or the accusative. Cf. the phrase with the approximation marker: p. 134, example 3.

13. (III, at the very end of Section B, p. 140.) Criteria for the direction of surface-syntactic dependencies are also discussed in Kunze and Ljudskanov (1975), where three criteria of this type are introduced: KI—KIII.

KI. Let there be a configuration C in the sense of Kulagina (1958) (roughly, a **configuration** is a wordform string that can, under certain conditions, be replaced by one wordform, called its **resultant**, without changing the grammaticality of the utterance including the initial string). Then criterion KI chooses as the syntactic head of C the wordform of C that is, from the viewpoint of grammatical properties, the closest to the resultant of C. It is easy to see that Criterion KI is similar to our main criterion, that is, to the criterion of the imposition of passive surface-syntactic valency (= B.I).

KII. Criterion KII stipulates that an obligatory complement of a wordform is its syntactic dependent. It is the predictability criterion in reverse. Because of this, KII is free of the most serious drawback of the predictability criterion: according to KII, a phrase introduced by a preposition or a conjunction is, as one would like it to be, a syntactic dependent of it.

KIII. Criterion KIII states that any omissible element is a syntactic dependent (this is the omissibility criterion in its pure form).

A more detailed analysis of KI—KIII is not appropriate here.

An in-depth discussion found in Robinson (1970b), particularly on pp. 272 ff., should be mentioned in particular. This article offers a detailed comparison of phrase structure systems and dependency systems, especially from the viewpoint of how the syntactic head of a phrase is determined. Some criteria are suggested for surface-syntactic governors, such as the criterion of the characterizing category, which picks up as governor the wordform that determines the syntactic properties (e.g., distribution) of the phrase that includes it. This criterion is also quite close to the criterion of imposition of the passive valency (our B.I).

Going into the history of the problem, it is necessary to name a short article Pittman (1948), where the author listed (probably for the first time) ten considerations that were used to determine the "satellite-nucleus" relation within all types of phrases. However, it seems impossible to review here all the works that set out to define syntactic dependency criteria, particularly criteria to determine dependency direction. I will limit myself to indicating the little-known note Revzin (1963).

14. (III, Criterion C.I, p. 141.) Let me remind the reader that a meaning-bearing gram-meme is DIRECTLY linked to the semantic representation of the utterance. Examples: the number of the noun ('one' or 'more than one'), the tense of the verb, and the degree of comparison of the adjective. On the contrary, such grammemes as the gender and the number of the adjective, the case of the noun, the person and the number of the verb are induced by syntactic context (agreement and government) and contribute to the full mean-ing of the utterance only INDIRECTLY, via the syntactic structure. Cf. p. 61.

15. (III, Criterion C.I, p. 141.) I prefer not to touch here the problem of the so-called "syntactic homonymy" (the case where the signantia of G_1 and G_2 are identical), for ex-ample, *John's invitation*, which gives rise to a double interpretation: either someone in-vited John, or John invited someone. The problem consists in distinguishing between am-biguity and vagueness, i.e., between the cases where it is necessary to postulate two different SS-relations and the cases where we are dealing with only one SSRel that has a rather broad and vague meaning (such as in *John's house*: the house where John lives, or that belongs to him, or that he built, etc.).

Part **III**

Syntactic Theory:
The Ergative Construction

One of the most hairy and challenging problems of modern syntax is the description and theory of the so-called "ERGATIVE CONSTRUCTION"; for an excellent summary of existing views and approaches see Catford (1976), Comrie (1978) and Dixon (1979) plus a collection of papers, Plank (1979). The ergative construction is so difficult to deal with and, at the same time, so fascinating to linguists for a very simple reason: it represents a crossing point of a number of important linguistic$_2$ notions, in particular of the following four: (1) Grammatical Subject (GS), as opposed to semantic "Agent", or "Actor", or simply to "Semantic Subject", (2) Transitivity of verbs, as opposed to their semantic and/or syntactic valency, (3) Case marking (of sentence nominal elements), as opposed to case forms, (4) Grammatical voice.

Each of these topics might require a whole volume, and what is even worse, cannot be seriously treated prior to, and independently from, the ergative construction. As so often happens in natural language, all these phenomena are tied up in a diabolic knot and so I must discuss them all together: proceeding by small steps, moving back and forth, sidetracking, using loose language and hoping, above all, that a benevolent reader will understand me properly, even if I do not state all my postulates and claims explicitly and formally.

I will not try to outline here a coherent theory of the Ergative Construction (EC). Instead, I offer two case studies: the EC in Dyirbal and in Lezgian; after that I propose a sketchy typology of predicative constructions, of which ergative construction is but a particular subclass. In so doing, I try to sharpen all the relevant notions and come up with more precise concepts than I have started with. (Later, in Part IV, I apply the descriptive tools developed in the process to a nuclear fragment of Alutor syntax in order to illustrate their applicability on new data.)

Accordingly, Part III comprises three chapters:

Chapter 4: Is there an Ergative Construction in Dyirbal?

Chapter 5: Is there an Ergative Construction in Lezgian?

Chapter 6: Toward a Definition of the Concept "Ergative Construction".

Before going ahead with my presentation, I need to clear up an important conceptual (or maybe terminological) point. Instead of the very general, broad and—because of that—fairly vague notion of "ergativity", which is the most frequently used term, I concentrate exclusively on a more specific and much narrower concept: "Ergative Construction". I do not discuss ergative languages, universal properties of ergativity and what not; I do discuss a particular syntactic configuration, trying to isolate it as fully as possible from all concomitant phenomena. Thus in this book **Ergative Construction** (and not **Ergativity**) is the key word.

Chapter *4*

IS THERE
AN ERGATIVE
CONSTRUCTION
IN DYIRBAL?

I. INTRODUCTORY REMARKS

The Dyirbal language of the rain-forest area in North Queensland, Australia, is often said to be a typical representative of the so-called "ERGATIVE LANGUAGES" (cf., for example, Hale 1970: 759). To make this claim more explicit, we need some traditional terms, which do not have clear-cut meaning. I will use double quotes to show that those terms are no more than provisional labels.

Let us take the most current predicative construction with a "transitive"[1] verb in Dyirbal and present it in accordance with the most current view:

(1) $N^1_{erg} + V_{(tr)} + N^2_{nom}$

where $V_{(tr)}$ stands for a "transitive" verb, and N_{erg} and N_{nom} are two nouns (in "ergative" and "nominative" case, respectively) syntactically dependent on it. (N. B.: The order of symbols in (1) by no means reflects actual word order in Dyirbal, see below, p. 159.) This construction is considered a classic example of ERGATIVE CONSTRUCTION and is traditionally analyzed as follows:

N^1, in the "ergative" case and indicating the "semantic subject" (the causer or the perceiver), is considered the grammatical subject (GS) of the sentence; N^2, in the "nominative" case and indicating the "semantic object", is considered the direct grammatical object (GO^{dir}). Thus we have

(2) GS   Main Verb GO^{dir}
                     [predicate]

     N_{erg} $V_{(tr)}$ N_{nom}
     by-man   *kill*   *eel*

that is, 'The man kills [or killed] the eel'.

Let me insist that the verb in (2) is by no means passive: it appears in the basic, lexicographic form. (Dyirbal does have a derived, morphologically marked verb form, which could be compared to English passive, but this is not the form that we find in structures of type (2); this derived form is marked by the suffix -*ŋay*, see below, IV, p. 176 ff., and VII.) Therefore, we are told that in Dyirbal the GS of a "transitive" verb is marked by the "ergative" case and its GO^{dir}, by the "nominative", i.e., the case that marks as well the GS of an "intransitive" verb. Thus (2) appears to be an ergative construction.

Yet such an analysis seems wrong to me. I came to this conclusion based on the excellent description of the Dyirbal language found in Dixon (1972). The book treats syntactic facts of Dyirbal comprehensively and very carefully; the presentation by Dixon is so explicit and lucid that it can easily be used by any researcher without mastery of Dyirbal or of Australian languages in general. Taking into account all the data in Dixon (1972) leads to a different analysis of (1), which will be given and argued for below.[2]

I must apologize for turning once again to Dyirbal: the language has been recently so extensively involved in linguistic discussions that there are now certainly far more linguists writing about Dyirbal than there are Dyirbal speakers (about two dozen). However, the language features such syntactic properties as are crucial to the general theory of predicative constructions; at the same time, Dixon's first-class description makes it readily available. So I think that my attempt to reconsider Dyirbal facts from a new stand is justified.

This is even more the case as the overall purpose of this chapter (as well as that of the following chapter on Lezgian) is by no means to discover new facts concerning the language in question. It is rather something different:

The main thrust of Chapters 4 and 5 is to contribute to the development of a consistent and adequate linguistic₂ metalanguage.

Therefore, the emphasis is on notions and definitions, as well as terminology, in a bid to lay the foundations of a system of formal notions for theoretical syntax (similar to that proposed for morphology in Mel'čuk 1982). Such notions as **grammatical subject**, "semantic subject/object", **transitivity**, **nominative case**, **ergative construction**, **grammatical voice**, in general, and the **passive** in particular, along with a few others, will be discussed at length. In this discussion, Dyirbal (and later on, Lezgian) data prove highly relevant.

II. A FEW FACTS ABOUT DYIRBAL

Here are some elementary data concerning Dyirbal (given strictly within the limits of what is needed to read and understand the examples).

1. Phonology

1) The transcription used does not call for explanations, with the exception of the following:

r is a semi-retroflex continuant [r]

n and d are laminoalveopalatal stops [n] and [d] (the blade of the tongue touches the hard palate or the alveolar ridge, or possibly both, with the tongue tip touching the teeth)

$ŋ$ is a dorsovelar stop (much like English -ng)

w and y are bilabial-velar and palatal semivowels.

2) Main stress occurs on the first syllable of any wordform, secondary stress —on all odd syllables; final syllables are never stressed.

3) The following morphophonemic operations are relevant to the discussion:

$$-y + d- \Rightarrow d(ŋay + da \Rightarrow ŋada)$$
$$-y + n- \Rightarrow n (balgal + ŋay + nu \Rightarrow balgalŋanu)$$
$$-l + n \Rightarrow n (balgal + n \Rightarrow balgan)$$
$$-l + ru \Rightarrow ru(dugumbil + ru \Rightarrow dugumbiru)$$

2. Morphology

1) The Dyirbal verb does not distinguish person, number, or nominal class (for nominal classes, see below): there is complete lack of verb agreement with verb actants.

The verb has only two tense forms: present-past in -n/-nu, the suffix being selected according to the last phoneme of the stem, and the future in -n. For the sake of simplicity, in the examples all verbs are given in the present-past tense only.

Since there are no person, number or class exponents in the verb, invocation of verb agreement is impossible when we consider SS-roles of Dyirbal nominals.

2) Dyirbal nouns are distributed among four nominal classes: (I) men, animals, winds, boomerangs, money; (II) women, fire, water (and anything to do with fire or water), birds, the sun, stars; (III) all wild fruit and vegetable foods; (IV) plants without edible fruit, stones, noises, languages, and other things.

Each class selects a specific form of the determiner (or **noun marker** in Dixon 1972)—a syntactic word with functions very much like those of the definite article in such languages as English, French, or German. Dyirbal has three determiners indicating the degree of the noun referent's remoteness from the speaker; my examples use only one of these, the most neutral and most frequent *bala-/ba-* 'that'. A determiner agrees with its noun in case and class; class suffixes of determiners are as follows: (I) -l, (II) -n, (III) -m, (IV) -∅. Omitting some morphophonemic complications (in the nominative of Class I), each determiner wordform can be said to consist of three components:

root + case suffix + class suffix

Thus for *bala-* we have in the instrumental of Class I $ba + ŋgu + l \; yaṛa + ŋgu$ 'by the man', in the dative of Class II $ba + gu + n \; dugumbil + gu$

Case	Suffixes
Nominative (the case of citation forms: answering the question 'What is this?')	-∅
Instrumental (denotes the instrument of an action as well as the agent, i.e., it has the "ergative" function also)	*-ŋgu, -gu, (-n)-du, (-ṇ)-ḍu, (-y)-ḍu, (-m)-bu, -ṛu* [the choice is determined by the phonemic composition of the stem]
Dative (denotes the addressee as well as the actant implicated by the situation in any way, perhaps in quite an oblique manner: 'with respect to . . .', 'in connection with . . .')	*-gu*

Table 4-1
The Three Relevant Dyirbal Grammatical Cases
and Their Suffixes

'to the woman', etc. In the nominative of Class I we find *ba* + *yi* instead of the expected **bala + l*.

Any noun in discourse is, as a rule, accompanied by its determiner, except for genitive, locative, allative and ablative forms. Determiners may also occur in discourse without nouns they characterize, and then they serve as 3rd person substitute pronouns: 'he, she, it, they'.

3) Dyirbal nouns, adjectives and determiners are declined according to one and the same formal pattern. Ten cases can be distinguished, of which only three are relevant for further discussion: nominative, instrumental, and dative; see Table 4-1 above.

Dyirbal pronouns (personal, interrogative and demonstrative) are declined according to a somewhat different pattern; the three case forms above for *ŋaḍa* (= *ŋay + da*) 'I', *waṇa* 'who', and *balagara* 'they' are as follows:

	ŋaḍa	**waṇa**	**balagara**
nominative	*ŋaḍa*	*waṇa*	*balagara*
instrumental	*ŋaḍa*	*waṇ + ḍu*	*bala + gara + gu,*
			ba + ŋgu + gara,
			ba + ŋgu + gara + gu

dative	ŋay + gungu	waṇ + ungu	bala + gara + gu,
			ba + gu + gara,
			ba + gu + gara + gu

First- and second-person pronouns of all numbers (singular, dual and plural) have homonymous forms in the nominative and instrumental; however, interrogative and demonstrative pronouns distinguish both cases formally. In addition, in Giramay, one of the three Dyirbal dialects, nominative and instrumental case forms are different in the 1st and 2nd person singular as well ('I': Giramay nom. *ŋayba*, instr. *ŋaḍa*; 'thou': Giramay nom. *ŋinba*, instr. *ŋinda*).

In connection with Dyirbal grammatical cases, two points call for additional discussion.

First, Dixon (1972) distinguishes, instead of my single instrumental, two cases: an ergative and an instrumental, which, in his opinion, just happen to have the same realization—as, for instance, do plural and genitive (= -*s*) in English (Dixon 1972: 42, 93–94). According to Dixon (I hope I do not misrepresent him), the facts about these two cases are as follows.

The instrumental and the ergative are never distinguished formally (that is, morphologically); they are distinguished exclusively by syntactic transformations. Thus, the passive transformation (with a -*ŋay*-form) may affect only an ergative NP, which becomes a GS in the "nominative", cf. (26)⇔(27), pp. 186–187. But the comitative transformation (with a -*mal*-form) may affect only an instrumental NP (which also becomes a GS), cf. (37b)⇔(37c), p. 191.

Dixon's conclusion is that if we mark both types of NPs with the same case label, like NP_2 and NP_3 in (3) below:

(3) NP_1 [= "nominative"] NP_2 [= instrumental] NP_3 [= instrumental] $V_{(tr)}$
      balan   ḍugumbil   baŋgul   yaṛaŋgu   baŋgu   yuguŋgu   balgan
      'The   woman   [by] the   man   [with] the   stick   is-being
                                                                         beaten

we would have no way of indicating that the passive transformation affects NP_2 but not NP_3, and that the comitative transformation affects NP_3 but of necessity leaves NP_2 untouched. Therefore, Dixon concludes, we are compelled to say that NP_2 and NP_3 stand in different cases, which automatically entails distinguishing the ergative and the instrumental cases.

Proceeding from the same data, I arrive, however, at a conclusion diametrically opposite to Dixon's: NP_2 and NP_3 in (3) reflect, in my view, a difference between the respective syntactic roles, i.e., between SURFACE-SYNTACTIC RELATIONS, rather than representing a difference in grammatical case. The surface-syntactic structure of (3) is roughly as follows (I anticipate here the results arrived at in Section III):

(3')

BALGAL-'beat'

predicative   agentive   instrumentive

NP₁   NP₂   NP₃

Accordingly, all syntactic transformations should be defined in terms of sur-face-syntactic structures (SyntSs) rather than in the terms of the morphological strings that implement those structures; furthermore, syntactically induced case-marking is absent from the SyntS: see pp. 61 and 83 above, and p. 276 below. This means that when stating the passive and comitative transformations, we need to specify the proper SS-relations; we cannot even mention the cases, for there are none in the SyntS. So the main argument in favor of positing instrumen-tal AND ergative cases in Dyirbal collapses, and I can safely keep classifying the forms in *-ŋu, -gu, -ɖu,* etc. (see Table 4-1, p. 156) as ONE case. The name of this case—"instrumental" or "ergative" or "instrumental-ergative"—is obvi-ously immaterial in this context. I prefer to reserve the term "ergative" for a case that marks either "transitive" grammatical subjects exclusively (much like the Georgian case in *-ma*) or GSs, agentive complements of passive forms, and even oblique objects (like the Dargwa case in *-li*, see Chapter 5) but not instruments, tools, or means. For this reason, I have chosen to call the Dyirbal case in ques-tion "instrumental": it readily marks instruments.

Second, along with the nominative, instrumental and dative, we find one case that proves very important for the present discussion: it will be temporarily called "accusative". This case denotes the "semantic object" of an action: something that changes its state as a result of causation, something that is perceived, etc. Note that pronouns have a special form for the "accusative": nom. *ŋaɖa*, "acc." *ŋay + guna* 'I'; nom. *ŋaliɖi*, "acc." *ŋaliɖi + na* 'we two'; nom. *ŋin + ɖa*, "acc." *ŋiṇ + una* 'thou'; nom. *waṇa*, "acc." *waṇ + una* 'who', etc. The "accusative" form serves only to refer to "semantic objects", and this role ex-cludes any other case form of the pronoun.

As for nouns, only some human nouns—namely, all proper names and a few common nouns (primarily kinship terms)—have a special form in the "accusa-tive"; but with such nouns the "accusative" forms are optional. In other words, if a man called Burbula is the "semantic object" of an action, his name can have one of two forms: either *Burbula* or *Burbula + ṇa*; *-ṇa*-forms can be used only for reference to "objects", so that in the "semantic subject" role only *Burbula*-form (without *-ṇa*) is possible.

Dixon does not recognize an accusative case for Dyirbal (1972: 60). I conclude from Dixon's presentation that he regards forms such as *ŋayguna, ŋaliɖina, ŋinuna*, etc. as variants of the nominative bearing the feature

[− actor] and forms such as *ŋaḍa, ŋaliḍi, and ŋinda* as other variants of the nominative with the feature [+ actor] (cf. 1972: 200), the difference between [− actor] and [+ actor] being one of syntactic roles. Yet, in my opinion, we cannot regard noun forms that clearly contrast in their syntactic roles as variants of the same case (see, in this connection, Chapter 10, Principle (5), and Mel'čuk (1986: 52-56)).

What has been said so far permits me to posit an "accusative" case for Dyirbal, which has obligatory special forms in pronouns, optional special forms in human Ns, and homonymous forms (coinciding with nominative forms) in all other Ns. A similar situation obtains in Russian, where the accusative has a special form only for first declension singular nouns in *-a/-ja: kniga* 'book'—*Ja vižu knigu* 'I see a book'; in other nouns the accusative form is identical to either the genitive (in animate masculine nouns and in animate plural nouns: *starik* 'an old man' —*Ja vižu starika* 'I see an old man'; *šljapa starika* 'the hat of the old man') or the nominative (in non-animate nouns and in animate singular non-masculine nouns: *dom* 'house'—*Ja vižu dom* 'I see a house').

To sum up, I am going to operate in Dyirbal with four cases: nominative, instrumental, dative and "accusative", ignoring the rest as irrelevant for our present purposes. ("Accusative" will be treated at some length in Section V.)

3. Syntax

The word order of Dyirbal is exceptionally free: in (4) and (5) below, all of the words, even determiners, may be permuted in an arbitrary order according to the needs of communicative structure (topic/comment, old/new information, and the like), emphasis, rhythm, etc. (Dixon 1972: 291).

As a result, one cannot rely on the word order when resolving problems of the surface-syntactic (SS-) role of sentence constituents in Dyirbal. Nonetheless, a sentence out of the context can feature a most natural, i.e., neutral, word order, which is presented in the examples.

III. GRAMMATICAL SUBJECT IN DYIRBAL

Let us begin by citing a number of typical Dyirbal sentences that constitute the data for further analysis:

(4)   **a.** *ba + yi yaṟa bani + ŋu*
      'The man came'.
    b. *bala + n ḍugumbil bani + ŋu*
      'The woman came'.
    c. *ŋaḍa bani + ŋu*
      'I came'.
    d. *waŋa ba + yi bani + ŋu?*
      'Who came?,'lit. 'Who this came?'
    e. *ba + yi Burbula bani + ŋu*
      'The Burbula [a man's name] came'.

(5) **a.** *bala + n ḏugumbil ba + ŋgu + l yaṟa + ŋgu balga + n*
'The woman the man hit',
i.e., 'The woman was hit by the man'.

  b. *ba + yi yaṟa ba + ŋgu + n ḏugumbi + ṟu balga + n*
'The man the woman hit',
i.e., 'The man was hit by the woman'.

  c. *ŋaḏa ba + yi yaṟa ⟨bala + n ḏugumbil⟩ balga + n*
'I the man ⟨the woman⟩ hit',
i.e., 'The man ⟨the woman⟩ was hit by me'.

  d. *ŋay + guna ba + ŋgu + l yaṟa + ŋgu ⟨ba + ŋgu + n ḏugumbi + ṟu⟩ balga + n*
'Me the man ⟨the woman⟩ hit',
i.e., 'I was hit by the man ⟨by the woman⟩'.

  e. *ba + yi yaṟa ⟨bala + n ḏugumbil⟩ waṇ + ḏu balga + n?*
'The man ⟨The woman⟩ who hit',
i.e., 'Who hit the man ⟨the woman⟩?'

  f. *waṇ + una ba + ŋgu + l yaṟa + ŋgu ⟨ba + ŋgu + n ḏugumbi + ṟu⟩ balga + n?*
'Whom did the man ⟨the woman⟩ hit?'

  g. *ba + yi yaṟa ⟨bala + n ḏugumbil⟩ ba + ŋgu + l Burbula + ŋgu balga + n*
'The man ⟨The woman⟩ the Burbula hit',
i.e., 'The man ⟨The woman⟩ was hit by Burbula'.

  h. *ba + yi Burbula/Burbula + ṇa ba + ŋgu + l yaṟa + ŋgu ⟨ ba + ŋgu + n ḏugumbi + ṟu⟩ balga + n*
'The Burbula the man ⟨the woman⟩ hit',
i.e., 'Burbula was hit by the man ⟨by the woman⟩'.

In the English glosses, words map first the Dyirbal order, and then, where necessary, a normal translation is also supplied.

Our main task is now to establish the GRAMMATICAL SUBJECT of these sentences.

1. Toward the Concept of Grammatical Subject

First of all, let us agree, tentatively at least, upon the use of the term **grammatical subject**. Adhering, more or less, to current usage, I propose to proceed from
the following four assumptions about what a grammatical subject is:

1. The Grammatical Subject (GS) is basically a SURFACE-SYNTACTIC item. To
define GS, neither purely semantic nor purely morphological terms should be
used.

  On the one hand, it is obvious that a GS may play different semantic roles
(Actor; Source; Location: **The box** *contains six bottles*; Object: **He** *was killed*;

Time: **3 o'clock** *saw them at Penn Station*; etc.), while a given semantic role may be filled by different syntactic items (cf. the Actor role in the following: **McCawley** *has described . . ., described* **by McCawley, McCawley's** *description, description* **of McCawley** or even **McCawleyan** *description*).

On the other hand, a syntactic item may have different morphological markings (i.e., different grammatical cases or different word order), while a given morphological device may be used to indicate different syntactic items. Thus, for example, in Georgian the grammatical subject may be marked by the nominative, the ergative or the dative (depending on the aspect-tense form of the verb: cf. (6) in Chapter 3, p. 110), while the nominative and the dative may also mark the direct object.

The GS is to be defined in terms of (surface-)syntactic properties, or, to be more precise, in terms of the following three types of properties centered around the (surface-)syntactic level of utterance representation (cf. Keenan 1976):

A. Surface-syntactic properties *sensu stricto*, i.e., BEHAVIORAL properties observed in surface-syntactic representations (deletability, relativizability, conjoinability and gapping, control of reflexivization, control of gerunds, control of floating quantifiers, etc.).

B. Morpho-syntactic CODING properties, i.e., properties describable in terms of relationships between the syntactic and the morphological representations (what agrees with what, what is governed by what, etc.; in short, what syntactic items impose what morphological dependencies). Note that when defining GS we should not mention its grammatical case (or, for that matter, its postposition). Case is a means of representing, or manifesting, the GS at a different and closer-to-surface level (namely, at the Deep-Morphological level), and, as such, it cannot represent one of the constituting properties of a GS. Case does for the GS exactly what a skirt does for a woman: a skirt does not make a woman a woman (women may wear dresses, trousers or nothing), but it marks one as such.

C. Semantico-syntactic INTERPRETATION properties, i.e., properties concerning relationships between the syntactic and the semantic representations (what influences or conditions, and in what way, the semantic interpretation of what).

In some languages, the coding properties of GSs may be irrelevant or even nonexistent, as is the case of Dyirbal (which completely lacks any number-person agreement in the main verb). However, the behavioral and interpretation properties are presumed to be valid for any language. (See the insightful analysis in Cole et al. 1980.)

2. Grammatical Subject is a nominal phrase that happens to be SYNTACTICALLY PRIVILEGED in the language examined. That is, a GS is an NP having (roughly) all properties of all other NPs and characterized in addition by a specific set of

surface-syntactic properties that it shares fully with no other NP in the language. To define GS in language $\mathcal{L}$, we must look for such syntactic properties of NPs in $\mathcal{L}$ that set off one type of NP, this type being GS.

3. The syntactically privileged status of NPs is LANGUAGE-SPECIFIC. Thus a syntactic property relevant in one language may turn out nonexistent or immaterial in another. For example, controlling the agreement of the main verb is a mark of privileged status in Russian or Italian, while it does not appear at all in Dyirbal, Lezgian or Japanese (where the main verb shows no mark of agreement with any NP). The ability of being topicalized may be a distinction bestowed upon a unique noun phrase in $\mathcal{L}_1$ but quite a common occurrence for any NP in $\mathcal{L}_2$, etc.

This means that the definition of GS is UNIVERSAL on an abstract level and is IDIOSYNCRATIC on a specific level: GS is an NP syntactically privileged in $\mathcal{L}$ (i.e., universal)—but what "syntactically privileged" means exactly can be answered solely with respect to $\mathcal{L}$ (i.e., idiosyncratic). As a result, lists of relevant surface-syntactic subjecthood properties are language-specific: see immediately below.

4. The GS in language $\mathcal{L}$ should be defined by INDUCTION, i.e., recursively:

   a. INDUCTION BASIS. We take the most current and simplest type of sentences in $\mathcal{L}$: "basic" sentences, consisting only of a semantically one-place (i.e., monovalent) verb in the least marked, lexicographic form (indicative mood, present tense, etc.) and a noun phrase, possibly a proper noun. In all probability it will be a sentence comprising two full wordforms (and maybe an auxiliary); something like *Mary died, John is-sleeping, Mother stands-up*, etc. The only nominal form or phrase in such basic sentences of $\mathcal{L}$ is taken to be the grammatical subject. It is called the **basic grammatical subject** and is considered as a prototypical GS, a GS par excellence, with which all other nominal elements that can claim the status of GS must be compared.

   b. INDUCTION STEP. All other sentence types in $\mathcal{L}$ are examined and a set $\{P_i\}$ of (surface-)syntactic properties is established such that these properties: (1) are relevant for the syntax of $\mathcal{L}$ in general and (2) characterize the GS of basic sentences, i.e., the basic GS. Then, for each type of sentence under analysis, each nominal susceptible of being recognized as a GS is compared to the basic GS according to the set $\{P_i\}$. The nominal that is more similar to the basic GS than any other nominal (i.e., shares with the basic GS more properties out of $\{P_i\}$ and shares them to a greater extent) is taken to be the grammatical subject in its turn.

Thus, the following definition of "grammatical subject" can now be formulated:

Grammatical Subject

> A **grammatical subject** in $\mathcal{L}$ is either a basic GS or any other nominal that is most similar to the basic GS from the viewpoint of relevant syntactic properties $\{P_i\}$.

I do not exclude the following logical possibility: In a language, there can be several nominals in a non-basic sentence that are EQUALLY similar to what is considered the basic GS. In other words, no nominal phrase depending on a polyvalent verb is syntactically more privileged than any other one; the language in question features syntactic democracy. In such a language, the non-basic GS has to be chosen more or less arbitrarily (e.g., by taking into consideration the relative importance of different P_i). But according to the definition proposed, there can be no language that lacks a grammatical subject altogether.

The above approach to the notion of "grammatical subject" has been developed since 1974 (Mel'čuk and Savvina 1974, Mel'čuk and Savvina 1978: 29–31, Mel'čuk 1979a: 33–37) and is closely related to the well-known proposal by Keenan (1976); see also Chvany 1975: 15–16, Blake 1976: 295, and Van Valin 1977. (For a general discussion of the problem, cf. Li 1976, Kibrik 1979 and Kozinskij 1983.)

After these preliminaries, let me get down to business, namely to the analysis of Dyirbal sentences in (4) and (5).

With sentences (4) everything is rather clear. They are minimal complete utterances of Dyirbal (Dixon 1972: 70) which do not contain simpler complete utterances. Nothing can be omitted from them without destroying their grammatical completeness and autonomy; they are obviously the "basic sentences" of Keenan (1976: 307 ff).[3]

If so, the only N occurring in (4a–e) should be considered, at the surface-syntax level, to be the grammatical subject: *yaṟa* 'man' in (4a), *ḍugumbil* 'woman' in (4b), *ŋaḍa* 'I' in (4c), *waṉa* 'who' in (4d), and *Burbula* in (4e). This is precisely the traditional view. The privileged status of GS in Dyirbal consists, particularly, in its obligatory character: GS is the only SS-actant that is necessary in any minimal, yet grammatically complete and contextually autonomous, sentence with a finite verb.

In (4), the GS is always in the nominative.

What, then, is the grammatical subject in (5)? Traditionally, it is taken to be the noun referring to the "semantic subject" of the action: i.e., *yaṟaŋgu* 'man' in (5a), *ḍugumbiṟu* 'woman' in (5b), *ŋaḍa* 'I' in (5c), etc. The GS of the verb *balgal* 'hit, kill' is believed to be the noun referring to the hitter, while the noun referring to the one receiving the blows, i.e., *ḍugumbil* 'woman' in (5a), *yaṟa* 'man' in (5b), etc., is analyzed as the direct grammatical object (GO^{dir}). In terms of such an analysis, GS in (5) and GS in (4) turn out to occur in different cases: in the latter GS is in the nominative; in the former it is in the instrumental. However, GO^{dir} in (5a–c), (5e) and (5g) has the form (with a zero suffix) identical with the form of GS in (4). That is why Australian linguists consider group (5) sentences as clear examples of the classical ergative construction.

Still, the traditional analysis of group (5) sentences leaves the following complication unresolved: in (5d) and (5f), the GO^{dir}, i.e., ŋayguna 'me' and waṇuna 'whom', has a form different from the GS of such verbs as baniy 'come' (ŋaḍa 'I' and waṇa 'who'). Moreover, in (5h) we have Burbulaṇa beside Burbula. This is the "accusative" just mentioned, and it compels realization of a new fact about Dyirbal: here, the GO^{dir} does not, generally speaking, coincide in case with the GS of baniy-type verbs—at least under certain lexical constraints on this GO^{dir}. Ergo, the ergative construction (EC) of Dyirbal is not quite the classical type: sometimes[4] the Dyirbal EC has its GO^{dir} in the "accusative", which is in sharp contrast to genuine classical ECs of Georgian, Dargwa, Alutor (see Chapter 7) or Chukchee, where GO^{dir} always occurs in the nominative, and where the accusative, as a special case of the grammatical direct object, is absent altogether.

In principle, there is nothing disconcerting about the last conclusion; on the contrary, purely theoretical considerations suggest that EC with GO^{dir} in the accusative—and with GS, clearly, not in the nominative—CAN occur. In terms of the traditional analysis pushed to its logical limits, Dyirbal yields a valid example of a deductively predicted phenomenon.

The real difficulty lies elsewhere: why, indeed, should N_{instr} in (5) be considered the grammatical subject? From what does this follow? Obviously, from the realm of semantics alone. However, when deciding on surface-syntactic (SS-) roles one cannot, as stated above, proceed from semantic considerations, i.e., one must not look for an actor or causer, or distinguish between an actor and something being in a state or changing its state as a result of causation. When we aim at establishing the SS-role of a sentence constituent, we should use only SS-considerations, i.e., we should take into account only SS-properties of this constituent. However, SS-properties such as linear position and verb agreement, which, generally speaking, are highly relevant, cannot be used at all in Dyirbal (see pp. 155 and 159). Therefore, we have to find other SS-properties P_i of nominal constituents that are relevant in this language. Thereafter, the problem of GS in (5) can be solved in the following manner, suggested in assumption 4 above (on page 162), i.e. recursively or by induction:

a. Any group (4) sentence has only one N (in the nominative); this N, as has been indicated above, is its GS. This is the basic GS of Dyirbal.

b. Any group (5) sentence has two Ns: one is in the instrumental, the other in the "accusative" (or nominative). Of these, GS is the N that, from the viewpoint of Dyirbal relevant SS-properties, is more similar to the basic GS (i.e., to N_{nom}) in group (4) sentences.

Note that the same idea for defining the GS in Australian languages is suggested in Blake (1976: 295): "The GS of the transitive verb is determined on the basis of which nominal constituent shares grammatical properties with the nominal constituent of an intransitive clause."

Thus the problem we face immediately is to find the set {P$_i$} of relevant SS-properties that will isolate in Dyirbal the priviledged N in "transitive" sentences. Proceeding from the facts cited in Dixon (1972), I can state seven such properties, which I will take now in turn. Two of them are BEHAVIORAL properties (p. 161, **A**), and in a sense, these are central when checking the similarity/dissimilarity of a candidate for GS with the accepted basic GS (in group (4) sentences): nondeletability and gapping-collapsibility. The five others are INTERPRETATION properties (p. 161, **C**).

2. Subjecthood Properties in Dyirbal

Property 1: BEING NONDELETABLE

Nondeletability (called also "indispensability," see Van Valin 1977: 690) is a powerful test for the priviledged status of an NP. More accurately, the property of nondeletability may be formulated as follows:

(6) | **1.** A noun phrase is said to be **nondeletable in a given sentence S** if and only if it cannot be deleted from the surface-syntactic structure of S without affecting its grammaticality or the degree of its independence from the broader linguistic context.
2. A noun phrase nondeletable in all[5] sentences of languages $\mathcal{L}$ is said to be **nondeletable in $\mathcal{L}$** .

It should be emphasized that what is meant by definition (6) is deletability in surface-syntactic structures, and not in actual sentences; cf., in this connection, Chapter 3, pp. 113 **(I)**, and 139.

Note that in English it is GS (and only GS) that is nondeletable, among all types of NP. To put it differently, if the surface-syntactic structure of a grammatical sentence in English includes only one NP it must be the GS.[6]

To make the meaning of definition (6) quite clear, we need a short terminological digression, which will allow us to avoid a confusion between two related phenomena: the (surface-syntactic) **ellipsis** of an item and the **deletion** of an item from the sentence.

Ellipsis

An item A is omitted only from the actual physical form of the sentence (i.e., from its DMorphS), but it is present in its surface-syntactic structure (as well as in its deep-syntactic structure) and contributes to its overall meaning. The elliptical omission is carried out according to language-specific rules, optional or obligatory, based on the syntactic context; therefore, A is always recoverable. A typical example of ellipsis (in addition to the grammatical subjects of imperative sentences, etc., see Note 6, p. 198) is as follows:

John kissed Ann, and Bob kissed Mary⇒John kissed Ann, and Bob Mary with the second *kissed* [i.e., 'Bob kissed Mary'] undergoing ellipsis (but appearing in the SSyntS of the sentence).

Deletion

An item *A* is omitted from the sentence altogether (i.e., from all its representations), so that it is not recoverable and does not contribute to the meaning:

John is sleeping in the kitchen⇒John is sleeping

with *in the kitchen* deleted.

What we are interested in now is deletion, and not ellipsis.

It was already indicated that in sentences (4) the GS [i.e., NP_{nom}] cannot be deleted without destroying grammatical completeness. In sentences (5), the nominal constituent that cannot be deleted is N_{nom}—or, in my terms, $N_{"acc"}$, i.e., the "semantic object" phrase:

(7) **a.** **ba + ŋgu + l yaṟa + ŋgu balga + n*
'The man hit' (cf.(5a)).
b. **ɲaḍa balga + n*
'I hit' (cf.(5c)).

Yet, any N_{instr} in (5) can be deleted with null effect on grammatical completeness and autonomy. Dixon (1972: 70) emphasizes that

(8) *bala + n ḍugumbil balga + n*
'The woman was-hit' (cf.(5a))

and

(9) *ŋay + guna balga + n*
'I was-hit' (cf.(5d))

are absolutely normal sentences and perfectly acceptable out of context (the actor in (8) and (9) is as unspecified as it is in the English glosses). The same holds concerning ANY Dyirbal sentence containing both a $NP_{"acc"}$ and a NP_{instr}: in Dyirbal, a NP_{instr} is deletable, while a $NP_{"acc"}$ is not.

We see that, with respect to nondeletability, $N_{"acc"}$, when used with verbs of the *balgal*-type in sentences (5), i.e., the NP referring to the "semantic object", is much more like the basic GS of sentences (4) than is N_{instr}—the "semantic subject" NP.

Another important terminological digression is now in order. I have to say a few words concerning the expressions "semantic subject" and "semantic object". These phrases are used throughout this book as handy labels, or abbreviations, whose content will be specified below. Note that they have nothing to do with the communicative structure of sentences (topicalization, emphasis and the like), but denote—somewhat unconventionally, I admit—deep-syntactic actants fulfilling specified semantic roles.

The "semantic subject" and "semantic object" of a verb are determined according to its basic, i.e., lexical, diathesis only. (For a discussion of diathesis see below, p. 176.) In non-basic, or derived, diatheses the "semantic subject" (SemSubj) or "semantic object" (SemObj) of a verb is the deep-syntactic actant that corresponds to the same variable in its semantic representation as the SemSubj/SemObj of the basic diathesis. For example, if the "semantic subject" of *(to) kill* is its 1st DS-actant (its GS at the level of surface syntax), then the "semantic subject" of *(to) be killed (by somebody)* is its 2nd DS-actant (its agentive complement—CO^{agent}—in surface syntax): in *John killed Mary* the SemSubj is *John*, and in *Mary was killed by John* the SemSubj is still *John*—the killer, or the causer of dying.

"Semantic Subject." If the meaning of the verb in question includes the component 'cause', then its "semantic subject" is the DS-actant that corresponds to the semantic Causer (or to the Cause); if the meaning of the verb does not include 'cause', then its "semantic subject" is the DS-actant that is treated (by the given language) in the surface-syntactic structure in exactly the same way as are the "semantic subjects" of the 'cause'-verbs. For example, Causers in English are normally implemented on the surface by GSs of verbs in their basic diathesis; Perceivers are also implemented by GSs; therefore, Perceivers are "semantic subjects" of English verbs of perception. In another language, however, the Causers may still be implemented by GSs while GSs of verbs of perception may be the Objects Perceived rather than the Perceivers. In such a language, the Perceivers are relegated to the status of indirect grammatical objects, that is, we get something like 'to-me he is-visible' meaning 'I see him'; the "semantic subject" of a similar perception verb is the Object Perceived, and not the Perceiver.

What this means is that "semantic subject" in our system is in no way a purely semantic and therefore universal concept; it is language-specific. A SemSubj is either the Causer or something that the language under analysis chooses to view in a similar manner at the surface-syntactic level.

"Semantic Object." The "semantic object" is defined in much the same way as the SemSubj, except for the following difference: instead of Causer or Cause, I isolate the 'actant changing its state as a result of the causation', or the Causee, so to speak. The SemObj of a 'cause'-verb is the DS-actant corresponding to the Causee; with other verbs the SemObj is the DS-actant that fulfills, in the surface-syntactic structure, the same role as the SemObj of 'cause'-verbs. Thus, what has been said of "semantic subjects" is also true of "semantic objects": the latter are language-specific as well.[7]

And now back to subjecthood properties in Dyirbal.

Property 2: BEING GAPPING-COLLAPSIBLE

This property is often referred to as "coordination possibility" (see, e.g., Comrie 1978: 346–348), "conjoinability" (Mel'čuk 1979a: 38), or "coreferential deletion across coordinate conjunctions" (Van Valin 1977: 691), but the newly coined term above now seems preferable to me. The reason will become clearer in the course of the subsequent account.

Let there be, in a given language $\mathcal{L}$, a surface-syntactic configuration

(10) $A \xleftarrow{\;r_1\;} X$ and $A \xleftarrow{\;r_2\;} Y$,

where the two As stand for two lexically and referentially identical nominal phrases, and r_1 and r_2 are two surface-syntactic relations whose identity is at stake. In other words, we would like to know whether $r_1 = r_2$ or $r_1 \neq r_2$. Note that the identity of morphological markings is not required for both As; cf. Chapter 5, p. 218–219, (23)–(25).

The syntactic operation transforming (10) into (10'):

(10') $A \xleftarrow{\;r_1\;} X$ and Y,

(10') being semantically (roughly) equivalent to (10), is generally called **conjunction reduction**, or **gapping**. If, in $\mathcal{L}$, gapping is applicable to all instances of a construction of type (10), the latter is said to be **conjunction-reducible**, or **gappable**; phrases X and Y are **conjoinable**; and both occurrences of A that are **collapsed** into one, under transformation (10) $\Rightarrow$ (10'), are called **collapsible under gapping**, or **gapping-collapsible**.

The following principle seems to hold:

(11) If, in language $\mathcal{L}$, two occurrences of the phrase A filling two surface-syntactic roles r_1 and r_2, i.e., $r_1(A)$ and $r_2(A)$, are gapping-collapsible, this constitutes an argument in favor of the identity of r_1 and r_2. If, on the contrary, $r_1(A)$ and $r_2(A)$ are not gapping-collapsible, this argues against the identity of r_1 and r_2.

It is obvious that (11) is no more than a heuristic principle; it should not be applied unwarily, like a precise criterion. $r_1(A)$ and $r_2(A)$ may seem gapping-collapsible even without $r_1 = r_2$: suppose, for instance, that the second occurrence of A is replaced by an anaphoric pronoun, which is obligatorily deleted by a surface ellipsis rule (a kind of Pro-Drop). On the other hand, $r_1(A)$ and $r_2(A)$ may not be collapsible in spite of $r_1 = r_2$, in particular, if the language does not admit collapsing two syntactic items that must have different morphological markings; such is the case in Russian.[8]

Let us try to conjoin Dyirbal sentences (4a) and (5a)—'The man came' and 'The man hit the woman'—and then to effect the gapping to obtain the sentence meaning 'The man came and hit the woman'. The noun phrase denoting 'the man', i.e., *bayi yaṛa* in (4a) and *baŋgul yaṛaŋgu* in (5a), is A of (10), X and Y being the verbs *baniṇu* 'came' and *balgan* 'hit'; and we are testing the gapping-collapsibility of both As. There are no logical connectives like English *and, or, if*, etc., in Dyirbal, and the conjunction is expressed here by simple juxtaposition of the two constituents to be conjoined (with appropriate adjustments in prosody). The resulting sentence in (12), however, turns out to be inadmissible in the above meaning:

(12) *ba + yi yaṛa bani + ṇu bala + n ḍugumbil balga + n.*

Note that sentence (12) is possible, but with a different meaning: 'The man came and SOMEBODY ELSE [≠ 'this man'] hit the woman'.[9]

Similarly, we cannot simply conjoin (5a) and (4a), in that order, and then gap to derive a sentence with the reading 'The man hit the woman and came':

(13) *bala + n ḍugumbil ba + ŋgu + l yaṛa + ŋgu balga + n bani + ṇu.*

Once again, sentence (13) is possible, but only with a different meaning: 'The man hit the woman, and SHE [i.e., this woman] came'.[10]

In contrast to this, (4a) 'The man came' and (5b) 'The woman hit the man' can be conjoined freely in either order and then gapped. Conjunction in the order (4a) + (5b) yields:

(14) *ba + yi yaṛa bani + ṇu ba + ŋgu + n ḍugumbi + ṛu balga + n*
'The man came [and by] the woman was-hit',

while the order (5b) + (4a) produces:

(15) *ba + yi yaṛa ba + ŋgu + n ḍugumbi + ṛu balga + n bani + ṇu*
'The man [by] the woman was-hit [and] came'.

Note that differences in case by no means block conjoining followed by gapping in Dyirbal: e.g., (4c) *ŋaḍa bani + ṇu* 'I came' with *ŋaḍa* in the nominative and (5d) *ŋay + guna ba + ŋgu + n ḍugumbi + ṛu balga + n*, lit. 'Me [by] the woman was-hit', with *ŋayguna* in the "accusative", conjoin freely, as in (16), where *ŋaḍa* appears in the nominative as required by the leftmost verb, *baniy*:

(16) *ŋaḍa bani + ṇu ba + ŋgu + n ḍugumbi + ṛu balga + n*
'I came [and by] the woman was-hit'.

And if we conjoin the same sentences in the inverse order, i.e., (5d) + (4c), we again get a grammatically well-formed sentence:

(17) *ŋay + guna ba + ŋgu + n ḍugumbi + ṛu balga + n bani + ṇu* 'I [by] the woman was-hit [and] came'.

This time *ŋayguna* occurs in the "accusative", since the left-most verb in (17), *balgal*, governs the "accusative" of its "semantic object" NP.

Examples (13)–(17) clearly show that $N_{\text{“acc”}}$ of *balgal*-type verbs rather than N_{instr} is syntactically isofunctional with our basic GS of the *baniy*-type verbs. From the viewpoint of gapping-collapsibility, the "semantic object" NP is much more similar to the basic GS than the "semantic subject" NP. Dixon himself asserts that "irrespective of realizational identities or differences [i.e., irrespective of grammatical case—I.M.], the . . . syntactic identification between simple sentences is always S(ubject) NP with O(bject) NP (or S with S, or O with O) and NEVER [emphasis Dixon's—I.M.] of an S or O NP with an A(gent) NP" (1972: 134). The statement about "syntactic identification" can be construed only as an assertion that the SS-roles of a Subject NP used with a $V_{(itr)}$ and of an Object NP are identical.

We see, then, that gapping-collapsibility also indicates that the $N_{\text{“acc”}}$ (i.e., NP referring to the "semantic object") in group (5) sentences is the GS.[11]

This fact has been noted repeatedly by Dixon (1977: 367–372; 1979: 62–65); he sums up as follows: "The rule for coordination in Dyirbal refers to the syntactic function of NPs, not their form: it demands that the common NP [i.e., the two NPs to be collapsed after gapping—I.M.] be in (surface) S [= NP_{nom}] or O [= $NP_{\text{“acc”}}$] function in each clause" (1979: 65). Given that conjoining and gapping, in order to form so-called "topic chains", is quite an important device in Dyirbal syntax (Dixon 1972: 71 ff.), we can safely conclude that gapping-collapsibility, along with nondeletability, is a crucial property of Dyirbal grammatical subjects.

In addition to these two behavioral properties of subjecthood—nondeletability of GSs and their gapping-collapsibility in conjoined clauses—Dyirbal has, as stated above, five more specific SS-properties that reveal the syntactive role identity of N_{nom} dependent on a $V_{(itr)}$ with $N_{\text{“acc”}}$ dependent on a $V_{(tr)}$— rather than with N_{instr} dependent on the same $V_{(tr)}$. SS-properties 1 and 2 concern the grammaticality (or well-formedness) of surface-syntactic structure (SSyntS) in Dyirbal. Nondeletability characterizes absolute grammaticality, and gapping-collapsibility reveals relative grammaticality, i.e., grammaticality with respect to a particular meaning. However, SS-properties 3–7 are connected with the correspondence between the SSyntS of a sentence and (in the ultimate analysis) its semantic representation; they are not a function of the SSyntS as such. These properties characterize the similarity of certain SS-items from the viewpoint of the mapping SSyntS ⇔ SemR. Properties 3–7 are as follows:

Property 3: BEING THE SEMANTIC TARGET OF THE VERBAL SUFFIX
        -*ḍay*

The verbal aspectual (≅ frequentative) suffix -*ḍay* may indicate large quantity of referent(s) of either NP_{nom} or $NP_{\text{“acc”}}$, but never of NP_{instr} (or NP_{dat}; Dixon 1972: 250):

(18) a. *ba+yi yaṟa* [N_{nom}] *ŋinan+ḍa+ŋu* [< *ŋinay+ḍay+nu*]
        'The man sat-down-many',
        i.e., 'Many men sat down'.

b. *bala + m miraṇ* [N‧‧acc‧‧] *ba + ŋgu + l yaṛa + ŋgu* [N$_{instr}$]
gundal + ḍa + ṇu
'The black-bean [by] the man was-gathered-many [= put in the dilly
bag]',
i.e., 'The man put lots of beans in his dilly bag' (but not *'Many men
put beans . . .').

c. *ba + yi yaṛa* [N$_{nom}$] *gundal + ŋa + ḍa + ṇu ba + gu + m*
miraṇ + gu [N$_{dat}$]
'The man gathered-many the black-bean',
i.e., 'Many men put beans in their dilly bags' (but not *'. . . put lots
of beans').

d. *ba + yi yaṛa* [N‧‧acc‧‧] *ba + ŋgu + n ḍugumbi + ṛu* [N$_{instr}$]
ba + gu + m wuḍu + gu [N$_{dat}$] *wugal + ḍa + ṇu*
'The man [by] the woman [to] the food was-given-many',
i.e., 'Many men were given food by the woman' (but neither *'. . .
were given lots of food' nor *'. . . by many women').

e. *ba + ŋgu + n ḍugumbi + ṛu* [N$_{instr}$] *bala + m wuḍu* [N‧‧acc‧‧]
wugal + ḍa + ṇu
'[By] the woman the food was-given-many',
i.e., 'The woman distributed lots of food' (but not *'Many
women . . .').

In (18c), we see a passive verb: *gundal-ŋay* vs. *gundal-*, so that the syntactic
roles of *yaṛa* 'man' and *miraṇ* 'beans' are inverted here with respect to (18b). In
(18d) and (18e) we have two different syntactic modifications of the verb *wugal*
'give', very much like English (*The man was given some food* vs. *The food was
given to the man*).

It is interesting to note that gapping-collapsibility (especially in connection
with the use of *-ŋay* and *ŋura*-forms) and the suffix *-ḍay* are also mentioned by
Blake (1976: 289) as important evidence substantiating the syntactic identification of N$_{nom}$ in an intrasitive clause with N‧‧acc‧‧ in a transitive clause.

Property 4: BEING THE SEMANTIC TARGET OF THE PARTICLE *wara*
The adverbial particle *wara* 'wrongly, badly' always qualifies the referent of
N$_{nom}$ or N‧‧acc‧‧ but never that of N$_{instr}$ or of the verb:

(19) **a.** *ba + yi yaṛa* [N$_{nom}$] *wara bani + ṇu*
'The man wrongly came',
i.e., 'The wrong man came' [e.g., the audience was waiting not for
him, but for somebody else].

b. *bala yugu* [N‧‧acc‧‧] *ba + ŋgu + l yaṛa + ŋgu* [N$_{instr}$] *wara nudi + n*
'The tree [by] the man wrongly was-cut',
i.e., 'The man cut the wrong tree' (but neither *'The wrong man . . .'
nor *'. . . cut in a wrong way').

Compare also the place name *Guṟawarabaḍanmi*, which occurs in Dyirbal myths (Dixon 1972: 390, Sentence 29). This name is built on the sentence *bala + n guṟa wara baḍ*an 'The woman's-sex-organ wrongly was-bitten', i.e., 'The wrong woman's sex organ was bitten' and means '[The place] where the wrong woman's sex organ was bitten' (but neither, say, *'. . . by the wrong man' nor *'. . . in a wrong way').

Property 5: CONTROLLING EQUI-NP DELETION
WITH THE INFINITIVE OF PURPOSE

Dyirbal has constructions with the infinitive of purpose, marked by -*i/-gu* ending (Dixon 1972: 160 labeled it "purposive inflection"), something like [*I came*] *to tell* [*him*], etc. This infinitive is SS-dependent on the main verb, and what should be its own dependents in the form of

$$N_{nom}(V_{(itr)inf}) \text{ and } N_{\text{"acc"}}(V_{(tr)inf})$$

are obligatorily deleted on the surface—in much the same way as the "semantic subject" of the infinitive in English: *He came to* [**he*] *listen to the music* or *He brought her to his place to* [**she*] *listen to the music*. But in contrast to English (and scores of other languages), where the actant (of the infinitive) to be deleted is the "semantic subject" of the infinitive and can be coreferential with both GS and GO^{dir} of the matrix verb [*he came—he listens* and *he brought her—she listens*], Dyirbal imposes two important restrictions on its infinitives. First, with an infinitive, only the dependent NP supposed to be in the nominative or in the "accusative" undergoes compulsory deletion; the "semantic subject" of the infinitive, if the former is in the instrumental, i.e. N_{instr}, may be present in the sentence, cf. *ḍugumbiṟu* in (20f). Second, the deleted actant of the infinitive may be coreferential only with either $N_{nom}(V_{(itr)})$ or with $N_{\text{"acc"}}(V_{(tr)})$—never with $N_{instr}(V_{(tr)})$, cf. (20c). See the examples:

(20)   **a.**   *bala + n ḍugumbil bani + ṇu miyanday + gu*
        'The woman came to-laugh'.
     b.   *bala + n*   *ḍugumbil*   *bani + ṇu*   *ba + gu + m*   *miraṇ + gu*[N_{dat}]
        babil + ṇay + gu
        'The woman came the black-beans to-scrape'.

In (20b), the verb *babil* 'scrape' is of necessity in the -*ṇay*-form (i.e., in the passive), since it must be intransitive, so that its "semantic subject" (= 'the woman') be in the nominative and its "semantic object" (= 'the beans'), in the dative. Otherwise, its "semantic object" would be in the "accusative": *bala + m miraṇ ba + ṇgu + n ḍugumbi + ṟu babi + n*, lit. 'The beans [by] the woman are-scraped'; therefore, this SemObj [= 'beans'] cannot stay with an infinitive (following the first restriction) and must be deleted—but it cannot be deleted, either (following the second restriction), since there is nothing in the sentence for it to be coreferential with. As a result, the sentence (20c)

c. *bala +n ḍugumbil bani+ ṇu bala+m miraṇ babil+i*

is totally ungrammatical; while if we delete *balam miraṇ* with a "transitive" infinitive anyway, the sentence will be grammatical but meaningless:

d. *bala+n ḍugumbil bani+ṇu babil+i*
'The woman came [for somebody] to-scrape [her]',
i.e., 'to be scraped'.

e. *bala+n ḍugumbil ba+ŋgu +l yaṟa+ŋgu wawu+n*
ŋayi+nba+gu [N_{dat}; *-nba* is a rare plural suffix] *balgal+ ŋay+gu*
'The woman [by] the man was-fetched girls to hit',
i.e., 'The man fetched the woman in order for her to beat up girls'.

f. *bala+n ŋayi+nba ba+ŋgu+l yaṟa+ŋgu wawu+n ba+ŋgu+n*
ḍugumbi+ṟu balgal+i
'The girls [by] the man were-fetched [for] the woman to-hit',
i.e., 'The man fetched the girls in order for the woman to beat them up'.

The following sentence:

g. *bala+n ŋayi+nba ba+ŋgu+l yaṟa+ŋgu wawu+n balgal+i*
'The girls [by] the man were-fetched to-hit'

does not overtly specify the agent who is to do the beating (although the context can make it obvious that it will be 'the man'), but leaves no doubt as to who will be the victims: the girls, since the deleted $N_{\text{"acc"}}$ actant of a transitive infinitive can be only coreferential with the N_{nom} or $N_{\text{"acc"}}$ actant of the main verb.

The meaning 'The man fetched the girls in order to beat them up' (implying that the man himself will be the beater) must be expressed by (20h):

h. *ba+yi yaṟa wawul+ŋa+ṇu ba+gu+n ŋayi+ nba+gu* [N_{dat}]
balgal+ŋay+gu

with two passivizations (*wawul+ŋa+ṇu* and *balgal+ŋay+gu*), necessary in order to have the agent—*bayi yaṟa*—both times in the nominative.

To put the matter differently, sentences (20) clearly suggest that the application of the Equi-NP deletion transformation involving a purposive infinitive is controlled by either N_{nom} or $N_{\text{"acc"}}$ but never by N_{instr}.

Property 6: DENOTING THE "INITIATOR"
IN INFINITIVE-AS-MAIN-VERB CONSTRUCTIONS

Infinitive-as-main-verb constructions in Dyirbal show close structural resemblance to their Russian counterparts (of the kind *A carica—xoxotat'* 'And the tsarina [began] to laugh madly' of *A Koljun'ka—nu celovat' Natašu* 'And our little Nick [began] to kiss Natasha madly') but have a considerably different meaning. In Russian such a construction conveys 'sharp beginning of an energetic activity' while in Dyirbal it indicates that 'the situation is implicated by the behavior or desires of one of its actants', which can be loosely called the Initiator. In an infinitive-as-main-verb construction, the Initiator may be the referent of only either $N_{nom}(V_{(itr)inf})$ or $N_{\text{"acc"}}(V_{(tr)inf})$ but not of N_{instr}, as shown by (21):

(21)   **a.** *bala + n ḏugumbil miyanda + ɳu*
'The woman is laughing'
vs.
b. *bala + n ḏugumbil miyanday + gu* [V_{inf}]
'The woman wants-to-laugh',
i.e., something has happened to make her want to laugh, and she will have to restrain herself to avoid doing so.
c. *bala + n ḏugumbil ba + ŋgu + l yaṟa + ŋgu balga + n*
'The man hit the woman'
vs.
d. *bala + n ḏugumbil ba + ŋgu + l yaṟa + ŋgu balgal + i*
'The man hit the woman complying with her desire',
i.e., 'The woman managed-to-be-hit [by] the man'.

Sentence (21d) clearly implies that the woman was willing, or at least voluntarily allowed herself, to be hit and, although fully grammatical, sounds odd (Dixon 1972: 69, 146).[12] With the verb *wadil-* 'screw' instead of *balgal-*, however, no difficulty would arise:

e. *bala + n ḏugumbil ba + ŋgu + l yaṟa + ŋgu wadil + i*
'The woman managed-to-be-screwed [by] the man'.

Cf. also the following pair:

f. *ba + yi yaṟa ba + gu + n ḏugumbil + gu balgal + ŋa + ɳu*
'The man hit the woman'
vs.
g. *ba + yi yaṟa ba + gu + n ḏugumbil + gu balgal + ŋay + gu*
'The man managed-to-hit the woman'.

In contrast to (21d), sentences (21e) and (21g) are semantically quite normal.

Property 7: BEING THE COREFERENTIAL ACTANT
OF THE -*ɳura* VERBAL ADVERB
The -*ɳura*-form and its usage are characterized in some detail below, in Note 10, p. 199. Suffice it to say here that the actant of the -*ɳura*-form which is

coreferential with an actant of the governing verb and thereby allows the use of the -ηura-form can only be N_{nom} or $N_{\text{"acc"}}$, but by no means N_{instr}. In other words, the shared actant of the -ηura adverb is N_{nom} or $N_{\text{"acc"}}$.

Let us summarize what has been established so far: N_{nom} and $N_{\text{"acc"}}$ have many surface-syntactic properties in common. Such properties are best stated by positing an identical SS-role for both; unless such a role is recognized, several syntactic statements must be repeated in a description of Dyirbal: once for N_{nom} and a second time for $N_{\text{"acc"}}$.[13] This common role of N_{nom} and $N_{\text{"acc"}}$ is privileged in Dyirbal: all and only those Ns fulfilling it 1) are nondeletable in all Dyirbal sentences, 2) are gapping-collapsible, 3) constitute targets of the suffix -day, 4) can be qualified by the particle *wara*, 5) control Equi-NP deletion, 6) implicate the situation described by an infinitive sentence and 7) can be the shared actant of a -ηura verbal adverb. Consequently, it would seem reasonable to call this role GRAMMATICAL SUBJECT. The general conclusion is obvious: the traditional view of the syntactic structure of sentences (5) is wrong. In (5) the GS is $N_{\text{"acc"}}$, i.e., the NP referring to "semantic object" rather than to "semantic subject". As for the NP referring to the "semantic subject" (i.e., N_{instr}), it constitutes an agentive complement at the level of surface syntax. (Note that being an exponent of agentive complements is one of the typical functions of the instrumental in many languages.) Thus the Dyirbal sentence

(5a)　　*bala* + *n ḍugumbil ba* + *ŋgu* + *l yaṛa* + *ŋgu balgan*

is—from the viewpoint of its structure—better rendered by a passive English sentence: *The woman was hit by the man*, since the grammatical subject in (5a) is its "semantic object"—*balan ḍugumbil*.[14]

Four important corollaries follow from the conclusion arrived at in Section III, namely, that the GS of the sentences in (5) is the NP in the "accusative", and not the NP in the instrumental. The corollaries involve the following topics:

1. "Transitive" verbs in Dyirbal, and transitivity in general.
2. "Accusative" in Dyirbal, and noun cases in general.
3. "Ergative Construction" (EC) in Dyirbal, and the notion of EC in general.
4. "Active" and "passive" voice in Dyirbal, and grammatical voice in general.

All these will be dealt with in subsequent sections.

IV. "Transitive" Verbs in Dyirbal

The Dyirbal verb *balgal-* 'hit' has (nearly) the same semantic representation (SemR) as its Indo-European equivalents, e.g., Russ. *udarjat'* 'hit', Eng. *hit*, etc.:

(22)   'X causes that X's hand or the object X is holding in X's hand comes sharply in contact with Y (with the purpose that it does harm to Y)'.[15]

However, even though the SemRs of *balgal-*, *udarjat'*, and *hit* are identical, *balgal-* differs radically from its Indo-European partners by its **diathesis**, that is, by the specific correspondence between its semantic and syntactic actants (Mel'čuk 1974a: 134–139 and 1982: 130–131, note 24; cf. also Note 1 in Appendix, Chapter 2, p. 101). Deep-syntactic (DS-)actant 1 of *balgal-* corresponds to Y in (22), while DS-actant 1 of *udarjat'* or *hit* corresponds to X.[16]

Below are the diatheses of the three verbs. The top row contains the semantic actants, and the bottom row, the deep-syntactic actants.

balgal-			*udarjat'* / *hit*	

X	Y
2	1

X	Y
1	2

It can be immediately seen that *balgal-* shows a converse diathesis with respect to *udarjat'* and *hit*, in much the same manner that English *like* [*Kolya likes Natasha*] is syntactically converse with respect to Russian *nravit'sja* [*Kole nravitsja Nataša*], which also means 'Kolya likes Natasha', the GS being, however, *Nataša*, and not *Kolja*. This converse relationship holds true for all "transitive" verbs of Dyirbal. This explains why, from the viewpoint of its Indo-European equivalents, a Dyirbal $V_{(tr)}$ seems to be "passive," so that in order to give a more literal rendering to its syntax, it is better translated by a passive form or by a verb with passive orientation (Dixon very frequently does so). Thus, *balgal-* is rather 'to be hit', 'to receive blows', *buṟal-* 'to be seen', 'to appear', and *wugal-* 'to receive', as in (18d), or 'to be given', as in (18e).

This feature of the basic, i.e., lexical, diathesis of Dyirbal "transitive" verbs is emphasized by Dixon (1972: 81–85) in his treatment of the habitative participle in *-muṇa*. If derived from a $V_{(itr)}$, this participle refers to a habitual "semantic subject" of the action: *miyanday + muṇa* means 'someone who always laughs'; but from a $V_{(tr)}$, the *-muṇa*-participle refers to the habitual "semantic object" of the action, and by no means the "semantic subject". From *ŋaṟnḍay-* 'watch, stare at' we derive *ŋaṟnḍay + muṇa* '(someone) who is always watched', and from *wadil-* 'screw' we get *wadil + muṇa* '(someone) [necessarily a woman, see Note 12] who is always screwed'. If we need to designate by a *-muṇa*-participle a habitual "semantic subject" of a $V_{(tr)}$ it can be achieved in one of two ways:

1) We may intransitivize the verb by attaching *-ŋay* to its stem: *ŋaṟnḍa + ŋay + muṇa* '(someone who always watches', *wadil + ŋay + muṇa* '(someone) who always screws [women]', etc.

2) Or we may intransitivize the verb by incorporating the object into the stem: *ḍugumbil* + *ŋaṟnḍay* + *muŋa* '(someone) who always watches women', 'a women-watcher', *ḍugumbil* + *wadil* + *muŋa*'(someone) who always screws women', 'a woman-screwer', etc.[17]

The same is true of the "normal" participle in -*ŋu* (Dixon 1972:99 describes this suffix as a special relative inflection; cf. below, p. 193). The -*ŋu*-participle of any $V_{(tr)}$ refers exclusively to its "semantic object": *ŋaṟnḍay*-'watch'~ *ŋaṟnḍay* + *ŋu* ⇒ *ŋaṟnḍaŋu* 'watched', *wadil*- 'screw' ~ *wadilŋu* 'screwed', etc. To make a -*ŋu*-participle refer to the "semantic subject" of the source $V_{(tr)}$, we have to intransitivize it by using -*ŋay* (as with -*muŋa*-participles): *ŋaṟnḍa* + *ŋa* + *ŋu* 'watching', *wadil* + *ŋa* + *ŋu* 'screwing', etc.

Nonetheless, the Dyirbal $V_{(tr)}$ looks passive only in comparison with its English or Russian equivalents; taken alone, it is not passive—until, clearly, -*ŋay* is added to the stem. There is nothing passive about the semantics of a Dyirbal $V_{(tr)}$; 'to see' and 'to be seen' are semantically identical ('I see you' = 'You are seen to/by me'), and so the corresponding verbs differ only by their diatheses. Nor is a Dyirbal $V_{(tr)}$ syntactically passive either. In effect, the passive verb form (in Indo-European and similar languages) has two specific features that oppose it to the active verb form:

—Passive is marked COMMUNICATIVELY, i.e., its use is dictated largely by context in a connected discourse, e.g., by a certain sequence of topics and comments, by old and new information, by the speaker's choices as to what has to be topicalized or highlighted etc., or by the desire of the speaker not to mention, to communicatively "demote" or, on the contrary, to "promote" a certain actant. The active, on the other hand, is communicatively neutral. This explains the fact that passive has a narrower domain than active (i.e., the use of the passive is usually more restricted than that of the active).

—As a general rule, passive is marked MORPHOLOGICALLY, i.e., passive is derived, while active is morphologically unmarked, or basic. The active form diathesis is assigned to the verb stem in the dictionary (i.e., in the speaker's brain), and the passive form diathesis is derived from the active by means of a special affix-operator.[18]

Passive differs from active by a PERMUTATION of its DS-actants (with respect to Sem-actants) such that it necessarily involves the DS-actant 1. The specific form of this permutation determines one of several possible types of passives:

$$1\ 2\ (3) \Rightarrow 2\ 1\ (3),\ 1\ 2\ 3 \Rightarrow 3\ 2\ 1,\ 1\ 2 \Rightarrow 2\Lambda,\ 1\ 2 = \Lambda\ 1,\ \text{etc.}$$

[Λ 'empty string' meaning here the deletion of the corresponding actant].

The lexical stem of a Dyirbal "transitive" verb is communicatively neutral and morphologically basic. But -*ŋay*-forms are morphologically derived and communicatively marked: for instance, they do not occur in the first sentence of a discourse (cf. Dixon 1972: 66). Therefore, forms with the lexical stems of a $V_{(tr)}$, such as *balga-n* '(he) hit', *buṛa-n* '(he) saw', etc., should be treated as active. The suffix *-ŋay*, which makes a $V_{(tr)}$ "intransitive" and changes its basic diathesis according to permutation 1 2 $\Rightarrow$ 2 1, is then an exponent of the passive. (On the terms "active" and "passive" as applied to Dyirbal, see Section V below for detailed discussion.)

Now the question arises as to whether we should continue in our use of the term "transitive" for such Dyirbal verbs as *balgal-* 'hit' (structurally, 'be hit', 'receive blows'), *buṛal-* 'see', 'be seen', 'appear'), *wadil-* 'screw' ('be screwed'), etc. Or, taking into account the fact that they are converse with respect to Indo-European transitive verbs, had we better coin a new term for them?

As is often the case where terminology is concerned, the answer depends on informal considerations, such as the convenience of a particular terminological system, or simply taste. I, for one, strongly oppose the practice of calling similar (though not necessarily identical) phenomena in different languages by different terms. I do not, for instance, like the way the term **compound word (compositum)** is generally used for German, while essentially the same unit in Chukchee is referred to as an **incorporative complex**; or that Sanskrit adjectives of the *śastra-pāṇi* type are called **bahuvrihi** (*śastrapāṇi* means literally 'sword-hand(ed)', i.e., 'having a sword in his hand') but adjectives such as Russian *sineglazyj* 'blue-eyed', which are built on exactly the same model, are never so called in Russian grammars. I believe that it is more commendable to use a linguistic$_2$ term to cover all similar phenomena quite independently of the language in which they are found. If necessary, additional modifiers (i.e., *differentiae specificae*) may be used to indicate some relevant differences. That is what I have done with the notion of "grammatical subject" in Section III.

If this tenet is accepted, then it becomes immediately clear that *balgal-*, *buṛal-*, *wadil-*, etc. SHOULD be called transitive verbs. Such a step entails redefining the term **transitive** to denote a very abstract notion having no direct correlation with any concrete semantic, syntactic or morphological properties of verbs in specific languages. It will also be necessary to shun the etymological meaning of the word **transitive**, as well as all of its Indo-European associations.

Transitive Verbs

We could proceed in the following manner: let the verbs of a given language be subdivided into two classes—$V_{(I)}$ and $V_{(II)}$—according to their relevant syntactic and morphological properties. Within each class, all members, when compared from the viewpoint of the whole set of properties under consideration, bear more resemblance to each other than to any member of the other class. Moreover, verbs in $V_{(I)}$ are mostly one-actant, which means that the majority take the construction N + V, or GS + MV (main verb), while those of $V_{(II)}$

are no less than two-actant and typically occur in the construction $N^1 + V + N^2$, i.e., GS + MV + GO.

It is important that $V_{(II)}$ should possess more specific properties than $V_{(I)}$:

—On the semantic plane, the meaning of all (or of at least most) members of $V_{(II)}$ includes the following component:
'$P_1(X, Y)$ causes that $P_2(Y)$',
were P_1 and P_2 are situations, and X and Y are actants.[19]

—On the syntactic and morphological planes, verbs of $V_{(II)}$ take a number of affixes, permit certain transformations (e.g. passivization), and, more generally, have various behavioral properties that are impossible for $V_{(I)}$ (even for $V_{(I)}$ verbs which have more than one actant, as English *depend on* or *strive for*).

—In general, the language has a means of transposing any verb of Class $V_{(II)}$ into Class $V_{(I)}$ without changing its meaning; the converse, however, is not true.

I suggest that we should call **transitive** all verbs of Class $V_{(II)}$ without regard to the morphological realization of their GSs and GOs.

It is well known that transitive verbs evince essential syntactic differentiation across various languages: a Russian $V_{(tr)}$ takes GO^{dir} in the accusative, while a Georgian $V_{(tr)}$ in the aorist series takes GO^{dir} in the nominative (with its GS in the ergative); in English the GS of a $V_{(tr)}$ is differentiated from its GO^{dir} only by linear order (commonly, GS + MV + GO^{dir}), etc. It is also well known that there is no one-to-one correspondence between verb semantics and verb transitivity: Russian transitive *blagodarit' kogo* 'thank whom' and *pozdravljat' kogo* 'congratulate whom' have as their semantic equivalents German intransitives *danken wem* and *gratulieren wem*, lit. 'thank to whom' and 'congratulate to whom'. We may go one step further and generalize the notion of transitivity to any class of (no less than) two-actant verbs distinguished in the language under consideration by a common set of semantic, syntactic and morphological properties, independent of the type to which their lexical diatheses belong.[20]

When speaking of such Dyirbal verbs as *balgal-*, *buṛal-* or *wadil-*, we no longer need to place double quotes around the adjective *transitive*. In terms of the expanded concept of transitivity proposed above, Dyirbal verbs of the *balgal-*type are clearly transitive, but with the following peculiarity: in contrast to an Indo-European $V_{(tr)}$ a Dyirbal $V_{(tr)}$ has in its active (i.e., basic) form a GS that refers to the "semantic object" of the action.

In resolving the problem of Dyirbal verb transitivity, the decisive role is played by a developed system of grammatical voices extant in the language in question (cf. pp. 223ff.). On the one hand, by involving verbal actants in some regular conversion operations Dyirbal voices convincingly demonstrate the poly-valency of the verb. Were it not for voices, one could maintain that all Dyirbal verbs are intransitive and semantically one-actant, denoting only states or processes rather than actions. (This would approximate the state of affairs in Lezgian, which altogether lacks grammatical voices; see the next chapter.) On the other hand, voices such as passive, middle or reciprocal transpose Vs of one class ($= V_{(II)}$) into Vs of the other class ($= V_{(I)}$) and indicate *eo ipso* which Dyirbal Vs are transitive.

Let me add, as a final touch to this discussion, that Dyirbal transitive verbs do not take "direct objects" (in whatever way this term may be used): they have GSs and agentive complements as their central actants. Thus we see that transitivity is not necessarily related to direct objects.

V. "ACCUSATIVE" IN DYIRBAL

As a rule, the term **accusative** is used to designate a grammatical case whose constitutive function is to mark the main grammatical object (of a $V_{(tr)}$). This object refers to the "semantic object" of the action and is called **direct** in Indo-European and similar languages. The accusative may have other functions as well, but the said function must necessarily be present.

If we agree on this characterization of the accusative, then we must admit that there is no such case in Dyirbal. The Dyirbal case that up to now has been called "accusative" for ease of exposition should not be so called, since it is by no means the case of the GO^{dir}; rather, it is the case of the GS($V_{(tr)}$). To be sure, it is a special, Dyirbal-style GS($V_{(tr)}$), i.e., one that refers to the "semantic object" rather than "semantic subject". Yet it is not a GO^{dir}, and, unlike the word *transitive*, we cannot drop double quotes around the word *accusative* and then apply it to Dyirbal: the term itself must be replaced.

The special (i.e., different from the nominative) case that marks a GS($V_{(tr)}$) referring to the "semantic subject" is usually called ERGATIVE. I suggest that the special case that marks GS($V_{(tr)}$) referring to the "semantic object" be called by analogy PATHETIVE[21] (or, in Latinized form, PATIENTIVE). To recall some of the pathetive forms in Dyirbal: *ŋay + guna* 'I' (nominative *ŋaɖa*), *waɲ + una* 'who' (nominative *waɲa*), and *Burbula/Burbula + ŋa* (nominative *Burbula*). All such forms can occur in only one surface-syntactic role: namely, that of GS($V_{(tr)}$). No other forms are possible in this role.

I cannot discuss here the issue of whether Dyirbal pathetive is a **full** or a **partial** case (in the sense of Zaliznjak 1973: 84–87; cf. Mel'čuk 1986: 61); that is, whether it should be distinguished in all nouns, or whether it is present only in the paradigms of pronouns and human nouns, while all non-human nouns that do not formally differentiate the pathetive from the nominative stand in the nominative when fulfilling the GS($V_{(tr)}$) role. Yet I would like to mention a syntactic phenomenon that seems to constitute a strong argument in favor of the hypothesis that the Dyirbal pathetive should be regarded as a full case.

A Dyirbal noun phrase can contain—in addition to the head noun or pronoun—a modifier or an attribute, i.e., an appositive noun, an adjective modifier or a participle. All nominal and adjective attributes necessarily agree with the head in case; this agreement constitutes a very general and virtually exceptionless rule of the Dyirbal language. Let us take a GS phrase with a pronominal head; the latter can occur in two different case forms: in the nominative when it is a $GS(V_{(itr)})$ or in the pathetive when it is a $GS(V_{(tr)})$. However, the nominal or adjectival attribute modifying the head remains in the same form while its head varies:

(23) **a.** *ŋaḍa bala + n ḍugumbil bani + ŋu*
        'I, the woman, came'
    and
    b. *ŋay + guna bala + n ḍugumbil balga + n*
        'I the woman, was-hit'

beside:
    c. *ŋaḍa ba + ŋgu + n ḍugumbi + ṛu bayi yaṛa balga + n*
        'I,the woman, hit the man'.

Consider also:

(24) **a.** *ŋaḍa wuygi bani + ŋu*
        'I, old [= no good], came'
    and
    b. *ŋay + guna wuygi balga + n*
        'I, old, was-hit'

beside:
    c. *ŋaḍa wuygi + ŋgu bala + n ḍugumbil balga + n*
        'I, old, hit the woman'.

In order to avoid an additional rule of case "disagreement" in sentences like (23b) and (24b), where the noun phrase head 'I' stands in the pathetive (such a rule would be completely isolated in Dyirbal), we must concede that the nominal apposition *balan ḍugumbil* and the adjective modifier *wuygi* also stand in the pathetive—although its form coincides here with the form of the nominative.[22]

As far as I know, a case like the pathetive (even under a different name) has never been considered in linguistics, neither in the theory of grammatical case nor in concrete linguistic descriptions. Yet the pathetive can be predicted on purely theoretical grounds following considerations of symmetry: if there exists a special case for $GS(V_{(itr)})$, i.e., nominative, and there exists a special case for $GS(V_{(tr)})$ = "semantic subject", i.e., ergative, why shouldn't there exist a special case for $GS(V_{(tr)})$ = "semantic object"? It is exactly such a case that is our pathetive, which, in a sense, is the converse of the ergative.

VI. NO ERGATIVE CONSTRUCTION IN DYIRBAL

Let us return to sentence (5a) and determine whether or not this construction is ergative (= EC):

(5a) *bala + n ḍugumbil ba + ŋgu + l yaṟa + ŋgu balga + n*
'The woman [by] the man was-hit'
or 'The man hit the woman'.

The answer obviously depends on the definition of EC from which one proceeds; *pour fixer les idées*, one could consider the precise definition of EC proposed by Trubetzkoy (1958: 73) and accepted by the majority of researchers working in the domain:

> EC is any predicative construction with a $V_{(tr)}$ where the $GS(V_{(tr)})$ is treated—by the language in question—differently from $GS(V_{(itr)})$.

According to this definition (and assuming the analysis of type (5) sentences put forth above to be correct), the Dyirbal construction

$$N_{path} + N_{instr} + V_{(tr)}$$
$$GS \quad CO^{agent} \quad MV$$

turns out to be ergative. $GS(V_{(tr)})$ is marked by the pathetive and is therefore treated differently from $GS(V_{(itr)})$, which is always in the nominative.

The same result obtains from what seems to be a natural generalization of Trubetzkoy's definition:

> EC is any predicative construction where GS is marked by a case other than the nominative (assuming the nominative to be the case of naming objects: the case of citation forms).

But linguistic[1] intuition tells us (or me, at least) that Dyirbal constructions with GS_{pathet} (as in sentences (5)) contrast sharply with genuine ECs in Georgian, Dargwa, Kurmanji, Alutor and Chukchee, such that it seems inadvisable to subsume sentences (5) under the notion of EC. This means that Trubetzkoy's definition as well as our generalization of it above are too broad; neither definition foresees the existence of a construction which is, in a sense, the converse of the EC.

On the basis of the Dyirbal data presented thus far, I would conclude that EC should be defined as a special subclass of non-nominative constructions according to the semantic role of GS. Namely:

Non-Nominative Construction

> A **non-nominative** construction is any predicative construction whose GS is marked by a case other than the nominative.

Ergative Construction

> An **ergative** construction is any non-nominative construction whose GS refers to the "semantic subject".

Let me emphasize that this is not a full-fledged definition of EC: such a definition is offered in Chapter 6, p. 259. To avoid cluttering up my presentation with too many details, I omitted from the definition of the non-nominative construction above the condition concerning grammatical cases that can alternate with the nominative without making the construction non-nominative. As for the notion of "semantic subject" (and "semantic object"), it has to be refined through the concept of 'causer', which in turn, is distinguished—on purely semantic grounds—by being, roughly, the first argument of the predicate '(to) cause' in the SemR of a given lexeme (cf. p. 167 and Note 7, p. 198). Later on, after having discussed the problem of EC in Lezgian (Chapter 5), I will propose a typology of predicative constructions and in this manner make the concept of EC more precise.

According to the definition above, there is no EC in Dyirbal, since a non-nominative GS in this language always refers to the "semantic object", and never to the "semantic subject". It seems to me that Dyirbal probably belongs to the many Australian languages (Lardil, Kayardilt, Yanggal and Ngarluma, to name but a few) that lack EC.[23]

However, Dyirbal also fails to meet the classificatory criteria for a normal nominative-accusative language of the Indo-European type, for Dyirbal features a quite specific non-nominative construction with GS = "semantic object". Such a construction, which has not been previously noted in linguistics, could naturally be called **pathetive**. In this manner, Dyirbal enlarges our conception of a universal calculus of possible predicative constructions, especially with regard to a typology of non-nominative constructions. And this is small wonder, since the ergative construction:

$$GS^{\text{'subject'}} + V_{(tr)} + GO^{dir}$$

and the pathetive construction of Dyirbal:

$$GS^{\text{'object'}} + V_{(tr)} + CO^{agent}$$

represent the two most important special subclasses of non-nominative constructions (cf. Chapter 6, Section III).

Thus the question asked in the title of this chapter is answered in the negative. The typical predicative construction of Dyirbal, namely, the one found in (5a):

bala+n	*ɖugumbil*	*ba+ŋgu+l*	*yaṛa+ŋgu*	*balgan+n*
the	woman	[by] the man		hit

is not an ergative construction. It is a non-nominative construction of a very specific type: with the GS of transitive verbs marked by a special case, the pathetive, and referring to the "semantic object" of the verb.

Note that the three core semantico-syntactic roles distinguished by practically everybody writing on the topic of ergativity, i.e., intransitive subject S, transitive subject (or actor) A and transitive object O (cf., for instance, Dixon 1979: 61 ff.) are marked by different cases in Dyirbal:

S by the nominative,
A by the instrumental,
O by the pathetive.

(Remember that for me, O in Dyirbal is but a transitive GS rather than a grammatical object, S being an intransitive GS, and A an agentive complement.) This situation is fairly rare in languages of the world although it is not unique to Dyirbal: the same triple distinction is known, for instance, in a few other Australian languages (in particular, Gabi).

VII. ACTIVE, PASSIVE AND OTHER VOICES AND "NEAR-VOICES" IN DYIRBAL

As noted above (cf. p. 177), the opposition between verbal forms without the -ŋay suffix and those with -ŋay is clearly related to grammatical voice; the -ŋay forms have, in fact, been called passive here. Now the meanings of both terms—**active** and **passive**—must be made more precise.

These terms are often understood in a literal, etymological sense according to the linguistic$_1$ meaning of *active* and *passive* as current words in everyday speech. Yet, even in Indo-European languages, the GS of a (grammatically) active verb is far from universally referring to something 'active' at the semantic level. Leaving aside such intransitive verbs as 'sleep', 'lie', 'stand', 'be sick', one can easily cite many transitive verbs whose GS in the active voice has an absolutely "passive" referent:

(25) *This morose, frozen, quite motionless landscape (actively)* **irritated** *me.*
Nick's look **moved** *Natasha.*
The speed of a blue whale **reaches** *twenty knots.*
The snow **covers** *the slope in a thick layer.*

Such examples show that the grammatical terms **active** and **passive** should not be equated with the semantic items 'active' and 'passive'. Terms are terms, that is, abstract labels assigned to concepts according to corresponding formal definitions.

Following a principle of terminology construction (stated on p. 178) that attempts to refine and generalize the meaning of an extant term rather than coin a new one, I will suggest a possible way toward a rigorous definition of active and passive.

We can speak about active/passive only when the language in question maintains voice distinctions; i.e., it has at least two different verbal forms with identical situational meaning but with different diatheses (i.e., correspondences between semantic and syntactic actants of the verb).

Active Voice

> **Active** is the basic voice, unmarked with respect to communicative structure and with respect to morphology (the second property is irrelevant for a few languages, e.g., for Semitic: cf. page 77 and Note 18, page 202).

The net result is that the lexical diathesis of a given verb stem always appears in the active, the exact nature of this diathesis being irrelevant. In a system of voices, the active is analogous to the nominative in a system of cases. In fact, if a language possesses at least two cases, one of these is necessarily nominative— the case of citation forms. In much the same manner, if a language possesses at least two voices, one of these is necessarily active—the voice that manifests a communicatively neutral and, as a rule, morphologically basic, diathesis; the active is the voice of the "most direct" and "simplest" denotation of a state of affairs by a finite verb. The parallelism between voice and case outlined here is by no means fortuitous; there is an essential connection between both categories, which, however, far exceeds the limits of our present subject.

Passive Voice

> **Passive** is a communicatively and morphologically marked voice that brings about the demotion of the deep-syntactic actant of the highest rank—i.e., the DS-actant 1.

There has been discussion in the literature about what should be considered the constitutive property of the passive: the demotion of the DS-actant 1 from its DS-place or the promotion of the non-first DS-actant into the first DS-place (with concomitant demotion of the DS-actant 1), cf. Comrie (1977). In this debate I take without hesitation the side of the demotion adherents, my reasoning being as follows: demotion is logically a more general operation, such that demotion can take place without promotion (which occurs, for example, in impersonal passives, as Comrie indicates; cf. Note 25, p. 205), while promotion without demotion is impossible. (For newer treatments of passive see Bresnan 1982a and Perlmutter and Postal 1983.)

With this abstract understanding of the terms **active** and **passive**, we see that such Dyirbal verb forms as *balgan, buṟan, wadin*, etc. are active, while *balgalŋaɲu, buṟalŋaɲu, wadilŋaɲu* are passive. However, it should be borne in mind that the Dyirbal $V_{(tr)act}$, when considered from the standpoint of diathesis, corresponds to the Indo-European $V_{(tr)pass}$ and, conversely, the Dyirbal $V_{(tr)pass}$ corresponds to the Indo-European $V_{(tr)act}$.

A different approach toward a definition of active and passive is also logically feasible: active can be defined through a specific diathesis rather than through any kind of basicness (i.e., non-markedness). Accordingly, active would be a voice in which the DS-actant 1 corresponds to the "semantic subject" ($\cong$ 'causer'), while passive would be a voice in which the DS-actant 1 corresponds to the "semantic object" ($\cong$ 'causee'). This definition obtains irrespective of basicness or derivedness of the verb form in question.

Such a semantics-based definition is not only nearer to the common interpretation of the terms **active** and **passive**, but also proves to be quite convenient: it permits us to speak of basic vs. derived passive and creates semantic equality between actives and passives in different languages. Nevertheless, a definition of this type would not be free of its own difficulties, for it would entail the claim that the Dyirbal passive is the basic (i.e., primitive) voice and that the active—or antipassive—is derivable from it by some sort of activization operation (the -ŋay suffix would then mark the active; etc). Worse yet is the fact that the Dyirbal verb would be transitive in the passive and intransitive in the active; there would be several different actives, one of which would turn out to approximate the middle voice. But perhaps there is nothing bad about this; in any event, a special study is needed.

The general definitions of active and passive sketched above do not claim a definitive character. I think that for my purpose, it is sufficient to state possible approaches and to point out some problems that arise. However, to be more specific, I will hereafter adhere to the abstract and broad interpretation of active and passive proceeding from the basicness of the active (stated on p. 185).

At this point, it seems advisable to supply a definition of voice (Mel'čuk and Xolodovič 1970).

Voice

Voice is an inflectional category whose elements (i.e., grammemes) specify modifications of the basic, i.e., lexical, diathesis of the lexeme in question.

Typically, voice does not affect that part of a verb's meaning that specifies the state of affairs described by the verb and can be called "situational meaning."[24]

Active and passive are "pure" voices, which do not (substantially) change the situational meaing of the verb. In addition to these, Dyirbal has two "mixed" voices: middle and reciprocal, and a voicelike category called comitative. Middle, reciprocal and comitative mark not only the change of the basic diathesis but a certain change in the verb meaning (i.e., in its SemS) as well. The three are similar to the passive in that they involve (roughly) the same change of diathesis.

Since diatheses, voices, and the like are very important for Dyirbal, it would perhaps not be out of place to survey briefly here its inventory of voices and "near-voices."

The four Dyirbal voices are as follows:

1. ACTIVE: zero exponent and basic (i.e., lexical) diathesis, such as in:

(26) *ba + yi ḍaban ba + ŋgu + l yaṛa + ŋgu waga + ṇu*
'The eel [by] the man is-speared'.

The V$_{(tr)}$ *wagay-* 'X spears an invisible Y' is in the active, with the following diathesis:

X	Y
2	1

The noun *ḍaban* 'eel' is the GS in the pathetive, and *yaṛa* 'man' functions as the agentive complement (CO^{agent}) in the instrumental.

2. PASSIVE: the exponent is -*ŋay* and the diathesis is derived:

(27) *ba + yi yaṛa ḍaban + du waga + ŋa + ŋu* [< *wagay + ŋay + ṇu*]
'The man [towards the] eel is-spearing'.

Here the verb *wagay-* is in passive, its diathesis being the converse of the active diathesis:

X	Y
1	2

yaṛa 'man' is the GS in the nominative, and *ḍaban* 'eel' is a GO^{indir} in the instrumental. The difference between (26) and (27) resembles the structural difference observed in Russian between *Kamni švyrjajutsja imi* 'The stones are being tossed by them' and *Oni švyrjajutsja kamnjami* 'They are tossing [with] stones'.[25]

Passive is formed from transitive verbs only, and the passive form itself is intransitive.

Note that the passive form admits also a different expression (on the surface) of its DS-actant 2, namely, by an oblique object (GO^{obl}) in the dative:

(28) *ba + yi yaṛa waga + ŋa + ṇu (ba + gu + l) ḍaban + gu*
'The man is-spearing [towards the] eel'.

The term **oblique object** denotes a sentence element that corresponds to a semantic actant of its governor but is syntactically linked to the latter in quite a loose way: this object can be easily omitted, does not participate in syntactic processes, etc. The GO^{obl} is very close to the 'chômeur' of Relational Grammar.

Dixon (1972: 66) points out a significant semantic distinction between (27) and (28): in (27), action, actor and goal are represented as comprising a whole event, while in (28) the event embraces only the action and the actor; the goal is described as a separate fact involved in this event or, better yet, as implicated by it. Relative remoteness of the goal in (28) is manifested by the dative of the GO^{obl} *ḍaban + gu* 'eel' and further emphasized by the word order. In a Dyirbal sentence that is neutral from the viewpoint of communicative structure, all GOs, as a rule, precede the verb; yet in (28), GO^{obl} = N$_{dat}$ follows it.

However, the contrast between the DS-actant $2 = GO_{instr}^{indir}$ and the DS-actant $2 = GO_{dat}^{obl}$ is not always possible. There are two instances where a GO dependent on a passive form (in -ŋay) cannot be assigned the instrumental:

1) When this GO is a pronoun, it must be marked by the dative. Thus, we have:

(29) **a.** *ŋaḍa* [N$_{nom}$] *ŋinun + gu* [N$_{dat}$] *balgal + ŋa + ṇu*
'I towards-you am-hitting'.
   b. **ŋaḍa* [N$_{nom}$] *ŋin + da* [N$_{instr}$] *balgal + ŋa + ṇu*.

2) The GO of a passive verb must also take the dative if this verb occurs in the infinitive rather than in a finite form, i.e., if the -ŋay form infinitive constitutes the head of a complete sentence (see Subjecthood Property 6 above, p. 173):

(30) **a.** *ŋaḍa ba + gu + l yaṛa + gu balgal + ŋa + gu*
'I [towards] the man to-be-hitting',
i.e., 'I want [am going, have] to hit the man'
vs.
   b. **ŋaḍa ba + ŋgu + l yaṛa + ŋgu balgal + ŋa + gu*.

3. MIDDLE VOICE (called "reflexive" by Dixon 1972: 89ff.). The exponents are:

-riy ~ yiriy ~ mariy ~ (-m)bariy

and the derived diathesis is quite similar to that of the passive:

X	Y
1	2

plus the following change in the situational meaning of the verb: if in the active a verb means 'P(X, Y)', than in the middle it means 'P(X, Y) in X's interest or with respect to X'. Consider, for example, the following sentences:

(31) **a.** *ba + yi yaṛa wagay + mari + ṇu ba + gu + l ḍaban + gu*
'The man spears-for-himself [toward] the eel' [cf. (28) on p. 187].
   b. *ba + yi yaṛa ḍaŋgay + mari + ṇu*
'The man eats-for-himself', i.e. 'The man is eating'.

The verb *ḍaŋgay-* 'eat' is transitive and cannot be used in the active without some indication of food appearing as the GS:

   c. **ba + ŋgu + l yaṛa + ŋgu ḍaŋga + ṇu*
'The man eats', 'The man is eating'.

d. *ba + yi yaṟa namba + yiri + ŋu*
'The man thinks', lit. 'listens to himself' (*nambal-* means 'listen').

When a *-riy*-form has no GO^{obl} and the verb's semantic content does not preclude a reflexive interpretation, it may have a genuine reflexive meaning. Dixon even draws a distinction between "true reflexives" and "false reflexives" such as those found in (31); the distinction though strikes me as being fully determined by context and hence linguistically irrelevant. Compare:

(32) **a.** *ba + yi yaṟa buyba + yiri + ŋu ba + gu yugu + gu*
'The man hides-for-himself the stick'
vs.
b. *ba + yi yaṟa buyba + yiri + ŋu*
'The man hides-himself'.

As is the case with the passive, the Dyirbal middle voice is formed exclusively from transitive verbs, transposing them into intransitives. This means, in particular, that a middle form has its GS in the nominative rather than in the pathetive.

The Dyirbal middle is a curious hybrid of voice (namely, passive) with the grammatical category found in many languages, in particular Georgian, and called **version** (namely, subjective version or version 'for oneself'). In this respect, it appears as an interesting typological parallel to the ancient Indo-European middle, which was more a version (in Ancient Greek, in particular) than a voice. The latter is shown in an insightful study by Barber (1975), who reveals the main points of contact between the middle and the passive and suggests a model for middle-to-passive transition.

The close connection between the middle and the passive in Dyirbal can be corroborated by the semantic proximity of sentences in such sentence pairs as:

(33) *ba + yi yaṟa ḍaban + ḍu wagay + mari + ŋu* [V$_{(tr)med}$].
(34) *ba + yi yaṟa ḍaban + ḍu waga + ŋa + ŋu* [V$_{(tr)pass}$].

Both sentences have approximately the same meaning—'The man spears (the) eels'—though with a minor semantic distinction: V$_{(tr)pass}$ refers to an immediate action, such that (34) contains the semantic component 'at this very moment' (the speaker sees the spearing or knows that it is taking place just now somewhere). V$_{(tr)med}$ refers, rather, to an impending action that is performed in the interests of the performer himself. Note that the SemR of (33) includes the component 'for oneself' but not the component 'at this very moment' (e.g., the man can be now out at the river looking for eels, but perhaps has not found any yet).

4. RECIPROCAL: the exponent is reduplication of the first two syllables of the verbal root plus the suffix *-(n)bariy*. The derived diathesis is:

X	Y
1	—

with the following change in the meaning of the verb: if a $V_{(tr)act}$ means 'P(X, Y)', then the meaning of the corresponding $V_{(tr)recipr}$ is 'P(X, Y) and simultaneously P(Y, X)', or roughly, 'P(X and Y one another)'. DS-actant 1 of a reciprocal form should necessarily denote a set of actors:

(35) **a.** *ba + yi yaṟa + rdi baral + baral + nbari + ŋu*
'The men [-*rdi* is a plural exponent, see above, p. 173, (20e)] are-fighting-each-other' [the transitive verb *baral-* means 'fight somebody'].

b. *ŋali ba + yi yaṟa baral + baral + nbari + ŋu*
lit. 'We-two [*ŋali* is the personal pronoun of 1st person dual] the man are-fighting-each-other', i.e., 'I am fighting the man'.

c. *ba + yi yaṟa + gara bala + n ḍugumbil + gara*
baral + baral + nbari + ŋu
lit. 'The man-one-of-the-pair the woman-one-of-the-pair are-fighting-each-other', i.e., 'The man and the woman are fighting'.

The reciprocal is also formed exclusively from transitive verbs, which are thereby transposed into intransitives.

Now comes the turn of the COMITATIVE. It is not a voice at all, yet syntactically it is close enough to passive to justify a cursory review here. The exponents of the comitative are *-mal/-mbal*, and its (derived) diathesis is:

X	(Y)	Z
2	(3)	1

plus the following change in the meaning of the verb: if 'V_{act}' = 'P(X, . . .)', then 'V_{comit}' = 'P(X, . . .) by means or with participation of Z'.

Unlike passive, middle, and reciprocal, the comitative is formed not only from transitive verbs but from intransitive ones as well—including those that have been derived by attaching voice suffixes to transitive stems (by the way, this is a strong argument against comitative being considered a voice). The comitative adds to the verb meaning the component 'by means or with participation of Z' (or 'involving Z in the situation') and provides, of necessity, a new semantic valence slot, i.e., a new semantic actant, to the verb. This means, in particular, that a $V_{(itr)}$ becomes a $V_{(tr)}$, which simultaneously demotes the DS-actant 1 of $V_{(itr)}$. That is, a $V_{(itr)}$ with diathesis:

X
1

becomes a $V_{(tr)}$ having the diathesis

X	Y
2	1

where X is expressed by the DS-actant 2, not 1. $V_{(tr)}$ with diathesis

X	Y
2	1

receives in the comitative a new diathesis:

X	(Y)	Z
2	(3)	1

Some examples are:

(36) **a.** *ba + yi yaṛa ḍana + n̠u*
'The man is-standing'
vs.

b. *bala yugu ba + ŋgu + l yaṛa + ŋgu ḍanay + ma + n*
lit. 'The stick ⟨a piece of wood, a tree⟩ [by] the man in-his-standing-is being-involved', i.e., 'The man is standing with a stick (in his hand)', or 'The man is standing on a piece of wood', or 'The man is standing under a tree (leaning against a tree)', etc.

(37) **a.** *bala + n ḍugumbil ba + ŋgu + l yaṛa + ŋgu balga + n*
'The woman [by] the man is-being-hit'
and

b. *bala + n ḍugumbil ba + ŋgu + l yaṛa + ŋgu ba + ŋgu*
yugu + ŋgu [N_{instr}] *balga + n*
'The woman [by] the man [with] the stick is-being-hit'
vs.

c. *bala yugu ba + ŋgu + l yaṛa + ŋgu balgal + ma + n ba + gu + n*
ḍugumbil + gu
lit. 'The stick [by] the man is-being-involved-in-his-hitting [towards] the woman', i.e. 'The stick is the thing with which the man hits the woman'.

Sentences (37b) and (37c) are synonymous up to the difference in communicative structure: (37b) answers the question of who is receiving the blows, and (37c) tells us about the tool of beating.[26]

The Dyirbal comitative is most remote from being a true voice, since it changes the verbal meaning in the most significant way, even to the point of adding a new valence slot. In this respect, the comitative resembles the causative. Curiously enough, Dyirbal, which lacks causative as a grammatical category, has a verbalizing suffix meaning 'to make Y X-en (X-ous)', i.e., 'to cause that Y becomes X-en/X-ous'. This suffix is homophonous with the comitative suffix *-mal/-mbal-*, cf. *waru-* 'crooked, bent' beside *waru-mal-* 'to bend', i.e., 'to cause to become bent'.

The five grammemes described above (pp. 186ff.) can be classified into two separate categories:

I. Active, passive, middle, and reciprocal are mutually exclusive within a verbal wordform, and so they constitute the category of GRAMMATICAL VOICE in Dyirbal. This solution requires broadening the notion of voice; namely, admitting, along with a change of diathesis, a change of meaning by the voice, with the condition that the latter (i.e., semantic change) not be too significant. (What a 'not-too-significant semantic change' means remains to be determined. Meanwhile, we can take as 'not too significant' those semantic changes that do not entail the addition of semantic actants.)

II. Comitative can be combined within a verbal wordform with active, passive or middle, such that the following forms are possible: *ŋugay +ŋay+ mba+ n* (*<ŋugay+ŋay+mbal+n*) 'is sitting together with those grinding (wild flour)' and *buyba+yiri+mba+n* (*< buybay+yiri+mbal+n*) 'is together with those hiding themselves'. The suffix of the middle may follow that of comitative: *ɲinay+ma+ri+ɲu* (*<ɲinay+mal+riy+ɲu*) 'is sitting down together with . . .', and even one more comitative suffix may be affixed to the result: *ɲinay +ma+ri+ma+n*(*< ɲinay+mal+riy+mal+n*) 'is sitting down together with those sitting down together'. This seems to show that the comitative is not a voice grammeme but a verbal derivateme, so that comitative belongs to derivation, rather than to inflection. Double comitatives are also possible (like double and triple causatives).

VIII. ANALYSIS OF POSSIBLE COUNTERARGUMENTS

To substantiate my proposal to consider the noun in the nominative or in the pathetive as the grammatical subject in Dyirbal, with all its far-reaching corollaries, I should examine at least the most important arguments ever advanced against this solution. I will discuss a stimulating paper by Van Valin (1977), where the problem of grammatical subject in Dyirbal arises once again. Van Valin indicates four syntactic properties of Dyirbal that identify the pathetive (**absolutive**, in Van Valin's terminology) NP as the grammatical subject in the respective sentences, and two subjecthood properties that accrue to Actor NPs (i.e., to NP_{instr}). His conclusion is that the splitting of subjecthood properties between (at least) two different sentence elements—between NP_{path} and NP_{instr}—cripples ". . . any attempt to give a unified definition of [grammatical—I.M.] subject" (1977: 694); therefore, Van Valin refuses to admit the existence of GS in Dyirbal. Were he right, my construction would collapse.

I would rather not discuss here the general problem of approaching the logically possible situation where subjecthood properties are really distributed in a language among DIFFERENT nominals. The only thing I will do is to analyze briefly Van Valin's arguments to the effect that it is the absolutive NP, or NP_{path}, that is GS and then concentrate on his arguments to the contrary, i.e., that NP_{instr} is GS.

There are, as noted above, four arguments to support the view that NP_{path} is GS:

1. Indispensability of NP_{path} (= nondeletability; see p. 165).
2. Coreferential deletion of NP_{path} across coordinate conjunctions (= gapping-collapsibility, p. 167).
3. Relativization, to which only NP_{path}s are susceptible in Dyirbal. (This means that in a relative clause the shared nominal, which is obligatorily deleted under coreference with the nominal that the relative clause modifies, occurs only in the pathetive.) Unfortunately, I must reject this argument altogether; the fact is that there are no relative clauses at all in Dyirbal. What is called a "relative clause" by Dixon (1972: 99–105) is not actually a clause, since its verb has no tense inflection, which constitutes the sole but obligatory marker of the finite verb in Dyirbal. The relativizing suffix -*ŋu*, when affixed to verbal stems, is a formant of the participle, the latter obligatorily agreeing in case with the modified noun—just as all Dyirbal adjectivals do (see above, V, p. 181). Thus, instead of relative clauses we get expanded participial constructions. Cf. above, p. 177. (Incidentally, one finds a complete lack of other types of subordinate clauses in Dyirbal. The relative clause, were it indeed present in the language, would therefore be completely unique as a syntactic phenomenon. It seems that Dyirbal does not readily admit complex sentences.)

   If such is the case, then relativization cannot be used as an argument in determining the surface-syntactic roles of nominals in Dyirbal.
4. Word order: NP_{path} occupies the leftmost position in the preferred arrangement of sentence constituents in Dyirbal. Van Valin believes that this position is typical for grammatical subjects "in most of the languages of the world" (1977: 693).

   But this argument cannot be accepted, either. Dixon repeatedly insists that word-order preferences in Dyirbal are too weak to be of any probative value in a syntactic description of the language. Furthermore, why must the leftmost position in a sentence be most typical for GSs? First of all, many Malayo-Polynesian languages (Malagasy, Toba-Batak, Fijian, Gilbertese, a number of languages of the Philippines), as well as Otomi (Mexico), Chumash (Californian Indian), Baure (Bolivia, Arawakan family) etc., place the grammatical subject in the communicatively neutral sentences in the right-most position. But even for the Indo-European or Ural-Altaic languages, would it not be more accurate to state instead that the GS most typically occurs preverbally in the position nearest to the verb? For example, the leftmost position in English and French clauses can be easily occupied by a circumstantial, although under normal conditions a nominal may not separate the grammatical subject from the finite verb.

Moreover, we should not invoke word order at all when determining syntactic roles. As established in Chapter 1, word order is a MEANS for encoding syntactic roles (much like grammatical cases), and correspondences or differences among the means used do not reveal anything about roles, since the same means can encode different roles, while the same role can be encoded by vastly different means.

Now let us turn to Van Valin's arguments in support of the NP_{instr} as GS. These are typical counterarguments I propose to refute in this section.

5. The Imperative Addressee Argument. "In English the addressee of an imperative is its subject [*(You) shave yourself!* vs. *(You) shave yourselves!*—I.M.] and in most languages the same holds true" (Van Valin 1977: 693). In Dyirbal, when the addressee of an imperative form is optionally expressed, it is always—as Van Valin says—the 2nd person pronoun, which with transitive verbs stands in the instrumental. That is, the addressee of a transitive imperative, if expressed, is the NP_{instr} and never the NP_{path}:

(38) *ŋinda bayi yaṛa balga!*
      'You [instrumental] the man [pathetive] hit!'

Thus "it is the first example of a major subject property [in Dyirbal] which is not associated with the absolute case NP [= NP_{path}]" (Van Valin 1977: 693)—but rather with the instrumental NP. This means that being the addressee of an imperative is considered to be an important subjecthood property.

However, there are two crucial points in this reasoning that at best seem unclear.

First, Van Valin apparently takes for granted the notion that in most languages the grammatical subject of an imperative NECESSARILY coincides with the addressee of that imperative, which by definition can be only the 2nd person. But I must point out that the facts simply do not warrant such an assumption. Take, for example, Spanish *¡Venga tu madre!*, lit. 'Come your mother!' or Polish *Niech cię moje oczy nie widzą!*, lit. 'Don't see you my eyes' (i.e., 'Get off!'): in both cases the addressee of the imperative (2nd person singular) and its GS (a noun: *madre* or *oczy*) are obviously distinct. Cf. also *Everybody stand up!* and the like in English, where the GS coincides with the addressee, but then both are 3rd person. Finally, in some languages—e.g., in Maori—imperative clauses are often

passivized: *Tuaina te taakan!*, lit. 'Be-felled the tree!' [= 'Fell the tree!'] etc.
Here the addressee of the imperative and its GS are distinct beyond any doubt.
Such a state of affairs is perfectly normal in a great number of languages possessing 3rd person imperatives. For instance, in Hungarian, where verbs in the
imperative distinguish all three persons of both numbers, sentences of the following type are quite common and illustrative of non-coreferentiality between
the GS (boldface) and the addressee in 3rd person imperatives: *Törjön*
[imperative, 3SG] *is* **mind** *ég felé!*, lit. 'Rise also everything heaven toward!'
(i.e., 'And let everything rise toward heaven!') or *Várjanak*[imperative, 3PL] *ez
az* **emberek***!*, lit. 'Wait these the people!' (i.e., 'Let these people wait!'). The
latter example is especially revealing: addressed, say, to a secretary, this sentence has 'these people' as its GS.

Second, contrary to Van Valin's statement, 1st person Actors with imperatives
are quoted in Dixon (1972: 120, 371) (the numbers in brackets are Dixon's):

(39)   [= 393] *ŋuri ŋaḏa wargiŋ wuga* [imperative], *ŋuri ŋinda yara wuga*
          [imperative]*!*
          'In-turn by-me boomerang be-given, in-turn by-you fishing-
          line be-given!', i.e., 'Let us exchange my boomerang for your
          fishing line!'

(40)   [= 14] *gaṇi ŋali waynḏi* [imperative]*!*
          'Come-on we-two let-us-go-uphill!', i.e., 'Come on, let us go
          up!'

(There are many examples similar to (14) on pages 368–382 in Dixon 1972.)

But if 1st person pronouns can be used as Actors with Dyirbal imperatives,
then the addressee and the Actor of an imperative need not be identical; even in
(39), the addressee of the first *wuga* is obviously 'you', while its Actor is 'I'. To
put the matter succinctly, the Dyirbal transitive imperative has the same diathesis
that all the non-imperative finite forms have. So when we say 'Beat this woman!'
in Dyirbal, we are in reality saying 'This woman be beaten!' where 'woman' is
the GS, and the addressee is always 'you'. If we do not specify by WHOM the
poor victim must be beaten, then—in conformity with the pragmatics of a normal dialogue—the utterance would most probably be taken to mean that it is the
addressee who is supposed to do the beating. Yet we can also, if we choose, indicate the beater explicitly by means of an agentive complement in the instrumental ('by you' or 'by him' or 'by Burbula').

To prove this point definitively, we need Dyirbal imperative sentences with
the Actor of the imperative form in the 3rd person. I was unable to find such sentences in Dixon (1972), but during my 1981 field trip to Queensland,[27] I readily
elicited a few from George Watson [ɲiyiḏa], Dixon's informant:

(41) a. **Rober+du** *bala+n ŋunḏa!*,
          lit. 'Robert kiss her!', i.e. 'Let Robert kiss her!'

b. ŋinda *bala yugu gunba,* **ba+ŋgu+l** ⟨**Rober+du**⟩ *bala yuguga-bun gunba!*
lit. 'You this tree cut, he ⟨Robert⟩ another-tree cut!'

An imperative sentence is quite all right, even without an overt Actor and without presupposing that the Actor is the addressee:

c. *bala yugu gunba!*
'Let this tree be cut!'

does not necessarily imply that you, who listens to me, must do the cutting.

So, as we see, the imperative counterargument must be abandoned altogether; it simply does not work for Dyirbal.

6. The Reflexivization Argument. Van Valin states that reflexivization is generally ("in most languages") triggered by GSs; by in Dyirbal it is the Actor NP (= NP_{instr}) that triggers reflexivization, as in (42a):

(42) a. *bayi yaṛa buyba+yiri+ṇu*
'The man hides-himself'.

Here reflexivization starts from an underlying transitive clause where the GS of (42a)—*bayi yaṛa* 'the man'—must be represented as a NP_{instr}. According to Van Valin, therefore, reflexivization triggering accrues to NP_{instr} (not to NP_{path}) and, as a presumably important property of the subjecthood, constitutes the second counter-example to the hypothesis "NP_{path} = GS".

However, one cannot agree with this conclusion, either.

First, in many languages reflexivization is triggered not by the GS (nor by any other SSynt-actant), but by the "Semantic Subject" (Causer, Perceiver = Actor, . . .), whatever its SSynt-role. Such is, for instance, the case in Lezgian (see Chapter 5, Note 4, p. 247). The semantic character of the reflexivization control makes it, generally speaking, an unreliable subjecthood property, which must be used with utmost care and only in a language in which it can be shown that in it reflexivization is not controlled semantically, but remains a syntactically driven process. (Such is, for instance, the case in Malayalam: Mohanan 1982: 566–567.)

Second, there is, as I have tried to show (pp. 188–189), no reflexivization proper in Dyirbal: neither reflexive pronouns nor reflexive meanings in the usual sense. Forms like *buybayiriṇu* are MIDDLE VOICE forms (meaning roughly 'be engaged in activity turned upon or concentrated around oneself', e.g., 'for oneself', 'to one's own profit', etc.) and—this is vital—admit objects that are lexically and referentially different from the Actor. Thus, every sentence of type (42a) can be supplemented with an object:

b. *bayi yaɽa buyba + yiri + ŋu ba + gu + m wudu + gu*[dative]
'The man hides-for-himself the fruit'.

Only in the absence of an explicit object and in a semantically favorable context can a middle voice form acquire a genuine reflexive meaning: 'do something to oneself'. On these grounds I must take exception to the reflexivization argument as well.

To summarize: If my objections are correct, Van Valin's analysis fails to add a further argument—beyond nondeletability and gapping-collapsibility of NP$_{path}$—in favor of NP$_{path}$ being the grammatical subject of all Dyirbal verbs; nor does it put forth a defensible counterargument, i.e., an argument in favor of NP$_{instr}$ being the GS of transitive verbs. Therefore, Van Valin's treatment does not necessitate any modifications in my description of the Dyirbal predicative construction.

What has been said above should by no means be construed as claiming that Van Valin's paper is devoid of positive content. Exactly the opposite is true: it is provocative and insightful in many respects, and for this reason deserves lengthy discussion here. (Cf. also the analysis of Dyirbal by Johnson (manuscript), which argues in favor of ergativity of the predicative transitive construction in this language.)

The conclusions obtained for Dyirbal are hopefully applicable to other languages as well: Australian, in the first place, but perhaps also American Indian languages. Thus, in Onondaga and Wichita, as far as one can judge from Chafe (1970) and Rood (1971), we find complicated relationships between GS and GO, on the one hand, and such semantic roles as 'agent', 'patient', 'perceiver', and 'beneficiary', on the other. Besides, the notions of transitivity, diathesis, voice, etc. seem to play an important role here. *Eo ipso*, my analysis of predicative constructions in Dyirbal, based upon Dixon (1972), may prove to be useful in solving some eternal linguistic problems. We will see whether this is true, at least, to some extent, when the results of this chapter are applied to Lezgian in Chapter 5.

NOTES

1. (I, p. 153.) Double quotes have been placed around the adjective *transitive* because it is used here with a provisional meaning: 'a (Dyirbal) verb such that its English translation equivalent is transitive'. Dyirbal "transitive" verbs include verbs whose meanings contain the component '(to) cause' (particularly, verbs of physical or psychic impact, such as 'cut', 'bind', 'kill', 'amuse', ...), verbs of perception ('see', 'hear', 'understand', ...), and some others. The notion of 'transitivity' will be elucidated below, cf. Section IV, p. 178 ff. In like manner, double quotes will be used for a few other expressions: "semantic subject", "semantic object", "ergative" case and "nominative" case, which have no claim to scientific status—as yet.

2. (At the end of I, p. 154.) For the present chapter, Dixon (1972) is the only source of information about Dyirbal. All facts cited in Dixon's book are accepted *bona fide*, and it is assumed that no relevant facts are omitted. Even if I have (involuntarily) distorted some linguistic$_1$ facts so that my description does not correspond to Dyirbal, this description is hopefully still of interest as a theoretical picture of a potential linguistic$_1$ phenomenon. In addition to well-established facts, a good linguistic$_2$ theory should also account for theoretically possible facts, and it is in this respect that the description of construction (1) in Dyirbal, proposed below, enriches the theory of syntax.

3. (III, p. 163.) In a favorable context we can have: (i) *ba + yi bani + ŋu* 'He came' and even (ii) *bani + ŋu* 'Came'. Dyirbal is highly prone to elliptical utterances of many kinds, but, as Dixon tells us, native speakers do not judge (i) and (ii) to be complete and autonomous sentences. Rather, (i) and (ii) are typical examples of contextual (more precisely, discourse) ellipsis.

4. (III, p. 164.) Or even always, if we assume that in (5a–c), (5e) and (5g) there are "accusative" forms that are homonymous with forms of the nominative. However, this is immaterial for the present discussion; but cf. below, Section V.

5. (III, Property 1, definition, p. 165.) I do not really mean *each* sentence of $\mathcal{L}$. It would be wiser to add here: ". . . perhaps, with the exception of some specific types of sentences that must be fully listed prior to application of the test."

6. (III, Property 1, p. 165.) Imperative sentences like *Read this book!* etc. do not contradict the last statement. Based on such cases as *Wash yourself/yourselves!* [the agreement of the reflexive pronoun with the deleted GS in number], *Don't you talk back to your mother!*, *Everybody stand up!* and the like, a GS—'you'—is postulated in their surface-syntactic structures, where this GS cannot be deleted. It does not appear in the actual sentence following rules of ellipsis. As for pseudo-imperative sentences of the type *Fuck you, you bastard!*, these are explained away in the penetrating essay by Quang (1971). The absence of overt GS in such sentences as Latin *Dum spiro, spero* 'While [I] breathe [I] hope' or Polish *Kocha ją* '[He] loves her', etc., is taken to be another case of surface-syntactic ellipsis.

7. (III, Property 1, by the end, p. 167.) It should be noted, however, that the notions put forth above in connection with causation are somewhat simplistic. In reality, the predicate 'cause' does not admit objects as arguments, but only other predicates: actions, processes, changes of state. In the sentence *John broke the window*, it is, properly speaking, an AC-TION of John's and not John himself that 'caused' the window to break. Therefore, the Causer is not actually the first argument of 'cause', but rather the first argument of the first argument of 'cause', the latter being necessarily an action:

$$\text{'cause'('action'}\underbrace{\text{('John');}}_{\text{Causer}}\text{'break'('window'))}$$

Consider also the sentence *John loves Mary*, where it is Mary who causes a specific feeling in John; but Mary is not a Causer in this case, because there is no action attributable to Mary that has an impact on John and causes a feeling of love in him. Observations such as these amount to distinguishing different types of causation: causation by immediate physical impact, causation by the very fact of existing and being perceived, logical causation, etc.

In view of the points raised above, it would be more accurate to say that the Causer is a semantic argument not simply of 'cause', but of a more complex semantic configuration, such as the one shown above.

8. (III, Property 2, Principle (11), p. 168.) Here is an obvious example: Let *A* in (10) be a noun phrase, *X* and *Y* two prepositions. It is beyond doubt that then $r_1 = r_2$. And yet gapping is possible in Russian only when both *X* and *Y* govern the same grammatical case but not otherwise:

  (i)   *pod*   *vodoj*   *i*   *nad*   *vodoj*   ⇒

        under water-INSTR   and above water-INSTR

        pod i nad vodoj 'under and above the water',

but

  (ii) *pod*   *vodoj*   *i*   *na vode*   ⇒

        under water-INSTR   and on water-PREP

        *pod i na vode 'under and on the water'.

  (iii) *iz-za*   *nego*   *i*   *radi*   *nego*   ⇒

        because.of he-GEN   and for[the] sake.of he-GEN

        iz-za i radi nego 'because of and for the sake of him',

but

  (iv) *iz-za*   *nego*   *i*   *blagodarja*   *emu*   ⇒

        because.of he-GEN   and thanks.to   he-DAT

        *iz-za i blagodarja emu 'because of and thanks to him.'

Cf. also:

  (v) **Marija* *byla*   *blagodarna*   *i*   *uvažala*   *Ivana*

        'Mary   was   grateful (to)   and respected   Ivan',

where *blagodarna* governs the dative and *uvažala* the accusative, and many similar examples.

[The correct way to say (v) would be (vi):

  (vi) *Marija* *byla*   *blagodarna*   *Ivanu* *i*   *uvažala*   *ego*

        'Mary   was   grateful (to)   Ivan   and respected   him'.]

9. (III, example (12), p. 169.) To express in Dyirbal the meaning 'The man came and hit the woman', we must affix to the verbal stem *balgal-* 'hit' a semantically void suffix *-ŋay*, which brings about the conversion of verb actants (*-ŋay* is the suffix of the passive; for more details, see pp. 187ff). With the verb form *balgal + ŋa + ŋu* [<*balgal + ŋay + ŋu*] the "semantic subject" NP stands in the "nominative" and is obligatory (i.e., it cannot be omitted), while the "semantic object" NP stands in the dative or instrumental and is optional. Thus, instead of (12) we should say (12'):

(12') *ba + yi yaṛa bani + ŋu ba + gu + n ḍugumbil + gu* [N$_{dat}$] *balgal + ŋa + ŋu*

      'The man came [and] toward the woman [he] hit'.

10. (III, example (13), p. 169.) The meaning of 'The man hit the woman and came' can be expressed by (13'):

(13') *bala + n ḍugumbil ba + ŋgu + l yaṛa + ŋgu balga + n bani + ŋura*

with a verbal adverb (of immediately following action) in *-ŋura*. A gloss that would capture the structure of (13') would be: 'The man hit the woman he-immediately-coming [after that]'.

    Given the theoretical importance of the *-ŋura*-form, it deserves a special discussion. I regard the *-ŋura*-form as a non-finite verb form (something like the English *-ing*-form), because *-ŋura* cannot be followed by a tense suffix, which is obligatory in any Dyirbal finite verb form. Rather, the ending *-ŋura* itself is a verbal adverb desinence that consists of a relativizing, or participial, suffix *-ŋu* and the locative suffix *-ra*, a pattern that many languages utilize to build verbal adverbs.

This -ηura-form is strictly syncategorematic in the following semantic sense: its deep-syntactic actant 1 (i.e., grammatical subject), which can, but need not, be manifested on the surface (Dixon 1972: 77), must be lexically and referentially identical with the "semantic subject" of the main verb. A similar situation obtains for Russian adverbial phrases such as *v polnom molčanii* 'in complete silence', which always bear semantically on the "semantic subject" of the governing verb, regardless of which surface-syntactic actant manifests this "semantic subject". Consider, e.g., Russian *Plotniki vozvodili pomost v polnom molčanii* 'The carpenters were constructing the scaffolding in complete silence' (where the GS is *plotniki* 'carpenters') vs. Russian *Pomost vozvodilsja plotnikami v polnom molčanii* 'The scaffolding was being constructed by carpenters in complete silence' (where the GS is *pomost* 'the scaffolding', and *plotnikami* is an agentive complement, as in English): in both sentences, *v polnom molčanii* bears on the SemSubj, *plotniki*. Because of the semantic orientation of the -ηura-form (it is, so to speak, controlled by a semantic, rather than a surface-syntactic, role of the governing verb's actant), I consider the control of the -ηura-form to be of little relevance to the subjecthood problem in Dyirbal and do not use it in my discussion. For further details on "semantics-based" syntactic properties, cf. Chapter 5, note 4, p. 243ff.

Dyirbal employs the -ηura verbal adverb primarily to join a sentence of the form $N'_{nom} + V_{(itr)}$ or $N''_{acc} + N_{instr} + V_{(tr)}$ (= Sentence 2) to a sentence of the form $N''_{acc} + N'_{instr} + V_{(tr)}$ (= Sentence 1, where ' denotes lexical and referential identity, shown in the sentences below with broken-line arrows); Sentence 2 becomes a nonfinite subordinate clause:

(i)   *bala yugu ba + ŋgu + l yaṟa + ŋgu nudi + n(bayi yaṟa)ba + ŋgu + l gamba + ṟu bidi + ŋura*
'The tree [by] the man was-cut [after which] (him) the rain moistened',
i.e., 'The man cut the tree until it started to rain'.

A sentence of the form $N''_{acc} + N'_{instr} + V_{(tr)}$ (= Sentence 2), however, cannot be immediately joined to a sentence $N''_{acc} + N'_{instr} + V_{(tr)}$ (= Sentence 1). To do this, Sentence 2 has to be passivized first such that the following situation obtains:

$$[N''_{acc} + N'_{instr} + V_{(tr)act}] \quad + \quad [N'_{nom} + N_{dat} + V_{(tr)pass}]$$
　　　Sentence 1　　　　　　　　　　　　Sentence 2

Now the verb of Sentence 2 (rendered intransitive because of passivization) must be transformed into the -ηura-form, which yields finally:

(ii)   *bala yugu ba + ŋgu + l yaṟa + ŋgu nudi + n (ba + yi yaṟa) ba + gu + l ṇalŋga + gu bundul + ŋa + ŋura*
'The tree [by] the man was-cut [after which] (he) the boy spanked',
i.e., 'The man cut the tree until he stopped to spank the boy'.

(The sentence *bala yugu ba + ŋgu + l yaṟa + ŋgu nudi + n ba + yi ṇalŋga bundu + n* would mean 'The man cut the tree and SOMEBODY ELSE spanked the boy'.)

That the -ηura verbal adverb is semantically oriented toward the "semantic subject" of the matrix verb (rather than toward its "semantic object") is quite typical of Dyirbal. The language possesses about two dozen adverbals, or verboids, that is, quasi-verbs that occur only jointly with a finite verb and describe the manner of action or process referred to by the latter. These adverbals form pairs such that one member is oriented only toward the "semantic subject" while the other is oriented toward the "semantic object". For instance, the "subject"-oriented adverbal *ganbil-* 'do badly/wrongly' means that the SemSubj of the matrix verb is somehow at fault, and the "object"-oriented adverbal *daral-* 'do badly/wrongly' implies that the event is unsatisfactory because of the SemObj. Thus, with *ḍaŋgay-* 'eat', *ganbil- ḍaŋgay-* means that there is something bad about the eater ('eat sloppily'), and *daral- ḍaŋgay-*, that the food is bad ('eat something stale'). For more details see Dixon (1972: 301–302).

11. (III, Property 2, at the end, p. 170.) Conjoining sentences with lexically and referentially identical grammatical subjects standing in different cases and subsequently gapping is possible in many languages with the ergative construction. Consider the following examples:

> **(i)** Georgian: *Is*[N_{nom}] *adga* 'He stood up' and *Man*[N_{erg}] *aiɣo çigni*[N_{nom}] 'He took a book' conjoin in either order, yielding *Is adga da aiɣo çigni* 'He stood up and took a book' and *Man aiɣo çigni da adga* 'He took a book and stood up'.

> **(ii)** Dargwa: *Nu*[N_{nom}] *duravxʿunra* 'I went out' and *Nuni* [N_{erg}] *žuz*[N_{nom}] *kasira* 'I [a] book took' result in two possible conjunctions: *Nu duravxʿunra va žuz kasira* 'I went out and took a book' and *Nuni žuz kasira va duravxʿunra* 'I took a book and went out'.

> **(iii)** Alutor: *ɣəmmə*[N_{nom}] *tətvaɣalək vaşqinujatikik* 'I sat-down into-other-sledge' and *ɣəmnan*[N_{instr}] *təʕalapən əlləɣən* [N_{nom}] 'I caught-up with-father' yield *ɣəmmə tətvaɣalək vaşqinujatikik to təʕalapən əlləɣən* 'I sat down into the other sledge and caught up with father' as well as *ɣəmnan təʕalapən əlləɣən to tətvaɣalək vaşqinujatikik*.

12. (III, Property 6, after example (21d), p. 174.) Neither masochism nor homosexuality is known among the Dyirbal people (Dixon 1972: 84).

13. (III, Property 7, p. 175.) Which is exactly what is done in Dixon (1972). Naturally, Dixon does not fail to notice the syntactic similarity of N_{nom} and $N_{"acc"}$ and because of this, he calls both constituents (i.e., Subject NP and Object NP) by the cover term **topic**. I believe, however, that topic is not a syntactic notion: it refers rather to communicative structure and should not be smuggled into syntactic description as such. Dixon himself does not use it in his argument, but only in informal explanations, so that this notion is of little help to him. In addition, it is hardly reasonable to call mechanically N_{nom} or $N_{"acc"}$ topic. In view of the freedom of word order in Dyirbal, the topic is probably expressed by linear position and/or prosodics. Later, Dixon switched to a better term: **pivot** (Dixon 1979: 62).

14. (End of Section III, p. 175.) An identical analysis of type (5) sentences is suggested in Keenan and Comrie (1977: 82–85); arguing along similar lines, the authors came to the following conclusion: "It turns out that the most subject-like NP in basic transitive sentences is the absolutive [my $N_{"acc"}$—I.M.] and does not express the agent" (84). Cf. also a remark in Hale (1970: 772, in 16(ii)), where he states that in Dyirbal "several syntactic rules identify the subject as the nominative NP in all sentences." However, Hale does not elaborate on this point any further, and regards Dyirbal as a "true ergative language." [Hale's nominative = my "accusative" in transitive clauses.]

15. (IV, (22), p. 176.) (22) disregards many semantic and syntactic subtleties that are irrelevant here. Dyirbal *balgal-* also means 'kill' and implies hitting with a long rigid instrument held in the hand, such as a spear. Russ. *udarjat'* admits two additional actants: *čem* 'with what' [N_{instr}] and *vo čto/po čemu* 'in/on what' (*dubinkoj v nos/po nosu* 'with a club on the nose'). Thus, *udarjat'* requires two additional semantic variables in its fully formed SemR. Also, one does not hit obligatorily with one's hand but can use the knee or head, etc.

16. (IV, after example (22), p. 176.) As stated in Chapter 1, p. 63, the number of a deep-syntactic actant is established in correspondence with its surface correlate: DS-actant 1 is mapped onto the surface-syntactic GS, and DS-actant 2 onto the main surface-syntactic GO, i.e., the one most closely connected with the verb.

17. (IV, 2, p. 177.) If the context of the discourse guarantees recoverability, the sequence -ŋay + muŋa is frequently shortened by the omission of -ŋay (Dixon 1972: 82). Thus, beside *balgalŋay + muŋa* 'habitual murder' we have the free variant *balgalmuŋa*. This shortening of -muŋa participles is a typical instance of the discourse (morphological) ellipsis which can always be restored *salva significatione*. (Out of context *balgalmuŋa* is clearly ambiguous, since it can mean either 'the one who is habitually murdered' or 'habitual murderer'.)

18. (IV, p. 177.) In Semitic languages active and passive voices are equally complex from the morphological point of view. A Semitic verbal root cannot be assigned any diathesis in the dictionary; both active and passive diatheses are shown explicitly in the verbal word form, each by its own transfix. For example, from the Arabic root *q-t-l* 'kill' we get *q-t-l* $\oplus$ *-a-a-* 'active' = *qatal + a* '(he) has killed' and *q-t-l* $\oplus$ *-u-i-* 'passive' = *qutil + a* '(he) has been killed'. Thus, the property of morphological markedness is irrelevant for Semitic passives.

19. (IV, p. 179.) Nichols (1974) makes some interesting observations concerning the relationships between transitivity and semantics in Russian verbs; the connections between verbal meaning and syntactic behavior are studied in a more general frame in Nichols (1975). See also Růžička (1970) and Růžička and Walther (1974). A classical study of transitivity as a quantifiable global property of clauses (rather than individual verbs) is found in Hopper and Thompson (1980); the authors treat transitivity as a continuum and supply a list of ten semantic factors that contribute to "high Transitivity" of a clause (such as: two or more participants; action vs. non-action; telic vs. atelic [action]; punctual vs. non-punctual; etc.). Tsunoda (1983) offers a scale of transitivity based on the "degree of effectiveness" of the corresponding verbal meaning: verbs of physical impact are more transitive than verbs of perception, the latter being more transitive than verbs of "pursuit" (*search, visit*), while these outtransitivize, in their turn, verbs of thinking, etc. Cf. also Tsunoda (1985).

20. (End of Section IV, p. 179.) EXCURSUS ON TRANSITIVITY.

The concept of transitivity is so crucial to this presentation that I really have to say a few words about it, although I by no means lay claim to a serious discussion. An interesting fact about transitivity deserves mention. Traditional grammar defines transitive verbs by two features:

1. They take an object in the accusative (or in the nominative in ergative languages), i.e., they have a (notorious) direct object.
2. They readily passivize, i.e. they form passive participles and participate in passive constructions.

However, generally speaking, these features are not sufficient or even necessary. Let us consider the transitive vs. intransitive opposition in Russian.

On the one hand, Russian has a number of verbs and verblike expressions that take an object in the accusative without being transitive, for that matter. Here are some examples (the accusative object is printed in boldface):

(i) *On boitsja* **učitel'nicu** ⟨**mamu, Borju**⟩ 'He's afraid of his teacher ⟨his mother, Borya⟩'.

(ii) The expressions such as **gore** *gorevat'* 'to grieve one's grief'; **zimu** *zimovat'* 'to pass the winter', **noč'** *nočevat'* 'to pass the night', as well as many similar constructions with the so-called "internal object."

(iii) So-called "predicatives" of the type *vidno* 'is seen', *slyšno* 'is heard', *zametno* 'is perceivable', *bol'no* 'it hurts', *sovestno* 'ashamed', *nado* 'need', *žal'* 'regret', etc.: *Mne bol'no* **ruku** 'My hand hurts', *Stalo vidno* **reku** 'The river became visible'; substandard *Mne sovestno* **Natašu** 'I'm ashamed of Natasha' (see Seidel 1983). Under negation, the accusative of GO^{dir} of such a predicative is replaceable with the genitive, as is the case of all Russian GO^{dir}s: *Mne nado knig***u**[acc] 'I necd a book' vs. *Mne ne nado knig***i**[gen] 'I don't need a book'.

(iv) A number of interjections having the meaning of a transitive verb, such as *bax!* 'hit', *šlëp!* 'spanking', *xvat'* 'grabbing', etc.: *I vdrug* **bednjažku** *cap-carap!* [Pushkin] 'And suddenly [he = the cat] grabs the poor thing [= the mouse]', *Nožičkom na meste čik* **Ljutogo pomeščika** [Majakovskij] 'With a knife on the spot [they] stab the cruel landlord', *Na(te)* **knigu** 'There is ⟨= Take⟩ the book'.

On the other hand, there are a few Russian verbs that are traditionally considered intransitive (they do not take a GO$_{acc}$) but nevertheless form passive participles and occur in passive constructions: *upravljat' čem* 'to guide, to drive' [lit. 'by something'], but *samolët, upravljaemyj avtopilotom* 'the plane guided by the autopilot'; *ugrožat' čemu* 'to menace' [lit. 'to something'], but (in the military parlance) *napravlenie, ugrožaemoe tankami protivnika* 'the direction menaced by the enemy's tanks'; *dostigat' čego* 'to reach' [lit. 'of something'], but *Vysota 16 km byla dostignuta im čerez 5 minut* 'The 16-km altitude was reached by him in 5 minutes'. At the same time, numerous verbs that traditionally are said to be transitive (because they take a GO$_{acc}$) have no passive participles and do not admit passive constructions: *minovat' (ugol doma)* 'to pass (a corner)'; *stoit' (odnu rupiju)* 'to cost (a rupee)'; *vesit' (odnu tonnu)* 'to weigh (a ton)'; *znat'* 'to know'; *žalet'* 'to pity'; *šeptat' (anekdot na uxo)* 'to murmur (a joke into one's ear)'; *dokonat'* 'to ruin, to destroy'; *naduvat'* 'to swindle, to dupe'; and many other verbs.

These examples clearly show that verbal properties such as the ability to take the GO$_{acc}$ or the ability to undergo passivization are logically independent of, and do not stand in one-to-one correspondence with, the notion of transitivity. When we call a verb "transitive", generally speaking, we thereby assign to it a whole complex of features. In Russian, for example, this complex includes such morphological properties as the absence of *-sja*, the presence of certain prefixes (*pro-, pere-, ob(o)-,* and the like), and membership in a certain stem class, e.g., *star-**i**-t'* 'to make old' vs. *star-**e**-t'* 'to become old', etc. One can distinguish among all V$_{(tr)}$s a kernel of "classic" transitives that embody a maximal number of possible transitivity properties. The remainder of V$_{(tr)}$s may lack some of these properties (i.e., they are, so to speak, less transitive), but they must still have a certain minimum of the transitivity properties that have been established for the language under consideration. (True, in certain languages the situation might be simpler; thus, in Melanesian Tok Pisin all transitive verbs and only transitive verbs have the suffix *-im* < English *him*.) Thus, in my opinion, transitivity is a typical CLUSTER CONCEPT.

21. (V, p. 180.) The term **pathetive** (in Russian: **pativ**) has been suggested in Zekox (1969: 58–59) for the so-called "absolutive" case in Adyghe, i.e., the case of citation forms, of GS(V$_{(itr)}$), and of GO^{dir}(V$_{(tr)}$).

22. (V, p. 181.) Bernard Comrie has drawn my attention to the fact that the data presented in (23) admit of an alternative description: it may be assumed that the appositive N agrees with its head in SS-role rather than in case. Under these circumstances no special statement about case "disagreement" would be necessary, and no conclusion could be drawn to the effect that this appositive N appears in the pathetive. Comrie compares

Dyirbal sentences of the type in (23) with Finnish *Otettiin ystävällisesti minut*[N_{acc}], *Kalle*[N_{nom}], *vastaan* 'They received [= *otettiin* . . . *vastaan*] me, Kalle, friendly', where the verb *otettiin* (in the subjective impersonal—a specific voice that precludes the expression of GS) requires as its GO^{dir} the accusative of a pronoun but the nominative of a noun. Nonetheless, such an approach seems appropriate only for appositive nouns and does not work for modifying adjectives, since it is obviously counterintuitive to speak of adjective-noun agreement in terms of SS-roles rather than cases. If this holds true, then examples (23)–(24) remain as valid evidence in favor of our proposal to consider the pathetive a full case in Dyirbal.

23. (VI, pp. 183.) Klimov (1973) enumerates many implications of the ergative structure of a language. If we take these into account, then we see immediately that Dyirbal does not satisfy the requirements for classification as a typical ergative language. Dyirbal maintains the opposition active ~ passive (as well as other voices), which is a deviation from the standpoint of ergative languages (see Klimov 1973: 104). Furthermore, Dyirbal has a genitive, which may be present in ergative languages, but is generally quite rare (Klimov 1973: 111). Dyirbal lacks suppletive verbal stems that differ only according to the singularity/plurality of the "object" of a $V_{(tr)}$ and the "subject" of a $V_{(itr)}$, a phenomenon that is common in ergative languages (Klimov 1973: 132–134). For a dissenting point of view concerning Dyirbal, see Hale (1970), who discusses the types of ergative constructions in Australian languages and formulates a hypothesis regarding their possible origin.

24. (VII, p. 186.) I think it is advisable, at this point, to answer the question that is asked very often: are the active and the passive constructions with the same verb synonymous? Strictly speaking, they are not: *John killed Mary* and *Mary was killed by John* have, in my opinion, different semantic representations.

In my approach (specified in the Introduction, Chapter 2, II, **2**, p. 53) a semantic representation (SemR) includes two different objects called "structures":

(i) The SEMANTIC STRUCTURE (SemS) is an arbitrary oriented graph (i.e., network) whose vertices, or nodes, are labeled with names of semantic units, and whose arcs, or arrows, show the predicate-to-argument relationships between these units. A SemS represents a given STATE OF AFFAIRS and does so more or less objectively and independently of the subjective attitude of the speaker toward his message: it lists all events and participants and records the relationships that link them. Clearly, *John killed Mary* and *Mary was killed by John* have the same SemS.

(ii) The SEMANTIC-COMMUNICATIVE STRUCTURE (Sem-CommS) is superimposed on the SemS and identifies the SUBJECTIVE ATTITUDE of the speaker toward the relation between this SemS and his message:

    a. what he takes for granted (presupposed) and what he wants to state as his own assertion;

    b. what he selects as his topic (i.e., the thing or event that he is mostly interested in and is going to discuss) and what will constitute his comment on this topic;

    c. what he wants to introduce as new information in a given sentence and what he will present as something that has already been mentioned within the same discourse;

    d. what he would like to emphasize and what he will leave neutral; etc.

In terms of the Sem-CommS, active and passive verbal constructions are different, for passivization changes the topicalization of the actants and thus shifts the main point of the speaker's interest from one actant to another one. In *John killed Mary* the topic is *John* (if neutral prosody is used); in *Mary was killed by John*, the topic is *Mary*.

Any grammatical voice that converts the actants of a verbal form also changes the Sem-CommS of the respective construction and thus the meaning (since the Sem-CommS is also a part of the meaning). So, to be absolutely precise, I should specify (in Section IV, page 176, and elsewhere) that two verbal forms manifesting different voices have identical SEMANTIC STRUCTURES rather than identical meanings; and whenever I refer to the identity of meaning among different voice forms, to "pure" voices not changing meaning, etc., the word *meaning* should be understood as 'semantic structure'. I have not replaced *meaning* by *semantic structure* only because I do not want to make the presentation still more cumbersome by introducing this distinction between meaning (i.e., SemR as a whole), semantic structure and semantic-communicative structure.

Note that the communicative non-identity of active and passive forms, i.e., the lack of full synonymy between them, has been advanced previously, e.g., by Jakobson in his 1966 paper entitled "Signatum and Designatum" (International Conference on Semiotics, Kazimierz-Dolny, Poland; see Padučeva 1967: 36–37). Cf. also Xrakovskij (1974) and excellent semantic characterization of passive in Wierzbicka (1980b: 49–69).

25. (VII, 2, p. 187.) Sentences (26)–(27) can also be compared to the following relationship well known in Dargwa: that between (i) and (ii) below.
In sentence (i)

(i) *Nu + ni žuz b + učul + ra*
'I [the] book read'

the pronoun *nu* 'I' is the GS in the ergative; *žuz* 'book' is the GO^{dir} in the nominative; the 1st person suffix *-ra* of the transitive verb *b + uč + es* 'to read' agrees with *nuni*, and its class prefix *b-* stands in agreement with *žuz*. But consider (ii):

(ii) *Nu žuz + li učul + ra* [from *v + učul + ra*] ⟨*r + učul + ra*⟩
'I-man ⟨I-woman⟩ [the] book read',

where *nu* 'I' is the GS as in (i) but in the nominative, while *žuz* 'book' is a GO^{obl} in the ergative. The verb *b + uč + es* is used intransitively and agrees with *nu* by means of both the suffix *-ra* and the class prefixes *v-* (masculine) and *r-* (feminine).

The Dargwa sentences (i) vs. (ii) resemble Russian *Oni švyrjajut kamni* 'They are tossing stones' vs. *Oni švyrjajutsja kamnjami* 'They are tossing [with] stones'.

Between (26) and (27) in Dyirbal we observe a typical active *vs.* passive distinction manifested by DSynt-actant conversion (whereby the DSynt-actant 1 and the DSynt-actant 2 are permuted). But the distinction between (i) and (ii) in Dargwa belongs exclusively to the surface-syntactic and morphological realizations. Both the GS and the GO retain their DS-roles; the SS-role of the GO, though, changes dramatically: from the GO^{dir}, it becomes a GO^{obl}, i.e., a "chômeur." (There is also a change in case assignment as indicated above.)

What we observe in (i) vs. (ii) is then also a voice distinction, but a different one: no actant permutation, only actant retrograding, or demotion; this is the distinction between the active (in (i)) and the so-called **objective impersonal** (in (ii)). The Dargwa objective impersonal has no segmental morphological marker—it is derived by conversion, namely, by changing its agreement pattern. For more about Dargwa objective impersonal see Chapter 5, p. 223.

26. (VII, after example (37), p. 191.) Dixon distinguishes two categories manifested by the *-mal/-mbal* suffix: instrumentive (formed only from a V$_{(tr)}$) and comitative (formed only from a V$_{(itr)}$ and having appreciably broader semantic possibilities). It seems, however, that this distinction is fully determined by semantic context, and therefore I regard the *-mal/-mbal* suffix as the exponent of a single comitative grammeme. This grammeme has a sufficiently broad and abstract meaning, such that the discourse situation can (when necessary) render it more specific:

(i) *ba + yi mugay ba + ŋgu + n ḍugumbi + ṛu nugay + ma + n*
'The grinding-stone [by] the woman in-her-grinding-is-being-involved', i.e., 'The woman is grinding (wild flour) by means of a grinding stone' [*nugay-* is a $V_{(tr)}$]

(ii) *ba + yi ŋalŋga ba + ŋgu + n ḍugumbi + ṛu nugay + ma + n*
'The boy [by] the woman in-her-grinding-is-being-involved', i.e., 'While grinding, the woman is nursing the boy', or 'The boy is sitting near the woman, watching her grinding', etc.

27. (VIII, after example (40), p. 195.) The trip was organized and provided for by R. M. W. Dixon, for which I owe him a pleasant debt of gratitude.

Chapter 5

IS THERE AN ERGATIVE CONSTRUCTION IN LEZGIAN?

I. INTRODUCTORY REMARKS

Lezgian is a language of Soviet Daghestan (Eastern Caucasus), the main representative of the Lezgian branch, which also includes Rutul, Tabassaran, Tsakhur, Agul, Kryz, Budug, Archi, Khinalug and Udi.

Lezgian surface syntax—more specifically Lezgian "transitive" constructions—will be our only concern here. By "transitive" construction, or "transitive" predication, linguists usually mean a tripartite formation composed of a finite verb denoting causation or perception (roughly equivalent to *cut, lift, kill, build,* . . . or *see, hear, understand,* etc.) and two nominal phrases denoting, respectively, the "(semantic) subject" and the "(semantic) object" of the action in question. Typical "transitive" constructions express such profound and provocative thoughts as

(1) **a.** 'Ali killed the dog'.
    b. 'A boy is eating an apple'.
    c. 'Mother bakes tasty bread'.
    d. 'The tractor is ploughing the field'.
    e. 'I see him'.
    f. 'He understands our question', etc.

Actually, the notions "transitive" verb, "semantic subject" and "semantic object," as traditionally applied to Lezgian, are far from being clear and explicit. However, after I have discussed them in the preceding chapter, they can be used safely, especially since I will not use them right now in any theoretical way, so there is no risk of dangerous confusion. (In this connection, see also Wilbur 1977.) Note that I am using here the same device of double quotes to indicate provisional labels as in Chapter 4.

All Lezgian sentences used to render the meanings of type (1a–d)[1] have the following form:

(2)	NP^1	NP^2	V
	Causer	Causee	Action

The nominal phrase NP^1, which denotes the causer and thus corresponds to the grammatical subject of active verbs in English, is obligatorily marked by a specific case in -*di*, used exclusively in this role. It is natural to call this case **ergative**, which is normally done.

The nominal phrase NP^2 denotes the thing changing its state (under the impact of causation; but see below, p. 209); it corresponds to the direct object in English. This phrase is marked by a case with a zero ending, which is also the citation form. I will call this form the **nominative** case. (The term **nominative** should be reserved—in any language—for the most unmarked case whose constitutive function is just to *name*—lat. *nominare*—objects. It is the only case that is normally used out of any syntactic context: as a label, in enumerations, etc. Many, however, choose to call such a form **absolute**, especially when discussing a non-Indo-European language. But I do not see sufficient reasons for this; cf. also Catford 1976: 47, note 1.)

Consider, for instance, (3):

(3)	*Ali* + *di*	*kʰiç*	+∅	*qe*	+ *na*
	Ali ERG	dog	NOM	kill	AOR

Note that in Lezgian the nominative may fulfill some further syntactic roles as well; among others, it marks the actor of an intransitive action or the subject of a state:

(4)	**a.**	*Ali* + ∅	*šeher* + *diz*	*fe*	+ *na*
		Ali NOM	town DAT	go	AOR

'Ali went to town'.

	b.	*Ali* + ∅	*kʰsa*	+ *nva*
		Ali NOM	sleep	RESULT

'Ali is asleep'.

Thus the "semantic object" of a "transitive" Lezgian verb and the "semantic subject" of an "intransitive" one are case-marked similarly, namely by the nominative. At the same time, the "semantic subject" of a "transitive" verb features a specific case-mark: the ergative. Therefore, the Lezgian construction of type (2), exemplified by sentences of type (3), is generally taken to be ergative. More than that: for some decades, the Lezgian construction under consideration has been cited as one of the most typical instances of the ergative construction.

However, in my opinion, this analysis, natural though it may seem at first glance, is wrong. Let me bluntly formulate my view of what really happens in Lezgian (the rest of this chapter is devoted to more fully substantiating it).

If the ergative construction is a specific SYNTACTIC phenomenon, then Lezgian has no ergative construction at all. The peculiarity of Lezgian sentences of type (3), when compared to, e.g., their English equivalents, resides not in syntax but rather is to be found on a much deeper level, namely, in their SEMANTICS. In such Lezgian sentences all the verbs denote states, not genuine "transitive" actions; action verbs simply do not exist in the language. Thus, instead of 'kill' Lezgian actually says 'die (maybe from somebody's hand)'; 'eat' is in Lezgian 'disappear swallowed', 'bake' is 'change [= become different] under the action of heat', and 'plow' is 'undergo plowing'. Accordingly, the agent phrase in the ergative is, from a syntactic viewpoint, the agentive complement (or even a circumstantial), and by no means the grammatical subject. Yet what is declared to be the direct object in sentences like (3), i.e., the nominal phrase in the nominative, is the grammatical subject. Semantically, k^hiç '(the) dog' in (3) denotes the thing being in the state of dying, so that a closer English rendering of (3) would be (3'):

(3')   'Caused-by-Ali the dog died'.
       Ali + di k^hiç   qena.

If this is the case, then (3) exhibits a quite common intransitive nominative construction, with no syntactic specificity at all—and the wind is taken out of the sails of those who would call it an ergative construction.

The above conclusion has been prompted by an examination of the data presented in two books by M. M. Gadžiev (1954, 1963), which offer a great number of well-chosen examples and clear explanations thereof. (However, most of the analyses and solutions put forth by Gadžiev himself run counter to what I am saying on the basis of his data.) Since I proceed only from the facts found in these books, many of my specific statements about the language may turn out wrong. Nevertheless, even if this should be the case my arguments still may be useful: they lay bare the structure of logical relations between some important linguistic phenomena (which, if absent from Lezgian, are still possible in human languages). All the assertions in this chapter are to be construed as implications: 'If the facts are such as presented, then the following holds.' And the truth of the logical implications seems to me more important than the truth of their factual premises. This is quite natural, given the preoccupation of the present book with linguistic$_2$ notions and terms, in short with a linguistic$_2$ metalanguage.

I start by proving (in section III below) that the agent NP in Lezgian sentences like (3) is by no means the grammatical subject: the grammatical subject is the nominative NP that represents the "semantic object"; then (in section IV) I argue against the idea that (3) is a specimen of an ergative construction.

II. A FEW FACTS ABOUT LEZGIAN

I give here only most elementary data necessary for the reading and under-standing of the examples.

1. Phonology

The Lezgian (and some other) examples are cited in an (almost) generally ac-cepted phonemic transcription. Some conventions:

$\underset{.}{C}$ = ejective consonant (pronounced with one's larynx closed)
C^w = labialized consonant
C' = palatalized consonant
C^h = aspirated consonant

(in most cases, Lezgian voiceless consonants *p, t, k* are strongly aspirated, so that their phonetic realization is rather [p^h], [t^h] and [k^h]; the lack of aspiration, not shown in conventional Lezgian spelling, may be phonemic, cf. /t^har/ 'the tara, a popular musical instrument' vs. /tar/ 'tree', both written *tar*; or /k^hal/ 'not ripe' vs. /kal/ 'cow', both written *kal*).

q^h is the uvular aspirated voiceless stop, χ is the uvular voiceless fricative, γ being the voiced counterpart of the latter. Thus *q* in *qena* 'died', which recurs so often in our examples, represents the uvular ejective voiceless stop.

2. Morphology

1) The Lezgian verb does not distinguish person, number, gender or nominal class. Much like the Dyirbal verb, the finite form completely lacks agreement with any nominal in the sentence. (See below, however, for the number agree-ment of the predicative participle: p. 221.) Therefore, just as in Dyirbal, the verb agreement in Lezgian cannot be recurred to as an argument when discussing the SS-roles of nominals.

Quite unlike Dyirbal, though, Lezgian possesses a plethora of tense forms: present, aorist, three imperfects, future, etc., some of which are listed in item 3 below.

2) The Lezgian noun has many cases; in the list of grammatical abbreviations I indicate only those that are needed in the examples.

3) An alphabetical list of grammatical abbreviations used is given below. (Only one or two of the several markers corresponding to a given grammeme are indicated.)

ABL	ablative case (*-divaj*)
ADES	adessive case ('near', 'at', 'by'; *-div*)

AOR	aorist (past tense denoting an accomplished punctual event; -*na*)
CAUS	causative (-*ar*-,-*ur*-)
DAT	dative case (-*diz*)
DEL	delative case ('from'; -*dilaj*)
ERG	ergative case (-*a*, -*di*)
FUT	future (tense denoting future or habitual events; -*da*)
GEN	genitive case
GER	gerund
HORT	hortative mood (-*n*)
IMPER	imperative mood
IMPF I	imperfect I (-*vaj*)
IMPF III	imperfect III (past tense denoting a prolonged or repeated event; -*daj*)
INES	inessive case ('in', 'within'; -*e*, -*da*)
INSTR	instrumental case (-*daldi*)
MASD	masdar (action nominal that plays the role of the infinitive; -*n*)
NOM	nominative case (-$\emptyset$)
OPT	optative mood (-*raj*)
PART	participle
PAST.GER	past-tense gerund (always homonymous with aorist; -*na*)
PL	plural
POSTES	postessive case ('behind', 'toward'; -*diq^h*)
PRES	present (-*(a/e/i)zva*)
RESULT	resultative (past tense denoting a past event whose results are present at the moment of speech; -*nava*)
SG	singular
SUBEL	subelative case ('from under'; -*dik^haj*)
SUBES	subessive case ('under'; -*dik^h*)
SUP	supine (roughly, 'with the purpose of'; -*iz*)
SUPERESS	superessive case ('on'; -*l*)

3. Syntax

Lezgian is a verb-final language. Except for that, its word order (outside the NP) is fairly free, but the nominative NP tends to be nearer to the verb (in communicatively neutral sentences).

III. GRAMMATICAL SUBJECT IN LEZGIAN

The theoretical approach to the concept of grammatical subject (GS) has been developed in Chapter 4, pp. 160–165. Here I take it for granted and proceed in three steps:

1. Three surface-syntactic properties of Lezgian are stated that point out NP$_{nom}$ (*k^hic* 'dog' in (3)) as GS.

2. The absence of some possible counterevidence is discussed.

3. Five counterarguments generally put forth against "NP_{nom} = GS" in Lezgian are analyzed and dismissed.

1. Subjecthood Properties in Lezgian

Let us consider a number of basic sentences in Lezgian:

(5)　**a.** *Ali + Ø*　　*aluqʰ + na*
　　　　Ali　NOM　fall　　　AOR
　　　　'Ali fell'.

　　　b. *Ali + Ø*　　*χta　 + na*
　　　　Ali　NOM　come　　AOR
　　　　'Ali came (back)'.

　　　c. *Ali + Ø*　　*kʰsa　+ nva*
　　　　Ali　NOM　sleep　　RESULT
　　　　'Ali is asleep'.

　　　d. *Ali + Ø*　　*elqʷ + ezva*
　　　　Ali　NOM　turn　　PRES
　　　　'Ali turns around'.

　　　e. *Ali + Ø*　　*kʰis　　+ na*
　　　　Ali　NOM　be.silent　AOR
　　　　'Ali became silent'.

In all these examples, the only nominal, *Ali* (that is, NP_{nom}), is the grammatical subject: the basic GS of my definition (p. 163). Thus, the basis for our inductive reasoning is set. Now we have to look for some surface-syntactic properties characterizing the privileged status of a nominal phrase in Lezgian from the viewpoint of its similarity to the basic GS. I know of three such properties: nondeletability, gapping-collapsibility and controlling the agreement of the nominalized participle in the predicative function.

Property 1: BEING NONDELETABLE

Applying to Lezgian the general definition of nondeletability given above (Chapter 4, III, (6), p. 165), we immediately find that in Lezgian it is NP_{erg}, or the agent NP (i.e., the traditionally presumed grammatical subject), that can always be omitted from the surface-syntactic structure of any sentence *salva correctione independentiaque*. (One problematic case has to be mentioned, though: sentences having as their main verb a one-actant, or monovalent, verb that takes its only actant in the ergative: cf. below, p. 227. I do not know whether or to what extent these N_{erg}s are omissible.) If, for instance, we omit *Alidi* from (3) we get (6), which is perfectly grammatical and context-independent:

(6) *Kʰič̣ q̇ena* 'The-dog died'.

There are a great number of examples like (3) vs. (6):

(7) a. *Ali + di   geṭe + ∅   χa   + na*
     Ali   ERG pot   NOM break   AOR
     'Ali broke the pot'.
  b. *Geṭe   χa + na*
     'The-pot broke'.

(8) a. *Ali + di   zi pʰerem + ∅   gazun + na*
     Ali   ERG my shirt   NOM tear   AOR
     'Ali tore my shirt'.
  b. *Zi   pʰerem gazun + na*
     'My shirt   got torn'.

Gadžiev (1954: 99–100) says that in (3) and in (6)–(8) we find a restricted class of verbs called **labile**, which are polysemous and possess (at least) a transitive and an intransitive sense. His examples include *q̇in* '(to) kill'/'(to) die'; *χun* '(to) break [trans.]'/'(to) break [intrans.]'; *kun* '(to) burn [trans.]'/'(to) burn [intrans.]'; etc. (see also below).

However, on the next pages of Gadžiev's book (1954: 100–101) we read that the agent phrase NP$_{\text{erg}}$ may be omitted in EVERY Lezgian sentence, the result being called by Gadžiev the "indefinite-human-agent construction":

(9) a. *Hažbuɣdajar + ∅   gatfariz cʰa + da*
     corn   NOM in.spring sow   FUT
     'Corn is sown [= they normally sow corn] in spring'.
  b. *Vilikdi čil + ∅   tʰürez   + daldi cʰa + daj,   gila*
     earlier soil NOM wooden.plow INSTR plow   IMPF III now
     kʰüten   + daldi cʰa   + zva
     metal.plow   INSTR plow   PRES
     'Earlier, soil was plowed with a wooden plow; now, it is plowed with a metal plow'.
  c. *pʰanbag + dikʰaj pʰarč̌ʰa + ∅   χra   + da*
     cotton   SUBEL cloth   NOM weave   FUT
     'Cloth is woven out of cotton'.

True, in (9) a human agent is necessarily understood; but this has nothing to do with the construction as such, i.e., with syntax: the human agent is imposed by the meaning of verbs 'sow', 'plow', or 'weave'. Let us take (10a):

(10) a. *Žive + di   reqʰ + ∅   basmiš + na*
      snow   ERG road   NOM block   AOR
      'The snow blocked the road'

and omit the NP_{erg};

b. *Req^h basmiš + na*

means 'The road got/became blocked' — not necessarily by people: it may have been by stones, blown-down trees, snow, a snowstorm, a flood, people or even animals.

Similarly,

(11) a. *Tar + ∅   jarχ + ar   + na*
tree   NOM fall   CAUS   AOR
'The tree toppled/was knocked down'.

does not imply a human agent: the tree might have been knocked down by a bear, a flood or by just a strong wind:

b. *Gar + u   tar + ∅   jarχ + ar   + na*
wind   ERG tree   NOM fall   CAUS   AOR
'The wind knocked down the tree'.

The situation is radically different, for example, with Russian indefinite-human-agent constructions featuring a zero lexeme in the capacity of the grammatical subject:

(12)
a. *Dorog + u   zasypal + i*
road   ACC   blocked   PL

means that it was done by people only, while

b. *Dorog + u   zasypal + o*
road   ACC   blocked   SG.NEUT

unmistakably indicates a "natural" agent, like the wind, snow, etc.

c. *Dorog + a   byl + a   zasyp + an   + a*
road   NOM was   SG.FEM block   PAST.PASS.PART   SG.FEM

is vague with respect to the agent: it could have been people, natural forces or animals. For more details about constructions of type (12a–b), featuring zero subject lexemes, see below, Chapter 8, pp. 314–320.

Note that Mejlanova and Talibov (1977) take exception with Gadžiev's statement about the restricted character of the class of labile, i.e., transitive-intransitive, verbs. The authors evaluate this class as comprising no less than 150 verbs and quote dozens of verbs belonging to it. Moreover, they point out the extreme productivity of the class in question: it tends to include all neologisms (in particular, Russian and international borrowings). On the other hand, they emphasize that it also includes the so-called "causative verbs" (with the suffix -r-, cf. below, p. 234), which argues, once again, for basic intransitivity of even causative verbs in Lezgian. Mejlanova and Talibov cite no "transitive" verb that could not be used intransitively; this implies that in their opinion all Lezgian "transitive" verbs are labile.

Let me summarize briefly what has been said thus far.

Any Lezgian sentence having the form

(13) 'X' 'Y' 'P'
NP^1_{erg} NP^2_{nom} Verb

means

(13′) 'X performs such actions that they cause that Y is in the state P'.

Thus, 'Ali kills the dog' = 'Ali performs such actions that they cause that the dog dies'; 'Ali tears my shirt' = 'Ali performs such actions that they cause that my shirt becomes torn'; etc.

In the surface-syntactic structure of any sentence of type (13), the phrase NP^1_{erg} denoting 'X' may be omitted without affecting its grammaticality or the degree of its dependence upon the preceding context. The result

(14) 'Y' 'P'
NP^2_{nom} Verb

is a complete and independent sentence, which means

(14′) 'Y is in the state P'.

If the above is correct, then we face the following dilemma: either we say that all Lezgian verbs admitting an agent phrase NP_{erg} are labile, i.e., (at least) two-way ambiguous, with a transitive and an intransitive sense; or we consider all Lezgian verbs nonambiguous and therefore only intransitive. Then all Lezgian verbs denote states or processes exclusively, never actions; and the semantic component '. . . perform(s) such actions that they cause that . . .' present in the sentences of type (13) is imparted by the ergative case of NP^1 rather than by the verb.

Economy of description obviously prompts us to adopt the second alternative. In this case, all the verbs cited by Gadžiev as labile turn out to be simply intransitive: *qin* means only 'die' (but never 'kill'), *χun* only 'get broken', *kun* only 'be consumed by fire', etc.[2]

Thus, the test of nondeletability indicates rather the nominative NP as the grammatical subject (with all kinds of verbs) in Lezgian: the ergative NP is deletable while the nominative NP in a non-basic sentence is not; I take this to be a sign of a privileged status of NP_{nom} with respect to NP_{erg}. As for the basic GSs in sentences (5), i.e., all the occurrences of *Ali*, these are obviously not deletable.

Remark 1

When I say that NP_{nom} is nondeletable in Lezgian, I by no means imply that a NP_{nom} can never be deleted from the surface-syntactic structure of a Lezgian sentence. It can be sometimes, but either such a deletion entails the sentence's incompleteness, as in (15b), or if it does not, then it is only possible under highly specific semantic circumstances that ensure the sentence's contextual autonomy, as in (16b) and (18b), but not in (17b) and (19b):

(15) **a.** *Gada + di   ktab + 0   qaču + na*
      boy   ERG book   NOM buy   AOR
      'The boy bought a book'.

    b. *Gada + di   qaču + na*
      'The   boy bought' [something that must have been mentioned before].

(15b), although grammatical in Lezgian, is not an autonomous sentence: it is strongly context-dependent.

(16) **a.** *Raq + ini   am   ku   + zva*
      sun   ERG he-NOM burn   PRES
      'The sun is burning him'.

    b. *Raq + ini   ku + zva*
      'The sun is burning'.

(16b) is a fully autonomous and grammatical sentence, while (17b) is not:

(17) **a.** *Buba   + di   ḳarasar + 0   ku   + zva*
      father   ERG wood   NOM burn   PRES
      'Father is burning wood'.

    b. **Buba + di ku + zva*
      'Father is burning'.

(The reason is that we probably have here three different senses of *kun*: roughly, 'to act upon with heat' (16a) vs. 'to produce heat' (16b) vs. 'to cause to be consumed by fire' (17a).)

The same thing happens with the next pair of examples:

(18)   **a.** *Evel aždahan + di   qür + ∅   ja   + na*
first   dragon   ERG hare   NOM strike   AOR
'At first, the dragon struck the hare'.
   b. *Evel aždahan + di ja + na*
'At first, the dragon struck' = 'The dragon struck first'.
(19)   **a.** *Evel aždahan + di qür gat^h + ana*
'At first, the dragon beat up the hare'.
   b. **Evel aždahan + di gat^h + ana*
'At first, the dragon beat up'.

Compare Note 3 in Chapter 4, p. 198.

Remark 2

Comparing NP_{nom} to NP_{erg}, I take into consideration only those NP_{nom}s that function as actants of a verbal form. All other uses of a Lezgian NP_{nom} are ignored here (such as in the role of a predicative complement: **student** *ja* 'is (a) student'; of an appositive: *p^{h}ahlivan* **Mahamed** 'the hero Mahamed'; of an apostrophe; of the nominal part in a compound verb: **p^{h}erevod** *ijizva* 'translation makes' = 'translates', cf. *Ada* [erg] *i stat'ja* [nom] **p^{h}erevod** [nom] *ijizva* 'He translates this article'; of an attribute: **ķaras** *ţur*, lit. 'wood spoon'; etc.). Cf. also Remark on p. 222 below.

Property 2: BEING GAPPING-COLLAPSIBLE

To quote Gadžiev (1954: 190): "Several main verbs may be conjoined in Lezgian only if all of them are either transitive or intransitive"—and, let us add, if all of them refer to the same actor or perceiver. That is, meanings such as in (20):

(20)   **a.** 'The boy returned and took the book'.
   b. 'The boy took the book and returned'.

cannot be expressed in Lezgian by (20′):

(20)   **a.** **Gada + ∅   χtana   va ktab + ∅   qačuna.*
            boy   NOM returned and book   NOM took
   b. **Gada + di ktab + ∅   qačuna va χtana.*
            boy   ERG book   NOM took   and returned.

Both sentences are bad only because of the union of the two conjuncts. Each conjuct as such is perfectly grammatical.

There are only two ways to express (20a) or (20b) in Lezgian: either by conjoining two complete sentences rather than two tensed verbs, which means using two occurrences of *gada* 'boy' (with the second one pronominalized), see (21); or by replacing the first finite verb with a gerund, in our case, with a past-tense gerund, see (22). Thus instead of 'The boy returned and took the book' Lezgian actually says 'The boy*i* returned and he*i* took the book' or 'The boy, having returned, took the book'. See examples:

(21) a. *Gada + ∅*   *χta*   *+ na,* *va* *ad + a*   *ktab + ∅*
      boy   NOM return   AOR and he   ERG book   NOM
      qaču + na
      take   AOR
      'The boy*i* returned, and he*i* took the book'.

    b. *Gada + di*   *ktab + ∅*   *qaču + na* *va* *am + ∅*
      boy   ERG book   NOM take   AOR and he   NOM
      χta   *+ na*
      return   AOR
      'The boy*i* took the book, and he*i* returned'.

(22) a. *Gada + di,* *χta*   *+ na,*   *ktab + ∅*   *qaču + na.*
      boy   ERG returned   PAST.GER book   NOM take   AOR
      'The boy, having returned, took the book'.

    b. *Gada + ∅,* *ktab + ∅*   *qaču + na,*   *χta*   *+ na*
      boy   NOM book   NOM take   PAST.GER return   AOR
      'The boy, having taken the book, returned'.

Such are the facts. What is their bearing upon the problem of the grammatical subject in Lezgian?

The gapping-collapsibility test, when applied to Lezgian, in the form of Principle (11) (see Chapter 4, p. 168), provides an argument against the identity of surface-syntactic roles of NP$_{erg}$ (i.e., agent phrase with a "transitive" verb) and NP$_{nom}$ (i.e., actor of an "intransitive" verb): they are not gapping-collapsible in Lezgian.[3] Let it be emphasized once again (cf. p. 201) that in languages where NP$_{erg}$ actually is the genuine grammatical subject both nominative and ergative NPs are readily gapping-collapsible; see examples from Georgian and Dargwa:

(23) Georgian

a. *Mama + m*   *gaigon + a*   *čemi xma + ∅*   *da adg + a*
    father   ERG hear   AOR my   voice NOM   and stand.up AOR
    'Father heard my voice and stood up'.

b. *Mama + ∅*   *adg + a*   *da gaigon + a*   *čemi xma + ∅*
    father   NOM stand.up AOR   and hear   AOR my   voice NOM
    'Father stood up and heard my voice'.

(24) Dargwa

    a. *Daud + li*   *Leila + ∅*   *lävriruli (saj) va* *murtalra*
      Daud   ERG Leila   NOM caressing (is) and always
      il   + ičil   *kajili saj*
      she   COMIT sitting is
      'Daud caresses Leila (a lot) and always is sitting with her'.

b. *Daud + Ø   Leila + či̯l   murtalra kajili (saj) va il   + Ø*
Daud   NOM Leila   COMIT always   sitting (is) and she   NOM
lävriruli saj
caressing is
'Daud is always sitting with Leila and caresses her a lot'.

The same thing happens in Chechen (Jakovlev 1940: 165–166).

GSs in different grammatical cases (nominative and pathetive) are also gapping-collapsible in Dyirbal (cf. examples (14)–(17) in Chapter 4):

(25) Dyirbal

a. *ŋaḑa   bani + ŋu ba + ŋgu + n   ḑugumbi + ṛu*
I-NOM   come-PAST the-INSTR-CLASS II woman-INSTR
balga + n
hit-PAST
'I came, and the woman hit me', lit. 'I came and was-hit by
the woman'.

b. *ŋay + guna ba + ŋgu + n   ḑugumbi + ṛu balga + n*
I-PATH   the-INSTR-CLASS II woman-INSTR hit-PAST
bani + ŋu
come-PAST
'The woman hit me, and I came', lit. 'I was-hit by the woman
and came'.

Thus chances are that in Lezgian $NP_{nom}(V_{(itr)})$ and $NP_{erg}(V_{(tr)})$ fulfill different surface-syntactic roles. But since $NP_{nom}(V_{(itr)})$—e.g., in (4)—is beyond any doubt the GS of its verb (in particular, it is nondeletable), this means that NP_{erg} in (2) is not: Q.E.D.

However, this is only the first half of the proof; it remains to be seen whether the gapping test favors the surface-syntactic identity of $NP_{nom}(V_{(itr)})$ and $NP_{nom}(V_{(tr)})$. To do so, it is sufficient to try to collapse them under gapping. Let us take (26):

(26) **a.** *Buba + di   Ahmed + Ø   viževaz gat^h + ana*
father   ERG   Ahmed   NOM   well   beat   AOR
'Father beat the hell out of Ahmed'.

  b. *Ahmed   q + fe + na*
Ahmed-NOM   away go AOR
'Ahmed went away'.

But these two sentences cannot be conjoined to produce (27):

(27) **Buba + di Ahmed viževaz gat^h + ana va q + fe + na*
'Father beat the hell out of Ahmed$_i$, and he$_i$ went away',

or more literally, 'From-the-father Ahmed got a tremendous beating and went away'; example (27) is judged ungrammatical. The best way to express the corresponding meaning is (27'):

(27')   *Buba* + *di*   *viževaz* *gat^h* + *aj*   + *la,*   *Ahmed* + *∅*
        Father   ERG   well   beat   PART   when   Ahmed   NOM
        q   + *fe* + *na*
        away   go   AOR

i.e., something like 'When beaten up by Father, Ahmed went away'. $NP_{nom}(V_{(itr)})$ and $NP_{nom}(V_{(tr)})$ are not gapping-collapsible in Lezgian, so that the collapsibility argument is only half valid there.

It must, however, be emphasized that the conjoining of full sentences is in general far from favored in Lezgian. Although sentences like (21), with the grammatical subject repeated in the second conjunct, are grammatically admissible and actually occur in literature (see examples in Note 3, p. 243), the informants perceive most of such sentences as "somewhat artificial," "possibly influenced by Russian usage" and strongly prefer various types of subordination. That is, the favored way of expressing, e.g., the meaning 'The father beat up the girl and she returned' is one of the two following sentences:

(28)   **a.** *Buba* + *di*   *gat^h* + *aj*   *ruš* + *∅*   *χta* +   *na*
               Father   ERG   beat   PART   girl   NOM   return   AOR
               'Beaten by Father, the girl returned'.
       b. *Buba* + *di*   *gat^h* + *aj*   + *la*   *ruš* + *∅*   *χta* + *na*
               Father   ERG   beat   PART   when   girl   NOM   return   AOR
               'After having been beaten by Father, the girl returned'.

Here are three more examples, all of them translations volunteered by a native speaker for conjoined sentences:

(29)   'I pushed him, and he fell' =
       Z + *a*   *ec^h* + *jaj* + *la,*   *am* + *∅*   *jarχ*   *xa*   + *na*
       I   ERG push   PART   when he   NOM lying become AOR
       i.e., 'After pushed by me, he fell'.
(30)   'Ahmed pushed the door, and it opened' =
       Ahmed + *a*   *c^hüq^w* + *ej* + *la,*   *rak* + *∅*   *ač^huχ* *xa*   + *na*
       Ahmed   ERG   press   PART   when door   NOM open   become AOR
       i.e., 'After pressed by Ahmed, the door opened'.
(31)   'Father heated the water, and it boiled' =
       a. *Buba* + *di*   *ce* + *l*   *zval* + *∅*   *γa*   + *na*
               Father   ERG   water SUPERESS   boiling NOM   bring.about AOR
               i.e., 'Father caused boiling on the water'.
               [*ce-* is a suppletive stem of *jad* 'water'.]

b. *Buba + di   jad + ∅   čʰimi   ijiz + ijiz, ada + l*
Father   ERG   water   NOM   hot   making   it   SUPERESS
zval + ∅   γa   + na
boiling   NOM   bring.about   AOR
i.e., 'Father, progressively making the water hot, caused boiling on it'.

c. *Buba + di   zval + ∅   γ   + iz   jad + ∅*
Father   ERG   boiling   NOM   bring.about   SUP   water   NOM
ecʰig + na
put   AOR
i.e., 'Father put the water [on fire] in order to bring about boiling on it'.

The ungrammaticality of (27) seriously cripples the gapping-collapsibility argument—but still does not kill it, since it remains valid against the claim that NP_{erg} is the grammatical subject.

Property 3: CONTROLLING THE AGREEMENT
OF PREDICATIVE COMPLEMENT PARTICIPLE

As was said above, Lezgian knows almost no agreement. The only vestiges of agreement can be found in the sentences with a copula that takes a nominalized participle in the role of the predicative complement. This participle may agree in number with the NP_{nom}, the agreement being obligatory if the NP_{nom} is animate and optional otherwise. But the participle in the complement position never agrees with the NP_{erg}. See examples:

(32)   a. *Z + az   i   tar + ar + ∅   naq*
I   DAT   this   tree   PL   NOM   yesterday
kʰutʰ +ur   + bur + ∅   *xiz   akʰʷ + azva*
plant   PART   PL   NOM   as   seem   PRES
'These trees seem to me as [if they had been] planted yesterday'.

b. *Zun   qsan ḳel + aj   + di + ∅   ja*
I-NOM   well   learn   PART   SG   NOM   be.PRES
'I am a well-educated person'.

c. *Čʰun   qsan ḳel + aj   + bur + ∅*
we-NOM   well   learn   PART   PL   NOM
⟨*ḳel + aj + di + ∅⟩   ja
                        be.PRES
'We are well-educated people'.

d. *Z + a   sa   ktab + ∅   ḳel + aj   + di + ∅*
I   ERG   one   book   NOM   read   PART   SG   NOM
⟨*ḳel + aj + bur + ∅⟩   ja
                        be.PRES
'I have read a book' (lit. 'By-me a book read is').

e. *Z* + *a*   *gzaf ktab* + *ar* + *∅*   ḳel + aj   + di + ∅ /
   I   ERG many book   PL   NOM read   PART SG   NOM
   ḳel + aj + bur + ∅   *ja*
     PL   NOM be.PRES
   'I have read many books' ('By-me many books read is/are').

f. *Zun*   *sa ktab* + *∅*   / *gzaf ktab* + *ar* + *∅*
   I-NOM one book   SG.NOM / many book   PL   NOM
   kel + aj   + di + ∅   ⟨*ḳel + aj   + bur + ∅⟩   *ja*
   read PART   SG   NOM read   PART   PL   NOM be.PRES
   'I am the person who read a book/many books'.

g. *Čʰn* + *a*   *sa ktab* + *∅*   ḳel + aj   + di + ∅
   we   ERG one book   NOM read   PART SG   NOM
   ⟨*ḳel +   aj   + bur + ∅⟩   *ja*
   read   PART PL   NOM be.PRES
   'We have read a book' ('By-us a book read is').

h. *Čʰn* + *a gzaf ktab* + *ar* ḳel + aj + di + ∅ /
   ḳel + aj + bur + ∅ *ja*
   'We have read many books' ('By-us many books read is/are').

i. *Čʰun sa ktab* / *gzaf ktabar* ḳel + aj + bur + ∅
   ⟨*ḳel + aj + di + ∅⟩ *ja*
   'We are those who read a book / many books'.

All these sentences show quite clearly that from the viewpoint of the only agreement relationship that obtains in Lezgian, $NP_{nom}(V_{(tr)})$ and $NP_{nom}(V_{(itr)})$ are treated as syntactically isofunctional items, both triggering the number agreement of the predicative complement; NP_{erg}, however, is excluded from this.

Remark

The only wrinkle to this excellently organized set of data seems to appear in examples (32f) and (32i), where we observe TWO noun phrases in the nominative: the GS *zun* 'I' or *čʰun* 'we' and the other one—*ktab/ktabar* 'book(s)'. But actually, there is no problem here: the second NP_{nom} is, so to speak, the "retained" GS of the participle. As Gadžiev points out (1963: 13–16, 68–69), in Lezgian all verbal nominalizations—the masdar (i.e., action nominal) and the participles—keep the full valence of the source verb so that what had been the GS of the verb may still stand in the nominative. (Cf. the insightful analysis of a similar phenomenon in Arabic by Comrie 1976b: 194–196.) Here are three more examples to illustrate this:

(33)   a. *Čʰun*   /*Zun*   *fe* + *ji*   + *bur* + *∅*   *kʰolχoz* + *din*
       we-NOM/I-NOM go   PART PL   NOM kolkhoz   GEN

> *baɣ* + *lar* + *∅*   *tʰir*
> orchard PL   NOM be-IMPF I
> 'The place we/I went was the collective farm's orchards'.

More literally, the sentence translates as 'Our/My goings were the collective farm's orchards', but with *we* / *I* as secondary grammatical subjects (of 'going').

b. *Oficer* + *di*   *vičʰ* + *∅*   *front* + *diqʰ*   *f* + *izva* + *j*   + *di* + *∅*
officer ERG he   NOM front POSTES go PRES PART SG   NOM
qil + *in*   *išarad* + *aldi*   *gal* + *ur*   + *na*
head   GEN nod   INSTR show   CAUS AOR
'With a nod, the officer showed that he was going to the front'.
Literally, 'The-officer showed with-a-nod of-head he going to-front'.

c. *Zi*   *murad* + *∅*   *vun* + *∅*   *han* + *iz*   *f* + *in*   + *∅*   *ja*
my wish   NOM   you NOM there DAT go MASD NOM be.PRES
'I wish you to go there', or, more literally, 'My wish is you going there'.

After all those deliberations, I am in a position to make the following state-ment, which will then be substantiated in the rest of the paper: nondeletability, gapping-collapsibility and control of participle agreement, all three being purely syntactic properties, indicate NP_{nom} as the GS in ALL Lezgian sentences; NP_{erg} is then relegated to the status of the agent complement (or maybe even a circum-stantial).[4]

2. Absence of Voice in Lezgian

An outstanding peculiarity of Lezgian is the complete absence of any voice system; there is not even the slightest trace of anything smelling of voice. How-ever, languages that possess "normal" transitive verbs and tripartite construc-tions GS + MV + GO^{dir} as a rule feature at least two voices, active and pas-sive, as in Dyirbal, or active and objective impersonal, as in Dargwa, where all transitive verbs admit two types of subject-verb-object construction (cf. Note 25, Chapter 4, p. 205):

(34) a. *Dudeš* + *li*   *gazet*   + *∅*   *b*   + *učuli*   *sa* + *j*
father   ERG newspaper NOM THING reading is   MASC
'Father is reading a newspaper'.

b. *Neš* + *li*   *gazet*   + *∅*   *b*   + *učuli*   *sa* + *ri*
mother ERG newspaper NOM THING reading is   FEM
'Mother is reading a newspaper'.

Here, NP_{erg} (*dudešli* and *nešli*) is the GS, and the auxiliary verb agrees with it in class, while NP_{nom} (*gazet*) is the direct object that conditions the agreement of the lexical part of the compound verb form (the class prefix *b-*); the verb is transitive. But in the nearly synonymous sentences (35) the grammatical structure is different:

(35) **a.** *Dudeš* + *∅* *gazet* + *li* *(w)* + *učuli* *sa* + *j*.
      father   NOM newspaper ERG MASC reading is   MASC
      b. *Neš* + *∅* *gazet* + *li* *r* + *učuli* *sa* + *ri*.
      mother NOM   newspaper ERG FEM reading is   FEM

The verb is intransitive; both its parts agree in class with the NP_{nom}, which is the GS. The NP_{erg} in (35) is an oblique object, a chômeur (which fills, however, the same "semantic object" valence slot as in (34)). The communicative emphasis in (35) is different from (34): it is the action itself that is in focus. (35) could be roughly translated as 'Father ⟨Mother⟩ is engaged in some reading, which involves a newspaper'.

The difference between (34) and (35) is a voice distinction: that between an active and an objective impersonal. These examples clearly show how Dargwa can manipulate both central actants of a transitive verb.

By and large, transitive verbs develop a kind of interplay among their syntactic actants, the latter being demoted or promoted in syntactic rank, etc. Nothing similar happens in Lezgian.

True, the absence of evidence is not reliable evidence. And yet the total lack of voice or voicelike distinctions in Lezgian strengthens the view that all Lezgian verbs are essentially intransitive and have just one obligatory actant; therefore all NP_{nom}s are GSs, both with $V_{(itr)}$ and presumed $V_{(tr)}$. The lack of voice would automatically follow from the intransitivity of all Lezgian verbs—or, more precisely, from the fact that they have only one obligatory syntactic actant. Otherwise, there is no feasible explanation for this circumstance.

3. Rejecting Possible Counterarguments

Now I will analyze five currently repeated counterarguments to the solution "NP_{nom} = GS, NP_{erg} = CO^{agent} (= agent complement)" in Lezgian.

1. Semantic Load on the Ergative Case

If my analysis (3′) of type (3) sentences is correct, then the semantic component '. . . performs such actions that they cause that . . .', which is so important for the meaning of the whole sentence, is carried not by the verb but by the ergative case of the agent phrase. The question immediately arises whether it is justified to load upon an apparently syntactic case (i.e., a case that marks one of the major surface-syntactic roles) such a heavy semantic cargo: the meaning of 'cause', which is, as a general rule, related to the verb rather than to a case form.

Normally, all grammatical cases of a language can be divided into two subclasses (obviously, with some intermediate phenomena hard to classify): (1) **con-**

crete, or **semantic**, cases which denote different locations (with meanings like 'on', 'over', 'under', 'along', 'into', . . .), comparison, possession, etc., and (2) **abstract**, or **syntactic**, cases, which mark surface-syntactic relations (mostly between the verb and its nominal dependents) and tend to carry no meaning at all. For example, Russian or German cases are all mainly syntactic, while in Hungarian or Finnish we find also (along with the syntactic cases like nominative and accusative) a number of semantic cases (e.g., inessive, illative, adessive, allative, etc.).

The ergative in Lezgian must be classified rather as an abstract, syntactic case—even in our analysis, where it marks the agent complement role (it is more so in the traditional analysis, which considers the ergative as the mark of the GS). So it may seem contrary to the spirit of Lezgian to hang the causation meaning onto a syntactic case.

However, to use syntactic cases as carriers for considerable semantic cargoes is very typical of Lezgian. Here are three obvious instances of this.

(i) In all sentences of type (3) the ergative may be replaced by the ablative, with the result that the sentence will mean what it means plus 'involuntarily, unwittingly, or in a very indirect manner':

(36) *Ali + divaj k^hiç + 0   qe + na*
     Ali   ABL dog   NOM die   AOR

which can be interpreted as 'Ali killed the dog involuntarily', 'Ali killed the dog accidentally', 'Ali somehow, but not on purpose, caused the dog's death'.

Thus the ablative of the agent NP conveys quite an involved meaning: '. . . performs such actions that, without his will or even his knowledge, they cause —maybe only indirectly—that . . .'

(ii) Verbs of giving or belonging normally govern the dative in Lezgian:

(37) **a.** *Ali + di   z + az   ktab + 0   vug + ana*
     Ali   ERG I   DAT book   NOM pass   AOR
     'Ali gave me a book [to be my property]'.

(or, literally, 'Caused-by-Ali, to-me a book passed'). (37a) means that the book in question is now my property: it was given as a gift—forever. But the dative (of the addressee phrase) may be replaced by the adessive, and then the sentence will imply only temporary contiguity in space:

     b. *Ali + di   z + av   ktab + 0   vug + ana*
     Ali   ERG I   ADES book   NOM pass   AOR
     'Ali gave me a book [on loan]'.

means that the book was given to be held for some time only, and is to be returned.

As is clearly seen, the dative of Beneficiary (or Addressee) carries the meaning '. . . as a permanent owner' (or '. . . to be the property of . . .'), while the contrasting adessive means '. . . as an interim user' ('. . . to be used or manipulated for some time and to be returned later').

(iii) Lezgian has a verbal construction of the form V_{supine} + *xun* 'become', which means roughly 'have V done', 'start and finish V'. But if the agent phrase of this construction is marked with the ablative (instead of the nominative or the ergative), the ablative adds to the meaning of the sentence the component 'can', 'possible':

(38) **a.** *Buba + Ø   šeher + diz   f + iz   xana + č*
             father NOM town   DAT go SUP became not
             'Father didn't go to town'
             vs.
    b. *Buba + divaj šeher + diz   f + iz   xana + č*
             father ABL town   DAT go SUP became not
             'Father couldn't go to town'.
    c. *Buba + di   ktab + Ø   ḳel + iz   xana*
             father ERG book   NOM read SUP became
             'Father read the book'
             vs.
    d. *Buba + divaj ktab + Ø   ḳel + iz   xana*
             father ABL book   NOM read SUP became
             'Father could read the book'.

We see, thus, that even such a typically verbal meaning as 'can' may be the target of a syntactic case in Lezgian.

To sum up the evidence presented in item 1: When we load a semantic component '. . . performs such actions that they cause that . . .' upon the ergative case, we do not thereby contradict the spirit of Lezgian. On the contrary, this solution fits closely into the general framework of Lezgian declension, where a high degree of semanticity is characteristic of grammatical cases—even those fulfilling typically abstract, syntactic functions like Actor or Beneficiary.

Let it be emphasized that in sentences like (36) Gadžiev himself considers the agent phrase in the ablative (*Ali + divaj*) to be the agentive complement rather than the grammatical subject: he assigns the latter role to the nominative NP (Gadžiev 1954: 98). This constitutes another argument (true, not a very cogent one) in favor of the above solution, namely, to treat the nominative NP as the grammatical subject and the ergative NP as the agentive complement. What is, indeed, the reason to analyze sentences (3) and (36):

(3) *Ali + di*   *kʰiċ ǧena* 'Ali killed the dog'.
(36) *Ali + divaj kʰiċ ǧena* 'Ali killed the dog involuntarily'.

from the syntactic standpoint in quite a different manner? SYNTACTICALLY they
seem to be identical. The only semantic difference ('caused' in (3), 'accidentally
or indirectly caused' in (36)) is obviously related to the different case markings
of the agentive NP. Cf. the same situation in English:

(39) **a.** *The book is* **on** *the desk.*
     b. *The book is* **above** *the desk.*

Both sentences are syntactically identical, and it is the semantically loaded preposition that is responsible for the conspicuous semantic distinction, in much the
same way as is the semantically loaded case in (3) vs. (36).

2. Verbs Taking Their Only Actant in the Ergative Case

Lezgian has a number of one-actant (traditionally, "intransitive") verbs whose
only actant must be in the ergative:

(40) **a.** *A + da*   *qsan + diz*   *k̫alax + izva*
       he   ERG good   ADVERB work   PRES
       'He works well'.
     b. *Ruš + a*   *ķel*   *+ izva*
       girl   ERG read/study PRES
       'The girl reads/studies'.
     c. *Gada + di*   *čʰukur + izva*
       boy   ERG run   PRES
       'The boy is running'.
     d. *Gada + di*   *zverna*
       boy   ERG up-and-ran
       'The boy started running'.

In many cases the reason for this is obvious: the verb is derived from the phrase
NP_{nom} + *avun* 'do', cf.:

k̫alax ijizva 'work do' (i.e., 'to do work') ⇒ *k̫alaxizva*
ķel ijizva 'reading do' (i.e., 'to do reading') ⇒ *ķelizva*, etc.

However, this circumstance does not simplify a synchronic and theoretical analysis of sentences of type (40). We face here the following alternative:

(i) Either we say that in (40) NP_{erg} is the grammatical subject (then verbs like
k̫alaxun 'work', *ķelun* 'read, study', *čʰukurun* 'run', *zverun* 'start running',
etc., must be lexically marked as taking the ergative in the grammatical subject
role). This solution does not logically contradict my claim that in type (3) sen-

tences NP$_{erg}$ is not the grammatical subject but no doubt weakens it. Moreover, many verbs of this type appear in two variants, "fused" as in (41a) and (41c) or "separate" as in (41b) and (41d):

(41)   **a.** *Ad + a*   *gužlu + z*   *ḳ^{w}alax + izva*
         he   ERG hard   ADVERB work   PRES
         'He works hard'.

       b. *Ad + a*   *gužlu ḳ^{w}alax ij + izva*
         he   ERG hard   work   do   PRES
         'He does hard work'.

       c. *Č^{h}n + a*   *ad + az*   *hürmet + zava*
         we   ERG he   DAT respect   PRES
         'We respect him [DATIVE!]'.

       d. *Č^{h}n + a*   *ad + az*   *(gzaf)*   *hürmet ij + izva*
         we   ERG he   DAT (much) respect do   PRES
         'We respect him (very much)'.

If NP$_{erg}$s in (41a), i.e., *ada*, and in (43c), i.e., *č^{h}na*, are grammatical subjects, but the same NP$_{erg}$s in (41b) and (41d) are—according to my claim—agentive complements (NP$_{nom}$s *ḳ^{w}alax* and *hürmet* being grammatical subjects), we get drastically different syntactic descriptions of sentences that are quite similar in their structure and semantically (nearly) synonymous.

    (ii) Or we admit that in (41a) and (41c) the grammatical subject is absent altogether, NP$_{erg}$ being the agentive complement, in complete conformity with what is supposed about this phrase in Subsection III.1. This would mean that (41a) and (41c) are **subjectless** sentences. They can be compared to Russian impersonal sentences of the well-known type (42):

(42)   **a.** *Skol'ko*   *nami*   *bylo*   *tut*   *xož + eno!*
         how-much we-INSTR (it-) was here walk-PART
         lit. 'How much was it walked by us here!'

       b. *Časten'ko*   *byvalo*   *im*   *na beregu*   *siž + eno,*
         often-DIMIN (it-)was he-INSTR on shore-LOC sit-PART
         lit. 'Pretty often was it sat by him on the shore'.

(An essential difference between the Russian impersonal and the Lezgian subjectless constructions is as follows: in Russian, specific morphological values of the copula verb—3rd person singular neuter—forces postulating a zero dummy subject, which triggers this agreement and is similar in function to the impersonal *it* in English, *il* in French, or *es* in German, see above, example (12b) and Chapter 8; while in Lezgian there is no grammatical subject at all.)

    Subjectless sentences denoting environmental, physiological and psychological states are quite common in Lezgian:

(43)   **a.** *Meqizva* ⟨ *= Meqida* ⟩
       'It is cold'.
    b. *Z + az*   *meqizva* ⟨ *= meqida* ⟩
       I   DAT cold
       'I am cold'.

(44)   **a.** *Čʰimida* ⟨ *Čʰimi*   *xana* ⟩
       'It is hot' ⟨ lit. 'Hot became', i.e., 'It got hot'⟩.
    b. *Z + az* *čʰimida* ⟨ *čʰimi*   *xana* ⟩
       'I am hot' ⟨'I became hot'⟩.

(45)   **a.** *(Ḳʷal + e)*   *mičida* ⟨ *= miči ja* ⟩
       room INES   dark-is   dark is
       'It is dark (in the room)'.
    b. *(Či xür*   *+ e)*   *aḳ luhud + ač*
       our village INES   so speak-not
       'They do not speak so (in our village)',
       lit. '(It is) not-spoken so . . .'
    c. *Ad + ak*   *χḳuna*
       he   SUBES hit
       lit. 'Under-him it-hit', i.e., 'He took offense', 'He felt hurt'.

Sentences (43)–(45) lack GS altogether; NP_{dat} (or NP_{iness} etc.) is but an oblique object or even a circumstantial: 'it is cold to me', 'it is getting hot to me', etc. We find interesting semantic contrasts, like the following ones:

(46)   **a.** *Gišinda* ⟨ *= Gišindi ja* ⟩
       'There is hunger'.
    b. *Z + az*   *gišinda*   ⟨ *= gišindi ja*   ⟩
       I   DAT hungry.be-PRES   hungry be-PRES
       'I am hungry'.
    c. *Zun*   *gišindi ja*
       I-NOM hungry be.PRES
       'I am a hungry fellow', i.e., 'I am always hungry'.

(47)   **a.** *Sad*   *xana*
       happy became
       'It became cheerful'.
    b. *Ruš + az*   *sad*   *xana*
       girl   DAT happy became
       'The girl became happy', i.e., 'cheered up momentarily'.
    c. *Ruš*   *sad*   *xana*
       girl-NOM happy became
       'The girl became a happy person'.

Gadžiev (1954: 66–67) considers (47b) and (47c) to be synonymous; I do not think so because of the difference he himself finds between (46b) and (46c).

The decision to take seems obvious to me: Lezgian verbs like $\underset{.}{k}^w alaxun$, $\underset{.}{k}elun$, etc. having their only actant in the ergative should be considered subject-less, and NP_{erg} modifying them should be treated as the agentive complement. Such a solution neatly corresponds to the general characteristics of Lezgian, which favors subjectless constructions of various types.[5] Note, however, that this solution predicts the absolute omissibility of N_{erg} with a one-actant verb. Such sentences as $\underset{.}{k}^w alaxizva$ 'Work takes place' or $č^h ukurizva$ 'Running takes place' ($\cong$ German *Es wird gearbeitet* ⟨*gelaufen*⟩) must be complete and independent utterances. Unfortunately, I do not know whether this is the case.

3. Imperative and Its Actor

A current argument against "NP_{nom} = Grammatical Subject" in Lezgian is the imperative construction (cf. the imperative counterargument in the Dyirbal chapter, p. 194). Let me first present the facts as they appear in Talibov 1966: 572–573 and then analyze them.

According to Talibov, the Lezgian imperative has three personal forms (that do not distinguish number):

> 1st person form in -*n*
> 2nd person form in -∅ (also, -*r*, reduplication of the last radical
>   consonant, or a suppletive stem)
> 3rd person form in -*raj*

See examples:

(48) **a.** *Z + a*   (*žuvan*) $\underset{.}{k}^w alax$ *iji + n!*
         I   ERG (my)   work-NOM do-IMPER
         'Let me do my work!'

b. *Vun + a* (*žuvan*) $\underset{.}{k}^w alax$ *aja!*
        you-ERG (your) work-NOM do-IMPER
        'Do your work!'

c. *Ad + a*   (*vič^h in*) $\underset{.}{k}^w alax$ *avu + raj!*
        he-ERG   (his)   work-NOM do-IMPER
        'Let him do his work!'

In (48a–c) we observe suppletive stems of the verb *avu + n* 'do': *iji-, aja-, avu-*.

This would mean that the Lezgian imperative presents personal agreement with the actor—in sharp contrast to all other verbal tensed forms, which lack agreement completely. The same thing seems to happen with the one-actant (i.e., "intransitive") verbs:

(49) a. *Zun* p^hak^ha $q^we + n!$
I-NOM tomorrow   come-IMPER
'Let me come tomorrow!'

     b. *Vun* p^hak^ha $at^hu!$
you-NOM tomorrow come-IMPER
'Come tomorrow!'

     c. *Am* p^hak^ha $at^hu + raj!$
he-NOM tomorrow   come-IMPER
'Let him come tomorrow!'

In (49a–c) we observe suppletive stems of the verb $at^hu + n$ 'come': q^we- and at^hu-.

Under Talibov's analysis, examples (48) and (49) would suggest that the actor NP triggers agreement of the main verb in the imperative and so acquires the privileged status that is necessary for an NP to be deemed grammatical subject (since no other NP does so). Thus the imperative construction in Lezgian would appear to be a counterargument when discussing the subjecthood of NP_{nom}: it is NP_{erg}, rather than NP_{nom}, that determines the form of the imperative verb in (48), exactly as NP_{nom} does in (49), i.e., with an "intransitive" verb.

However, all of the above deliberations are wrong. What makes Talibov's statements concerning the imperative suspect is a well-known typological consideration: imperative forms are highly specific in comparisons to all other verbal forms; in particular, as a rule, imperative forms do not distinguish more categories than the forms of all other moods (see, e.g., Jakobson 1971b). Therefore, it seems highly improbable that in a language where no verbal finite form shows personal agreement, it would be exclusively the imperative form that agrees with its "grammatical subject." I propose, then, the following explanation of the facts presented in (48) and (49).

In actual practice, Lezgian possesses three different "command" moods: an **imperative**, an **optative** and a **hortative**.

The **imperative** means roughly 'speaking to you [= my addressee], I want you to (cause that) . . .'; that is, using an imperative form the speaker URGES his listener TO DO something. Because of this meaning the Lezgian imperative is semantically incompatible with actors of persons other than 2nd: 'let me' or 'let him' cannot be rendered in Lezgian by an imperative form. The meaning 'Prepare a book for me!' must be expressed in Lezgian as (50):

(50) *Vun + a*   *z + az*   *ktab*   *hazura!*
you-ERG   I-DAT   book-NOM   prepare-IMPER

which means, strictly speaking, 'I want you to cause that a book get ready for me'.

The **optative** means 'speaking to you [= my addressee], I want that . . . take place' — WITHOUT the component '[want] YOU TO CAUSE [that]', that is, without trying to urge the listener to cause anything. Therefore, the optative admits actors or perceivers of all three persons, 2nd person included:

(51) **a.** *Čʰun   jašamiš + raj!*
          we-NOM   live-OPT
          'Long may we live!'
      b. *Vun   giligʰ + raj, dušman!*[6]
          you-NOM die-OPT   enemy-NOM
          'May you drop dead, enemy!'
      c. *Ad + a   zi   ktab   qaču + raj!*
          he-ERG   my   book-NOM take-OPT
          'May he take my book!'

Telling semantic contrasts are possible; compare (52), featuring an imperative, with (53), with an optative, both addressed to the 2nd person singular:

(52) *V + az   buba   ḳan   xux!*
      you-DAT   father-NOM beloved   become-IMPER
      'Love your father!'

which, in a more explicit form, means

(52′) 'I want you to cause that your father become beloved to you';

that is, I hold you responsible for the feeling in question and try by my words to induce it in you. On the other hand,

(53) *V + az   buba   ḳan   xu + raj!*
      you-DAT   father-NOM beloved   become-OPT
      'May you love your father!'

means

(53′) 'I want that (it happens that) your father become beloved to you'.

Uttering (53), I do not try to urge my interlocutor to do something; I simply express my desire.

Note in passing that the negative form of the imperative is built by suffixing *-mir* to the positive form, while in the optative the negative form is built by prefixing *tʰ-*. Thus, *-mir* occurs only in the 2nd person forms, and *tʰ-* co-occurs with all three persons.

The above analysis explains why the Lezgian more readily says 'Don't be afraid!' in the imperative and 'Don't be hot!' in the optative, although structurally both sentences are identical—something like 'Don't let it be frightening/hot to you':

(54) a. *V + az*   *kʰiče*   *že + mir!*
       you-DAT   frightening   become-not-IMPER
       [*že-* is a suppletive stem of *xun* 'become']
      b. *V + az*   *čʰimi tʰa + xu + j / tʰa + xu + raj!*
       you-DAT   hot   not-become-OPT

In (54a), I ask you TO DO something, if only on a moral or psychological level, to avoid fear; in (54b) I simply express my desire that heat be not excessive, while you are not supposed to do anything. The imperative and the optative can be exchanged in (54a) and (54b), resulting in the following grammatical sentences:

(54′) a. *V + az* *ḳʰiče tʰa + xu + raj!*
       'Let there be nothing frightening to you!' [= 'I wish that you meet nothing frightening'].
      b. *V + az* *čʰimi ijiz že + mir!*
       'Do something to avoid being overheated!' [e.g., put on lighter clothes, open a window or switch on a fan].

The **hortative** means 'speaking to you, I want you to agree that . . . takes place' and, like the optative, is compatible with actors of all three persons (2nd person being semantically slightly less plausible, since it is strange to invite someone to agree to one's own actions):

(55) a. *Z + a* *ḳʷalax*   *iji + n!*
       I-ERG   work-NOM   do-HORT
       'Let me do [my] work!'
      b. *Vun*   *pʰakʰa*   *qʷe + n!*
       you-NOM   tomorrow   come-HORT
       'Let you come tomorrow!'
      c. *Fahum + fikir iji + n*   *vičʰ + i!*
       reasoning-NOM do-HORT   himself-ERG
       'Let him reason himself!'
       [Suleiman Stal, a famous Lezgian poet]

To sum up: What we see in examples (48) and (49) is by no means verb agreement. These examples clearly show three different verbal moods: hortative in (a), imperative in (b) and optative in (c).

If my analysis of Lezgian command sentences is correct, then the imperative counterargument can be safely disposed of.

4. Causatives

The next argument to be weighed is the existence in Lezgian of so-called "causative verbs" with suffixes -*ar*-, -*ur*-, -*ür*- and -*ud*-:

(56) **a.** *aqʷaz* + *un* 'to stop' [intr.]
  acʰuq + *un* 'to sit down'
  qʰür + *ün* 'to laugh'
  kʰus + *un* 'to sleep'
  galatʰ + *un* 'to get loose'

  b. *aqʷaz* + *ar* + *un* 'to stop somebody or smth'
  acʰuq + *ar* + *un* 'to seat somebody' (or 'to settle somebody')
  qʰür + *ür* + *ün* 'to make laugh'
  kʰus + *ur* + *un* 'to put to sleep'
  galud + *un* < *galatʰ* + *ud* + *un* 'to detach'

The verbs listed in (56b) strike the observer as seemingly transitive and thus contradicting my claim that there are no transitive verbs in Lezgian. But in fact they are not. Actually *aqʷaz* + *ar* + *un* means 'cease moving because of some external efforts', *acʰuq* + *ar* + *un* 'sit (or settle) down because of some external efforts', etc. The best proof of this is the fact that sentences with (56b)-type verbs are both perfectly grammatical and fully autonomous and self-sufficient without any mention of the causer, i.e., with no NP$_{erg}$:

(57) **a.** *Ajal* + *∅*   *kʰus* + *ur* + *na*
  child   NOM sleep   CAUS AOR
  'The child was put to bed'.

  b. *Taxirkar* + *diz*   *vigovor* + *∅*   *malum* + *ar* + *na*
  guilty   DAT reprimand NOM known   CAUS AOR
  'The guilty one was publicly reprimanded'
  [lit. 'To-the-guilty-one, a-reprimand was-declared].

It would be helpful to add three more facts about Lezgian causatives.

(i) The following pair of sentences seems to clearly show that the causative suffix imparts to the meaning of the stem the semantic component '. . . because of some external efforts':

(58) **a.** *Z* + *az*   *pʰul* + *∅*   *žɣa* + *na*
  I   DAT money NOM find   AOR
  'I found some money—quite accidentally, without having looked for it'.

  a. *Z* + *a*   *pʰul* + *∅*   *žuɣ* + *ur* + *na*
  I   ERG money NOM find   CAUS AOR
  'I found the money I was looking for'.

In both sentences, the form of *zun* 'I' may be omitted, and then (58a) means 'Some money appeared ⟨happened to be found⟩' while (58b) means 'The money was discovered (by somebody who had been looking for it)'.

(ii) It is repeatedly stated (Gadžiev 1954: 117, Talibov 1966: 570) that Lezgian causative verbs derived from "transitive" verbs do not differ in meaning from their noncausative partners. Currently cited examples include:

(59) *degiš + un* / *degiš + ar + un* 'exchange'
  aldatmiš + un / *aldatmiš + ar + un* 'cheat, dupe'
  tamam + un / *tamam + ar + un* 'fulfill, comply with'
  etc.

But in my opinion the above statement is wrong in general, although the examples given are basically correct. The causative suffix always brings with it the meaning '. . . because of some external efforts' but verbs denoting 'exchanging', 'cheating' or 'fulfilling' already have this semantic component since their meanings necessarily presuppose some external efforts; and therefore no apparent difference in meaning is perceived.

The fact that a Lezgian causative suffix when added to a "transitive" verb does not visibly change the meaning of the latter is a good argument to the effect that the causative suffixes do not mean 'to cause', but rather 'because of some external efforts'. The verb *degiš + ar + un* could in principle mean 'to cause to exchange' [= 'to make somebody exchange something for something'] but it does not; this is true about any so-called "causative verb" in Lezgian derived from "transitive" stem X: it never means 'to cause to X', but just simply 'X'. In languages such as Turkish, that possess true causative suffixes, the situation is exactly the opposite: Turkish *unut* 'forget'/ *unut-tur-* 'cause to forget'; *yaz-* 'write'/ *yaz-dir-* 'cause to write'; *oku-* 'read'/ *oku-t-* 'cause to read'; etc. Even multiple causative suffixes are possible, each one adding the meaning of a new causation: *piş-* 'be cooked'/ *piş-ir-* 'cook [trans]/ *piş-ir-t-* 'cause to cook', as in *Karım eti aşçya piş-ir-t-ti* 'My-wife meat to-the-cook caused-to-cook', i.e., 'My wife had the cook to cook the meat'. Nothing of the kind can happen in Lezgian.

(iii) Lezgian has numerous basic (i.e., simple) verbs that do not admit the agent NP$_{erg}$; at the same time, the causatives derived from such verbs can be used both ways: without or with NP$_{erg}$. For instance, taking a verb like *ҫur-un* 'melt' we get the following:

(60) a. *Živ + ∅*   *ҫr + azva*
    snow NOM melt PRES
   b. **Raq + ini*   *živ + ∅*   *ҫr + azva*
    sun   ERG   snow NOM   melt PRES

c. *Živ + 0   çur + ur   + izva*
   snow NOM   melt   CAUS PRES
   'Snow is being melted'.

d. *Raq + ini   živ + 0   çur + ur   + izva*
   sun   ERG   snow NOM   melt   CAUS PRES
   'The sun is melting the snow'.

The meaning '. . . because of some external efforts' is expressed in (60d) twice: by the ergative case of *raɣ* 'sun' and by the causative suffix *-ur-* in the verb.

(60a) and (60c) contrast semantically, as shown by their English glosses: in (60a), the snow melts, so to speak, by itself ['becomes water'], while in (60c) it undergoes an action by an external agent ['is made water'].

For verbs that do not take NP_{erg} see Note 2, p. 242.

Thus the Lezgian causatives do not contradict the claim that all Lezgian verbs are basically intransitive. Rather, they show quite well how genuine transitive verbs could eventually emerge in Lezgian—for instance, if the causative verbs cease to admit a free omission of the causer phrase in the ergative.

5. Passive (?) Character of the "Transitive" Predication

Now comes the main thesis put forth by those who propose to consider NP_{erg} as the grammatical subject in sentences like (3), (7a), (8a), etc. It runs approximately as follows (adapted from Gadžiev 1954: 83ff.).

If in (3) the phrase NP_{erg} is taken to be the agentive complement and NP_{nom} the grammatical subject, then (3) turns out to be an analogue of the passive construction of English, Latin, Russian, etc. (Note that older investigators, P.K. Uslar, for instance, actually spoke of (3) as of a passive construction.) Then all Lezgian verbs must be equated with passive forms of the corresponding Indo-European verbs, and the Lezgian ergative, with the Latin ablative, the Russian instrumental or the English agentive phrase introduced with *by*. Yet this is unacceptable at least for two reasons:

(i) The linguistic[1] intuition of the Lezgian people seems to perceive type (3) constructions as active. More precisely, any Lezgian with a firm command of all the subtleties of Russian (or English, for that matter) will translate (3) by an active construction and is likely to protest against a passive-construction equivalent.

(ii) The Lezgian ergative is not equivalent to the instrumental of Indo-European languages: it denotes the agent only, while for designating tools of an action a separate instrumental (more precisely, a supralative, with the basic meaning 'onto') is available, cf.:

(61) *Buba + di   jaḳʷ + aldi   ḳaras + ar + ∅   aṭ + uzva*
father   ERG ax   INSTR wood   PL   NOM cut   PRES
'Father cuts wood with an ax' [the ergative of 'ax' being *jaḳʷ + u*].

However, the above objections are due to nothing more than a misunderstand-ing. Nobody (including Uslar) ever seriously maintained that the Lezgian type (3) construction actually is a passive construction. Reference to the passive con-struction was (and sometimes is) used exclusively as a handy comparison — to demonstrate to English (French, Russian, . . .) readers formal peculiarities of Lezgian "transitive" sentences. It is obvious that *Ali + di kʰič ǥena* should not be seriously analyzed as 'By-Ali the dog was-killcd'. The passive construction is always communicatively non-neutral (and in most cases, morphologically sec-ondary). It is but a stylistic or communicative variant of the active construction, normally with a restricted domain of usage: not in informal speech, not in the first utterance of a discourse, etc., while the active construction knows no such restrictions (cf. Kurilovič 1946). Yet in Lezgian the construction NP_{erg} + NP_{nom} + MV is the only construction available, and it is used with no restric-tions whatsoever. Therefore, it is perceived as basic and neutral, i.e., closer to the English (or Russian) active construction. For speakers of a language, the pri-mary character, the basicness of a linguistic[1] item constitutes a highly relevant property immediately perceptible by the native linguistic[1] intuition. At the same time, all formal details of speech (like syntactic constructions, etc.) are not per-ceived (or are quite poorly perceived) by native speakers in normal linguistic[1] communication. Small wonder, then, that for Lezgian speakers their construc-tion of the type (3) is much nearer to the basic and neutral English active transi-tive construction. But all this by no means prevents type (3) constructions from being built, as far as their formal structure is concerned, more like a passive con-struction of English.

I think that the oldest analysis of (3), by Uslar, is the correct one: NP_{nom} is the grammatical subject and NP_{erg} the agentive complement, without the verb being passive; it only reminds an Indo-Europeanist of passive forms. The Lez-gian ergative case need not be equated with the Indo-European instrumental, and thus the above objections miss their target.

6. Three Pseudo-Transitive Constructions

In order to bring this section to a long overdue end, let me emphasize the fol-lowing important point. Gadžiev himself quite convincingly shows, for at least three types of Lezgian constructions that are traditionally taken to be transitive (perhaps by a superficial analogy with those of some other Daghestanian lan-guages), that they are intransitive, so that their NP_{nom} is the grammatical sub-ject, not the direct object, as many believe.

(i) Constructions with verbs of perception or feeling
Gadžiev argues that in (62):

(62) $Z + az$ $balkan + \emptyset$ $ak^hu + na$
I   DAT horse   NOM see   AOR
'I saw a horse'.

the grammatical subject is *balkan* 'horse' and the sentence is construed as 'To-me (a) horse became visible'; cf.

(63) $Da\gamma$ $+ din$ $k^huk^w + alaj$ $viri$ $dugun + \emptyset$ $ak^{hw} + ada$
mountain GEN summit DEL all   valley   NOM see   FUT
'From the summit of the mountain, all the valley is visible'.

The same holds for such verbs as 'hear' (= 'the sound comes'), 'smell' (= 'the smell comes'), 'know' (= 'is known'), 'love' (= 'is beloved'), etc. See pairs of sentences quoted by Gadžiev (1954: 103–110):

(64) a. $Z + az$ $ra\chi un$ $+ rin$ $van + \emptyset$ $at^ha + na$
I   DAT conversation GEN sound NOM come   AOR
'I heard the conversation' [lit. 'To-me sound of-conversation came'].
b. $Z + az$ $muhman + \emptyset$ $at^ha + na$
I   DAT guest   NOM come   AOR
'To me a guest came'.

(65) a. $Gada + diz$ $t^hars + \emptyset$ $č^hi$ $+ da$
boy   DAT lesson   NOM known be.PRES
'The boy knows his lesson'.
b. $Gada + diz$ i $k^har + \emptyset$ $malum$ ja
boy   DAT this business NOM known be.PRES
'To the boy, this business is known'.

(66) a. $Gada + diz$ i $ruš + \emptyset$ $\underset{.}{k}an$ $+ da$
boy   DAT this girl   NOM beloved be.PRES
'The boy loves this girl'.
b. $Gada + diz$ i $ruš + \emptyset$ $\underset{.}{k}an$ xa $+ na$
boy   DAT this girl   NOM beloved become AOR
'The boy fell in love with this girl'.

(66b) is a regular past form of (66a); cf. (67):

(67) I $ruš + \emptyset$ $qsan$ xa $+ na$
this girl   NOM good become AOR
'This girl recovered/improved/became good',

which is built syntactically just like (66b).

Thus, according to Gadžiev, there is no affective, or dative, construction in Lezgian: sentences presented in (62) through (67) all feature the most trivial intransitive nominal construction. (The traditional and officially accepted view in

Soviet Lezgianistic studies—see, e.g., Mejlanova 1967: 539—holds the NP$_{dat}$ in (62), (64a), (65a) and (66a) to be the GS, with the NP$_{nom}$ being considered the direct object.)

(ii) The stative, or resultative, construction
Consider sentences of type (68):

(68) **a.** *Rak^h + 0   aq^{h}a + jnava*
door   NOM open   RESULT
'The door is/has been opened (obviously, by somebody)'.

b. *I   rajon + da   plan + 0   behem + ar + nava*
this district INES plan   NOM fulfill   CAUS RESULT
'In this district, the plan is/has been fulfilled'.

c. *Klub + 0   agal + nava*
club   NOM closed + RESULT
'The club is/has been closed'.

Here the NP$_{nom}$ is, Gadžiev insists, the grammatical subject and not, as Lezgianists traditionally say, the GO^{dir}, the GS being absent but understood as indefinite human agent [$\cong$ 'they'].

(iii) Modal constructions meaning 'by accident' or 'possibility'
In (36):

(36) *Ali + divaj k^{h}iç + 0   qe + na*
Ali   ABL dog   NOM die   AOR
'Ali killed the dog accidentally'

Gadžiev attributes the role of grammatical subject to *k^{h}iç*; likewise in all similar cases where an NP$_{abl}$ denotes an involuntary, or indirect, causer.
He proposes the same analysis for (69):

(69) *Dide + divaj ajal + 0   sek^{h}in + riz   žez   + (va   + čir)*
mother ABL child   NOM quiet   SUP become RESULT not
'The mother could not still the child'.

He says that *dide + divaj*, although semantically the actor, is grammatically no more than an indirect object, while the grammatical subject is the NP$_{nom}$ *ajal* 'child'.

Nonetheless, having so resolutely stripped the semantic actor (or causer, or perceiver) of its privileged syntactic status as the grammatical subject in the three specific aforementioned cases, Gadžiev stops as if frightened before the general case

(3)   *Ali + di kʰiç̣ q̇e + na* 'Ali killed the dog'.

Here, he repeats, in complete accordance with the most widespread modern view, that *Alidi* is the grammatical subject, and *kʰiç̣* the direct object. He claims even more: if a NP$_{erg}$ is added to a sentence of type (68), this NP$_{erg}$ becomes the grammatical subject and the NP$_{nom}$ becomes the direct object (1954: 121)! The only explanation I have for this strange logical aberration is pressure from Russian grammar. It seems to be too difficult for linguists who either are Russian or do all their scientific thinking and writing in Russian to accept such a drastic digression from the Russian pattern. One readily recalls the terrible burden of the Latin grammatical tradition that has so strongly influenced the description of European vernaculars for so many centuries. Let me add that it has been repeatedly stated in Soviet linguistic literature that the description of national languages of the USSR should bring them nearer to the grammar of Russian, in order to facilitate for the nationals the assimilation and mastery of the latter.[7]

Summing up the evidence discussed in Subsections III. 1, III. 2 and III. 3, I can definitively state my final conclusion:

In all constructions of type (2) and (3):

(70)

NP$_{erg}$	NP$_{nom}$	MV
Alidi	*kʰiç̣*	*q̇ena*

'Ali killed the dog'

the grammatical subject is NP$_{nom}$, and NP$_{erg}$ is no more than the agentive complement.

IV. NO ERGATIVE CONSTRUCTION IN LEZGIAN

With my subsequent deliberations strongly anchored in statement (70), I will now set out to answer the question whether or not constructions of the type illustrated in (2) and (3) in Lezgian are ergative.

It is obvious that the answer is fully dependent on the definition of ergative construction that we proceed from, or, more precisely, on the meaning of the linguistic$_2$ term **ergative**. I take for granted the provisory definition formulated in Section VI of Chapter 4, which is repeated here for the reader's convenience:

An ergative construction (EC) is any non-nominative construction [i.e., a predicative construction where GS is marked by a case other than the nominative] whose grammatical subject refers to the "semantic subject" [i.e., roughly, 'causer'].

If we agree with this definition, it becomes immediately clear that the type (2) construction in Lezgian—*Alidi kʰiç̣ q̇ena* 'Ali killed the dog'—cannot be an EC. In all probability, there are no ECs at all in Lezgian. Lezgian and, say, English (as a typical representative of the so-called "nominative languages") are contrasted on a far deeper level than that of surface syntax, where the ergative construction occurs: these languages differ on the semantic level, since the semantics of Lezgian verbs (all of them being intransitive descriptions of STATES) is sharply distinct from what we find in English. Syntactically, (3) is an instance of the most trivial intransitive nominative construction.

In the next chapter I will deal in greater detail with the term **ergative**, distinguishing its various senses. That will, I hope, make the contents of our discussion of the Ergative Construction much clearer. But before proceeding to the analysis of the term **ergative**, I would like to compare the results obtained for Lezgian with those obtained in the preceding chapter for Dyirbal.

DYIRBAL:	LEZGIAN:
1. Has transitive verbs, whose meanings roughly approach those of their Indo-European equivalents, but whose diatheses are converse with respect to those of these equivalents.	1. Does not have transitive verbs at all: a Lezgian verb denotes a state or a process, never an action. (But there is a difference between two types of Lezgian verbs; some of them are "more intransitive" than the others: they do not admit the expression of the external Causer, while the others do.)
2. Has a well-established system of voices, which manipulate major syntactic actants of a transitive verb and detransitivize it, making the contrast "transitive *vs.* intransitive" much more visible.	2. Has no voices or voicelike categories at all; syntactic actants cannot be permuted, demoted or promoted.
3. Has a non-nominative construction: the GS of a transitive verb must be in the pathetive rather than in the nominative; but this GS never denotes the "semantic subject" (only the "semantic object").	3. Has only a nominative construction: the GS of any Lezgian verb must be in the nominative.

In my analysis of surface syntax of Dyirbal and Lezgian, I have arrived at the conclusion that neither language possesses an EC. However, the reasons for the respective conclusions are different: Dyirbal features a non-nominative construction that fails to be ergative because of semantics—its GS does not refer to the "semantic subject"; while Lezgian does not even have a non-nominative construction.

NOTES

1. (I, p. 208.) Verbs of perception, feeling and thinking manifest quite a different construction in Lezgian; see below, pp. 237–238.

2. (III, Property 1, after example (14′), p. 215.) Curiously enough, all Lezgian verbs that Gadžiev (1954: 100) lists as labile happen to have two different equivalents in Russian:

qin	= *umirat′* 'die' or *ubivat′* 'kill'
kun	= *goret′* 'burn, intrans' or *žeč′* 'burn, trans'
rugun	= *kipet′* 'boil, intrans' or *kipjatit′*, *varit′* 'boil, trans'
qurun	= *soxnut′* 'dry, intrans' or *sušit′* 'dry, trans'
χun	= *razbivat′sja* 'break, intrans' or *razbivat′* 'break, trans'
čʰurun	= *peč′sja*, *pospet′* 'be baked, get ready' or *peč′* 'bake'
aṭun	= *porvat′sja* 'get torn/divided' or *porvat′* 'tear/divide', *rezat′* 'cut'
qazunun	= *porvat′sja* 'get torn' or *porvat′* 'tear'

For other verbs, such as *basmišun* 'crush, flood, block', *čʰun* 'plow, sow', *χurun* 'weave', *qačun* 'take', *jarχarun* 'fell, knock down', etc., which behave in quite the same way, Russian lacks such an obvious "proof" of ambiguity. This is, I am afraid, the only reason for distinguishing in Lezgian a small class of labile verbs — while in fact either all Lezgian verbs that take an agent NP_{erg} are labile, or none of them is. (For another instance of Russian influence on Lezgian linguistic$_2$ thought, see below.)

Notice, however, that by no means all Lezgian verbs can take an agent NP_{erg} contributing the meaning 'caused by. . . .'. For instance, to express the meaning 'Caused by Ali, the girl left', the Lezgian does not say

(i) **Ali + di   ruš + Ø   qfena*;
     Ali   ERG   girl   NOM   left

we have to have recourse to a different verb ('chase', 'send away', . . .) or to an analytical causative construction V_{supine} + *tun* 'let, make, force' (i.e., 'Ali made the girl leave'). Another such verb is *çur + un* 'melt' in (60b) or *xun* 'become': cf.

(ii) *Gada + diz   čʰimi   xana*
     boy   DAT   warm   became
     vs.
     Buba + di   gada + diz   čʰimi   avuna ⟨*xana⟩
     father   ERG   do
     'The father made the boy warm'.

Thus there are, after all, two classes of verbs distinguished in Lezgian. Both are intransitive; but the verbs of the first class are, so to speak, absolutely intransitive and do not admit an expression of the causer (of the event described), while the verbs of the second class can (although need not) be combined with the causer (= agent) NP_{erg}. I think that the name **labile** could be applied to this second class, which is by no means small or otherwise restricted. It is this class that could eventually develop into a class of genuinely transitive verbs.

3. (III, Property 2, after example (22), p. 218.) In both of his books, Gadžiev warns against collapsing NP_{erg} and NP_{nom} under gapping (1954: 191; 1963: 54–56), and stigmatizes some examples of this kind he finds in the Lezgian press and literature as contradicting the spirit of Lezgian, "careless and ugly style" — induced possibly by Russian usage. It may be helpful, for the reader, to have here some more examples of actual Lezgian sentences with non-collapsible NP$_{nom}$s and NP$_{erg}$s (in boldface):

(i) **Alimehamed** *vič^{h}in lit^h + inin qene haq + na*
Alimehamed-NOM his coat GEN inside get.into PAST.GER
ač^{h}uq + navaj, **ad + a** *k^{h}ifil jaγiz + vaj*
sit RESULT II he ERG reed.pipe-NOM play IMPF I
va zajif van + č^{h}eldi mani + jar luhuz + vaj
and weak voice INSTR song PL-NOM sing IMPF I
'Alimehamed sat, wrapped in his woolen coat, played the reed-pipe, and sang songs in a low voice'.

(ii) **Sekretar** *ad + aq^h elq^w + ena va* **ad + a** *sa vuč^h*
secretary$_i$-NOM he$_i$ POSTES turn-AOR and he$_i$ ERG one what
žibin + din knižka + da kx + ena
pocket GEN book INES write AOR
'The secretary turned to him and wrote something in his notebook'.

Let it be emphasized that in (ii), it is the secretary who wrote, not 'he': *ada* refers to the secretary, not to *adaq^h*.

(iii) **Rabijat + a** *storož raγkur + na va* **vič^{h}ni**
Rabijat ERG watchman-NOM send.away AOR and she-NOM-also
ha + dan güγünal alaz eqeç + na javaš + javašdi fena
that GEN behind being go.out PAST.GER without.hurry go-AOR
'Rabijat sent the watchman away and, having gone out after him, she also went there in no hurry'.

4. (III, end of 1, p. 223.) There is probably a further syntactic property that could throw some light on the problem of the grammatical subject in Lezgian: the use of the reflexive pronouns *žuv* 'myself/yourself', *vič^h* 'himself/herself' and *č^{h}eb* 'themselves'. Cf.:

(i) *Gada + di* **vič^h + iz** *č^{h}ekme + jar + ∅ zakaz + ∅ ij + izva*
boy ERG himself DAT boot PL NOM order NOM do PRES
'The boy orders boots for himself'.

as opposed to (ii):

(ii) *Gada + di* **ad + az** *č^{h}ekmejar zakaz ijizva*
'The boy orders boots for him', i.e., for somebody else.

See further (iii) and (iv):

(iii) *Vun + a* **žuv + an** *k̦^{w}alax avu + raj!*
you ERG your work do OPT
'May you do your work!'

(iv) *Ad + a* **vic^h + in** *k̦^{w}alax avu + raj!*
he ERG his work do OPT
'May he do his work!'

However, the data about these pronouns are so scanty in Gadžiev (1954) and (1963) that it proved impossible to draw any sound conclusions. But after Mel'čuk (1981b), which underlies this chapter, had been published, I came across interesting data concerning the control of EQUI-Deletion, reflexivization and pronominalization in a dialect of Lezgian, namely the Khlut dialect (Kibrik 1979–80: issue 129, pp. 41–45). Given the importance of these data and their inaccessibility (because of the highly restricted character of the publication), I will quote them here. Note that the dialect in question is relatively distant from the Standard Lezgian, which explains several observed differences (*riš* 'girl' vs. standard *ruš*, *kʰatʰ* 'beat' vs. standard *gatʰ*, etc.). Kibrik's examples are given here with slight modifications in order to facilitate their presentation in my framework. I also added the indication of SSynt-roles of the NPs.

Only the examples bearing on the following surface-syntactic configuration are quoted:

—There are two verbs such that the one is a dependent of the other.
—One of the actants of the one verb is coreferential with one actant of the other.

Notations: V^1 stands for the higher verb, and V^2 for its dependent: $V^1 \rightarrow V^2$; actants of a verb V are notated as A(V). Coreference is shown with a broken-line arrow: $A(V^1) \dashrightarrow A(V^2)$; an actant participating in the coreference relation is notated $A_{coref}(V)$. The triangle ▲ stands for the noun elided under coreference (= the result of EQUI-Deletion). X/Y means that X is preferable to Y.

Let it be emphasized that to describe the data observed in (v)–(x) below, I am using my own interpretation of Lezgian syntax and my terminology, proposed in this chapter.

A. The verb *kan* 'want'

The $GO^{indir}(kan)$ denotes the experiencer of the desire and is marked with the dative: ≅ 'to-him desire-is'; in the examples, this is *gada + diz* 'boy' [= 'The boy wants . . .']. The target of EQUI-Deletion and reflexivization under *kan* is the $A_{coref}(V^2)$, i.e. the actant of the dependent verb that is coreferential with 'boy'. The three dependent verbs used in all the examples are: an intransitive verb (*kʰlig* 'look at'), a traditionally "transitive" verb (*kʰatʰ* 'beat'), and a perception verb (*akʰw* 'see' [= 'be visible to']).

(v) **a.** *gada + diz* ▲ *riš + az* *kʰlig + iz* *kan + zava*
  boy DAT NOM girl DAT look SUP want PRES
  GS GO^{indir}
  'The boy wants to look at the girl'.

 b. *gada + diz* ▲ *riš +* *0* *kʰatʰ + az* *kanzava*
  ERG girl NOM beat SUP
  CO^{agent} GS
  'The boy wants to beat the girl'.

 c. *gada + diz* ▲ *riš + 0* *akʰw + az* *kanzava*
  DAT girl NOM see SUP
  GO^{indir} GS
  'The boy wants to see the girl'.

(vi) **a.** *gada + diz* *riš + 0* *üčʰ + üz* *kʰlig + na* *kanzava*
  boy DAT girl NOM self DAT look AOR wants
  GS GO^{indir}
  'The boy wants that the girl look at him'.

b. *gada + diz   riš + a   üčⁿ + ∅   kʰatʰ + ana   kanzava*
 girl   ERG   self   NOM   beat   AOR
 CO^{agent} GS
 'The boy wants that the girl beat him'.

c. *gada + diz   riš + az   üčⁿ + ∅   akʰʷ + ana   kanzava*
 girl   DAT   self   NOM   see   AOR
 GO^{indir} GS
 'The boy wants that the girl see him'.

A clear picture emerges: if A$_{coref}$(V²) is either our basic GS, or the CO^{agent}, or else the GO^{indir} denoting the perceiver, then V² takes the supine form (which corresponds roughly to the English infinitive) and A$_{coref}$(V²) is elided. Otherwise, that is, if A$_{coref}$(V²) is either a GO^{indir} = perceiver or a non-basic GS, then V² takes the form of the aorist (which, in this context, corresponds to the English subjunctive) and A$_{coref}$(V²) is reflexivized. Thus from the viewpoint of EQUI-Deletion and reflexivization under *kan* 'want', it is CO^{agent} and GO^{indir} = perceiver, rather than our non-basic GSs, that pattern with the basic GS.

B. The verb *kʰče* 'be afraid of'

The GO^{indir}(*kʰče*) denotes the experiencer of the fear and is also marked with the dative: ≅ 'to-him fear-is'; in these examples, it is again *gada + diz* 'boy' [= 'The boy is afraid . . .']. The target of EQUI-Deletion and reflexivization under *kʰče* is, as in A, the A$_{coref}$(V²).

(vii) **a.** *gada + diz   ▲ / üčⁿ + ∅   riš + az   kʰlig + iz*
 boy   DAT NOM self   NOM   girl   DAT   look   SUP
      GS   GO^{indir}

kʰčezava
be.afraid-PRES
'The boy is afraid to look at the girl'.

b. *gada + diz   ▲ / üčⁿ + ü   ris + ∅   kʰatʰ + az   kʰčezava*
    ERG   self   ERG   girl   NOM   beat   SUP

      CO^{agent} GS
'The boy is afraid to beat the girl'.

c. *gada + diz   ▲ / üčⁿ + üz   riš + ∅   akʰʷ + az   kʰčezava*
    DAT   self   DAT   girl   NOM   see   SUP

      GO^{indir} GS
'The boy is afraid to see the girl'.

(viii) **a.** *gada* + *diz*   *riš* + *∅*   *üčʰ* + *üz* / ▲ *kʰlig* + *iz*   *kʰčezava*
       boy   DAT girl   NOM self   DAT DAT look   SUP

                 GS   GO^{indir}
      'The boy is afraid that the girl will look at him'.

     b. *gada* + *diz*   *riš* + *a*   *üčʰ* + *∅* / ▲ *kʰatʰ* + *az*   *kʰčezava*
               girl   ERG self   NOM NOM beat   SUP

            CO^{agent} GS
      'The boy is afraid that the girl will beat him'.

     c. *gada* + *diz*   *riš* + *az*   *üčʰ* + *∅* / ▲ *akʰw* + *az*   *kʰčezava*
               girl   DAT self NOM NOM see   SUP

         GO^{indir} GS
      'The boy is afraid that the girl will see him'.

Once again, the sentence elements that pattern with the basic GS are the CO^{agent} and GO^{indir} = perceiver: the corresponding A$_{coref}$(V²) is preferably elided (by EQUI-Deletion), although reflexivization remains possible; but if A$_{coref}$(V²) is either a GO^{indir} not denoting a perceiver, or a GS, then it is rather reflexivized, although ellipsis is possible as well (but less current).

C. A finite verb governing a circumstantial gerund

In sharp contrast to A and B above, the target of EQUI-Deletion and pronominalization in this construction is the A$_{coref}$(V¹), i.e. the actant of the governing verb that is coreferential with the actant of the gerund.

(ix) **a.** *gada* + *di*   *harajar* + *iz*,   ▲   *riš* + *az*   *kʰlig* + *zava*
       boy   ERG shout   GER.PRES NOM girl   DAT look   PRES
                                      GS   GO^{indir}
      'The boy$_i$ shouting, (he$_i$) looks at the girl'.

     b. *gada* + *di*   *harajar* + *iz*, ▲   *riš* + *∅*   *kʰatʰ* + *azava*
            ERG shout   ERG girl   NOM beat   PRES
                              CO^{agent} GS
      'The boy$_i$ shouting, (he$_i$) beats the girl'.

     c. *gada* + *di*   *harajar* + *iz*, ▲   *riš* + *∅*   *akʰw* + *azava*
            ERG shout   DAT girl   NOM see   PRES
                              GO^{indir} GS
      'The boy$_i$ shouting, (he$_i$) sees the girl'.

(x) **a.** *gada* + *di*   *harajar* + *iz*, *riš* + *∅*   *an* + *daz* *kʰlig* + *zava*
      boy   ERG   girl   NOM he   DAT look   PRES
                               GS   GO^{indir}
      'The boy$_i$ shouting, the girl looks at him$_i$'.

b. *gada + di   harajar + iz, riš   + a   ama + ∅   kʰatʰ + azava*
　　　　　　　　　　　girl　　　　　ERG　he　　NOM　beat　　PRES
　　　　　　　　　　　CO^agent　　　　　　　GS

'The boy$_i$ shouting, the girl beats him$_i$'.

c. *gada + di   harajar + iz, riš   + az   ama + ∅   akʰʷ + azava*
　　　　　　　　　　　girl　　　　　DAT　he　　NOM　see　　PRES
　　　　　　　　　　　CO^indir　　　　　　　GS

'The boy$_i$ shouting, the girl sees him$_i$'.

Here, as in the two previous cases, EQUI-Deletion vs. pronominalization is controlled by our basic GS, the CO^agent or the perceiver GO^indir: if $A_{coref}(V^1)$ is one of these three, it is elided; otherwise it is pronominalized.

To sum up: let me call the control of the three syntactic operations mentioned—EQUI-Deletion, reflexivization, and pronominalization—PRO-Control, for short. Generally speaking, PRO-Control is, beyond any doubt, an important syntactic property, relevant for the decision about subjecthood. And according to Kibrik's data, this property indicates the N_{erg} and N_{dat} (with verbs of perception) as the GS, thereby contradicting my solution to consider as the GS the N_{nom} with all types of verbs.

True, Kibrik's data come from a dialect that differs considerably from Standard Lezgian, so that the phenomenon in question might not occur in the latter (I am not in a position to check and to establish whether this is the case). However, my main purpose is theoretical, not descriptive; therefore, I cannot hide behind the excuse of different dialects; instead, I have to face the situation and decide what is to be done if the said phenomenon existed in Standard Lezgian.

I would still say that in Lezgian, the N_{nom} of all verbs is the grammatical subject etc., that is, I would stand my ground anyway. The reason is that, to me, in Lezgian the property of PRO-Control is motivated SEMANTICALLY: the PRO-Controller is here the Actor, the Causer, the Perceiver or the Experiencer, or, to use an obvious abbreviation for this disjunction, the Agent, regardless of its actual surface-syntactic role. In other words, the rule for EQUI-Deletion and pronominalization in case C must be written without even mentioning SSynt-roles. Cf.:

Similar rules are needed for cases A and B.

We see, then, that the capacity to effect PRO-Control accrues in Lezgian to obvious, clear-cut semantic roles (or, using Kibrik's term, to a semantic hyperrole), rather than to semantically diffuse and vague syntactic roles. Therefore, I consider the property "being a PRO-Controller" as less weighty or less relevant than the three previously considered subjecthood properties, which have no unifying semantic substratum.

Let it be emphasized that what I am actually doing here is introducing a new parameter to be used in subjecthood discussions: relative WEIGHT, or IMPORTANCE, of properties P_i according to which different candidates to the GS role are compared with the basic GS. I also propose that underlying semantic regularity is, so to speak, a demerit point for a SYNTACTIC property. This topic, however, cannot be pursued here any longer. (Cf., in this connection, Nichols et al. 1980, where it is clearly shown how communicative structure —topicality and the like—influences syntactic processes independent of the SSynt-roles of the corresponding sentence elements.)

Notice, by the way, that in Dyirbal, the control of verbal adverbs in -ŋura (roughly similar to the -ing-form in English) is also typical of a semantic, rather than a SSynt-, unit: the -ŋura phrase bears on the "Semantic Subject" (= N_{instr}, i.e. CO^{agent}) of the main verb, not on its GS (although the coreferential actant of the -ŋura- form must necessarily be its GS, whatever its semantic interpretation: something like 'By-the-man$_i$ the-tree was-cut, he$_i$ immediately leaving' = 'The man cut down the tree and left immediately'). Therefore, I do not consider the control of -ŋura-forms as an important subjecthood property in Dyirbal, either, and for the same reason as PRO-Control in Lezgian: this is a syntactic phenomenon that is fully motivated semantically. Cf. Chapter 4, Note 10, pp. 199ff.

5. (III, 3, end of **2**, p. 230.) A short terminological note seems not to be out of place here. The following three notions should be kept strictly apart:

Subjectless sentence, or a sentence that has no GS at all, e.g., (43)–(45).
Zero subject sentence, or a sentence that has a zero grammatical subject, e.g., (12a—b) and (42).
Impersonal sentence, or a sentence that has a dummy grammatical subject (overt or zero) and therefore does not admit an actual actor or perceiver in the subject role, e.g., *It rains* or *It's getting dark.*

As we see, an impersonal sentence has a grammatical subject, even if only a dummy; on the other hand, a subjectless sentence is not necessarily an impersonal one, like (43b) and (44b), for example, where a human perceiver is explicitly mentioned. (A similar distinction was proposed in Jakovlev 1940: 14–15.)

6. (III, 3, **3**, example (51b), p. 232.) Two further examples of the 2nd person optative form are the current formula of saying 'goodbye', 'farewell', 'thank you':

(i) *De,   vun saγ   + raj!*
    well you healthy   OPT

and the current formula of cursing:

(ii) *Vun   qazun + raj!*
     you   tear   OPT
     'May you be cut open (after your death)!'

7. (End of III, p. 240.) It is interesting to quote, in this connection, some passages from Jakovlev (1940). Jakovlev fights the opinion that NP_{nom} in Chechen sentences (structurally quite close to the Lezgian sentences of type (3)) is the grammatical subject. But his only argument is as follows: "Such an interpretation of the Chechen transitive construction [i.e., that the NP_{nom} is the GS − I.M.] leads not only to theoretical confusion but had and still has serious practical consequences. Due to this explanation of the Chechen structure . . . , the correct acquisition of Russian is most strongly impeded for a vast majority of Chechen people. . . . All this sabotage is a direct result of the shortsightedness and purposeful russification policy [*sic*!] of Chechen bourgeois nationalists . . . this "theory" [that the NP_{nom} is the $GS(V_{(tr)})$ − I.M.] is no more than a front for the larcenous policies of the capitalist powers; that is why it is shared and supported by all these saboteurs, the worst enemies of the Soviet people" (1940: 46–47); "if we were to accept that in Chechen the direct object [= $NP_{nom}(V_{(tr)})$] is the grammatical subject, . . . then the Chechen people would be deprived of the possibility to correctly acquire Russian and other European languages. . . . In a word, it would mean that we follow the dangerous path of the people's enemies, the bourgeois nationalists. Therefore, the only correct, scientific solution is to call grammatical subject in Chechen exactly that which is called grammatical subject in all other standard [*sic*!] languages" (1940: 50–51). It is really difficult to stop quoting arguments like these. . . .

Chapter 6

TOWARD
A DEFINITION
OF THE CONCEPT
"ERGATIVE
CONSTRUCTION"

I. INTRODUCTORY REMARKS

As indicated on the introductory pages of Part III, the topic of ergative construction is very popular with linguists today, and for good reason. The number of studies dedicated to its different aspects, even if we take only those that have been published in the last decade, runs into hundreds—actually, we are facing a real ergative boom, so that a survey of relevant literature, be it however cursory, is out of the question here. I refer the reader to the best and clearest reviews available, already mentioned at the beginning of Part III: Catford (1976), Comrie (1978) and Dixon (1979) (they also contain full bibliographies), to which I can add a few more special works: Comrie (1973), Klimov (1973, 1977), Tchekhoff (1978), Plank (1979), Kibrik (1979–80, 1985). Avoiding any polemics, I propose to try a purely logical analysis of some central concepts—along the lines sketched in Mel'čuk 1978. In this way I hope to bring more order into the discussion, which I feel is plagued by notional and terminological vagueness. It goes without saying that I proceed from the theoretical framework outlined in Part I, i.e., from the Meaning-Text theory. Given the limitations of the present chapter, I have to be satisfied with simply stating the key points, without substantial argumentation. I will also draw heavily on the results obtained in Chapters 4 and 5.

II. THE TERM **ERGATIVE**

First of all, I pledge to avoid the currently used term **ergativity**—an abstract noun, multiply ambiguous and having no well-defined content: cf. the last paragraph of the introduction to Part III. I allow only the terminological use of the adjective *ergative* (and of its derivation, *the ergative*) exclusively in the following three senses:

1. The **ergative case**, or simply **the ergative**, denotes a morphological case whose main function is to mark, generally speaking, the grammatical subject of a transitive verb or an agentive complement (in sharp contrast with the nominative, the ergative is not used to name things; in contrast with the instrumental, the ergative does not mark instruments or means). As we have seen, Dyirbal has no ergative (Chapter 4, p. 158), while Lezgian has one: the case in *-di* (Chapter 5). Further examples of the ergative include the Georgian ergative (the case in *-ma*) and the Basque ergative (the case in *-k*).[1]

2. The **ergative construction** (EC): the term applies exclusively to (surface) syntactic formations; more specifically, it denotes a particular subclass of predicative (bipartite: GS + MV) or predicative-objective (tripartite: GS + MV + GO^{dir}) constructions. The *differentiae specificae* of this subclass reside in the relationships between the EC and its representations at the neighboring levels: on the one hand, case marking of its nominal components on the deep-morphological level (the GS is marked by a non-nominative case); and on the other hand, semantic interpretation of the situational roles of the same components on the semantic level (the GS denotes the "semantic subject"). See the definition of EC below.

3. An **ergative language**, with two possible subsenses:
   a. Ergative₁ language = 'a language where ergative constructions predominate'. This is obviously a quantitative concept. The degree to which a language may be called ergative₁ depends on how often and consistently it uses ECs. The ergativity₁ index of language $\mathcal{L}$ varies (at least, in theory) continuously from 0 to 1; to have this index equal to 1, $\mathcal{L}$ must have ALL its predicative (including predicative-objective) constructions to be ergative in the above sense. If the ergativity₁ index is less than 1 (but more than 0), the expression **ergative split** (Comrie 1978: 350 ff., Dixon 1979: 79–98) is used. The appearance/non-appearance of an EC may be conditioned semantically (voluntary vs. involuntary action) or grammatically (present vs. past tense of the main verb, pronominal vs. nominal actant).

   b. Ergative₂ language = 'a language possessing a bundle of particular features having to do with subject-object relations: (i) its verbs are object-, rather than subject-, oriented (they have object agreement; they have suppletive stems as a function of the grammatical number or class of the object); (ii) it has no voice; (iii) the object of V(tr) and the subject of a V(itr) have the same case-marks, while the subject of a V(tr) has a different case-mark; (iv) it has no accusative, the $GO(V_{(tr)})$ and $GS(V_{(itr)})$ being marked by the nominative ($GS(V_{(tr)})$ may have any case-mark other than the nominative); etc.' (see Klimov 1973 for a fuller list of ergativity$_2$ features). Since all these features are quantitative, the ergativity$_2$ index of $\mathcal{L}$ also varies continuously from 0 to 1.

Let it be most strongly emphasized that these three concepts — the ergative case, the ergative construction and the ergative$_{1/2}$ language — are logically independent.

For one thing, the ergative case is not necessarily connected with EC in a one-to-one way: A language can have a full-fledged and widespread EC but no ergative case at all, its "transitive" GSs being marked by the instrumental (like Alutor, see Chapter 7, pp. 280), the genitive (Lak), the oblique (Kurmanji), the locative, the dative, etc. A language can also have the ergative case with no EC, its ergative obligatorily marking the causer [= SemSubj], which, on the SSynt-level, appears as an agentive complement or even a circumstantial rather than as the grammatical subject (such is the case of Lezgian).

Furthermore, a language may have an ergative construction without, however, being to a sufficient degree ergative$_1$ (e.g., because its EC has a very limited range) or without being ergative$_2$ (because it does not possess enough properties typical of genuine ergative$_2$ languages). Take, for instance, Aronson (1970) who states that Georgian is not an ergative$_2$ language (i.e., not a language with typical ergative$_2$ properties) and quotes three arguments to support this view: "Firstly, the agent of a transitive verb can be marked in Georgian not only by an ergative case but also by a dative-accusative and by a nominative. Secondly, the substratum [= GS − I.M.] of middle verbs is marked generally by the ergative and not by an 'absolute' case (nominative). Thirdly, the presence of a whole set of passive paradigms is a feature typical of 'nominative' languages rather than of 'ergative' languages" (Aronson 1970: 295). I share Aronson's opinion, but this by no means prevents me from saying that the most current Georgian transitive predicative construction (in the aorist series) is quite a typical instance of EC:

(1) Georgian *mama* + *m*   *çeril* + *i*   *daçer* + *a*
        father   ERG letter   NOM write   AOR
        'Father wrote the letter'.

[*mamam* is the grammatical subject and *çerili*, the grammatical direct object; I must abstain from substantiating this analysis here, which is, by the way, the generally accepted one; cf., e.g., Chanidzé (1963) and Harris (1981)].

The term **ergative$_2$ language** seems, however, infelicitous and cannot be recommended in spite of the fact that it enjoys wide currency. In fact, if the term **ergative construction** is retained, then it will be necessary to be able to say that some ergative$_2$ languages do not possess ergative construction, etc., which might lead to harmful confusions. It is wiser to save the terms **ergative construction** and **ergative$_1$ language** and coin a new term for ergative$_2$ languages (of

Lezgian type). One could have recourse to a modifier and distinguish **syntactically ergative** [= ergative$_1$] and **semantically ergative** [= ergative$_2$] languages. But our point here is clearly not this terminological problem. (This complication with the term arose because by the time the usages of the adjective *ergative* were being established in general linguistics (by Dirr 1928), no clear-cut distinction had been drawn between Georgian-type and Lezgian-type languages, *ergative* being used indiscriminately for both in two basically different senses. Let it be added that to make things even more confused, the following terminological usage is widespread in the literature (cf. Comrie 1978: 337–350):

Ergative$_1$, i.e. Georgian-type, languages are being called **morphologically ergative**.

Ergative$_2$, i.e. Lezgian-type, languages are being called **syntactically ergative**.

However, I cannot agree to such wording, since it runs counter to the intuitive interpretation of morphology and syntax: selection of a particular case for the grammatical subject belongs to syntax rather than morphology; having a GS that never expresses the 'causer' is a feature of semantics rather than syntax. So, to the extent that I have to speak of ergative$_{1/2}$ languages, I will use the expressions **syntactically** vs. **semantically ergative**.)

In what follows, as in the preceding two chapters, I concentrate on the concept of ergative construction; the concepts of ergative case and of ergative$_{1/2}$ language have been simply touched upon in order to better delineate the former.

III. LEVELS OF REPRESENTATION IN THE STUDY OF THE ERGATIVE CONSTRUCTION

When speaking of the ergative construction, (at least) the following three levels of linguistic$_1$ representation should be postulated and kept strictly apart:

—SEMANTIC (Sem-) level. Here the meaning of the verb appears as a (complex) predicate configuration, 'predicate' being taken in the logico-semantic sense; the meanings of its dependent NPs are arguments of this predicate. In slightly different terms, these NPs are **semantic actants** of the verb, identifiable by the positions (= argument slots) they occupy in the predicate: 'causer' [= first argument of 'cause'], 'perceiver', 'moving body', 'causee' [= 'changing its state under the impact of a causation'], '(the) perceived', 'experiencer' [of an internal psychological or physiological state], etc.

—SURFACE-SYNTACTIC (SSynt-) level, where the verb and its dependents appear as nodes in a linearly unordered dependency tree—lexemes, with no direct access to their meanings and stripped of their syntactically induced morphological markings (so that, among others, the NPs bear no case-marks). The NPs related to the verb in a particular, lexically specified ways are its **surface-syntactic actants**: grammatical subject GS, grammatical objects GO and complements. There are also various circumstantials ($\cong$ adverbials: temporal, spatial, conditional, etc.), which should not interest us in this book.

—DEEP-MORPHOLOGICAL (DMorph-) level: the verb and its dependent NPs appear as a string of lexemes provided with all morphological characteristics. Here grammatical cases are most relevant, namely **case marking** of NPs.

Remark 1

To avoid notional complications, the deep-syntactic level is not considered here. It is quite important in discussing, e.g., grammatical voices, but can be safely bypassed in a study of the ergative construction. True, the omission of this level forces more simplistic formulations.

Remark 2

Interestingly, the same three levels (although under different names: Deep, Shallow and Surface Structures) are distinguished in Dixon (1979: 65). There are crucial differences between Dixon's approach to these levels and mine, in the first place in the formalisms used; nevertheless, the main idea, namely, that EC concerns SIMULTANEOUSLY semantics, syntax and morphology, is the same.

Note that the terms **subject, object** and **agent**, used frequently in discussions concerning EC and related matters, are by no means genuine semantic entities: there are no such semantic units as 'being the subject/the object/the agent of' in our SemR, of which these elements could be arguments. Neither are they surface-syntactic entities; all in all, their status is vague and dubious, and this is why I consistently avoid them. The terms "semantic subject" and "semantic object" that I have been using in Chapters 4 and 5 are not semantic units themselves but arbitrary labels, used as handy abbreviations for two disjunctions:

"semantic subject" = any semantic actant that is treated by the language in question in the same way as the 'causer';

"semantic object" = any semantic actant that is treated by the language in the same way as the 'causee'.

Thus, consider *I cannot endure this pain* = 'I experiencing this pain causes that I cannot behave properly'; 'I' is by no means a 'causer', neither is 'pain' a 'causee'; however both elements pattern exactly as 'causers' and 'causees' do in English: *I cannot cut this wire, He cannot cook this meat*, etc., and therefore the NP *I* is the "semantic subject" of *endure*, while *this pain* is its "semantic object." (Cf. similar remarks in Dixon 1979: 106–107.)

In this book I use for the said three levels the formalisms adopted within the Meaning-Text theory (and introduced in Chapters 1 and 2). These need not necessarily be accepted by the reader: other formalisms would probably not do worse; but one cannot fruitfully discuss the ergative construction without exactly these three levels: semantics, syntax, morphology.

To make the distinction between them absolutely clear, let me illustrate it by means of three corresponding representation of a Russian transitive sentence:

(2)   Russian *Ja ubil ego* 'I killed him'.

The **Semantic Representation** of (2), expressed verbally and drastically simplified, appears as (3):

(3)   'I acted physically upon him [= I did something to him]; this act caused that he died; the temporal and spatial distance between my act and his death is small' (cf. Wierzbicka's discussion of *kill* vs. *cause to die*: 1975).

Here, 'I' is the 'causer', and 'he', the 'causee'.
The **Surface-Syntactic Structure** of (2) is as follows:

(4)

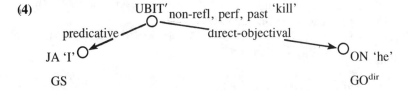

Let it be recalled that in our framework the SSynt-structure is a labeled dependency tree where the linear order of nodes is quite immaterial. Labels on branches are SS-relations of the (Russian) language. The subscripts on UBIT′ stand for non-reflexivity, perfective aspect, and past tense: all morphological values (= grammemes) that convey meaning. Syntactically conditioned morphological categories, such as (person and) number of the main verb or grammatical case of the nominals, are not shown at this level (much like word order).

The **Deep-Morphological Structure** of (2) is shown below:

(5)   JA $\boxed{\text{nom}}$ 'I' UBIT′ $_{\text{non-refl, perf, past,}}$ $\boxed{\text{sg, masc}}$ 'kill' ON $\boxed{\text{acc}}$ 'he'

(5) is a string formed by lexeme names provided with all morphological subscripts necessary to derive actual wordforms. (Subscripts which were absent in (4) but added in (5) are boxed for the reader's convenience.)

Comparing noun phrases that appear on the same level of representation, we can establish the most important NP, the one that is somehow privileged from the viewpoint of this particular level.

On the semantic level, it is the 'causer' NP and all the others that are treated by the language much like it, i.e., our "SEMANTIC SUBJECT."

On the syntactic level, it is the GRAMMATICAL SUBJECT NP, defined in the way sketched in Chapters 4 and 5.

On the morphological level, it is the NOMINATIVE NP. The nominative case is universally the most privileged one in that it is used out of any context to name objects; therefore, it is supposed to be present in any language that has cases.

Then our main building blocks in putting together a definition for Ergative Construction are the 'Causer' (or, more generally, "Semantic Subject"), the grammatical subject and the nominative case. Let us see what can be done with these blocks.

IV. TYPOLOGY OF PREDICATIVE CONSTRUCTIONS

A verb that means 'kill', for example, necessarily has the same two Sem-actants in any language: 1) X, who causes the situation of dying by means of physical impact on . . . [= 'causer'] and 2) Y, whose life is taken away [= 'causee']. But SSynt-actants of such a verb and their DMorph-marking need not be the same in two different languages:

—the 'causer' X can be implemented at the SSynt-level either as GS or as a different sentence element, a non-GS.
—GS, in its turn, can be marked, at the DMorph-level, either by the nomina-tive or by an oblique case, a non-nominative.

We are interested in predicative constructions distinguished at the SSynt-level, and especially in their most privileged component: the GS. Starting with GS and using the aforementioned elements of the two adjacent levels, the SemSubj and the nominative case, we obtain exactly four logical possibilities for the predica-tive construction of the type illustrated in (2):

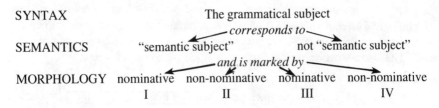

SYNTAX   The grammatical subject
                              corresponds to
SEMANTICS   "semantic subject"   not "semantic subject"
                          and is marked by
MORPHOLOGY nominative non-nominative nominative non-nominative
                   I   II   III   IV

All these possibilities are actually manifested in natural languages, so that we find four (sub)classes, or types, of predicative construction:

Type I: the GS expresses the "semantic subject" (i.e., at least in some occur-rences of this predicative construction the GS denotes the 'causer') and is marked by the nominative. Such predicative constructions are the only pos-sible in Germanic, Slavic, Romance, Semitic, Ural-Altaic and many other languages.

Type II: the GS expresses the "semantic subject" but is marked by a non-nominative (but see the proviso in the definition of EC in Section V below). This type of construction is widespread in Kartvelian (Georgian and Zan), in Dargwa, in Chukchee, Koryak and Alutor, in Eskimo, in Hindi and several other Indian languages, in Pashto, Kurmanji, Burushaski, Basque, etc.

Type III: the GS does not express the "semantic subject", i.e., it never expresses the 'causer' (it may but need not express the "semantic object"); nonetheless, this GS is marked by the nominative. The predicative constructions in Lezgian, Chechen, etc. are exclusively of this type.

Type IV: the GS does not express the "semantic subject" and is not marked by the nominative; such are all predicative transitive constructions in Dyirbal, where the "transitive" GS is marked by the pathetive.

This classification applies only to constructions (and languages) that have grammatical case. To cover languages that lack it, a generalization of our approach is needed, cf. below.

The types of predicative construction established are the most general subclasses possible; they presuppose a number of finer distinctions to be introduced. For instance, for Type II predicative constructions the following features are relevant:

i. Are all GSs marked by a non-nominative case—or only the "transitive" (or "active") GSs?

ii. Does the case marking of the GS depend on the meaning or the form (tense, aspect, . . .) of the main verb?

iii. Are the "transitive" GSs marked the same way or differently as the "intransitive" GSs?

iv. Is the case marking of GOs somehow related to the case marking of GSs —or is it fully independent in this respect?

And so forth.

In this condensed presentation I will not touch on these topics. Instead, I proceed to discuss the term **ergative construction** in more detail and to formulate a rigorous definition.

V. THE ERGATIVE CONSTRUCTION: ATTEMPT AT A DEFINITION

The term **ergative** is at present widely used to refer to two-nominal predicative constructions of Types II through IV. But this is clearly a misleading usage since in this way two quite different phenomena are being subsumed under the same term:

1. A purely SEMANTIC property of some constructions that use GS to express the 'causee' rather than the 'causer' (Lezgian or Chechen); the crucial point here is the semantic content of the GS.

2. A purely SURFACE-SYNTACTIC property of some other constructions that mark their GS by a case other than the nominative (Georgian, Chukchee, etc.); the point here is the morphological marking of the GS. Note, however, that the predicative transitive construction in Dyirbal combines both properties.

Since the very term **ergative construction** implies a **syntactic** construction, only expressions that possess genuine syntactic peculiarities deserve the name of EC. Languages of a pure Daghestanic type, like Lezgian, Chechen or Avar, have no EC at all: all of their "abnormality" (if compared with English, Russian, etc.) resides, as Uslar used to emphasize a century ago (1888, 1889), not in the realm of their syntax, but rather in the realm of their semantics.

Based on this consideration, the most logical procedure to construct a good definition of EC would be to define first the broadest possible class of surface-syntactic constructions that includes EC: non-nominative constructions.

NON-NOMINATIVE CONSTRUCTION

(6) || A **non-nominative construction** is a predicative construction GS + MV where GS is marked at the DMorph-level by a case other than the nominative, this marking being not induced by the semantic content of the GS itself.

The last restriction is necessary since in several languages the case of the GS may be conditioned by the semantics of the latter: whether it is definite/indefinite, taken in its totality/partially etc., without involving the relation between the GS and the main verb. Thus in Finnish (and quite similarly in Estonian) the GS denoting 'some X' must be in the partitive rather than in the nominative:

(7) Finnish **a.** *Lapsi + a   juokse + e   pihalla*
child   PL.PART run   PRES.IND.3SG in-courtyard
'Some children are [lit.: is] running in the courtyard'
vs.

b. *Lapse + t   juokse + vat   pihalla*
child   PL.NOM run   PRES.IND.3PL
'The children are running in the courtyard'.

c. *Leipä + ä   on pöydällä*
bread   SG.PART is on-table
'There is some bread on the table'
vs.

d. *Leipä + Ø   on pöydällä*
bread   SG.NOM
'The bread is on the table'.

Such constructions will be considered nominative, the partitive in (7a) and (7c) being treated as a semantic "partner" of the nominative.

The same happens in Russian, where with some negated verbs a non-referential GS appears in the genitive:

(8) Russian

a. *Odnako   nikakix   mer   + ∅   prinjat + o*
however no   measure   PL.GEN taken   SG.NEUT
ne   byl + o
not was   NEUT.3SG
'However, no measures were [lit.: was] taken'.

b. *Odnako èti   mer   + y   prinjat + y   ne byl + i*
           these   measure   PL.NOM taken   PL not was   PL
'However, these measures were not taken'.

In similar way, the construction (8a) is also considered nominative.

Now EC is naturally defined as a subclass of non-nominative constructions:

ERGATIVE CONSTRUCTION

(9)   ‖An **ergative construction** is a non-nominative construction where the
         ‖GS denotes the "semantic subject."

Along the same lines may be defined the pathetive construction founa in
Dyirbal:

PATHETIVE CONSTRUCTION

(10) ‖A **pathetive construction** is a non-nominative construction where the
         ‖GS denotes the "semantic object."

Similarly, we can quite naturally define further subclasses of non-nominative
constructions, e.g., as follows:

ACTIVE / AFFECTIVE/ . . . CONSTRUCTION

(11) ‖An **active/affective/. . . construction** is a non-nominative construc-
         ‖tion where the GS does not denote the "semantic subject" or the "se-
         ‖mantic object" (i.e. neither the 'causer' nor the 'causee'), but the
         ‖'actor'/'experiencer'/. . . .

Definitions of type (11) are needed for languages where "intransitive" 'actors'
or 'experiencers', etc. do not pattern like 'causers' or like 'causees' and therefore
cannot be subsumed under "semantic subject" or "semantic object."

As we see, EC cannot be defined in exclusively syntactic terms. Its syntactic
peculiarity (a non-nominative marking of its GS) is a necessary but by no means
sufficient condition: to distinguish between ergative and pathetive (active, affective, . . .) constructions, we need semantic terms (correlation between GS and
'causer'/'causee'). What is essential for a proper understanding of EC is just this
double correspondence of GS: with the morphological marking and with semantic actants.

Under definition (9), the most typical examples of EC are given by Georgian,
Dargwa, Chukchee and Koryak, a number of Indo-Iranian languages, etc. Many
narrower subclasses of EC can be naturally distinguished, e.g.:

i. Two-member vs. three-member EC. In some languages (e.g., Georgian), binary (= intransitive) predicative constructions are found where $GS(V_{(itr)})$ is a non-nominative (e.g., the ergative) case and denotes the "semantic subject" (not a 'causer' but an element that patterns like one in Georgian):

(12) Georgian   **a.** *Bawšw + ma*   *gamoiɣwiʒa*
              child   SG.ERG   awoke
              'The child awoke'
              vs.
         b. *Bawšw + ma gamoaɣwiʒa*   *deda*   *+ Ø*
                                      mother   SG.NOM
              'The child awoke Mother'.
         c. *Bawšw + ma icoca ⟨ gaiɣima ⟩*
              'The child started to crawl ⟨ smiled ⟩'.
         d. *Sicive + m*   *imaṭa*
              cold   SG.ERG
              'The cold grew stronger'.

(Georgian intransitive sentences with GSs in the ergative case are discussed in Fähnrich 1967.)

In Bats, the 1st or 2nd (but not 3rd) person GS is in the ergative with most intransitive verbs in all tenses:

(13)   Bats   **a.** *As*   *vujtas*
              I-ERG
              'I go'.
         b. *Atxo*   *bakxbalinŏ*
              we-ERG
              'We became adults'.
         c. *Aiš*   *belir*
              you-ERG
              'You [pl] were laughing'.

These GS also denote the "semantic subjects," so that in (13) we see a good example of EC.

ii. ECs with different cases that mark GS: a special case (= ergative) vs. one of the oblique cases present in the language (instrumental, dative, genitive, . . .).

The well-known and universally accepted definition of EC by Trubetzkoy (1958), based both on 1) different treatment of $GS(V_{(tr)})$ and $GS(V_{(itr)})$ and 2) identical treatment of $GS(V_{(itr)})$ and $GO^{dir}(V_{(tr)})$ by the respective language, seems to be too narrow: it characterizes only a particular subclass of constructions related to EC, which cannot be justified from the logical point of view (true, linguistically$_1$ it is the most widespread subclass). This definition fails to deal properly both with bipartite constructions having $GS(V_{(itr)})$ not in the nominative (see (i) above) and tripartite constructions having $GS(V_{(tr)})$ not in the nominative but with $GO^{dir}(V_{(tr)})$ treated differently from $GS(V_{(itr)})$—as in Motu (New Guinea), where the $GS(V_{(tr)})$ is in the ergative, the $GS(V_{(itr)})$—in the active (a special case marking only "intransitive" GSs!), and the GO^{dir} in the nominative (i.e., the case of citation forms):

(14) Motu
    a. *mero* + *na*   *e*   + *giminu*
         boy   ACT   3SG.SUBJ   stand
         'The boy is standing'
         vs.
    b. *mero* + *ese*   *amiani* + *∅*   *e*   + *eni* + *go*
         boy   ERG   food   NOM   3SG.SUBJ   give   1SG.OBJ
         'The boy gives me [some] food'.

The Meghrel ergative construction (with aorist series verb forms) is also a challenge for Trubetzkoy's definition; here all the GSs, "transitive" as well as "intransitive", are marked by the ergative case and denote the "semantic subject":

(15) Meghrel **a.** *ḳoč* + *k*   *komortu*
                  man   ERG   arrived
                  'The man arrived'.
             b. *ḳoč* + *k*   *doǰaru*   *kaɣard* + *i*
                           wrote   letter   NOM
                  'The man wrote a letter'.
             c. *ǰim*   + *as*   *keesuru*   *sumar* + *k*
                   brother   DAT   came   guest   ERG
                  'A guest came to [my] brother'.

Definition (9), however, properly treats as ergative the predicative constructions found in (14b) and (15), but not the one in (14a), which is an active construction. On the other hand, our definition does not apply to related phenomena found in languages without grammatical case.

For caseless languages that encode SSynt-roles of actants in the verb (such as Abkhaz or Mayan languages), we need two additional concepts: **quasi-nominative** and **quasi-ergative construction**. The latter concept should be based on the way in which the dependent NPs are cross-referenced within the verb form (rather than on grammatical cases). A rough sketch of the corresponding definitions might look like (16) below.

Let the verbal affixes that cross-reference the GS of a one-argument [≅ intransitive] verb be called **subjectal affixes**; then:

(16)
> A predicative construction
>
> $$GS + MV_{(tr)}$$
>
> is called **quasi-nominative** if and only if its GS is cross-referenced within the $V_{(tr)}$ by a subjectal affix, and **quasi-ergative** otherwise.

(Which NP is the GS must be determined independently, using surface-syntactic subjecthood properties, as specified in Chapters 4 and 5.)

VI. ORIGINS OF THE ERGATIVE CONSTRUCTION

There seem to be only three main ways in which Ergative Construction can arise independently (i.e., not as a borrowing) in a language: either from a basically intransitive [= stative] construction, or from a basically transitive but passive construction, or else from a transitive nominative construction via change of case-marking (induced, for instance, by phonological or purely morphological development): through transitivization, through depassivization and through case-mark change.

1. Through Transitivization

The noun phrase that has been before a free agentive determination (= an agentive complement or circumstantial) to a semantically single-actant stative verb (in the above sense) becomes a full-fledged semantic and syntactic actant, in particular, when it begins to be reflected by an exponent in the verb form, i.e. cross-referenced. It becomes somehow "attached" to the verb, adds a new semantic valence slot to it, and hereby makes it transitive; then it becomes GS by analogy with "active" GSs of $V_{(itr)}$ but keeps its original oblique form—and we get an EC. Such a way is clearly attested in Dargwa (perhaps in Georgian, too). Something like the following happens:

(17)

state of affairs attested in Lezgian

X dies vs. X[= GS] dies caused-by-Y[= CO^{agent}] >
> X dies vs. X dies-caused by-Y['dies-caused' $\cong$ 'is-killed'] >
> X dies vs. X is killed/kills by-Y >
> X dies vs. by-Y[= GS] kills X[= GO^{dir}]

ergative construction

What matters here is the semantic change in originally stative, single-argument verbs.

2. Through Depassivization

A tripartite passive construction (with a past participle) that plays the role of a missing perfective form within an active verb paradigm (something like *I kill him ~ I'll kill him ~ to-me is killed he/him*) is reinterpreted by analogy with other elements of the paradigm as an active transitive construction, the former agentive circumstantial (or complement) becoming the GS but preserving its oblique form (as in Indo-Iranian, e.g. Kurmandji or Pashto):

(18)   X is-killing Y vs. to-X[= GO^{indir}] is-killed Y[= GS] >
     > X is-killing Y vs. to-X[= GS] killed Y[= GO^{dir}_j]

ergative construction

Here we find a profound syntactic modification with no semantic change in verbs. (For details and facts about how EC arose in Indo-Iranian see Pirejko 1968 and Zakharyin 1979.) A slightly different development from a passive construction to an active, but ergative one is postulated for some Polynesian languages (Chung 1978): in Tongan and Samoan, the (historical) agent phrase modifying the passive verb has gradually acquired all the surface-syntactic properties of GS, while the (historical) subject of this verb lost them and thus became the direct object.

3. Through Case-mark Change

Phonological and/or morphological changes entail coincidence of case-marks on the "intransitive" GS and the GO^{dir}, so that the "transitive" GS becomes distinguished from the "intransitive" one on the DMorph-level; or such changes bring about the identity of personal pronoun forms marking the "intransitive" GS and the GO^{dir}; etc. This event, in its turn, determines a complete restructuring of syntax. Development of this type is proposed for several Australian languages in Dixon (1977).

There is, obviously, a fourth way: through direct borrowing of EC from a language where it existed before; it is of no interest in the present framework.

Section VI should not be construed to imply that EC always arises replacing a previous "non-ergative" state, i.e., that syntactic development always goes toward EC. I do not mean that: examples are known of the opposite trend, when EC is progressively replaced by a nominative construction; this, however, falls beyond our limits. (For more about constructions turning into ergative see Anderson 1977 and Cole et al. 1980.)

NOTE

1. (II, **1**, p. 251.) The Japanese case in *-ga* presents an interesting problem: it is used solely for grammatical subjects, and it is different from the zero-ending nominative and the instrumental in *-de*; should it be called ergative? I do not think so. I would rather propose calling this case **subjective** (since it marks indiscriminately all subjects), so that the term **the ergative** be reserved, in accordance with tradition, for the case marking "transitive" GSs (and maybe a few "intransitive" GSs, but then in specific contexts only).

Part *IV*

SYNTACTIC DESCRIPTION: SURFACE-SYNTACTIC MODELS AND NOTIONS

Part IV touches on two general problems of surface syntax: surface-syntactic models, or grammars (in more familiar parlance); and surface-syntactic notions.

In connection with the first problem, Chapter 7 presents a fragment of a particular surface-syntactic model, specifically, for Alutor. It sets out to demonstrate how some concepts, introduced and discussed in Part III ('grammatical subject', 'ergative construction', etc.), work when applied to the raw data of an actual language.

Dealing with the second problem, Chapter 8 discusses the concept of syntactic zero, or zero lexeme, this concept being crucial for the analysis of voice and related matters. The discussion is based on Russian data.

Thus, this part is characterized by a DESCRIPTIVE ORIENTATION. It is intended to demonstrate how observed linguistic$_1$ phenomena could be presented in the framework adopted in this book.

Chapter 7

TOWARD A FORMAL MODEL OF ALUTOR SURFACE SYNTAX: PREDICATIVE AND COMPLETIVE CONSTRUCTIONS

I. A FEW FACTS ABOUT ALUTOR

1. Introductory Remarks

Alutor is a language of the Chukchee-Kamchatka stock, which, besides Alutor, includes Chukchee, Kerek, Koryak and Kamchadal (= Itelmen). Alutor is considered by some to be only a dialect of Koryak. Since this matter is irrelevant to the present study, we will confine ourselves to the by now official opinion expressed in *Jazyki Narodov SSSR*, vol. V, 1968, p. 235 ff., which grants Alutor the status of an independent language in its own right.

Spoken by about a thousand people in some remote villages of Northern Kamchatka (Vyvenka, Tiličiki, Anapka, Rekinniki, etc.), Alutor possesses neither monographic descriptions published so far, nor any lexicons or collections of texts. There exist two unpublished descriptions of Alutor (Mel'nikov 1940 and Vdovin 1956), which we were unable to obtain. The only previous scientific sources available are an informative, though brief outline, Žukova (1968), and a pioneering paper Stebnickij (1938). And as scant as the general information on Alutor is, it is, as is the case with many languages, its syntax that remains the least studied aspect. Consequently, we have tried to develop a formal model of Alutor surface syntax using data gathered during two field trips to Kamchatka, organized and supported by Moscow University (in 1971 and 1972). Our linguistic team worked in the village of Vyvenka under the supervision of A.E. Kibrik;

the Alutor informants who have contributed most to the present chapter include T. Qupqə (Kosova), M. Mulitka, M. Tinangawut and M. Volkova.[1]

The linguistic data we have at our disposal permit us to undertake no more than a tentative description of Alutor syntax; the elaboration thereof has resulted in some fifty rules of the form discussed in Section III. We first investigated predicative and completive constructions, which make up the "predicative kernel" of any Alutor sentence—its verbal predicate (= main verb) together with the grammatical subject and the grammatical objects. It is these constructions that reveal many syntactic peculiarities characteristic of Alutor as a representative of the Chukchee-Kamchatka stock (in particular, the **ergative construction**, so typical of the languages of the stock). And it is these constructions that will be described below.

Before starting our description, it seems advisable to cite here some pertinent data about Alutor that appear frequently in the examples. (I supply more details here than I did for Dyirbal and Lezgian, because of paucity of published materials on Alutor.)

2. Phonology

The phonemic pattern of Alutor is as follows:

VOWELS

i		u
	ə	
e		o
	a	

CONSONANTS

Type of artic-ulation \ Point of articulation	Labial	Pre-velar Non-pala-talized	Pre-velar Palata-lized	Velar	Uvular	Laryn-geal
Obstruents Voiceless	p	t	ç/ş	k	q	ʕ,ʔ
Obstruents Voiced	v			γ		
Sonants Nasal	m	n	ņ	ŋ		
Sonants Non-nasal		l̦ r	ļ			
Glides	w	j				

ʕ is an emphatic (≅ pharyngealized) glottal stop, and ʔ is a simple glottal stop; ç and ʂ are free variants, mostly in different idiolects, ç being a very "soft" /č'/, and ʂ a very "soft" /š'/. (The above phonemic pattern of Alutor has been established by S.V. Kodzasov; there are some minor differences between it and the pattern appearing in Žukova 1968: 295, which cannot be discussed here.)

Stress is automatic and always falls on the second syllable from the beginning of a wordform, except if it is the last syllable or if it is open and contains an /ə/: then the stress is on the leftmost, i.e. first syllable.

3. Morphology

1) The Alutor verb conjugation is organized according to the following five categories (for more details see Mel'čuk 1973a):

Mood	indicative, imperative, and conjunctive.
Tense	present (with the exponent -*tkən*) and aorist (with a zero exponent).
Aspect	resultative (see immediately below, item 2) and non-resultative.
Person	1st, 2nd, and 3rd.
Number	sg, du, and pl.

For simplicity's sake, we ignore here the sequential (with the *ta-* . . . -ŋ exponent), the imperfective-inchoative form with the suffix -*lqiv*-, and all non-finite forms.

The most essential fact within the present frame of reference is that the Alutor transitive verb is BI-PERSONAL; that is, a transitive main verb in a clause obligatorily agrees in number and person both with its grammatical subject and its direct object. Thus, we have in effect two grammatical variables for number in transitive verbs: subjectal number (sg_s, du_s, pl_s) and objectal number (sg_o, du_o, pl_o). The same holds for person: there is subjectal person (1_s, 2_s, 3_s), as well as objectal person (1_o, 2_o, 3_o).

Below, the paradigm of an intransitive (= mono-personal) verb, *jəlqat + ək* 'to sleep', in the aorist of the indicative is given in full, while the paradigm of a transitive verb, *pəŋlu + k* 'to ask (questions)', also in the aorist of the indicative, is cited only partially (because of its size: it has 63 different forms!).

JƏLQAT-ƏK 'to sleep'

tə + jəlqat + ək	'I-slept'		*mət + jəlqan + mək*	'we[du]-slept'
∅ + jəlqat + i	'thou-slept'		*∅ + jəlqat + tək*	'you[du]-slept'
∅ + jəlqat + i	'he/she-slept'		*∅ + jəlqat + γəʔət*	'they[du]-slept'
		mət + jəlqal + la + mək	'we[pl]-slept'	
		∅ + jəlqal + la + tək	'you[pl]-slept'	
		∅ + jəlqal + la + t	'they[pl]-slept'	

PƏŊLU-K 'to ask'

tə	+ pəŋlu + na	+ wwi		'I-asked-them[pl]'
∅	+ pəŋlu + na	+ wwi		'thou-asked-them[pl]'
∅	+ pəŋlu + nina	+ wwi		'he-asked-them[pl]'
na	+ pəŋlu + γəm			'they[du/pl]-asked-me'
na	+ pəŋlu + γət			'they[du/pl]-asked-thee'
na	+ pəŋlu + n			'they[du/pl]-asked-him'
mət	+ pəŋlu + na	+ wwi		'we[du/pl]-asked-them[pl]'
∅	+ pəŋlu + tki			'you[du/pl]-asked-them[pl]'
na	+ pəŋlu + na	+ wwi		'they[du/pl]-asked-them[pl]'
na	+ pəŋlu + mək			'they[du/pl]-asked-us[du]'
na	+ pəŋlu + tək			'they[du/pl]-asked-you[du]'
na	+ pəŋlu + na	+ t		'they[du/pl]-asked-them[du]'

2) The Alutor resultative is a verb category very similar to the Indo-European perfect. Like the latter, the resultative depicts observable results of a past action rather than the action itself. This fact imparts to the resultative its specific flavor of non-evidentiality and brings it nearer to the well-known obviative category (of, e.g., Algonquian languages), so that resultative forms (marked by the prefix γa-) are used mostly to refer to events or facts not witnessed by the speaker or the addressee; therefore, they are rarely used in the 1st or 2nd person.

Formally, resultative forms are very much like English past participles (*gone, sprung, written, asked, . . .*). When derived from transitive verbs, they have obvious passive meaning and can be used as passive participles. Their most salient feature in the main-verb function is that a resultative form (even of a transitive verb) agrees only with one of its surface-syntactic actants, which constitutes a sharp contrast to all non-resultative forms of transitive verbs, where a double (subject-object) agreement is, as we have just noted, without exception.

We will return to this peculiarity later, while discussing the problem of grammatical subject in Alutor.

3) The Alutor noun distinguishes three grammatical numbers: singular (sg), dual (du), and plural (pl).

As for grammatical case, the case system of Alutor includes four central (= syntactic, see below) cases and five peripheral ones (= semantic cases with more specific meanings). Non-human nouns neutralize the three numbers in all oblique cases, while human nouns neutralize all oblique cases in the dual and the plural.

We give here the central part of the paradigms of the nouns *mənγəlŋən* 'hand' and *Miti* (feminine proper noun), i.e., their syntactic cases only:

MƏNГ-ƏLŊƏN

	SG	DU	PL
NOMINATIVE	mənγ + əlŋən	mənγ + ət	mənγ + uwwi
INSTRUMENTAL		mənγ + a	

DATIVE $\qquad$ $m\partial n\gamma + \partial\eta$

LOCATIVE $\qquad$ $m\partial n\gamma + \partial k$

MITI

	SG	DU	PL
NOMINATIVE	*Miti*	*Miti + na + t*	*Miti + na + wwi*
INSTRUMENTAL	*Miti + na + ta*		
DATIVE	*Miti + na + ŋ*	*Miti + tək*	
LOCATIVE	*Miti + na + k*		

For the form *Mitinata* see below, page 290.

There is no accusative in Alutor, which is quite natural, given its ergative₁ syntax (for **ergative₁** see Chapter 6, p. 251); nor is there a genitive, its function being fulfilled by the denominal adjective.

Notice the following three important properties of the Alutor declension:

First, the suffix of the instrumental has two allomorphs: *-a* after a consonant (like in *mənγ+a* 'by the hand'), and *-ta* after a vowel (like in *qura+ta* 'by the reindeer', cf. the nominative *qura + ŋa* '(a) reindeer'). Other case and number suffixes also have different allomorphs depending on the stem: *-əŋ/-ŋ* in the dative, *-ək/-k* in the locative, *-uwwi/-wwi* in the plural, and so on (the first allomorph being used after a consonant, the second, after a vowel).

Second, most of the human proper names and most of the kinship terms insert before oblique case suffixes and number suffixes the determinacy marker *-na*, which never appears on non-human nouns; cf., e.g. the locative case: *rara + k* 'in the house', *wajam + ək* 'in the river', *arγiŋ + ək* 'on the shore' vs. *Qəmavə + na + k* 'at Qamav's', *Marina + na + k* 'at Marina's', etc.

Third, the set and composition of Alutor syntactic cases is a controversial issue. What we present here is, in our opinion, the most plausible analysis. A rather sketchy discussion of the problem and alternative solutions will follow (pp. 289–291).

4. Syntax

I. Verb-noun agreement in Alutor, or the agreement of the main verb X with the noun phrase Y, its grammatical subject or its direct object, can best be described by Table 7-1 on page 272. (On grammatical subjects and direct objects in Alutor see below, pp. 286 ff.)

Some comments to Table 7-1

1. The table consists of two halves, the top half (I) specifying the person of the verb, the bottom half (II), its number, depending on the agreement-triggering noun. Since it is necessary to distinguish person and number of the subject from person and number of the direct object ($\mathbf{p_s}$, $\mathbf{n_s}$ vs. $\mathbf{p_o}$, $\mathbf{n_o}$, see p. 269), it seems expedient to use variables π and ν, which stand respectively for person and number alone: $\pi = \mathbf{p_s}$ or $\mathbf{p_o}$, $\nu = \mathbf{n_s}$ or $\mathbf{n_o}$. When the condition part of a surface-

Noun Y (= noun) / Verb X	Features of Y (= noun)	Context of Y (= noun)		
		$Y \xrightarrow{\textbf{not coord}} Z$	$Y \xrightarrow{\text{coord}} Z^1 \xrightarrow{\text{coord}} Z^2 \dots Z^{k-1} \xrightarrow{\text{coord}} Z^k \mid k \geq 1$	
			$(A)_{i\mid 1\leq i\leq k}\ (Z^i = \textbf{non pers})$	$(\exists_{i\mid 1\leq i\leq k})\ (Z^i = \text{pers}, \textbf{p})$
		I	II	III
I. $\pi(X)$ (= the person of the verb)	$Y_{(\text{pers}, \textbf{p})}$	① $\pi(X) = \textbf{p}(Y)$		② $\pi(X) = \min(\textbf{p}(Y), \textbf{p}(Z^i))\mid 1\leq i\leq k$
	$Y_{(\textbf{non pers})}$	③ $\pi(X) = 3$		④ $\pi(X) = \min(\textbf{p}(Z^i))\mid 1\leq i\leq k$
II. $\nu(X)$ (= the number of the verb)	Y_{sg}	⑤ $\nu(X) = \textbf{n}(Y)$	⑥ $\nu(X) = \begin{cases} 1)\ \text{du}\mid k = 1, \textbf{and } \textbf{n}(Z^1) = sg \\ 2)\ \text{pl}\mid k \neq 1, \textbf{or } \textbf{n}(Z^i) \neq sg \end{cases}$	
	$Y_{\textbf{not } sg}$		⑦ $\nu(X) = \text{pl}$	

Table 7-1
Verb-Noun Agreement in Alutor

syntax rule—see below, page 277—contains the **standard function** AGREE, it is explicitly specified there whether π and v in the above agreement table should be read as $\mathbf{p_s}$ and $\mathbf{n_s}$ or as $\mathbf{p_o}$ and $\mathbf{n_o}$.

2. The person and number of the verb depend on: (i) certain features of the controlling noun—its inherent (lexicographic) properties as well as its morphological values and (ii) its surface-syntactic context. The first dependency is reflected in rows of the table, and the second, in its columns. The first column (I) covers the cases when the noun does not belong to a conjoined noun phrase, the second (II) and the third (III), the cases with conjoined subject or object ($X\xrightarrow{\text{coord}}Y$ means that there exists a coordinate surface-syntactic relation between X and Y); more specifically, the second column provides for conjoined noun phrases having no personal pronoun among the conjuncts added to the subject X, while the third column admits a personal pronoun among such conjuncts.

N.B.: it should be emphasized that personal pronouns are considered here to be a subclass of nouns (with the feature "pers").

3. As can be seen from the table, four types of person agreement and three types of number agreement can be distinguished:

Person

1. The subject or object is a personal pronoun, and the subjectal or objectal person of the verb is identical to that of this pronoun:

(1)   **a.**   *γəmmə*[Y] *tə*   + *levətku*   + $\emptyset$ + *k*
          I-NOM   1SG.SUBJ   go.for.a.walk   AOR   1SG.SUBJ
          nuta + *k*
          tundra   SG.LOC
          'I went for a walk in the tundra'.
       b. *γəm* + *nan*   *tə*   + *laʔu* + $\emptyset$ + *γət*   *γəttə*[Y]
            I   INSTR 1SG.SUBJ   see   AOR   2SG.OBJ   thou-NOM
            'I saw thee'.

2. The subjectal or objectal person of the verb is identical to that of the corresponding pronominal conjunct whose person has the lowest value:

(2)   **a.** *ənnu*[Y]   *to*   *γəmmə*[Z^1]
          he-NOM   and   I-NOM
          mət   + *levətku* + $\emptyset$ + *mək*   *nuta* + *k*
          1DU.SUBJ   1DU.SUBJ
          'He and I we-went-two-of-us for a walk in the tundra'.
       b. *γəm* + *nan tə* + *laʔu* + $\emptyset$ + *tək*   *ənnu*[Y] *to γəttə*[Z^1]
                                    2DU.OBJ   he-NOM   thou-NOM
            'I saw-two-of-you him and thee'.

3. The verb is in the 3rd person (Y is not a personal pronoun, 3rd person pronouns being accounted for in item 1):

(3) **a.** *γəmnin + ∅   tumγətum + ∅*[Y]
    my   SG   friend   SG.NOM
    ∅   *+ levətku + ∅ + j*   *nuta + k*
    3SG.SUBJ   3SG.SUBJ
    'My friend went for a walk in the tundra'.

    b. *tumγ + a   ∅   + lə?u + ∅ + nina   + wwi*
        friend   SG.INSTR 3SG.SUBJ see   3SG.OBJ   PL
        γərnik + u[Y]
        animal   PL.NOM
        '(My) friend he-saw-them animals'.[2]

    4. The same as in 2, the only difference being that Y itself is not a pronoun but there is at least one pronoun among the nominals conjoined with Y:

(4) **a.** *Əmka + ∅*[Y], *Miti + ∅*[Z^1] *to γəmmə*[Z^2]
                            I-NOM
    mət   + levətku + la + ∅   + mək   nuta + k
    1DU.SUBJ   PL   AOR   1DU.SUBJ
    'Amka, Miti and I we-went-all-of-us for a walk in the tundra'.

    b. *əlla?   + a   na   + la?u + la + ∅   + mək*
        mother   SG.INSTR 3SG.SUBJ see   PL   AOR   1DU.OBJ
        Əmka + ∅[Y], *γəttə*[Z^1] *to γəmmə*[Z^2]
                   thou-NOM   I-NOM
        'Mother she-saw-all-of-us Amka, thee and me'.

Number

    5. The number of the verb is identical to that of the noun the verb agrees with:

(5) **a.** *γəmnin tumγətum + ∅   ŋalvəl? + ək*
    my   friend   SG.NOM   herd   SG.LOC
    ∅   + vitatə + tkən
    3SG.SUBJ   work   PRES
    'My friend works in the herd'.

    b. *tumγə + t   γa + şγitkəşav   + lina   + t*
        friend   DU.NOM   RES   lose.one's way   3SG.SUBJ   DU
        nuta + k
        tundra   LOC
        'The two friends lost their way in the tundra'.

    6. a) The number of the verb is dual if there are only two conjoined nominals, both singular, to agree with:

(6)   *əlləγə + n*[Y]   *to əlla? + ∅*[Z^1]
       father   SG.NOM and mother SG.NOM

$\emptyset$ + *vi$^{?}$ə* + $\emptyset$ + *γə$^{?}$ət*
3SG.SUBJ   die   AOR   DU
'Father and mother they-two-died'.

b) The number of the verb is plural if there are more than two conjoined
nominals with which the verb agrees or if the second conjunct is dual or plural:

(7)   **a.** *Miti* + *na* + *k* $\emptyset$ + *lə$^{?}$u* + $\emptyset$ + *nina*   + *wwi*
               LOC 3SG.SUBJ see   AOR   3SG.SUBJ   PL
         qajuɲuɲu + $\emptyset$[Y],   *ŋavəşqatpiḷ* + $\emptyset$[Z^{1}]   *to* ʕətʕə + *n*[Z^{2}]
         boy   SG.NOM girl   SG.NOM dog   SG.NOM
         'Miti she-saw-all-of-them (a) boy, (a) girl and (a) dog'.

     b. *ənɲin* + *ra* + *k* $\emptyset$ + *il* + *la* + *tkə* + *t*
         this   house SG.LOC 3SG.SUBJ be   PL   PRES PL
         qajuɲuɲu + $\emptyset$[Y] *to*   *ɲitaq ŋavəşqatpiḷa* + *t*[Z^{1}]
         boy   SG.NOM two   girl   DU.NOM
         'In this house, there are (a) boy and two girls'.

7. The number of the verb is plural if *Y* is dual or plural and there are other
nominals conjoined with it:

(8)   *aktəka*   *mə*   + *nmənavə* + $\emptyset$ + *na*   + *wwi*
         impossible 1SG.SUBJ.IMPER   bring   AOR   3SG.OBJ   PL
         wuttaku + *wwi qajuɲuɲu* + *wwi*[Y] *to* *ŋavəşqatpiḷ* + *u*
         this   PL   boy   PL.NOM   girl   PL.NOM
         'It is impossible (that) I bring (here) these boys and girls' [*aktəka*
         governs the imperative].

II. Word order in Alutor is quite free: linear arrangement of phrases is determined by communicative organization of the sentence (topic vs. comment, given
vs. new, emphasis and the like). Therefore, very much like Dyirbal or Lezgian,
word order in Alutor is irrelevant for the determination of major sentence elements: grammatical subject and grammatical objects.

II. FORMALISM AND NOTATIONS USED

The model for a small fragment of Alutor surface syntax that we suggest in
this chapter lies within the framework of the Meaning-Text linguistic$_2$ theory. A
brief survey of the theory has been offered in the Introduction, so we need not repeat it here. However, for the reader's convenience, we will recall the concepts
of surface-syntactic structure and deep-morphological structure, since it is exactly with these two structures that our surface-syntactic rules given below operate. We will totally ignore other components of surface-syntactic and deep-morphological representations.

The SURFACE-SYNTACTIC STRUCTURE (SSyntS) of a sentence is an unordered dependency tree each of whose branches is labeled with one of the surface-syntactic relations (SSRel) of the language and each of whose nodes is labeled with the name of a lexeme of the sentence, this name having subscripts for the values of all relevant meaning-bearing, or semantic, morphological categories: see above, Chapters 1 and 2.

It was already emphasized that the MT-approach introduces, for its syntax, a powerful descriptive device quite alien to the classical PS (phrase-structure) formalism: we mean labeled SS-relations, i.e., the explicit marking of different syntactic dependencies. In what follows, three SS-relations are used: the PREDICATIVE SSRel, the DIRECT-OBJECTIVAL SSRel, and the INDIRECT-OBJECTIVAL SSRel.

The DEEP-MORPHOLOGICAL STRUCTURE (DMorphS) of a sentence is a string consisting of deep-morphological representations (DMorphR) of all the word-forms in the sentence. The DMorphR of a wordform is the name of the corresponding lexeme (spelled out in uppercase letters) having subscripts for the values of *all* morphological categories of the lexeme, needed for the synthesis of the corresponding actual wordform—semantic categories as well as syntactic ones. The linear order of DMorphRs of the wordforms in the DMorphS of the sentence is the same as the order of the actual wordforms in the output sentence.

Let us present here the SSyntS and the DMorphS of an Alutor sentence:

(9) **a.** *uŋuŋu* + *tək*   *na*   + *nəşvişşavə* + *n*
      child   PL.INSTR 3PL.SUBJ   pitch   3SG.OBJ
      maniwra + *n*
      tent   SG.NOM
      'The children pitched the tent'.

b. The SSyntS of Sentence (9a):

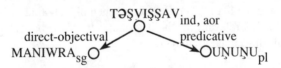

c. The DMorphS of Sentence (9a):

UŊUŊU$_{\text{pl}, \boxed{\text{instr}}}$ TƏŞVIŞŞAV$_{\text{ind, aor}, \boxed{3_s, \text{pl}_s, 3_o, \text{sg}_o}}$ MANIWRA$_{\text{sg}, \boxed{\text{nom}}}$

Morphological values boxed in (9c) are syntax-induced; they do not appear in the SSyntS and are added by the rules of surface syntax, which are given in Section III.

Having briefly touched upon those two components of the SSyntR and the DMorphR of a sentence that are important for our purpose, that is, the SSyntS and the DMorphS, we will now concentrate on the rules specifying the correspondences between the two.

These rules, called SURFACE-SYNTAX RULES, have the form

$$P \Leftrightarrow Q|C,$$

where:

1) P is a minimal subtree of the SSyntS tree: a pair of lexical nodes M_1 and M_2 connected by a SSRel r, i.e. $M_1 \overset{r}{\to} M_2$, and, perhaps, other nodes and branches constituting the context that controls the applicability of the rule; M_1 and M_2 have subscripts for semantic morphological categories.

2) Q is the same pair of nodes M_1 and M_2, perhaps with some morphological subscripts added, these latter referring to those syntactic morphological categories that express the SSRel r between such nodes in a sentence. (Naturally, besides M_1 and M_2, Q also contains all context nodes and branches out of P, if there are any.) M_1 and M_2 in Q are linearly ordered as prescribed by r and by their own syntactic properties.

3) C is the set of Boolean conditions that must be met by P, or Q, or both in order for the rule to apply. C may be null; obviously, C is the only optional component of a rule.

Component C of a surface-syntax rule is intended to include the type of information that cannot be expressed (at least, in a natural and compact manner) in either the left-hand or the right-hand part of the rule: e.g., "negative" tree context (a requirement that such and such a subtree be absent); or else a complicated correspondence between some morphological values of nodes in P or Q given by a rather sophisticated Boolean formula (e.g., complicated cases of grammatical agreement: pp. 273–275); etc.

When all minor and secondary complications are relegated to conditions, the number of surface-syntax rules may be reduced and their generality increased. Essentially similar syntactic facts may be covered by one rule, which could otherwise not capture useful generalizations about the language in question.

4) The two-headed double arrow $\Leftrightarrow$ means 'corresponds', by no means 'replaces' or 'is rewritten as': our rules are not substitutions or other type of transformations (in wider, non-Chomskyan sense of the latter term); they are simply correspondences. When they apply to the SSyntS of a sentence to produce the DMorphS of this sentence, the initial SSyntS is not changed: the surface-syntax rules construct the corresponding DMorphS using the SSyntS as a blueprint, without dismantling it. The same happens if they apply in the opposite direction: to a DMorphS to produce the corresponding SSyntS. In fact, being essentially static rather than dynamic, our surface-syntax rules are neutral with respect to orientation. We present them, however, in the syntax$\Rightarrow$morphology shape, since we believe that this orientation is basic, in accordance with the general principle adopted in this book: Chapter 2, I, Postulate 2, 3, p. 46.

We assume that such rules as characterized above are formally adequate for expressing all of the relevant information about the syntax of any natural language, i.e., for explictly showing which grammatical means—morphological categories and/or word order—serve for expressing or manifesting which syntactic relationships in which contexts.

Specific conventions used in our surface-syntax rules:

1. Roman capitals X, Y, Z, W stand for lexeme variables, i.e., variables ranging over the set of (Alutor) lexemes. These variables are used to label the nodes of surface-syntactic trees.

2. The parenthesized subscript to a lexeme variable represents the **syntactics** of the respective lexeme. (See Note 1 in Chapter 1, p. 39.) In the present chapter the following seven types of syntactic data, or seven syntactics features, are used for Alutor:

(1) Part of speech (V — verb; N — noun; . . . recall that personal pronouns are treated as a subclass of N: page 273).

(2) Proper/common nouns (prop/non-prop).

(3) Human/non-human nouns (hum/non-hum).

(4) Grammatical person (for pronouns only; $p = 1, 2, 3$).

(5) The government pattern of the verb, for instance: 1[instr], 2[nom], 3[dat], 2[CLAUSE]. The digit before brackets stands for the number of the respective deep-syntactic actant, and the symbol inside the brackets stands for the morphological shape of its surface-syntactic counterpart. "Instr" means 'the instrumental or the locative case of the grammatical subject in the ergative construction' (for details, see below, p. 289); "nom" is nominative; "dat" is dative; and "CLAUSE" means an object clause. The correspondence between deep-syntactic and surface-syntactic actants is, in this case, rather simple: the first deep actant of a verb is always mapped onto its grammatical subject, the second deep actant onto its first grammatical object (which may be direct or not, depending on the verb) and the third, onto its second grammatical object. For instance, $X_{(V,2[nom])}$ means that the lexeme substituted for X must be a verb taking as its first grammatical (surface) object a noun in the nominative case, i.e., a direct object.

(6) Verbs of perception (perc).

(7) Indirectly transitive/not indirectly transitive verb (ind-tr/non-ind-tr); for details on indirectly transitive verbs see below, Section IV, p. 294.

3. The subscripts assigned to a lexeme variable outside the parentheses that enclose its syntactics represent its inflectional (morphological) variables (boldface type) or values thereof:

(1) Grammatical number of the noun: n = sg, du(dual), pl.

(2) Grammatical case of the noun: c = nom(inative), dat(ive), instr(umental), loc(ative).

(3) Grammatical person and number of the verb in agreement with its grammatical subject (subjectal person and number): $p_s = 1_s, 2_s, 3_s$; $n_s = sg_s$, du_s, pl_s.

(4) Grammatical person and number of the verb in agreement with its direct object (objectal person and number), $\mathbf{p_o} = 1_o, 2_o, 3_o; \mathbf{n_o} = sg_o, du_o, pl_o$.

(5) Aspect of the verb: res(ultative), non-res.

4. The plus symbol (in the right-hand part of a rule) denotes the linear (left-to-right) ordering of lexeme occurrences in the text, its absence indicating the possibility of arbitrary ordering. Three dots show that the occurrences in question may be separated by arbitrary lexical material. Thus:

X + Y means 'X immediately precedes Y'.

X + . . . + Y means 'X precedes Y, perhaps not immediately'.

X . . . Y means 'X precedes or follows Y, perhaps not immediately'.

5. The topmost rightmost ordinary arrow (which may be the only arrow used) in the left-hand part of a rule, linking the nodes labeled X and Y, represents the surface-syntactic relation described by this particular rule. All other ordinary arrows (if any) in the left-hand part constitute the tree context and are therefore repeated in the right-hand part of the rule.

6. The symbol AGREE in the condition part of rules is the name of a special **standard function**, which provides for person and number agreement of the verb with both its grammatical subject and its direct object, according to the agreement table given above. (For standard functions, see Note 14, Chapter 2, p. 91.)

III. NINE SURFACE-SYNTAX RULES OF ALUTOR

1. Predicative constructions (Rules 1–3)

Nominative construction with an intransitive verb or with a transitive verb in the resultative (for resultative, see below, p. 298); all and only such verbs take their grammatical subject in the nominative.

Rule 1

X
○(V,1[nom])/(V,1[instr])res
|
predicative ⇔ Yn, nom...X$\mathbf{p_s}$, $\mathbf{n_s}$ |AGREE($\mathbf{p_s}$, $\mathbf{n_s}$(X); $\mathbf{p}$, $\mathbf{n}$(Y))
|
▼
○
Y

(N,**p**)n

(10) *kətawət   Qutkəṇṇaqu*[Y]   *kəteṇaş^{ʔ}u + j*[X]
'Suddenly Qutkinyaqu[nom] he-quickly-looked[subject-3sg]
tənuɣərŋə + ŋ
at-smoke-outlet'.

(11) *γəmnin qəlavul*[Y] *ŋalvəlʔək*   *vitatəlqivətkən*[X]
'My   man[nom]   in-the-herd(of-reindeer)he-goes-to-work[subject-3sg]'.

(12) *ŋanina + wwi uraşik + u*[Y]   *Avaməlqakinak*
'Those   servants[nom,pl] by-Avamilqaki
γa + kmil + laŋ[X]
they-were-taken[resultative; subject-3pl]'.

(13) *oro   ənŋin ənpəŋav*[X]   *γa + viʔə + lin*[Y]
'Soon this   old-woman[nom]   she-died[resultative; subject-3sg]'.

Ergative construction with a transitive verb in the non-resultative; all and only such verbs admit the ergative construction.

A common noun or a non-human proper name as grammatical subject

Rule 2

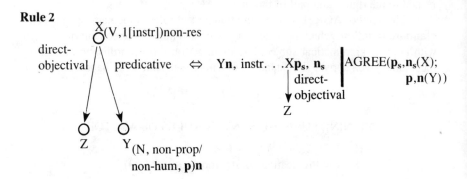

Notice that in Rule 2, the grammatical subject is marked by the instrumental.

The direct-objectival branch issuing from the top node X in Rules 2 and 3 shows that both rules are applicable only in the presence of a direct object, which means that in Alutor, the ergative construction necessarily presupposes the direct object.[3] The converse is also true: in all rules that describe completive constructions with direct objects, we find the predicative SSRel as necessary context.

In Alutor, a nearly obligatory rule of pronoun ellipsis (= Pro-Drop) is operational, so that sentences like (14) and (15) are quite normal:

(14) *qolin   ənpəʔəllaʔa inivi*
'One-day grandmother she-told-me'.

(15) *γəmnan təŋvun   talaʔuŋək*
'I   I-started-it to-look-for [it] [i.e., for a spou̇ꞏ that has been mentioned in the preceding sentence]'.

Here, we find grammatical subjects in the instrumental—*ənpəʔəllaʔ+a* and *γəm+nan*—but no direct object at all. It is so because the pronominal grammatical objects in the nominative—*γəmmə* 'I' (*ivək* 'to say, tell' is transitive in Alutor, see Section IV, on *ivək* 2) in (14) and *ənnu* 'it' in (15)—should not be used on the surface if there is no special emphasis on them. However, such pronouns do appear in the SSyntS, where they trigger the agreement of the main verb. Thus, the requirement stated by the presence of the context direct-objectival branch in Rules 2 and 3 is satisfied for (14) and (15): the direct object pronoun is present in the SSyntS thereof.

(16) *γəm + nan*[Y]   *ətγina + t   pujγə + t*[Z]   *nuta + ŋ*
'I[instr]'   their   two-spears   into-tundra
tə + tallaŋ + əna + t[X]
I-will-carry-them-away-two[subject-1sg]'
= 'I'll carry their two spears away into the tundra'.

(17) *ənpəŋav + a*[Y]   *ləʔuṣqiv + nin*[X]   *qəlavul*[Z]
'Old-woman[instr]   she-went-to-see-him[subject-3sg]   man[nom]'
= 'An old woman went to see (her) man'.

A human proper name as grammatical subject

Rule 3

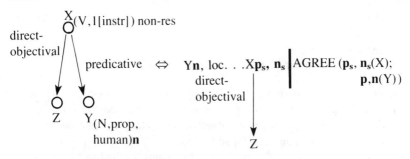

Here the grammatical subject is marked by the locative; cf. the discussion below, p. 289 ff.

(18) *taqəkjita ṣəvitku + nin*[X]   *murγin ŋalla*[Z]
'Why   he-divided-it[subject-3sg]   our   herd
Rənnəŋalpəlʔən + na + k[Y]
Rannangalpal'an[loc]'
= 'Why did Rannangalpal'an divide our herd?'

(19) *Miti + nak*[Y]   *ləʔuṣqiv + nin*[X]   *qəlavul*[Z]
'Miti[loc]   she-went-to-see-him[subject-3sg]   man[nom]'
= 'Miti went to see (her) man'.

2. Completive constructions with a finite transitive verb in the non-resultative (Rules 4–9)

Nominal direct object

Rule 4

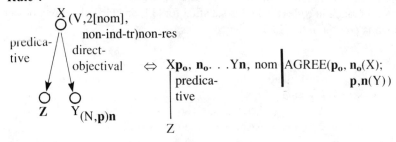

(20) *na + nutkə + na + wwi*[X] *ənpəqlavul + ətək*[Z]
'They-eat-them[object-3pl]   old-men
wapaqa + wwi[Y], *ənki?ak   jəlqəlqiv + latkət*
fly.agarics[pl,nom], then   they-go-to-sleep'
= 'The old men eat some fly agarics, and then go to sleep'.

(21) *ənpəŋav + a / Miti + na + k*[Z] *lə?uşqiv + nin*[X]
'Old-woman / Miti   she-went-to-see-him-[object-3sg]
qəlavul[Y]
man[sg, nom]'
= 'The old woman/Miti went to see (her) man'.

Note that the predicative branch stemming from the top node X in Rules 4–9 is our way to show that these rules are applicable to the main verb, i.e., a finite form, only. Infinite forms such as infinitives or participles have no agreement with their direct objects and call for separate rules.

At the same time, this predicative context accounts for the fact that in Alutor a direct object is possible only in the presence of an ergative subject (see the above comment after Rule 2).

Much like a pronominal object, a pronominal subject also may not appear in actual sentences, as in (22):

(22) *kulta + wwi*[nom, pl]   *mət + ənpətkə + na(+ wwi)*
'The-soles   we-sew-them-on'.

where the subject in the instrumental—*murɣənan* 'we'—is elided by the afore-mentioned Pro-Drop rule. Yet it is present in the SSyntS, in conformity with Rules 4–9.

Sentential direct object with a verb of perception

Verb agreement with the grammatical subject of the object clause
Rule 5

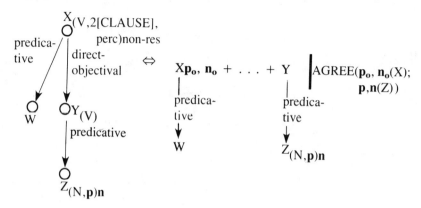

(23)   *Qəmavə + na + k   na + laʔutkəni + γət*[X]   *γən + annə*[Z]
      'Qamav   he-sees-you[object-2sg]   you[sg, instr]
      kəlγatətkən + a[Y]   *qura + wwi*
      you-harness-them[object-3 pl]   reindeer[pl, nom]'
      = 'Qamav sees that you are harnessing the reindeer'.

Note that in Rules 5–7 the order of elements in the DMorph is rigid: a sentential object must obligatorily follow its matrix verb. Nominal objects and grammatical subjects may both precede and follow the main verb; therefore, there are
no plus signs in the right-hand parts of Rules 1–4 and 8 and 9.

Verb agreement with the direct object of the object clause

Rule 6

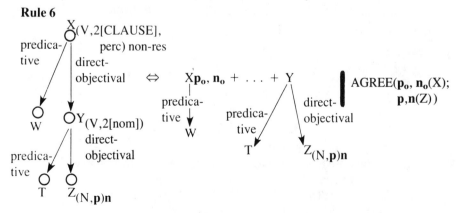

(24) *Qəmavə + nak   ləʔutkə + nina*[X]   *γən + annə*
      'Qamav   he-sees-them[object-3 pl]   you[sg,instr]
      kəlγatətkə + na[Y]   *qura + wwi*[Z]
      you-harness-them[object-3pl]   reindeer[pl,nom]'.

Verb agreement with the object clause as a whole

Rule 7

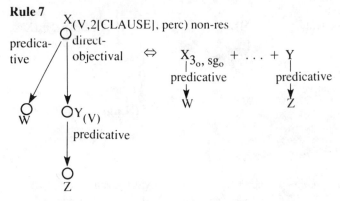

(25) *Qəmavə + nak   ləʔutkə + nin*[X]   *γən + annə*[Z]
      'Qamav   he-sees-it[object-3 sg]   you[sg,instr]
      kəlγatətkə + na[Y]   *qura + wwi*
      you-harness-them[object-3pl]   reindeer[pl,nom]'.

Verb agreement with the direct object

Rule 8

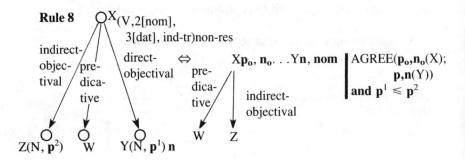

(26) *əlləγ + a   jəl + nina*[X]   *ənəkə + ŋ*[Z]
      'Father[instr]   he.gave.as.wives.them[object-3pl]   to-him[dat]
      şininkina ŋavakka + wwi[Y]
      his   daughters[pl, nom]'
      = 'Father gave him his daughters as wives'.

Verb agreement with the indirect (= dative) object

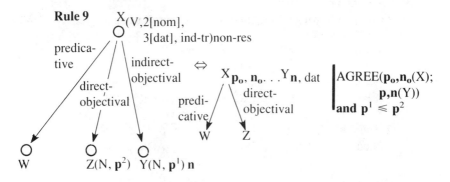

(27) $\partial ll \partial \gamma + a \quad ina + j \partial l + i[X]$
 'Father[instr]   he.gave.as.wife-me[ina- is the exponent of 1sg obj]
 $\gamma \partial m \partial k \partial + \eta[Z] \quad \gamma \partial t t \partial[Y]$
 to-me[dat]   thou[nom]
 = 'Your father gave thee to me as a wife'.

IV. DISCUSSION OF PREDICATIVE AND COMPLETIVE CONSTRUCTIONS IN ALUTOR

The rules cited in Section III exemplify two interesting phenomena of Alutor surface syntax:

1. **Ergative construction**, which raises the problem of the grammatical subject and that of its case.
2. Special cases of **object agreement** of the main verb.

We will analyse them in turn.

1. The Ergative Construction in Alutor

We proceed from the definition of ergative construction argued for in Chapters 4 and 5 and finally formulated in Chapter 6: see (9), p. 259. It is immediately obvious that Rules 2 and 3 above describe an ergative construction: first, the dependent element of the predicative SSRel, i.e., the GS (Y in both rules), is not marked with the nominative (it is marked with the instrumental in Rule 2, and with the locative in Rule 3); second, this GS expresses the 'Causer', i.e. it is the "semantic subject". This happens in all moods and tenses: the GS of any Alutor transitive verb is invariably marked either with the instrumental or (only if it is a human proper name) with the locative. So far, so good: Alutor seems to feature a classical type of ergative construction. However, two questions arise to trouble the peace of the researcher's soul:

(i) How do we know that what we think is a GS in Alutor is indeed a GS (and not an agentive complement as, for instance, in Lezgian)?

(ii) What about grammatical cases that mark this suspect sentence element?

Let us answer these questions.

(i) Subjecthood Properties in Alutor.

Consider the following set of Alutor basic sentences using the verb JƏLQAT- 'sleep' in the aorist of the indicative:

(28)

SINGULAR

1 $\gamma\partial mm\partial$ + $\emptyset$ $t\partial$ + $j\partial lqat$ + $\emptyset$ + ∂k
   I   NOM   1SG   AOR   1SG

2 $\gamma\partial tt\partial$ + $\emptyset$ $\emptyset$ + $j\partial lqat$ + $\emptyset$ + i
   thou   NOM   2SG   AOR   2SG

3 $u\underaccent{}{n}u\underaccent{}{n}u$ + $\emptyset$ $\emptyset$ + $j\partial lqat$ + $\emptyset$ + i
   child   SG.NOM   3SG   AOR   3SG

DUAL

1 mur + i $m\partial t$ + $j\partial lqan$ + $\emptyset$ + $m\partial k$
   we   DU.NOM   1DU   AOR   1DU

2 tur + i $\emptyset$ + $j\partial lqat$ + $\emptyset$ + $t\partial k$
   you   DU.NOM   2DU   AOR   2DU

3 $u\underaccent{}{n}u\underaccent{}{n}u$ + t $\emptyset$ + $j\partial lqat$ + $\emptyset$ + $\gamma\partial^{?}\partial t$
   child   DU.NOM   3DU   AOR   3DU

PLURAL

1 mur + $uwwi$ $m\partial t$ + $j\partial lqal$ + la + $\emptyset$ + $m\partial k$
   we   PL.NOM   1DU   PL   AOR   1DU

2 tur + $uwwi$ $\emptyset$ + $j\partial lqal$ + la + $\emptyset$ + $t\partial k$
   you   PL.NOM   2DU   PL   AOR   2DU

3 $u\underaccent{}{n}u\underaccent{}{n}u$ + wwi $\emptyset$ + $j\partial lqal$ + la + $\emptyset$ + t
   child   PL.NOM   3DU   PL   AOR   PL

The only nominal in these sentences, comprising a one-actant intransitive verb, is—in accordance with our postulate (Chapter 4, p. 162)—the GS. And we see that it triggers the person-number agreement of the verb, the agreement being shown by affixes (more specifically, circumfixes), which we will call **subjectal affixes**; the set of subjectal affixes in Alutor will be denoted A_{subj}.

In sharp contrast to Dyirbal and Lezgian, verb-noun agreement plays an important role in Alutor and should be taken into account in the first place when discussing subjecthood in this language.

Consider now a series of transitive sentences using the verb TƏTKƏŊAVAT- 'scold' (also in the aorist of the indicative):

9)

γəm	+nan	γəttə	+ ∅	tə	+ nətkəŋavat	+ ∅	+ γət	
I	INSTR	thou	NOM	1SG		AOR	2SG	
"	"	tur	+ i	tə	+ nətkəŋavat	+ ∅	+ tək	
		you	DU.NOM	1SG		AOR	2DU	
"	"	tur	+ uwwi	tə	+ nətkəŋaval	+ la	+ ∅	+ tək
		you	PL.NOM			PL	AOR	2DU
"	"	uɲuɲu	+ ∅	tə	+ nətkəŋavatə	+ ∅	+ n	
		child	SG.NOM			AOR	3SG	
"	"	uɲuɲu	+ t	tə	+ nətkəŋavan	+ ∅	+ na	+ t
		child	DU.NOM			AOR	3SG	DU
"	"	uɲuɲu	+ wwi	tə	+ nətkəŋavan	+ ∅	+ na	+ wwi
		child	PL.NOM			AOR	3SG	PL

uɲuɲu	+ ta	γəmmə	+ ∅	ina	+ nətkəŋavat	+ ∅	+ i[4]	
child	SG.INSTR	I	NOM	1SG		AOR	3SG	
"	"	mur	+ i	na	+ nətkəŋavan	+ ∅	+ mək	
		we	DU.NOM	3SG		AOR	1DU	
"	"	mur	+ uwwi	na	+ nətkəŋaval	+ la	+ ∅	+ mək
		we	PL.NOM	3SG		PL	AOR	1DU
"	"	ənnu	+ ∅	∅	+ tətkəŋavan	+ ∅	+ nin	
		he/she	SG.NOM	3SG		AOR	3SG	
"	"	ətt	+ i	∅	+ tətkəŋavan	+ ∅	+ nina	+ t
		he/she	DU.NOM	3SG		AOR	3SG	DU
"	"	ətt	+ uwwi	∅	+ tətkəŋavan	+ ∅	+ nina	+ wwi
		he/she	PL.NOM	3SG		AOR	3SG	PL

This (incomplete) paradigm suffices to show that an Alutor transitive verb agrees with or cross-references both its actants by means of two sets of affixes: A_1 —prefixes cross-referencing $NP_{instr/loc}$, and A_2—suffixes cross-referencing NP_{nom} (with the exception of lsg object forms mentioned in Note 4). Now let us compare A_1 and A_2 of the transitive verb with A_{subj} of the intransitive verb in order to see which one of the two is more similar to it in composition.

Leaving aside nine resultative forms derivable from all verbs, intransitive and transitive as well (because the resultative forms show some peculiarities in agreement, see below, Note 5), we obtain the following:

a. An Alutor intransitive verb has 72 finite forms manifesting purely SUBJECT AGREEMENT by subjectal affixes A_{subj}, consisting each of a prefixal and a suffixal part.

b. An Alutor transitive verb has 504 finite forms manifesting double, viz. SUBJECT-OBJECT, AGREEMENT by two sets of affixes: prefixes A_1 and suffixes A_2. The question is whether A_1 or A_2 cross-reference the grammatical subject.

c. A prefix from A_1 is identical with the prefixal part of a circumfix from A_{subj} expressing the same number and person in 320 our of 504 instances (63 percent of coincidences), while a suffix from A_2 is identical with the suffixal part of a circumfix from A_{subj} expressing the same number and person only in 70 out of 504 instances (13.5 percent of coincidences). The ratio—almost 5:1 (63 percent vs. 13,5 percent)—leads to the conclusion that in the subject-object forms the prefix-set A_1 is far more similar to A_{subj} than the suffix-set A_2. In other words, in subject-object forms it is the prefix of the verb that systematically cross-references the grammatical subject, while the suffix reflects the direct object. A_1 are **subjectal prefixes**.

d. But the subjectal prefixes of the Alutor transitive verb cross-reference $NP_{instr/loc}$: therefore, the NP_{instr} is the GS of Alutor $V_{(tr)}$, since it triggers its subjectal agreement.

Thus the main subjecthood property in Alutor is control of the verb's subjectal agreement; is it the only one? We must admit that we do not know: we have not carried out the supplementary research necessary to establish the presence of further subjecthood properties, should they exist. Let us remark, though, that nondeletability cannot be invoked since neither of the two actants of an Alutor $V_{(tr)}$ can be deleted from the sentence without making it strongly context-dependent or ungrammatical; as a consequence, nondeletability is not diagnostic for GS. Gapping-collapsibility does not contradict our solution: a $NP_{instr/loc}$ functioning as the $GS(V_{(tr)})$ is readily gapping-collapsible a with NP_{nom} functioning as the $GS(V_{(itr)})$, and that in both directions, cf.:

(30) **a.** *Qutkəŋŋaqu + nak*   *∅*   *+ lə?u + ∅*   *+ nin*
     Qutkinyaqu   SG.LOC   3SG.SUBJ   see   AOR   3SG.OBJ
     ŋav?an + ∅   *to Qutkəŋŋaqu + ∅*
     wife   SG.NOM   and   SG.NOM
     ∅   *+ tinmə*   *+ vi?*   *+ ∅*   *+ i*   ⇒
     3SG.SUBJ   pseudo   die   AOR   3SG.SUBJ
     Qutkəŋŋaqunak lə?unin ŋav?an to tinməvi?i 'Q. saw [his] wife and pretended to be dead'.

    b. *əlla? + a*   *∅*   *+ tu + ∅*   *+ nina*   *+ wwi*
     mother   SG.INSTR   3SG.SUBJ   eat   AOR   3SG.OBJ   PL
     wapaq + u   *to əlla? + ∅*
     fly.agaric   PL.NOM   and   mother   SG.NOM
     ∅   *+ jəlqəlqiv*   *+ ∅*   *+ i*   ⇒
     3SG.SUBJ   go.to.sleep   AOR   3SG.SUBJ
     əlla?a tuninawwi wapaqu to jəlqəlqivi 'Mother ate the fly agarics and went to sleep'.

(31) **a.** *Jattiɣən + ∅*   *∅*   *+ semav*   *+ ∅*   *+ i*
     Yattigen   SG.NOM   3SG.SUBJ   come.closer   AOR   3SG.SUBJ
     Qəmavə + naŋ   *to Jattiɣən + nak*
     Qamav   SG.DAT   SG.LOC
     ∅   *+ kenan + ∅*   *+ nin*   *nanqə*   *+ k*   ⇒
     3SG.SUBJ   kick   AOR   3SG.OBJ   stomach   SG.LOC

Jattiɣən semavi Qəmavənaŋ to kenannin nanqək 'Y. came closer to
Q. and kicked [him] in the stomach'.

b.   ∅   + ŋətu + ∅   + lat   inaral? + u   to
3SG.SUBJ   go.out   AOR   PL.SUBJ   neighbor   PL.NOM
inaral?ə + tək   na   + ŋvu + ∅   + n
PL.INSTR   3PL.SUBJ   begin   AOR   3SG.OBJ
tanŋu ləŋki ənpəŋav   + ∅   ⇒
ridicule   old.woman   SG.NOM
ŋətulat inaral?u to naŋvun tanŋu ləŋki ənpəŋav
'Neighbors went out and began to ridicule the old woman'.

However, as we have already pointed out (p. 280), pronouns are almost oblig-
torily elided in Alutor, except if they carry strong emphasis or contrastive stress.
Therefore, it can be maintained that in (30) and (31) we do not have gapping
after conjunction reduction but rather anaphoric pronominalization—with the
pronoun appearing in the SSyntS but elided on the surface (so that instead of
'Qutkinyaqu saw his wife and pretended to be dead' we have in Alutor—in the
SSyntS—'Q. saw his wife, and HE pretended to be dead'; or instead of 'Yatti-
gen$_i$ came closer to Qamav$_j$ and kicked him$_j$' we actually have 'Y.$_i$ came closer
to Q.$_j$ and HE$_i$ kicked HIM$_j$'). That is why we have to stick to the only more or
less obvious property of Alutor GSs: control of subjectal agreement.[5]

(ii) In What Case is the GS in Alutor?
The ergative construction in Alutor exhibits the following interesting property.
The noun in the role of grammatical subject of a transitive verb (not in the
resultative) has one of two case forms depending on its own features: if it is a human proper name (like *Qutkəiŋŋaqu* or *Mulitka*) it takes the suffix *-(ə)nak*, otherwise, the suffix *-ta/-a* (in the singular). But *-(ə)nak* is known to be a locative suffix, which with human proper names has the meaning 'in the house of':

(32)   *əɣəv*   *ənnu   Qilivŋawut + ənak   ɣatkivlin*
'Yesterday   he   at-Qilivngawut's   has-passed-the-night',

while *-ta/-a* is the instrumental suffix of common nouns:

(33)   *jənakjita*   *ənannə ɣapkavlin ɣərnik milɣər + a*
'Because-of-mist   he   couldn't   animal   with-rifle[INSTR]
tanmənki
kill'.

This fact opens the way for the following three competing solutions:

SOLUTION I. In Alutor, the surface-syntactic role of grammatical subject may
be fulfilled by nouns in two different cases: either in the instrumental, for com-

mon nouns and non-human proper names, or in the locative, for human proper names. This is the solution we adopt, and our rules are written accordingly: cf., in particular, Rules 2 and 3. (A similar treatment was proposed by Volodin 1967 for nouns and pronouns in Kamchadal, also one of Chukchee-Kamchatka languages.)

A striking typological parallel can be found also in some languages of Soviet Daghestan. Thus, in Tsakhur the subject of a transitive verb is in the in essive (= locative), if it is a human noun, and in the genitive case otherwise; in Lak, the transitive GS is marked by the nominative, if it is a 1st or 2nd person pronoun, and by the genitive otherwise; etc.

SOLUTION II. *-(ə)nak* can be taken to be not only a locative case suffix, but also a homonymous instrumental case suffix of human proper names. (We find just such a description of the related Chukchee suffix *-ne/-na* in Inènlikèj and Nedjalkov 1967: 258–260.) Then any Alutor noun in grammatical subject role with a transitive verb will exhibit only one case, i.e., the instrumental.

The latter description is supported by the obvious lack of instrumental forms in *-(ə)nata* for proper names: such forms are not attested either in published accounts of Alutor or in our own data. Yet this argument does not seem convincing. The point is that a human proper name standing in the instrumental but not being the subject of a transitive verb should denote an instrument or a tool,[6] and it is extremely difficult to imagine an actual situation where a human would be manipulated like an instrument. It may be just this inherent anomaly of such situations that accounts for the complete absence of sentences with proper names in *-(ə)nata* in the corpus. We believe, however, that such sentences are probably not absolutely excluded, if even only as purely potential utterances.

If in an Alutor translation of a (say, English) sentence meaning 'He broke the window with John' a native were to employ a proper name in *-(ə)nata* (however odd the meaning itself would seem to him) but would not employ a form in *-(ə)nak*, then the first alternative would be clearly preferable. And we possess some positive evidence that such expressions can be forced in Alutor: one of our informants, Marina Tinangawut (18 years old), when asked (in a letter) what the sentence *Qəmavə ojitkən Marinanata* could mean, answered that strange as it is, it means 'Qamav feeds on Marina', while the sentence *Qəmavə ojitkən Marinanak* would necessarily mean 'Qamav feeds (himself) at Marina's'. Based on this evidence, we reject Solution II.

SOLUTION III. For all nouns in Alutor, three rather than two cases (along with all other cases that are not under analysis here) should be differentiated, namely:

(1) An instrumental (in *-ta/a*) with instrumental or objective meaning (semantically excluded in proper nouns).

(2) A locative (in *-k*) with purely locative meaning.

(3) An ergative, or the exclusive case of the grammatical subject in ergative constructions with transitive verbs and of the agentive complement with the resultative of transitive verbs (see Note 5, p. 298).

The form of the ergative always coincides, then, either with that of the locative (for human proper names) or with that of the instrumental (of all other nouns), which means that such an ergative would be in Alutor a morphologically **non-·autonomous** case. (The term is from Zaliznjak 1973: 69, q.v. also for more on problems connected with this type of case and some ways to solve them.)

We do not accept Solution III, either, because of the following methodological principle:

Principle of Internal Autonomy of Cases

(34) ‖ A morphologically non-autonomous case should be postulated in a language if and only if otherwise the SSynt-rules that describe the selection of cases would have to mention individual properties of the lexeme to be declined.

Since in our instance, Rules 2 and 3, which state the distribution of the instrumental vs. the locative, do not need to address any individual properties of lexemes in GS role, postulating in Alutor a morphologically non-autonomous ergative would violate Principle (34).[7] For more about this principle see Mel'čuk (1986: 66–68).

2. Special Cases of Object Agreement of the Main Verb

Surface-syntax rules of Alutor demonstrate two types of deviation from the ordinary pattern of object agreement:

(i) Object agreement of the main verb (in a matrix clause) with its object clause, i.e., with a sentential object (Rules 5–7).

(ii) Object agreement of the so-called "indirectly transitive" verbs.

We will take up these types in turn.

(i) Object agreement of the main verb (in a matrix clause) with its object clause.

Alutor transitive verbs of perception that can take as their direct object an object clause (i.e., verbs whose syntactics contains the feature "2[CLAUSE]") show, generally speaking, three types of object agreement.

If the object clause (OC) has as its own main verb a two-actant (transitive) verb forming an ergative construction, then the object agreement of its governing, or matrix, verb may be as follows (to facilitate the comparison, we have boxed the agreeing verb forms).

TYPE I: The object agreement of the matrix verb is with the grammatical subject of the OC:

(35)	Qəmavə	+ nak	na	+ laʔu +	tkəni	+ γət
	Qamav	SG.LOC	3SG.SUBJ	see	PRES	2SG.OBJ

γən	+ *annə*	*∅*	+ *kəlγatətkə*	+ *na*	+ *wwi*
thou	INSTR	2SG.SUBJ	harness	3SG	PL

qura	+ *wwi,*
reindeer	PL.NOM

lit. 'Qamav sees-**thee thou** art-harnessing reindeer' = 'Q. sees you harnessing the reindeer'.

TYPE 2: The object agreement of the matrix verb is with the direct object of the OC:

(36) *Qəmavə* + *nak*

∅	+ *ləʔu* + *tkə*	+ *nina*	+ *wwi*
3SG.SUBJ	see	PRES	3SG.OBJ	PL

γən + *annə ∅* + *kəlγatətkə* + *na* + *wwi qura* + *wwi,*

lit. 'Qamav sees-**them** thou art-harnessing **reindeer**' = 'Q. sees you harnessing the reindeer'.

TYPE 3: The object agreement of the matrix verb is with the OC as a whole; the OC is treated then as a singular noun so that the matrix verb has an object exponent of 3 sg:

(37) *Qəmavə* + *nak*

∅	+ *ləʔu* + *tkə*	+ *nin*
3SG.SUBJ	see	PRES	3SG.OBJ

γən + *annə ∅* + *kəlγatətkə* + *na* + *wwi qura* + *wwi,*

lit. 'Q. sees-**it thou art-harnessing reindeer**' = 'Q. sees you harnessing the reindeer'.

If the main verb of the object clause is intransitive, then type 2 agreement is obviously excluded while types 1 and 3 remain possible:

(38) **a.** *Qəmavə* + *nak*

∅	+ *ləʔu* + *tkə*	+ *nina*	+ *wwi*
3SG.SUBJ	see	PRES	3SG.OBJ	PL

SG.LOC

arγiŋ + *əŋ*	*∅*	+ *təla* + *la* + *tkə*	+ *t*	*ʕətv* + *uwwi,*
shore	DAT	3SG.SUBJ come PL	PRES	PL boat PL.NOM

lit. 'Q. sees-**them** to-the-shore are-coming **boats**' = 'Q. sees boats come/coming to the shore'.

b. *Qəmavə* + *nak*

∅	+ *ləʔu* + *tkə*	+ *nin*
3SG.SUBJ	see	PRES	3SG.OBJ

arγiŋ + *əŋ ∅* + *təla* + *la* + *tkə* + *t ʕətv* + *uwwi,*

lit. 'Q. sees-**it to-the-shore are-coming boats**' = 'Q. sees boats come/coming to the shore'.

We know of no formal conditions determining the choice among these various possibilities of object-clause agreement: sentences (35)–(37) and (38) seem to be free syntactic variants. Even if there are some minor semantic differences these would probably be no more than differences in emphasis.

A caveat: some speakers of Alutor do not readily accept or produce sentences like (37) or (38b)—i.e., sentences showing object agreement of the matrix-clause main verb with the object clause as a whole. Perhaps this could be explained by the difficulty of making the verb agree not with an actual noun but with a pure abstraction of a clause. More generally, object clauses with verbs of perception (at least of the type just mentioned) are not favored by Alutor speakers. Although sentences (35)–(38) have been volunteered by native informants and, if produced, are not objected to, in spontaneous speech an Alutor will usually express what would be an object clause in English by a participle (with incorporated object, if any). For example, a more common way to render the meaning of (35) seems to be (39):

(39) *Qəmavə* + *nak na*   + *laʔu* + *tkəni* + *γət*
              3SG.SUBJ   see   PRES   2SG.OBJ
      qura   + *kəlγat* + *əlʔu*   + *γət,*
      reindeer   harness   PARTICIPLE   2SG
      lit. 'Q. sees you reindeer-harnessing'.

In much the same manner, (38a) and (38b) could be expressed instead as (40):

(40) *Qəmavə* + *nak* ∅   + *ləʔu* + *tkə*   + *nina*   + *wwi*
              3SG.SUBJ   see   PRES   3SG.OBJ   PL
      arγiŋ   + *əŋ*   *təla* + *lʔu*   *ʕətv* + *uwwi,*
      shore   DAT   come   PARTICIPLE   boat   PL.NOM
      lit. 'Q. sees to-the-shore coming boats'.

The reluctance of Alutor to use genuine object clauses with verbs of perception may necessitate a description different from ours. In case the governing matrix verb agrees with the grammatical subject or the direct object of its object clause—as in (35), (36) and (38)—it can be maintained that the whole sentence is COMPOUND rather than complex, i.e., it is made up of a conjunction of two simple sentences, the first one having its pronominal object omitted by the pronoun ellipsis rule repeatedly mentioned above:

(41) *Qəmavə* + *nak na* + *laʔu* + *tkəni* + *γət* [*γəttə*],
                                     thou
      γən + *annə*   ∅ + *kəlγatə* + *tkə* + *na* + *wwi qura* + *wwi,*
      thou   INSTR
      lit. 'Q. sees thee, thou art-harnessing reindeer'.

This solution provides a very simple statement for object agreement of the main verb in supposedly complex sentences: 3sg only (since only cases like (37) and (38b) will be considered to be complex sentences). The surface ellipsis of personal pronouns reflected in verb agreement is, as has been said, a common process in Alutor, which seems to be a further argument in favor of the latter solution. However, to definitively answer the question of how sentences with this verb agreement should be described, we need more data.[8]

For the present, our model implements the former solution, i.e., the three variant agreements in complex sentences. It is this solution that Rules 5–7 embody.

(ii) Object agreement of the verb with its indirect (dative) object in the presence of a direct (nominative) object.

As a general rule, an Alutor transitive verb obligatorily shows object agreement with its direct object only—see above, p. 269, and elsewhere. However, Alutor may have a few verbs admitting object agreement with their indirect objects (in the dative) rather than their direct objects. So far we have found in Alutor only one verb exhibiting object agreement with its dative object. It is JƏLƏKKI: (1) 'to give s.t. to s.o.'; or (2) 'to give s.o. [= a woman] as a wife to s.o.'. Object agreement of JƏLƏKKI with one of its two objects, either nominative (= direct) or dative (= indirect), is determined by the following two rules:

a. If the direct and the indirect objects of JƏLƏKKI are of the same person (which Alutor admits only if both are of the 3rd person)[9], then the verb exhibits object agreement with its direct object:

(42) əlləγ+ a   ∅   + jəl +nina   + wwi
father SG.INSTR   3SG.SUBJ give 3SG.OBJ PL
⟨*∅ + jəl + nin   ⟩ ənək + əŋ şininkina + wwi
      3SG.OBJ   he   DAT his   PL.NOM
ŋavakka + wwi
daughter   PL.NOM
'Father gave his daughters as wives to him'.

[The object agreement of the verb with the indirect object 'to him', i.e. featuring the singular objectal suffix, is ungrammatical.]

b. If the direct and the indirect objects of JƏLƏKKI are of different persons, then the verb agrees with one of the objects in the following order of preference:

first person > second person > third person.

1st vs. 2nd

(43) əlləγ + a ∅   +ina   + jəl + i
        3SG.SUBJ 1SG.OBJ   give   3SG.SUBJ

⟨*∅ + jəl + γət ⟩ γəmək + əŋ γəttə + ∅
    2SG.OBJ I   DAT thou   NOM
'Father gave thee as a wife to me'.

[The object agreement of the verb with the direct object 'thee', i.e., in the 2nd person singular, is ungrammatical.]

(44) *əlləγ + a ∅ + ina + jəl + i ⟨*∅ + jəl + γət⟩*
    γənək + əŋ γəmmə + ∅
    thou   DAT I   NOM
    'Father gave me as a wife to thee'.

1st vs. 3rd

(45) *əlləγ + a ∅ + ina + jəl + i ⟨*∅ + jəl + nin⟩*
         1SG.OBJ   3SG.OBJ
    γəmək + əŋ şininkin + ∅   ŋavakək + ∅
         his   SG.NOM daughter   SG.NOM
    '[Her] father gave me his daughter as a wife'.

(46) *əlləγ + a ∅ + ina + jəl + i ⟨*∅ + jəl + nin⟩*
    ənək + əŋ γəmmə + ∅
    he   DAT I   NOM
    '[My] father gave me as a wife to him'.

2nd vs. 3rd

(47) *əlləγ + a ∅   + jəl + γət   ⟨*∅ + jəl + nin⟩*
        3SG.SUBJ give   2SG.OBJ
    γənək + əŋ şininkin + ∅ ŋavakək + ∅
    thou   DAT
    '[Her] father gave thee his daughter as a wife'.

(48) *əlləγ + a ∅ + jəl + γət ⟨*∅ + jəl + nin⟩*
    ənək + əŋ γəttə + ∅
    he   DAT thou   NOM
    '[Your] father gave thee as a wife to him'.

The verbs of the JƏLƏKKI type (if indeed there exist more in Alutor; so far we are unaware of others) might be called **indirectly transitive** and should be marked "ind-tr" in the dictionary.

Object constructions with indirectly transitive verbs are described by Rules 8 and 9.

Rule 8 makes an "ind-tr" verb agree with its direct object if the person of the latter has a number less than or equal to that of the person of its indirect object (see in the condition part: $\mathbf{p}^1 \leqslant \mathbf{p}^2$).

Rule 9 provides for the agreement of the verb with the indirect object if its person is strictly lower-numbered than that of the direct object (i.e., $\mathbf{p}^1 < \mathbf{p}^2$).[10]

In connection with what has been said above, the following interesting fact about the verb IVƏK 'to tell; to say' seems worth mentioning. In Alutor such sentences as (49) are quite common:

(49) **a.** *∅*   + *in*   + *iv* + *i*   : *γəmnina* + *t*
2SG.SUBJ   1SG.OBJ   say   2SG.SUBJ   my   DU.NOM
qələqtumγə + *t*   *mən*   + *ənmə* + *na*   + *t*
brother   DU.NOM   1DU.SUBJ.CONJ   kill   3SG.OBJ DU
'Thou said to me: Let us both kill my two brothers'.

     b. *γəm* + *nan*   *t*   + *iv* + *γət*   *γəttə* + *∅:*
I   INSTR   1SG.SUBJ   say   2SG.OBJ   thou   NOM
kətvəl   *mən* + *ənmə* + *na* + *t*
shouldn't
'I said to thee: Both of us shouldn't kill both of them'.

The forms *in* + *iv* + *i* 'thou-said-to-me', *t* + *iv* + *γət* 'I-said-to-thee' and the like, where *ivək* has object agreement with the addressee, might prompt the conclusion that here we are dealing with another instance of indirectly transitive verbs: according to Indo-European linguistic[1] intuition, the noun phrase denoting the addressee with **verba dicendi** should perforce be an indirect object (in the dative case in languages like Russian or German, or with preposition like English *to*, French *à*, etc. in caseless languages). In Alutor there is little relevant data: pronominal reference to the addressee is usually omitted (see p. 280), so that one cannot determine its case form. However, such a conclusion would be wrong: *ivək* is not an indirectly transitive verb. Actually, Alutor has, roughly speaking, two different verbs *ivək* with different government patterns (but probably having the same or nearly the same meanings):

IVƏK 1, or a verb syntactically similar to English *say*, which can be used intransitively or transitively. If used intransitively, IVƏK 1 takes the addressee as an indirect object, i.e. in the dative, and never agrees with it; the "intransitive" IVƏK 1 has only subject agreement like all intransitive verbs, and its GS is in the nominative:

(50) **a.** *Qilivŋawut* + *∅* | *∅*   + *ivəlqiv*   + *i* |
Qilivngawut   NOM | 3SG.SUBJ   begin.to.say   3SG.SUBJ |
qəlavul + *əŋ*
husband   *SG.DAT*
'Q. said [= lit. 'began to say'] to her husband'.

     b. *Qilivŋawut* + *∅* | *∅* + *ivəlqiv* + *i* | *qələqtumγ*   + *əŋ*
                                      brothers[du or pl]   DAT
      'Q. said to her brothers'.

IVƏK 2, or a transitive verb syntactically similar to English *tell* and taking the addressee of speech as a direct object, i.e. in the nominative (its own grammatical subject is in the instrumental or the locative):

(51) $\gamma \partial m$ + *nan*

t	+ iv + $\gamma \partial t$
1SG.SUBJ	say 2SG.OBJ

$\gamma \partial tt \partial$ + $\emptyset$

  I   INSTR   1SG.SUBJ say   2SG.OBJ   thou   NOM
'I told thee'.

Sentences such as (52):

(52)

qolin   ənpə^ʔəlla^ʔ + *a $\emptyset$ + in   + iv + i*
one.day grandmother   SG.INSTR 3SG.SUBJ 1SG.OBJ say   3SG.SUBJ
'One day, Granny told me . . .'

also exemplify the use of IVƏK 2 since the grammatical subject in the instrumental case (*ənpə^ʔəlla^ʔ* + *a*) must signal the presence, in the surface-syntactic structure of (52), of a direct object *γəmmə* 'I' elided by a nearly obligatory rule (Pronoun Ellipsis, or Pro-Drop; cf. p. 280).

The present chapter reproduces, with modifications and additions, the paper Mel'čuk and Savvina (1978).

NOTES

1. (I, p. 268.) As a result of these trips, three studies concerning Alutor have been published by members of the expedition. Given the scarcity of available literature on Alutor, I feel it will be helpful to list them here: Mel'čuk (1973a), Barulin (1978) and Kodzasov and Murav'ëva (1980) (plus Mel'čuk and Savvina 1978).

2. (II, example (3b), p. 274.) In Alutor, the dual and the plural in verb forms are expressed by separate dual and plural markers added to singular and/or dual exponents which cross-reference the subject and the object. Thus, the singular 3rd person object form $\emptyset$ + *lə^ʔu* + *nin* 'he-saw-him' is dualized and pluralized as follows: $\emptyset$ + *lə^ʔu* + *nina* + l 'he-saw-two-of-them', $\emptyset$ + *lə^ʔu* + *nina* + **wwi** 'he-saw-many-of-them'; the dual 1st person subject form *mət* + *levətku* + *mək* 'we-went-two-of-us' is pluralized as *mət* + *levətku* + **la** + *mək* 'we-went-many-of-us', etc.

3. (III, Rule 2, p. 280.) This is in sharp contrast, for instance, with Georgian, where a whole class of intransitive verbs admits the ergative construction in the aorist series, i.e., a verb of this class takes its GS in the ergative case without any direct object: cf. Chapter 6, example (12), p. 260 ff. One-place (= monovalent) verbs having their GS—their only actant—in the ergative are known in Lezgian as well: Chapter 5, p. 227.

4. (IV, (29b), p. 287.) Forms with the lsg object are exceptional in the sense that they cross-reference the object by means of the prefix *ina-* and the subject by means of a suffix, while in all other subject-object forms, as we will immediately see, the prefix reflects the subject and the suffix reflects the object.

5. (IV, 1,(i), p. 289.) Grammatical Subject in the Resultative.

The resultative creates an additional problem for the determination of subjecthood in Alutor; since, however, the solution thereof has no direct bearing on our description of Alutor ergative construction, we could afford bypassing it in the main body of our discussion. Nonetheless, it is interesting in itself and deserves a few lines.

A resultative form, essentially a conjugated past participle, agrees with only one actant (as indicated above), thus deviating from double, subject-object agreement of all non-resultative forms.

With intransitive verbs, the only (agreement-triggering) actant of a resultative form corresponds to the GS of the non-resultative form:

(i)   **a.** *uṇuṇu*   *γa + retəlqiv + lin*   '(The) child has-gone-home'.
         uṇuṇu + t   *γa + retəlqiv + lina + t* 'Both-children have-gone-home'.
         uṇuṇu + wwi *γa + retəlqiv + laŋ*   'Children have-gone-home'.
     vs.
   b. *uṇuṇu*   *retəlqiv + i*   '(The) child went-home'.
         uṇuṇu + t   *retəlqiv + ye ʔət*   'Both-children went-home'.
         uṇuṇu + wwi retəlqiv + la + t   'Children went-home'.

In (ia), *uṇuṇu* is the GS; it is in the nominative, as GSs of intransitive verbs regularly are.

However, transitive verbs display another pattern. The resultative form of a transitive verb happens to agree with the actant that constitutes the direct object of the corresponding non-resultative form and does not agree at all with the other actant, i.e., with the actant that is the grammatical subject of the non-resultative form. Cf.:

(ii)   **a.** $\left\{\begin{array}{ll} uṇuṇu + ta \\ \text{child} \quad \text{SG.INSTR} \\ uṇuṇu + tək \\ \text{child} \quad \text{DU/PL.INSTR} \end{array}\right\}$ $\begin{array}{l} γa + nəṣviṣṣav + lin \quad maniwra + n \\ \text{RES} \quad \text{pitch} \qquad \text{3SG} \quad \text{tent} \qquad \text{SG.NOM} \end{array}$

$\left\{\begin{array}{l} \text{The child} \\ \text{Both-children} \\ \text{Children} \end{array}\right\}$ has/have pitched the tent'.

$\left\{\begin{array}{l} uṇuṇu + ta \\ uṇuṇu + tək \end{array}\right\}$ $\begin{array}{l} γa + nəṣviṣṣav + lina + t \quad maniwra + t \\ \qquad\qquad\qquad \text{3SG} \quad \text{DU} \qquad\qquad \text{DU.NOM} \end{array}$

$\left\{\begin{array}{l} \text{The child} \\ \text{Both-children} \\ \text{Children} \end{array}\right\}$ has/have pitched two tents'.

$\left\{\begin{array}{l} uṇuṇu + ta \\ uṇuṇu + tək \end{array}\right\}$ $\begin{array}{l} γa + nəṣviṣṣav + laŋ \quad maniwra + wwi \\ \qquad\qquad\qquad \text{3PL} \qquad\qquad \text{PL.NOM} \end{array}$

$\left\{\begin{array}{l} \text{The child} \\ \text{Both-children} \\ \text{Children} \end{array}\right\}$ has/have pitched the tents'.

     vs.
   b. *uṇuṇu +*   *ta*   ∅   *+ təṣviṣṣav +*   *nin*   *maniwra +*   *n*
               ŞG.INSTR   *3SG.SUBJ*   pitch   *3SG.OBJ*   SG.NOM
       'The child pitched the tent'.

uŋuŋu + tək   na   + nəṣviṣṣavə + n
    DU/PL.INSTR   DU/PL.SUBJ   3SG.OBJ
maniwra + n
'Both children/Children pitched the tent'.

Let it be emphasized that, unlike (iib), in (iia) the N_{instr}, i.e., uŋuŋu + ta / uŋuŋu + tək, can be readily deleted without affecting the grammaticality or contextual autonomy of the sentence:

  c. γa + nəṣviṣṣav + lin maniwra + n

is a complete and self-contained sentence, meaning 'The tent has been pitched'; the N_{instr} can be so amputated in ANY resultative sentence.
    The question is, then, which of the two nominal elements in (iia) and all such sentences is the grammatical subject. Two competing solutions present themselves.

SOLUTION I: N_{nom} is the GS of a resultative form, N_{instr} being its agentive complement.
SOLUTION II: N_{instr} is the GS of a resultative form, N_{nom} being its direct object.

Let us compare these solutions with regard to different SSynt-properties of Alutor.

- *Agreement-triggering* argues, as we have already pointed out, in favor of Solution I. However, with the resultative, this factor is not as compelling as with non-resultative forms: instead of 504 finite non-resultative forms, the resultative distinguishes only 9 forms (3 persons × 3 numbers), so that the role of agreement is here not as important.
- *Nondeletability* also argues, and with no reserve, in favor of Solution I: N_{nom}, and not N_{instr}, is nondeletable.
- Solution I treats resultative forms of transitive verbs as passive. It corresponds to the obviously passive meaning of the γa-participle, underlying the resultative, and to the widespread usage of Alutor agentless resultative sentences as passives:

(iii) **a.** əninnə uŋuŋu + ∅   Piŋinaŋ   + ∅
        his   child   SG.NOM Pinginang   SG.NOM
        γa + tkal + lin   mra + məny   + ək
        RES wound 3SG   right hand/arm   SG.LOC
        'His son Pinginang has been wounded in the right arm'.
  b. ət^ʔəmt   + ək   nəməlʔən jiləjil + ∅
        Karagin-island   SG.LOC   Alutor   language SG.NOM
        γa   + javalqiv + lin
        RES   use   3SG
        'On the Karagin island, the Alutor language has been used'.

- *The gapping-collapsibility test* is of no use with the resultative forms. Due, probably, to free omission of anaphoric pronouns on the surface, we actually get here all logically possible conjoinings, so that no safe judgment can be based on it. Cf.:

(iv) **a.** ənnəʔə + n   γa + ŋinməṣʔatəlqiv + lin,
       fish   SG.NOM RES begin.to.speak   3SG
       təlɣələŋə +n   γa + ttil   + lin, γa + ral + lin,
       finger   SG.NOM RES let.loose 3SG RES fall   3SG

lit. 'Fish has-started-to-speak, finger has-been-let-loose, [fish] has-fallen' = 'The fish started to speak, let [his = main character's] finger loose and fell'.

b. *to   vitγa   tanŋ + a   γa + qatvə + lin*
and immediately enemy SG.INSTR RES spear   3SG
əşşaŋjuş?ə   + n   to   γa + vi? + lin,
younger.brother SG.NOM and RES die   3SG
lit. 'And immediately by-enemy has-been-speared younger-brother and has-died' = 'And then the enemy speared the younger brother, and [the latter] died'.

c. *pujγə + n   γa + niŋli + lin   Əmka + nak   to*
spear   SG.NOM   RES throw   3SG Amka   SG.LOC and
?ala?al + ∅   γe + tu + lin   [<γa + jtu + lin],
ax   SG.NOM   RES grab 3SG
lit. 'Spear has-been-thrown by-Amka and ax has-been-grabbed' = 'Amka threw his spear and grabbed his ax'.

● *The person-number suffixes* of the resultative are the same as the person-number suffixes of predicative nominals (noun and adjectives), i.e. they are subjectal suffixes, cf.:

(v)   **a.** *γa + piŋku + jγəm* 'I have jumped'
RES jump   1SG

vs.

γəm + ŋaŋŋuş   ŋavakke + γəm [*<ŋavakka + jγəm*] 'I am the only
I   only   daughter   1SG   daughter'.
b. *γa + tkal + iγət* 'Thou hast been wounded'.
RES wound 2SG

vs.

nə + mis?e + γət 'Thou art beautiful'.
beautiful 2SG
c. *γa + ŋivə + laŋ* 'The have been sent'.
RES send   3PL

vs.

nə + lilə + laŋ 'They are green'.
green   3PL

● Solution I entails a passivelike inversion of actants in the resultative form (with respect to the corresponding transitive non-resultative verb), while Solution II avoids this unpleasant claim. However, a passivelike conversion of actants in perfect and related formations is quite plausible typologically, so that it should not bother us too much.
● Under Solution I, NP$_{instr}$ is, as indicated above, an agentive complement. But note that if this CO^{agent} is a human proper name, then it must be in the locative; in other words, the distribution of grammatical cases in the CO^{agent} is exactly the same as in a transitive GS (the locative for human proper names, the instrumental elsewhere):

(vi)   **a.** ⎧*uŋuŋu +   ta*⎫
⎪child   SG.INSTR⎪ *γa + nəşvişşav + laŋ   maniwra + wwi,*
⎨*Qəmavə + nak*⎬ RES pitch   3PL   tent   PL.NOM
⎩Qamav   SG.LOC⎭
'⎧By-child⎫
lit. ⎨   ⎬ have-been-pitched the tents'.
⎩By-Qamav⎭

vs.[1]

b. $\left\{ \begin{array}{l} u\underline{\eta}u\underline{\eta}u \ + \ ta \\ Q\partial mav\partial + \ nak \end{array} \right\}$ $\emptyset$ $+ \ t\partial \c{s}vi\c{s}\c{s}av + \ nina \ + \ wwi \ \ maniwra + wwi,$

$\qquad\qquad\qquad\qquad$ 3SG.SUB $\quad$ pitch $\qquad$ 3SG.OBJ $\;$ PL

$\qquad$ lit. $\left\{ \begin{array}{l} \text{Child} \\ \\ \text{Qamav} \end{array} \right.$ $\Big\}$ he-pitched-them tents'.

Solution I entails, consequently, the repetition of the same syntactic rule (i.e., the one that states the distribution of cases in GSs and CO^{agent}s), while Solution II avoids it (by considering the $NP_{instr/loc}$ with resultative forms as GS). Therefore, this fact argues in favor of Solution II.

Taking into account available evidence, we choose Solution I, which is superior to Solution II in all respects but the last one. Therefore, the GS of a resultative verb is taken to be the NP_{nom}; in the resultative, all verbs are intransitive and have no direct objects.

6. (IV, **1**,(**ii**), Solution II, p. 290.) With a few verbs the Alutor instrumental case may mark an indirect object rather than an instrument of some action. However, the verbs governing an object in instrumental case usually have meanings that pragmatically preclude a human object: e.g., OJIK 'to feed (on s.t.)' [not 'to eat (s.t./s.o.)'].

7. (IV, **1**, (**ii**), Principle (34), p. 291.) Principle of Internal Autonomy of Cases is, in a certain sense, the converse of the Principle of External Autonomy of Case Forms, which is introduced below, in Chapter 10, Principle (5), p. 360.

8. (IV, **2**, (**i**), at the end, p. 294.) A case of the main verb object agreement with the object of a transitive object clause even across the subordinate conjunction is briefly mentioned in Inènlikèj and Nedjalkov (1973: 182) for Chukchee (closely related to Alutor). Cf.:

(i) $\quad$ Chukchee *ənan* $\qquad$ *qəlɣiļu ləŋərkə + nin, iŋqun* $\qquad$ *rətəmŋəv + nen*

$\qquad\qquad\qquad\qquad$ 'He[instr] regrets-it[3sg], $\qquad$ that $\;$ [he] $\;$ he-lost-it

$\qquad$ *qora + ŋa*

$\qquad$ [the] reindeer[sg,nom]'

$\qquad$ vs.

(ii) $\quad$ *ənan qəlɣiļu / ləŋərkə + nin + et,* $\qquad$ *iŋqun* $\qquad$ *rətəmŋəv + nen + at*

$\qquad$ 'He $\;$ regrets-them [3pl], $\qquad\qquad$ that $\;$ [he] $\;$ he-lost-them

$\qquad\qquad$ *qora + t*

$\qquad$ [the] reindeer[pl,nom]'.

9. (IV, **2**, (**ii**), before example (42), p. 294.) Note that to express a situation when the subject and the object of a verb are of the same person and referentially identical (i.e., to express "reflexivity"), Alutor uses the noun *uvik*, lit. 'body', as an object, which is in this context equivalent to the English *myself, yourself, himself*, etc.; the verb has the same object agreement with this noun as with any other object noun: 3sg. Cf. also Mel'čuk 1973a: 27–28.

10. (IV, **2**, (**ii**), before example (49), p. 296.) In Chukchee, the verb *jəl-* (etymologically related to Alutor *jəl + əkki* but lacking the sense 'give in marriage') shows a very similar pattern of object agreement: it agrees with its indirect object (in the dative case) if this is 1st or 2nd person, but with the direct object (in the nominative case) if the indirect object is 3rd person. (The Chukchee *jəl-* does not currently permit 1st or 2nd person direct objects.) Most interestingly, in Djaru (Western Australia), the verb *yung-/yiny-* 'give; give in marriage' agrees with its indirect object rather than the direct one according to the same person hierarchy: 1st > 2nd > 3rd (Tsunoda 1981: 65–67); cf.:

(i) Djaru

    a. *lamparra*   + *lu*   *ŋa*   + *∅*   + **yi**   *yiny* + *a*
        father-in-law   INSTR   AUX   3SG.SUBJ   1SG.OBJ   give   PAST
        kujarra + *∅*   *ŋumpirr* + *∅*   *ŋani* + *ŋa*
        two   NOM   wife   NOM   I   DAT
        '[My] father-in-law gave me two wives'.

    b. *ŋa*   + *rna*   + **ŋku**   *yiny* + *a kujarra* +*∅*
        AUX   1SG.SUBJ   2SG.OBJ
        ŋumpirr + *∅*   *nyunu* + *ŋa*   'I gave thee two wives'.
                         thou   DAT

But, unlike Alutor, in Djaru, if both the direct and the indirect objects are 3rd person, then the object agreement is governed by another hierarchy, namely, that of number: plural > dual > singular; cf.:

(ii) Djaru

    a. *lamparra* + *lu ŋa* + *∅*   + **anu**   *yiny* + *a*
                          3SG.SUBJ   3PL.OBJ
        yampa + *∅*   *murrkun* + *ku*   *ŋumpirr* + *ku*
        child   NOM   three   DAT   wife   DAT
        'Father-in-law gave a child to three wives'.

    b. *lamparra* + *lu ŋa* + *∅* + **anu** *yinya*   *murrkun* + *∅*
                                        three   NOM
        yampa + *apa* + *∅*   *ŋumpirr* + *ku*
        child   PL   NOM
        'Father-in-law gave three children to (a) wife'.

See Faltz (1978) for more data concerning indirect objects in different languages.

Chapter 8

SYNTACTIC, OR
LEXICAL, ZERO

La langue peut se contenter de l'opposition
de quelque chose avec rien.
F. de Saussure, *Cours de linguistique générale*, 1962: 124.

I. THE PROBLEM STATED: QUESTIONS 1–3

Working on a theory of grammatical voice, on the description of the voice system in a particular language or on the notorious problem of grammatical subject, the linguist cannot avoid asking and answering many crucial questions, of which the following three will retain our attention in this chapter.

Question 1
What is the relationship of voice to such syntactic constructions as the Russian so-called **indefinite-personal agent construction** of (1) or the Russian **impersonal construction** of (2)?

(1) Russian *Ivan + a   priglasil + i   k   trëm   časam*
              Ivan   ACC   invited   PL   to   three   o'clock
              lit. '[They] invited Ivan for three o'clock' = 'Ivan was
              invited . . .'

(2) Russian *Ivan + a   oprokinul   + o*
              Ivan   ACC   knocked.over   SG.NEUT
              lit. '[It] knocked Ivan over' = 'Ivan got knocked over'.

Question 2

Are constructions (1) and (2) grammatically subjectless? The same question may be asked of the Ukrainian construction (3) and the Spanish construction (4):

(**3**) Ukrainian *Bul* + *o*   *organizovan*   + *o*
         was   SG.NEUT   organized[pass. part.]   SG.NEUT
         èkspedycij   + *u*
         expedition[fem]   ACC
         lit. '[It] was organized an expedition' = 'An expedition was organized'.

(**4**) Spanish *Aquí se   vend* + *e   periódico* + *s*
         here   itself sell   3SG   newspaper   PL
         lit. 'Here, [it] sells itself newspapers' = 'Newspapers are sold here'.

Question 3

Why don't we posit an unspecified human agent in Russian sentences such as (5) in order to treat them as indefinite-personal constructions?

(**5**) Russian *Ivan   byl   priglašën* + *∅*
         Ivan-NOM   was-SG.MASC   invited [pass.part]   SG.MASC
         k trëm časam
         to three o'clock
         'Ivan was invited for three o'clock'.

Constructions such as in (5) are traditionally considered to be agentless passives. But (5) is perfectly synonymous with (1), and (1) is a classic example of the indefinite-personal construction.

To answer these questions requires, first of all, clarification of the concept "syntactic, or lexical, zero." But such a clarification presupposes, in turn, a theoretical account of linguistic$_1$ zero in general.[1] Even more than that, it presupposes an account of sentential incompleteness, which includes ellipsis (omission of some lexical nodes from the DMorphS of the sentence), missing arguments, unfinished utterances, etc. Since these problems could not be fully investigated in this chapter, I will restrict myself here to the problem of zero in syntax. In the absence of a unified theory of syntactic incompleteness, my conclusions are of a preliminary and programmatic character.

To avoid overburdening the exposition, I have refrained from reviewing the question and have provided only minimal references. For a detailed presentation of the problem of zeroes in language and copious references, see Meier (1961); several important points are made in Godel (1953); my main source of inspiration is the excellent analysis of Haas (1957). On zero affixation in word derivation see Lopatin (1966) and Kastovsky (1969); remarks pertinent to zero expression of morphological categories are found in Aschmann and Wonderly (1952). An insightful analysis of zeroes in syntax is provided by Wierzbicka (1966).

The exposition is organized as follows.

In Section II, the **zero wordform** or (better) **zero lex**[2] and **zero lexeme** are introduced by analogy with such morphological zeroes as zero morphs and zero morphemes. (The concept of zero morph and zero morpheme are sufficiently clear and intuitively accessible to be taken as basic.) Zero lex and zero lexeme are called **syntactic**, or **lexical**, **zeroes**; this double qualification is explained below, on page 312.

In Section III, the concepts of zero lex and zero lexeme are tested on certain types of Russian sentences.

In Section IV, I discuss a use of the term **zero verb** (the concept is logically a particular instance of the concept "syntactic, or lexical, zero") current in linguistic[2], particularly Russian, literature; the goal is an improved organization of terminology for zeroes. Some of the uses of this term correspond not to the notions I propose but to phenomena sharply distinct from zero—in particular, ellipsis.

In Section V, answers to the three above questions are proposed, and several connections are noted between the theory of grammatical voice and the approach to zero lexes and lexemes outlined here.

II. FROM MORPHOLOGICAL TO SYNTACTIC ZEROES

1. Morphological Zeroes

A generally recognized example of a linguistic[1] zero is morphological zero: namely, a zero ending in paradigmatic forms of a (highly) flective language, such as in Russian wordforms *ruk* 'hand, PL.GEN' [cf. *ruka* 'hand, SG.NOM'] or *kryš* 'roof, PL.GEN' [*kryša* 'roof, SG.NOM']. The zero ending here signals cumulatively the plural and the genitive (in much the same manner as non-zero endings signal other combinations of number and case: $ruk + á$ SG.NOM, $ruk + í$ SG.GEN, . . ., $rúk + i$ PL.NOM, . . ., $ruk + áx$ PL.PREPOS). This zero ending is a zero morph, a concept that I want to analyze in greater detail.

A **morph** X is an elementary segmental[3] (linguistic[1]) sign. To put it into a more developed form, a morph is an ordered triplet

$$\mathbf{X} = \langle \text{'X'}; /X/; \Sigma_x \rangle,$$

where:

'X'   is the **signatum** [= **signifié**] of the morph, that is, a complex of symbols representing its meaning (whatever we agree to understand by meaning);

/X/   is the **signans** [= **signifiant**] of the morph, that is, a string of phonemes (possibly supplied with a complex of prosodemes);

Σ_x is the **syntactics** of the morph, that is, the set of all data about the combinatorial possibilities of the morph **X**; syntactics includes part of

speech, grammatical gender (in nouns), declension or conjugation
type, phonological and/or morphological environments, selectional
restrictions of all kinds, etc. (Cf. Chapter 1, Note 1, p. 39.)

The morph sign, being, by definition, elementary, is not representable (or quasi-
representable) in terms of other signs of the language. (I cannot enter into substantial explanations here, so my presentation of many crucial notions is of necessity sketchy. For a rigorous treatment of such concepts as "linguistic₁ sign",
"morph", "representable", etc. see Mel'čuk 1982: 40 ff.)

Let me give now several examples of morphs written in the standard form.

(6) Russian non-zero genitive plural endings:
  a. -ej = ⟨'plural genitive'; /ej/; Σ = noun suffix, after a palatalized or
          hushing consonant, . . .⟩
      Cf. /júnoša/ 'youth'—/júnoš + ej/; /kón'/ 'horse'—/kon' + éj; /nóž/
      'knife'—/nož + éj/; /mór' + e/ 'sea'—/mor' + éj/; /krovát'/ 'bed'
      —/krovát' + ej/; /nóč/ 'night'—/noč + éj/.

Note that the syntactics of this morph, as well as those of other morphs in examples (6)–(8), is approximate: it does not fully specify the distribution of the
corresponding morph and is quoted only as illustration.

  b. -ov = ⟨'plural genitive'; /of/; Σ = noun suffix, IInd declension,
          masculine gender, **not** after a palatalized or hushing
          consonant, . . .⟩
      Cf. /stól/ 'table'—/stol + óf/; /t'ígr/ 'tiger'—/t'ígr + of/;
      /tr'eugól'n'ik/ 'triangle'—/tr'eugól'n'ik + of/.

(7) English past indefinite endings:
  a. -d = ⟨'past'; /d/; Σ = verb suffix, in weak verbs, after a vowel, a
          sonant or a voiced consonant other than /d/, . . .⟩
      Cf. *echo + ed, care + d; struggle + d, comb + ed; dubb + ed, rage + d.*
  b. -ed = ⟨'past'; /ɨd/; Σ = verb suffix, in weak verbs, after /d/ or
          /t/, . . .⟩
      Cf. *fade + d, patt + ed.*
  c. -t = ⟨'past'; /t/; Σ = verb suffix, either in weak verbs after a
          voiceless consonant other than /t/ or in lexically specified
          strong verbs, . . .⟩
      Cf. *miss + ed, stopp + ed; slep + t, mean + t.*

Now, a **zero morph** is a morph whose signans is an empty string (of phonemes). Let Λ stand for the empty string and **∅** for zero; then our Russian zero
suffix can be written as follows:

(8) Russian $-\emptyset_{\text{PL.GEN}}$ = ⟨'plural genitive'; /Λ/; Σ = noun suffix, Ist/ IInd declension, **not** after a palatalized or hushing consonant, . . .⟩

Like any regular non-zero morph, a zero morph has, as we see, both a non-empty signatum and a non-empty syntactics. The signatum in the case of (8) is identical with that of the non-zero morphs of (6); the syntactics of $-\emptyset_{\text{PL.GEN}}$ provides for the fact that this zero morph is restricted to certain types of Russian noun stems.

There are several other zero suffixes in Russian inflection; for example:

$-\emptyset_{\text{SG.NOM}}$ in IInd declension masculine nouns (*stol* 'table', *tigr* 'tiger', . . .).

$-\emptyset_{\text{SG.MASC}}$ in past tense verbs (*vstal* '[X = a masculine noun] rose', *čital* '[X = a masc. noun] read', . . .).

$-\emptyset_{\text{SG.MASC}}$ in short adjectives (*zdorov* '[X = a masc. noun] is healthy', *krasen* '[X = a masc. noun] is red', . . .).

Morphs having identical signata and distributed according to some phonological and/or morphological conditions are united into one **morpheme**, of which they are **allomorphs**.[4] Thus the English morphs of (7) are allomorphs of the morpheme {PAST}; the Russian morphs -**ej**, -**ov** and $-\emptyset_{\text{PL.GEN}}$ are allomorphs of the morpheme {PL.GEN}, $-\emptyset_{\text{PL.GEN}}$ being its zero allomorph.

As is well known, there are morphemes with only one allomorph. For example, in Russian the morpheme {PL.PREP} for adjectives contains only one allomorph, -**ix**. The sole allomorph of a morpheme can also be zero: a morpheme that has only a zero allomorph is naturally called a **zero morpheme**; e.g., the nominal and adjectival singular morpheme in Spanish, {SG}, contains just one allomorph: zero.[5]

It follows that the expression **morphological zero** can be understood only in one of two precise senses: either (i) it is a zero morph, i.e., a morph whose signans is an empty string; or (ii) it is a zero morpheme, i.e., a morpheme having a zero morph as its sole allomorph. We can make the following generalization:

A linguistic₁ zero either is a zero sign, i.e., a sign whose signans is an empty string; or it is the corresponding zero "-eme," i.e., the set of equivalent signs that contains only one zero "allo-" (one zero sign).

2. Formal Nature of (Morphological) Zeroes: Their Place in the System of Linguistic₁ Representations

The morphological considerations used so far and the syntactic considerations of interest in this chapter are two very different things. In order to relate them I must resort to a more abstract level of analysis.

In morphology, the set of wordforms is considered as given. A wordform is a linguistic$_1$ sign: its signatum will be represented by a formal expression called **deep-morphological representation** (DMorphR), which has already been mentioned in this book on several occasions; and its signans is a string of phonemes (plus, probably, prosodemes). The DMorphR of a given wordform **w** consists of the name of the corresponding lexeme subscripted for all morphological values (i.e., grammemes) of **w**. (The syntactics of the wordform is irrelevant for the moment.) The task of morphology is to describe the set of all wordforms of a language in a more concise manner than by simply listing them. This goal can be achieved to the extent that wordforms are COMPLEX signs, i.e., insofar as their signata have recurring components corresponding to recurring components in their signantia. Here is one generally accepted approach to the construction of such morphological description.

Consider the following set of signantia of Russian wordforms:

(9)   Russian **a.** /rúk/ 'of hands', /st'én/ 'of walls', /l'ín'ij/ 'of lines', . . .
/nočéj/ 'of nights', /put'éj/ 'of ways', /nožéj/ of knives', . . .
/stvolóf/ 'of (gun) barrels', /ostrovóf/ 'of islands', /bojcóf/ 'of soldiers', . . .

and the corresponding set of deep-morphological representations depicting the signata of the same wordforms:

b. RUKA$_{pl, gen}$,   STENA$_{pl, gen}$,   LINIJA$_{pl, gen, \cdots}$
NOČ$'_{pl, gen}$,   PUT$'_{pl, gen}$,   NOŽ$_{pl, gen, \cdots}$
STVOL$_{pl, gen}$,   OSTROV$_{pl, gen}$,   BOJEC$_{pl, gen, \cdots}$

We must establish correspondences between sets (9a) and (9b) in the most economical way possible, without simply recopying all the pairs. To accomplish this, the following morphs are introduced:

(10)   Russian **ruk**   = ⟨'RUKA'; /ruk/; Σ = noun stem, fem, I decl, . . .⟩
sten   = ⟨'STENA'; /st'en/; Σ = noun stem, fem, I decl, . . .⟩
ostrov = ⟨'OSTROV'; /ostrov/; Σ = noun stem, masc,
II decl, . . .⟩
bojec = ⟨'BOJEC'; /bojec/; Σ = noun stem, masc,
II decl, . . .⟩
.
.
.
-Ø$_{PL.GEN}$ = ⟨'plural genitive'; /Λ/; Σ = noun suffix, I/II decl,
. . .⟩ (see (8) above)
-ej   = ⟨'pl, gen'; /ej/; . . . ⟩ ⎫
-ov   = ⟨'pl, gen'; /of/; . . . ⟩ ⎬ (see (6) above)

The morphs of the language described must be specified by a list. Obviously this list will contain far fewer items than the full list of wordforms. (For instance, if we take into account regular word formation rules of Russian, the list of Russian wordforms is at least one hundred times the size of the list of morphs.) The correspondence of (9a) and (9b) can then be described in a trivial manner: in the transition from (9a) to (9b), the signans of the wordform is broken into signantia of the appropriate morphs in accordance with their syntactics; then the signata of these morphs are combined to produce the deep-morphological representation of the wordform. Conversely, in the transition from (9b) to (9a) the underlying deep-morphological representation of the wordform is broken into the signata of the morphs in accordance with their syntactics, then the signantia of these morphs are combined to produce the signans of the wordform. (This description of the correspondence between signantia of wordforms, i.e. their phonetic representations, and their deep-morphological representations is very tentative: e.g., accentuation and morphonological alternations have not even been mentioned.) By following this approach, we arrive at an INTERMEDIATE representation of wordforms—a representation in terms of morphs. Thus from morphological point of view, we need at least three levels for representation of wordforms:

—An upper, or $(n + 1)$th, level, which is closer to text—the signans of the wordform in question, a string of phonemes, or its deep-phonetic representation.
—An intermediate, or nth, level—a string of morphs.
—A lower, or $(n - 1)$th, level, which is closer to meaning—the deep-morphological representation of the wordform.

For example:

$(n + 1)$th level	/noč éj/	/stvol óf/	/rúk/	
	⇕ ⇕	⇕ ⇕	⇕ ⇕
nth level	**noč + ej**	**stvol + ov**	**ruk + ∅**PL.GEN
	⇕ ⇕	⇕ ⇕	⇕ ⇕
$(n - 1)$th level	NOČ´‿‿ pl, gen	STVOL‿‿ pl, gen	·RUKA‿‿ pl, gen

The two-headed double arrow symbolizes, as it does elsewhere in this book, correspondence in both directions.

This schema makes explicit the distinctive formal property of zero morphs: a zero morph is the symbol in an intermediate linguistic₁ representation of the nth level such that:

—In the transition $n \Rightarrow (n - 1)$ it corresponds to some (usually) non-empty symbol or complex of symbols.
—In the transition $n \Rightarrow (n + 1)$ it corresponds to an empty string.
—On its own nth level it combines with other symbols of the same level ac-

cording to fully specified rules of the language that are captured in its syntactics.

A similar formal property must be inherent in any zero sign in language. We can, then, formulate a definition.

ZERO SIGN

A **zero sign** is a symbol of the nth level of linguistic$_1$ representation that on the $(n + 1)$th, more surface, level always corresponds to an empty string and that is justified either "from below" (it corresponds to non-zero symbols on the $(n - 1)$th level) or on its own level (its behavior is governed by well-specified rules of co-occurrence with other symbols of the nth level).[6]

To complete the picture, let me introduce the last complication: In the Meaning-Text theory, as in several other theories, a further level of morphological representation of wordforms is postulated, called surface-morphological representation (SMorphR): Chapter 2, p. 71. It lies between the nth and $(n - 1)$th levels and will be notated n'. The n'th level is the "-emic" level, where a wordform is represented as a set of morphemes; thus **nočej** appears as {NOČ'}, {PL.GEN}; **ruk** as {RUKA}, {PL.GEN}; and so forth. (Remember that a morpheme is a set of all morphs having an identical signatum and distributed as a function of the phonological or morphological context.) Therefore, a full-fledged representation of a wordform **w** is as follows:

$(n + 1)$th   level: string of signantia of morphs—a phonemic string
      nth   level: string of morphs
     n'th   level: set of morphemes ($=$ the SMorphR of **w**)
$(n - 1)$th   level: the DMorphR of **w**

Now we are ready to construct syntactic analogs of zero morphs and zero morphemes. Note, however, that the analogy between syntax and morphology cannot be perfect: the differences between the two are so fundamental that the parallels I will draw are little more than heuristic considerations.

3. Morphology-to-Syntax Analogy

Before discussing the zeroes of a syntactic level n we must determine the $(n + 1)$th and $(n - 1)$th levels of sentence representation. I emphasize that from the viewpoint of the problem of zeroes these levels must be taken as axiomatic—the levels $n + 1$ and $n - 1$ must be postulated independently of and prior to an inquiry into the question of zero on the nth level. In syntax, the set of sentences is considered as given (thus a sentence is to syntax what a wordform is to morphology). A sentence is a complex of linguistic$_1$ signs, one that has a signans and a signatum (but lacks syntactics).[7] The signans of a sentence is a phonemic string plus relevant prosody (intonation contour, stresses, pauses); it constitutes the upper, or $(n + 1)$th level of sentence representation. The signatum of a sentence

—its semantic representation—is a network introduced to represent the meaning of the sentence; it is the lower, $(n - 1)$th, level. What are then levels n and n' in sentence representation?

The closest syntactic analogs to morphs, these ultimate building blocks of the wordform, are wordforms, or **lexes**, the ultimate building blocks of the sentence. (Note that henceforth I will use instead of wordform the term **lex**; although it is not synonymous to **wordform**, it is preferable in that it makes explicit the important proportion **morph : morpheme = lex : lexeme**. Cf. Note 2.) Therefore, an intermediate sentence representation on the level n must be a string of lexes, each of them represented by its respective deep-morphological representation. Thus for (11):

(11)   Russian *Matros   snova   polez   na   mačtu*
               sailor   again   began.to.climb   on   mast
               'The sailor began to climb the mast again'.

the representation of level n will be (11′):

(11′)

$\text{MATROS}_{\text{sg, nom}}\ \text{SNOVA}\ \text{POLEZT}'_{\text{non-refl,perf,past,sg,masc}}\ \text{NA}\ \text{MAČTA}_{\text{sg, acc}}$

(11′) is the deep-morphological structure (DMorphS) of sentence (11); cf. Chapter 2, p. 71. Let me emphasize that DMorphS of a sentence is the upper limit where syntax (= syntax rules) operates, so that this level can be very loosely treated as "syntactic."

Pursuing our analogy, on the syntactic level n' we must have as units sets of lexes possessing an identical lexical signatum, i.e., **lexemes**. The sentence is then represented as an unordered set of lexemes linked by surface-syntactic relations (SSyntRels), or, to put it in more familiar terms, as a surface-syntactic structure (SSyntS), defined in Chapters 1 and 2. We have already discussed this notion repeatedly; therefore, without any further ado, I will demonstrate the SSyntS of (11):

(11″)

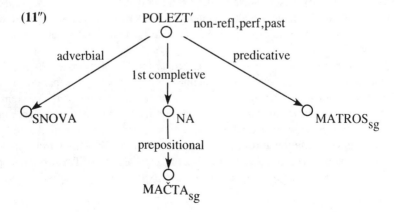

In the surface-syntactic structure there are, by definition, no other means to describe interword connections than labeled SSyntRels. This fact will prove essential in the subsequent argumentation.

The four-level representation of a sentence **S** is then as follows:

$(n + 1)$th level: signans of **S**—a string of lex signantia, i.e., a phonemic
string, with all appropriate prosodemes ($=$ DPhonR of **S**)
nth level: string of lexes, i.e., of their DMorphRs ($=$ DMorphS of **S**)
n'th level: SSyntS ($=$ dependency tree) of **S**
$(n - 1)$th level: semantic representation of **S** ($=$ SemR of **S**)

4. Syntactic Zeroes

Now the notion "syntactic zero" can be made explicit. A **zero wordform**, or **zero lex**, which has as its signans an empty string of phonemes, is the syntactic analogue of a zero morph. It is a symbol on level n of the representation of a sentence such that it always disappears on movement upward, toward the text; it corresponds to an empty string on level $n + 1$ (i.e., in phonemic representation). Conversely, on movement downward, toward the meaning, the zero wordform corresponds to an identifiable complex of symbols on level $n - 1$ (i.e., in semantic representation).

A **zero lexeme**, a one-element set of lexes that contains only a zero lex, is the syntactic analogue of a zero morpheme. Symbols for zero lexemes, together with the symbols for other lexemes, label the nodes of the syntactic tree on the n'th level of sentence representation (i.e., in the SSyntS of a sentence).

As was true for zero morphs, a zero lex is "deficient" only with respect to its signans: normally it has a full-fledged signatum and a full-fledged syntactics— that is, a specific, identifiable meaning and specific, identifiable possibilities of combination with other words.

A zero lex either belongs to a lexeme that has other, non-zero lexes as well, or it is the sole allolex of a zero lexeme. An example of a zero lex of a nonzero lexeme is the zero present tense form of the Russian lexeme BYT' 'be' (copula and locational verb), which also includes several nonzero lexes; cf. Evreinov (1973). An example of a zero lexeme is the indefinite-personal agent of Russian, discussed below.

As zero morphemes should be contained in the list of morphemes of a language, so zero lexemes should be contained in its dictionary as separate entries. Zero lexes should also be mentioned in the dictionary entries of their lexemes, just as zero morphs of nonzero morphemes are indicated in morphological rules. While being essentially lexical units, zero lexes and lexemes might also be loosely called **syntactic zeroes**, in view of the fact that they are introduced and motivated at the syntactic levels of linguistic₁ representation. This explains both the title of this chapter and my use of the two expressions.

III. SYNTACTIC, OR LEXICAL, ZEROES IN RUSSIAN

1. Zero lexes

A clear example of zero lex in Russian is the present tense form of the verbs BYT'1 'be [copula]' and BYT'2 'be located'. Cf. (12) and (13):

(12) Russian *Durak ty, bocman, i šutki tvoi durackie*
fool   thou boatswain and jokes thy foolish
'Boatswain, you **are** a fool and your jokes **are** foolish'.

(13) Russian *Kolja v sosednej komnate*
Kolya in next   room-SG.PREP [= locative]
'Kolya **is** in the next room'.

In these sentences, no overt form of BYT' may appear in the present, while such a form is compulsory in the past, in the future, in the subjunctive and in the imperative:

(12′) Russian **a.** *Durak ty   byl, bocman!* 'Boatswain, you were a fool'.
fool   thou was boatswain
b. *Durak ty   budeš'* 'You will be a fool'.
fool   thou will-be
c. *Durak ty byl by*   'You would be a fool'.
would-be
d. *(Ne) bud' durakom!* 'Do(n't) be a fool!'
not   be   fool

For (12), we have the lexeme BYT'1 in the SSyntS and the zero lex BYT'1$_{\text{ind, pres, 2sg}}$ in the DMorphS:

(12″) **a.** The partial SSyntS of (12):

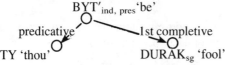

BYT'$_{\text{ind, pres}}$ 'be'

predicative   1st completive

TY 'thou'   DURAK$_{\text{sg}}$ 'fool'

b. The partial DMorphs of (12):
DURAK$_{\text{sg, nom}}$ TY$_{\text{nom}}$ BYT'1$_{\text{ind, pres, 2sg}}$

Then this zero lex disappears on the phonemic surface:

c. /durák ti/

2. Zero lexemes

For examples of zero lexemes consider (14) vs. (15):

(14) Russian   *Ulic* + *u*   *zasypal* + *i*   *pesk* + *om*
                street   SG.ACC   strewed   PL   sand   SG.INSTR
                'The street was strewed with sand (by somebody)'.
(15) Russian   *Ulic* + *u*   *zasypal* + *o*   *pesk* + *om*
                           strewed   SG.NEUT
                lit. '(It) strewed the street with sand' = 'The street got strewed with sand'.

There is a clear difference in meaning between the two sentences. For (14), it is unquestionably people who strewed the street with sand (although just who these people were is not specified), while (15) implies that it was some elemental force (wind, sandstorm, etc.). Thus the meanings of (14) and (15) may be conventionally represented on level $n - 1$ (i.e., in the semantic representation of the sentence) as:

(14′) '«people» strewed the street with sand',
(15′) '«elements» strewed the street with sand',

where '«people»' and '«elements»' designate the understood agents. These are complex, highly specific meanings distinct from those of the ordinary Russian nouns LJUDI 'people' and STIXII 'elements'. I will not analyze these meanings here[8] but, taking them for granted, I will try to answer a more relevant question:

‖ What expresses the meanings '«people»' and '«elements»' in (14) and (15)?

My answer is that (14) and (15) contain zero nominal lexes (i.e., wordforms), respectively $\mathbf{0}^{\mathbf{PEOPLE}}$ and $\mathbf{0}^{\mathbf{ELEMENTS}}$ or, more precisely, that these symbols are present on the nth level of sentence representation—i.e., in the DMorphS of both sentences. The corresponding nodes in the n'th level—in the SSyntSs of (14) and (15)—are labeled then with the symbols of the corresponding lexemes, which turn out to be zero lexemes (since they contain no other, nonzero lexes).

I know of two arguments to support my claim that the two zero lexemes have to be postulated in Russian in order to account for sentences of the type illustrated in (14) and (15).

Argument 1: *ad semanticam*

If sentences (14) and (15) do not contain different zero lexes and corresponding zero lexemes do not appear in their surface-syntactic structures, then evidently the sole source of the meanings '«people»' and '«elements»' would be the verb. But then we would have to admit that almost every Russian verb, taken by itself in a single well-specified sense, is always two-way ambiguous in the 3rd person plural and the 3rd person singular neuter. For instance, the form *tašč* + *at*

[3pl] '[they] drag' would mean either simply 'drag' with an open slot for any 3pl grammatical subject or '«people» drag' with no overt subject possible. Similarly, *tašč* + *it* [3sg, neut] 'drags' would be ambiguous between 'drags' and '«elements» drag', the second reading appearing, e.g., in (16):

(16) *Ego*　　　*taščil*　+ *o*　　　　　*po*　　*kamnjam*
　　　　he-ACC　dragged　SG.NEUT　along　rocks
　　　　i　　*udarjal* + *o*　　　　*o*　　*bereg*
　　　　and　smash　　SG.NEUT　against　shore
　　　　'He got dragged along the rocks and smashed against the shore', lit.
　　　　'[It] dragged him . . . and smashed him . . .'].

This solution has at least three drawbacks.

1. Supplementary homophonous forms with the meanings '«people»' and '«elements»' (and possibly others mentioned below) would be posited for all Russian verbal paradigms. It is bad enough that we would then have to augment every verb paradigm by eight forms: six in the indicative ('«people»' and '«elements»' in the three tenses) plus two in the subjunctive.

2. Forms such as *taščat* and *taščit* are not actually perceived as ambiguous by native speakers; and in fact Russian verbal forms are never ambiguous (with a single exception: the ambiguity of indicative and imperative second person plural forms of a few second conjugation verbs such as *spite* 'you sleep' or 'sleep!').

3. We would have to ascribe to grammatical forms (or endings) very complex and specific meanings of the type carried by no other Russian grammatical ending. It is more plausible to postulate two strongly marked and unique lexemes than to posit several homophonous, strongly marked and unique grammatical endings.

Note that we cannot avoid the said drawbacks by simply claiming that the indefinite-personal ('«people»') and the impersonal ('«elements»') meanings are present only in certain constructions, namely those where the grammatical subject is materially absent and not recoverable from context. If we do so, we would claim that the meanings '«people»' and '«elements»' are expressed by the construction as a whole, i.e., by the verb in the given form PLUS THE ABSENCE of an overt grammatical subject. But this is tantamount to attributing these meanings to the absence of the grammatical subject, which in turn implies that in a formal description of the construction a symbol should be present to point to the absence of grammatical subject. And such a symbol is, in essence, exactly what I am calling a zero lex (functioning as grammatical subject).

Argument 2: *ad syntaxem*

If sentences (14) and (15) do not contain different zero lexes and corresponding zero lexemes do not appear in their SSyntSs, then we have no natural way of accounting for the number, person and (in the past tense) gender of the finite (main) verb in these sentences. As has been noted in this book, the morphology of agreement is not expressed in surface-syntactic structure. Therefore, in the SSyntSs of (14) and (15) the lexeme ZASYPAT′ 'strew' cannot have subscripts of person, number, and gender, since these are determined solely by the grammatical subject, and the grammatical subject (on this assumed analysis) is not present.

Rather than resort to ad hoc means, a zero grammatical subject as the source of verb agreement should be posited here, and agreement provided for by the usual mechanism. In (14) the zero grammatical subject is the lexeme $\emptyset^{PEOPLE}$, which triggers 3rd person plural agreement (it is a **plurale tantum**). In (15) the lexeme $\emptyset^{ELEMENTS}$ triggers 3rd person singular neuter agreement (it is a neuter **singulare tantum**).

Thus the two zero lexemes allow us to easily avoid both of the difficulties: the semantic and the syntactic ones. This, in turn, leads to the conclusion that $\emptyset^{PEOPLE}$ and $\emptyset^{ELEMENTS}$ should appear in a dictionary of Russian, provided with semantic definitions and detailed descriptions of their syntactic behavior.[9] The latter point is especially important, since $\emptyset^{PEOPLE}$ and $\emptyset^{ELEMENTS}$ have highly specific signata and syntactics, as illustrated below.

Since zero lexemes are not something very familiar I think it is advisable to briefly review their properties (cf. also Kozinskij 1983: 35–41).

First, the Russian signatum '«people»' is more than simply the negation of the signatum '«elements»', and vice versa: the two are not logical complements. Neither (17a) nor (17b) can refer to animals or machines as actors:[10]

(17) Russian **a.** *Ego   vsego   iscarapal   + i*   [$\emptyset^{PEOPLE}$]
      he-ACC all-ACC scratched.up   PL
      'He was all scratched up [by someone]'.

   b. *Ego vsego iscazapal + o*   [$\emptyset^{ELEMENTS}$]
                           SG.NEUT
      'He got all scratched up [by something]'.

Second, $\emptyset^{PEOPLE}$ and $\emptyset^{ELEMENTS}$ have no synonyms in Russian. This means that the corresponding signata cannot be adequately and naturally expressed in Russian by any other single means. Curiously, neither $\emptyset^{PEOPLE}$ nor $\emptyset^{ELEMENTS}$ coincides in meaning with French *on* and *il* or German *man* and *es*. Expressions with *on* and *man* are not always translatable into Russian by expressions with $\emptyset^{PEOPLE}$ (see Clas 1970 for English and German translation equivalents of *on*). The same is true of *il* and *es* with respect to $\emptyset^{ELEMENTS}$

Third, zero lexemes have limited distribution (possibly due to the nature of their signata; much further research remains to be done here). Thus, generally speaking, the lexeme $\emptyset^{PEOPLE}$ cannot be the grammatical subject of a passive; active (18a) is correct while passive (18b) is not:[11]

(18) Russian

  a. *Tam rasstreljal + i   geroev   - partizan*
     there shot   PL heroes-ACC guerillas-ACC
     [the grammatical subject = $\emptyset^{\text{PEOPLE}}$]
     lit. 'There [they] shot the guerilla heroes' = 'The guerilla
     heroes were shot there'.

  b. **Tam byl + i   rasstreljan   + y palačami*
     there was   PL shot [past part.]   PL by-the-executioners
     [the grammatical subject = $\emptyset^{\text{PEOPLE}}$] 'There they were shot by
     executioners'.

However, $\emptyset^{\text{PEOPLE}}$ can appear as the GS of the passive form of a few verbs:

  c. *V ministerstve uže   byl + i preduprežden   + y*
     in ministry   already was   PL warned[past part.]   PL
     ⟨ *izveščen*   + y,   *proinformirovan* + y   , . . . ⟩
     notified[past part.] PL   informed[past part.] PL
     o našem priezde,
     about our   arrival
     lit. 'In the ministry, [they] were already warned ⟨ notified,
     informed, . . . ⟩ about our arrival'.

But $\emptyset^{\text{PEOPLE}}$ becomes unacceptable with the passive even of these verbs, if there is an agentive phrase:

  d. ?**V ministerstve uže byli predupreždeny* **Ivanom** *o našem priezde.*
                                               by-Ivan

The lexeme $\emptyset^{\text{PEOPLE}}$ does not combine with certain verbs, such as *naxodit'sja* 'be situated', *suščestvovat'* 'exist', *snit'sja* 'appear in dreams':

(19) **Mne vsë vremja snjatsja*
     me   all time   appear.in.dreams-3PL

Nonetheless, it combines freely with reflexive and reciprocal verbs:

(20) **a.** *Tam umyvajutsja*
       there wash.up-3PL
       '«people» are washing up there'.

    b. *Tam celujutsja*
         kiss-3PL
       '«people» are kissing there'.

Presumably this behavior depends on the signatum, which must contain a component 'action' or 'actor' excluding the use of $\emptyset^{\text{PEOPLE}}$ with "passive", "actionless" predicates.

Fourth, the lexes of $\emptyset^{\text{PEOPLE}}$ and $\emptyset^{\text{ELEMENTS}}$ are marked for case as well as for person, number and gender. However, they can have only the nominative case, since they appear only in the role of grammatical subject, and in Russian the grammatical subject is normally nominative. (Nouns having only one case are attested elsewhere in Russian. Cf. the **pluralia tantum** *ščec* 'some endearing cabbage soup', *drovec* 'some endearing firewood', *drožžec* 'some endearing yeast', which have only the partitive.)

In much the same way, French *on* end German *man* can only be grammatical subjects. Consider, for instance, (21):

(21) Russian *On*   *byl*   *ves'*   *iscarapan*
        he-NOM   was-SG.MASC   all-NOM   scratched.up-SG.MASC
        'He was all scratched up'.

This sentence is by no means synonymous with (17a) or (17b): nothing in (21) alludes to who or what scratched him. However, (21) is the syntactic converse of both (17a) and (17b). What happens here is that in this case passivization brings about an important loss of information: namely, the reference to the agent is lost. If under passivization the reference to the agent has to be retained for some reason, then the demoted grammatical subject must appear as the agentive complement in the instrumental—which is impossible with a zero lexeme, since it has no instrumental. This explains the non-synonymity of (21) and (17).[12]

Fifth, both $\emptyset^{\text{PEOPLE}}$ and $\emptyset^{\text{ELEMENTS}}$ control the gerund just as any ordinary grammatical subject does. It is one of the strictest laws of Russian syntax that a gerund may be used only if its "semantic subject" (which cannot be overt) coincides, semantically and referentially, with the grammatical subject of the governing verb:

(22) *Uvidja*   *nas, on vyšel*
        seeing [gerund] us   he went.out
        'Seeing us, he went out' [= 'he$_i$ saw us, and he$_i$ went out'].

(23) is a famous jocular example (A.P. Chekhov) of a typically non-Russian, ungrammatical construction with a "dangling" gerund:

(23) **Pod''ezžaja k   stancii, u   menja sletela šljapa*
        riding.up   to station by me   fell.off hat
        'Riding up to the station, my hat fell off'.

Yet with zero subjects, gerunds are perfectly acceptable:

(24) *Sjuda každyj den' privozjat   kirpič, razgružaja   ego*
here   every day   bring-3PL brick unloading [gerund] it
u   dorogi
by road
'Every day [they] bring bricks here, unloading them by the road'.

It is not stated explicitly who brings bricks: it is $\emptyset^{PEOPLE}$. But those who bring them are necessarily the same as those who unload them.

The same is true of (25):

(25) *Liš'   v   avguste 1539 goda, special'no   izmeniv*
only in August 1539 year, specially   having-changed [gerund]
dlja ètogo pravila, Kardano prinjali   v   kollegiju
for this   rules   Cardano accepted-3PL into collegium
vračej   Milana
of-doctors of-Milan
'Only in August 1539, having specially changed the rules for it, [they] admitted Cardano to the collegium of doctors of Milan'.

Likewise, with $\emptyset^{ELEMENTS}$:

(26) *Iz   èlektrorevol'vera xlopnulo,   osvetiv*
from electric.revolver cracked-SG.NEUT lighting[gerund]
vsë vokrug zelënym   svetom [Bulgakov]
all around with-green light
'From the electric revolver (it) cracked, throwing green light on everything around'.

Again, we do not know what produced the cracking noise from the revolver, but it was the same mysterious 'it' that lighted the environment in green.

Sixth, the lexeme $\emptyset^{PEOPLE}$ controls reflexivization as all other Russian GSs do (for $\emptyset^{ELEMENTS}$ it is impossible for purely semantic reasons):

(27)
a. *Svoi   grjaznye noski na stol   ne kladut,*
oneself's dirty   socks on table not put -3PL
lit. '[They] don't put their dirty socks on the table' = 'One shouldn't put one's dirty socks on the table'.
b. *U   nas rabotajut, v osnovnom, na svoix   učastkax ⟨ dlja sebja ⟩*
by us work-3PL mostly   on oneself's lots   for oneself
'In our country, they [= people] work mostly on their own lots ⟨for themselves⟩'.

Seventh, there is a suggestive parallel between word order adjustments caused by a zero lex in a sentence, and morphophonemic adjustments caused by a zero morph in a wordform. The zero morph in Russian cannot carry word stress, for obvious reasons. Thus paradigms with fixed ending stress show automatic retraction of stress onto the stem-final syllable when the ending is zero:

(28)   *durák* + ∅   'fool' (*durak* + ∅̸ would be phonetically impossible)
      durak + *á*
      durak | *ú*
      durak + *á*
      durak + *é*
      durak + *óm*

In much the same fashion, the zero lex cannot fill a word-order position in the phonemic shape of the sentence, and another wordform will automatically be moved to the slot of the zero lex. Russian has the following general syntactic rule: if the grammatical subject is overt and precedes the main verb, then in a stylistically neutral sentence, the direct object normally follows the verb (especially if this GO^{dir} is a pronoun). Cf.:

(29) a. *Neožidannyj tolčok*   *sbil*   *ego*   *s*   *nog* ⟨. . .$^?$ *ego sbil* . . .⟩
      unexpected   push-NOM knocked him   from feet
             GS   MV   GO^{dir}
      'An unexpected push knocked him off his feet'.

But where no overt subject precedes the main verb—either the subject is non-overt or it follows the verb—the direct object is preverbal. (Other orders are possible but strongly marked.) Thus we have (29b), with the zero subject:

b. *Neožidannym tolčkom*   *ego*   *sbilo*   *s*   *nog*
      unexpected   push-INSTR him   knocked-SG.NEUT from feet
                                    GO^{dir} MV
      ⟨. . .$^?$ *sbilo ego* . . .⟩
      'idem' [= (29a)].

Thus the zero subject affects the normal position of the direct object, just as the zero ending affects the normal position of stress in (28).

A zero lexeme meaning 'something indefinite' has been proposed for Polish and Russian in Wierzbicka (1966), on the basis of the so-called "impersonal" sentences of both languages. Wierzbicka's zero must serve as grammatical subject in sentences of the type *Svetaet* '[It] dawns', *Morozit* '[It] freezes'; in sentences like *U menja stučit v viskax* 'My temples are pounding', lit. 'By me [it] pounds in temples', *Skrebët v glotke* '[It] scratches in [the] throat'; and, finally, in sentences like *Polja pobilo gradom* '[It] crushed [the] crops with hail', *Ego ranilo oskolkom*, lit. '[It] wounded him with a shell splinter', etc.

3. Other Zero Lexemes in Russian?

In addition to $\emptyset^{\text{PEOPLE}}$ and $\emptyset^{\text{ELEMENTS}}$, there further appears to be a zero lexeme $\emptyset^{\text{ANY}}$, whose sole (zero) lex has the signatum 'anyone', often in the sense of 'everyone'. $\emptyset^{\text{ANY}}$ would be a singular pronoun capable of appearing either as the direct object (with verbs governing the accusative case) or as an indirect object (with words governing the dative case), see the examples:

(30) The lexeme $\emptyset^{\text{ANY}}$ as the direct object

Russian **a.** *Podobnye poručenija očen' obremenjajut*
such errands very burden-3PL [trans.verb]
'Such errands are very burdensome',
lit. '. . . burden [everyone] very much'.

b. *V internate zastavljajut spat' posle obeda*
in boarding.school force-3PL sleep-INF after lunch
'In boarding school [they] make [everyone] take a nap after lunch'.

c. *Takoe otnošenie očen' raduet*
such attitude very makes.happy
'Such an attitude makes [everyone] happy'.[13]

(31) The lexeme $\emptyset^{\text{ANY}}$ as an indirect object

Russian **a.** *Izvestno, čto Zemlja vraščaetsja vokrug Solnca*
it is known that earth revolves around sun
'It is known [to everyone] that the Earth revolves around the sun'.

b. *Nel'zja tak govorit'*
mustn't so talk-INF
'No one should talk that way',
lit. '[One] mustn't . . .

c. *Kurit' vospreščaetsja*
smoke-INF is.forbidden
'Smoking is not allowed',
lit. 'It is forbidden [to all] to smoke'.

[*Izvestno, nel'*zja and *vospreščaetsja* govern the dative: *mne izvestno*, lit. 'to me [it] is known'; *mne nel'zja* 'I shouldn't', lit. 'to me [it's] impossible'; *mne vospreščaetsja*, lit. 'to me [it] is forbidden'; all these expressions feature the dative *mne* 'to me'.] $\emptyset^{\text{ANY}}$ cannot be the dependent of a preposition or the grammatical subject. In this latter respect it resembles the reflexive pronoun *sebja* 'self', which also has only oblique cases and therefore cannot be the grammatical subject.

So far I have postulated three zero lexemes for Russian: the pronouns $\emptyset^{\text{PEOPLE}}$ (nominative only), $\emptyset^{\text{ELEMENTS}}$ (nominative only), and $\emptyset^{\text{ANY}}$

(dative and accusative). In addition, the verb BYT′ 'be' presents a zero wordform: the present tense zero lex, cf. above. This list of zero lexemes and lexes is in principle open-ended, so that more zero lexemes may prove necessary. Two likely candidates come to mind: $\emptyset^{EGO}$ in impersonals such as *mne* ⟨*tebe, emu, . . .*⟩ *xolodno* ⟨*bol′no, smešno . . .*⟩ 'I'm ⟨you are, he is⟩ cold ⟨in pain, amused⟩' = 'My ⟨your, his, . . .⟩ ego experiences cold ⟨pain, humor⟩'; and $\emptyset^{SURROUNDINGS}$ in impersonals such as *Zdes′ xolodno* ⟨*grjazno, nakureno, . . .*⟩ 'Here it's cold ⟨dirty, smoky⟩' = 'Here the surroundings are cold ⟨dirty, smoky⟩'. Nothing prevents the discovery of further syntactic, or lexical, zeroes; cf., for instance, Note 15, p. 335. A number of syntactic zeroes have actually been proposed by other investigators; to gain a clearer picture of the relevant constructions I need first provide a substantive discussion of linguistic$_2$ terminology pertaining to zeroes, in order to bring some more logical order into this troubled zone.

IV. "ZERO" TERMINOLOGY IN LINGUISTICS

The different uses of the term **zero** that have appeared in linguistic$_2$ literature are largely based on Bally (1922) and Jakobson 1971c [1939], and can be divided into two classes:

(a) 'zero' as applied to linguistic$_1$ items: **zero phoneme, zero sound, zero affix, zero ending, zero sign, . . ., zero article, zero verb, . . ., zero predicate, zero grammatical subject, zero grammatical object, . . .**

(b) 'Zero' as applied to entities other than linguistic$_1$ items: **zero paradigm, zero contrast, zero word order, zero stylistic characteristics, zero predicative link, zero valence, . . .**

As a rule, the uses of type (b) constitute metaphors. They lack a precise common meaning and are replaceable in any particular instance by a different expression. For example, zero paradigm = unmarked paradigm; zero word order = neutral word order; zero valence = absence of valence; etc. Such terminology should be avoided if the meaning of the term *zero* is not to become completely obscured (cf. Haas 1957: 43, note 1).

We must also introduce some order into the uses of type (a) above by assigning a standard and precise meaning to the term *zero*. In accordance with Sections II and III I suggest applying the term *zero* only in the following way: either to linguistic$_1$ signs (e.g., morphs, lexes) or to sets of synonymous signs distributed according to simple rules (e.g., morphemes, lexemes). Adopting this proposal entails two consequences.

First, expressions such as **zero sound, zero phoneme, alternation of phoneme** /x/ **with zero, zero signatum, zero meaning**, etc. refer neither to signs nor to sets of signs. In these instances the word **zero** designates simply 'absence', and thus has a meaning completely different from its meaning in, e.g., **zero af-**

fix. Note that in the morphological representation of a text zero morphs are shown obligatorily (a zero morph is *not* equal to the absence of a morph), while zero phonemes or phones are never written in phonological or phonetic transcription; similarly, a zero lex is by no means simply the absence of any lex.

Second, terms such as **zero grammatical predicate, zero grammatical subject, zero grammatical object, zero verb, zero noun, zero article, zero syntactic element, zero variant of a word** can be used only to designate zero lexes or lexemes. Thus a zero grammatical predicate is a predicate expressed by a zero lex; a zero verb is a zero verbal lexeme; a zero variant of a word is a zero lex of the word; etc.

At the very end of Section II, I actually proposed a criterion for evaluating the usefulness of particular zero signs and corresponding zero "-emes". This criterion is the researcher's readiness to include the given zero sign or zero "-eme" in the same list that contains all similar nonzero signs or "-emes", and to provide the sign or the "-eme" under consideration with a complete description of its combinatorial possibilities. Just as a zero affix appears in the inventory of affixes of the languages, a zero lexeme, together with its dictionary entry, should appear in the dictionary.

Although this criterion is far from formal, it can obviously be formalized. To do this we need only establish the conditions for the willingness (or lack thereof) of the researcher to include such items in inventories as part of the description of the language. These conditions are probably nothing more than maximal compactness and standardness of inventories; as a rule, linguists try not to enlarge inventories unless it is absolutely necessary. They also seek to avoid duplicating items in such inventories and to avoid grouping unlike items together. The more precise formulation of these conditions is a separate task that I will not deal with here. At present it suffices to correlate the abstract, intuitively non-obvious question of the existence of a zero item to the concrete and much more obvious question of the inclusion of a zero item in the appropriate inventory.

Now we have the apparatus necessary to analyze utterances in the search for syntactic zeros. I have shown that linguists, when speaking about "zero X" on the syntactic level, have actually been speaking either of a zero lex or a zero lexeme; and the motivation for postulating a zero lexeme can be verified by the linguist's willingness to include it in the dictionary.

Let us ask, at this point, to what extent linguists would be willing to include in dictionaries the "zero verbs of motion" proposed by Galkina-Fedoruk (1962). She proposes zero verbs of motion as grammatical predicates (= main verbs) in such sentences as (32). (Here and below, the English words without overt Russian correspondents are capitalized.)

(**32**)   Russian   *Tat'jana v   les,   medved' za   neju* [Pushkin]
          T.   into forest bear   after her
          'Tatyana RAN into the forest, the bear FOLLOWED her'.

However, Širjaev (1967, 1973) has demonstrated that carrying this proposal to its logical limit would require postulating "zero verbs of assault" for sentences that are fully analogous to (32) in structure:

(33) Russian   *A   my eë   po   tolstym mjasam*
               and we her-ACC across fat   behind
               'She's GONNA GET IT on her fat behind', lit. 'And we're
               GONNA GIVE IT to her on [her] fat behind'.

In much the same way, there will be need for "zero verbs of communication" (as in (34)) and "zero verbs of playing" (as in (35)):

(34) Russian   *Pro   svoi deliški on mne   ni   slova*
               about his   affairs he me-DAT not word-GEN
               'He didn't SAY a word to me about his affairs'.
(35) Russian   *My s   nej uže   vtoruju partiju*
               we with her already second game-ACC
               'She and I are already PLAYING the second game'.

Evidently there are few, if any, verbal meanings that could not be expressed by such a "zero verb". Even DIFFERENCIROVAT' 'differentiate' (in the mathematical sense), for example, is replaceable by a "zero verb":

(36) Russian   *A   my èto sejčas po* **t**
               and we this now   by *t*
               'Now we will DIFFERENTIATE this by *t*'.

It follows that if we understand the expression **zero verb** (of motion, speech, assault, etc.) as a zero lex or zero lexeme we will face the following alternative. Either we include a zero lex (which does not distinguish person, number or tense) in practically every verbal lexeme of Russian; or we introduce a great number of zero word synonyms for almost every verb lexeme in the Russian lexicon. However, those who speak of "zero verbs" would hardly agree to this. Thus it is clear that in (32)–(36) there are no "zero verbs" that could be analogous to the zero nouns (or pronouns) $\emptyset^{PEOPLE}$, $\emptyset^{ELEMENTS}$, and $\emptyset^{ANY}$. The word **zero** in the phrase **zero verb** is used by Galkina-Fedoruk and Širjaev in a completely different sense than it carries in such phrases as **zero affix, zero lexeme**, etc.

For (32)–(36) we would do better to speak of ELLIPSIS (as proposed by Popova 1963: 55–63). The surface syntactic structures of these sentences need to include a top node (as in (11″)) labeled by the symbol of a specific lexeme. This lexeme carries an essential part of the sentence's meaning; and it determines the form (preposition or case) of the governed noun. Note that case and prepositional government is an exclusively lexical matter: it is conditioned by a lexeme rather than simply by its meaning. Compare two (nearly) synonymous sentences in (37):

(37) Russian **a.** *A   on nam   matematiku*
              and he we-DAT mathematics-ACC
              'He TEACHES math to us'.

           b. *A   on nas   matematike*
              and he we-ACC mathematics-DAT
              'He INSTRUCTS us in math'.

Clearly the surface-syntactic structure of (37a) must contain, as its top node, PREPODAVAT' 'teach' (Y = 2[acc], Z = 3[dat]), while that of (37b) contains UČIT' or OBUČAT' 'teach' (Z = 2[acc], Y = 3[dat]), where the expressions in parentheses represent the government pattern of the corresponding lexeme, cf. Chapter 2, p. 69.

However, on level $n + 1$, i.e., in actual sentences such as (37), the top-node verbal lexeme is not overtly represented. We cannot consider it to be represented by its zero lex: otherwise, as established above, we would have to introduce zero lexes as members of virtually all Russian verbal lexemes.

We must therefore accept that before the mapping from surface-syntactic structure to deep-morphological structure of the sentence is carried out, the top lexeme is omitted from the SSyntS of (37):

(38)

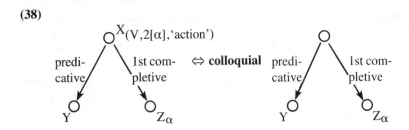

Informally stated, in surface-syntactic structure the topmost verb, if it denotes an action rather than a state and governs a first object, may be eliminated; the resulting sentence exhibits a colloquial (and expressive) character. But note that this rule can apply only to previously morphologized SSynt-structures, i.e., the predicate lexeme may be eliminated from the SSynt-structure only after the surface morphological markings of the grammatical objects are specified. In (38), this is indicated by the subscript α to node Z, which corresponds to the case-mark α appearing in the government pattern of X.

Rule (38) is a rule of ELLIPSIS, one of many ellipses possible in Russian. Some details have been omitted from its presentation: the rule is probably not applicable to all verbs designating actions, nor is it always applicable when only a first object is present. For present purposes, however, it suffices simply to characterize ellipsis as a particular type of linguistic$_1$ rule.

A somewhat different type of ellipsis is observed in imperatives of many languages. In (39) the grammatical subject is not a zero lex or lexeme, but a deleted second person pronoun:

(39) **a.** *Stand up!*
  b. *Behave yourselves!*

Sometimes, for example under contrast or emphasis, the second person pronoun as the grammatical subject of the imperative can be retained:

(40) **a.** **You** *stand up, and* **you** *remain seated.*
  b. *Don't* **you** *talk back to your mother!*

A still more different type of ellipsis appears in (41):

(41) **a.** *Upon arriving, you should go to the passport office*
    [= 'upon **your** arrival'].
  b. *I met a friend* [= 'a friend **of mine**'].
  c. *She wants to see the film* [= 'she wants that **she** should see the film'].

In sentences (41) there are no identifiable zero lexes, which would be distinct from all other English lexes and which would convey specific meanings not attributable to other lexes. Nor can we speak of deletion of surface lexical material that has left syntactic traces in the form of agreement, nonsaturated valence slots, etc. Rather sentences of type (41) involve (obligatory and optional) non-appearance in surface-syntactic structure of specific deep-syntactic actants.

These examples are far from exhausting the logically possible types of ellipsis; but they clearly show the difference between syntactic, or lexical, zeroes and ellipses.

Syntactic zero and ellipsis contrast in language. ZERO is a sign or a set of signs—either a particular sign that has an empty string as its signans, or a one-element set that contains such a sign. ELLIPSIS is a rule that eliminates certain signs in certain surface contexts (where they are essentially redundant). Generally, zero conveys meaning, i.e., bears information of some kind. Ellipsis normally does not convey meaning but is required by grammatical or stylistic considerations.

Both zero and ellipsis belong to *langue* rather than *parole*. Evidence that ellipsis belongs to *langue*, not *parole*, is the fact that different languages have different rules of ellipsis. For example, ellipsis of the grammatical subject *ja* 'I' is stylistically obligatory for Russian performative verbs: *Prošu vas* 'please', lit. 'Am asking you'; *Pozdravljaju vas* 'congratulations', lit. 'Am congratulating you', etc. cannot include *ja*. This is not possible in English. Therefore it is incorrect to contrast ellipsis and zero as respectively a phenomenon of *parole* and a unit of *langue* (see Bally 1922): both belong to *langue*. (For zero vs. ellipsis see also Skovorodnikov (1973: 118–119); a logical analysis of the triple opposition "zero vs. ellipsis vs. non-saturation of an obligatory valence slot" is offered in Apresjan et al. 1978: 304–308.)

While syntactic zeroes go into the dictionary, ellipses are instead included in the grammar among other syntactic rules (a similar argument for including rules of ellipsis in the grammar is found in Shopen 1972, an excellent study of sentence incompleteness). Note, however, that syntactic zero and ellipsis as described here do not cover the entire range of phenomena traditionally connected with syntactic incompleteness of sentences; but this is a subject rather marginal to the present discussion.

V. ANSWERS TO QUESTIONS 1–3

I will now return to the questions asked at the beginning of this chapter; that is, I will explain how my conclusions apply to the problem of grammatical voice in the world's languages.

Question 1
From the viewpoint of voice, sentence (1)

(1) Russian   *Ivana*   *priglasili*   *k*   *trëm*   *časam*
              Ivan-ACC invited-PL for three o'clock

is an ordinary active construction with $\emptyset^{\text{PEOPLE}}$ as its grammatical subject. Syntactically, (1) is in no way distinguished from Russian constructions with nonzero grammatical subjects.

Sentences such as (2) are not as straightforward, however:

(2) Russian   *Ivana*   *oprokinulo*
              Ivan-ACC knocked.over-SG.NEUT
              'Ivan got knocked over'.

If, as proposed here, (2) contains the zero grammatical subject $\emptyset^{\text{ELEMENTS}}$, then we must assign such sentences to the active voice. This is the solution I favor, although the following difficulty must be pointed out: if (2) is active it will be necessary to consider the following (a) and (b) sentences nonsynonymous (since active verbs in both are synonymous while the (a) sentence contains a full lexeme—$\emptyset^{\text{ELEMENTS}}$—absent from the (b) sentence).

(42) Russian **a.** *Polja*   *pobilo*   *gradom*
                 fields-ACC crushed-SG.NEUT hail-INSTR
                 'The crops were destroyed by hail'.
          b. *Grad*   *pobil*   *polja*
                 hail-NOM[masc] crushed-SG.MASC fields-ACC
                 'Hail destroyed the crops'.

DEPENDENCY SYNTAX: THEORY AND PRACTICE

328 DEPENDENCY SYNTAX: THEORY AND PRACTICE

(43) a. *Glaza   rezalo   na svetu*
eyes-ACC irritated-SG.NEUT in light
'[My] eyes were bothered by the light'.
b. *Svet   rezal   glaza*
light-NOM[masc] irritated-SG.MASC eyes-ACC
'The light bothered [my] eyes'.

(44) a. *Sil'nym udarom   ego   sbilo   s   nog*
strong blow-INSTR he-ACC knocked.off-SG.NEUT from feet
'He got knocked off his feet by a strong blow'.
b. *Sil'nyj udar   sbil   ego   s   nog*
strong blow-NOM[masc] knocked-SG.MASC he-ACC from feet
'A strong blow knocked him off his feet'.

The (a) sentences must be understood as '«elements» destroyed the crops with hail', etc., and the (b) sentences as 'hail destroyed the crops', etc. In other words, the relationship between the (a) and (b) sentences in (42)–(44) is the same as that between (45a) and (45b):

(45) a. *Karandaš   provël   tonkuju liniju*
pencil-NOM[masc] drew-SG.MASC thin   line-ACC
'The pencil drew a fine line'.
b. *Ivan   provël   karandašom   tonkuju liniju*
Ivan-NOM drew-SG.MASC pencil-INSTR thin   line-ACC
'Ivan drew a fine line with the pencil'.

(45b) has, with respect to (45a), an additional overt actant—*Ivan*—corresponding to '«elements»' of (42)–(44).

I am prepared to accept the interpretation of the pairs (42)–(44) as nonsynonymous. (42a *vs.* b) might appear to be a counterexample, since these two sentences are perceived by native speakers as semantically identical. However, since hail is an '«element»' itself, both of these (actually nonsynonymous) sentences have one and the same real-world referent and therefore seem to have identical signata. That (44a *vs.* b) are not synonymous is more readily apparent: (44a) indicates that what struck him was something unclear or incomprehensible, while there is no such meaning in (44b). This difference underlies the unacceptability of (46) vs. the acceptability of (47):

(46) *Soldaty brosilis' na Ivana, i   srazu že   ?sil'nym*
soldiers rushed   at Ivan   and immediately strong
udarom   ego   sbilo   s   nog
blow-INSTR he-ACC knocked-SG.NEUT from, feet
'The soldiers rushed at Ivan and immediately he got knocked off his feet
by a strong blow'.

(47)   *Soldaty brosilis' na Ivana, i srazu že sil'nyj   udar*
                                                    blow-NOM[masc]

sbil   *ego s nog*
knocked-SG.MASC
'The soldiers rushed at Ivan and immediately a strong blow knocked him
off his feet'.

Likewise, the nonsynonymity of the second (conjunct) clauses is evident in (48)
and (49):

(48)   *Ivan   otkryl   kran,   i   ?vodoj   srazu že*
           I.-NOM opened faucet and   water-INSTR immediately
           zalilo   plastinu
           flooded-SG.NEUT plate
           'Ivan turned on the faucet, and the plate was immediately flooded with
           water'.

(49)   *Ivan otkryl kran, i voda   srazu že zalila*
                                water-NOM[fem]   flooded-SG.FEM
           plastinu
           'Ivan turned on the faucet, and water immediately flooded the plate'.

The alternative to this solution [i.e., that sentences of type (2) are "normal"
active sentences] is to consider the (a) and (b) sentences of a pair synonymous.
This would entail positing for Russian, and assigning to (2) and (42a), a special
voice: "impersonal" or "subjective impersonal." Then the forms *oprokinulo* in
(2), *pobilo* in (42a), and *rezalo* in (43a) would cease to be personal active forms
requiring agreement. The zero subject would no longer be needed to provide for
their morphological shape, since they would simply be impersonal voice forms
that lack personal conjugation (much like the Estonian subjective impersonal
voice of (52) below). There are at least two unpleasant consequences to this alternative solution. First, all third person singular neuter verb forms in Russian
would become ambiguous between '3sg, neut, active' and 'impersonal voice'.
Second, there would be no natural way to explain the ungrammaticality of (46)
and (48).

Question 2
(1)–(4) are not subjectless sentences: each contains a grammatical subject in
the form of (an occurrence of) a zero lexeme that figures in their surface-syntactic structures but does not materialize in the transition to the actual sentence.
Moreover, for Russian and all other languages where the main verb obligatorily
agrees with the grammatical subject (Spanish, English, etc.) there can be no subjectless complete sentences with a finite verb at all (elliptical sentences without
GS are of course possible). If a sentence contains a finite verb, the verb must
agree with something, and this can only be the grammatical subject, including

one expressed by a zero lexeme. The following Russian sentences are bipartite, i.e., they consist of (zero) GS + VP:

(50)   **a.** *Cypljat   po oseni sčitajut*
chicks-ACC in fall   count-3PL
[a proverb, roughly 'Don't pass judgment prematurely'].
   b. *Morozit*
freeze-3SG
'It is freezing'.

much as Russian lexes such as *ruk* 'of hands' (gen, pl) or *nos* 'nose' (nom, sg) are bimorphic. In light of this, (50b) is not subjectless; it is, however, impersonal—in that its grammatical subject can only be $\emptyset^{\text{ELEMENTS}}$.[14] (Cf. Chapter 5, Note 5, page 248.)

Similarly, sentence (3) is not subjectless, since it is also bipartite:

(3)   Ukrainian
   Bulo   organizovan + o   èkspedycij + u
was-SG.NEUT organized   SG.NEUT expedition   ACC
'An expedition was organized'.

Namely, (3) consists of a GS manifested by a zero neuter pronoun, and a VP including a verb form in neuter singular (agreeing with the GS) plus a GO^{dir}. From the viewpoint of voice, (3) features the so-called "subjective impersonal" (Mel'čuk and Xolodovič 1970: 118), where the meaning 'human agent' is imparted by the verbal form in *-t+o* / *-n+o* (cf. Ukrainian *zavezeno* '[they] have brought', etc.). The Spanish example (4) is also a subjective impersonal, rather than a passive, construction.

Note that constructions such as (3) and (4) contain an unusual kind of zero grammatical subject. It is a semantically empty zero lexeme, i.e., a zero lexeme with an empty signatum. Empty lexemes are attested in many languages: strongly governed prepositions and conjunctions, various auxiliaries and dummy (or expletive) subject pronouns. Examples of the latter are English *it*, French *il*, German *es* as in (51):

(51)   **a.** English **It** *is evident that the parser shouldn't . . .*
   b. French **Il** *s'agit ici de trois difficultés suivantes,*
lit. 'It is dealt here with three following difficulties'.
   c. German **Es** *wird hier viel Ski gefahren*
'People ski here a lot', lit. 'It is skied here very much'.

It in (51a) has the signans /it/ and a very complex syntactics, but its signatum is an empty set of semes:

it = $\langle$ 'Λ'; /it/; Σ = anticipatory pronoun in such constructions as . . .$\rangle$

The same holds of French *il* and German *es* in (51b-c). The Ukrainian dummy grammatical subject in (3) is likewise empty; but unlike *it*, *il*, *es*, it is also materially zero. The only component spared this mutilated pronoun is its syntactics, which includes the following specifications: it is singular neuter as shown by the verb agreement, it can be used only in a strictly limited type of construction, etc.

The mere presence of syntactics as manifested in agreement is, as we see, sufficient basis for postulating a zero lex and the corresponding lexeme. However, such signs, simulataneously empty and zero, represent a degenerate case and are rarely encountered.[15]

It should be emphasized that no zero lex in a capacity of grammatical subject may be postulated where the verbal form does not exhibit agreement. Thus in Estonian, verb forms in *-takse* (subjective impersonal voice) are not inflected for person or number at all:

(52) Estonian **a.** *Kuulatakse   muusikat*
is.listened.to music-ACC
'Music is listened to'.

b. *Haalikut* [o] *haaldatakse   nii*
sound-ACC is.pronounced so
'The sound [o] is pronounced like this'.

Therefore, no zero subject can be posited here.[16]

Question 3

A zero agentive complement with indefinite-personal meaning is not postulated for sentences such as (5):

(5) *Ivan   byl   priglašën   k   trëm   časam*
I.-NOM was-SG.MASC invited-SG.MASC for three o'clock
'Ivan was invited for three o'clock'.

because the meaning '«people»' is not expressed in these constructions (see the discussion of (21)). Likewise, in (21) and (53) there is no reference whatsoever to who or what scratched him or knocked him over—it could be people, the elements or else animals or machines:

(21) *On byl ves' iscarapan*
he was all scratched.up[pass. part.]
'He was all scratched up'.

(53) *On byl oprokinut*
knocked.over[pass. part.]
'He was knocked over'.

(53) is not synonymous with either (54a) or (54b):

(54) **a.** *Ego*   *oprokinuli*
he-ACC   knocked.over-PL
'He was knocked over [by people]'.
b. *Ego*   *oprokinulo*
he-ACC   knocked.over-SG.NEUT
'He got knocked over [by the elements]'.

In addition to the lack of semantic basis, there is also no natural syntactic basis to justify a zero agent in such constructions as (5), (21) and (53): the presence of a zero agent would never be manifested in surface phenomena such as agreement or government. It is true that the agent is perfectly recoverable in (5), and that it is identifiable as 'people', i.e., (5) is synonymous with (1):

(1) *Ivana*   *priglasili*   *k*   *trëm*   *časam*
I.-ACC invited-PL for three o'clock
'[They] invited Ivan for three o'clock'.

However, this synonymity depends on the particular meaning of the verb *priglašat'* 'invite' and on our knowledge of the real world. Insofar as only people (including people in a broad sense—collectives, institutions, organizations, etc.) can be engaged in the activity of inviting, the meaning 'people' (as agent) in (5) emerges from the semantics of the verb *priglašat'*. This accounts for the synonymity of (1) and (5). As we have seen, verbs that do not describe specifically human actions lack such synonymity (see (53) and (54) above).

Chapter 8 is based on Mel'čuk (1974b), a paper that originated as an attempt to answer some of the questions posed by A.A. Xolodovič in connection with the elaboration of a consistent theory of grammatical voice. Aleksandr Aleksandrovič Xolodovič, one of the leading Russian theoretical linguists and a brilliant Japanologist and Koreanologist (his partial bibliography is found in *Narody Azii i Afriki*, 1966, No 3: 215–217; 1976, No 6: 229) died of heart failure in 1977. For more than twenty years he had been my linguistic guru and, more important, a close friend. May the present chapter be a modest contribution to preserving his memory.

NOTES

1. (I, after example (5), p. 304.) Remember (Introduction, Note 5, p. 11, that **linguistic₁** stands for 'pertaining to language(s)' and **linguistic₂**, for 'pertaining to linguistics'. Let it be emphasized that I am interested only in linguistic₁ zeroes—entities that I claim EXIST in language and as such are stored in the brains of speakers. I will completely leave out the question of linguistic$_2$ zeroes—descriptive devices introduced by the researcher in order to make his description look more homogeneous, more compact or more elegant.

2. (I, near the end, p. 305.) A lex is a (grammatical) form of a lexeme; it can be either a wordform or a phrase representing an analytical form of the lexeme in question. Some lexes of the English lexeme SEE: *see, sees, will see, was seen, has been seen,* . . .

3. (II, near the beginning, p. 305.) **Elementary X** = 'X that cannot be represented or quasi-represented in terms of other Xs'; **segmental X** = 'X that (or whose signans) consists of a string of phonemes (plus maybe prosodemes)'.

4. (II, after example (8), p. 307.) Note that in my use of the term, a morpheme (or a lexeme, cf. below) is not a sign but a set of signs.

5. (II, after example (8), p. 307.) For insightful remarks about zero suffix morphs in English see Smirnickij (1959: 20–23). As regards the much discussed zero morpheme of singular in English nouns, I think it is a zero morph but not a zero morpheme, since beside zero (as in *house* + $\emptyset$, *bird* + $\emptyset$, *leg* + $\emptyset$) we also find some nonzero morphs (*phenomen* + *on*, *alumn* + *us*, *formul* + *a*). Although the latter are few in number and found only in Latin borrowings (most in carefully written texts), I feel their presence justifies postulating a nonzero morpheme for English: {SG} = -$\boldsymbol{\theta}_{SG}$, **-on**, **-us**, **-a**, . . .

6. (II, in the definition, p. 310.) In Section V we will see that "justification from below" is, logically speaking, not necessary: semantically empty zero signs, i.e. signs whose both signatum and signans are empty, with only the syntactics nonempty, are possible. Conditions on postulating zero forms are discussed at length and clearly in Haas (1957).

7. (II, **2**, p. 310.) See in this connection the well-known paper by Benveniste (1964).

8. (III, **2**, after example (15), p. 314.) For English, *something* may be a more felicitous rendition of the second zero than *elements*, the literal translation of Russian *stixii*. This is also what Wierzbicka suggests (1966: 188, 191, 193). More about meaning and syntactic behavior of the Russian zero lexemes will be said below; cf. especially note 12.

9. (III, **2**, **Arg. 2**, p. 316.) This conclusion fully coincides with the opinion of Panov (1960: 11): "The grammatical subject can be zero, there being in Russian several homonymous zero grammatical subjects, as in *Svetaet* '[It] dawns', *Cypljat po oseni sčitajut* '[They] count chicks in the fall', etc." Cf. corresponding nonzero subjects in other languages, e.g., German *es*, *man*, French *il*, *on*.

10. (III, **2**, example (17), p. 316.) There remain, however, some complications connected with the zero lexeme $\emptyset^{PEOPLE}$. Consider such normal sentences as the following:

(i)   *Nado že,*   *vsë*   *sklevali*
     it's   incredible everything-ACC pecked.up-PL
     'I can't believe everything got pecked up',
     lit. '. . . [they] pecked everything up'.

(ii)   *Bednen'kij, kak tebja*   *pokusali!*
     poor.thing   how thou-ACC bit-PL
     'Poor thing, you got all bitten up!',
     lit. '. . . [they] bit you all up'.

In these sentences the zero grammatical subject would designate birds and insects, respectively. But compare the following unacceptable sentences:

(iii)   **Takoj silos*   *ne edjat*
     such   sileage-ACC not eat-3PL
     'Such sileage [they] don't eat' [where 'they' = 'cows'].

(iv) *U nas pasutsja   na bol'šom lugu*
　　at us   graze-3PL in big   pasture
　　'We have [them] grazing in the big pasture', '[They]'re grazing . . .'

Nonovert subjects can be understood to refer to birds or insects, but not to cattle. It is not unlikely that there is ellipsis of the grammatical subject, rather than a zero lexeme, in (i) and (ii).

11. (III, **2**, before example (18), p. 316.) Sentence (18b) may be correct if read as elliptical, i.e., the result of deleting the grammatical subject *oni* 'they' by coordinate reduction:

(i) *Tam byli   sxvačeny geroi-partizany. Tam byli   rasstreljany palačami.*
　　there were captured heroes-guerrillas there were shot   by-executioners
　　'It was there that the guerrilla heroes were captured. There they were shot by executioners'.

12. (III, **2**, after example (21), p. 318.) For interesting data about the semantics and syntax of the lexeme $\emptyset^{\text{PEOPLE}}$ see Nakhimovsky (1979), especially Ch. 3 ("Syntactic zeroes"), and (1983: 105–109). Although Nakhimovsky disagrees with the introduction of this zero lexeme, his claims may be roughly summarized as the two relevant semantic properties of it, rather than as arguments against its existence.

First, $\emptyset^{\text{PEOPLE}}$ behaves semantically much like the Russian indefinite pronouns *kto-nibud'*, *kto-to* 'someone', etc. For instance, in a particular context $\emptyset^{\text{PEOPLE}}$ may force the epistemic reading on what would elsewhere be ambiguous sentences with *moč'* 'can, may', just as indefinite pronouns do. For instance,

(i) *On možet   priglasit' Dimu   k   obedu.*
　　he can/may invite   D.-ACC for dinner

means either 'he is physically able/allowed to invite Dima to dinner' [= deontic reading] or 'it is possible ⟨it may happen⟩ that he will invite Dima to dinner' [= epistemic reading]. With $\emptyset^{\text{PEOPLE}}$ or *kto-nibud'* in an independent clause only the epistemic reading is possible:

(ii) *Kto-nibud'   možet   priglasit' Dimu k obedu.*
　　someone   may-3SG
(iii) *Dimu mogut   priglasit' k obedu.*
　　may-3PL

Both (ii) and (iii) can be understood only as 'it is possible that someone will invite Dima to dinner', or (for iii) 'Dima just may get invited to dinner'.

Note, however, that in the appropriate semantic setting, both $\emptyset^{\text{PEOPLE}}$ and *kto-nibud'* accept the deontic reading of *moč'* [= 'have the ability/ the possibility'] as well:

(iv) *Za èto tebja   uže   mogut   posadit',*
　　for this you-ACC already can-3PL jail
　　lit. 'For this, [they] can already jail you' [= 'they have the right, the pretext, etc.'].
(v) *Ja ne mogu èto sdelat',   a kto-nibud' navernjaka možet*
　　I not can this make/do but someone certainly can-3SG
　　'I cannot do this, but somebody certainly can'.

Second, $\emptyset^{\text{PEOPLE}}$ may refer not only to many people but also to a single person, including the speaker or the hearer:

(vi) *Karaul, grabjat!* 'Help! I'm being mugged!',
help   mug-3PL
lit. '**They** are mugging!', uttered when there is only one mugger around.

(vii) *Utrom zě tebe   žrat' davali* . . . *Ili net, èto   ja tebe*
in-morning thou-DAT to-eat gave-PL   or no   it('s) I
včera   daval
yesterday gave-SG.MASC
'You were fed in the morning, weren't you . . . [lit. '**They** fed you, didn't
they . . .'] Actually you weren't—it was yesterday that I fed you' [man speaking to his cat; quoted from Nakhimovsky (1979: 109)].

However, reference to the speaker is excluded in contexts like the following:

(viii) *Ja obeščaju, čto Dimu   priglasjat   k   obedu*
I   promise   that D.-ACC will.invite-3PL for dinner
'I promise that Dima will be invited to dinner'.

(viii) can only mean that someone other than the speaker will invite Dima. The same is probably true of French *on* and German *man*.

Nevertheless, for all the similarity of their behavior, $\emptyset^{\text{PEOPLE}}$ and *kto-nibud'* are by no means synonymous.

A fairly exhaustive review of the various uses of the Russian indefinite-personal construction is offered by Gasparov (1971). Many interesting examples and penetrating remarks on the meaning and contrastive use of French *on*, German *man*, and English *one*, *anybody*, *people* and the passive construction are found in Clas (1970).

13. (III, example (30), p. 321.) I consider the direct objects of the transitive verbs of (30) as strictly obligatory. The nonovert status of the direct object conveys specific information and is thus treated as a zero lex of the zero lexeme $\emptyset^{\text{ANY}}$. This is not true of verbs such as *čitat'* 'read', *verit'* 'believe', *pet'* 'sing', and others: for these the direct object is syntactically facultative, and its absence conveys no specific information. In the following sentence nothing is said about what he is reading:

(i) *On sidel i   čital*
he sat   and read
'He was sitting and reading'.

(In this connection, cf. also Lehrer 1970.)

14. (V, example (50), p. 330.) Interestingly enough, all the claims made in this paragraph were stated in explicit form as early as 1935 by Jakobson (1971a[1935]: 21): "The Russian norm does not know personal sentences without grammatical subject. The so-called impersonal sentences exhibit a zero subject. Russian has lost all types of unipartite indicative sentences." Jakobson even offers a diachronic explanation, relating the appearance of the zero lexeme subject in Russian to the disappearance of inflected enclitics in all the Northeastern Slavic languages. Cf. also the insightful remark of Hetzron (1969: 141): "In Italian *piov + e* 'it rains' the grammatical subject is zero rather than simple absence, since its presence is signalled indirectly by the suffix of the verb [3sg]."

15. (V, after example (51), p. 331.) Here are three further examples of empty zero lexes (and, correspondingly, empty zero lexemes).

1. Hetzron (1969: 152–153) reports an empty zero object in some Hungarian idiomatic expressions:

(i)   *X megjár* + **ja**   *Y* + *kel*   'X has trouble with Y'.
(ii)   *X beér* + **i**   *Y* + *kel*   'X satisfies himself with Y'.
(iii) *X megér* + **i**   *Y* + *nek*   'X is worth doing for Y'.

Here all the verbs are in the so-called "objective" form, shown by the boldface 3sg object suffix (cf. Chapter 3, p. 128). The Hungarian objective form obligatorily indicates agreement in number and person with a definite direct object, but in expressions (i)–(iii) no direct object is overtly present. The verb agreement leads Hetzron to postulate a zero direct object—a dummy definite noun that is semantically empty. It does not contribute any specific meaning to the above expressions, yet its presence is crucial for their idiomatic meaning: *megjár* means 'pass by', while *megjár* + $\emptyset^{\text{dirert object}}$ means 'have trouble'; *beér* means 'catch up with', while *beér* + $\emptyset^{\text{direct object}}$ means 'satisfy oneself with'; *megér* means 'cost', while *megér* + $\emptyset^{\text{direct object}}$ means 'be worth doing'.

2. Constructions with an empty zero subject, similar to (3), are typical of North Russian dialects:

(iv) *Molodu ženščinu*   *sxvačen*   + *o*   *medvedicej*
     young   women-ACC taken[pass.part.] SG.NEUT she.bear-INSTR
     'A young woman has been carried off by a she-bear'.

(v)   *Babušku*   *-to gde*   *poxoronen*   + *o*?
     Grandma-ACC ptc where buried[pass. part.]   SG.NEUT
     'Where is Grandma buried?'

(vi) *Otpravlen*   + *o*   *byl* + *o*   *syna*
     sent.off[pass.part.] SG.NEUT was SG.NEUT son-ACC
     '[My] son was sent away'.

(quoted from Babby and Brecht 1975: 347). In all these sentences a zero empty subject (functionally equivalent to English expletive *it*) may be posited to account for the neuter gender of the predicate. (For more such examples see Kuz'mina and Nemčenko 1971: 27–106.) This is, however, not the only possible analysis. Another approach is suggested by Timberlake (1976): in the following sentences the prepositional phrase *u* + noun is taken as grammatical subject:

(vii) *U nas byl* + *o*   *telënka*   *zarezan*   + *o*
     at us was SG.NEUT calf-ACC slaughtered[pass.part.] SG.NEUT
     'We have slaughtered a calf'.

(viii) *Vodu*   *u ej*   *nanesen*   + *o*
     water-ACC at her brought[pass.part.] SG.NEUT
     'She has brought water '.

The verb agreement rule is as follows: if the grammatical subject is the phrase "*u* + noun", then the main verb is in the singular neuter gender. But too many things remain unclear to pass definite judgment.

3. It is possible that an empty zero lexeme exists in Standard Russian as well; namely a dummy zero subject found in sentences of the type (ix):

(ix) *V ego pis'me govorilos'*   *o*   *priezde Koli.*
     in his letter was-spoken-SG.NEUT about arrival Nick
     lit. 'In his letter, IT was-spoken of Nick's arrival' = 'His letter spoke of Nick's arrival'.

It should be a third zero subject lexeme: $\emptyset^{dummy}$. Its range or usage is, however, highly restricted: only a few verbs of speech admit it (*ukazyvalos' na* 'it was pointed to', *prizyvalos' k* 'it was called on to', *namekalos' na* 'it was hinted at', . . .).

16. (V, the end of Question 2, p. 331.) To avoid possible misunderstandings, I would like to insist on the fundamental difference between my zero subject (= a zero lexeme in the role of GS) and what is called **null subject** in the transformational approach. The term **null subject** frequently appears in numerous transformational works, where the corresponding notion became a hot issue; see, e.g., Rizzi (1982). However, this null subject has nothing to do with my zero lexeme subject: the transformationalist's null subject is by no means a specific lexeme having its own meaning and syntactic properties, but simply an abstract symbol representing the result of nonappearance or deletion of a pronoun. Cf. the following typical examples of null subjects in Rizzi (1982):

(i) Italian **a.** *Verrà*, lit. 'Will come' = NullSubj + *verrà* 'He will come'.
b. *Chi$_i$ credi che* NullSubj$_i$ *verrà?*,
lit. 'Who$_i$ do-you-think that will-come?'

Under the heading of null subject, then, particular types of ellipsis or extraction are being discussed, irrelevant for my purposes here. The transformational null subject is a typical linguistic$_2$, rather than linguistic$_1$, zero. (Nevertheless, the discussion of null subjects in Rizzi (1982) contains some points related to the problem of zero lexemes: cf., for instance, dummy subjects in meteorological sentences, such as Italian *Piove* 'It rains' vs. *Essendo piovuto, siamo rimasti a casa*, lit. '[It] having rained, [we] have remained at home', etc.; or logical dependencies between transformationalists' null subjects and verb personal inflection:

(ii) Hebrew **a.** (*'Ata*)   *'axal* + *ta*   *'et ha-banana*
thou.MASC   ate   2SG.MASC   the banana
'You[sg] ate the banana' ['*et* is a preposition introducing direct objects; '*ata* is optional]
vs.
b. *'Ata 'oxel* + $\emptyset$ *'et ha-banana*
        eat   SG.MASC
'You[sg] eat the banana'
vs.
c. **'Oxel 'et ha-banana* ['*ata* is obligatory].)

Part V

SYNTACTIC METHODOLOGY: SOME THORNY QUESTIONS OF RUSSIAN SYNTAX

The three chapters of Part V raise the following three problems:

1. How to choose among the competing descriptions of a peculiar Russian construction where direct speech is introduced by a verb of emotion or of gesture? (Something like *'Is it you?'* —*John became glad.*)
2. How to choose among the competing descriptions of differing forms of Russian adjectives and numerals in the accusative (of a given gender and number)? (As in *Ja vižu* **bol'šogo** *slona* vs. **bol'šoj** *stolb* 'I see a big elephant' vs. 'a big pole'.)
3. How to choose among the competing descriptions of a Russian numeral phrase governed by a 'quantitative' preposition? (For instance, *na* **tri rebënka** *bol'še* 'three children more'.)

This part has an obvious METHODOLOGICAL ORIENTATION: it discusses ways of choosing, in a principled manner, between competing descriptions and postulates principles to be guided by in such choices. For better coherence, its three chapters deal with just one language taken at just one level (i.e., syntactic); namely, they deal with Russian syntax on the borderline between syntax and semantics (in Chapter 9) and between syntax and morphology (in Chapters 10 and 11). At the end of the part, I offer an inventory of methodological principles introduced and applied in the preceding chapters.

Chapter **9**

ON A CLASS OF RUSSIAN VERBS THAT CAN INTRODUCE DIRECT SPEECH: LEXICAL POLYSEMY OR SEMANTIC SYNTAX? (CONSTRUCTIONS OF THE TYPE *"OSTAV'TE MENJA!" —ISPUGALSJA BUFETČIK*)

Napišet avtor:
  "—Kak vy smeete!—vspyxnula Elena".
A Zobov popravit:
  "—Kak vy smeete!—**vspyxnuv, skazala** Elena" [emphasis added—I.M.].
—Začem vy vstavljaete slova?—zlitsja avtor.—Kto vas prosit?
—A kak že?—s dostoinstvom otvečaet Zobov.—Vy pišete, čto Elena vspyxnula, a kto skazal frazu: "Kak vy smeete"—ostaëtsja neizvestnym. . . .

N. Tèffi, "Trubka" ['The Pipe'], in:
N. Tèffi, *Rasskazy,* Moscow, 1971:113.[1]

I. RUSSIAN DIRECT SPEECH SENTENCES WITH VERBS OF EMOTION

Consider the Russian sentence (1), quoted in the subtitle:

(1) *"Ostav'te menja!" —ispugalsja bufetčik*
"Leave me alone!"—said the bartender, frightened
[literally: 'became frightened the bartender'].

The peculiar thing about this sentence is that direct speech is introduced not by a verb of speech (such as 'said', 'answered', 'asked', 'yelled', 'exclaimed', etc.) but rather by a verb of emotion: 'became frightened.'[2]

On the one hand, this type of sentence is quite characteristic of Modern Standard Russian, being widespread in literary texts from the second half of the nineteenth century well into our time; cf., e.g., Levin (1960: 410–411), where constructions "Direct Speech + Verb of Emotion" (and several related structures) are described at some length.

On the other hand, sentences like (1) are highly specific, since they manifest a syntactic construction completely absent from, or minimally represented in, many other languages (such as French or English). Most Russian sentences of this type cannot be translated into French or English without a substantial change in the syntactic structure. Let us cite here some examples from *The Idiot*, by F. Dostoyevsky, and *The Master and Margarita*, by M. A. Bulgakov, along with their French and English equivalents.[3]

(2)   **a.**   *—Da . . . kak že èto?—udivilsja do stolbnjaka i čut' ne vypučil glaza činovnik* [Dostoyevsky].

      b.   *—Oui . . . comment cela?—Le fonctionnaire fut frappé d'étonnement jusqu'à en rester médusé, les yeux hors de la tête.*

      c.   *"But . . . how is that?" The official was petrified with amazement, and his eyes seemed almost starting out of his head.*

(3)   **a.**   *—Nu ladno,—smjagčilsja artist,—kto staroe pomjanet . . .* [Bulgakov].

      b.   *—Enfin bon, dit l'artiste en s'adoucissant, ne parlons plus du passé.*

      c.   *"All right," the artist relented slightly, "since you have owned up we'll be lenient."*

(4)   **a.**   *—Vot eščë novosti!—opjat' zatrevožilsja general* [Dostoyevsky].

      b.   *—En voilà des nouvelles!—lança le général, de nouveau alarmé.*

      c.   *"Here's something new!" said the general, uneasy again.*

(5)   **a.**   *—Nu, pošla!—rasserdilas' general'ša* [Dostoyevsky].

      b.   *—Allons, la voilà partie! dit la générale, fâchée.*

      c.   *"Get along with you," said her mother* [= *general'ša* = *la générale*], *getting angry.*

(6) **a.** *—Očen' blagodaren-s,—udivljalsja general* [Dostoyevsky].
   b. *—Je vous remercie bien, fit le général, étonné.*
   c. *"I am very much obliged to you," said the general, surprised.*

(7) **a.** *—Ostav'te menja, Xrista radi,—ispugalsja bufetčik i provorno sprjatal den'gi* [Bulgakov].
   b. *—Laissez-moi tranquille, par le Christ!—dit le buffetier effrayé, et il cacha promptement son argent.*
   c. *"Leave me alone, for Christ's sake!" said the bartender and promptly hid the money.*

As examples (2)—(7) show, the Russian construction "Direct Speech + Verb of Emotion" cannot normally be translated by an identical French or English construction:[4]

(2′) **b.** **—Oui . . . comment cela?—fut frappé d'étonnement le fonctionnaire.*
   c. ** "But . . . how is this?" the official was petrified with amazement.*
(4′) **b.** **—En voilà des nouvelles!—s'alarma le général.*
   c. ** "Here's something new!" the general became uneasy again.*
(5′) **b.** **—Allons, la voilá partie!—se fâcha la générale.*
   c. ** "Get along with you", her mother [= la générale] became angry.*

Note that English glosses (2′c), (4′c) and (5′c) use the appropriate [i.e., English] word order in the clause that introduces direct speech; we do this in order to show that the translation problem lies not in an impossible inversion of the grammatical subject but just in the choice of the introductory verb.

When translating Russian sentences like (2a)–(7a) into French or English, one must employ one of the following three methods in order to make the Russian structure comply with the rules of French or English grammar. (We use self-explanatory terms: **direct speech clause**, or **DS-clause**, meaning 'a clause that conveys direct speech'; **direct speech sentence**, or **DS-sentence**, meaning 'a sentence that contains a DS-clause'; **direct speech introductory clause**, or **DSI-clause**, meaning 'the main clause of a DS-sentence, which introduces the DS-clause'. Thus, a DS-sentence = DS-clause + DSI-clause.)

A. A single Russian DS-sentence is broken up into two independent sentences, with no direct syntactic links between them. The first of these sentences conveys direct speech, the second the introductory expression, cf. (2b) and (2c).

B. The unity of the Russian DS-sentence is preserved in translation, but the syntactic status of the DSI-clause is dramatically changed: it becomes a parenthetical clause within the DS-clause, i.e., it loses its syntactic governor role to assume the more modest one, that of sentential modifier, cf. (3c). This new status is marked by a specific prosody and linear insertion of such a parenthetical clause into the DS-clause. The same kind of relation can be observed in Russian between (8a) and (8b):

(8) **a.** *Estestvenno,→čto on otkazalsja* 'It is natural that he refused'.
   b. *On, estestvenno,←otkazalsja* 'He, naturally, refused'.
(As throughout the book, the arrows indicate syntactic dependency, X→Y meaning 'Y is an immediate syntactic dependent of X'.)

C. The DSI-clause undergoes the following transformation: the Russian verb of emotion that introduces the DS-clause is replaced by a verb of speech (as, e.g., French *dit, fit* or English *said,* etc.), which assumes the syntactic governor role, while the emotion is expressed by means of a separate lexical item syntactically dependent on the verb of speech (directly—as an adverbial modifier, or indirectly—as an appositive, a disjoined adjectival modifier etc.; see (3b), (4)–(7)). In other words, instead of, for instance, Russian *rasserdilas'* '[she] became angry' the French or English equivalent must contain '[she] said angrily', 'said, angry', 'said in anger', etc. The secondary character of the expression denoting emotion in French and English DS-sentences is attested to by (*inter alia*) its deletability, assuming the translator does not judge its meaning to be particularly relevant (with respect to the information conveyed by the DS-sentence as a whole).

These three methods of translating Russian DS-sentences containing a verb of emotion that introduces the DS-clause make more explicit the following three properties of those sentences:

1. (2a)–(7a) are single sentences displaying an overall syntactic hierarchy. The DS-clause is syntactically linked to the verb of emotion, this link being marked by a particular word order and a particular prosody:
   a. The DSI-clause necessarily follows the DS-clause, and the main verb of the DSI-clause, i.e. the verb of emotion, necessarily precedes its grammatical subject.
   b. Full pause between the DS- and DSI-clauses is impossible, and the pitch level falls continuously from the DS-clause to the end of the sentence.
The syntactic unity of the Russian DS-sentences under consideration becomes still more evident if we compare one such sentence with a pair of syntactically autonomous sentences expressing the same meaning. For instance, for (2) we get (9):

(9) *"—Da . . . kak že èto?" Činovnik udivilsja do stolbnjaka i čut' ne vypučil glaza.*
   "But . . . how is that?" The official was petrified with amazement and his eyes seemed almost starting out of his head.

Here, the second sentence (= *Činovnik udivilsja* . . .) shows different word order and prosody than those observed in the DSI-clause in (2a).

2. In (2a)–(7a) the DS-clause plays the role of a dependent syntactic element while the verb of emotion assumes the role of its syntactic governor (i.e., the emotion verb is the top node of the whole DS-sentence).

3. In (2a)–(7a), the DSI-clause expresses the meaning 'utter the given utterance', which is rendered by a separate verb of speech in French or English translations.

Based on these three properties, we can now attempt a more formal description of the Russian sentences (2a)–(7a).

First of all, it should be pointed out that the construction under study admits not every verb of emotion (a fact not indicated in Levin 1960) but only verbs that denote emotions involving reactions: like *vozmutit'sja* '(to) become indignant', *ispugat'sja* '(to) become frightened', *udivit'sja* '(to) become astonished', *obradovat'sja* '(to) become happy', *ogorčit'sja* '(to) become upset', *vstrevožit'sja* '(to) become anxious', *obidet'sja* '(to) become offended', . . . as opposed to verbs that denote emotions linked to attitudes, like *uvažat'* '(to) respect', *prezirat'* '(to) despise', *ljubit'* '(to) love', *nenavidet'* '(to) hate', *simpatizirovat'* '(to) sympathize', . . . Cf. (10):

(10) **a.** *—Nado že!—proiznosit s udivleniem Kolja.*
       "That's something!" Kolya mutters with astonishment.
       —Nado že!—udivljaetsja Kolja.
       [lit.] "That's something!" Kolya becomes astonished.
       b. *—Nado že!—proiznosit s uvaženiem Kolja.*
       "That's something!" Kolya mutters with respect.
       vs.
       *—Nado že!—uvažaet Kolja.
       [lit.] "That's something!" Kolya respects.

Now we can turn to the construction itself. As stated before, we proceed from the representation of surface-syntactic structures adopted in Meaning-Text theory. Using the corresponding formalism, the construction in question can be diagramed as follows:

(11) V·'emotional reaction' —*r*→ DS-clause,

where *r* stands for the specific type of SSRel that subordinates (the syntactic top node of) the DS-clause to the verb of emotion.

II. THE PROBLEM STATED

The question immediately arises: what SSRel is r in (11)? Does r, in particular, coincide with the SSRel that subordinates a DS-clause to a true verb of speech? With the latter, we treat the DS-clause as a direct object and use the first-completive SSRel:

(12) a. *On skazal* —1st-compl→ *pravdu* 'He told the truth'.
　　　b. *On skazal,* —1st-compl→ *čto pridët* 'He said he would come'.
　　　c. *On skazal:* —1st-compl→ *"Pridu"* 'He said: "I'll come" '.

(see Mel'čuk 1974a: 222, Iomdin and Percov 1975: 25–31).

There are three possible answers: r in (11) may be the first-completive SSRel; it may be some other member of the set of SSRels proposed so far for Russian (Mel'čuk 1974a: 221–235); or there may be grounds (naturalness, elegance, productivity) to posit a new SSRel.

A second question comes to mind once we start looking for the linguistic₁ element in (2a)–(7a) that carries the meaning 'utter the given utterance'. Is the verb of emotion this element? If so, this verb acquires a new semantic component, and therefore perhaps a new sense. Or is the meaning 'utter the given utterance' expressed through the syntactic construction itself, i.e., by the corresponding SSRel?

The answer to this second question is intimately connected to the answer we provide for the question about the type of SSRel appearing in our construction. The rest of this chapter attempts to answer both these interrelated questions as they pertain to the Russian DS-sentences in (2a)–(7a):

(13) a. What type of SSRel subordinates the DS-clause to the verb of emotion?
　　　b. Which sentence element carries the meaning 'utter the given utterance'?

III. ALTERNATIVE SOLUTIONS: LEXICAL VS. SYNTACTIC

There are two possible solutions to the problems stated under (13): a lexical one and a syntactic one.

SOLUTION I: **lexical**. The meaning 'utter the given utterance' is ascribed to the verb of emotion; then any Russian verb denoting a reaction-implying emotion E possesses one additional lexicographic sense, namely, 'Experiencing E, utter the given utterance'. For instance, under Solution I, ISPUGAT'SJA '(to) become frightened' turns out to be two-way ambiguous:

ISPUGAT'SJA 1. *X ispugalsja Y-a* 'X became frightened of Y' [we do not define the corresponding meaning here since this is irrelevant for our purpose].

ISPUGAT'SJA 2. *"Z", —ispugalsja* X Y-*a* = *'Ispugavšis'* 1 Y-a [= having been frightened of Y], X uttered the utterance Z'.

Accordingly, sense 2 of any verb of emotion implying reaction should be considered a verb of speech; the DS-clause should be subordinated to it via the same SSRel as in the case of all 'normal' verbs of speech. In our system, we would use here the first-completive SSRel. The semantic correlation 'experience emotion E' ~ 'experiencing emotion E, utter the given utterance' then emerges as a new type of regular polysemy in Russian (for an inventory of such types see Apresjan 1974: 193–215).

SOLUTION II: **syntactic**. The meaning 'utter the given utterance' is ascribed to the syntactic structure of (11) itself, specifically, to the type *r* of the SSRel connecting its members, rather than to the verb of emotion.

Under this solution, *r* cannot be the same SSRel that subordinates the DS-clause to a normal verb of speech (i.e., *r* ≠ first-completive SSRel), since the first-completive SSRel does not carry this specific meaning (all the completive SSRels are in principle fully asemantic). Moreover, no SSRel in the existing inventory carries the meaning 'utter the given utterance'. Therefore, *r* must be a new SSRel, which could be dubbed, e.g., **quotative**. On the deep-syntactic level, the meaning rendered by the quotative SSRel will be represented by a fictitious lexeme "VYSKAZAT'" '(to) utter' (for fictitious lexemes, see Chapter 2, p. 60). The corresponding deep-syntax rule has the following form:

(14)

See also rule (33) below.

With Solution II, the deep-syntactic structure and the surface-syntactic structure of sentence (1) are (15) and (16), respectively:

(15)

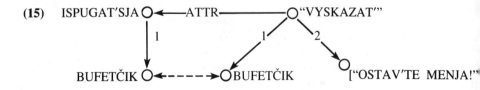

(16)

(For deep-syntactic rules as well as for deep- and surface-syntactic structure see above, Chapter 2, pp. 60ff., 68–69, 79ff.)

IV. THREE ARGUMENTS AGAINST THE LEXICAL SOLUTION

Comparison of the two solutions leads us to choose the second, i.e. the syntactic one. We can present three arguments in favor of our choice—all three being against the lexical solution.

Argument 1

The lexical solution increases unlimitedly the class of verbs of speech, adding to it all the assumed speech senses attributed to verbs of emotion. However, these new verbs of speech (let us call them hypothetical) differ from normal verbs of speech in their syntactic properties.

First, the normal verbs of speech that can introduce DS-clause always admit the construction with indirect speech as well:

(17)   **a.**   *"Vsë ob "jasnju potom"*,—*skazala mat'*.
       "I'll explain everything later," the mother said.
      b.   *Mat' skazala, čto vsë ob "jasnit potom.*
       The mother said that she would explain everything later.
(18)   **a.**   *"Net, ty tuda ne pojdëš'!*—*serdito kriknul on.*
       "No, you are not going there!" he exclaimed angrily.
      b.   *On serdito kriknul, čto ja tuda ne pojdu.*
       He exclaimed angrily that I was not going there.

Unlike normal verbs of speech, no hypothetical verb of speech admits the construction with indirect speech:

(19)   **a.**   *"Vsë ob "jasnju potom"*,—*smjagčilas' mat'*.
       "I'll explain everything later," the mother relented.
      b.   **Mat' smjagčilas', čto vsë ob "jasnit potom.*
       The mother relented that she would explain everything later.
(20)   **a.**   *"Net, ty tuda ne pojdëš'!" *—*rasserdilsja on.*
       [lit.] "No, you are not going there!" he became angry.
      b.   **On rasserdilsja, čto ja tuda ne pojdu.*
       He became angry that I was not going there.

(The sentence (20b) is possible, but in a different meaning: if the completive clause does not convey the utterance of the experiencer of anger but rather denotes the reason for his anger, as is also true of the English translation. On the grammatical reading, (20b) describes a situation that is opposite to that of (20a), namely, in (20b) the experiencer of anger wants me to go there.)

Thus the transformation "direct speech⇒indirect speech" is typical of normal verbs of speech but it is impossible for hypothetical verbs of speech.

Second, the lexical solution creates a difficulty with the SSRel linking the speech sense of a verb of emotion with the DS-clause. In the case of normal verbs of speech, the first-completive SSRel is used, as indicated above; it would be natural to use the same SSRel for emotion verbs in the speech sense, too. This solution cannot work, however, since the first-completive SSRel with any verb of emotion is already occupied by the object (= reason, or source) of the emotion, as in *udivit'sja* $\xrightarrow{\text{1st-compl}}$ *ètoj novosti* '(to) be astonished by the news', *is-pugat'sja* $\xrightarrow{\text{1st-compl}}$ *otca* '(to) be frightened by the father', etc. As a result, we face the following dilemma:

—We may insist upon subordinating the DS-clause to a verb of emotion in its speech sense by means of the first-completive SSRel (as we would do with normal verbs of speech). The object of emotion, which is still possible with the speech sense, would have to be subordinated to it by, say, the second-completive SSRel. This decision makes the speech sense the converse of the emotion sense and destroys the natural parallelism in the valence of all Russian emotion verbs used to introduce DS. Thus in (21) *ètoj novosti* 'by the news' is the first complement in **a** but the second complement in **b**:

(21) **a.** *Tanja udivilas'* $\xrightarrow{\text{1st-compl}}$ *[ètoj novosti]*
    'Tanya was astonished by the news'.
  b. [*"Kak?"*,—] $\xleftarrow{\text{1st-compl}}$ *udivilas'* $\xrightarrow{\text{2nd-compl}}$ *[ètoj novosti] Tanja*
    'How is that?—Tanya exclaimed, astonished by the news'.

—Or we may retain the first-completive SSRel for the object of emotion in the speech sense as well, in which case the DS-clause would have to be subordinated to the verb by the second-completive SSRel. This decision destroys the natural parallelism with normal verbs of speech.

The lexical solution entails, therefore, an obvious embarassment in the description of the syntactic structure of our construction.

Argument 2

At the same time, the lexical solution runs into an even greater difficulty, this one of a purely semantic nature. Russian has a number of expressions that characterize the actual delivery of an utterance:

(22) *vysokim* ⟨*gnusavym, piskljavym, vizglivym, . . .*⟩ *golosom* 'in a high-pitched ⟨nasal, squeaky, squealing, . . .⟩ voice', *kriklivo* 'screaming', *tixo* 'in a low voice', *ele slyšno* 'hardly audible', *skvoz' zuby* 'through clenched teeth', . . .

With the exception of some obvious semantic contradictions (of the type **šë-potom zavopil* 'shouted in whisper' or **kriklivo prošeptal* 'whispered shouting'), the expressions in (22) freely co-occur with all verbs of speech:

(23)   **a.**   *—Vot eščë novosti!—tixo ⟨skvoz' zuby, šëpotom⟩ skazal general.*
"Here's something new!" said the general in a low voice ⟨through clenched teeth, in whisper⟩.

     b.   *—Nu, pošla!—vizglivym ⟨piskljavym, vysokim⟩ golosom voskliknula general'ša.*
"Get along with you," said her mother [= general's wife] in a squealing ⟨squeaky, high-pitched⟩ voice.

     c.   *—Pospeem li za cvetami zaexat'!—kriklivo ⟨piskljavo⟩ sprašival malen'kij.*
"But do we have enough time to go to fetch some flowers?" said the little one almost shouting ⟨in a squeaky voice⟩'.

However, none of the expressions in (22) can co-occur with a verb of emotion used in the hypothetical speech sense:

(24)   **a.**   **—Vot eščë novosti!—tixo ⟨skvoz' zuby, šëpotom⟩ zatrevožilsja general.*
"Here's something new!" the general became uneasy in a low voice ⟨through clenched teeth, in whisper⟩.

     b.   **—Nu,   pošla!—vizglivym   ⟨piskljavym,   vysokim⟩   golosom rasserdilas' general'ša.*
"Get along with you," her mother became angry in a squealing ⟨squeaky, high-pitched⟩ voice.

     c.   **—Pospeem li za cvetami zaexat'?—kriklivo ⟨piskljavo⟩ bespokoilsja malen'kij.*
"But do we have enough time to go to fetch some flowers?" the little one was anxious shouting ⟨in a squeaky voice⟩.

We do not see any natural way to preclude the expressions of (24) if we accept the lexical solution. According to the syntactic solution, however, (24) will be barred automatically because of semantic incompatibility: the meaning 'the . . . manner in which the utterance is uttered' cannot be combined with the meaning 'experience a . . . emotion'.

Argument 3

There is yet another fact that argues against the lexical solution. So far we have discussed only verbs of emotion, but in fact our construction admits some other verbs as well. More precisely, a DS-clause can be introduced by practically any verb that denotes (whether usually, occasionally or in certain contexts only) a specific manifestation of an emotional reaction. Specifically, these comprise facial expressions (*naxmurit'sja* '(to) frown', *ulybnut'sja* '(to) smile', *oskalit'sja* '(to) grin', *ustavit'sja* '(to) stare', . . .), emotional gestures (*potirat' ruki* '(to) rub one's hands' [a gesture of satisfaction], *sxvatit'sja za golovu* '(to) clutch one's head' [a gesture of despair], . . .), and movements (*vstat'* '(to) stand up', *povernut'sja* '(to) turn', . . .). Here are some examples from *The Idiot:*

(25) **a.** *—T'fu tebja!—spljunul černomazyj.*
   "Hang you!" the dark man spat.
b. *—Nu-s, nu-s, teper' zapoët u nas Nastas'ja Filipovna!—potiraja ruki, xixikal činovnik.*
   "Well, well, now N. F. will sing another tune," the official chuckled, rubbing his hands.
c. *Ex! Ux!—krivilsja činovnik.*
   "Ech! Ugh!" the official wriggled.
d. *—To, stalo byt' , vstavat' i uxodit'?—pripodnjalsja knjaz', kak-to daže veselo rassmejavšis'.*
   "Nothing but to get up and go?" the prince got up, laughing with positive mirthfulness.

As (25) shows, the set of verbs participating in the construction under analysis is open-ended: a most unexpected verb can appear in it if there is an appropriate semantic context. Cf. also (26):

(26) *"Ja budu vas ždat' . . . budu rad . . . Ja vas vstreču . . ."—zatoropilsja on, kak-to stranno pjatjas'.*
   "I'll wait for you . . . I'll be happy . . . I'll pick you up . . . ," he said in a hurry [lit. 'he hurried'], stepping backwards in a strange way [B. Okudžava].

If we were to accept the lexical solution, we would have to attribute the additional speech sense to an enormous number of verbs, and, what is more, for many of them (for instance, *vstat'* '(to) stand up', *zatoropit'sja* '(to) hurry') this sense would be potential, i.e. appearing in highly specific contexts only. We feel that introducing potential senses is an unnatural device, which should be avoided. The syntactic solution, on the other hand, does not call for any particular lexical marking of verbs admitted in the construction under study; the semantic condition that accompanies the corresponding deep-syntax rule (see (33) below) is sufficient: ANY verb whatsoever can be used in our construction provided this verb denotes a manifestation of an emotional reaction.

As for arguments against the syntactic solution, none is known to us so far. Nonetheless, one could foresee some objections to the ascription of meaning to a SSRel, i.e., admitting such a highly specific, semantically loaded SSRel as the quotative into the inventory of Russian SSRels. These objections can be laid to rest by pointing out that Russian possesses similar SSRels beyond any doubt. Let us cite some examples.

(i) The approximative-quantitative SSRel, carrying the meaning 'approximately':

(27) *prošël kilometrov*$\overset{\text{approx-quant}}{\longrightarrow}$ *dvadcat'* 'covered about 20 km',
sobralos' čelovek$\overset{\text{approx-quant}}{\longrightarrow}$*pjat' desjat*'there gathered about 50 people'.

(ii) The approximative-ordinal SSRel, carrying the same meaning ('approximately'):

(28) $\overset{\text{approx-ord}}{\overset{\frown}{den'\ na\ šestoj}}$ 'on approximately the sixth day',
$\overset{\text{approx-ord}}{\overset{\frown}{stranicy\ s\ desjatoj}}$ 'from approximately the tenth page'.

(iii) The identificative-appositive SSRel, carrying the meaning 'be':
(29) $\overset{\text{ident-appos}}{\overset{\frown}{divan\text{-}krovat'}}$, lit. 'sofa-bed,' i.e. 'a sofa which is a bed';

znak $\overset{\text{ident-appos}}{\longrightarrow}$ *plus* 'plus sign'.

(iv) The nominative-appositive SSRel, carrying the meaning 'called', 'having the name':

(30) *gorod* $\overset{\text{nom-appos}}{\longrightarrow}$ *Moskva* '[the] city of Moscow',
funkcija $\overset{\text{nom-appos}}{\longrightarrow}$ *P(a)* 'function P(a)'.

(v) The modal-infinitive SSRel, carrying the meanings 'be able', 'be desirable' and 'have to' (depending on the syntactic context):

(31) **a.** $\overset{\text{mod-inf}}{\overset{\frown}{Nam\ ne}}$ *naučit'sja ètomu* 'We won't be able to learn this' ['be able' —when the infinitive is negated and the modal particle *by* is absent].

b. $\overset{\text{mod-inf}}{\overset{\frown}{Nam\ by}}$ *naučit'sja ètomu* 'We would like to learn this' ['be desirable' —when the modal particle *by* is present].

c. $\overset{\text{mod-inf}}{\overset{\frown}{Nam\ eščë}}$ *učit'sja ètomu* 'We still have to learn this' ['have to'— when both the negation and the particle *by* are absent].

More syntactic constructions with a semantically loaded SSRel are found in colloquial Russian:

(32) **a.** *Besplatno ne besplatno, no dёšẹvo* 'Free it is not, but it's cheap' ['**Although** it is not free . . .'].

concessive

b. *Besplatno, ne besplatno, ja beru* 'Free or not free, I take it' ['**Independently of the fact** whether it is free . . .']; etc.

"irrelevantive"

[The concessive and the "irrelevantive" phrases are uttered with different prosody: (32a) *Besplatno ne besplatno* vs. (32b) *Besplatno ne besplatno* .]

We see that surface-syntactic relations carrying a specific meaning are characteristic of Modern Russian, so that the quotative SSRel we propose is far from being unique or unprecedented. Note, however, that meaning-bearing surface-syntactic relations, at least of the type illustrated, are alien to English: not even one of the Russian examples cited can be rendered by an isomorphic syntactic structure in English, where we have to add words in order to express meaning encoded by Russian constructions.

Thus, our answer to the question raised in the subtitle of the chapter is as follows:

> Constructions of the type (1) should be described in terms of a semantically loaded SSRel, rather than in terms of polysemy of the verb that introduces the DS-clause.

The construction (1) provides, then, another example of "semantic syntax" in Russian.

In conclusion we present a formal description of the construction in question by means of a deep-syntactic (33) and a surface-syntactic (34) rule.

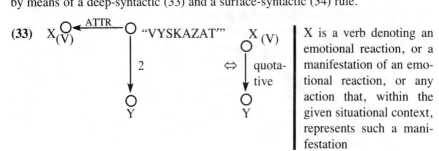

(33) X is a verb denoting an emotional reaction, or a manifestation of an emotional reaction, or any action that, within the given situational context, represents such a manifestation

(34)

Comments on Rule (34)

1. $\widetilde{Y}$ means 'the node Y and all the nodes that depend on it', i.e. a full subtree with the top node Y.
2. The condition (to the right of the vertical bar) indicates that the verb [= X] that introduces the DS-clause must precede its own grammatical subject [= Z].

V. A RESIDUAL CASE: VERBS OF EMOTION HAVING A SPEECH COMPONENT

When arguing for the syntactic solution we deliberately avoided considering the following six verbs of emotion:

(35) *udivljat'sja* '(to) be astonished', *izumljat'sja* '(to) be amazed', *vosxiščat'sja* (to) be delighted', *vostorgat'sja* '(to) be enraptured', *vozmuščat'sja* '(to) be indignant', *negodovat'* 'idem'.

The fact is that all those verbs, besides denoting an emotion, can also mean '(to) utter an utterance that expresses this emotion'. This is possible both in the construction with direct speech and, what is most important, outside that construction. See (36), where the presence of the semantic component 'utter an utterance . . .' is proved by the contrast with *molčat'* '(to) keep silent' or the co-occurrence with modifiers of the type (22):

(36) **a.** *Gosti počitali objazannost'ju vosxiščat'sja psarnej Kirilla Petroviča—odin Dubrovskij molčal i xmurilsja* [Pushkin], lit. 'All the guests considered it their duty to be delighted with K. P.'s kennel—only D. kept silent and frowned'.
   b. *Vse gromko ⟨šëpotom⟩ udivljalis' ⟨izumljalis'⟩ ètoj novosti,* lit. 'Everybody was loudly ⟨in whisper⟩ astonished ⟨amazed⟩ by this piece of news'.
   c. *Vse napereboj ⟨gromko⟩ vozmuščalis' ego povedeniem,* lit. 'In eager rivalry ⟨loudly⟩ everybody was indignant with his behavior'.
   d. *Vse xorom ⟨vpolgolosa⟩ negodovali po povodu ego poslednej vyxodki,* lit. 'Everybody was in chorus ⟨under breath⟩ indignant with his latest escapade'.
   e. *Staruška piskljavym golosom vostorgalas' pirogami,* lit. 'The old lady was in a squeaky voice enraptured with the cookies'.

But similar sentences with any other verb of emotion are impossible: cf. examples (24).

Now, how does this fact affect our proposal to describe the construction (1) in terms of a special surface-syntactic relation? Would it not be more natural, at least for the above six verbs, to regard the direct-speech clause as a syntactic actant of the verb in question and to subordinate the former to the latter via the first-completive SSRel?

We do not think so. Even in that case the syntactic solution seems preferable to us by virtue of our first argument in Section IV: the six verbs in (35) do not admit the transformation of the DS-clause into indirect speech, either, and they present the same difficulty in using the first-completive SSRel as all other verbs of emotion do.

Therefore, the meaning 'utter an utterance . . .' carried by the six verbs does not change anything in our reasoning. Simply, this meaning can be expressed TWICE in the case of those verbs: lexically, by the verb itself, and syntactically, by the quotative construction. As is widely known, the 'duplication' of meaning, that is, simultaneous expression of a given meaning by different linguistic₁ means, is highly typical of natural languages.

The last problem, only tangentially related to our topic, is the choice of a lexicographic description for the verbs in (35): Should we split each of those verbs into two lexicographic senses, i.e., the emotion sense and the speech sense, or should we include the speech meaning as an optional component into the only sense of the verb? We vote for the second solution since the hypothetical speech sense does not exhibit any particularities if compared to the emotion sense (neither the morphological properties nor the government pattern nor the restricted lexical cooccurrences are different). Thus, e.g., our lexicographic definition of the verb VOSXIŠČAT'SJA runs as follows:

(37) *X vosxiščaetsja Y-om* [X is delighted with Y] = 'X is in a fairly intensive positive emotional state caused by the fact that X believes that Y, perceived by X, is very good (and X utters an utterance which expresses this state)'.

The present chapter reproduces, with minor modifications, the paper Iordanskaja and Mel'čuk (1981).

NOTES

1. (Epigraph, p. 341.) Since the epigraph exemplifies a linguistic phenomenon that does not exist in English (or, if so, only on a much more restricted scale), its literal translation must be given.

An author writes:
—How dare you!—[lit.] flared up Elena.
And Mr Zobov corrects:
—How dare you!—exclaimed Elena, flaring up.
—Why do you insert words?—[lit.] becomes mad the author.—Who is asking you?
—Well,—answers Mr Zobov with dignity.—You have written that Elena flared up, all right, but you leave it unclear who pronounced the sentence "How dare you!" . . .

2. (I, p. 342.) This chapter concentrates on the contrast only between verbs of speech and verbs of emotion (in the capacity of an element introducing direct speech). The actual picture, however, is more complex. In addition to the verbs of speech, we find a number of verbs that are, in a sense, semantically related to them: verbs of thought (*podumat'* '(to) think', *rešit'* '(to) decide', *zakolebat'sja* '(to) hesitate', . . .), verbs characterizing the course of a dialogue and the process of speech (*vozrazit'* '(to) object', *podtverdit'* '(to) confirm', *načat'* '(to) begin', *oborvat'* '(to) interrupt', . . .) and some other types (see, e.g., Levin 1960: 408 ff.). All of these will be ignored here.

3. (I, p. 349.) These equivalents have been borrowed from the following published translations:

Idiot, 1977. Paris: Garnier [tranduit par Pierre Pascal]; *The Idiot*, 1962. New York: Modern Library [translated by Constance Garnett].

Le maître et Marguerite, 1968. Paris: Laffont [traduit par Claude Ligny]; *The Master and Margarita*, 1967. New York–Evanston: Harper & Row [translated by Michael Glenny].

4. (I, after examples (2) - (7), p. 343.) Note that in some cases (at least in French) a construction identical with the Russian one can be found. For instance:

(i) —*Pas pour cette affaire? s'étonna le magicien étranger.*
"It is not this business?" said the magician, astonished [lit. 'the magician became astonished'].

(ii) —*Quelle bassesse! s'indigna Woland.*
"That's mean!" said Woland indignantly [lit. 'W. became indignant'].

Chapter **10**

ANIMACY IN RUSSIAN CARDINAL NUMERALS AND ADJECTIVES AS AN INFLECTIONAL CATEGORY: A PROBLEM OF AGREEMENT

I. INTRODUCTORY REMARKS

Most of existing descriptions of Modern Standard Russian (e.g., Vinogradov 1947: 182, 291 ff.; Vinogradov et al. 1960: 312ff., 369ff.; Isačenko 1962) usually introduce three inflectional categories for (all or some) cardinal numerals, which they share with adjectives (Russian ordinal numerals being, from the grammatical viewpoint, simply adjectives): gender, number, and case.

(a) **Gender**: masculine, neuter, feminine. Only four Russian cardinal numerals differentiate gender at all: ODIN 'one', POLTORA 'one-and-a-half', DVA 'two', and OBA 'both'. But POLTORA and DVA do so only in the nominative and accusative cases (the latter when they do not modify animate nouns), and they differentiate materially only feminine vs. non-feminine (masculine and neuter have identical expression); OBA differentiates genders in all cases, but once again, has only two forms: feminine vs. non-feminine; finally, only ODIN materially differentiates all three genders, but that as with POLTORA and DVA, only in the nominative (and inanimate accusative): *odin* [masc], *odna* [fem], *odno* [neu]. Nevertheless, for uniformity of description, I consider POLTORA, DVA, and OBA to have separate neuter forms, which are always homonymous with masculine forms: thus, in *dva doma* 'two houses', *dva* = DVA$_{masc, nom}$, since DOM is masculine; but in *dva okna* 'two windows', with neuter OKNO, *dva* =

DVA$_{neu, nom}$. (In *dve izby* 'two peasant houses', we have, obviously, *dve* = DVA$_{fem, nom}$.)

(b) **Number**: singular, plural. Number is differentiated only in ODIN: *odin voz* 'one cart' vs. *odni sani* 'one sledge' (SANI is a plurale tantum). The plural form *odni* is used exclusively for automatic agreement with pluralia tantum, like SANI, ČASY 'watch' (literally, the plural form of ČAS 'hour'), OČKI 'eyeglasses', etc. Note that the absence of inflection in number is a constitutive characteristic of Russian cardinal numerals—unlike nouns denoting numbers, such as TYSJAČA 'thousand', MILLION 'million', all of which are inflected for number.[1]

(c) **Case**: nominative, accusative, genitive, dative, instrumental, prepositional.

Traditionally, Russian linguistics allows no other inflectional categories of cardinal numerals and adjectives. (Naturally, I exclude here such purely adjectival categories as attributiveness, which opposes short and long forms, or degrees of comparison.)

II. THE PROBLEM STATED

But the three aforementioned categories are insufficient for deep-morphological representation of Russian cardinal numerals and adjectives.[2] This becomes clear if we look at examples showing the simplest and most current types of Russian sentences:

(1) **a.** *Ja vižu ČETYRE*   *sosny* 'I see four pine trees'.
  b. *Ja vižu ČETYRËX*   *devušek* 'I see four girls'.
(2) **a.** *Ja vižu KRASIVYJ*   *dom* 'I see a beautiful house'.
  b. *Ja vižu KRASIVOGO* *junošu* 'I see a handsome youth'.

What should be the deep-morphological representations of the numerals and adjectives printed in capitals?

If we have nothing more than gender, number, and case, we can answer this question only as follows: in (1), we have ČETYRE$_{acc}$ 'four'; in (2), KRASIVYJ$_{masc,sg,acc}$ 'beautiful, handsome'. Then *četyre* and *četyrëx* are different forms of the same accusative case of the numeral ČETYRE, while *krasivyj* and *krasivogo* are different forms of the same accusative case of the adjective KRASIVYJ. This is the traditional answer.[3] But such a solution cannot be accepted in this precise formulation, for the following reasons:

The forms *četyre* and *četyrëx, krasivyj* and *krasivogo* are by no means in free variation. The choice between them is determined entirely by the animacy of the modified noun: with an inanimate noun, *četyre* and *krasivyj*; with an animate noun, *četyrëx* and *krasivogo*. So, if we accept that suspect forms are in the accusative, it follows that different forms of the same case are complementarily distributed depending on external context. But I refuse to admit that the choice of the FORM (or, more precisely, the MARKER) OF A CASE **c** within the wordform **w** of some lexeme L₁, i.e. within **w**(L₁), taken in a definite context, depends on some other wordform **w**(L₂) syntactically connected with **w**(L₁). The wordform **w**(L₂) may control only the choice for **w**(L₁) OF THE CASE ITSELF, never of its form; whereas the EXPRESSION of the chosen case **c**(**w**(L₁)) by a specific morphological MARKER, i.e. the choice of the case FORM, must be solely dependent upon the wordform **w**(L₁) as such. When I say 'dependent upon a wordform **w**', I mean dependent upon the following of its features:

(a) The grammemes that it expresses, other than the grammeme under discussion. (A grammeme is any elementary unit of grammatical meaning—roughly, a specific morphological value.) In particular, the marker of case **c** can express not only case but, at the same time, number (as with Russian nouns) or both number and gender (as with Russian adjectives).

(b) The type of its stem.

(c) The presence in it of some specific morphological markers, e.g., affixes. Thus consider the choice between -*aja* and -*yj* in (3):

(3) [*Stoit*] *krasiv***aja** *devuška* vs. *krasiv***yj** *junoša* 'A pretty girl/A handsome youth [is standing]'.

This choice is determined by the difference in the morphological values of the respective wordforms: *krasivaja* is 'fem, sg, nom' while *krasivyj* is 'masc, sg, nom'. A further example is the following choice between -*yj* and -*oj*:

(4) [*Stoit*] *krasiv***yj** *mužčina* vs. *molod***oj** *mužčina* 'A handsome man/ A young man [is standing]'.

Here the controlling factor is the type of the stem: with *krasiv-*, the stress is always on the stem (*krasívyj, krasívogo, krasívomu, . . .*), but with *molod-*, it falls on the ending (in all the full forms: *molodój, molodógo, molodómu, . . .*); -*yj* and -*oj* are distributed accordingly.

Suppose now that somebody argues against this and tries to convince me that, as a general rule, a case form may be selected according to the external context as well, i.e., in response to a different wordform. But if that were so, then it could be maintained that any forms of different syntactic cases are actually forms of the same case, distributed in accordance with different surface-syntactic contexts.[4] Thus the Russian wordforms *kamnja* [sg, gen] 'of the rock' and *kamnju* [sg, dat] 'to the rock' could be considered forms of the same case. *Kamnja* would be used when dependent on the prepositions *ot* 'from', *dlja* 'for', *u* 'by' etc., on nouns (*ves kamnja* 'weight of the rock'), on negated transitive verbs (*Ja ne vižu kamnja* 'I don't see the rock') etc.; and *kamnju* would be used when dependent on the prepositions *k* 'to', *po* 'along', *blagodarja* 'thanks to' etc., on verbs of the type *pridavat'* 'to impart', *prinadležat'* 'to belong' (*pridavat' kamnju* 'impart to the rock'), etc. Along these lines, one could even come to the far-fetched conclusion that, in any language, all syntactic cases are really a single case, whose various forms are determined by their syntactic context, i.e. by wordforms syntactically connected with the wordform under consideration. (To prevent misunderstandings, let it be clearly stated that, everywhere in this book, grammatical case is taken to be a SURFACE category, not to be confused with deep or semantically oriented cases as introduced and used in Charles Fillmore's case grammar.)

What has been said above can be stated as the PRINCIPLE OF EXTERNAL AUTONOMY OF CASE FORMS. This principle has been observed in linguistics, although implicitly, for a long time, at least in more or less obvious cases. Thus suppose that R is a nominal stem; $w_i(R)$ are wordforms with the stem R; c is a grammatical case; and $m_j(c)$ are morphs expressing the case c [m_j may express not only case but other grammemes as well, i.e. they may be CUMULATIVE markers]. Then the following must hold:

Principle of External Autonomy of Case Forms

(5) If a language displays two nominal wordforms $w_1(R)$ and $w_2(R)$ such that $w_1(R)$ contains $m_1(c)$ and $w_2(R)$ contains $m_2(c)$, then either $w_1(R)$ and $w_2(R)$ are in free variation, or the choice between $w_1(R)$ and $w_2(R)$ depends only upon their own properties [i.e., upon the grammemes that they express and/or the morphological processes that they include].

Remark 1

This is a simplified formulation of the principle in question: it does not mention a marginal phenomenon irrelevant for our purposes here. For a full formulation and more detailed discussion see Mel'čuk (1986: 53–56).

Remark 2

In requiring that the choice of a case marker within a wordform be independent from other wordforms, Principle (5) purposely abstracts from various phenomena of *Satzphonetik*, e.g., the purely phonological and morphonological transformations at wordform junctures or external sandhis. The variation of a case marker because of general sandhi rules (of the language in question) does not contradict Principle (5). Thus, in Sanskrit *Nalo nama* 'Nalas name', i.e. 'named Nalas', where *Nalo* < *Nal* + *as*, the nominative marker *-as* changes to *-o* before a voiced consonant beginning the immediately following wordform. In Sanskrit, however, ANY final *-as*, regardless of its morphological role, changes to *-o* before a voiced consonant, so that here we do not observe the choice of a case marker depending on other wordforms.

The principle of external autonomy of case forms is also not contradicted by such phenomena as the different case forms in the Russian pronouns ON 'he', ONA 'she', ONO 'it', and ONI 'they', which depend upon the presence or absence of a preposition or certain comparatives before the pronoun:

—*dala EMU* [dative] 'she gave him' vs. *spešila k NEMU* [dative] 'she rushed to him'.

—*sil′nee EGO* [genitive] 'stronger than he' vs. *vyše NEGO* [genitive] 'taller than he'.

Here the preceding wordform does not determine the choice of the case-marker, but rather the stem variant of the pronoun: /n′-/ after a preposition (or a specific comparative), and /j-/ elsewhere. The case marker remains the same: /-omu/ in the dative (/n′omú/, /jomú/, written *nemu, emu*), /-ovo/ in the genitive (/n′ovó/), /jovó/, written *nego, ego*). (Cf., however, a different description in Zaliznjak 1967: 52–54.) In addition, here a single phonetic wordform is formed by the preposition and the pronoun; i.e., this phenomenon is clearly related to *Satzphonetik*.

Remark 3

Principle (5) seems to lend itself to a still more general formulation. It might be true not only of grammatical case, but also of other grammemes marking surface-syntactic dependencies. Such a generalization, however, would require special research; therefore, I limit myself here to a more cautious statement.

Principle (5) means that, for a given stem, two different markers of the same case can be in the following relationship only:

(a) They may always replace one another, independent of context, without affecting meaning or grammaticality. For example, Russian *rukoj* vs. *rukoju* 'with the hand', *toboj* vs. *toboju* 'with you', [*s*] *molodoj* vs. [*s*] *molodoju* 'together with the young female one', where *-oj* and *-oju* are in free variation (with perhaps a slight stylistic difference). German *am Tag* vs. *am Tage* 'on the day' or *im Haus* vs. *im Hause* 'in the house', i.e., *-∅* vs. *-e*, also in free variation.

(b) They may be distributed depending upon something else within the same wordform: other grammemes expressed by it (e.g., Russian *-aja* vs. *-yj* in (3), *-aja* 'fem, sg, nom' vs. *-ye* 'pl, nom') or other morphological devices contained in it. (A hypothetical example might be as follows: **c** is marked with m_1 after a zero singular marker, and with m_2 after both the dual marker *-um* and the plural marker *-lar,* so that we get wordforms R + m_1 but R + *um* + m_2 and R + *lar* + m_2.)

If the choice between two case markers depends upon the surface-syntactic context of a wordform—upon its syntactic role with relation to some other wordform, or simply upon another wordform syntactically connected with it, i.e., upon something OUTSIDE it—then the two case markers belong to two different cases.

Perhaps it was Principle (5) that led Jakobson (1936) (following A.A. Šaxmatov and N.S. Trubetzkoy) to insist that the Russian wordforms like [*na*] *mostú* 'on the bridge', [*v*] *lesú* 'in the forest', [*v*] *kroví* 'in the blood', on the one hand, and [*nemnogo*] *čaju* 'a little tea', [*daj mne*] *saxaru* 'give me some sugar', on the other, are by no means mere 'variants' of the prepositional and the genitive cases, respectively, but forms of two separate cases in their own right: locative (or second prepositional) and partitive (or second genitive). Note the following pairs of examples (cf. Jakobson 1936: 62, 1958: 174):

(6) a. *Ne sleduet nastaivat' na ètom* $\left\{\begin{array}{l} \text{*}mostu \text{ [loc]} \\ moste \text{ [prep]} \end{array}\right\}$
     'One shouldn't insist on this bridge'.

   b. *Avarija proizošla na ètom* $\left\{\begin{array}{l} mostu \text{ [loc]} \\ \text{*}moste \text{ [prep]} \end{array}\right\}$
     'The accident happened on this bridge'.

(7) a. *pačka* $\left\{\begin{array}{l} čaja \text{ [gen]} \\ čaju \text{ [part]} \end{array}\right\}$ 'a pack of tea'

   b. *cvet* $\left\{\begin{array}{l} čaja \text{ [gen]} \\ \text{*}čaju \text{ [part]} \end{array}\right\}$ 'the color of tea'

(8) a. *nedostatok* $\left\{\begin{array}{l} čaja \text{ [gen]} \\ čaju \text{ [part]} \end{array}\right\}$ 'shortage of tea'

   b. *nedostatok* $\left\{\begin{array}{l} čaja \text{ [gen]} \\ \text{*}čaju \text{ [part]} \end{array}\right\}$ 'the defect of [this] tea'

(9) a. *On ne pil kon'jaku* [part] 'He did not drink cognac' (on a particular occasion).

   b. *On ne pil kon'jaka* [gen] 'He drank no cognac' (as a rule, e.g., since he did not like it).

Further examples include such phrases as *mesjac SROKU* [part] ⟨*sroka⟩ [gen] 'one-month term', lit. '[one] month of-term', *dva časa XODU* [part] ⟨*xoda [gen]⟩ 'two hours of-walking', *so STRAXU* [part] ⟨*straxa⟩ [gen] 'from fear', etc.[5]

Essentially, Principle (5) requires the following: if w_1 and w_2—two different case forms derived from the same nominal stem—are not in free variation, then their respective deep-morphological representations should be different. Observing Principle (5), we must make sure, in examples (1) and (2), that *četyre* (accusative form with inanimate noun) vs. *četyrëx* (accusative form with animate noun), as well as *krasivyj* vs. *krasivogo,* have DIFFERENT deep-morphological representations. It is at this point that the problem addressed in this chapter can be finally formulated:

(10) ‖ What is to be done to ensure that the DMorphRs of both numerals in (1a) vs. (1b) and of both adjectives in (2a) vs. (2b) be different?

III. ALTERNATIVE SOLUTIONS: ANIMACY VS. A SPECIFIC CASE

The question asked in (10) can be answered in one of two ways: either by introducing another inflectional category to distinguish members of the pairs under analysis, or by considering the members of each pair to be in different cases. Let us formulate both solutions in more precise terms, and then compare them.

SOLUTION I. We introduce for Russian cardinal numerals and adjectives a fourth inflectional category: **animacy,** composed of two grammemes: {an(imate), inan(imate)}. This solution was proposed by Zaliznjak (1967: 183–184, 187), apparently the first linguist to approach the problem of deep-morphological representation of adjectival and numeral forms in contexts like examples (1) and (2).[6] Then our forms are described at the deep-morphological level as follows:

(11) *četyre* = $\text{ČETYRE}_{\text{inan, acc}}$
      četyrëx = $\text{ČETYRE}_{\text{an, acc}}$
      krasivyj = $\text{KRASIVYJ}_{\text{masc, inan, sg, acc}}$
      krasivogo = $\text{KRASIVYJ}_{\text{masc, an, sg, acc}}$

SOLUTION II. We consider the adjective and the numeral in (1b) and (2b), respectively, to be in a special grammatical case different from the accusative; this could be called the animate-accusative case. Then we have:

(12) *četyre* = $\text{ČETYRE}_{\text{acc}}$
      četyrëx = $\text{ČETYRE}_{\text{an-acc}}$
      krasivyj = $\text{KRASIVYJ}_{\text{masc, sg, acc}}$
      krasivogo = $\text{KRASIVYJ}_{\text{masc, sg, an-acc}}$

Thus a new case will have to be added to the inventory of Russian grammatical cases—relevant, however, for adjectival and cardinal-numeral lexemes only.[7] Solution II was put forth as a tentative proposal in Es'kova et al. (1971).

Both solutions allow all the observable and relevant facts of Russian to be described in an exhaustive and consistent manner; the resulting descriptions are about equally complex. This gives us a typical case of non-uniqueness: the non-uniqueness of a morphological solution (cf. Mel'čuk 1971).

Yet an INFORMAL comparison of Solutions I and II allows us to make a principled choice. Solution I is preferable, since it fits in more closely with the overall characteristics of the Russian language as a whole, and corresponds better to the language's 'spirit' (whatever one means by the word).

IV. SEVEN ARGUMENTS TO SUPPORT THE ANIMACY SOLUTION

Let me list seven advantages of introducing the inflectional category of animacy for Russian numerals and adjectives, rather than an extra (= animate-accusative) case. First, I offer four arguments FOR THE INTRODUCTION OF ANIMACY.

Argument 1

Animacy in Russian cardinal numerals and adjectives happens to be quite similar, as a grammatical category, to grammatical gender, at least in the following three respects:

(a) Like gender, animacy is a component of the syntactics of nouns (in Zaliznjak's terms, it is a nominal "classifying category"), but an inflectional category for cardinal numerals and adjectives. (Nouns are MARKED in the lexicon for gender and animacy; cardinal numerals and adjectives are INFLECTED for gender and animacy, which they borrow from the nouns they modify.)

(b) Like gender, which in numerals is relevant only for four lexemes, animacy is morphologically relevant in numerals for a rather restricted number of lexemes: ODIN, DVA, TRI, ČETYRE, OBA and collective (or personal) numerals of the type DVOE, TROE etc. Other Russian cardinal numerals do not differentiate animacy morphologically, as they do not differentiate gender.

(c) Like gender, animacy in adjectives characterizes all the lexemes, but not in all the case-number forms: the opposition of the three genders is neutralized in the plural, and that between the masculine and the neuter in all the cases of the singular except the nominative and the accusative; in much the same way, the animacy opposition is neutralized in all cases except the accusative.

Argument 2

With the category of animacy present, Russian cardinals and adjectives agree with accusative nouns to an even greater extent: not only in gender, number and case, but also in animacy.

Argument 3

Russian nouns exhibit, in fact, TWO different animacy categories: morphological animacy, which is responsible for the accusative form of the noun (in morphologically animate nouns, the accusative form coincides with the genitive form; in morphologically inanimate nouns, with the nominative), vs. syntactic animacy, which controls the animacy in agreeing adjective and numeral lexemes which are syntactically dependent on the noun. Let us consider examples of all four possible combinations of morphological and syntactic animacy.

—MALČIK 'boy' is both morphologically and syntactically animate:

(13) *Ja vižu mal'čika, koto***rogo**[animate, because of *mal'čik*] *my vstretili včera*
'I see the boy whom we met yesterday'.

—ON 'he' is morphologically always animate, but its syntactic animacy depends on that of its antecedent:

(14) a. *Ja vižu ètot jaščik*[inanimate]; **ego**[= ON$_{acc}$] *privezli včera* **ves' razlomannyj**[inanimate] 'I see this box; they brought it yesterday all broken up'.
   b. *Ja vižu ètogo mal'čika*[animate]; **ego**[= ON$_{acc}$] *privezli včera* **vsego perepačkannogo**[animate] 'I see this boy; they brought him yesterday all dirtied up'.

—MEŠOK S DER'MOM 'bag of shit'[= 'a disgusting person'] is morphologically inanimate and syntactically animate:

(15) *Ja ne mogu videt' ètot mešok s der'mom* ⟨**ètogo meška s der'mom*⟩, *koto*rogo[animate] *ja dolžen opekat'* 'I can't stand that bag of shit I have to take care of'.

—JAŠČIK 'box' is both morphologically and syntactically inanimate:

(16) *Ja vižu jaščik, kotor***yj**[inanimate, because of *jaščik*] *my privezli včera* 'I see the box which we brought yesterday'.

A rather similar split of the animacy category is also observed in Russian cardinal numerals. Morphological animacy, as has been indicated, is relevant only for "small" numerals—up to PJAT' 'five'. Starting with PJAT', higher numerals do not distinguish animate and inanimate forms in the accusative:

(17) a. *Ja vižu desjat' jaščikov*[inanimate] 'I see ten boxes'.
   b. *Ja vižu desjat' mal'čikov*[animate] 'I see ten boys'.

Yet higher numerals are sensitive to syntactic animacy in the nouns they modify: a cardinal numeral is, so to speak, transparent to this animacy, and transfers it to the preceding adjective (if any) which syntactically depends on it (rather than on the noun):[8]

(18) a. *Ja vižu vse* ⟨*èti, moi*, . . .⟩/*vsex ⟨*ètix, moix*, . . .⟩ *desjat' jaščikov* 'I see all ⟨these, my, . . .⟩ ten boxes'.
   b. *Ja vižu vsex* ⟨*ètix, moix*, . . .⟩ /*vse ⟨*èti, moi*, . . .⟩ *desjat' mal'čikov* 'I see all ⟨these, my, . . .⟩ ten boys'.

Nothing comparable happens with Russian adjectives.

This should by no means be construed as a suggestion to introduce two different animacy categories for Russian numerals (as is done for Russian nouns). On the contrary, I am against such a suggestion. The point I am trying to emphasize here is that animacy in numerals is much like animacy in nouns: numerals have morphological animacy (exactly like adjectives) and some traces of syntactic animacy, which corresponds pretty well to the position of Russian cardinal numerals, intermediate between nouns and adjectives.

Argument 4
Introducing the inflectional category of animacy for Russian numerals helps provide a concise and elegant description of those "strange" constructions where a numeral phrase with an animate noun in the accusative, i.e. [Num + N]$_{(an)acc}$, appears in the inanimate form:

(19)　**a.** *V každuju palatu položili po* **troe bol'nyx** ⟨**troix bol'nyx*⟩ 'They put three patients in each room' [as opposed to . . . *položili* **troix bol'nyx** 'put three patients'].
　　b. *siloj v* **tri lošadi** ⟨**trëx lošadej*⟩, lit. 'with the power of three horses' [= 'three horsepower . . .'; as opposed to *Ja vižu* **trëx lošadej** 'I see three horses'].
　　c. *Kol'čuga stoit* **tri belki** ⟨**trëx belok*⟩ 'The chain mail costs three squirrels' [as opposed to *On pojmal* **trëx belok** 'He caught three squirrels'].

In these and many similar constructions, I postulate DISAGREEMENT in animacy between the numeral and the noun, which is triggered by a very restricted and specific class of contexts ('quantitative' prepositions and verbs, etc.); cf. Mel'čuk (1980a) and (1985: 183–184, 440ff). I see no satisfactory alternative to this analysis.

I will now cite three arguments AGAINST THE ANIMATE-ACCUSATIVE CASE.

Argument 5
The animate-accusative case would appear only in adjectival-type paradigms, i.e. in the paradigms of adjectives and cardinal numerals, but not in the paradigms of nouns. This situation seems inadequate from a typological standpoint: in natural languages, it is much more normal for nouns to differentiate more cases than adjectives or numerals; i.e., the noun may possess cases absent in the adjective and numeral, but not vice versa. Thus the Russian noun has a partitive, a locative and possibly an adnumerative,[9] which Russian adjectives and Russian numerals both lack. The introduction of an animate-accusative case in adjective and numeral paradigms would create a typologically suspicious precedent.

Argument 6
In Russian, all cases of nouns are determined by GOVERNMENT (of verbs, prepositions, adjectives, other nouns etc.); but all cases of adjectives are nor-

mally controlled by AGREEMENT with the nouns modified, namely by their "substantive" case. Yet all the adjectival cases can also be governed, even if rarely and in rather specific contexts—in particular, when an adjective is nominalized by ellipsis of the noun that it modifies (under referential identity): e.g., *On stal činit' sinij karandaš, a ja zanjalsja krasnym* 'He started sharpening the blue pencil while I was busy with the red [one]', where the instrumental of the adjective form *krasnym* 'red' is governed by the verb *zanimat'sja* 'be busy with'. The animate-accusative case would be the only exception in this respect: it can never be governed, its only possible source being the agreement with an $N_{(an)acc}$. This is because, basically, the animate-accusative would globally encode the governable accusative together with agreement-triggering animacy.

Argument 7

The animate-accusative would be the only partial case in Russian adjectives and numerals, i.e., the only case relevant for a mere SUB-class of a given nominal lexemic class, rather than for the whole class. Partial cases are characteristic of Russian nouns—e.g., the partitive, locative and adnumerative; but Russian adjectives and numerals possess no other partial case.

Arguments 1 through 7 force me to accept Solution I, i.e., Zaliznjak's proposal. Thus, my answer to (10) is as follows:

> A new category must be added to the traditional three inflectional categories of Russian numerals and adjectives, namely **animacy**, with two grammemes: animate, inanimate.

V. IMPORTANT RESIDUAL CASES

Two further problems remain to be discussed: 1) the relationship between animacy and other inflectional categories of Adj and Num in Russian, and 2) the relevance of animacy for Adj and Num lexemes. Let us take these in turn.

1. In What Inflectional Forms of Adj and Num is Animacy Relevant?

For numerals and adjectives (as for nouns), morphological animacy is relevant only in the accusative case: either for the masculine gender in the singular, or for all genders in the plural. But in order to achieve greater consistency and compactness of description, I choose to consider animacy relevant for ALL forms of the accusative in adjectives and numerals—although, materially, animate and inanimate forms are opposed in a more restricted situation, as stated above. This leaves us with homonymy of forms in the singular feminine and neuter:

(20)   **a.** *[Ja vižu] ODNU [komnatu]*   = $ODIN_{fem, inan, sg, acc}$
       b. *[Ja vižu] ODNU [devušku]*   = $ODIN_{fem, an, sg, acc}$
       c. *[Ja vižu] ODNO [otverstie]*   = $ODIN_{neu, inan, sg, acc}$
       d. *[Ja vižu] ODNO [čudovišče]*   = $ODIN_{neu, an, sg, acc}$

The description suggested is similar for all cardinal numerals characterized by animacy, and also for all adjectives.

I find no linguistic$_1$ evidence to substantiate this kind of treatment (as opposed to saying that *odnu* and *odno* are not marked for animacy at all, and must be represented as ODIN$_{fem,sg,acc}$ and ODIN$_{neu,sg,acc}$, respectively). But I feel that there is a helpful METHODOLOGICAL consideration to guide our choice in cases like this; it could be called THE PRINCIPLE OF SIMPLEST RESTRICTION (to be imposed upon the relevance of a given inflectional category).

Suppose that a given language possesses an inflectional category C_1 such that it is materially differentiated only in a proper subset Π' of all forms of a given paradigm Π. We have to choose between the following two alternatives: should we somehow single out Π' and declare C_1 relevant only for Π' and thereby make C_1 a partial category, or should we consider C_1 relevant for the whole Π, and thereby make all forms in the difference $\Pi - \Pi'$ homonymous in respect to C_1? To resolve this dilemma, I posit the following principle:

Principle of Simplest Restriction

(21) We should prefer to restrict the relevance of C_1 to Π' if and only if we can specify Π' in terms of (elements of) just one other inflectional category C_2; otherwise we should prefer to make C_1 relevant for the whole Π, thereby admitting homonymy into the difference $\Pi - \Pi'$.

Obviously, this principle should not be applied unwarily: it is not a rigorous criterion, but rather a guiding idea. (Among other problems, the extent to which homonymy might be tolerated is not stated explicitly.) In any event, my decision to take animacy in adjectives and numerals to be relevant in all forms of the accusative is in accordance with Principle (21): Π', here the accusative case, is specified in terms of just one inflectional category, i.e., the case.

Note that, with animacy of Russian adjectives and numerals restricted to the accusative case, we get an obvious asymmetry: the deep- and the surface-morphological (i.e., morphemic) representations of all adjective and numeral forms in the accusative would drastically differ from the respective representations for the rest of the cases; e.g.:

(22)   **a.** *krasivomu* [*junoše*] = KRASIVJ$_{masc,sg,dat}$ '(to a) handsome youth';
      b. [*Ja vižu*] *krasivogo* [*junošu*] = KRASIVYJ$_{masc,an,sg,acc}$ 'I see (a) handsome youth'.

Accordingly, on the surface-morphological (morphemic) level, we have:

(23)   **a.** {KRASIV-} $\oplus$ {MASC.SG.DAT}
      b. {KRASIV-} $\oplus$ {MASC.AN.SG.DAT}

However, this asymmetry cannot be taken as a counterargument. The fact is that such asymmetry is generally characteristic of Russian adjectives, since gender is not relevant for them in the plural:

(24)   **a.** *krasivomu [junoše]*   =   KRASIVYJ$_{\text{masc,sg,dat}}$ '(to   a)   handsome youth';

   b. *krasivym [junošam]*   =   KRASIVYJ$_{\text{pl,dat}}$ '(to) handsome youths'.

Correspondingly,

(25)   **a.** {KRASIV-} $\oplus$ {MASC.SG.DAT}
   b. {KRASIV-} $\oplus$ {PL.DAT}

2. For What Lexemes of Adj and Num is Animacy Relevant?

The animacy category is obviously relevant for all adjectives; i.e., every Russian adjective lexeme differentiates (in the accusative) the animate from the inanimate form. But what about numerals? As stated above, morphologically only ODIN, DVA, OBA, TRI, ČETYRE and the collective numerals reflect animacy. However, all of them convey animacy from the nouns they modify to the adjectives that modify them:

(26)   **a.** *Emu ne xotelos' vysekat'* **ètix** *dvenadcat´ apostolov* 'He had no desire to carve those twelve apostles'.

   b. *Maškov obrjadil* **vsex** *dvadcat' pjat' zaverbovannyx v standartnuju formu* 'Mashkov dressed up all twenty-five hired people in standard uniforms'.

To account for this phenomenon, I see the following three possibilities:

(a) We may generalize the animacy category to all the cardinal numerals and thus admit the homonymy of animate/inanimate forms in the majority of numerals. Then *dvenadcat'* in (26a) would be animate (because APOSTOL'apostle' is animate), but in *vysekat èti dvenadcat' figur* 'to carve these twelve figures', it would be inanimate (since FIGURA'figure' is inanimate).

(b) We may introduce two animacy categories for cardinal numerals (but not for adjectives), so that morphological animacy will be relevant only for lower and collective numerals, while syntactic animacy will characterize all the numerals, in order to ensure the correct description of constructions like (26).

(c) We may be satisfied with animacy in lower and collective numerals only, providing more sophisticated syntactic rules of adjective-numeral agreement for constructions like (26). Being context-sensitive, these rules could account for the construction in question by transferring the value of animacy directly from the noun modified by the numeral to the adjective, as in Figure 10-1.

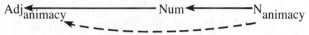

[Solid arrows show syntactic dependencies; the broken-line
arrow metaphorically represents the transfer of animacy.]
Figure 10-1

I strongly support solution (c). Since examples like (26) provide the only reason for creating overall homonymy or introducing a new category in Russian numerals, it seems much more natural to describe a purely syntactic complication by a specific syntactic rule. Otherwise this rather restricted and infrequent peculiarity of Russian syntax would spread over the whole of numeral morphology, where it does not belong at all. I believe that it is better to localize difficulties as much as possible, i.e., to try to overcome them with the most specific descriptive means possible. This is, in point of fact, another methodological principle—the Principle of Maximal Localization, which will be fully stated in the next chapter (p. 383).

But even beyond this general consideration, two concrete facts contribute to refuting solutions (a) – (b). First, note that (27a) is ungrammatical, while (27b–e) are correct:

(27) **a.** *On   vstretil   četyrëx   — pjat'   znakomyx
           he-NOM   meet-PAST   four-AN.ACC   five-ACC   acquaintance-PL.AC
           'He met four or five acquaintances'.

      b. On vstretil dvux   — trëx   znakomyx
                        two-AN.ACC   three-AN.ACC
           'He met two or three acquaintances'.

      c. On vstretil pjat   — šest'   znakomyx
                        five-ACC   six-ACC
           'He met five or six acquaintances'.

      d. On vstretil četveryx   — pjateryx
                        four.collective-AN.ACC   five.collective-AN.ACC
           znakomyx 'He met four or five acquaintances'.

      e. On vstretil četyre   — pjat'   mašin
                        four-INAN.ACC   five-ACC   car-PL.GEN
           'He met four or five cars'.

The restriction to be imposed on the Num_1 — Num_2 approximative construction, to preclude combinations like (27a), is obvious and natural:

(28) If Num_1 is animate, then Num_2 must also be animate.

Thus we get agreement of numerals in animacy. But had we accepted the animacy category for all numerals and therefore admitted that *pjat'* in (27a) is also animate, what would become of our elegant statement (28)? The only way out of the cul-de-sac, then, is to say the following:

(29) If both Num₁ and Num₂ are animate, and Num₁ is a lower or collective numeral, then Num₂ must also be a lower or collective numeral.

Compare (29) with (28) and make your choice! I feel that this takes care of solutions of type (a).

Second, quantitative phrases of the type illustrated in (30) are all ungrammatical:

(30) *Terroristy otpustili *vsex/*vse sto tridcat' četyre založnika* 'The terrorists released all 134 hostages'.

In Russian, even the lower numerals do not agree in animacy with the animate noun when they occur in a compound numeral. Thus Russian has:

(31) **a.** . . . *otpustili (sto) tridcat' četyre*[inan] ⟨**četyrëx*⟩ *založnika* '. . . released (1)34 hostages'

    vs.

    b. . . . *otpustili četyrëx*[an] ⟨**četyre*⟩ *založnikov*.

The head of a compound numeral that contains a lower numeral as its terminal component and modifies an animate noun does not allow as its own modifier either an animate or an inanimate adjective. In other words, phrases like 'release **all (these)** 134 ⟨23, 62, . . .⟩ hostages' cannot be rendered in Russian by an analogous structure because of the boldfaced adjectives.

If we take the numeral *sto* in (30) or *tridcat'* in (31a) to be syntactically animate, in accordance with solution (b), then we still must formulate an involved context-sensitive rule to state the ungrammaticality of (30). This rule will override the effect of syntactic animacy in numerals, and thus make it superfluous. So solution (b) seems also to be ruled out.

With all this in mind, I can now state the result of my ultimate analysis:

‖The inflectional category of animacy is relevant in the accusative case for all ‖Russian adjectives, but only for lower and collective numerals.[10]

NOTES

1. (I, p. 358.) Russian cardinal numerals constitute a special word-class, sharply distinguished by morphological and syntactic properties from nouns that denote numbers or sets of a given cardinality. Thus STO 'hundred' is a cardinal numeral, while SOTNJA '(a) hundred' or MILLION '(a) million' are nouns. Except for the four numerals ODIN,

POLTORA, DVA and OBA, cardinal numerals, as opposed to nouns, do not differentiate gender or number; they combine with quantified nouns in a specific way (whereas no 'numeral' noun does so); they participate in the so-called 'approximative' construction; etc. Cf. Mel'čuk (1985: 35 ff., 265–270).

2. (II, p. 358.) As stipulated in Chapter 2, pp. 69, 71, I suggest two levels of morphological representation for linguistic$_1$ items: a surface-morphological and a deep-morphological representation. To help the reader, I will illustrate them here once again.

First, the surface-morphological representation (SMorphR) of a wordform shows its morphemic composition:

(i) SMorphR(English *smiling*) – {SMILE} $\oplus$ {GER} / {SMILE} $\oplus$ {PRES.PART}
(ii) SMorphR(Russian *ulybajuščixsja* 'of those who smile') =
 {ULYB-} $\oplus$ {TH.E} $\oplus$ {PRES.ACT.PART} $\oplus$ {PL.GEN} $\oplus$ {REFL}

Here, {ULYB-} is the stem of *ulybat'sja* 'smile'; {TH.E} is the so-called "thematic" element (/aj/, /a/, /e/, /i/ etc.); {PRES.ACT.PART} is the present active participle suffix; {PL.GEN} is the genitive plural suffix; and {REFL} is the suffix of reflexivity.

Second, deep-morphological representation (DMorphR) of a wordform shows the corresponding lexeme and the values of all its grammatical variables (= its grammemes):

(iii) DMorphR(*smiling*) = SMILE$_{(V)ger / part,pres}$
(iv) DMorphR(*ulybajuščixsja*) = ULYBAT'SJA$_{(V)refl, part, pres, act, pl, gen}$

SMorphR characterizes essentially the physical shape and morphological structure of the item, while DMorphR reflects its semantic content and syntactic behavior.

3. (II, p. 358.) Let it be emphasized that, to the best of my knowledge, no standard description of Modern Russian published before 1980 formulates this answer explicitly, because the very question concerning the inflectional categories of forms *krasivyj* and *krasivogo* in contexts like (2) usually does not arise (the only exception known to me is Zaliznjak 1967: 83). The traditional answer as I tentatively formulate it is drawn from implicit information: above all, from full adjectival paradigms cited in various textbooks, where forms in *-yj* and *-ogo* are found in the row of the masculine singular accusative with no comment; and also from the complete failure to mention the problem. In particular, this problem is not brought up even in such basic reference works on Russian as Vinogradov (1947) or Isačenko (1962). More than that, Vinogradov et al. 1960: 312 bluntly says that "full adjectives are inflected for gender, number, and case"; the contrast *vižu krasivyj dom* vs. *krasivogo junošu* is totally ignored. The situation changed in 1980. Garde (1980: 206) indicates animacy (called **subgender**) as an agreement category of Russian adjectives and mentions its existence for "small" numerals (236–237); so does Švedova (1980: 545–546, 575–576).

4. (II, p. 359.) A syntactic case, as opposed to a semantic case, is one that marks exclusively passive surface-syntactic roles of a noun, but does not itself carry meaning. This means that a syntactic case is fully determined by the context. A typical syntactic case —more precisely, a typical syntactic case OCCURRENCE—is any instance of a strongly governed object or complement. For more details about the difference between syntactic and semantic cases, see in particular Mel'čuk (1977: 18–19) and (1986: 56ff., 60–61).

5. (II, after the examples (6) - (9), p. 362.) In connection with Principle of External Autonomy, let it be recalled that in Dyribal (cf. Chapter 4) personal pronouns have contrasting forms such as *ŋaḍa* [<*ŋay + da*] vs. *ŋayguna* (both from *ŋaḍa* 'I'). According to

Dixon (1972: 50), the first may refer only to the "semantic subject" of the action, the second only to the "semantic object". In my analysis, the first form is possible only as the grammatical subject of an intransitive verb, and the second one only as the grammatical subject of a transitive verb. In Dyirbal, all transitive verbs are CONVERSE with respect to their Indo-European semantic equivalents, so that the GS of a Dyirbal $V_{(tr)}$ expresses its "semantic object": Chapter 4, pp. 179ff.) Dixon considers ŋaḍa and ŋayguna to be forms of the same case, namely nominative, which are in complementary distribution depending on their syntactic role (1972: 60, 200). However, for me such a solution is excluded: Principle (5) requires us to assign ŋaḍa and ŋayguna to different cases, as I have done, considering ŋaḍa to be the nominative, and ŋayguna a special case called the pathetive. The form ŋaḍa represents as well the instrumental and can express the agentive complement of a transitive verb, but this is immaterial here.

6. (III, p. 363.) But cf. a brief remark in Vinogradov et al. (1960: 367) that anticipates Zaliznjak's solution (in the domain of numerals only): "The animacy category finds its expression only in numerals *dva, tri, četyre*, . . . However, these numerals are often excluded from this category when combined with names of animals . . . : *Pojmal dve rybki* '(He) caught two small fishes' etc."

7. (III, p. 363.) Note that, on purely formal grounds, the forms *četyrëx* and *krasivogo* could—within the framework of the 'case' solution—be relegated to the genitive case: cf. the genitive forms *u četyrëx devušek*, lit. 'at four girls' or *u krasivogo junoši*, lit. 'at a handsome youth'. However, the inadequacy of this approach seems quite obvious: if we take *četyrëx* in (1b) and *krasivogo* in (2b) to be genitive case-forms, then the rules for case agreement become unnecessarily involved—a genitive numeral and adjective would agree with an accusative noun, a phenomenon never observed elsewhere in Russian.

8. (IV, before example (18), p. 365.) Consider phrases like these:

(i) *moi* ⟨*èti*, . . .⟩ *desjat' knig* 'my ⟨these, . . .⟩ ten books';
(ii) *desjat' moix* ⟨*ètix*, . . .⟩ *knig* 'ten of my ⟨these, . . .⟩ books'.

These are obviously different in form and in meaning: (i) refers to a DEFINITE set of books that must have been specified for both interlocutors before, and implies that I have no other books, at least in the situation under discussion; but (ii) denotes SOME ten books, probably out of a larger stock of my books, and therefore does not carry the implication of (i). That is why I choose to say that in (i) the adjective is syntactically dependent on the numeral, but in (ii) on the noun. In spite of the importance of the problem, I cannot substantiate my proposal in this book; cf. Mel'čuk (1985: 95–98, 102).

9. (IV, Argument 5, p. 366.) A hypothetical adnumerative case in Russian might be postulated for a few nouns, in order to account for such forms as *časá* or *šagá* in *dva časá* ⟨*šagá*⟩ 'two hours ⟨steps⟩', the genitive of respective nouns being *čása, šága*. For more about this case see Mel'čuk (1985: 435–436).

10. (At the very end of the text.) For animacy in Russian, see now the comprehensive work Klenin (1983).

Chapter **11**

THE GRAMMATICAL CASE OF THE NUMERICAL EXPRESSION IN RUSSIAN PHRASES OF THE TYPE (*BOL'ŠE*) *NA DVA MAL'ČIKA* OR *PO TROE BOL'NYX*: A PROBLEM OF GOVERNMENT

Kiberdvornik djadja Fedja,
Siloj rovno **v tri medvedja**,
[Iz svoej prjamoj kiški
Polivaet kamuški!]
'Uncle Fedya,
Our **three bear-power** robot janitor,
[Is watering pebbles
From his straight hose ⟨or: his rectum⟩!']
A. and B. Strugackij, *Polden'*.
XXII vek ['Noon. 22nd Century'],
Moscow, 1975: 118.[1]

I. CONSTRUCTIONS WITH "DIFFICULT" CASE FORMS

Let me refer to any expression of the type "numeral + noun" as a Numerical Expression (NE). Now, consider the following type of Russian prepositional phrases comprising a NE:

(1) **a.** [*siloj rovno*] *v tri medvedja* 'with the power of exactly three bears' ['three bear-power . . .'];

    b. [*bol'še*] *na dva mal'čika* 'two boys more';

    c. [*Apel'siny končilis'*] *za četyre čeloveka* [*do menja*] 'The organges ran out four people ahead of me' [speaking of a waiting line].

    d. [*On stojal v očeredi*] *čerez četyre čeloveka* [*ot menja*] 'He stood in line four people away from me'.

    e. *po troe bol'nyx* [*v palatu*] 'three patients in each room';

    f. *dve ženy tomu nazad* 'two wives ago'.

A prepositional phrase of the type illustrated in (1) consists of a preposition (belonging to a very small subset of all Russian prepositions) and a numerical expression.

The preposition is one of the following five: VI 'in', NAI 'on', ZAI 'behind', ČEREZ 'through, away' and POIII 'each' [the Roman numeral I is used here to distinguish the directional prepositions governing the accusative from their locative counterparts governing the locative case; the numeral III marks the distributive sense of PO]; instead of a preposition, there can also be the complex postposition TOMU NAZAD 'ago', also governing the accusative. All these lexemes have—in the contexts such as in (1)—a specific "quantitative" meaning: they obviously imply quantity, measurement and the like. I will call them for short "quantitative" prepositions.

The numerical expression NE, in its turn, includes:

—Either a "small" numeral Num (DVA 'two', TRI 'three', ČETYRE 'four'), or a personal-cardinal numeral (also called collective numeral: DVOE, TROE, . . .).

—An animate noun.

In what follows we will be interested exclusively in such NEs because they have distinct nominative and accusative forms: *Dva mal'čika*[nominative] *prišli* 'Two boys came' vs. *Ja vižu dvux mal'čikov*[accusative] 'I see two boys', and that presents a problem (see immediately below). NEs with Num from PJAT' 'five' on or with an inanimate noun do not present the same problem, since they do not have distinct nominative and accusative forms: [*V ètom lesu živut*] *pjat' medvedej*[nominative] 'In this forest, there live five bears', [*siloj v*] *pjat' medvedej*['difficult' case form] 'five bear-power . . .' and [*Ja vižu*] *pjat' medvedej*[accusative] 'I see five bears'; or [*V ètom lesu rastut*] *tri sosny*[nominative] 'In this forest, there grow three pine trees', [*vysotoj v*] *tri sosny*['difficult' case form] 'three pine trees high' and [*Ja vižu*] *tri sosny*[accusative] 'I see three pine trees'.

II. THE PROBLEM STATED

The following question can be (and in fact has often been) asked:

(2) What is the grammatical case of the Russian NE in the phrases of type (1)?

Since, generally speaking, the prepositions in (1) govern the accusative case, the traditional answer to question (2) is that numerical expressions in phrases of type (1) are in the accusative; in other words, that in (1) we have the following:

case(*tri medvedja*) = acc;
case(*dva mal'čika*) = acc;
and so on.

As an example of this answer one may consult Vinogradov (1947: 694, item 19).

There is, however, a catch to this simple answer. It is a well-known fact that Russian NEs of the type shown in (1), when in standard accusative contexts, such as the direct object of a transitive verb, must have a different form from that in (1):

(3)   **a.**   *Oxotnik ubil ètix trëx medvedej* ⟨**èti tri medvedja*⟩ 'The hunter killed these three bears in the Zabaikalye Region' [cf. (1a)].

   b.   *V naš klass prinjali eščë ètix dvux mal'čikov* ⟨**eščë èti dva mal'čika*⟩ 'The administration admitted also these two boys to our class' [cf. (1b)].

   c.   *Vrač osmotrel troix bol'nyx* ⟨**troe bol'nyx*⟩ 'The doctor examined three patients' [cf. (1e)].

   d.   *On očen' ljubil svoix dvux žën* ⟨**svoi dve ženy*⟩ 'He loved his two wives very much' [cf. (1f)].

If the above answer is to be accepted, one must assume that a Russian NE of the type under discussion (i.e., consisting of a 'small' or personal-cardinal Num plus an animate N) can have two distinct forms in the accusative, the choice between them being determined exclusively by the surface-syntactic context of this NE. Thus, the NE TRI MEDVEDJA would have two different accusative forms:

trëx medvedej vs. *tri medvedja*.

The first form appears as the direct object of a transitive verb, as well as in a number of other contexts; while the second appears only in the role of a complement to the said prepositions in special 'quantitative' contexts.

However, the proposal that different forms for a single grammatical case of a given nominal expression may be conditioned only by its EXTERNAL surface-syntactic (SS-) context, is unacceptable: it contradicts the Principle of External Autonomy of Case Forms, postulated in Chapter 10, p. 360.

III. ALTERNATIVE SOLUTIONS:
NOMINATIVE VS. INANIMATE ACCUSATIVE

Accepting Principle of External Autonomy of Case Forms almost automatically implies the following two competing solutions to the problem stated in (2) (I omit several trivially recoverable logical links).

SOLUTION I: In a phrase such as *v tri medvedja, na dva mal'čika* and *po troe bol'nyx*, the NE is in the NOMINATIVE case (the 'counter-traditional' solution).

SOLUTION II: In a phrase of this type, the NE is in the accusative case, but between Num and the animate N ANIMACY NON-AGREEMENT takes place, i.e., Num here remains inanimate, the animacy of the noun notwithstanding. It is this circumstance that gives rise to such expressions as *tri medvedja* instead of *trëx medvedej* (the 'protraditional' solution).[2]

Under Solution II, the selection of the correct accusative form for a Russian NE of type (1) is determined not by its external context, but rather by an internal property of this NE: the agreement or lack of agreement of Num with N according to animacy. Only this last property of NEs directly depends on their external context (in particular, on the presence of 'special' prepositions).

I adopt Solution II. The reasons for my choice are offered below; the consequences of each solution are stated and compared.

The primary consideration in favor of Solution I is its simplicity. In order to surmount all the obstacles involved in giving the numerical expressions in (1) the right form, it suffices to assume that five Russian prepositions (*v, na, za, čerez, po*), when used in highly specific 'quantitative' senses, and the postposition *tomu nazad* may govern the nominative. The NEs at issue will then simply be assigned the nominative case by the syntactic component of Russian grammar, and the morphological characteristics of their constituents will be determined by the very same rules which apply to all Russian NEs in the nominative.

It turns out, however, that the matter is far more complicated. A more careful analysis of all the relevant phenomena reveals several arguments against Solution I. None of them is decisive, since they each can be challenged, with varying degrees of difficulty. Taken as a whole, however, it seems that these arguments bear convincing witness to the advantages of the second, 'pro-traditional' solution. In order to maintain Solution I, assumptions that are overly cumbersome and unnatural would need to be made. These assumptions are presented below (see p. 385), after the arguments in favor of Solution II, in as far as that they represent the converse of those arguments.

IV. FOUR ARGUMENTS IN FAVOR OF THE ACCUSATIVE SOLUTION

In increasing order of significance, I will discuss four arguments against Solution I, and hence in favor of Solution II.

Argument 1

The nominative case in Russian may not be governed by a preposition. This statement is a generally accepted META-STATEMENT about Russian (i.e., a statement about existing descriptions of Russian), and as such merits serious consideration. From a purely intuitive point of view, it seems convincing, and the possibility that it reflects certain fundamental properties of Russian—some kind of principle corresponding to its 'spirit'—should not be excluded. (Despite the informality and the elusiveness of the concept 'spirit of a language', it is, in my opinion, extremely important.)

However, the thesis that the nominative after prepositions is precluded (in Russian) is neither self-evident, nor strictly proven. Moreover, it rests (psychologically, if not logically) on the thesis of absolute syntactic independence for the nominative—in the study of Russian it has always been traditionally assumed that N_{nom} may not depend syntactically on anything, i.e., that the nominative case is in general never syntactically governed. However, this more general thesis is simply false. I cite a number of facts that contradict the absolutely ungoverned status of the Russian nominative in a separate *Excursus*, which concludes this chapter, pp. 386 ff. (It is better to relegate all the data concerning the syntactic dependencies of nominative noun phrases in Russian to the Excursus because, on the one hand, these data are of independent interest and deserve independent discussion, while, on the other hand, they are peripheral with respect to the major logical line of this inquiry.) This Excursus disproves the thesis that N_{nom} in Russian never depends syntactically on anything, and it thereby weakens the asssertion that the nominative case can never follow a preposition.

Nevertheless, it remains an argument. In point of fact, there is not a single known example of the Russian nominative being dependent on a preposition that is completely beyond dispute; expressions such as in (5) do not exist:[3]

(5) **v (odna) tonna* 'in one ton', **na (odna) sanitarka* 'on one nurse', **čerez (odna) nedelja* 'in one week'.

Argument 2

A subclass of NEs after several "quantitative" prepositions (in phrases of type (1)) *are obviously in the accusative.* More specifically, if the numerical expression after the prepositions VI, NAI, ZAI and ČEREZ (but not POIII) contains the Num ODIN 'one' or a compound Num ending in ODIN (such as DVADCAT′ ⟨TRIDCAT′ . . .⟩ ODIN 'twenty-one ⟨thirty-one, . . .⟩'), then this NE is obligatorily in the accusative case:

(6) [*siloj*] *v odnu lošad′* ⟨*v odnogo medvedja*⟩ 'one horse-⟨bear-⟩power . . .' ['with the power of one horse ⟨bear⟩'];
[*vesom*] *v dvadcat′ odnu tonnu* ⟨*v dvadcat′ odnogo medvedja*⟩ 'having a weight of twenty-one tons ⟨bears⟩';

[*bol'še*] *na odnu delegatku* ⟨*na odnogo mal'čika*⟩ 'one lady delegate ⟨one boy⟩ more';
[*Oni stojali*] *čerez odnogo čeloveka* [*ot menja*] 'They stood one man away from me'.

The situation is identical, if in the contexts of (1) or (6), the N has no overt numeral modifier at all (in which case the sense of 'one' is understood):

(7) [*siloj*] *v lošad'* ⟨*v medvedja*⟩ 'one horse-⟨bear-⟩ power . . .'; [*vesom*] *v tonnu* 'having a weight of one ton'.

Once we admit that the NEs in (1) are in the nominative case, we have to accept that the Russian prepositions Vɪ, NAɪ, ZAɪ and ČEREZ, taken in a single sense and in a single type of context, govern two different cases: either the accusative, if N is not quantified at all or has a modifying quantifier ending with the numeral ODIN; or the nominative otherwise, i.e., if N is modified by a numeral not ending with ODIN.

Such multiple governement of Russian quantitative prepositions is an undesirable consequence of Solution I and therefore constitutes an argument against it. If, indeed, some NEs in phrases of type (1) are in the accusative beyond doubt, then it would be far more elegant to say that all NEs in strictly the same context are in the accusative as well—especially since we have no explanation for this being not so.

However, Argument 2 is not too cogent. The trouble is that there are no general grounds to ban multiple prepositional government of the kind implied by Solution I. No logical considerations prevent a preposition, taken in a specific sense, from governing different cases of a dependent NP as a function of the internal structure of the latter. Moreover, such a situation does actually exist in Russian: the preposition POɪɪɪ governs three different cases in the same ('distributive') sense: it takes either the dative—for a N without Num or with a Num ending in ODIN, or the accusative (or the putative nominative?)—for a N accompanied by any other Num; if Num is "large" (from *pjat'* 'five' on), the genitive is also possible (in free variation with the accusative):

(8) **a.** *po (odnomu) čeloveku, po (dvadcat' odnoj) tonne, po času,* . . . 'one person each, twenty-one tons each, an hour each, . . .'[dative];

   b. *po dva čeloveka, po tri tonny, po pjat' rublej* ⟨*čelovek,* . . .⟩ 'two persons each, three tons each, five rubles ⟨persons⟩ each, . . .'[accusative];

   c. *po pjati rublej* ⟨*čelovek*⟩, *po soroka kopeek,* . . . 'five rubles ⟨persons⟩ each, forty kopecks each, . . .'[genitive].

Therefore, we cannot simply dismiss Solution I only because it entails multiple government of several "quantitative" Russian prepositions. Nevertheless, this multiple government remains an undesirable property and constitutes some weight on the balance against Solution I. And POⅢ does not provide sufficient counterweight since it is dissimilar to "quantitative" prepositions in too many respects.

First, the preposition PO governs both the dative (*Oni razošlis' po domam* 'They dispersed to their homes') and the accusative (*po pojas v vode* 'up to one's waist in water') independently of the Num + N construction (true, it does so in two different senses); whereas the hypothetical dual government of the prepositions VI, NAI and so forth (accusative vs. nominative) arises only in the presence of a "small" numeral. Consequently, the grammatical-case problem posed by constructions of type (1) is more likely connected with Num than with the preposition; therefore, a solution that localizes the exotic quality of these constructions in the numeral (i.e., Solution II: nonagreement of Num and N in animacy in particular contexts) seems to be more logical; cf. the Principle of Maximal Localization below, on p. 383.

Second, only after POⅢ so many odd case variants are possible, as seen in *po tonne*[dative] vs. *po tri tonny*[accusative] vs. *po pjat'sot*[accusative]/*pjatisot* [genitive] *tonn* ⟨**po pjatisot/pjatistam*[dative] *tonnam*⟩; only after it do the adverbs MNOGO 'many', SKOL'KO 'how many', and NESKOL'KO 'several' allow a special form in -*u*: *po mnogu, po skol'ku, po neskol'ku*; only after POⅢ is the conjunction of two numerals in different cases possible—a phenomenon which is extremely atypical for Russian conjunction in any other circumstances: *po odnomu*[dative]—⟨*ili*⟩ *dva*[accusative] *čeloveka* 'one or two people each', *po odnoj*[dative]—⟨*ili*⟩ *dve*[accusative] *posetitel'nicy* 'one or two female visitors each'.

Third, only POⅢ (but no other 'quantitative' preposition) can introduce a grammatical subject or direct object: *V každuju komnatu vošlo* **po čeloveku** [subject] 'One person walked into each room' or *Deti s"eli* **po jabloku**[direct object] 'The children ate an apple each'; cf. below, (23a).

To put it bluntly, the preposition POⅢ is quite unique in Russian and its properties should not be taken as a model when judging of "quantitative" prepositions.

Summing up the contradictory evidence presented so far, I conclude that the presumed multiple government of VI, NAI, etc. in contexts of (1) argues against Solution I, although not very forcefully.

Argument 3

"Questionable" case forms for numerical expressions (with non-agreement in animacy between the numeral and the noun) *are possible not only in the context of "quantitative" prepositions VI, NAI, ZAI and ČEREZ, but in the role of direct object as well.*

In the following five instances, "questionable" forms of the numerical expression may occur as direct objects of transitive verbs:

1) A "small" Num is the final (rightmost) component of a compound number:

(9) **a.** *Ona obslužila včera (sto)* **dvadcat' dva klienta** ⟨**dvadcat' dvux kli-entov*⟩ 'She served (a hundred) twenty-two clients yesterday'.
b. *Ona obslužila včera* **dvux klientov** ⟨**dva klienta*⟩ 'She served two clients yesterday'.

2) A Num + N phrase appears as a complement to a "quantitative" verb to indicate quantity, price, etc.:

(10) **a.** *Uroven' zagružennosti personala prevyšaet* **tri čeloveka** ⟨**trëx če-lovek/ljudej*⟩ *v čas* 'The staff work load is greater than three people per hour'.
b. *Kol'čuga stoit* **dve belki** ⟨**dvux belok*: if (10b) is simply a statement of the price⟩ 'The chain mail costs two squirrels'.
c. *On zaplatil za ètu jurtu* **tri ovcy** ⟨**trëx ovec*⟩ 'He paid three sheep for this yurt'.

3) A Num + proper name phrase appears with a verb of (visual?) perception (and the two different forms of the NE contrast semantically):

(11) *On uvidel srazu* **tri Kati** 'He saw three Katyas at once' [three representations of one and the same girl]
vs.
On uvidel srazu **trëx Kat'** 'He saw three Katyas at once' [three different girls with the same first name].

Note, however, that with the great majority of transitive verbs of the type *tri Kati* are not possible as direct objects:

(12) **Emu neobxodimo poslat' èti tri Kati* [even on the reading 'three representations of Katya'; in both senses, the phrase should read: . . . *ètix trëx Kat'*] 'It is necessary to send him these three Katyas'.

4) An N refers to a (living) being prepared as a foodstuff, or to a dish made from this being:

(13) **a.** *On zakazal* **tri cyplënka tabaka** 'He ordered three tabaka chickens'.
b. *Im podali* **dve indjuški s jablokami** 'They were served two turkeys with apples'.

5) A Num + N phrase is used non-referentially (and moreover certain factors facilitating the appearance of a "questionable" case form are present in the sentence):

(14) **a.** *Im privozili každyj den'* **tri korovy** 'They were brought three cows each day'.

b. *Udačlivyj rybak berët za čas* **dve-tri ščuki** 'A lucky fisherman will catch two or three pikes in an hour'.

c. *Každyj iz nix deržit doma* **dve ili tri sobaki** 'Each of them has two or three dogs at home'.

d. *Vožd' možet imet'* **celyx četyre ženy,** *a rjadovoj voin—tol'ko dve* 'A chief may have as many as four wives, but a rank-and-file soldier is allowed only two'.

If Solution I is accepted for constructions of type (1), then we would have to claim that the phrase Num + N is in the nominative in (9)–(14) as well for our description to be consistent. It would then turn out that all (or, in any case, a significant portion of) transitive verbs in Russian sometimes govern the accusative, and sometimes the nominative for direct objects, and that the choice of the case depends on the semantic contents of the direct object and its internal syntactic structure. Are we prepared to accept such a conclusion?

The notion that the case of a verbal object or complement be dependent on its own characteristics (in particular semantic ones: referentiality, definiteness, partiality, etc.) is, in and of itself, entirely plausible typologically. Thus, in Turkic languages, the direct object is marked by the accusative case if it indicates a definite entity (the only conceivable in the given situation), and by the nominative otherwise. In Estonian the genitive case is used for definite direct objects (totally involved by the action) in the singular, the nominative for the same objects in the plural, and the partitive for indefinite or mass objects. Even in Russian itself analogous facts are completely typical:

(15) a. —*Prinesi* **vino**[acc]*!* 'Bring the wine!' [definite, known to speaker and hearer]

vs.

—*Prinesi* **vina**[part]*!* 'Bring some wine!'

b. *Ja ne vižu* **Kolju**[acc] 'I can't see Kolya' [Kolya is here, but something prohibits my seeing him: someone hid him or my eyes are not functioning properly]

vs.

Ja ne vižu **Koli**[gen] [Kolya is, in all probability, not here].

(Cf. also Chapter 6, Definition 6, pp. 258 ff., on the choice of case for the grammatical subject as a function of the semantic characteristic of the latter.)

But as far as the numerical expressions in (9)–(14) are concerned, there are at least two difficulties in the way of admitting the nominative for them. First, in Modern Standard Russian an unambiguously nominative case never serves as a marker of the direct object (which was possible in Old Russian and is possible even now in North Russian dialects: cf. Section V below, item 6, page 391).

Second, "questionable" case forms are only possible with "small" numerals. This fact compels me to try to localize all the difficulties connected with describing type (1) constructions within the numerals themselves. I consider it judicious to observe the following methodological principle:

Principle of Maximal Localization

Let there be a linguistic$_1$ phenomenon **p** and its two competing descriptions $D_1(\mathbf{p})$ and $D_2(\mathbf{p})$; **p** is implied by the class **U** of certain linguistic$_1$ units (i.e., **p** is admissible or obligatory only in the presence of **U** units).

(16) | In choosing between descriptions $D_1(\mathbf{p})$ and $D_2(\mathbf{p})$, we should prefer the one that is based on units of class **U** and touches on as few units of other classes as possible.

In other words, I propose to consider the best that description of a phenomenon **p** that maximally concentrates all its complexity and 'strangeness' in, so to speak, the nearest neighborhood of **p**, hereby avoiding, as far as possible, to involve distant levels of the language.

In the present instance, the Principle of Maximal Localization demands Solution II: the "questionable" case forms are implied by the presence of the "small" numerals; consequently, it is better to link all the difficulties in the description of these forms to the behavior of the numerals (by having enumerated the standard situations where there is no agreement of Num in animacy with the quantified N) than to permit the problem to escalate to all transitive verbs in Russian. It is more natural to account for the specific forms of a NE like *(privozili) tri korovy* '[they] used to bring three cows' and *(arestovali) dvadcat' dva demonstranta* '[the police] arrested twenty-two demonstrators' (instead of *trëx korov* and **dvadcat' dvux demonstrantov*) in a description of the surface syntax of the Russian numerals, rather than in a description of the surface syntax of Russian transitive verbs. For these reasons, I consider facts of the type in (9)–(14) to constitute a serious argument in favor of Solution II.

Argument 4

A postposed adjective in the nominative case is impossible with Num + N phrases in contexts of the type in (1):

(17) **a.** *Naša kompanija uveličilas' na tri studenta, *perevedënnye* [should read: . . . *perevedënnyx*] *so vtorogo kursa* 'Our group was augmented by three students transferred from the second year'.

  b. . . . *siloj v tri medvedja, xorošo *raskormlennye i otdoxnuvšie* [should read: . . . *raskormlennyx i otdoxnuvšix*] 'with the strength of three well-fed and rested bears'.

  c. *Každomu dali v pomoščnicy po dve sanitarki, *prislannye* [should read: . . . *prislannyx*] *iz goroda* 'As assistants, each was given two nurses, sent from the city'.

There is, however, an exception:

    d. *Im podali po dve indjuški, zažarennye ⟨zažarennyx⟩ v duxovke* 'They were each served two turkeys roasted in an oven',

where the postposed adjective may be (and even is preferred) in the nominative. This is possible only if in the Num + N phrase the noun denotes a dish prepared from a being.

At the same time, if a Num + N phrase appears as the grammatical subject, i.e., it is unambiguously in the nominative, a postposed adjective, dependent on that N, may either be in the nominative or the genitive (the choice has to do with the grammatical number of the main verb and is determined, in the final analysis, by the communicative structure of the sentence, in particular, by the division into 'old' and 'new' information):

(18)   **a.** *Tri studenta, perevedënnye so vtorogo kursa, ne byli dopuščeny k èkzamenu* 'The three students transferred from the second year were not let into the exam'.

    or

    K èkzamenu ne bylo dopuščeno tri studenta, perevedënnyx so vtorogo kursa 'Three students transferred from the second year were not let into the exam'.

  b. *Tri medvedja, raskormlennye i otdoxnuvšie, rezvilis' v vol'ere* 'The three bears, well-fed and rested, romped in the open-air cage'.

    or

    V vol'ere rezvilos' tri medvedja, raskormlennyx i otdoxnuvšix 'There were three well-fed and rested bears romping in the open-air cage'.

  c. *V bol'nice rabotali dve sanitarki, prislannye iz goroda* 'The two nurses, sent from the city, worked in the hospital'.

    or

    V bol'nice našlos' vsego dve sanitarki, prislannyx iz goroda 'In the hospital, there were only two nurses sent from the city'.

However, if a NE Num + N appears (in this same "questionable" form!) as a direct object, postposed adjectives cannot be in the nominative:

(19)   *Oni prinjali dvadcat' tri studenta, perevedënnyx ⟨*perevedënnye⟩ so vtorogo kursa* 'They accepted 23 students transferred from the second year'.

Items (17)–(19) provide evidence that [*na*] *tri studenta* and all the similar NEs are, as I propose, in the accusative, not the nominative, i.e., they argue again in favor of Solution II.

Unfortunately, however, Argument 4, like the previous ones, is inconclusive. One might attempt to reject it, asserting that in (17) a special case of agreement between the postposed adjective and N_{nom}, occurring in specific environments (after "quantitative" prepositions, for example), is observed. A similar assertion is by no means absurd, for there do exist in Russian context-dependent restrictions on the agreement of a postposed adjective with its head N in a Num + N phrase. These have just been demonstrated in the examples of (18). Thus, if the main verb is in the singular and precedes its Num + N subject (the subject is 'new'), then a postposed adjective most likely bears the genitive case:

(20)   **a.**   *U nas v gruppe pojavilos' tri studenta, perevedënn*yx ⟨?*perevedënn*ye⟩ *so vtorogo kursa* 'There appeared in our class three students who had been transferred from the second year'.

   b.   *V bol'nice našlos' vsego dve sanitarki, prislann*yx ⟨?*prislann*ye⟩ *iz goroda* 'In the hospital, there were only two nurses sent from the city'.

There is also a correlation between the grammatical cases of a preposed and a postposed adjective depending on the same N in a Num + N phrase; as a rule (although this too is not without exception), these cases must be identical. By analogy with the similar dependencies of the case of a postposed adjective on its environment, it is also possible to acknowledge the nominative in phrases of the type in (17). To do so, it would be sufficient to stipulate that if a N_{nom} depends on a "quantitative" preposition (in such contexts as in (1)), then the postposed adjective dependent on it is obligatorily in the genitive case.

However, in all other instances where the case of a postposed adjective in a nominative Num + N phrase is context-dependent, the genitive is at least more desirable (the nominative remaining possible), whereas in (17a–c) and (19) the genitive is the only case possible—precisely as with a N in the accusative.

To sum up, if we were to adopt Solution I and consider the Numerical Expression of the type *tri medvedja* in the context of the type *siloj rovno v . . .* to be in the nominative, then we would have to make the following four assumptions about Russian:

1. The nominative may follow a preposition, although this only occurs in type (1) situations.
2. A preposition appearing in the same environment and having the same meaning may exhibit double case government (nominative and accusative), although this only occurs in the presence of the "small" numerals DVA 'two', TRI 'three', and ČETYRE 'four' in the governed phrase.
3. A significant proportion of transitive verbs may govern their direct objects not only in the accusative, but in the nominative as well, although this only occurs when the direct object contains a "small" numeral.
4. Agreement between a postposed adjective and a NE_{nom} may vary in accordance with the surface-syntactic role of this NE_{nom}: if it is a subject, then the adjective may be either in the nominative or the genitive; if, however, it is the complement to a "quantitative" preposition, then the adjective is obligatorily in the genitive (once again, only when the NE contains a "small" numeral).

(These are the undesirable assumptions that were mentioned earlier, on p. 377.)

It seems that all that has been said above permits to answer question (2), as posed in the very beginning of the chapter:

> The numerical expression *tri medvedja* in the context *siloj rovno v* . . . is in the accusative case; the difference between the form *tri medvedja* and another accusative form *trëx medvedej* (as in the context of the verb *vižu* 'I see', etc.) is explained by the fact that in the latter instance the numeral TRI agrees with MEDVED' in animacy, whereas in the former it does not.

In other words, we have the following deep-morphological representations for the two accusative forms *tri medvedja* vs. *trëx medvedej*:

(21) [*siloj rovno v*] $\text{TRI}_{\text{inan,acc}}$ $\quad \text{MEDVED}'_{\text{(an)sg,gen}}$

vs.

[*vižu*] $\qquad\quad \text{TRI}_{\text{an,acc}}$ $\quad\;\; \text{MEDVED}'_{\text{(an)pl,acc}}$

The rules for establishing morphological correspondences between N and Num inside numerical expressions are, basically, surface-syntax rules, and they take into consideration the external surface-syntactic environment of the NE: for example, with prepositions like VI, NAI, ZAI, and ČEREZ (in "quantitative" senses), numerals remain inanimate even if the N is animate; exactly the same situation obtains, if N denotes a being prepared as food (i.e., a dish); or if N is used nonreferentially with a transitive verb; and so forth.[4]

The inanimacy of the Num determines both its own form, i.e., *tri* rather than *trëx*, and that of the quantified N: with the inanimate TRI we get $N_{\text{sg, gen}}$ (= *medvedja*), rather than $N_{\text{pl, acc}}$ (= *medvedej*).

In this way, the paradoxical quality of the Russian Num + N phrases in (1) and (9)–(14) enters into the description of Russian in connection with precisely those elements that create the paradox—that is, in describing the agreement between a "small" Num and its quantified N.

V. EXCURSUS: THE NOMINATIVE NOUN AS A SYNTACTICALLY DEPENDENT ELEMENT IN RUSSIAN

Six basic situations where a N_{nom} may be a syntactically dependent element in Russian are enumerated below. In other words, I indicate the situations where the nominative may be syntactically governed, i.e., where it serves to mark the dependent status of a noun in a specific surface-syntactic role. To avoid misunderstanding, let it be emphasized that we are dealing with ANY KIND of nominative government, and not only with strong government (where the governed item corresponds to a semantic valence slot of the governing lexeme).

1. In those schools of contemporary linguistics where a dependency tree is used to depict surface-syntactic structure, the grammatical subject is universally considered to be SYNTACTICALLY DEPENDENT on the predicate verb (although

MORPHOLOGICALLY the subject may subordinate the predicate, the latter agreeing with the former, for example, in person and number: cf. Chapter 3, p. 134). Rather than attempting to substantiate this point of view here, I simply accept it as a postulate. The basic consideration in favor of the surface structure

$$V_{\overline{\text{finite}}}\text{predicative SSyntRel}\longrightarrow N$$

(*Devočka*◄—predic—*plačet: šarik*◄—predic—*uletel* 'A girl is crying: the balloon flew away' [B. Okudžava] and so on)

is the following: the passive surface-syntactic (SS-)valency of a predicative pair (= Grammatical Subject + Main Verb) is completely determined by the predicate, but it does not depend at all on the subject.[5]

If, however, the predicate (= main verb) syntactically subordinates, or governs, the subject, then the subject's nominative case indicates a passive SS-role of the corresponding noun phrase, in much the same manner all other cases do. Let us note here the following two facts.

On the one hand, the grammatical subject in Russian is by no means always in the nominative case. It can be, according to some syntactic theories, a noun in the genitive or partitive case (depending on several different factors—(22)) or even a prepositional phrase (23):

(22) a. **Druzej** *u neë tak i ne zavelos'* 'She just didn't have any friends', lit. 'Of friends at her did not appear'.
   b. **Deneg** *nam xvataet* 'We have enough money', lit. 'Of money suffices us'.
   c. **Nikakix pisem** *polučeno ně bylo* 'No letters were received'.
   d. **Ètogo količestva** *budet dostatočno* 'This amount will be enough'.
   e. **Vody** *pribylo* 'The water rose', lit. 'Of-water became-more'.
(23) a. *S derev'ev upalo* **po gruše** (cf. Sidorov and Il'inskaja 1949) 'A pear fell off each tree'.
   b. *Muzej poseščalo v den'* **ot pjatisot do tysjači čelovek** 'Five hundred to a thousand people visited the museum daily'.
   c. *V ètom rajone obitaet* **okolo tridcati volkov** 'About thirty wolves live in this region'.[6]

On the other hand, in Russian by no means every verb can govern its subject in the nominative: for example, *xvatat'* 'suffice' (*Deneg* ⟨**Den'gi*⟩ *xvataet* 'There is enough money') and *ne dostavat'* 'lack' (*Emu ne dostaët mužestva* ⟨**mužestvo*⟩ 'He lacks courage') can only take a genitive/partitive subject; some of the so-called "impersonal" verbs, like *tošnit* 'is nauseated', *nejmëtsja* 'is bent on doing something', and *nezdorovitsja* 'feels unwell', can't have a genuine N as a subject at all; etc. Consequently, government of the nominative must, in principle, be indicated in dictionary entries for Russian verbs, just as is the government of any other case.

2. The second example of a governed N_{nom} in Russian is the nominal constituent, or the subjective-copredicative complement, with the verb BYT′ 'be', in particular when in its identifying sense (cf. Apresjan 1980: section 4b):

(24)   **a.** **Kto** *byla èta zenščina?* 'Who was that woman?'
   b. *Vot tot čelovek*—**moj brat** [with the zero copula] 'That man there is my brother.'
   c. *Da* **kto** *že vy budete?* 'And who might you be?'

3. Syntactic dependence of a noun in the nominative in Russian (i.e., its susceptibility of being subordinated) may further be observed in a number of constructions with comparative conjunctions (Mel′čuk 1979a: 109–115). If a comparative conjunction itself indirectly depends on an N′, then the conjunction governs its immediately subordinate N in the nominative:

(25)   **a.** *Ja znaju ljudej*[N′] *bolee* ← *vysokix*, **čem** → **Alik**[N_{nom}]
      'I know people [who are] taller than Alec'.

(Both here and in (25b) I disregard the second possible reading of these sentences: 'I know people who are taller than anybody Alec knows'.)

   b. *Oni tjanutsja k ljudjam*[N′] *takim že,* **kak** → **Alik**[N_{nom}]
      'They strive after people like Alec'.

   c. . . . *o ljudjax*[N′], *stol′ že ostroumnyx*, **skol′**→**Alik**[N_{nom}]
      'about people who are as witty as Alec';

   d. *s devuškoj*[N′] *strojnoj,* → **kak** → **topol′**N_{nom} 'with a girl slim like a poplar tree'.

In (25), the second comparate (the nominal phrase denoting the item that the first comparate is being compared to) depends on the comparative conjunction; at the same time, the second comparate can only be in the nominative, which thus is imposed (i.e., governed) by the conjunction.

4. The fourth class of situations where the nominative may be governed in Russian obtains with dependent noun phrases of the following four types (a–d), which are all related, in one way or another, to NEs:

(a) A NE_{nom} fills in a semantic (and syntactic) valency slot with measure nouns (colloquial variants):

(26)   **a.** *pri vese* **odna tonna** 'with a weight of one ton';
    b. *čeln dlinoj* **dvadcat′ odna sažen′** 'a twenty-one-sagene-long dugout';
    c. . . . *razvivaet skorost′* **tysjača sem′sot kilometrov (v čas)**
      '[It] has a speed of seventeen hundred kilometers (per hour)'.

In this SS-role the NE$_{nom}$ is synonymous to a V'in' + NE$_{acc}$ phrase:

(26′)   **a.** *pri vese* **v odnu tonnu**;
    b. *čeln dlinoj* **v dvadcat′ odnu sažen′**;
    c. . . . *razvivaet skorost′* **v tysjaču sem′sot kilometrov**.

  (b) The name of a unit of measurement is in the nominative with NEs indicating monetary sums, as in constructions of the type in (27), meaning 'specific cost':[7]

(27)   **a.** [*po sto rublej*] **(odna) tonna** 'a hundred rubles per ton';

    b. [*po šest′ tysjač tugrikov*] **(každaja) ustanovka** 'six hundred thousand tugriks each plant';

    c. [*Jabloki stojat zdes′ 2 rublja*] **kilogramm** 'Apples cost two rubles a kilogram here'.

    d. [*Koljun′ka kuril sigary po ⟨za⟩ 25 peso*] **štuka** 'Kolyunka smoked twenty-five-peso cigars'.

In this SS-role, the name of the unit of measurement is, first, synonymous with a ZA 'for' + N$_{acc}$ phrase:

(27′)   **a.** *po sto rublej* **za odnu tonnu**;
    b. *po šest′ tysjač tugrikov* **za (každuju) ustanovku**; . . .

and, second, omissible without destroying grammaticality:

(27″)   **a.** *cement po sto rublej (tonna)* 'cement at a hundred rubles a ton';
    b. *ustanovki po šest′ tysjač tugrikov* 'plants at six thousand tugriks each';
    c. *Jabloki stojat zdes′ dva rublja* 'Apples cost two rubles here'.
    d. *On kuril sigary po ⟨za⟩ 25 peso* 'He smoked twenty-five-peso cigars'.

  (c) A NE$_{nom}$ appears as a dependent component of a compound ordinal numeral and, in the colloquial language, of compound cardinals as well (I take the rightmost component of a compound numeral to be its syntactic head):

(28) a. *v* **odna tysjača devjat'sot tridcat'** *sed'mom godu* 'in 1937';
 b. coll. *so vsemi ètimi* **dva milliona sorok odna tysjača devjat'sot** *dvadcat'ju sem'ju dollarami* 'with all these 2,041,927 dollars'.

The tendency not to decline compound numerals, and by the same token whole NEs, using them in various passive SS-roles in the 'basic' (= dictionary) form, i.e., in the nominative, is becoming more and more widespread in Russian (foremost in professional speech). Already Vinogradov (1947: 302) remarked that "the case function of the nominative has been destroyed for numerals: for them the nominative is by no means in the domain of meaning, but in that of conventional syntactic use." It is thus especially natural to find the governed nominative in numerals and NEs, i.e., in precisely type (1) expressions.

(d) The very same tendency to invariance of NEs apparently appears in the following marginal use of NE$_{nom}$ as a temporal adverbial modifier (colloquial):

(29) *Poezd otxodit* (**dvadcat'**) **odna minuta devjatogo** 'The train leaves at eight twenty-one'.

5. Let us point out, at last, three more particular cases of the use of a noun in the nominative in a SS-dependent role.

(a) The second, or objective-copredicative, complement of verbs like *nazyvat'(sja)* 'to name (to be named)', *zvat'(sja)* 'to call (to be called)', *veličat'(sja)* 'to call (to be called)', and so on:

(30) a. *Svoju dočku oni nazvali* **Svetlana** 'They named their daughter Svetlana'.
 b. *Eë sestra zvalas'* **Tat'jana** [Pushkin] 'Her sister was called Tatyana'.

Verbs that appear in constructions of this type bear a metalinguistic function: they introduce the names of objects. The nominative case here is equivalent to quotes.

(b) Various types of naming appositives:

(31) *na ostrove* **Java** 'on the island of Java'; *na beregax reki* **Volga** 'on the banks of the river Volga'; *s avianoscem* **"Saratoga"** 'with the aircraft-carrier *Saratoga*'; *otnositel'no porody* **"russkaja gončaja"** 'with respect to the Russian foxhound breed'; and so forth.

Here again we see a phenomenon connected with a metalinguistic function (for more on Russian appositives see Uryson 1981).

(c) The first (leftmost) element in constructions like *X nad X-om* 'X over X', *X za X-om* 'X behind X', *X k X-u* 'X to X' etc. and also in the pronominal expressions *odin . . . odin* 'each . . . other' and *odin . . . drugoj* 'idem':[8]

(32) **a.** *I možno pridat' im porjadok takoj,*
Čtob stroki stojali **stroka** *nad strokoj*[Ju. Levitanskij]
'And they could be given an order so fine,
That all the lines stood line upon line'.

b. *On prosmotrel vsju rukopis'* **stranica** *za stranicej* 'He examined the entire manuscript page by page'.

c. *On uložil svoë bogatstvo v čemodan* **pačka** *k pačke* 'He lay all his wealth into the suitcase bundle to bundle'.

(33) **a.** *On plotno ustavil knigi na polke* **odna** *k odnoj* 'He placed the books on the shelf flush against each other'.

b. *On udobno uselsja, položiv nogi* **odna** *na druguju* 'He crossed his legs and sat down comfortably'.

Note that the nominative in (30) freely alternates with the instrumental (*nazvali* **Svetlanoj**, *zvalas'* **Tat'janoj**), and in (32) and (33) it does so with the accusative (but only in the appropriate contexts: *prosmotrel rukopis'* **stranicu** *za stranicej*; *ustavil knigi* **odnu** *k odnoj*).

6. Although somewhat marginal in the framework of the present chapter, it is a highly curious fact that the nominative was used to mark direct objects and adverbial circumstantials of duration in Old Russian and still is in contemporary North Russian dialects:

(34) **a.** *I korolju byla* **ta ruxljad'** *dati* [15th c.] 'And the king had to give up this possession'.

b. *. . . čtoby emu sobě* **dočer'** *tvoja vzjati* [15th c.] 'in order that he take your daughter to himself'.

c. *Ino dostoit' mužu* **žena svoja** *nakazyvati* [14th c., "Domostroj"] 'For it is up to the husband to punish his wife'.

d. *Nait'* **noc'ka** *spat' perva* [contemporary dialect] 'After all, first the night must be slept'.

(The examples in (34) are due to Timberlake 1974.)

As Timberlake (op. cit.) showed, marking direct object and circumstantials of duration with the nominative case is characteristic of constructions with infinite forms, i.e., in situations where the object or circumstantial can in no way be mistaken for the subject. This means that the nominative is inclined to appear in a dependent position instead of other cases if it is impossible to have a declensional contrast in that position.

In conclusion, the following two comments of a general nature, summarizing, in a certain sense, the content of the present Excursus:

Comment 1

It is obvious that the answer to the question of absolute syntactic independence for the nominative case in Russian is entirely determined by whatever general theory of SS-representation is assumed. In the framework of the approach to which I personally subscribe, a full sentence always has only one syntactic top node—the finite form of the verb, from which all its remaining wordforms depend, either directly or indirectly. Consequently, all N_{nom} must be dependent— that is to say, by definition. An independent N_{nom} is possible only in incomplete utterances: titles, nominal sentences, and so on.

As far as the traditional approach accepted in Russian grammar is concerned (cf., in particular, Peškovskij 1934: 48–55), this is a somewhat, although not entirely, different matter. The top node of the sentence is considered to be its grammatical subject, on which all the other wordforms depend. In this way, corresponding to even the most traditional viewpoint, only a single type of N_{nom} is independent, and all the remaining ones must all the same be recognized as dependent and thus governed! As we have seen, the traditional thesis of absolute independence for the nominative in Russian contradicts the equally traditional doctrine of syntactic dependence and must be rejected (not to mention that the position of absolute syntactic supremacy of the subject may be successfully disputed).

Comment 2

The instances of nominative government enumerated include also instances of STRONG government, where a N_{nom} fills in the semantic valency slot of the governing expression. Such is the state of affairs in items 1 (grammatical subjects), 2 (predicate complements), 4a (names of measures), 4b (names of units of value), and 5a (complement nouns with verbs of naming). However, with the exception of the completely antiquated or highly dialectal usages of the type in item 6, a N_{nom} in Russian never appears in the role of a genuine object or complement (the subjective-copredicative complements with *byt'*, the objective-copredicative complements with *nazyvat'*, and others like them, are very special phenomena). In particular, one does not find a N_{nom} as a SS-dependent with prepositions or prepositional collocations. Therefore, although our analysis of Russian removes from the nominative case the aura of absolute independence, it does not provide DIRECT evidence against the thesis of the impossibility of a N_{nom} with a preposition.

NOTES

1. (The epigraph, p. 374.) This quotation from Strugackijs' science-fiction novel is a slightly altered children's rhyme. *Prjamaja kiška*, lit. 'a straight gut/hose' (since *kiška* is ambiguous between 'gut' and 'hose'), is an idiom meaning 'rectum'; it is the word play that makes the rhyme funny.

2. (III, p. 377.) There is yet another logically conceivable variant to Solution II: consider that the noun itself, here used non-referentially, becomes inanimate in phrases of the type in (1). This, however, is contradicted by two kinds of facts.

First, the morphological animacy of the N in these phrases is proven by its own declension in combinations with ODIN:

(i)   *siloj v (dvadcat') odnogo* **medvedja** ⟨**v (dvadcat') odin medved'*⟩,

where the lexeme *medved'* is unambiguously animate, although it is used non-referentially. Compare:

(i') *siloj v (dvadcat') odin* **kilogramm** ⟨**v (dvadcat') odnogo kilogramma*⟩ 'with the force of 21 kilograms'.

Second, the syntactic animacy of the N is shown by the declension of the partially agreeing lexemes KOTORYJ 'which' and KAŽDYJ (*iz*) 'each (of)' (cf. Zaliznjak 1967: 71–72):

(ii) *V našem klasse stalo bol'še na dva* **mal'čika, kotoryx** ⟨**kotorye*⟩ *privezli iz Leningrada* 'Two more boys, who had been brought from Leningrad, were in our class'.
Otrjad medrabotnikov rajona, čislennost'ju v četyre **vrača, každogo** ⟨**každyj*⟩ *iz kotoryx prixoditsja zagružat' sverx mery* . . . 'The ranks of the region's medical workers, which number four doctors, each of whom has to take on an excessive work load . . .'

Compare:

(ii') *U nas stalo bol'še na dva* **jaščika, kotorye** ⟨**kotoryx*⟩ *privezli iz Leningrada* 'We got two more boxes brought from Leningrad'.
. . . *čislennost'ju v četyre* **stanka, kotorye** ⟨**kotoryx*⟩ *prixoditsja zagružat' sverx mery* '. . . numbers four lathes, which must be excessively loaded with work'.

Therefore, it is impossible to consider the N in phrases like *(siloj) v dva medvedja* inanimate. (For morphological vs. syntactic animacy see Chapter 10, p. 364.)

3. (IV, **Argument 1**, p. 378.) Let me point out three cases, which can give the wrong impression that a N_{nom} after a preposition is possible in Russian (although in reality this is not so).
1) Sentences with the expression *čto za* 'what (kind of)', after which the nominative case is typical:

(i)   *A èto čto za* **figura***?* 'What kind of figure is that?'
Čto za **idiot***!* 'What an idiot!'
A čto on za **čelovek***?* 'What kind of person is he?'

However, the expression *čto za* is a non-decomposable semantico-syntactic idiom, and the element *za* in it can in no way be considered a preposition. To what part of speech the expression *čto za* does belong is a separate question. I propose that it is an invariable pronoun, not unlike the possessive pronouns *ego* 'his', *eë* 'her', and *ix* 'their'. Compare the German expression *was für* . . . , which has the same properties.
2) Constructions of type (ii):

(ii) *idti v* **lëtčiki** 'become a pilot', *brat' v* **njan'ki** 'take as a nurse', *pročit' v* **artisty** 'intend [for someone] to be an actor', *prolezt' v* **načal'niki** 'make one's way into the ranks of the bosses', *kandidat v* **posly** 'a candidate for ambassador', *xotet' v* **Napoleony** 'want to become somebody like Napoleon', . . .

which have already been discussed more than once. A comprehensive summary of the existing points of view and possible solutions can be found in Zaliznjak (1967: 50–52), where the following is proposed (as one of two competing descriptions): the N in constructions of the type *idti v lëtčiki* is in the nominative. (The alternative proposal has it that *lëtčiki* is a form of the accusative, but not of the animate noun lexeme LĖTČIK 'pilot'; instead, it is a form of a special inanimate noun LĖTČIKI, i.e., a **plurale tantum** meaning 'aggregate of pilots'.) Relying on Zaliznjak's reasoning, I attempted to summarize the existing arguments concerning the form of N in constructions of type (ii) in Mel'čuk (1980c) (cf. also Mel'čuk 1985: 461–488). My conclusion: the case of the plural noun in the construction of (ii) is accusative, but the noun, although it remains the same lexeme, loses its morphological animacy. Therefore, expressions of type (ii) cannot serve as an argument in favor of the nominative after a preposition in Russian.

3) The appearance of nouns in the nominative case after the words PLJUS 'plus' and MINUS 'minus':

(iii) *On posetil vsex svoix druzej pljus ⟨minus⟩* **Maša** 'He visited all his friends plus ⟨minus⟩ Masha'.
Mandel'štam vsegda kazalsja soveršenno otdel'nym čelovekom pljus **bespomoščnyj i milyj brat Šura** [N. Mandel'štam, *Vtoraja kniga*, 1972: 568–569] 'Mandelstam always seemed to be a completely separate person plus his nice, helpless brother Shura'.

Expressions of this type are also discused in Mel'čuk (1980c), where it is shown that the lexemes PLJUS and MINUS in constructions (iii) cannot be recognized as prepositions; most likely these are nouns in the nominative, typical of scientific (in particular, mathematical) texts, and as such they determine the nominative case for the noun phrases that follow them.

4. (The very end of Section IV, p. 386.) Let me note here a curious fact. The lack of animacy agreement of Num with N, as proposed, and the resultant formal distinctions in a Num + N phrase (*tri medvedja* vs. *trëx medvedej*) are relatively superficial phenomena. For the most part, they pertain to the morphological representation of a sentence and are introduced when establishing correspondences between surface-syntactic structure and its morphological realization. Nevertheless, this lack of animacy agreement is in many cases rather directly related to semantic distinctions: 'a being' vs. 'a being as a unit of measure'; 'a being' vs. 'dish prepared from this being'; etc. The tendency to exploit semantically any formal distinctions is extremely characteristic of natural languages.

5. (V, 1, p. 387.) Let me recall (Chapter 3, I, B, p. 134) that a predicative pair (as well as a finite verb alone—without an overt subject!) may by itself constitute a grammatically complete and autonomous sentence. It may also depend on a subordinate conjunction, thus forming a subordinate clause. However, a subject noun phrase cannot appear in such SS-roles:

(i) *On skazal,* **čto** $\left\{\begin{array}{l}\textit{Maša ne pridët}\\ \textit{pridët}\\ \textit{smerkaetsja}\end{array}\right\}$ 'He said that $\left\{\begin{array}{l}\text{Masha wouldn't come}\\ \text{[he] would come}\\ \text{it was getting dark}\end{array}\right\}$',

but not

(ii) **On skazal,* **čto** *Maša* 'He said that Masha' [except, of course, for elliptical sentences].

In essence, the criterion of imposing, by the SS-head, its passive SS-valency on the construction as a whole is being used here. This is discussed in more detail in Chapter 3, pp. 132ff.

It is interesting to note that in a number of languages grammatically complete sentences, normal in all respects, need not have a subject: in order to attain sentential status, a grammatical predicate, i.e., a finite verb, is sufficient. Such a state of affairs is typical of Japanese or Vietnamese, for example. The opposite situation does not hold: there is no language in which full-fledged sentences can exist without a predicate. Therefore, the grammatical predicate is the constitutive element of the sentence.

There are other arguments supporting the view that the role of the grammatical subject is subordinate, such as the mutual grammatical transformability of subject and object (passives of various types), but it would be impossible to examine them here.

6. (V, 1, example (23), p. 387.) For the D-representation of the boldface GS phrases in (23b—c) see Mel'cuk (1985: 362ff). An insightful analysis of Russian genitive and prepositional subjects is found in Babby (1980: 30ff.) Babby objects to the subjecthood of genitive noun phrases of the type represented in (22) on the grounds that their syntactic behavior is radically different from that of the unquestionable subjects: 'genitive subjects' do not conjoin with nominative subjects (i.e., the latter and the former are not gapping-collapsible), etc. Cogent though Babby's arguments are, I do not think they are final —since I have in mind a broader notion of grammatical, or surface-syntactic, subject. In any event, even if examples (22) may be felt somewhat dubious, examples (23) are okay. Moreover, typologically, a case-mark diversity of grammatical subjects is a well-established fact. On the one hand, in the ergative construction of a number of languages (Kartvelian, some Daghestanian such as Dargwa, Chukchee and Koryak, Burushaski, several Indo-Iranian, among others) the grammatical subject appears in different cases, often as a function of the type or grammatical form of the finite verb. On the other hand, in such languages as Finnish or Estonian, the grammatical subject admits different cases (nominative vs. genitive or partitive) as a function of its own referentiality, definiteness etc. (cf. Chapter 6, p. 258).

In addition, Russian (as many other languages) features several types of grammatical subjects that are not noun phrases at all. Thus a Russian GS can be, for example:

- **(i)** an infinitive:
  Kurit' *byvaet očen' prijatno* 'To smoke may be very pleasant';
- **(ii)** a phrase headed by a quantifying adverb:
  Mnogo detej *perebyvalo v ètom lagere* 'Many kids have been in this camp';
- **(iii)** a clause:
  Menja očen' bespokoit, **čto eë do six por net** 'It worries me a lot that she isn't here yet';
- **(iv)** a phrase with an obligatory denotation of a monetary sum (= English '. . . worth of . . .'):
  Sjuda bylo privezeno **knig na sem'sot rublej** 'Seven hundred rubles' worth of books were brought here'.

See Iomdin et al. (1975) for a discussion of possible kinds of grammatical subjects in Russian.

7. (Excursus, **4b**, p. 389.) In expressions such as in (27), the semantic valency slot for an item of merchandise is not inherent to the name of the monetary unit, taken separately. This valency slot appears with freely created phrases of the form "Num + name of a monetary unit" in the scope of the prepositions PO and ZA, the verb STOIT' 'cost', the noun CENA 'price' (*Cena im byla 8 rublej korzinka* 'Their price was 8 rubles a basket'), and so on.

8. (Excursus, **5c**, p. 390.) The SS top node, or head, of such expressions is considered to be the preposition, and when it is missing—the right-hand component. The left-hand

component depends on the right-hand one as a part of a compound word: *stroka za →*
strokoj 'line by line', *odin ← drugogo* 'each other', etc., just like *ni dlja → kogo* 'for no
one' or *drug . . . druga, drug . . . drugu* etc. 'one . . . another'. Note that even if this
SSynt-structure for an expression of the type of *stroka za strokoj* is not accepted and the
N_{nom} is taken to be its SS-head, we still have here a case of a syntactically dependent
N_{nom}: the whole phrase depends on the verb via its SS-head, i.e., N_{nom}.

FOUR METHODOLOGICAL PRINCIPLES OF SYNTACTIC DESCRIPTION

For a better surveyability of the methodological principles stated and discussed above, in Chapters 7, 10, and 11, I repeat them here in the order of decreasing generality.

1. The **Principle of Maximal Localization** bears on linguistic$_1$ description in general. Informally, it necessitates localizing all the difficulties and peculiarities observed when describing a linguistic$_1$ phenomenon within its narrowest "neighborhood," that is, to avoid to the greatest extent possible the spreading of these difficulties to distant spheres and levels of the language in question.

Let there be a linguistic$_1$ phenomenon **p** and its two competing descriptions $D_1(\mathbf{p})$ and $D_2(\mathbf{p})$; **p** is implied by the class **U** of certain linguistic$_1$ units.

In choosing between $D_1(\mathbf{p})$ and $D_2(\mathbf{p})$, we should prefer the one that is based on **U** and touches on as few units of other classes as possible.

Cf. Chapter 11, (16), p. 383.

2. The **Principle of Simplest Restriction** operates in morphology, and more specifically, when deciding on inflectional categories of a particular word class. It says that if a category is physically distinguished only in some morphological forms of the class under analysis, then we should declare it **partial**, i.e., relevant exclusively for these forms, if and only if the latter can be specified by just one other inflectional category; otherwise, the category in question is considered **full** and the forms where it is not distinguished are said to be homonymous with respect to this category. Thus in Russian adjectives, the gender is never distinguished in the plural: therefore, gender is considered to be a partial category of adjectives, relevant in the singular only. But the masculine and the neuter are not distinguished in the singular except in the nominative: that is, we need to mention two categories (number and case) to specify the problematic forms. Therefore, we do not consider masculine + neuter in Russian adjectives as a partial subgender, so that forms such as *milomu* 'lovely' are said to be homonymous with respect to gender:

$$milomu = \begin{cases} \text{MILYJ}_{\text{masc,sg,dat}} \\ \text{vs.} \\ \text{MILYJ}_{\text{neut,sg,dat}} \end{cases}$$

Let there be an inflectional category C_1 applicable to a word class with the paradigm Π. C_1 is materially differentiated only in a proper subset Π' of Π, so that the following dilemma ensues: Should we declare C_1 relevant for Π' only and thereby make C_1 a partial category, or should we consider C_1 relevant for the whole Π and thereby make all the forms in the difference $\Pi - \Pi'$ homonymous with respect to C_1?

> In choosing between the two alternative solutions, we should prefer to restrict the relevance of C_1 to Π' if and only if we can specify Π' in terms of (elements of) just one other inflectional category C_2; otherwise we should prefer to make C_1 relevant for the whole Π, thereby admitting homonymy into the difference $\Pi - \Pi'$.

Cf. Chapter 10, (21), p. 368.

The following two principles are the least general: they apply to grammatical cases only.

3. The **Principle of External Autonomy of Case Forms** requires that two different case forms (of a noun or a noun phrase) never be distributed as a function of the external (subordinating or governing) surface-syntactic context: the latter determines the choice, for a given noun (or a noun phrase), only of a case as such, while the selection of the form (= the marker) of this case depends entirely on internal properties of the noun (phrase).

Let there be a nominal stem R and wordforms w_i (R) comprising the stem R; c is a specific case and $m_j(c)$ are different morphs expressing c (m_j may express other grammemes as well, i.e., they may be cumulative markers).

> If a language displays two nominal wordforms $w_1(R)$ and $w_2(R)$ such that $w_1(R)$ contains $m_1(c)$ and $w_2(R)$ contains $m_2(c)$, then either $w_1(R)$ and

> $w_2(R)$ are in free variation, or the choice between $w_1(R)$ and $w_2(R)$ depends only upon their own properties.

See Chapter 10, (5), p. 360.

Remember that this is a simplified formulation; the full-fledged one adds a proviso accounting for rather exceptional situations where the choice between $w_1(R)$ and $w_2(R)$ may be contingent upon the presence of a particular syntactic dependent or codependent thereof. Thus, strictly speaking, the Principle of External Autonomy of Case Forms actually means autonomy from the SUPERORDINATED (= governing) syntactic external context; but I cannot go here into the details.

4. The **Principle of Internal Autonomy of Cases** excludes postulation of a **non-autonomous** case, i.e., a case such that all of its forms are physically identical to forms of other cases, if there are no strong syntactic reasons for that.

> A morphologically non-autonomous case should be postulated in a language if and only if otherwise the SSynt-rules that describe the selection of cases would have to mention individual properties of the lexeme to be declined.

For instance, in Lak the transitive GS selects the nominative, if it is a 1st or 2nd person pronoun, and the genitive otherwise; the rules that state this distribution mention no individual properties of corresponding lexemes, and therefore the Principle of Internal Autonomy of Cases disallows postulating in Lak an ergative whose forms would be identical either to these of the nominative (for 1st and 2nd person pronouns) or to these of the genitive (for nouns and 3rd person pronouns). However, the Russian partitive (*melu* '[some] chalk', *pesku* '[some] sand', . . .) is a legitimate non-autonomous case whose forms always coincide with those of the dative: without partitive, the rules describing the case-marking in terms of dative would have to address individual properties of lexemes, cf. *Prinesi peska* [gen] / *pesku* [part] 'Bring some sand', but *Prinesi uglja /*uglju* 'Bring some coal' (the lexeme UGOL' 'coal' lacks partitive), etc.

See Chapter 7, (34), p. 291.

It goes without saying that this is by no means a serious and systematic study of linguistic$_2$ research principles: I did not supply any justification of the four principles nor any analysis of their applicability, and so forth. My only goal here is to outline, be it in a fairly rough way, some of the basic rules a linguist should abide by during his decision making. This is still a far cry from even a tentative inventory of rigorous principles that should underly our research endeavor. (Cf., in this connection, a few principles for linguistic$_2$ description stated in Hudson 1984: 16–18, 29.)

REFERENCES

Abbreviations used

AJL	*Australian Journal of Linguistics*
BLS n	*Proceedings of the* n-*th Annual Meeting of the Berkeley Linguistics Society*
BPTJ	*Buletyn Polskiego Towarzystwa Językoznawczego* [= Bulletin of Polish Linguistic Society]
BSLP	*Bulletin de la Société de Linguistique de Paris*
CLS n	*Papers from the* n-*th Regional Meeting, Chicago Linguistic Society*
FoL	*Foundations of Language*
IJAL	*International Journal of American Linguistics*
IRSL	*International Review of Slavic Linguistics*
IULC	*Indiana University Linguistics Club*
LI	*Linguistic Inquiry*
LInv	*Linguisticae Investigationes*
NTI	*Naučno-texničeskaja informacija* [Scientific and Technological Information]
OLJa	*Otdelenie literatury i jazyka* [Division of Literature and Language]
PK	*Problemy kibernetiki* [Problems of Cybernetics]
PP PGÈPL	*Predvaritel′nye Publikacii. Problemnaja gruppa èksperimental′noj i prikladnoj lingvistiki* [= Preprints. Research Group in Experimental and Applied Linguistics]
VJa	*Voprosy jazykoznanija* [Questions of Linguistics]
WSA	*Wiener Slawistischer Almanach*

Anderson, Stephen R. (1977) 'On Mechanisms by Which Languages Become Ergative,' in Ch. N. Li (ed.), *Mechanisms of Syntàctic Change*, Austin—London: University of Texas Press, 317–363.

Apresjan, Jurij D. (1974) *Leksičeskaja semantika* [Lexical Semantics], Moscow: Nauka.

———. (1980) *Tipy informacii dlja poverxnostno-semantičeskogo komponenta modeli "Smysl ⟺ Tekst"* [Types of Information for Surface-Semantic Component of the Meaning-Text Model], Vienna: WSA.

Apresjan, Jurij D., Igor' M. Boguslavskij, and Leonid L. Iomdin (1984) *Lingvističeskoe obespečenie sistemy francuzsko-russkogo avtomatičeskogo perevoda ÈTAP-1. III. Francuzskij sintaksičeskij analiz* [Linguistic Software for the ETAP-1 System: French-to-Russian Automatic Translation. III. Syntactic Analysis of French], Moscow: Institut Russkogo jazyka AN SSSR [*PP PGÈPL*, 155].

Apresjan, Jurij D., Leonid L. Iomdin, and Nikolaj V. Percov (1978) 'Ob"ekty i sredstva modeli poverxnostnogo sintaksisa russkogo jazyka' [Objects and Means of a Model for Surface Syntax of Russian], *IRSL*, 3:3, 249–312.

Aronson, Howard I. (1970) 'Towards a Semantic Analysis of Case and Subject in Georgian,' *Lingua*, 25:3, 291–301.

Aschmann, H., and W. L. Wonderly (1952) 'Affixes and Implicit Categories of Totonac Verb Inflection.' *IJAL*, 18:3, 13–45.

Babby, Leonard H. (1980) *Existential Sentences and Negation in Russian*, Ann Arbor, MI: Karoma.

Babby, Leonard H., and Richard D. Brecht (1975) 'The Syntax of Voice in Russian,' *Language*, 51:2, 342–367.

Bally, Charles (1922) 'Copule zéro et faits connexes,' *BSLP*, 23:1, 1–6.

Barber, E. J. W. (1975) 'Voice—Beyond the Passive,' *BLS 1*, 16–24.

Barulin, Aleksandr N. (1978) 'Model' sklonenija ličnyx mestoimenij aljutorskogo jazyka' [A Model for Declension of Alutor Pronouns], in *PP PGÈPL*, 107, Moscow: Institut Russkogo jazyka AN SSSR, 3–8.

Baumgartner, Karl (1965) 'Spracherklärung mit den Mitteln der Abhängigkeitsstruktur,' *Beiträge zur Sprachkunde und Informationsverarbeitung*, 5, 31–53.

Bazell, Charles (1950) 'The Fundamental Syntactic Relations,' *Časopis pro moderní filologii*, 33:1, 9–15.

Beleckij, Mixail I. (1967) 'Beskontekstnye i dominacionnye grammatiki i svjazannye s nimi algorifmičeskie problemy' [CF-grammars and Domination Grammars: Some Decision Problems], *Kibernetika* (Kiev), 4, 90–97.

Beleckij, Mixail I., Vladimir M. Grigorjan, and Isaak D. Zaslavskij (1963) 'Aksiomatičeskoe opisanie porjadka i upravlenija slov v nekotoryx tipax predloženij' [Axiomatic Description of Order and Government between Words in Some Types of Sentences], *Matematičeskie voprosy kibernetiki i vyčislitel'noj texniki* (Erevan), 1, 71–78.

Benveniste, Émile (1964) 'Les niveaux de l'analyse linguistique,' in *Proceedings of the 9th International Congress of Linguists*, London etc.: Mouton, 266–275.

Blake, B. J. (1976) 'On Ergativity and the Notion of Subject (Some Australian Cases),' *Lingua*, 39:4, 281–300.

Bloomfield, Leonard (1933) *Language*. New York: Holt, Rinehart and Winston.

Boguslavskij, Igor' M. (1978a) 'Otricanie v predloženijax s obstojatel'stvami v russkom jazyke' [Negation in Russian Sentences with Circumstantial Complements], *Studia Gramatyczne II*, Wrocław etc.: Wydawnictwo PAN, 122–136.

―――. (1978b) O ponjatii smeščennogo otricanija [On the Notion of Displaced Negation], in *PP PGÈPL*, 107, Moscow: Institut Russkogo jazyka AN SSSR, 9–20.

―――. (1985) *Issledovanija po sintaksičeskoj semantike: sfery dejstvija logičeskix slov* [Studies in Syntactic Semantics: Scopes of Logical Words], Moscow: Nauka.

Bresnan, Joan (1980) 'Polyadicity: Part I of a Theory of Lexical Rules and Representations,' in T. Hoekstra, H. van der Hulst and M. Moortgat (eds.), *Lexical Grammar*, Dordrecht—Cinnaminson: Foris, 97–121.

―――. (1982a) 'The Passive in Lexical Theory,' in Bresnan (1982b), 3–86.

―――. (1982b) (ed.) *The Mental Representation of Grammatical Relations*, Cambridge, MA—London: MIT Press.

Bresnan, Joan, Ronald M. Kaplan, Stanley Peters, and Annie Zaenen. (1982) 'Cross-serial Dependencies in Dutch,' *LI*, 13:4, 613–635.

Catford, John C. (1976) 'Ergativity in Caucasian languages,' *Recherches linguistiques à Montréal* [Actes du VIme Congrès de l'Association linguistique du Nord-Est, 31 oct.–2 nov. 1975], 6, 37–48.

Chafe, Wallace L. (1970) *A Semantically Based Sketch of Onondaga*, Baltimore: Waverly Press [= *IJAL*, 36:2, Part II, Supplement].

Chanidzé, Akaki (1963) 'Le sujet grammatical de quelques verbes intransitifs en géorgien,' *BSLP*, 58:1, 1–27.

Chomsky, Noam (1970) *Le langage et la pensée*, Paris: Payot.

―――. (1982) *Lectures on Government and Binding: The Pisa Lectures*, Dordrecht: Foris.

Chung, Sandra D. (1978) *Case Marking and Grammatical Relations in Polynesian*, Austin: University of Texas Press.

Chvany, Catherine V. (1975) *On the Syntax of* be-*Sentences in Russian*, Cambridge, MA: Slavica.

Clas, André (1970) 'Le système du pronom indéterminé *on*: problèmes de traduction,' *Lebendige Sprachen*, 25:1, 13–16.

Cole, Peter, Wayne Harbert, Gabriella Hermaon, and S. N. Sridhar (1980) 'The Acquisition of Subjecthood,' *Language*, 56:4, 719–743.

Comrie, Bernard (1973) 'The Ergative: Variations on a Theme,' *Lingua*, 32:3, 239–253.

―――. (1976) 'The Syntax of Action Nominals: A Cross-Language Study,' *Lingua*, 40:2/3, 177–201.

―――. (1977) 'In Defense of Spontaneous Demotion: The Impersonal Passive,' in P. Cole and J. M. Saddock (eds.), *Syntax and Semantics, 8: Grammatical Relations*, New York: Academic Press, 47–58.

―――. (1978) 'Ergativity', in W. Lehman (ed.), *Syntactic Typology: Studies in the Phenomenology of Language*, Austin: University of Texas Press, 329–394.

Cooper, William E., and John R. Ross (1975) 'World Order,' in *Papers from the Parasession on Functionalism*, Chicago: University of Chicago, 63–111.

Dahl, Östen (1980) 'Some Arguments for Higher Nodes in Syntax: A Reply to Hudson's 'Constituency and Dependency',' *Linguistics*, 18:5/6, 485–488.

Dirr, A. L. (1928) *Einführung in das Studium der kaukasischen Sprachen*, Leipzig.

Dixon, Robert M. W. (1972) *The Dyirbal Language of North Queensland*, Cambridge: Cambridge University Press.

―――. (1977) 'The Syntactic Development of Australian Languages,' in Ch. N. Li (ed.), *Mechanisms of Syntactic Change*, Austin—London, University of Texas Press, 365–415.

————. (1979) 'Ergativity,' *Language*, 55:1, 59–138.

Dougherty, Ray C. (1970–1971)'A Grammar of Coordinate Conjoined Structures, I–II,' *Language*, 46:4, 850–898, 47:2, 298–339.

Dolinina, Inga B. (1969) 'Sposoby predstavlenija sintaksičeskoj struktury predloženija' [Methods of Representing the Syntactic Structure of a Sentence], in A. A. Xolodovič (ed.), *Tipologija kauzativnyx konstrukcij*, Leningrad: Nauka, 294–310.

Dönnges, Ulrich and Heinz Happ (1977) *Dependenz-Grammatik und Latein-Unterricht*, Göttingen: Vandenhoeck & Ruprecht.

Es'kova, Natal'ja A., Igor' A. Mel'čuk, and Vladimir Z. Sannikov (1971) *Formal'naja model' russkoj morfologii. I: Formoobrazovanie suščestvitel'nyx i prilagatel'nyx* [A Formal Model of Russian Morphology. I: Inflection of Nouns and Adjectives], Moscow: Institut Russkogo jazyka AN SSSR [*PP PGÈPL*].

Evreinov, Irina A. (1973) 'Die Semantik einer Nullform: Versuch einer neuer Definition der Kopula im Russischen,' *Linguistics*, 98, 41–57.

Fähnrich, Heinz (1967) 'Georgischer Ergativ im intransitiven Satz,' *Beiträge zur Linguistik und Informationsverarbeitung*, 10, 34–42.

Faltz, Leonard M. (1978) 'On Indirect Objects in Universal Syntax,' *CLS 14*, 76–87.

Fillmore, Charles (1968) 'The Case for Case,' in E. Bach and R. T. Harms (eds.), *Universals in Linguistic Theory*, New York etc.: Holt, Rinehart and Winston, 1–88.

Fitialov, Sergej Ja. (1962) 'O modelirovanii sintaksisa v strukturnoj lingvistike' [On Modeling Syntax in Structural Linguistics], in S. K. Šaumjan (ed.), *Problemy strukturnoj lingvistiki*, Moscow: Academy of Sciences, 100–114.

————. (1968) 'Ob èkvivalentnosti grammatik NS i grammatik zavisimostej' [On the Equivalence of PS- and D-grammars], in S. K. Šaumjan (ed.), *Problemy strukturnoj lingvistiki-1967*, Moscow: Nauka, 71–102.

Gadžiev, M. M. (1954) *Sintaksis lezginskogo jazyka. I. Prostoe predloženie* [Syntax of Lezgian. I. The Clause], Maxačkala: Dagest. Filial AN SSSR.

————. (1963) *Sintaksis lezginskogo jazyka. II. Složnoe predloženie* [Syntax of Lezgian. II. The Complex Sentence], Maxačkala: Dagest. Filial AN SSSR.

Gaifman, Haim (1965) 'Dependency Systems and Phrase Structure Systems,' *Information and Control*, 8:3, 304–337.

Galkina-Fedoruk, Evdokija M. (1962) 'O nulevyx formax v sintaksise' [On Null Forms in Syntax], *Russkij jazyk v škole*, No 2, 6–12.

Garde, Paul (1977) 'Ordre linéaire et dépendance syntaxique: contribution à une typologie,' *BSLP*, 72:1, 1–19.

————. (1980) *Grammaire russe. I. Phonologie—Morphologie*, Paris: Institut d'Études slaves.

Gasparov, Boris M. (1971) 'Neopredelënno-sub"ektnye predloženija v sovremennom russkom jazyke' [Indefinite-Subject Sentences in Modern Russian], *Trudy po russkoj i slavjanskoj filologii*, XIX, Tartu University, 3–58.

Gazdar, Gerald, Ewan Klein, Geoffrey K. Pullum, and Ivan Sag. (1985) *Generalized Phrase Structure Grammar*, Oxford: Basil Blackwell.

Gazdar, Gerald, and Geoffrey K. Pullum (1981) 'Subcategorization, Constituent Order, and the Notion "Head",' in M. Mortgat, H.v.d. Hulst, and T. Hoekstra (eds.), *The Scope of Lexical Rules*, Dordrecht—Cinnaminson: Foris, 107–123.

Gladkij, Aleksej V. (1966) *Lekcii po matematičeskoj lingvistike dlja studentov NGU* [Lectures on Mathematical Linguistics for Students of Novosibirsk University], Novosibirsk: Novosibirsk State University.

————. (1968) 'Ob opisanii sintaksičeskoj struktury predloženija' [On Describing the Syntactic Structure of a Sentence], *Computational Linguistics* (Budapest: Computing Centre of the Hungarian Academy of Sciences), 7, 21–44.

————. (1971) 'Opisanie sintaksičeskoj struktury predloženija s pomošč'ju sistem sintaksičeskix grupp. I. Formal'nyj apparat' [Describing the Syntactic Structure of a Sentence by Means of Syntactic Group Systems. I. The Formal Apparatus], *NTI*, series 2, No 9, 35–38.

————. (1973) *Formal'nye grammatiki i jazyki* [Formal Grammars and Languages], Moscow: Nauka.

————. (1981) 'Opisanie sintaksičeskoj struktury predloženija s pomošč'ju sistem sintaksičeskix grupp. (Lingvist* interpretacija)' [Describing the Syntactic Structure of a Sentence by Means of Syntactic Group Systems (Linguistic Interpretation)], *Slavica Debrecenensia*, 17, 5–38; 18, 21–49.

Gladkij, Aleksej V., and Igor A. Mel'čuk (1969) *Tree Grammars*. International Conference on Computational Lingistics [preprint 1], Stockholm.

————. (1974) 'Grammatiki derev'ev. II. K postroeniju Δ-grammatik dlja russkogo jazyka' [Tree Grammars. II. Constructing Δ-Grammars for Russian], *Informacionnye voprosy semiotiki, lingvistiki i avtomatičeskogo perevoda*, 4, 4–29.

————. (1975) 'Tree Grammars: I. A Formalism for Syntactic Transformations in Natural Languages,' *Linguistics*. 150, 47–82.

————. (1983) *Elements of Mathematical Linguistics*. Berlin etc.: Mouton.

Godel, Robert (1953) 'La question des signes zéro,' *Cahiers F. de Saussure*, 11, 31–41.

Goralčiková, Alla (1973) 'On One Type of Dependency Grammar,' in W. Klein and A. von Stechow (eds.), *Functional Generative Grammar in Prague*, Kronberg: Skriptor, 64–81.

Haas, William (1957) 'Zero in Linguistic Description,' in W. Haas, *Studies in Linguistic Analysis*, Oxford: Basil Blackwell, 33–53.

Hale, Kenneth L. (1970) 'The Passive and Ergative in Language Change: The Australian Case,' in S. A. Wurm and D. C. Kaycok (eds.), *Pacific Linguistic Studies in Honor of A. Capell*, Canberra: Linguistic Circle of Canberra, 757–781.

Hale, Kenneth L., and Chisato Kitagawa (1976–1977) 'A Counter to Counter Equi,' *Papers in Japanese Linguistics*, 5, 41–61.

Happ, Heinz (1976) *Grundfragen einer Dependenzgrammatik des Griechischen*, Göttingen: Vandenhoeck und Ruprecht.

————. (1977) 'Syntaxe latine et théorie de la valence,' *Les études classiques*, 45: 337–366.

————. (1978) 'Théorie de la valence et l'enseignement du français,' *Le français moderne*, 46:2, 97–134.

Harris, Alice C. (1981) *Georgian Syntax. A Study in Relational Grammar*, Cambridge, etc.: Cambridge University Press.

Hartenstein, Klaus, and Peter Schmidt (1983) 'Kommentierte Bibliographie zum "Smysl ⇔ Tekst"-Modell,' *WSA*, 11, 355–409.

Hawkins, John A. (1984) 'Modifier-Head or Function-Argument Relations in Phrase Structure? The Evidence of Some Word Order Universals,' *Lingua*, 63:1, 107–138.

Hays, David G. (1960) *Basic Principles and Technical Variations in Sentence Structure Determination*, Santa Monica, CA: RAND Corporation (Mathematical Division. P-1934). [Reprinted in: Collin Cherry (ed.), *Information Theory*, 1961, Washington: Butterworths, 367–374.]

————. (1961) 'Grouping and Dependency Theories,' in H. P. Edmundson (ed.), *Proceedings of the National Symposium on Machine Translation*, Englewood Cliffs, NJ: Prentice-Hall, 259–266.

————. (1964a) 'Connectability Calculations, Syntactic Functions and Russian Syntax,' *Mechanical Translation* 8, 32–51. [Reprinted in: David G. Hays (ed.), *Readings in Automatic Language Processing*, 1966, New York: American Elsevier, 107–125.]

————. (1964b) 'Dependency Theory: A Formalism and Some Observations,' *Language*, 40:4, 511–525.

Heringer, H.-J. (1970) 'Einige Ergebnisse und Probleme der Dependenzgrammatik,' *Der Deutschunterricht*, 4, 42–98.

Hetzron, Robert (1969) 'Des compléments obligatoires en hongrois,' *Word*, 25:1, 2-3, 140–154.

Hirschberg, Lydia (1961) 'Le relâchement conditionnel de l'hypothèse de projectivité,' in *Discussions sur l'hypothèse de projectivité*. [Rapport no. 35 du Centre de Traitement de l'information scientifique]. Ispra: EURATOM.

Hockett, Charles F. (1958) *A Course in Modern Linguistics*, New York: Macmillan.

Hopper, Paul J., and Sandra A. Thompson (1980) 'Transitivity in Grammar and Discourse,' *Language*, 56:2, 51–99.

Hudson, Richard A. (1976) *Arguments for a Non-transformational Grammar*, Chicago; University of Chicago Press.

————. (1980a) 'Constituency and Dependency,' *Linguistics*, 18:3/4, 179–198.

————. (1980b) 'A Second Attack on Constituency: A Reply to Dahl,' *Linguistics*, 18:5/6, 489–504.

————. (1984) *Word Grammar*, Oxford—New York: Basil Blackwell.

Humesky, Asya (1964) *Majakovskij and His Neologisms*, New York: Rausen.

Inènlikèj, Petr I. and Vladimir P. Nedjalkov (1967) 'Iz nabljudenij nad èrgativnoj konstrukciej v čukotskom jazyke' [Some Observations Concerning the Ergative Construction in Chukchee], in V.M. Žirmunskij (ed.), *Èrgativnaja konstrukcija predloženija v jazykax različnyx tipov*, Leningrad: Nauka, 246–260.

————. (1973) 'Glagoly čuvstva v čukotskom jazyke [Verbs of Emotion in Chukchee],' in S. D. Kacnelson (ed.), *Lingvističeskie issledonanija-1972*, čast' I, Moscow: Institut jazykoznanija AN SSSR, 175–203.

Iomdin, Leonid L. (1979) *Eščё raz o sintaksičeskom soglasovanii v ruskom jazyke* [Once Again on Syntactic Agreement in Russian], Moscow: Institut Russkogo jazyka AN SSSR [*PP PGÈPL*, 122].

Iomdin, Leonid L., Igor' A. Mel'čuk, and Nikolaj V. Percov (1975) 'Fragment modeli russkogo poverxnostnogo sintaksisa. Predikativnye sintagmy' [A Fragment of a Surface Syntax Model for Russian: Predicative Syntagms], *NTI*, Serija 2, No 7, 30–43. [See also a French translation in: M. Borillo and J. Virbel (eds.), *Analyse et validation dans l'étude des données textuelles*, Paris: Éditions du CNRS, 1977, 83–122].

Iomdin, Leonid L., and Nikolaj V. Percov (1975) 'Fragment modeli ruskogo poverxnostnogo sintaksisa. II. Kompletivnye i prisvjazočnye konstrukcii' [A Fragment of a Surface Syntax Model for Russian: II. Completive and Copulative Constructions], *NTI*, serija 2, No 11, 22–32.

Iordanskaja, Lidija N. (1963) 'O nekotoryx svojstvax pravil'noj sintaksičeskoj struktury (na materiale russkogo jazyka)' [On Some Properties of Correct Syntactic Structure (on the Basis of Russian)], *VJa*, No 4, 102–112.

————. (1964) 'Svojstva pravil'noj sintaksičeskoj struktury i algoritm ee obnaruženija (na materiale russkogo jazyka)' [The Properties of Correct Syntactic Structures and an Algorithm for their Detection (on the Basis of Russian)], *PK*, 11, 215–244.

――――. (1967) *Avtomatičeskij sintaksičeskij analiz. Tom II: Mežsegmentnyj sintak-sičeskij analiz* [Automatic Syntactic Analysis. Volume II: Intersegmental Syntactic Analysis], Novosibirsk: Nauka.

――――. (1982) 'Le placement linéaire des clitiques pronominaux non-sujets en français contemporain,' *LInv*, 6:1, 145–188.

Iordanskaja, Lidija, and Nadia Arbatchewsky-Jumarie (1982) 'Lexicographic Applications of Lexical Functions: Two Sample Lexical Entries from an Explanatory Combinatorial Dictionary,' *BLS 8*, 364–372.

Iordanskaja, Lidija, and Igor Mel'čuk (1981) 'On a Class of Russian Verbs Which Can Introduce Direct Speech (Constructions of the Type *"Ostav'te menja!"*―*ispugalsja bufetčik*: Lexical Polysemy or Semantic Syntax?),' in P. Jacobsen and H. L. Krag (eds.), *The Slavic Verb (An Anthology Presented to H.Ch. Sørensen 16th December 1981)*, Copenhagen: Rosenkilde and Bagger, 51–66.

Isačenko, Alexander V. (1962) *Die russische Sprache der Gegenwart*, Halle/Saale: Niemeyer.

Jakobson, Roman (1936) 'Beitrag zur allgemeinen Kasuslehre: Gesamtbedeutung der russischen Kasus,' *Travaux du Cercle Linguistique de Prague* 6:240–288 [Reprinted in his *Selected Writings*, II. The Hague: Mouton, 1971, 23–73].

――――. (1958) 'Morfologičeskie nabljudenija nad slavjanskim skloneniem (sostav russkix padežnyx form)' [Morphological Observations on Slavic Declension (The Composition of Russian Case Forms)], in *American Contributions to the 4th International Congress of Slavists*, The Hague: Mouton. 127–156 [Reprinted in his *Selected Writings*, II, The Hague: Mouton, 1971, 154–183].

――――. (1960) 'Linguistics and Poetics,' in T. A. Sebeok (ed.), *Style in Language*, New York—London: M.I.T. and John Wiley, 350–377.

――――. (1966) *Signatum and Designatum*, International Conference on Semiotics, Kazimierz-Dolny, Poland.

――――. (1971a) [1935] 'Les enclitiques slaves,' in *Selected Writings*, II, The Hague: Mouton, 16–22.

――――. (1971b) 'Stroj ukrainskogo imperativa [Structure of the Ukrainian Imperative],' in *Selected Writings*, II, The Hague: Mouton, 190–197.

――――. (1971c) [1939] 'Signe zéro,' in *Selected Writings*, II, The Hague: Mouton, 211–219.

Jakovlev, Nikolaj F. (1940) *Sintaksis čečenskogo literaturnogo jazyka* [Syntax of Standard Chechen], Moscow—Leningrad: AN SSSR.

Jelitte, Herbert (1973) 'Modelle der Konstituenten- und Dependenzgrammatik im Russischen,' *Die Welt der Slaven*, 18, 216–235.

Johnson, David E. (unpublished) *Ergativity in Universal Grammar*.

Kastovsky, Dietrich (1969) 'Wortbildung und Nullmorphem,' *Linguistische Berichte*, 2, 1–13.

Keenan, Edward (1976) 'Towards Universal Definition of 'Subject',' in Li (1976), 301–333.

Keenan, Edward and Bernard Comrie (1977) 'Noun Phrase Accessibility and Universal Grammar,' *LI* 7:1, 63–99.

Kibrik, Aleksandr E. (1979) 'Podležaščee i problema universal'noj modeli jazuka'

[Grammatical Subject and a Universal Model of language], *Izvestija AN SSSR. OLJa*, 38:4, 309–317.

──────. (1979–1980) *Materialy k tipologii èrgativnosti* [Materials for a Typology of Ergativity], Moscow: Institut Russkogo jazyka AN SSSR. [*PP PGÈPL*, 126–130].

──────. (1985) 'Toward a Typology of Ergativity,' in J. Nichols and A. C. Woodbury (eds.), *Grammar Inside and Outside the Clause*, Cambridge: Cambridge University Press, 268–323.

Klenin, Emily R. (1983) *Animacy in Russian: A New Interpretation*, (UCLA Slavic Studies. Vol. 6), Los Angeles: UCLA.

Klimonow, Gerta A., S. Nündel, and Ingrid Starke (1969) 'Syntaktische Analyse,' in *Automatische Sprachübersetzung. Deutsch-Russisch*, Berlin: Akademieverlag, 66–123.

Klimov, Georgij, A. (1973) *Očerk obščej teorii èrgativnosti* [General Theory of Ergativity in Outline], Moscow: Nauka.

──────. (1977) *Tipologija jazykov aktivnogo stroja* [Typology of Active Languages], Moscow: Nauka.

Kodzasov, Sandro V., and Irina A. Murav'ëva (1980) 'Slog i ritmika slova v aljutorskom jazyke' [Syllable and Word Rythm in Alutor], in *Aktual'nye voprosy strukturnoj i prikladnoj lingvistiki*, Moscow: Moscow University Press, 103–128.

Korhonen, J. (1977) *Studien zu Dependenz, Valenz und Satzmodell. Teil I: Theorie und Praxis der Beschreibung der deutschen Gegenwartssprache*, Frankfurt am Main: Peter Lang.

Koutsoudas, Andreas (1978) *The Question of Rule Ordering: Some Common Fallacies*, Bloomington, IN: IULC.

Koutsoudas, Andreas, and Gerald A. Sanders (1974) *On the Universality of Rules and Rule-Ordering Constraints*, Bloomington, IN: IULC.

Kozinskij, Icxak S. (1983) *O kategorii "podležaščee" v russkom jazyke* [On the Subject Category in Russian], Moscow: Institut Russkogo jazyka AN SSSR [*PP PGEPL*, 156].

Kulagina, Olga S. (1958) 'Ob odnom sposobe opredelenija grammatičeskix ponjatij na baze teorii množestv' [On a Method for Defining Grammatical Concepts on the Basis of the Set Theory], *PK*, 1, 203–214.

──────. (1970) *Algoritm sintaksičeskogo analiza v sisteme francuzsko-russkogo mašinnogo perevoda* [An Algorithm for Syntactic Analysis in the French-to-Russian Machine Translation] (Preprint No. 13), Moscow: Institut Prikladnoj matematiki AN SSSR.

Kunze, Jürgen (1972) 'Die Komponenten der Darstellung syntaktischen Strukturen in einer Abhängigkeitsgrammatik,' *Prague Bulletin of Mathematical Linguistics*, 18, 15–27.

──────. (1975) *Abhängigkeitsgrammatik*. Berlin: Akademieverlag.

Kunze, Jürgen, and Aleksandr Ljudskanov (1975) 'Die Anwendung von Unterordnungskriterien im Bulgarischen,' *SERDICA, Bulgaricae mathematicae publicationes*, 1, 144–157.

Kunze, Jürgen, and W. Priess (1967–1971) 'Versuch eines objektivierten Grammatikmodells,' *Zeitschrift für Phonetik, Sprachwissenschaft und Kommunikationsforschung*, 20, 415–448, 21, 421–466, 23, 347–378; 24, 373–402.

Kurilovič, Jurij [= Kuryłowicz, Jerzy] (1946) 'Èrgativnost' i stadial'nost v jazyke'

[Ergativity and Stadiality in Language], *Izvestija AN SSSR. OLJa,* 5, 387–394. [French: Kuryłowicz, J. *Esquisses linguistiques* I, Munich: W. Fink Verlag, 1973.]

————. (1960) 'Les structures fondamentales de la langue: groupe et proposition,' in J. Kuryłowicz, *Esquisses linguistiques,* Wrocław—Kraków: Wydawnictwo PAN, 35–40.

Kuz'mina, Irina B., and Elena V. Nemčenko (1971) *Sintaksis pričastnyx form v russkix govorax* [Syntax of Participial Forms in Russian Dialects], Moscow: Nauka.

Lamb, Sydney (1966) *Outline of Stratificational Grammar,* Washington: Georgetown University Press.

Lecerf, Yves (1960) 'Programme des conflits, modèle des conflits,' *Traduction automatique,* 1:4, 11–18; 1:5, 17–36.

Lehrer, Adrienne (1970) 'Verbs and Deletable Objects,' *Lingua,* 25:3, 227–253.

Levin, Viktor D. (1960) 'Prjamaja, kosvennaja i nesobstvenno-prjamaja reč'' [Direct, Indirect and Quasi-Direct Speech], in *Grammatika russkogo jazyka. II. Sintaksis, čast'* 2, Moscow: AN SSSR, 402–432.

Li, Charles (ed.) (1976) *Subject and Topic,* New York etc.: Academic Press.

Lopatin, Vladimir (1966) 'Nulevaja affiksacija v sisteme russkogo slovoobrazovanija' [Null Affixation in Russian Derivation], *VJa,* No. 1, 76–87.

Lynch, Irina (1961) 'Suggestions for Modification of Lecerf Theory of Projectivity and of his Stemmas, for the Purpose of their Application to "Non-projective" Russian Sentences,' in L. Hirschberg and I. Lynch, *Discussions sur l'hypothèse de projectivité* [Rapport no. 35 du Centre de Traitement de l'information scientifique], Ispra: EURATOM.

McCawley, James D. (1973) 'William Dwight Whitney as a Syntactician,' in J. D. McCawley, *Grammar and Meaning,* Tokyo: Taishukan, 320–332.

Machová, Svatava (1975) 'Die Abhängigkeitsgrammatiken,' in *Einführung in die generative Grammatik (Prager Autorengruppe),* Kronberg: Skriptor, 146–154.

Malkiel, Yakov (1959) 'Studies in Irreversible Binomials,' *Lingua,* 8:2, 113–160. [Reprinted in: Y. Malkiel, *Studies on Linguistic Themes,* 1968, Oxford: Basil Blackwell, 311–355].

Marcus, Solomon (1965a) 'Sur la notion de projectivité,' *Zeitschrift für mathematische Logik und Grundlagen der Mathematik,* 11, 181–192.

————. (1965b) 'Sur une description axiomatique des liens syntaxiques,' *Zeitschrift für mathematische Logik und Grundlagen der Mathematik,* 11, 291–296.

Martin, Philippe (1977) *Syntax and Intonation: An Integrated Theory,* Toronto, Ontario: Victoria University [Toronto Semiotic Circle: Monographs, Working Papers and Prepublications, No. 2].

————. (1978) 'Problèmes de phonosyntaxique et de phonosémantique en français,' *LInv,* 2:1, 93–125.

Matthews, P. H. (1981) *Syntax,* Cambridge, etc.: Cambridge University Press.

Megen, van, J. (1985) 'Dependency Grammar, Valence and the Bilingual Lexicon,' in G. A. J. Hoppenbrowers, P.A.M. Seuzen, A.J.M.M. Weijters (eds.), *Meaning and the Lexicon,* Dordrecht—Cinnaminson: Foris, 170–178.

Meier, Georg F. (1961) *Das Zero-Problem in der Linguistik,* Berlin: Akademie-Verlag [Schriften für Phonetik, Sprachwissenschaft und Kommunikationsforshung, 2].

Meisel, Jurgen M., and Martin D. Pam (eds.) (1979) *Linear Order and Generative Theory,* Amsterdam: Benjamins.

Mejlanova, Unejzat A. (1967) 'Lezginskij jazyk' [Lezgian], in *Jazyki narodov SSSR*, IV, Moscow: Nauka, 528–544.

Mejlanova, Unejzat A., and Bukar B. Talibov (1977) 'Konstrukcii predloženija s perexodno-neperexodnymi glagolami v lezginskom jazyke' [Constructions of Sentences with Transitive-Intransitive Verbs in Lezgian], in T. X. Kuaševa and X. T. Taov (eds.), *Voprosy sintaksičeskogo stroja iberijsko-kavkazskix jazykov*, Nalchik: Institut Istorii, Filologii i Èkonomiki, 265–272.

Mel'čuk, Igor' A. (1962) 'Ob algoritme sintaksičeskogo analiza jazykovyx tekstov (obščie principy i nekotorye itogi)' [On an Algorithm for Syntactic Analysis of Natural Texts: General Principles and Some Results], *Mašinnyj perevod i prikladnaja lingvistika*, 7, 45–87.

——. (1963) 'Avtomatičeskij analiz tekstov (na materiale russkogo jazyka)' [Automatic Analysis of Texts (on the Basis of Russian)], in *Slavjanskoe jazykoznanie*, Moscow: Nauka, 477–509.

——. (1964a) *Avtomatičeskij sintaksičeskij analiz. Tom I: Obščie principy. Vnutrisegmentnyj sintaksičeskij analiz* [Automatic Syntactic Analysis. Volume I: General Principles. The Intrasegmental Syntactic Analysis], Novosibirsk: Nauka.

——. (1964b) 'Tipy svjazej meždu èlementami teksta i tipologija jazykov' [Types of Links Between the Elements of a Text and Linguistic Typology], in *Materialy konferencii "Aktual'nye voprosy sovremennogo jazykoznanija i lingvističeskoe nasledie E. D. Polivanova"*, 1, Samarkand: Samarkand University, 57–59.

——. (1967) 'K postroeniju dejstvujuščei modeli jazyka' [Towards a Functional Linguistic Model], in *Problemy jazykoznanija*, Moscow: Nauka, 82–89.

——. (1970) 'Towards a Functioning Model of Language', in M. Bierwisch and K. E. Heidolph (eds.), *Progress in Linguistics*, The Hague: Mouton, 198–207 [Janua Linguarum, Series maior, 43].

——. (1971) 'K probleme vybora opisanija pri needinstvennosti morfologičeskix rešenij' [Problem of Choice in the Case of Non-uniqueness of Morphological Solutions], in *Fonetika, fonologija, grammatika (K semidesjatiletiju A. A. Reformatskogo)*, Moscow: Nauka, 211–220.

——. (1972) 'Urovni predstavlenija vyskazyvanij i obščee stroenie modeli "Smysl ⟺ Tekst"' [Levels of Utterance Representation and General Structure of the Meaning-Text Model], in *PP PGÈPL*, 30, Moscow: Institut Russkogo jazyka AN SSSR, 3–37.

——. (1973a) *Model' sprjaženija v alutorskom jazyke* [A Model of Alutor Conjugation], Moscow: Institut Russkogo jazyka AN SSSR [*PP PGÈPL*, 45–46].

——. (1973b) 'On the Possessive Forms of the Hungarian Noun,' in F. Kiefer and N. Ruwet (eds.), *Generative Grammar in Europe*, Dordrecht: D. Reidel, 315–332.

——. (1973c) 'Towards a Linguistic Meaning ⟺ Text Model,' in F. Kiefer (ed.), *Trends in Soviet Theoretical Linguistics*, Dordrecht: D. Reidel, 33–57.

——. (1974a) *Opyt teorii lingvističeskix modelej "Smysl ⟺ Tekst"* [Toward a Theory of Meaning-Text Linguistic Models], Moscow: Nauka.

——. (1974b) 'O sintaksičeskom nule' [On Syntactic Zero], in A. A. Xolodovič (ed.), *Tipologija passivnyx konstrukcij. Diatezy i zalogi*, Leningrad: Nauka, 343–361.

——. (1976) *Das Wort*, München: W. Fink.

——. (1977) 'Le cas,' *Revue des études slaves*, 50:1, 5–36.

——. (1978) 'Toward a Definition of the Concept 'Ergative Construction',' in

W. U. Dressler and W. Meid (eds.), *Proceedings of the XIIth International Congress of Linguists, Vienna, 1977*, Innsbruck: Universität Innsbruck, 384–387.

———. (1979a) *Studies in Dependency Syntax*, Ann Arbor, MI: Karoma.

———. (1979b) 'Syntactic, or Lexical, Zero in Natural Language,' *BLS* 5, 224–260.

———. (1980a) 'O padeže čislovogo vyraženija v russkix slovosočetanijax tipa *(bol'še) na dva mal'čika* ili *po troe bol'nyx*' [On the Case of the Numerical Expression in Russian Phrases of the Type *(bol'še) na dva mal'čika* or *po troe bol'nyx*], *Russian Linguistics*, 50:1, 55–74.

———. (1980b) 'Animacy in Russian Cardinal Numerals and Adjectives as an Inflectional Category,' *Language*, 56:4, 797–811.

———. (1980c) 'O padeže suščestvitel'nogo v russkoj konstrukcii tipa *Idti v soldaty*' [On the Case of the Noun in the Russian Construction of the Type *Idti v soldaty*], *Svantevit*, 5:1/2, 5–32.

———. (1981a) 'Meaning-Text Models: A Recent Trend in Soviet Linguistics,' *Annual Review of Anthropology*, 10, 27–62.

———. (1981b) 'Grammatical Subject and the Problem of the Ergative Construction in Lezgian,' in B. Comrie (ed.), *Studies in the Languages of the USSR*, Carbondale—Edmonton: Linguistic Research, 229–276.

———. (1981c) 'The Grammatical Case of Rusian Numerical Expressions of the Type *(bol'še) na dva mal'čika* or *po troe bol'nyx*,' *Forum Linguisticum*, 6:2, 117–140.

———. (1982) *Toward a Language of Linguistics*, München: W. Fink.

———. (1985) *Poverxnostnyj sintaksis russkix čislovyx vyraženij* [Surface Syntax of Russian Numeral Expressions], Vienna: WSA.

———. (1986) 'Toward a Definition of Case,' in R. Brecht and J. Levine (eds.), *Case in Slavic*, Columbus, OH: Slavica, 35–85.

Mel'čuk, Igor' A., Lidija N. Iordanskaja, and Nadia Arbatchewsky-Jumarie (1981) 'Un nouveau type de dictionnaire: le Dictionnaire explicatif et combinatoire du français contemporain (Six articles de dictionnaire),' *Cahiers de lexicologie*, 38:1, 3–34.

Mel'čuk, Igor' A., Nadia Arbatchewsky-Jumarie, Léo Elnitsky, Lidija N. Iordanskaja, and Adèle Lessard (1984) *Dictionnaire explicatif et combinatorie du français contemporain. Recherches lexico-sémantiques. I*, Montréal: Les Presses de l'Université de Montréal.

Mel'čuk, Igor' A., and Nikolaj V. Percov [= Pertsov] (1973a) 'Fragment modeli anglijskogo poverxnostnogo sintaksisa (predvaritel'noe soobščenie)' [A Fragment of an English Surface Syntax Model (Preliminary Report)], in *PP PGÈPL*, 35, 3–18.

———. (1973b) *Poverxnostno-sintaksičeskie otnošenija v anglijskom jazyke* [Surface-Syntactic Relations in English], Moscow: Institut Russkogo jazyka AN SSSR [*PP PGÈPL*, 43].

———. (1975) *Model' anglijskogo poverxnostnogo sintaksisa. Perečen' sintagm, č. I i II; Priloženija k perečnju sintagm* [A Model of English Surface Syntax. The Inventory of Syntagms, I and II; Appendix to the Inventory of Syntagms], Moscow: Institut Russkogo jazyka AN SSSR [*PP PGÈPL*, 64–66].

———. (1987) *Surface Syntax of English. A Formal Model within the Meaning-Text Framework*, Amsterdam: Benjamins.

Mel'čuk, Igor' A., and Elena N. Savvina (1974) 'O formal'noj modeli sintaksisa aljutorskogo jazyka' [On a Formal Model of Alutor Syntax], in *PP PGÈPL*, 55, Moscow: Institut Russkogo jazyka AN SSSR, 15–32.

————. (1978) 'Toward a Formal Model of Alutor Surface Syntax: Predicative and Completive Constructions,' *Linguistics*, Special Issue, 5–39.

Mel'čuk, Igor' A., and Aleksandr A. Xolodovič (1970) 'K teorii grammatičeskogo zaloga. (Opredelenie. Isčislenie)' [Toward a Theory of Grammatical Voice. A Definition and a Calculus], *Narody Azii i Afriki*, No 4, 111–124.

Mel'čuk, Igor' A., and Alexander K. Zholkovsky (1984) *Tolkovo-kombinatornyj slovar' sovremennogo russkogo jazyka. Opyty semantiko-sintaksičeskogo opisanija russkoj leksiki* [Explanatory Combinatorial Distionary of Modern Russian. Semantico-Syntactic Studies of Russian Vocabulary], Vienna: WSA [Sonderband 14].

Mel'čuk, Igor' A., and Aleksandr K. Žolkovskij [= Zholkovsky] (1970) 'Towards a Functioning 'Meaning-Text' Model of language,' *Linguistics*, 57, 10–47.

Mel'nikov, G. I. (1940) *Fonetika aljutorskogo i karaginskogo dialektov korjakskogo jazyka na osnove èksperimental'nyx dannyx* [Phonetics of the Alutor and Karaga Dialects of Koryak Based on Experimental Data], unpublished. Leningrad: Institute of Linguistics, Academy of Sciences of the USSR.

Miller, George A., and Philip N. Johnson-Laird (1976) *Language and Perception*, Cambridge etc.: Cambridge University Press.

Mohanan, K. P. (1982) 'Grammatical Relations in Malayalam,' in Bresnan (1982b), 504–589.

Nakhimovsky, Alexander (1979) *Voice and the Indefinite-Personal Construction in Russian* (Ph.D. thesis, Cornell University), Ithaca, NY.

————. (1983) *Meaning-Text Linguistics and the Problem of Voice*, Carbondale—Edmonton: Linguistic Research.

Nichols, Johanna (1974) *Transitivity and the Russian Verb*, Paper read at the Soviet-American Conference on the Russian Language, Cambridge, MA.

————. (1975) 'Verbal Semantics and Sentence Construction,' *BLS 1*, 343–353.

————. (1978) 'Secondary Predicates,' *BLS 4*, 114–127.

————. (1979) 'The Meeting of East and West: Confrontation and Convergence in Contemporary Linguistics' *BLS 5*, 261–276.

————. (1981) *Predicate Nominals: A Partial Surface Syntax of Russian*, Berkeley: University of California Press.

————. (1986) 'Head-marking and Dependent-marking Grammar,' *Language*, 62:1, 56–119.

Nichols, Johanna, Gilbert Rappaport, and Alan Timberlake (1980) 'Subject, Topic, and Control in Russian,' *BLS 6*, 372–386.

Ohmann, Richard (1971) 'Grammar and Meaning,' in W. Morris (ed.), *The Heritage Illustrated Dictionary of the English Language*, New York: American Heritage and Houghton Mifflin, XXXI-XXXIV.

Padučeva, Elena V. (1964) 'O sposobax predstavlenija sintaksičeskoj struktury predloženija' [On Methods of Representing the Syntactic Structure of a Sentence], *VJa*, No 2, 99–113.

————. (1967) 'Meždunarodnaja konferencija po semiotike v Pol'še' [An International Conference on Semiotics in Poland], *NTI*, No 2, 35–44.

Panov, Mixail V. (1960) 'O častjax reči v russkom jazyke' [On Parts of Speech in Russian], *Filologičeskie nauki*, No 4, 3–14.

Percival, W. Keith (1976) 'On the Historical Sources of Immediate Constituent Analysis,' in J. D. McCawley (ed.), *Notes from the Linquistic Underground* = *Syntax and Semantics*, 7, New York: Academic Press, 229–242.

Percov, Nikolaj V., and S. D. Polovko (1978) *Naxoždenie aktantov neličnyx glagol'nyx form pri avtomatičeskom analize francuzskogo teksta* [Identifying the Actants of Non-finite Verb Forms in Automatic Analysis of French], Moscow: Institut Russkogo jazyka AN SSSR [*PP PGÈPL*, 108].

Perlmutter, David M. (ed.) (1983) *Studies in Relational Grammar I*, Chicago: University of Chicago Press.

Perlmutter, David M., and Paul M. Postal (1983) 'Toward a Universal Characterization of Passivization,' in Perlmutter (1983), 3–29.

Peškovskij, Aleksandr Ja. (1934) *Russkij sintaksis v naučnom osveščenii* [Russian Syntax: A Scientific Approach], Moscow: Učpedgiz.

Pirejko, Lija A. (1968) *Osnovnye voprosy èrgativnosti na materiale indoiranskix jazykov* [Basic Problems of Ergativity in Indo-Iranian], Moscow: Nauka.

Pittman, Richard S. (1948) 'Nuclear Structures in Linguistics,' *Language*, 24:2, 287–292.

Plank, Frans (ed.) (1979) *Ergativity: Toward a Theory of Grammatical Relations*. London etc.: Academic Press.

Popova, Irina A. (1963) 'Nepolnye predloženija v sovremennom russkom jazyke' [Incomplete Sentences in Modern Russian], *Trudy Instituta Jazykoznanija Akademii Nauk SSSR*, II, 3–136.

Pullum, Geoffrey K. (1979) *Rule Interaction and the Organization of a Grammar*, New York and London: Garland.

Quang, Phuc Dong [= James D. McCawley] (1971) 'English Sentences without Overt Grammatical Subject,' in A. M. Zwicky et al. (eds.), *Studies out in Left Field: Defamatory Essays Presented to James D. McCawley*, Carbondale—Edmonton: Linguistic Research, 3–10.

Revzin, Isaak I. (1963) 'Ob odnoj sintaksičeskoj modeli' [On a Syntactic Model], *VJa*, No 2, 148–150.

Rizzi, Luigi (1982) 'Negation, *Wh*-movement and the Null Subject Parameter,' in L. Rizzi, *Issues in Italian Syntax*, Dordrecht—Cinnaminson: Foris, 117–188.

Robinson, Jane J. (1970a) 'A Dependency-based Transformational Grammar,' in *Actes du Xme Congrès international des linguistes (Bucareste, 1967)*, 2, Bucharest, 807–813.

———. (1970b) 'Dependency Structures and Transformational Rules,' *Language*, 46: 2, 259–285.

Rood, David S. (1971) 'Agent and Object in Wichita,' *Lingua*, 28:1/2, 100–107.

Rozencvejg, Viktor Ju. (ed.) (1974) *Essays on Lexical Semantics*, Vol. I–II. Stockholm: Skriptor.

Růžička, Rudolf (1970) 'Semantik des Verbs und Syntax des Satzes,' *Zeitschrift für Slawistik*, 15:5, 627–644.

Růžička, Rudolf, and G. Walther (1974) 'Beziehungen zwischen Bedeutung und Syntax,' *Zeitschrift für Slawistik*, 19:4, 460–474.

Sanders, Gerald A. (1972) *Equational Grammar*, The Hague—Paris: Mouton.

Sannikov, Vladimir Z. (1979–1980) 'Sočinitel'nye i sravnitel'nye konstrukcii: ix blizost', ix sintaksičeskoe predstavlenie. I–II' [Coordinate and Comparative Constructions: Their Proximity and Their Syntactic Representation], *WSA*, 4, 413–432; 5, 211–242.

Seidel, Hans-Eberhard (1983) '*Mne vas ne slyšno*: Zur Syntax der transitiven Prädikative im Russischen,' in R. Lauer und B. Schulz (eds.), *Slavisches Spektrum. Festschrift für Maximilian Braun zum 80. Geburtstag*, Wiesbaden: Otto Harrassowitz, 472-490 [= *Opera Slavica*, Neue Folge: B 4].

Sgall, Petr (1967) *Generativní popis jazyka a česká deklinace* [Generative Description of Language and Czech Declension]. Praha: Academia.

Shopen, Timothy (1972) *A Generative Theory of Ellipsis*, Bloomington, IN: IULC.

Sidorov, Vladimir N., and Irina S. Il'inskaja (1949) 'K voprosu o vyraženii sub″ekta i ob″ekta dejstvija v sovremennom russkom jazyke' [On Expression of the Subject and Object in Modern Russian], *Izvestija AN SSSR. OLJa*, 8:4, 343–354.

Skovorodnikov, A. P. (1973) 'O kriterii èlliptičnosti v russkom sintaksise' [On the Criterion of Ellipsis in Russian Syntax], *VJa*, No 3, 114–123.

Smirnickij, Aleksandr I. (1959) *Morfologija anglijskogo jazyka* [Morphology of English], Moscow: Izdatel'stvo Literatury na Inostrannyx Jazykax.

Starosta, Stanley (1975) 'Case in the Lexicon,' in L. Heilmann (ed.), *Proceedings of the XIth International Congress of Linguists, Bologna-Florence, 1972*, Bologna: Il Mulino, 805–813.

――――. (1981) *The End of Phrase Structure as We Know It* [unpublished manucript; a new version of 1985 is available].

Stebnickij, S. N. (1938) 'Aljutorskij dialekt nymylanskogo (korjakskogo) jazyka' [The Alutor Dialect of Koryak], *Sovetskij Sever*, No 1.

Sussex, Roland (1974) 'The Role of Transformational Generative Grammar in Modern Slavonic Linguistics,' in R. D. Brecht and C. V. Chvany (eds.), *Slavic Transformational Syntax*, Ann Arbor, MI: University of Michigan Press, 3–20.

Suxotin, Boris V. (1973) 'Issledovanie struktury prostogo predloženija s pomošč'ju ÈVM' [Studying the Structure of Clauses by Means of a Computer], in S. K. Šaumjan (ed.), *Problemy strukturnoj lingvistiki-1972*, Moscow: Nauka, 429–488.

――――. (1976) *Optimizacionnye metody issledovanija jazyka* [Optimization Methods in Linguistic Research], Moscow: Nauka.

Širjaev, Evgenij N. (1967) *Nulevye glagoly kak členy paradigmatičeskix i sintagматičeskix otnošenij (na materiale sovremennogo russkogo jazyka)* [Null Verbs as Terms of Paradigmatic and Syntagmatic Relations (in Modern Russian)]. Avtoref. kand. diss., Moscow.

――――. (1973) 'O nekotoryx pokazateljax nezameščённyx pozicij v vyskazyvanijax razgovornoj reči i nulevye glagoly-predikaty' [On Certain Markers of Unfilled Slots in Colloquial Speech and Null Verbs as Predicates], in E. A. Zemskaja (ed.), *Russkaja razgovornaja reč'*, Moscow: Nauka, 288–317.

Švedova, Natal'ja Ju. (ed.) (1980) *Russkaja grammatika* [Russian Grammar], I–II, Moscow: Nauka.

Talibov, Bukar B. (1966) 'Grammatičeskij očerk lezginskogo jazyka' [A Grammatical Outline of Lezgian], in B. Talibov and M. Gadžiev, *Lezginsko-russkij slovar'*, Moscow: Sovetskaja Ènciklopedija, 537–603.

Tchekhoff, Claude (1978) *Aux fondements de la syntaxe: l'ergatif*, Paris: Presses Universitaires de France.

Tesnière, Lucien (1959) *Éléments de syntaxe structurale*, Paris: Klincksieck [Second edition, revised and corrected, 1969].

Timberlake, Alan (1974) 'The Nominative Object in North Russsian,' in R. D. Brecht and C. V. Chvany (eds.), *Slavic Transformational Syntax*, Ann Arbor, MI: University of Michigan Press, 219–243.

———. (1976) 'Subject Properties in the North Russian Passive,' in Li (1976), 545–570.

Trubeckoj, Nikolaj S. (1958) [1937] 'Mysli ob indoevropejskoj probleme' [Thoughts on the Indo-European Problem], *VJa*, No 1, 65–77 [published posthumously].

Tsunoda, Tasaku (1981) 'Interaction of Phonological, Grammatical and Semantic Factors: An Australian Example,' *Oceanic Linguistics*, 20:1, 45–92.

———. (1983) 'A Re-Definition of 'Ergative' and 'Accusative',' in Sh. Hattori and K. Inoue (eds.), *Proceedings of the XIIIth International Congress of Linguists, Tokyo, 1982*, Tokyo, 962–966.

———. (1985) 'Remarks on Transitivity,' *Journal of Linguistics*, 21, 385–396.

Uryson, Elena V. (1981) 'Poverxnostno-sintaksičeskoe predstavlenie russkix appozitivnyx konstrukcij' [Surface-Syntactic Representation of Russian Appositive Constructions], *WSA*, 7, 155–216.

———. (1982) 'Napravlenie sintaksičeskoj zavisimosti v russkix appozitivnyx konstrukcijax' [Syntactic Dependency Direction in Russian Appositive Constructions], *BPTJ*, 39, 97–107.

Uslar, Petr K. (1888) *Čečenskij jazyk* [Chechen], Tiflis.

———. (1889) *Avarskij jazyk* [Avar], Tiflis.

Van Valin, Robert D., Jr. (1977) 'Ergativity and the Universality of Subjects,' *CLS 13*, 689–706.

Van Valin, Robert D., Jr., and William A. Foley (1980) 'Role and Reference Grammar,' in E. Moravcsik (ed.), *Syntax and Semantics, 13: Current Approaches To Syntax*, New York: Academic Press, 329–352.

Vater, H. (1975) 'Toward a Generative Dependency Theory,' *Lingua*, 36:2/3, 121–145.

Vdovin, I. S. (1956) *Aljutorskij dialekt korjakskogo jazyka* [The Alutor Dialect of Koryak], Unpublished. Leningrad: Institute of Linguistics, Academy of Sciences of the USSR.

Vinogradov, Viktor V. (1947) *Russkij jazyk* [Russian], Moscow—Leningrad: Učpedgiz.

Vinogradov, Viktor V., E. S. Istrina, and Stepan G. Barxudarov (eds.) (1960) *Grammatika russkogo jazyka* [A Grammar of Russian], Moscow: Academy of Sciences of the USSR.

Volodin, A. P. (1967) 'Èrgativnaja konstrukcija v itel'menskom jazyke' [Ergative Construction in Itelmen], in V. M. Žirmunskij (ed.), *Èrgativnaja konstrukcija predloženija v jazykax različnyx tipov*, Leningrad: Nauka, 240–245.

Ward, Dennis (1973) 'Appositional Compounds in Russian,' *The Slavonic and East European Review*, 51 (No 122), 7–10.

Wells, Rulon S. (1947) 'Immediate Constituents,' *Language*, 23:1, 81–117.

Wierzbicka, Anna (1966) 'Czy istnieją zdania bezpodmiotowe' [Subjectless Sentences, Do They exist?], *Język polski*, 46:3, 177–196.

———. (1972) *Semantic Primitives*, Frankfurt am Main: Athenäum.

———. (1975) 'Why "kill" Does not Mean "cause to die": The Semantics of Action Sentences,' *FoL*, 13:4, 495–528.

———. (1980a) *Lingua Mentalis: The Semantics of Natural Language*, Sydney etc.: Academic Press.

———. (1980b) *The Case for Surface Case*, Ann Arbor, MI: Karoma.

———. (1982) 'Why Can You *have a drink* when You Can't **have an eat*?,' *Language*, 58:4, 753–799.

————. (1984a) '*Apples* Are Not a "Kind of Fruit": The Semantics of Human Categorization,' *American Ethnologist*, 11:2, 313–328.

————. (1984b) 'Cups and Mugs: Lexicography and Conceptual Analysis,' *AJL*, 4:2, 205–255.

————. (1985) *Lexicography and Conceptual Analysis*, Ann Arbor, MI: Karoma.

————. (To appear) *A Dictionary of English Speech Act Verbs*, New York—Sydney: Academic Press.

Wilbur, T. M. (1977) 'Transitive, Intransitive, Ergative: a Terminological Autopsy,' in *Acten der 2. Salzburger Frühlingstagung für Linguistik*, Tübingen: G. Narr, 119–126.

Xolodovič, Aleksandr A. (1970) 'K voprosu o dominante predloženija' [On the Element Dominating the Clause], in R. Jakobson and Sh. Kawamoto (eds.), *Studies in General and Oriental Linguistics. Presented to Sh. Hattori on the Occasion of His Sixtieth Birthday*, Tokyo: TEC, 318–324. [Reprinted in Xolodovič, A. A., *Problemy grammatičeskoj teorii*, 1979, Leningrad: Nauka.]

————. (1971) 'Nekotorye voprosy upravlenija v japonskom jazyke' [Some Government Problems in Japanese], in I. F. Vardul (ed.), *Voprosy japonskojo jazyka*, Moscow: Nauka, 113–132.

————. (ed.) (1974) *Tipologija passivnyx konstrukcij: Diatezy i zalogi* [Typology of Passive Constructions: Diatheses and Voices], Leningrad: Nauka.

Xrakovskij, Viktor S. (1974) 'Problemy sinonimii i konversnosti passivnyx i aktivnyx konstrukcij' [Problems of Synonymy and Conversivity of Passive vs. Active Constructions], in *Universalii i tipologičeskie issledovanija. Meščaninovskie čtenija*, Moscow: Nauka, 80–91.

Xrakovskij, Viktor S. (ed.) (1978) *Problemy teorii grammatičeskogo zaloga* [Problems in the Theory of Grammatical Voice], Leningrad: Nauka.

————. (1981) *Zalogovye konstrukcii v raznostrukturnyx jazykax* [Voice Constructions in Languages of Different Structure], Leningrad: Nauka.

Zakharyin, Boris (1979) 'On the Formation of Ergativity in Indo-Aryan and Dardic,' *Osmania Papers in linguistics*, 5, Hyderabad: Osmania University, Dept. of Linguistics, 50–71.

Zaliznjak, Andrej A. (1967) *Russkoe imennoe slovoizmenenie* [Russian Nominal Inflection], Moscow: Nauka.

————. (1973) 'O ponimanii termina "padež" v lingvist1českix opisanijax. I' [On Interpreting the Term 'Case' in Linguistic Descriptions, I], in A. A. Zaliznjak (ed.), *Problemy grammatičeskogo modelirovanija*, Moscow: Nauka, 53–87.

Zekox, U. S. (1969) *Sistema sklonenija v adygejskom jazyke* [System of Declension in Adyghe], Majkop.

Zwicky, Arnold M. (1978) 'Arguing for Constituents,' *CLS 14*, 503–512.

Žolkovskij, Aleksandr K. (1964) 'O pravilax semantičeskogo analiza' [On Rules for Semantic Analysis], *Mašinnyj perevod i prikladnaja lingvistika*, 8, 17–32.

————. (1971) *Sintaksis somali* [Somali Syntax], Moscow: Nauka.

Žolkovskij, Aleksandr K., Nina N. Leont'eva, and Jurij S. Martem'janov (1961) 'O principial'nom ispol'zovanii smysla pri mašinnom perevode' [On Fundamental Use of Meaning in Machine Translation], in *Trudy Instituta Točnoj Mexaniki i Vyčisl. Texniki AN SSSR*, 2, 17–46.

Žolkovskij, Aleksandr K., and Igor' A. Mel'čuk (1965) 'O vozmožnom metode i instrumentax semantičeskogo sinteza' [On a Possible Method and Instruments for Semantic Synthesis (of Texts)], *NTI*, No 6, 23–28.

————. (1967) 'O semantičeskom sinteze' [On Semantic Synthesis (of Texts)], *PK*, 19, 177–238.

Žukova, A. N. (1968) 'Aljutorskij jazyk' [Alutor], in *Jazyki narodov SSSR*, V, Leningrad: Nauka, 294–309.

INDEXES

INDEX OF NAMES

INDEX OF LANGUAGES

INDEX OF SUBJECTS
AND TERMS

Boldfaced numbers identify the pages on which the definition (or at least a substantive discussion) of the term in question is found.